SO-AWD-502

TURTLES

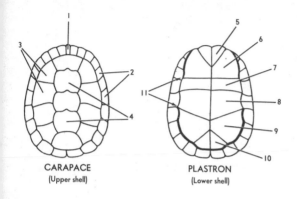

CARAPACE
(Upper shell)

PLASTRON
(Lower shell)

THE SCUTES

1. Nuchal
2. Marginals
3. Costals
4. Vertebrals
5. Gular
6. Humeral
7. Pectoral
8. Abdominal
9. Femoral
10. Anal

11. Bridge

LIZARDS

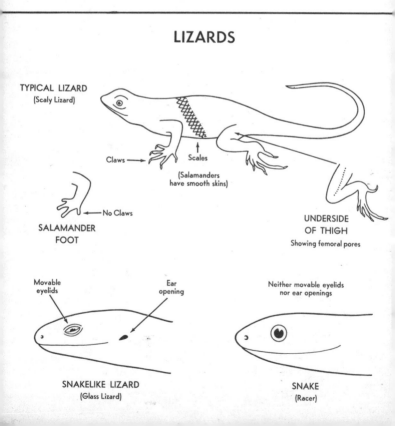

TYPICAL LIZARD
(Scaly Lizard)

Claws

Scales

(Salamanders
have smooth skins)

SALAMANDER
FOOT

No Claws

UNDERSIDE
OF THIGH

Showing femoral pores

Movable
eyelids

Ear
opening

SNAKELIKE LIZARD
(Glass Lizard)

Neither movable eyelids
nor ear openings

SNAKE
(Racer)

SNAKES

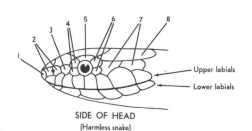

SIDE OF HEAD
(Harmless snake)

Upper labials
Lower labials

HEAD SCALES

1. Rostral
2. Nasals
3. Loreal
4. Preoculars
5. Supraoculars
6. Postoculars
7. Temporals
8. Parietals
9. Internasals
10. Prefrontals
11. Frontal
12. Mental
13. Chin shields

14. Ventrals

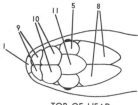

TOP OF HEAD

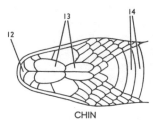

CHIN

SECTIONS
OF
BODIES

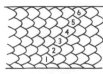

Counting
scale
rows

Keeled scales

Smooth scales

Scale pits
present

No scale
pits

UNDERSIDES OF TAILS

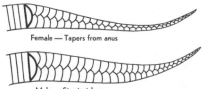

Female — Tapers from anus

Male — Stout at base

Single anal plate

Divided anal plate

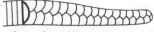

Stump-tail — part lost through accident

A Field Guide
to Reptiles and Amphibians
of Eastern and Central
North America

THE PETERSON FIELD GUIDE SERIES

EDITED BY ROGER TORY PETERSON

THE PETERSON FIELD GUIDE SERIES

A Field Guide to Reptiles and Amphibians

of Eastern and Central North America

BY ROGER CONANT

Adjunct Professor, Department of Biology
University of New Mexico
and
Director and Curator of Reptiles Emeritus
Philadelphia Zoological Garden

Illustrated by

ISABELLE HUNT CONANT

SECOND EDITION

Sponsored by the National Audubon Society
and National Wildlife Federation

HOUGHTON MIFFLIN COMPANY BOSTON

1975

Copyright © 1958, 1975 by Roger Conant
All rights reserved. No part of this work may be
reproduced or transmitted in any form by any means,
electronic or mechanical, including photocopying and re-
cording, or by any information storage or retrieval system,
without permission in writing from the publisher.

Library of Congress Cataloging in Publication Data
Conant, Roger, 1909–
    A field guide to reptiles and amphibians of Eastern
and Central North America.

    (The Peterson field guide series, 12)
    First published in 1958 under title: A field guide
to reptiles and amphibians of the United States and
Canada east of the 100th meridian.
    Bibliography: p.
    1. Reptiles—North America. 2. Amphibians—North
America. 3. Reptiles—Identification. 4. Amphibians
—Identification. I. Title.
QL651.C65 1975   598.1′097   74-13425
ISBN 0-395-19979-4   ISBN 0-395-19977-8 (pbk.)

Printed in the United States of America

V   10   9   8   7   6   5   4   3   2   1

This book is dedicated to

ISABELLE
without whose talents as
photographer and artist
it never
would have been attempted.

Editor's Note

THE AMATEUR naturalist who is interested in herpetology, the science of reptiles and amphibians, has a distinct advantage over his fellows. Unlike most bird watchers, he can catch and handle his animals, and unlike botanists and entomologists, who must dry and mount their specimens in order to preserve them, the herpetologist can keep his captives alive, often for long periods of time. He can study them and enjoy them as pets. The keeping of live reptiles and amphibians has become an important adjunct of the biology classroom and of the summer camp.

Roger Conant, keenly aware of this because of the thousands of questions he has received, has included a section in this book on how to house and feed reptiles and amphibians, and sprinkled through his text are numerous other hints. Hence this *Field Guide* serves a double purpose—it enables the reader to identify his specimen and then tells him how to care for it if he wants to keep it. The section on snakebite and what to do about it is also an important feature, providing the latest information about starting emergency treatment in the absence of a doctor.

The magnitude of the problem of obtaining live specimens of virtually every reptile and amphibian species and subspecies in eastern and central North America is staggering. The assistance of scores of friends and colleagues was required to accomplish this part of the project. Keeping the animals alive and healthy, sometimes for months, while the photographic illustrations were being prepared was another demanding task. During virtually all this time Roger Conant continued in his capacity as Curator of Reptiles at the Philadelphia Zoological Garden and then also as its Executive Director. Because of his long experience in communicating with the layman (he was Public Relations Director of the Zoo for 30 years) this book is far from being strictly technical. It contains information that the professional herpetologist needs to identify species and subspecies, but its language will be clear to everyone. He has now retired to the Southwest where he serves as an Adjunct Professor in the Department of Biology at the University of New Mexico. In recognition of his contributions to herpetology and his distinguished zoo work he has been awarded the degree of Doctor of Science by the University of Colorado.

Dr. Conant has written three books, a long monograph on the water snakes of Mexico, and more than 150 technical and semipopular papers on reptiles and amphibians. Recently he rewrote the *Reptile Study* merit badge pamphlet for the Boy Scouts of America, an organization with which he has been associated since boyhood and which kindled his early interest in natural history.

Isabelle Hunt Conant, the illustrator, who is Mrs. Roger Conant, was official photographer at the Philadelphia Zoo for ten years. Scores of popular and technical publications have reproduced her pictures. She has accompanied her husband on field trips throughout a large part of the United States and in every state of Mexico. Many of the trips were made expressly to obtain specimens to be illustrated in this book.

Standardization of vernacular names of North American birds was begun in 1886 (and is only now reaching stabilization), but herpetological names have long been in a state of confusion. Dr. Conant has served as Chairman of the Committee on Herpetological Common Names for the American Society of Ichthyologists and Herpetologists. This committee has prepared a list that will aid in standardizing the names of reptiles and amphibians. These names, except for a few updatings and emendations, are used throughout this book.

Many colleges and universities selected the First Edition of the Conant *Field Guide* as a text for their courses in herpetology. It has also served as a stimulus to amateur herpetological societies, members of which have provided Dr. Conant with a great deal of new information on range extensions, maximum sizes, etc.

Inasmuch as there had been a hiatus between the area covered by the First Edition of this *Field Guide* and Stebbins' *Field Guide to Western Reptiles and Amphibians,* it seemed advisable in this edition to close the gap by including western Texas as well as the western parts of the states to the north and adjacent Canada. This involved three seasons of intensive field work for the Conants in the Big Bend region of Texas where many Mexican species occur. These, the addition of a number of West Indian lizards that are now established in Florida, and the discovery of several new species increase the number of full species covered in this Second Edition to 331. The distribution maps have all been updated and redrawn, and the research devoted to them alone involved nearly three years (for the two editions combined).

It is certain that in the years ahead, North America will adopt the metric system of measurements so widely used elsewhere in the world. This edition of Conant's *Field Guide* is one of the first books in the series to include measurements both in inches and the metric equivalents.

Roger and Isabelle Conant have produced a *Field Guide* that we are very proud to have in the series. Do not leave it on the library shelf when you travel about the countryside. Put it in the glove compartment of your car, in your knapsack, or in the pocket of your jacket.

ROGER TORY PETERSON

Acknowledgments

SINCE the publication of the first edition of this *Field Guide* in 1958 I have received more than a thousand letters, a great many of them from strangers, offering information on range extensions, new maximum lengths (especially for snakes), and a wealth of other data. All this has been grist for the mill, so to speak, and a large portion of the refinements and improvements in this second edition are the result of the interest and thoughtfulness of colleagues, their students, and a host of amateur herpetologists who have made contributions to the cause. I apologize for insisting that many of them send me firm evidence or specimens to substantiate their claims and for demanding to see alleged record-breaking animals so I could measure them myself. Not a single person complained because of this extra effort on his part as I sought accuracy and strove for perfection.

Because our territory had to be moved much farther westward to include all of Texas and the states north of it, as well as Manitoba and Keewatin, we were confronted with the problem of obtaining living examples of a large number of additional species. They were needed for making photographs for our plates or for guidance in preparing line drawings. Also, several more West Indian species are now firmly established in Florida. Users of this book are apt to encounter them, so those, too, have been added in text and picture. Many of the desired reptiles and amphibians I collected myself during three summers in the Big Bend region of Texas and during a brief excursion to southern Florida in 1966, but the bulk of the new material was accumulated through the efforts of friends and professional colleagues.

To all those persons who have helped I am deeply grateful, but I also am embarrassed. Space limitations preclude the listing of all their names. Their contributions, however, are carefully recorded in my workbooks, my files, and on my base maps, and their findings, properly accredited, are available on request.

Some persons have contributed literally scores of man-hours, however, and others have invested heavily in time and effort in responding to my requests for information, reading portions of the text, checking preliminary maps submitted for their critical review, or rendering other favors.

While we were in the Big Bend region Roland H. Wauer and

James F. Scudday were extremely helpful. A number of other persons who were resident or working in that area assisted in a variety of ways; among them were Perry Brown, Luther T. Peterson, Jr., David A. Easterla, Jerry A. Johnson, Samuel Sikes, Felix Hernandez III, Charles E. Babcock, Ted L. Brown, and Wayne Baize.

A considerable number of herpetologists generously sent me copies of their unpublished manuscripts, so I could preview them and, in many cases, incorporate taxonomic changes they were proposing. Others provided detailed information that was helpful in revising or completely rewriting accounts of various genera and species. Among this group were Ralph W. Axtell, Richard M. Blaney, Joseph T. Collins, George W. Folkerts, Laurence M. Hardy, David Haynes, W. Ronald Heyer, Richard Highton, John M. Legler, Carl S. Lieb, John D. Lynch, Ronald R. McKown, D. Bruce Means, John S. Mecham, William W. Milstead, Charles W. Myers, Craig E. Nelson, R. Earl Olson, Ann E. Pace, George R. Pisani, William H. Stickel, Samuel S. Sweet, Stephen G. Tilley, Kenneth L. Williams, Larry David Wilson, and John W. Wright.

In the preparation of the distribution maps I have had help from innumerable people, especially from those who were compiling records for specific states or areas or who had spent much time afield near their homes or favorite vacation spots. Among this group special credit must be given to: Robert H. Mount (Alabama), Richard L. Timken (the Dakotas, Nebraska, and Montana), Charles H. Wharton (Georgia), Sherman A. Minton (Indiana), Harold A. Dundee and Douglas A. Rossman (Louisiana), Herbert S. Harris, Jr. (Maryland), David S. Lee (Maryland and Florida), Max A. Nickerson (Missouri and Wisconsin), Jeffrey H. Black (Montana), Timothy S. Doyle, Terry E. Graham, Allen E. Greer, James D. Lazell, Jr., and C. Robert Shoop (New England), William G. Degenhardt, John S. Applegarth, and Kirkland L. Jones (New Mexico), Edgar M. Reilly, Jr. (New York), William M. Palmer (North Carolina), Clarence J. McCoy and Neill D. Richmond (Pennsylvania), George W. Folkerts (the Southeast in general and Alabama in particular), Frederick R. Gehlbach and Gerald G. Raun (Texas), and Albert Schwartz (West Indies).

Dr. Raun gave me his documented map workbook on Texas early during the preparation of this *Field Guide* and thereby saved me hundreds of hours of searching for references. Francis R. Cook accelerated his survey of the zoogeography of Canadian reptiles and amphibians so the information would be available for my use. Franklin J. Tobey, Jr., who serves as coordinator and cartographer for the Virginia Herpetological Society, supplied me with detailed copies of maps for his state.

Samuel S. Sweet and Albert E. Sanders very kindly prepared detailed sketches of amphibians from which Mrs. Conant executed the line drawings in Figures 88 and 102. Ruth G. Endy typed the manuscript, and Georgette and Edmond V. Malnate posed for the photographs on Plate 2. The information and illustrations concerning first aid for snake bite were reviewed by Findlay E. Russell, Sherman A. Minton, and William F. Blank. Franklin Williamson helped with some of the photographic details.

A number of good friends and colleagues have repeatedly assisted in a variety of ways, offering advice and data for text and maps and responding to the many problems I referred to them for their professional opinions. These include Charles M. Bogert, Howard K. Gloyd, Edmond V. Malnate (who also read the entire manuscript), Hobart M. Smith, Philip W. Smith, and Richard G. Zweifel.

For a wide variety of favors, including the gift or loan of living specimens, the loan of museum specimens, supplying miscellaneous information or locality records, reading parts of the manuscript or checking maps, rendering assistance in the field, or helping in other ways, I am indebted not only to the persons mentioned above but also to the following: Ross Allen, Ronald Altig, James D. Anderson, Paul K. Anderson, Rudolf G. Arndt, Ray E. Ashton, Jr., Walter Auffenberg, Daniel F. Austin, Joseph R. Bailey, Richard J. Baldauf, Royce E. Ballinger, Roger W. Barbour, A. James Barton, John L. Behler, Robert L. Birch, John D. Black, Albert P. Blair, W. Frank Blair, H. T. Boschung, Jr., Ernest Bostelman, Jr., J. Kevin Bowler, Arden H. Brame, Ronald A. Brandon, Bayard H. Brattstrom, Walter J. Breckenridge, William E. Brode, Richard C. Bruce, A. J. Bullard, Jr., Ray D. Burkett, Charles C. Carpenter, Archie Carr, Allan H. Chaney, Steven P. Christman, Charles J. Clarke, J. William Cliburn, Charles J. Cole, Roger K. Conant, Miles Cook, John E. Cooper, James Court, Walter R. Courtenay, Jr., Ronald I. Crombie, Hector S. Cuellar, Donald M. Davis, William K. Davis, Ralph W. Dexter, James R. Dixon, James L. Dobie, Herndon G. Dowling, William E. Duellman, Arthur C. Echternacht, Richard A. Edgren, Carl H. Ernst, James H. Everitt, Robert C. Feuer, Clyde B. Fisher, Henry S. Fitch, Wayne Frair, Richard Franz, Richard S. Funk, Carl Gans, H. Carl Gehrhardt, Jr., Glenn Gentry, J. Whitfield Gibbons, John Gilhen, Coleman J. Goin, Robert E. Gordon, Stanley W. Gorham, N. Bayard Green, Harry W. Greene, William L. Grogan, Jr., Frank Groves, Sheldon I. Guttman, Jack P. Hailman, Jack Hamilton, Julian R. Harrison III, Max Hensley, Barry Hinderstein, Richard L. Hoffman, J. Alan Holman, René Honegger, Gordon Hubbell, Donald G. Huggins, Philip S. Humphrey, Victor H. Hutchison, Joe Ideker, Robert F. Inger, John B. Iverson III, Crawford G. Jackson, Jr., James F. Jackson, James S. Jacob, Pauline James, Ted Joanen, W. J. W. Johnson, O. Ray Jordan, Ralph Jordan, Jr., Jack K. Kappel, the late Carl F. Kauffeld, J. P. Kennedy, A. Ross Kiester, F. Wayne King, Arnold G. Kluge, Lionel A. Landrey, Jr., Gerald S. Lentz, Hague L. Lindsay, Jr.,

Ernest A. Liner, Richard B. Loomis, David V. Mandley, Bernard S. Martof, T. Paul Maslin, Clayton J. May, William ,L. McClure, Roy W. McDiarmid, Philip A. Medica, Greg Mengden, Dean E. Metter, Gary Meyer, Richard R. Montanucci, James M. Moulton, Ken Nemuras, Lewis D. Ober, John C. Ogden, Harry M. Ohlendorf, Dennis R. Paulson, Ray L. Pawley, George B. Pendlebury, the late James A. Peters, Jack R. Pierce, Dwight R. Platt, Louis Porras, Peter C. H. Pritchard, Gerald T. Regan, John Rindfleish, William B. Robertson, Michael D. Robinson, Francis L. Rose, Janis A. Roze, Norton M. Rubenstein, Michael D. Sabath, James D. Saxon, Frederick C. Schlauch, Michael E. Seidel, Wayne Seifert, Otto M. Sokol, Robert C. Stebbins, Henry M. Stevenson, William H. Stickel, Arthur Stupka, Charles D. Sullivan, Paul L. Swanson, Wilmer W. Tanner, the late Ernest C. Tanzer, Sam R. Telford, Richard Thomas, Robert A. Thomas, Donald W. Tinkle, Thomas M. Uzzell, Jr., Barry D. Valentine, Philip F. Van Cleave, Thomas R. Van Devender, Robert V. Wade, David B. Wake, Charles F. Walker, Rhea Warren, Aaron O. Wasserman, Robert G. Webb, George C. Wheeler, Ernest E. Williams, Gary M. Williamson, Michael A. Williamson, Richard D. Worthington, Harry Yeatman, and George R. Zug.

The editorial staff of Houghton Mifflin Co. has been most co-operative. Virginia Ehrlich has responded promptly to a large volume of correspondence and has repeatedly demonstrated her skill and thoroughness not only as a copy editor but also in supervising the preparation of this book for its trip through the press. We are also indebted to Morton H. Baker, Helen Phillips, and Katharine R. Bernard, all of whom have had a part in bringing this work to its final fruition.

Credit must also be given to the hundreds of herpetologists whose published works have been consulted, often repeatedly, and whose names would appear frequently if this were a documented, scientific publication. I am deeply grateful to them, but there is room to list only relatively few of their works on the pages devoted to references.

ROGER CONANT

Contents

Illustrations

Line drawings

Plates (grouped after page 205)

By Way of Definition

What Is a Reptile? And What Is an Amphibian?

UNTIL about a century ago it was customary to classify all the animals listed in this book simply as "reptiles," and some people still think of them in that way. Actually they form two natural groups, the Classes Reptilia and Amphibia among the vertebrates (backboned animals), and they are placed below the birds and mammals and above the fishes. They are cold-blooded, deriving heat from outside sources and controlling their body temperatures by moving to cooler or warmer environments as necessary.

The following definitions will apply to all the species found in our area:

REPTILES are clad in scales, shields, or plates, and their toes bear claws. (The clawless Leatherback sea turtle is an exception. Softshell turtles have only a few scales on their limbs.) Young reptiles are miniature replicas of their parents—in general appearance, if not always in coloration and pattern. To this Class belong the crocodilians, turtles, lizards, amphisbaenians, and snakes. Extralimital is the only surviving member of another group, the tuatara, now confined to tiny islets off the coast of New Zealand.

AMPHIBIANS have moist, glandular skins and their toes are devoid of claws. Their young pass through a larval, usually aquatic stage (tadpoles among the frogs) before they metamorphose into the adult form. The word "amphibious" is based upon Greek words and means "living a double life." Belonging to the Class Amphibia are the salamanders (including newts) and the toads and frogs. A third group occurs in the tropics, consisting of the burrowing, or aquatic, snake-shaped caecilians.

Map of eastern and central North America showing the area
covered by this *Field Guide*. All reptiles and amphibians
known to occur in the *unshaded* portions of the United
States and Canada are included. Since these animals lack
the mobility of birds and rarely leave their normal habitats,
geography can be of considerable importance in making
accurate identifications. Maps showing the ranges of all the
species (and subspecies) are grouped together at the back
of the book (pp. 363 to 412, inclusive).

I

Introduction

INTEREST in herpetology continues to proliferate on two broad fronts — among scientists who are using reptiles and amphibians ever more frequently for studies such as those on life histories, behavior, demography, and life functions of the animals themselves, and among amateurs who derive pleasure and knowledge from observing these animals in the field or keeping them in home terrariums. For both groups accurate identification of species is essential, and it is largely for them and the field naturalist in general that this book has been written.

The second edition of the *Field Guide to Reptiles and Amphibians* is substantially larger than its predecessor. We have extended our territory farther westward (see opposite page), many additional West Indian lizards are now established in Florida, and several new species and subspecies have been described or discovered since the first edition was published in 1958. We are now concerned with 331 species distributed as follows: Three crocodilians, 45 turtles, 61 lizards, one amphisbaenian, 86 snakes, 74 salamanders, and 61 toads and frogs. When all species *and* subspecies are counted, 574 different kinds of reptiles and amphibians are included, and the vast majority of these are illustrated. There are 472 reproductions of photographs in full color and 174 in black and white on 48 plates grouped at the center of the book. In addition, to show features that are useful in the identification of various species and subspecies, there are 353 line drawings, which appear on the endpapers or are scattered through the text and legend pages. There are also 311 distribution maps arranged near the back of the book. Counting all these, the frontispiece map, and two decorative figures, the illustrations in this *Field Guide* total 1313.

Time was when the only good snake was a dead one, but that unfortunate attitude is now almost a thing of the past except among ignorant, intolerant, or older people and the pitiful, sadistic vandals who kill anything that moves. Most young persons, as a result of exposure to reptiles at summer camps or in science classrooms, have discovered that the snake is a useful creature and, in most varieties, quite harmless. The new attitude has also helped to reduce the antipathy toward lizards and frogs and other scaly or slimy animals. There is now conclusive proof that fear of these animals has to be learned by children, usually from parents or other persons, some of whom may be prejudiced.

Using This Book: Anyone familiar with Roger Tory Peterson's *Field Guide to the Birds* will have no trouble consulting this book, for the general approach is the same. Nine times out of ten, however, the reader will have his specimen at hand before he attempts identification. The Boy Scout with his lizard, the biology student with her frog or salamander, or the sportsman with his freshly killed snake will bring book and animal together for comparison. Except for the basking turtle and an occasional other specimen, the techniques employed in bird watching will have little application. The vast majority of reptiles and amphibians are hiders, not likely to be seen at all by day unless one goes hunting for them. Even those that prowl are apt to be mere streaks in the grass. Accurate identification, for the most part, depends on a careful, close-range check.

Naturally, you will turn to the pictures first, and many times your specimen will closely match one of them. If it doesn't, then select the illustration it most nearly resembles and consult the text for that species — page references appear directly opposite each plate. Read about the key characters, the points of difference that are diagnostic of each separate kind, and also check the subentry **Similar species** to eliminate others that may resemble the one in hand. Details of anatomy and pattern are shown in the line drawings to which there are references in the text. Time spent studying the illustrations on the endpapers of this book will be well invested, for it will help you to understand the things for which to look.

In trying to make identifications remember that animals are not cut out by die-stamping machines or patterned by a trip through a printing press. Variation is a normal part of nature, and some species may show bewildering modifications of coloration and pattern. Occasional specimens may lack one or more of the pigment components of the skin and may be reddish, yellowish, bluish, or even albinistic (white or whitish) instead of exhibiting their normal colorations. Melanistic (all black) specimens are also occasionally found. Bear in mind, also, that frogs and lizards may change colors; a brown one, for example, may turn to green a short time later. I have tried to include the major variations by mentioning them in the text, especially in the cases of those species that are illustrated in black and white instead of color. Aberrant specimens or hybrids between species are found occasionally, and they may even confound the experts. If you have real trouble in trying to make sure what you have caught, take it to the nearest natural history museum, zoo, or university supporting a zoology department and ask for help.

Only a few of the snakes are dangerous, and all venomous species known from within our area are illustrated on Plates 30,

34, 35, and 36. Learn to recognize them on sight and let them strictly alone unless you are of age and have been given professional coaching on how to handle them. Also be cautious about picking up most turtles and large harmless snakes; they can and will bite in self-defense. Suggestions on how to handle big turtles are shown on Plate 1.

Unfortunately there is no short, well-established, collective designation for reptiles and amphibians in the English language. Such coined words as "herptiles" and "herpetozoa" have not been widely accepted. For brevity and because it is a word often used by herpetologists, I make frequent use of the slang expression "herps" in referring to members of both groups in these introductory pages.

Area: The area covered by this book includes all of the United States and Canada from the Eastern Seaboard to the western limits of Texas, Oklahoma, Kansas, Nebraska, the two Dakotas, Manitoba, and the District of Keewatin (see map, p. xx). This is an artificial boundary, but it was designed to meet the eastern edge of the territory embraced by Robert C. Stebbins' *Field Guide to Western Reptiles and Amphibians*. Our area has thus been expanded to include a large part of the Great Plains as well as a portion of the Chihuahuan Desert in Trans-Pecos Texas, in which latter there is a strong representation of Mexican species.

Range: Knowing where a specimen was collected can be of great importance in making identifications. Reptiles and amphibians lack the mobility of birds and seldom wander far from their natural habitats. Some of them, like salamanders, would die from desiccation if they left their caves or mountain streams. So note the origin of your specimen. If you take it to a professional herpetologist and ask his help, his first question probably will be "Where did it come from?"

The ranges are stated in brief at the end of each species or subspecies discussion, but they are shown in detail on the maps grouped on pages 363 to 412. Since geography is such an important crutch on which to lean, references to the maps are given in two places — opposite the plates and in the text.

Maps: The general range of each species and subspecies is shown by a pattern of dots, cross hatching, etc., on the maps grouped at the back of this book, but don't expect to find any reptile or amphibian evenly distributed throughout the areas indicated. A water snake, for example, seldom wanders far from stream or pond or brook, and, toward the west, where rivers are far apart, many miles may separate localities in which to look for specimens. Obviously, on maps small enough to fit into a *Field Guide* it would be impossible to show all details.

You may chance upon a specimen outside the known range of its species. There are several reasons why this may happen. For example:

1. People have a well-meaning but misguided habit of turning loose any pets that become a burden. Turtles and "horned toads" often fall into this category, and so do an astounding number of other herps. Most die quickly in their new and alien environments, but sometimes the waifs establish themselves in their new locations, at least for a time. The Red-eared Turtle has done so in a number of states, the Western Diamondback Rattlesnake in Wisconsin, and the Texas Horned Lizard in Florida and elsewhere. A number of tropical species have been introduced, most of them accidentally, into Florida or other southern states, and some kinds have developed temporary colonies only to die out after periods of heavy frost or other adverse conditions. The exotic species that seem now to be well established are included in this book.

2. You may discover a bona fide range extension. Many herps are so secretive they are readily overlooked, and, although herpetology has acquired a legion of new adherents in recent years, there are still many areas that have not been collected at all, or only sketchily. If your outlander seems to be in a proper habitat and especially if it occurs in colonies, you may have something worth reporting.

3. On rare occasions you may find a specimen that tends to look like a distant subspecies instead of matching the race you would expect in your immediate vicinity. This phenomenon is an expression of relationship. Related subspecies theoretically have had common ancestors, and it is not surprising to find the inherited characteristics of one race appearing occasionally in populations of another. Actually this type of phenomenon may be commonplace within areas of intergradation — where two subspecies of the same species share a common boundary. There may be a nearly perfect blending of the two races with some individual specimens showing one or more characteristics of *both* subspecies. Care must be taken in trying to identify such specimens, and it is perfectly correct to refer to them as intergrades or intermediates. The areas of intergradation vary greatly in size; they are usually narrow in regions of sharp physiographic changes, such as along an escarpment, where grasslands give way to forests, etc. But they may be very wide where changes in the environment are less pronounced. Only a few of the broader areas of intergradation are shown on the distribution maps, and these are indicated by the overlapping of patterns (spotting, hatching, etc.). Bear in mind that intergradation may take place for varying distances on both sides of any common boundary between subspecies. In some cases subspecies that once were probably connected through intergrades now occupy completely separate ranges, but they still retain sufficient similarity to be considered as races rather than as distinct species.

At this point, some comment should be made about hybrids. Crosses between species occur occasionally in nature, but such mismatings are almost always between animals of closely related species, and they may take place at various localities within their common ranges. The products of hybridization are frequently infertile, like a mule — the cross between a horse and an ass. Intergrades, on the other hand, are members of freely interbreeding populations, and are restricted to geographical regions where the ranges of two or more subspecies come together.

Introgression is a word that has come into wide use among students of animal populations during recent years. It describes a phenomenon that, in a sense, is the next step beyond hybridization. In some cases the hybrid offspring *are* fertile and hybrid swarms develop that combine characteristics of both parental species and pass them along to their own progeny. As a result animals are produced that defy exact identification. In some swarms no two hybrids look alike; they carry genes from both parental species but in different combinations. Introgression is likely to occur where habitats have been seriously altered by human activities or by such natural disturbances as hurricanes that sweep ashore and cause great destruction. Such changes may permit one animal species to invade the range of another closely related species, whereas they previously had occupied mutually exclusive territories. Under such circumstances introgression may develop. This phenomenon is well known among the toads (*Bufo*). Other examples occur between two of the water snakes (*Natrix sipedon* and *N. fasciata*) in the Carolinas, and among some of the turtle complexes of the genera *Graptemys* and *Chrysemys*.

Much time and effort were expended toward making the maps as complete and accurate as possible. Approximately three years of research time and correspondence were required to draft and document them. They were submitted to many specialists for checking and criticisms, and scores of herpetologists have reviewed them at meetings or at my home laboratory. I make no claim to perfection, however, for it would take several lifetimes to run down every possible locality reference and to check the vast numbers of specimens preserved in museums. Some states have been much more thoroughly explored herpetologically than others or the data about their reptiles and amphibians are much better organized or more readily accessible. As I predicted in the first edition of this *Field Guide* in 1958, the appearance of my distribution maps resulted in literally hundreds of range extensions being reported in the scientific literature or to me personally. Such a smoking-out process is a healthy sign of interest, and is the usual by-product whenever a large collection of range maps appears in print.

The maps may be used to prepare a personal check list. Just tabulate or check off the species occurring in your own state or region. They also may be used for a life list by placing a check mark after the name of each species or subspecies you encounter.

Illustrations: We have illustrated this book the difficult way. Instead of making paintings, we have depended on photography,

an art in which Mrs. Conant is singularly skilled. She made all
the pictures, did all the darkroom work, and then, having prepared
and toned a black and white print, she colored it by hand, using
the living animal as a model. This was a time-consuming task,
but it enabled us to record the colors with great accuracy. Also,
by enlarging the original black and white prints to the proper
dimensions before coloring them, it was relatively simple to group
all the animals on any one plate (or portion of a plate) to the
proper scale so that comparisons between large and small animals
is facilitated.

My part of the job was to pose the animals, inventing tricks
to render them motionless for a few seconds, and then keeping
them alive and healthy until the print was colored or retouched
(for the black and white plates). At one time we had in excess
of 200 snakes, lizards, turtles, frogs, toads, and salamanders in our
house. (Not all were of different species!)

This book is the only one of the *Field Guides* concerned with
zoology to be illustrated directly from life. There is only one dead
animal portrayed in the entire lot of photographs — a Leatherback Turtle, a marine species that few herpetologists have ever
seen alive. For the picture of it we are indebted to The American
Museum of Natural History. We have borrowed one other, that
of the Tennessee Cave Salamander, from Dr. Edward McCrady.
Some of the rattlesnake pictures were made through the close
cooperation of the late Carl F. Kauffeld.

Obtaining the animals alive has given me the extraordinary
opportunity of getting acquainted with them firsthand, and I have
not had to depend nearly so much on faded, stained, or distorted
pickled specimens for data as might otherwise have been the case.

The photographs for the black and white plates were prepared
with as much care as those for the color plates. Again, live animals
were used for models whenever retouching was needed to restore
pattern details that were obscured by highlights on shiny amphibians, turtle shells, etc.

The plates are supplemented by more than 100 sets of line
drawings showing for the most part key characters that are useful
in distinguishing between genera or between species or subspecies.
These also were executed by Mrs. Conant. Many are original, but
others have been adapted from figures appearing in numerous
scientific publications.

Scientific Names: It will be quickly apparent to longtime users
of this book that there have been many changes in scientific names
since publication of the first edition in 1958. Herpetological nomenclature is still a long way from achieving stability. Some of
the groups of reptiles and amphibians have not yet been subjected
to intensive investigation, and there is considerable disagreement
on how some of them should be classified.

Changes come about in a variety of ways. Careful study may

reveal that what once appeared to be single species may actually be two, as in the case of the Gray Treefrog (p. 323). Conversely, two or more apparently different species or subspecies are now obviously one. Hurter's and the Eastern Spadefoot, which were previously thought to be distinct, are now known to be subspecies of a single species. Another example concerns the variously colored and patterned members of the Appalachian Woodland Salamander (*Plethodon jordani*) complex. They have been shown to intergrade in so many different ways and in so many different localities that they must be defined as one extremely variable species rather than as a collection of numerous subspecies. Alterations in nomenclature resulting from such studies usually receive wide acceptance among herpetologists.

In other cases as soon as changes are proposed (published) by one or more herpetologists they are vigorously opposed by others. This is particularly true at the generic level (the first unit of any scientific name and the one that is always capitalized). Should it be *Natrix* or *Regina* for one of the subgroups of the water snakes? Should the snake genus *Liodytes* be combined with *Natrix?* Should the Texas Earless Lizard be split off from *Holbrookia* and placed in another genus (*Cophosaurus*) by itself? One of the problems is that there is no general agreement on the definition of a genus, and the net result is often a switching back and forth of names that may cause endless confusion. The situation is acute in the enormous snake family, the Colubridae (pp. 138–224), and particularly in the subdivision of it that includes the water snakes and their allies. This group still defies classification even though many competent taxonomists have worked on it on a worldwide basis for decades.

Some generic name changes are not in dispute. For example, the newts are now *Notophthalmus* instead of *Diemictylus* as a result of a decision by The International Commission on Zoological Nomenclature, a sort of Supreme Court to which problems concerning taxonomy may be referred for action. There are additional changes that are not in controversy and which the majority of herpetologists have accepted.

Other changes are still being debated. Future study and appeals to the International Commission may result in settling some of them, but others are likely to be argued pro and con for years. Rather than try to anticipate the outcome, and in order to preserve some semblance of stability, I have taken the conservative view in this book and have retained the same generic names that appeared in the first edition in those cases where there is controversy and confusion.

Generic names in this second edition that differ from those used in the first edition are as follows: *Abastor* has been combined with *Farancia; Diemictylus* is changed to *Notophthalmus; Haldea* to *Virginia; Lygosoma* to *Leiolopisma; Manculus* combined with

Eurycea; and *Pseudemys* combined with *Chrysemys.* Also, several species have been transferred to other genera: *Eleutherodactylus augusti* (Barking Frog) is now *Hylactophryne augusti; Ficimia cana* (Western Hooked-nosed Snake) is now *Gyalopion canum; Hyla baudini* (Mexican Treefrog) is now *Smilisca baudini;* and *Hyla ocularis* (Little Grass Frog) is now *Limnaoedus ocularis.*

Common Names: In general, the common names used in this book follow those published in 1956 by the American Society of Ichthyologists and Herpetologists in its journal *Copeia,* but a few adjustments have been made, based on common usage and the urging of experts on certain groups. Where such changes occur, however, the names used in the first edition are also mentioned in order to avoid confusion.

In many instances the common names of the animals honor a herpetologist or general naturalist who is now deceased; for example, Dunn's Spring Salamander and Blanding's Turtle. In each of such cases there is a brief statement about the person in question, who he was, or what he did.

Subspecies: The problem of what to do about subspecies had to be resolved early in the planning stages of the first edition of this book.

In the case of birds only a relatively few subspecies can be identified with accuracy through binoculars. The detection of minor details is difficult, especially since many avian subspecies are based on differences that require examination in the laboratory rather than in the field. The situation with reptiles and amphibians is quite another matter, for, with the specimen at hand, accurate identification to subspecies is normally quite possible.

A uniformly black snake, a yellow one with dark stripes, and others with bold spotted patterns look quite different, but all the serpents on Plate 28 from the Black Rat Snake to the bottom of the page, inclusive, are members of the same species. To illustrate just one and bury the others in the text would be unfair — both to the amateur naturalist and to these distinctively marked animals.

There are many other examples. Some of the subspecies (races) of the harmless Milk Snake strongly resemble the Coral Snake, and one is almost a perfect visual mimic of that dangerous species (Plate 30). Some of the races of the Fence Lizard are striped longitudinally; others have wavy dark crossbands and no well-defined stripes.

So subspecies are in — and the problems that go with them. Some subspecies are separated from their closest relatives by minutiae that will bore the field man, but the data are briefly summarized for those who wish to know. We have tried to include, on the plates or among the line drawings, illustrations of the species *and subspecies* that are visually different and can be told apart without recourse to the microscope, complicated scale counts, checks on internal anatomy, or sophisticated laboratory techniques.

If a subspecies is visually distinct enough to warrant inclusion on the plates, it also rates a separate main entry in the text. Less easily defined subspecies (and a few rare ones) are included under those they most closely resemble. My methods of presenting or listing subspecies are variable and unorthodox, but all races are included. It should be borne strongly in mind that most persons will refer to the illustrations first and the text afterward. Hence, the text has been made to fit the pictures and *not* vice versa.

Zoological taxonomists (persons who classify animals) are far from agreement as to what constitutes a subspecies. It is the general practice to recognize those races that have been defined as such by the author of a review or monograph of a genus or species. In less well-studied groups, opinions tend to differ. It is well known that most animal populations are subject to clinal variations. A cline is a geographical trend in which a certain structural, color, or pattern characteristic shows a gradual change from one part of the range to another. For example, Wood Frogs have long hind legs in the northeastern states, but very short ones in northern Canada and Alaska. The populations at opposite ends of the range are so different that they easily could be classified as different subspecies or even distinct species — if it were not for the gradually changing populations in between them. Often two or more clines are involved, and these may manifest themselves in different directions, one cline progressing from south to north, while another *in the same species* progresses from east to west. Many of the disputes concerning subspecies result from differences of opinion in the interpretation of clines. One taxonomist might consider all Wood Frogs as belonging to a single full species devoid of subspecies; a less conservative one might divide them into two or three or even more subspecies.

Suffice it to say, without becoming deeply involved in this controversial subject, that no two books or lists that include subspecies are likely to be quite in agreement. More stability will undoubtedly be achieved as study material accumulates from critical localities and becomes available to the research worker. In preparing this *Field Guide* I have endeavored to bear the layman's problems in mind, and have stressed the subspecies that *look* different to him. This means that from the taxonomic point of view I have been quite conservative in many instances but distinctly radical in others.

The subspecies, carefully defined and backed by detailed study, is a useful taxon (a classification unit). It provides a name for distinctive populations, and helps point out evolutionary trends and the responses of species to habitats that may differ distinctively in concordance with the various physiographic regions inhabited by the species as a whole. The subspecies has been abused in the past, with a tendency for some taxonomists to assign names to fragmentary or splinter populations. Such extremism has now largely disappeared. On the other hand, I strongly disagree with the handful of herpetologists who would ignore subspecies entirely and who refer to annectent populations as that portion of the species which is black in coloration, the one that has a distinctive spotted pattern, the variety that possesses a larger number of scales than other members of the same species, etc. How much simpler it is to refer to each fraction of the full species by a subspecific name that is applicable to the animals in question.

For those readers of the *Field Guide* who are being exposed to subspecies for the first time, the following should be borne in mind: the scientific name is the clue. If there are three parts to the name (a trinomial), then there are one or more additional related subspecies, each of which bears the same first two names. For example, *Lampropeltis getulus niger* (Black Kingsnake), *Lampropeltis getulus holbrooki* (Speckled Kingsnake), and *Lampropeltis getulus getulus* (Eastern Kingsnake) are all subspecies of the same species. The repetition of *getulus* in the name for the Eastern Kingsnake shows that it was the first member of the group to receive scientific description. In this book the words "subspecies" and "race" are considered to be synonyms and are used interchangeably. If there are only two parts to a scientific name (a binomial), then no subspecies are known or recognized. The term "form" is used to designate any population of reptiles or amphibians that bears a scientific name and regardless of whether a species or subspecies is involved.

Size: Reptiles and amphibians *may* continue to grow as long as they live, rapidly at first but more slowly after maturity. Hence, giant specimens *may* be encountered on very rare occasions. The greatest length that I believe to be *authentic* is given for each animal included in this book. Longer measurements will be called to my attention, no doubt, and some of these may be accurate. Evaluating claims is not easy, for some snake hunters are as notorious as certain anglers. Serpents, like fishes, shrink remarkably in size when stretched along a rule or measuring tape. Hearsay "evidence" about big snakes is not difficult to find. The longest serpent native to the United States is the Eastern Indigo Snake, with a maximum known length of 103½ inches, or a little less than 9 feet (2.629 meters).

Because reptiles and amphibians do not attain standard lengths and then stop growing, their sizes, in most instances, are expressed in this book by three measurements. For the Ringed Salamander, to use an example, the following figures (omitting metric measurements for the moment) appear directly after **Identification:** 5½–7; record 9¼, and they indicate that average adults vary from 5½ to 7 inches in length, whereas the largest specimen on record had a total length of 9¼ inches. In the cases of lizards, which so frequently lose their tails and then grow new but *shorter* ones, the maximum head–body lengths are also included. Among certain species, notably some of the turtles, females not only grow bigger than males but they also look different, so for them there are separate measurements for the two sexes. Approximate sizes of young reptiles at the time of hatching or birth are also given in most instances. Sizes at transformation of amphibians from the larval to adult form are not included for two reasons: there is a dearth of such information for many species, and variations in size are considerable and subject to environmental conditions. If a pond dries up, for example, tadpoles may transform into toadlets or froglets at a much smaller size than if the pond remained filled with water.

The proper methods of taking measurements of animals in each major group are illustrated on the back endpapers. For use in the field there is a metric conversion rule on the back cover of this book (in the hardbound edition).

The Metric System: The United States is planning to convert to the metric system within the next several years. The measurements in this book are therefore given in both the U.S. system and the metric system.

In preparing the metric equivalents a number of problems had to be borne in mind. The measurements of average specimens are rounded to the nearest inch (or half inch) or foot in the U.S. system. Thus, in the case of the Ringed Salamander, used as an example above, the average sizes for adults (5½ to 7 inches) are rounded, whereas the record length (9¼ inches) is an accurate dimension. It can be converted to the nearest tenth of a centimeter (cm), i.e., to the nearest millimeter (mm), but to convert the other measurements in the same fashion would imply more accuracy than exists. So the metric figures for average adults are also rounded to the nearest centimeter or, in some instances, to the nearest half centimeter. Thus, for the Ringed Salamander the metric equivalents of 5½–7 inches; record 9¼ inches are 14–18 centimeters; record 23.5 centimeters.

Tiny animals, however, such as some geckos and many of the frogs, are so small that rounding off their measurements would be impractical. Adults of the Ashy Gecko, for example, have a spread in size of only 2¾ to 2⅞ inches, which would become 7 to 7 centimeters if the two extremes were rounded in the metric system. Because of such problems I have arbitrarily selected 4 inches (10.2 centimeters) as a cutoff point. Any animal in which the largest *average* adult size is less than 4 inches has all of its measurements given to the nearest tenth of a centimeter. Just hatched or newborn young also follow the same 4-inch rule; those species or subspecies in which the young do not exceed 4 inches have their measurements converted to the nearest tenth of a centimeter whereas those that are longer are rounded.

All *record* sizes are also given to the nearest tenth of a centimeter. Bear in mind, however, that record sizes in many parts of the text are implied rather than specifically designated. Among the lizards, where the head–body maximums appear in addition to the total lengths, the longer total length in each case is the record for the species (or subspecies) in question. The measurements of the Broad-headed Skink, for example, are 6½–12¾ (head–body max. 5⅝) inches. The 12¾ inches is the maximum known length for a specimen with a full original tail. Thus, among the lizards the last two figures are converted to the nearest tenth of a centimeter, but the first figure is rounded.

Among those turtles in which separate measurements are listed for the two sexes, the larger figure indicated for males and the larger one for females are *the* records for their respective sexes. Also, if only two figures appear for any animal, such as 5 to 6¾, the larger represents the maximum known size; in such cases the record specimen is only slightly greater in length than the biggest average adults and is lumped with them.

Large measurements are converted to meters (m), such as those for the crocodilians and for which most of the measurements in the U.S. system are given in feet. These are rounded to the nearest tenth of a meter. In converting altitudes from feet, the metric equivalents are rounded to the nearest hundred meters, except that low altitudes are converted to the nearest ten meters. Average weights of large turtles are also rounded off to the nearest kilogram; records are shown to the nearest tenth of a kilogram. Temperatures are given in degrees Fahrenheit followed by degrees Celsius (Centigrade), and both are rounded to the nearest degree.

Voice: Toads and frogs are quite vociferous, at least in season, but only a few other herps of our area produce vocal sounds. The crocodilians grunt, roar, and bellow, and some of the geckos make mouselike squeaks. Kissing, squeaking, popping, and yelping noises have been reported occasionally in salamanders, but the sounds in this last group are usually produced when air is suddenly exhaled through the lips.

Each kind of toad or frog has its own distinctive call, and nearly all can be readily identified by ear after a little practice. The calls normally are associated with the breeding season when males of most species assemble in or near shallow water and start singing lustily for their mates. Some choruses are enormous and may be composed of several species all singing at the same time. Local weather conditions are of paramount importance in stimulating frogs into calling and breeding, and even human activities may start them off, such as when areas are flooded during irrigation and temporary ponds or puddles are formed. Choruses, usually weak, without the enthusiasm of mating time, and composed largely or wholly of young frogs, may sometimes be heard out of season. A few southern species may be vocal at almost any time of year, and treefrogs call intermittently throughout the summer months. The onset and duration of the breeding season varies greatly, depending on locality, latitude, and weather conditions. The times mentioned in the text are only approximations. Certain migratory birds arrive at any given locality on almost the same day every year, but toads and frogs, which are cold-blooded animals and at the mercy of the weather, are highly irregular.

Describing the calls of animals of any kind presents many obstacles, but I have been greatly aided by a large number of recordings made in the field and given to me by W. Frank Blair, Charles M. Bogert, Pauline James, John C. Wottring, and Richard G. Zweifel. Listening to the records mentioned on page 361 will aid you in learning to recognize the calls of many of the species of toads and frogs.

Conservation: As is the case with so many kinds of animals, the reptiles and amphibians are under great pressure, and they are rapidly disappearing from many areas where formerly they were abundant. The senseless slaughter that still continues, the massive destruction of habitats resulting from the activities of mankind, and the exploitation of these animals for the pet trade all take heavy toll.

Despite educational efforts in their behalf and the realization by great numbers of people that they are useful creatures, herps are still destroyed because of human ignorance or vandalism. Snakes are bombarded by rocks or clubbed to death, basking turtles are used for target practice, and so are frogs and lizards by small boys with slingshots. The plight of the alligator, which was relentlessly poached so thoughtless, wealthy persons could brag about owning a fancy wallet, handbag, or pair of shoes, made national headlines.

Ruination of habitats and pollution are probably the worst enemies of reptiles and amphibians. Every new housing, factory, or shopping center development in rural areas decimates the local wildlife populations. The dumping of solid wastes in swamps or marshes also destroys habitats. So does the pollution of streams with industrial and organic sewage. For years we sprayed the countryside with deadly DDT and other long-lasting chlorinated hydrocarbons.

An aroused public, now keenly aware of the ecological-environmental crises that plague so many parts of the world, is bringing pressure to bear that may halt or at least decelerate many of these abuses, but the proliferation of the human population with its attendant demands for land may soon relegate many reptiles and amphibians to wildlife reservations and probably bring about the extinction of many species, or at least exterminate them in and near every megalopolis.

Another, insidious threat is the pet trade. During one year in the early 1970's 2,000,000 reptiles and nearly 600,000 amphibians were imported legally, a very large percentage for sale as pets. The pressure on our native species is even greater. Whatever their source, they are handled in such great numbers that individual care is impossible, and many vendors treat them as so much merchandise, like cans or boxes on a grocer's shelf. Many buyers acquire them as novelties or on sudden impulse, and the losses, in general, are appalling. There is no harm in keeping herps as pets, at least those which are not rare or endangered in nature, but the lay pet owner is usually totally unprepared to cope with the needs of his new purchase. To help you — and them — I have included a chapter on Care in Captivity (pp. 22–29).

In response to these various problems many laws have been passed protecting reptiles and amphibians. Even mere possession of a protected species may earn you a heavy fine or jail sentence. Don't collect any rare or endangered species, and steadfastly refuse to buy specimens of such kinds from anyone.

Concentrate on studying reptiles and amphibians in the field. You can make valuable contributions about behavior and population dynamics through a program of continuous observations of local populations. Also, if you employ techniques for harmlessly marking individual specimens for future positive identification, data on rates of growth, longevity, and movements from one habitat to another can be accumulated. (Similar work with birds, by placing numbered bands on their legs, has yielded an enormous amount of information on migration, duration of life, etc.) If you are seriously interested in undertaking such a project, any competent curator of reptiles in a zoo or museum, or university professor who does research in herpetology, can give you references on how to mark reptiles and amphibians, and perhaps might even be willing to help you get started.

Another subject that has been neglected, except by a few specialists, is the photographing of snakes and frogs and all the others under field conditions. By comparison with the vast array of extraordinarily fine bird pictures that are now available, herpetology is far behind. If you have skill with a camera, here lies a big opportunity for you. Even an average lensman can soon accumulate a collection of reptiles and amphibians in his photo album, a collection that is permanent, needs no cleaning or feeding, and is not destructive to wild populations.

Don't maintain these animals as pets just for the novelty of having them. If you keep them in captivity, initiate a program of study or observation and make records of what you see.

Be kind to habitats. Some species, such as certain salamanders, occur only in restricted areas. By ripping up all the rocks and other shelters, you may do irreparable damage or even exterminate the colony. Replace rocks, logs, and boards after you overturn them. Mind your outdoor manners, and leave the countryside in the same or better condition than you find it. If you discover a colony of any rare or unusual species, keep the information to yourself. Like telling a secret, the news may soon reach the ears of an unscrupulous person who, for private gain, may raid the colony for the pet market.

Introductions: Our herpetological fauna is changing. Besides the several destructive factors mentioned in the paragraphs above, there is the insidious problem of the introduction of exotic species or the transplantation of some of our native herps into areas where they do not naturally occur. The Giant Toad and the Bullfrog are now well established in many localities where they don't belong, and their large size and voracious appetites have resulted in their decimating or even extirpating some of our native species. A great many herps have been introduced into Florida, a number of which are reproducing and thriving. An effort has been made to include all of these in this book, as of the date of going to press. Others may become established, or colonies that apparently had vanished may be found to have survived. For example, the introduced Mexican iguana, *Ctenosaura pectinata,* may still occur at Brownsville, Texas, even though it apparently had disappeared from there some years ago. If you find an exotic that seems to be doing well, report it to the nearest zoo or museum or to me at the Department of Biology, University of New Mexico, Albuquerque.

For the Serious Student: If you have a deep interest in herpetology you may wish to read further on the subject or even join one of the organizations devoted to the study of reptiles and amphibians. Reference books and papers are listed on pp. 355–361. If there is a report available on any or all of these animals for your own state or region, get a copy and keep it handy for ready reference. Reptile clubs have been established in many cities, and information about them can be obtained by inquiring at your local zoo or natural history museum or by writing to the Secretary, Division of Reptiles and Amphibians, National Museum of Natural History, Washington, D.C. 20560. From the latter you can also obtain a pamphlet entitled "Opportunities for the Herpetologist" and information on college courses in herpetology.

There are three major American professional societies concerned with herpetology. These are: The American Society of Ichthyologists and Herpetologists, publishers of *Copeia;* the Herpetologists' League, publishers of *Herpetologica;* and the Society for the Study of Amphibians and Reptiles, publishers of the *Journal of Herpetology.* For information about these or the *Catalogue of American Amphibians and Reptiles* write to the Department of Herpetology, American Museum of Natural History, Central Park W   St., New York, N.Y. 10024, or to the Washington paragraph above.

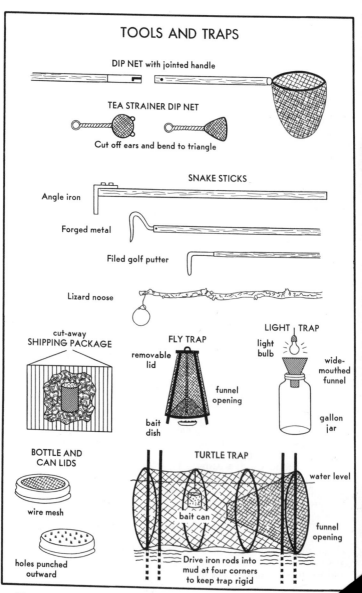

TOOLS AND TRAPS

DIP NET with jointed handle

TEA STRAINER DIP NET

Cut off ears and bend to triangle

SNAKE STICKS

Angle iron

Forged metal

Filed golf putter

Lizard noose

cut-away
SHIPPING PACKAGE

FLY TRAP

removable
lid

funnel
opening

bait
dish

LIGHT TRAP

light
bulb

wide-
mouthed
funnel

gallon
jar

BOTTLE AND
CAN LIDS

wire mesh

holes punched
outward

TURTLE TRAP

water level

bait can

funnel
opening

Drive iron rods into
mud at four corners
to keep trap rigid

Fig. 1. Tools used in catching and transporting reptiles and amphibians. (See also Plate 1.) Fly and light traps are useful for gathering live insects to feed captive lizards, toads, treefrogs, etc.

II

Making and Transporting the Catch

YOUR OWN two hands are the best tools for catching reptiles and amphibians. Most kinds can just be grabbed, but you had better be quick about it, for they are adept at slipping away. But *never try to catch a poisonous snake without proper tools*. Learn to recognize the dangerous species instantly.

Large harmless snakes can be caught without equipment after a little practice. One method is to immobilize the snake by stepping on it gently while you reach for the nearest stick with which to pin down its head. Or you can use your other foot instead of a stick — if you are good at balancing yourself. Once the head is under control, you can pick up the serpent by grasping it firmly but gently just behind the jaws. Use your thumb and middle finger to do the grasping, and place your index finger on top of the snake's head. Another method requires more skill and nerve. This consists of seizing the snake by tail or body and slinging it quickly, but gently, between your legs, meantime clamping your legs together to hold the reptile as in a vise. By pulling the snake slowly forward — tail first, of course — you will eventually come to the head and can grasp it in the approved fashion. Wear bluejeans or clothe yourself in some other tough fabric before you try this, however. Some nonvenomous snakes can bite hard, and you will be exposed to attack from the rear.

A slapping-down technique can be used for those lizards and frogs that freeze in place instead of dashing away. This consists of slapping your flattened hand over them and pinning them down while you grasp a leg (or legs) with your other hand. Don't slap too hard, or there will be casualties. You will have less difficulty in stalking your quarry if you *don't look directly at it*. Move in at an angle, watching it out of the corner of your eye.

Numerous other tricks are used to catch herps by hand, and you may invent some of your own. Tools are essential for some purposes, though, and particularly since considerable field work consists of overturning rocks and other objects beneath which reptiles and amphibians may have taken shelter. Each herpetologist has his own opinion about what implements are best. Here are some of the important tools and their uses.

Snake Stick (or Snake Hook): This is an L-shaped instrument with the long arm serving as a handle; the short arm consists of a piece of metal flattened at the bottom and suitable for pinning a snake to the ground (Fig. 1, p. 16). A golf putter that has been filed down makes a good snake stick. So also does a forged and tempered metal hook securely fastened to a wooden handle. A more simple and easily constructed type consists of an angle iron screwed to the end of a square stick, but it may break or bend if you use it for turning rocks. You will want to experiment, especially in deciding what handle length is best suited to your own stature and techniques. The traditional forked stick is of little value. If the fork is too large, small snakes will slip right through it; if too small, it may severely injure the neck of a large snake.

Snake Tongs: A mechanical device 3 or 4 feet (90 cm or 1.2 m) long that depends upon spring action. By pressing a hand grip, jaws can be made to grasp the body of a snake. Releasing the grip frees the snake. Such tongs are available commercially.

Potato Rake and Stevedore Hook: See Plate 1 for use of these tools.

Collecting Bags: Just a few years ago flour, salt, and sugar came in cloth sacks that made ideal collecting bags, although their loosely sewn edges required restitching on a sewing machine before they could be used with safety. Nowadays you may have to make your own bags, in all probability with the aid of a distaff member of your family. Unbleached muslin or any other sturdy kind of fabric will do. It is well to have two or three different sizes of bags: a large one measuring roughly 20 by 36 inches (50 by 90 cm), a medium one of perhaps 12 by 24 inches (30 by 60 cm), and a small one of about 8 by 16 inches (20 by 40 cm). Pillow cases are acceptable, but beware of castoffs that may have worn thin and which will rip the instant they touch a briar or any other snag in the field.

Loop one or two large bags through your belt to have them handy, and carry little ones in your pocket. Bagging small snakes is generally easy, but with large ones it is best to have your companion hold the bag while you drop in your catch. If the snake is poisonous be sure to carry it in the manner shown on Plate 1. Incidentally, it is prudent practice never to go snake hunting alone. Trying to bag a venomous snake all by yourself is *not* recommended. You will need someone else to help and render first aid if you should be bitten.

After a specimen has been caught and placed inside a cloth bag the simplest way to confine it is to tie an overhand knot in the top (Plate 1). Be careful not to tie the knot around the neck of a snake that may be crawling upward in its efforts to escape! The use of string for tying bags is not recommended — it is something extra to carry with you, it might work loose, and small snakes, in struggling to get out, have been known to push string right off the neck of a bag.

If you catch amphibians, wet the bottoms of the bags and throw in a handful of moss, wet leaves, or other damp vegetation. Putting these animals in plain bags will dry them out, and they will die of desiccation. Even reptiles will survive better if their environment is slightly moist. Remove all livestock from bags as soon as possible; otherwise they may develop sore noses and feet from trying to escape. Wash bags thoroughly before using them again.

Plastic bags are favored by some field men — not the type you use in a refrigerator, but bags fashioned from heavy, sturdy plastic. These are translucent (even almost transparent) so you can see your catch, and lizards cannot climb upward as they frequently do in cloth bags. Canvas bags are too heavy and too closely woven for most purposes. Burlap is useless for almost all herps; the weave is so open and loose they can get through it with little effort.

Glass Jars and Cans: Punch holes in lids with the points *aimed outward*. A tidier job can be done by soldering wire screening to the inner side of a screw-top lid, the kind that is open in the center and is little more than a rim. Both jars and cans have advantages and disadvantages. Glass jars can be broken, but you can see their contents. Cans will stand being dropped, but they will rust (unless they are made of aluminum), and you cannot tell in advance whether an animal is ready to leap out the moment you remove the lid. Jars made of opaque plastic are also dangerous for the same reason.

Dip Net: An ordinary crabbing net will do as a starter, but a deeper, finer-mesh bag will be necessary for holding baby turtles. Cut the handle in half and provide it with a ferrule and locking device for quick assembling or dismounting (Fig. 1, p. 16). The original handle will be too long to fit comfortably into the average automobile.

Tea Strainer Dip Net: An ordinary tea strainer, bent to triangular shape and with its ears lopped off or folded out of the way, makes a handy gadget for catching salamanders. These slippery and elusive amphibians, which normally hide or scurry away when rocks are overturned along tumbling brooks, can often be worked into a tea strainer dip net. When one gets in, clap your hand over the top and you've made your capture.

Turtle Trap: There are several different ways to trap turtles, but a simple, efficient device can be made from three sturdy wire hoops and a supply of stout corded fisherman's netting with a 1-inch (2.5 cm) mesh or slightly smaller. Make the hoops 30 inches (75 cm) in diameter, give or take a little. (Measure the trunk of your car or your storage closet to see what size will fit conveniently.) Tie netting to the hoops to form a collapsible barrel-shaped trap about 4 or 5 feet (1.2 or 1.5 m) long. At one end fashion a narrow slitlike throat extending into the trap and through which a turtle can enter readily (Fig. 1, p. 16). The other end of the barrel can be netted over solidly or another throat can be installed. For the bait, select a can with a tight-fitting lid and about the same size as an ordinary drinking tumbler. Punch numerous holes through the can, through lid, sides, and bottom. Fill the can with freshly chopped raw fish or chicken entrails and hang it from the top of the trap so the bait is completely submerged. The trap can be kept rigidly in place by driving iron bars or rods (the rods used for reinforcing concrete are ideal) down through the ends of the trap and into the mud. As an alternate the trap can be made to float by attaching it to two logs or two pieces of timber, one along each side. When placing the trap, be sure its top extends above the surface of the water. Unless they can get air, turtles entering it may drown.

Headlamps: Amphibians, especially frogs and toads in chorus, are easily found after dark with the aid of a flashlight. So are aquatic snakes, salamanders, and certain other herps. For many purposes a headlamp, strapped around your forehead and powered by batteries fastened to your belt, is superior, particularly since it leaves both hands free for grabbing. Headlamps can be purchased from sporting goods stores or camp outfitters.

Lizard Catchers: Slingshots, rubber-band guns, or large rubber bands shot from the fingers can be used to stun lizards, but some risk is involved; a few may be killed or permanently injured instead of just being temporarily immobilized. Noosing lizards is safer. Attach a small noose of horsehair or fine thread or wire to the end of a pole measuring a few feet in length. (If you use cotton or nylon thread, rub the noose frequently with paraffin to keep it stiff while you are in the field.) Slip the noose over the lizard's head and let it come to rest around the neck. Jerk the pole quickly upward and the lizard is yours! This method requires practice, but is quite efficient when mastered.

Shipping Containers: It occasionally may be necessary to send specimens to a friend or an institution such as a zoo or museum. Large snakes or turtles should be bagged and then placed inside a strong wooden box provided with numerous small holes to permit the flow of air to the inmates. In the case of venomous snakes, wrapping the entire container in stout wire hardware cloth provides a safeguard against escape if the box should be crushed or broken in transit. Snakes of all kinds are barred from the mails. They must be sent by express or some other common carrier. Large turtles are best shipped the same way.

Smaller herps require special packing. Use a can or glass jar with vent holes in the lid (as described on page 19), nearly fill it with slightly damp paper towels (moister for amphibians than for reptiles), and place the animals inside. The towels not only will prevent desiccation but will keep the travelers from getting shaken up too much. Nest the can or jar in the center of a cardboard box or styrofoam container filled with excelsior (Fig. 1, p. 16), shredded paper, or crumpled newspapers. Allow at least 3 inches of packing material on *all* sides of the can or jar. This material will help serve as insulation against heat or cold, and the space between its components becomes a reservoir of air during shipping. The package may be sealed on the outside if desired. Mark it "perishable" and use air service if the recipient is some distance away. To insure prompt delivery pay the extra postage for special handling.

Before attempting any extensive collecting, be sure to check with your state fish or game commission or conservation department. Aside from the restrictions imposed to protect rare and endangered species (see p. 14), there may be other laws you will need to observe. Closed seasons may be stipulated for turtles and frogs in some states, turtle traps (because they also catch fish) may be restricted or even prohibited in others, and catching frogs through the use of lights at night may be forbidden in still others. You may have to apply for a collecting permit. Reptiles and amphibians enjoy far more protection now than they used to get.

As a good conservationist you will sort your catch in the field, select only the specimens you need for your studies, and liberate the others. Don't be a game hog!

Be sure to keep a record of the source of your material. If you should find something unusual or wish to tell a professional herpetologist about it, he will need certain basic information — the exact locality in which it was found, the date, collector's name and address, a description of the habitat, notes on the animal's behavior, and other pertinent data.

III

Care in Captivity

AFTER YOU catch a snake or frog or turtle, what do you do with it? If you are the average outdoor enthusiast you will hold it briefly, check its identity, admire its coloration and pattern, perhaps photograph it, and then turn it loose. But you may wish to keep it for a time. Most reptiles and amphibians are relatively easy to maintain in captivity. They are fun to watch, and the surest way to learn something about them is to keep them close at hand, but, unless you plan special studies or observations, they should be liberated *where you found them* in not more than two or three weeks.

Housing the Catch: The most versatile of all cages is a home aquarium. Perhaps you have one left over from a former interest in mollies, guppies, or other tropical fishes. If not, aquariums are inexpensive to buy. Get a roomy one — 15 inches (38 cm) or more in length and at least 8 to 10 inches (20 to 25 cm) in both width and depth. Then make a heavy or tight-fitting lid of wire screening tacked onto a wooden frame. This is very important, for reptiles and amphibians can crawl, leap, or push their way out with startling agility. Even salamanders, because of the natural adhesion of their wet bodies against the glass, can readily walk up and out. If you are planning to keep lizards or treefrogs, build two hinged doors into the lid so you can get your hand inside to service half their quarters at a time (Fig. 2, p. 24). Don't try to catch these little animals and remove them every time their cage needs cleaning. And that brings up an important rule: Don't handle any specimens more than is necessary. Most of them will settle down and thrive best when they are undisturbed.

Once it is equipped with a lid, your aquarium is ready to serve as a terrarium, a cage, or as a true aquarium for aquatic species.

Preparing a Terrarium: Attractively planted terrariums make excellent homes for many kinds of amphibians, lizards, and small turtles. Fill the bottom of an aquarium with small clean pebbles to a depth of an inch (2.5 cm) to provide drainage. Cover them with a ¼-inch (.5 cm) layer of charcoal chips to help keep the soil sweet. Then add about an inch of loamy or sandy soil. Small plants can be rooted in this, but it is easier and much more practical simply to put the plants in a flower pot, and place the pot (or pots) in the terrarium with its base resting on the charcoal or pebble layer. When you clean up, you lift out the pot instead of having to uproot the plants each time. Frogs and lizards of some kinds like to cling to the sides of a pot. Typical hothouse plants should be selected and ones that will stand watering every day. When they are sprinkled the lizards will lap up the drops. (Many lizards will *not* drink regularly from a water dish.) Other terrarium residents, such as frogs and toads, need a shallow water container made of glass, plastic, or nonrusting or noncorroding metal. Small branches may be placed in the cage for specimens that like to climb.

For lizards from arid habitats the terrarium should be floored with fine gravel or plain, clean, dry sand (no pebbles or charcoal), and potted cactus plants may be used as an appropriate decoration. Such plants cannot stand a daily sprinkling, but water for the lizards can be provided by filling a shallow container to the brim and letting a little of the water spill over to provide a circle of damp sand or gravel around the dish.

Snakes normally do not make good terrarium animals, for they may burrow down out of sight and uproot plants, pebbles, and charcoal. Many toads and turtles may do likewise. Such specimens, if they are to be seen at all, are best kept on bare pebbles, but potted plants and shelters may be added.

Hiding places are a necessity. A piece of bark with its concave side down makes a good shelter under which the residents may secrete themselves; natural cork bark, procurable from most first-class florist shops, is ideal. Small flat stones may be piled up to make a miniature cave, but they must be stacked carefully so they will not collapse on the animals. Small flattish cardboard boxes, with their lids in place and with holes cut through their sides, may also be used, but in the damp environment of a terrarium they may disintegrate; they are better suited for dry cages.

The Semiaquatic Terrarium: Water-loving turtles, newts, and the more aquatic types of frogs often do best if they have a choice of wet and dry environments. This can be accomplished by inserting a partition across the center of the aquarium and piling pebbles on one side of it. The partition can be of stone or slate, or, if these are not at hand, a piece of wood may be used with its ends held firm by inserting small wooden wedges between them and the glass. The pebbles provide a beach on which a potted plant and a shelter may be placed; the other half of the aquarium may be left in open water. Baby turtles may need a ramp, perhaps a small rough stone or piece of bark, on which to climb ashore. Young crocodilians require similar but much larger accomodations. Their pens should be big enough so they can stretch out straight both in the water and out of it.

The True Aquarium: Only a few kinds of reptiles and amphibians can live in water in straight-sided aquariums with no place to crawl out. These include mud, musk, and softshell turtles, rainbow, mud, and swamp snakes, aquatic newts, sirens, amphiumas, mudpuppies, waterdogs, and hellbenders. All of these should have a stone cave at the bottom of the aquarium to serve as a retreat. Aquatic vegetation may be used with most of them, and, in fact, some plant growth to furnish resting and hiding places is almost essential for the smaller kinds.

The Cage: The simplest type of cage is, once again, the home aquarium. For snakes, fold or cut sheets of newspaper (about six to eight pages in thickness) to fit the bottom of the aquarium exactly. These will serve to absorb excess moisture, and when they become soiled they are easily discarded and replaced. More substantial cages are not difficult to construct. The one illustrated in Fig. 2 (below) has wooden sides, back, and bottom, a glass front, and a screened top. The top is hinged at the back and is provided with hasp and staple for a lock. No air holes are necessary at the sides if the top is completely screened; in fact, snakes will rub their noses sore on any rough objects, such as wire tacked over air holes, at cage-floor level.

Install a water dish large enough for the snake to submerge itself completely but heavy enough so it cannot be tipped over. Also provide a hiding place. Bark or stones will do, but here is where the cardboard box with a hole in its side serves to perfection. With the snake inside the box it is a simple matter to lift out the serpent and its house while the cage is cleaned. Most snakes, including

Pool and beach for turtles and frogs

Locked cage for snakes

Terrarium for lizards and treefrogs

Temporary quarters in gallon jar

Fig. 2. Living quarters for the smaller kinds of reptiles and amphibians are easily made from old aquariums, wooden boxes, and glass gallon pickle, mustard, and mayonnaise jars.

water snakes, thrive best if their quarters are kept completely dry except for the contents of the water dish. When conditions are too damp snakes often develop blisters and infections.

Temporary Quarters: A gallon wide-mouthed glass jar can serve as a temporary home for almost any small or medium-sized reptile or amphibian. This can be equipped with stones, sticks, etc., but plain crumpled paper towels are more practical. These can be dampened slightly (for lizards and snakes) or wet thoroughly (for amphibians and turtles). Not only do the towels supply moisture but they also serve as hiding places. The jar should be cleaned at least every other day, and before replacing the towels a small amount of cool (not cold) water should be poured in to give the animals a chance to get a drink. In general, temporary quarters should not be used much more than a week or so. Transfer their inmates to permanent cages or terrariums as quickly as possible.

Outdoor Turtle Pens: Large turtles are scarcely household pets, but they are easily accommodated if you have a spacious backyard where you can construct a turtle pen. Surround an area measuring 5 feet by 8 feet (1.5 m by 2.5 m), or larger, with a wire fence or a masonry wall, making sure that the wire or the foundations descend into the ground for about a foot (30 cm) to discourage burrowing. This depth is adequate for most turtles, but if you keep such efficient diggers as gopher tortoises you will need a stone floor in your pen covered by a foot or more of well-packed soil. The sides of the enclosure should rise about 30 inches (75 cm); the exact height can be determined by testing just how high a wall you can step over comfortably, for stepping over eliminates any need for a door. The outer walls *must* bend well inward or have a substantial overhang, for otherwise the more agile turtles, stinkpots and snappers especially, will climb up and out. A shallow pool of stone or concrete, built so water will not leak out of it, should cover not more than half the pen. This must have gently sloping sides so that even a box turtle can walk out at any point, and it should not be more than about 12 or 15 inches (30 or 40 cm) deep. If at all possible, install a drain at the lowest spot and connect this with a sewer or tile line. (In summertime you may need to clean your pool almost daily, and baling it out with a bucket soon becomes a burdensome chore.) Shelters in the form of logs or stumps should be provided, both in the water and out, for those reptiles that wish to hide, but keep all such objects away from the outer walls or they will serve as ladders for would-be escapers.

Don't try to keep large snappers with other turtles, or babies of any aquatic kinds with adults of their own or other species. During the excitement of feeding time the smaller specimens may be seriously injured or even decapitated by their more voracious elders.

The turtle pen also serves as an excellent place in which to let

turtles hibernate over winter. After nightly temperatures begin
to drop regularly into the low fifties (10° to 12°C), scrub the pool
thoroughly and fill it with fresh water. Then fill the pen to the
brim with wet leaves, tossing them over land and water alike and
atop the turtles. If the weather stays cool the turtles will remain
quiescent under their blanket, but if it turns warm some of them
will burrow upward to the surface to bask briefly before their
winter sleep. Occasionally they may be active enough to walk out
of their enclosure; to be sure they don't, string wire mesh horizontally a foot (30 cm) or more in width around the perimeter of
the pen and well above the leaves, or roof it over completely if it
is small. If the leaves tend to dry out, they should be sprinkled to
keep the hibernators from dying from desiccation.

In summer camps, where large and elaborate turtle pens make
interesting adjuncts to the nature department, it is best to liberate
any native turtles at the end of the season, especially since most
camps close long before the reptiles are ready to retire for the
winter. Exotic turtles or those not occurring locally should be
given to a zoo or museum. Don't turn them loose in a strange
environment.

Temperatures: Reptiles and amphibians are cold-blooded animals whose temperatures, unless they are exposed to sunlight or
heat lamps, closely approximate the temperatures of the room or
cages in which you keep them. When they are cold, body functions slow down and appetites are poor or nonexistent. When they
are too warm they suffer distress; too much heat will kill them.
Temperatures of about 75° to 85° Fahrenheit (24°C to 30°C) are
best for the majority of reptiles; most amphibians will thrive
under somewhat cooler conditions, usually below 70°F (21°C).

In summertime, specimens may be kept in any comparatively
cool place, such as a well-ventilated camp building or in the base-
ment of your home. Some sunshine is usually essential for lizards
and turtles; snakes can get along without it if they eat well and
are given good food. In any event, provision must be made so
that the animals can bask or retreat to the shade in accordance
with their own desires. Hence, outdoor cages should be roomy and
supplied with hiding places. Never set a cage wholly in the sunshine or in a spot where the sun may strike it later in the day
and roast your captives.

In wintertime, normal room temperatures (without too much
nightly chilling) are suitable for most amphibians. Reptiles, if
they are to be active, need to be kept warmer. During the cooler
months your herpetological collection should be installed in a
warm part of the house, and the best location can be determined
by running a few tests with a thermometer for a day or two. Check
for the ideal temperatures mentioned above. Avoid too much drop
at night. For example, don't place cages in a bedroom where the
window normally would be opened at night.

Supplementary heat may be needed, especially for lizards, and this can be supplied by placing an electric lamp (with reflector) atop the cage in such a way as to direct the heat downward. If the cage is large, the lamp should be mounted at an end or side so the reptiles may retreat to a cooler spot if they wish. If the cage is small, then the lamp should be left on only for limited periods of time. Many lizards enjoy temperatures of 95°F (35°C) for a few hours daily, but such readings are too high for most other reptiles and amphibians. Test with a thermometer and adjust your heat source by moving it closer or farther away to produce the proper temperature. Basking places for most lizards, in the form of twigs or small branches, should be provided. Feed the lizards when they are well warmed up.

Don't expect your captives to eat with the same avidity in the wintertime as they do in warm weather, even when they are well supplied with heat. Some of them, turtles and crocodilians in particular, will go off feed for weeks or months at a time. When hunger strikes are long continued, it is often best to transfer the fasters to cooler quarters — to temperatures in the fifties (10° to 15°C) — until spring, but they must be kept moist.

Food: The very large majority of reptiles and amphibians are carnivorous or insectivorous. A few eat vegetable matter.

A good basic food for crocodilians, aquatic salamanders, and virtually all kinds of turtles is canned dog food, but be sure to choose a brand that is nearly all meat. It is advisable to add vitamins and minerals even though the label on the can may indicate the contents have been fortified. The simplest method is to use a drop or two of a vitamin-mineral concentrate (as in baby bottles) and a pinch of bone meal or oyster shell flour (for extra calcium) to the dog food or to lean ground meat, and then stir it in thoroughly. Mold the mixture into small rounded pellets and place them at the water's edge — not in it. The animals will then take a piece at a time. (Of course, if they are in straight-sided aquariums, you will have to drop the food right in with them, but do it sparingly and with due regard for their appetites. There is no point in fouling the water unnecessarily.) Most of these animals will also eat chopped fish (be sure to include the entrails) and any natural food such as insects, worms, or freshly killed tadpoles or crayfish (crack the shells thoroughly).

Turtles of almost all kinds will also eat some vegetable matter. A piece of lettuce or other leafy vegetable should be given at least once each week. Lawn cuttings are savored by some. Tortoises and box turtles should have greens as well as a variety of soft fruits and berries. Even though they may show a preference for vegetable matter (tortoises especially) they should be given a chance to eat meat occasionally.

A good labor-saving practice is to train your turtles to eat in a feeding bowl or pan supplied with shallow water. Place the turtles gently in it and then drop the food near their mouths. Once they get used to this procedure they will eat and strew their food around in an easily cleaned container rather than in their home aquarium. Rinse the turtles off with tepid water before putting them back.

Some kinds of reptiles and amphibians require live insects or other invertebrates. Toads and frogs and most lizards are in this category, and the motion of their prey serves as a triggering mechanism that induces them to spring into action. Some of these animals will starve to death even if surrounded by platoons of dead insects. Drop in a live one and it is seized at once.

Supplying live insects is not difficult during the warmer months. Examine window screens at night for beetles and moths attracted by the lights inside. The simplest method for collecting them consists of placing a jelly glass over the insect, and then sliding a card between the rim and the screen. The same apparatus can be used for imprisoning the spiders you may find in basements, under eaves, or other lurking-places. A light trap is an efficient way of getting nocturnal insects in quantity. Get a gallon glass jar and solder a wide-mouthed kitchen funnel to a large hole cut through its lid. Screw on the lid, place the jar on the ground outdoors at night, and set an electric light bulb an inch or two (2.5 to 5 cm) above the mouth of the funnel (Fig. 1, p. 16). Insects will fly to the light and then tumble into the jar. A fly trap, for use in daytime, can be made on the same general pattern, but upside down and of wire (also see Fig. 1). This is set an inch (2.5 cm) or so above a dish of meat or fish. The flies are attracted to the bait, but in leaving it they fly upward. They strike the wire funnel, walk up it, pass through its neck, and then enter the wire cage above. *Never* use insects that have been exposed to fly sprays or other chemicals. Your captives may be killed if they eat them.

Obtaining insects in wintertime is another matter, at least if you live in Canada or the northern states. If you are plagued with roaches, consider it a blessing in disguise, for here is a readily available food. Live crickets may be purchased from bait supply houses. If you intend keeping lizards and frogs in any quantity you will have to raise flies and meal worms or other insects, and you will have to start weeks or months ahead of time. Consult any experienced reptile keeper or your government department of entomology for instructions.

Small salamanders and frogs will eat tubifex worms, which you can buy from most tropical fish dealers. Larger amphibians eat earthworms, which you can probably dig up for yourself except in the coldest weather. Snakes have specialized feeding habits, and their food is mentioned in the text for each group or species.

A Suggestion: Keeping reptile and amphibian pets is an interesting pastime, but it does take time and effort. In most instances you will find it practical to hold specimens for only a few days or weeks, studying them until you grow quite familiar with them and then liberating them where you caught them. Do not turn them loose in a strange environment. In any event do not keep them after it is obvious they are deteriorating for lack of food or for some other reason.

Pet Store Turtles: If you buy a pet store turtle, pick out a lively one and one that has some weight. Sometimes they are kept so long and improperly that they are virtually starved or desiccated before they are sold at retail. The commercial, so-called turtle food, consisting largely of dried ant "eggs" (really pupae), is not recommended. Turtles with soft shells or whose eyes are closed or which show evidences of a cheesy exudate, are usually suffering from a dietary deficiency.

Many state and local governments have regulations prohibiting the sale of turtles unless they are guaranteed to be free from salmonella. This is a wise precaution, but you also should establish personal procedures to prevent or control salmonella in your own collection. Keeping the water clean by frequent changes is helpful. Don't let children play with turtles, especially if they are still young enough to cram all sorts of objects into their mouths. Wash your hands thoroughly after handling turtles. If you follow these rules, there is little likelihood of having trouble. Keeping water turtles in dry bowls is not recommended.

Larval Amphibians: Tadpoles and salamander larvae are fairly easy to maintain in aquariums. Tadpoles are largely vegetarian during their early stages, and they should be supplied with freshly-boiled lettuce daily. Older tadpoles and salamander larvae are carnivorous and will usually thrive on canned dog food or ground beef that has been fortified with vitamins and minerals. As the time approaches for transformation to the adult stage, a floating object, such as natural cork bark, should be placed in the aquarium so the animals can crawl out when they so desire.

Words of Caution: Remember that many persons dislike reptiles, snakes especially. Your neighbors may resent your keeping such creatures unless you can assure them that your pets are under strict control at all times. Lock all snake cages to forestall escapes and to prevent the younger members of your family from getting into mischief. *Under no circumstances should venomous snakes be kept in a private home or apartment.*

IV

What About
the Snakebite Problem?

THE BEST answer to that question is not to get bitten. Most bites result from the careless handling of venomous snakes by amateurs or by failure to follow proper precautions in the field.

Don't keep venomous snakes in captivity unless you have had experience and use escape-proof cages. It is well to let all poisonous snakes alone. Even while trying to kill them people have been bitten and died. Snakebite can be an extremely serious thing. If complications develop you may be hospitalized for weeks and the experience may cost you thousands of dollars.

In the field wear protective clothing in those districts where poisonous snakes are known to occur. Rubber or knee-high leather boots are of some help. Wear sturdy high shoes for hiking or climbing, not sneakers or other low shoes. Watch where you put your hands when you climb. Don't thrust hands or feet under rock ledges, logs, or stumps that might harbor serpents. Use tools to overturn rocks or logs. Stay on paths or trails and watch where you walk. Never go off alone, and always remain within call of your companions.

Fortunately, snake venom poisoning is rather rare in the U.S., and with prompt, proper, and energetic treatment 99 percent of the victims recover. Your chances of being killed by a snake are considerably fewer than being struck by lightning.

Snake venom is a liquid, usually yellowish in color, secreted by glands on the sides of the head and injected into a victim through grooved or hollow fangs (Fig. 3, p. 31). Venoms, which vary from species to species, are complex mixtures of chemicals capable of producing many destructive changes in various tissues of the body, sometimes in many different places and ways at the same time. Some venom components attack the blood cells and vessels, whereas others have their chief effect on the nervous system, but almost all snake poisons have multiple modes of actions. The venoms of the rattlesnakes, copperheads, and cottonmouths are similar enough so the same first-aid treatment can be used for all, even in the case of the exceptionally dangerous Mojave Rattlesnake. A bite from a snake of that species, which has a powerful neurotoxic venom, can pose a difficult problem for the attending physician, who should be alerted about the possible development of serious generalized manifestations even though there may be only a comparatively mild local reaction.

Fig. 3. VENOM MECHANISM
OF A PIT VIPER

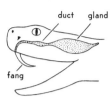

Diagram showing location
of venom gland, duct,
and fang

Bony structure of the
head in striking
position

Position of mouth
and fangs just
before impact

The seeking of competent medical help should be the preeminent objective after any snakebite accident, but if that obviously cannot be achieved within a half hour, first aid should be initiated quickly — provided you are positive a venomous snake was involved. The accepted procedure consists of: (1) use of a constriction band; and (2) incision and suction. (See Plate 2 for detailed first-aid instructions.)

Antivenin, a commercially available snake venom serum, is highly useful in treating snakebite. It should never be administered by anyone except a doctor, however, or a person acting under a doctor's instructions. By federal regulation it can be dispensed only through prescription, and it is not always available. If you have a summer home or cabin, or if you intend to camp where poisonous snakes are prevalent, seek the cooperation of your personal physician. Having serum to take with you might save a life if it should be necessary to rush someone (and the Antivenin) to the nearest hospital, clinic, or doctor's office. Although the serum comes dehydrated and can be kept at temperatures below 90° Fahrenheit (32° C), it should be refrigerated (not frozen) whenever possible.

To relieve pain after a bite, ice cubes can be placed on the wound for one to four hours following the initial incision-suction period — if there is a delay in getting to a doctor. The use of large amounts of ice or other chilling or freezing agents in treating snakebite (cryotherapy), which has received wide notoriety, is *not* recommended.

Was the Snake Really Poisonous?

Any *poisonous* snakebite must be treated as a medical emergency. But suppose a harmless species is involved? Most persons have difficulty making accurate identifications, especially under the emotional stress that usually develops, and many nonpoisonous species do look superficially like certain of the dangerous kinds. Many thousands of persons are bitten by harmless snakes every year with little damage, except for scratches and temporary worry. It is foolish and could even be dangerous to initiate first-aid treatment when no envenomation is involved. Don't start wielding a knife or razor blade unless you are positive such treatment is necessary and medical help is far away.

So learn to identify all your local snakes on sight. Study Plates 30, 34, 35, and 36, and the text from pages 224 to 238. Compile a check list of dangerous snakes occurring in your own vicinity by consulting maps 173 to 184. You may need to make an identification — and quickly — someday on whether a snake is poisonous or not. Bear in mind that it is not always easy to determine whether a venomous or harmless snake is involved just by examining the bite. The puncture marks from the fangs are not always clearly evident. The bites of many harmless snakes may show a whole series of scratches (tooth marks) and they may be far more bloody, at least at first, than bites by poisonous species, but there are no infallible rules.

Most persons can identify a rattlesnake if it is clearly seen, but in the case of the other dangerous species the descriptions of eye witnesses, under the stress of excitement, may be erroneous and misleading. If there is doubt, some member of your party should kill the snake. An examination of the carcass will show for certain whether a venomous species was involved. You can check it for facial pits and a single row of scales (anteriorly) under the tail, characteristics that are common to all the pit vipers (copperheads, cottonmouths, and rattlesnakes) found within our area. (Don't forget that on rare occasions rattlers may have stub tails and no rattles!) You may learn from the dead serpent whether a coral snake did the biting or one of its harmless "mimics." Take the remains to the hospital or doctor's office with you for positive identification.

But a few words of caution! *Handle the dead snake with extreme care.* Reflex action may last a long time, and supposedly dead pit vipers have been known to bite. Use a stick or long-handled tool to pick up and box or bag the remains of any poisonous serpent.

Starting Treatment

If you can get the victim to a hospital or clinic within 30 minutes simply remove rings and bracelets, apply a constriction band as indicated opposite Plate 2, wash the area around the wound to remove any unabsorbed venom, and omit cutting and sucking. Do not permit the victim to move or exercise more than is necessary, and immobilize the bitten limb or part in a natural position. When the doctor takes charge he can test the victim for serum sensitivity, be on the watch for such emergencies as shock and respiratory failure, arrange for transfusions, if necessary, and be prepared to administer antibiotics and various drugs. If the doctor has not previously treated a snakebite case, he can get information and often find an experienced physician with whom to consult by calling the nearest Poison Control Center.

If there is no chance of getting medical help within 30 minutes then incision and suction should be started as soon as possible, especially if there is evidence of the signs and symptoms of pit viper envenomation: (1) *numbness and discoloration* at the site of the bite, (2) marked *swelling,* and (3) the development of *pain* that may become severe. Be careful in cutting fingers or toes so as not to injure superficial blood and nerve structures. If the bite occurs anywhere on a hand or foot, apply a constriction band at the wrist or ankle, moving it as directed opposite Plate 2, but maintaining pressure until medical aid is obtained.

The bite of a coral snake — fortunately extremely rare — presents special difficulties. The venom attacks the nervous system, especially that portion which controls breathing, and the patient may die from respiratory failure. Ordinary first-aid treatment is largely ineffective, and more reliance must be placed on Antivenin and medical aid. A doctor can obtain the specific serum for treatment of a coral snake bite by telephoning the Center for Disease Control, U.S. Public Health Service, Atlanta, Georgia, day or night.

In case of bites by exotic venomous snakes, which sometimes occur in zoos or research stations or because of the extraordinarily risky practice of keeping cobras, vipers, and other dangerous foreign serpents as personal pets, the doctor can call the Antivenin Index Center of the American Association of Zoological Parks and Aquariums at the Oklahoma Poison Control Center. This center, operated through the Oklahoma City Zoo, maintains a current list of foreign antivenins stored at all zoos in the United States and Canada and has a 24-hour telephone answering service.

Prepare for snakebite in advance by studying the directions that come with your suction kit. Review them and practice with the kit at least once a year.

Antivenin for American pit vipers, procurable through prescription as mentioned, is a product of Wyeth Laboratories, a Division of American Home Products Corporation, New York City. A variety of good snakebite suction kits may be obtained through any first-class drugstore.

V

Crocodilians
Order Crocodylia

HUGE lizardlike reptiles that occur in many of the warmer parts of the world. Twenty-one species are known to science, but only two, the American Alligator and the American Crocodile, are native to the United States.

Crocodile: Family Crocodylidae

AMERICAN CROCODILE *Crocodylus acutus*   **Pl. 3**
Identification: 7½–12 ft. (2.3–3.7 m); record 15 ft. (4.6 m) in U.S. to 23 ft.(7.0 m) in S. America. The long tapering snout is the hallmark of the American Crocodile. General overall coloration gray to tannish gray or dark greenish gray with dusky markings. A large tooth (4th) in lower jaw shows prominently when mouth is closed (Fig. 46, opp. Pl. 3). This is visible only at close range and is not well developed in young individuals. *Young:* Gray or greenish gray with narrow black crossbands or rows of spots; about 8½–10 in. (21.5–25.5 cm) when hatched.

The Crocodile, now rare in the United States, is confined chiefly to Florida Bay in the Everglades National Park, Biscayne Bay, and the Florida Keys. Any crocodilian seen in salt or brackish water from Miami southward and along the Keys will *probably* be this species. The Alligator rather rarely leaves fresh water, but is known to occur on Big Pine and other Keys. Although neither of these big reptiles normally attacks human beings, large adults should not be approached. Wounded ones are very dangerous, especially the Crocodile, which is a savage fighter when aroused or captured. Eggs are buried in sand or marl, which may be scooped into low mounds; nests normally are left unguarded, although the females may return to them more or less regularly at night.
Similar species: (1) Alligator has broadly rounded snout and no boldly conspicuous tooth in lower jaw. (2) Spectacled Caiman has curved bony ridge in front of eyes.
Voice: *Male:* A low rumble or growl, less intense than and without penetrating power of the Alligator's roar. *Young:* A high-pitched grunt.

Range: Extr. s. Florida and the Keys, but occasionally wandering north along Florida's w. coast at least to Sarasota Co. Greater Antilles; s. Mexico to Colombia and Ecuador. Map 1

Alligator and Caiman: Family Alligatoridae

AMERICAN ALLIGATOR   Pl. 3
Alligator mississippiensis
Identification: 6–16½ ft.   (1.8–5.0 m);   record   19 ft.   2 in. (5.84 m). The broadly rounded snout will distinguish this big reptile from the American Crocodile of s. Florida, the only species with which a large adult Alligator could possibly be confused in the field. General coloration black, but light markings of young may persist (not too conspicuously) into adulthood. *Young:* Bold yellowish crossbands on black ground color; about 9 in. (23 cm) at hatching.

The Alligator is a characteristic resident of the great river swamps, lakes, bayous, marshes, and other bodies of water of Florida and the Gulf and Lower Atlantic Coastal Plains. All sizes bask. Watch for eyes, heads, or snouts protruding from water surface of 'gator holes along wilder waterways of the South. Nests, mounds of vegetable debris 4 to 7 ft. (1 to 2 m) in diameter, 18 in. to 3 ft. (45 to 90 cm) high, and in which the eggs are buried, should be approached with caution from spring to early autumn, when there may be a guarding female in attendance nearby.

Similar species: (1) American Crocodile has tapering snout and, except in small individuals, the 4th lower jaw tooth protrudes conspicuously upward near snout (Fig. 46, opp. Pl. 3). (2) Spectacled Caiman has curved, bony, crosswise ridge in front of eyes (Fig. 46, opp. Pl. 3).

Voice: *Adult male:* A throaty, bellowing roar with great carrying power. *Adult female:* Bellows like the male but less loudly; grunts like a pig in calling to her young, which she may actively protect from other predators. Under some circumstances the young may remain with her until the spring after they hatch. *Young:* A moaning grunt, like saying *umph-umph-umph* with mouth closed and in a fairly high key. Alligators of all sizes hiss.

Range: Coastal se. N. Carolina to extr. s. Florida and sporadic on the Keys; west to cen. Texas and introduced (?) in the lower Rio Grande Valley. Extermination over large areas, because of poaching and the drastic alteration of habitats by human activities, makes preparation of an accurate range map impossible.

When given protection, the Alligator prospers and soon reoccupies wild areas where it has long been absent.   Map 1

SPECTACLED CAIMAN *Caiman crocodilus*   **Pl. 3**
  Identification: 3½–6 ft. (1.1–1.8 m); record 8 ft. 8 in. (2.64 m).
  Not native, and included here only because juveniles were long
  sold in the pet trade. Escaped or liberated specimens may
  occasionally be met in the field. Ground color greenish-, yellow-
  ish-, or brownish gray with dark brown crossbands. Bony ridge
  in front of eyes (Fig. 46, opp. Pl. 3) may be broken or irregular,
  but it is by far the best means of identification. *Young:* About
  8 in. (20 cm) at hatching.
  Similar species: Young Alligators are *black* with yellowish
  crossbands.
  Range: S. Mexico to n. Argentina.

VI

Turtles
Order Testudines

TURTLES occur in all the continents except Antarctica. They rove the open seas, survive in arid deserts, and are particularly abundant in eastern North America. Worldwide there are well in excess of 200 species.

Some have good field characters that are visible through binoculars, but a great many kinds must be caught for positive idenification. Check the number and arrangement of the scutes on the plastron and whether or not it is hinged. The markings of the soft parts may also require examination. To get a bashful turtle to stick out its neck and legs, put it temporarily in an aquarium or large glass jar full of water and wait quietly; usually the head and neck will soon be extended.

Bear in mind that turtles often turn up in strange places, sometimes far outside their normal ranges. Pets escape, and turtles may be caught, transported, and subsequently liberated unwisely by well-meaning persons.

Snapping Turtles:
Family Chelydridae

LARGE freshwater turtles with short tempers and long tails; of economic value and ranging collectively from Canada to South America.

SNAPPING TURTLE *Chelydra serpentina*   **Pls. 5, 11**
   Identification: 8–12 in. (20–30 cm); record 18½ in. (47.0 cm). Weight of average adults 10–35 lbs. (4.5–16 kg), but to 86 lbs. (39.0 kg) for fattened captive ones. Ugly both in appearance and disposition, this freshwater "loggerhead" is easily recognized by its large head, small plastron, and long tail, which is saw-toothed along the upper side. Carapace in adults varies from almost black to light horn-brown. *Young* (Plate 5): Blackish or dark brown, a light spot at edge of each marginal scute. Carapace very rough and with 3 fairly well defined longitudinal keels. (The rugose condition becomes less prominent as turtle grows

older; adults tend to become smooth, but usually retain traces of the keels.) Tail as long as carapace or longer. Carapace about 1-1¼ in. (2.5-3.2 cm) at hatching.

Any permanent body of fresh water, large or small, is a potential home for a snapper; it even enters brackish water. Snappers *rarely bask* as most other turtles do. Under water they are usually inoffensive, pulling in their heads when stepped on. They often bury themselves in mud in shallow water with only eyes showing. On land they may strike repeatedly; a favorite maneuver is to stand with hind quarters elevated and jaws agape and then lunge forward. Small and medium-sized specimens may be carried by their tails (Plate 1). Keep plastron side toward your leg. Omnivorous — food includes various small aquatic invertebrates, fish, reptiles, birds, mammals, carrion, and a surprisingly large amount of vegetation. Economically important; large numbers are caught for making soups and stews.

Similar species: (1) Alligator Snapper has an extra row of scutes between marginals and costals. (2) Mud and Musk Turtles have short tails and (adults) smooth shells.

Range: S. Canada to Gulf of Mexico; Atlantic Ocean to Rocky Mts., and introduced farther west.

Subspecies: COMMON SNAPPING TURTLE, *Chelydra s. serpentina* (Plates 5 and 11). As described above and with range as stated. FLORIDA SNAPPING TURTLE, *Chelydra s. osceola*. Similar, but with the knobs on the keels more toward the centers of the large scutes; uppersurface of neck with long pointed tubercles (rounded, wartlike tubercles on neck of Common Snapper). *Young:* Chestnut-brown; keels and ridges very prominent. Peninsular Florida and extr. s. Georgia. Additional subspecies occur from s. Mexico to Ecuador.   Map 3

ALLIGATOR SNAPPING TURTLE   Pls. 5, 11
Macroclemys temmincki

Identification: 15–26+ in. (38–66+ cm). Weight 35–150 lbs. (16–68 kg); record 219 lbs. (99.3 kg). Look for the huge head with its strongly hooked beaks, the prominent dorsal keels, and the *extra row of scutes* on each side of the carapace. Likely to be confused only with Common Snapper. *Young* (Plate 5): Brown, shell exceedingly rough; tail very long. About 1¾ in. (4.4 cm) at hatching.

This gigantic freshwater turtle, our largest and one of the largest in the world, often lies at bottom of lake or river with mouth held open. A curious pink process on floor of mouth resembles a worm, wriggles like one, and serves as a lure for fish.

Similar species: Common Snapper has a saw-toothed tail, a smaller head, and also lacks the extra row of scutes between costals and marginals.

Range: Sw. Georgia and n. Florida to e.-cen. Texas; north in Mississippi Valley to Kansas, Iowa, and extr. sw. Indiana.

Map 2

Musk and Mud Turtles:
Family Kinosternidae

THESE are the "stinkpots," the "skillpots," and the "stinking-jims" that often take the fisherman's hook. Such inelegant names derive from a musky secretion exuded at the time of capture from two glandular openings on each side of the body. These are situated where the skin meets the underside of the carapace.

"Bottom crawlers" would be a good way to describe these reptiles. They are strongly aquatic, the musk turtles especially, and rarely leave the water except during rains or in the nesting season. They bask in the open occasionally, but are more likely to take the sun in shallow water with only part of the shell exposed above the surface. Try to catch them if you can, for identification is difficult without flipping them over for a look at the plastron. Use a net or hold the shell far back — their jaws are strong, necks long, and many are very short-tempered.

The musk turtles (*Sternotherus*) have relatively small plastrons that offer little protection for the legs. The anterior lobe is movable on a transverse hinge situated between the 2nd and 3rd *pairs* of plastral scutes (Fig. 4, below), but the hinge usually is not apparent to the eye. It may be demonstrated, however, by moving the front tip of the plastron gently up and down. The pectoral scutes are squarish. This genus ranges from southern Ontario south to and through the Gulf States.

The mud turtles (*Kinosternon*) have much larger plastrons equipped with *two readily discernible* transverse hinges (Fig. 4, below). (The hinges are not developed in the young of either genus.) The pectoral scutes are usually triangular in shape in most of our species. *Kinosternon* ranges from New England to northern Argentina.

The two genera share the following characteristics: (a) there are

Fig. 4. PLASTRONS OF MUD AND MUSK TURTLES

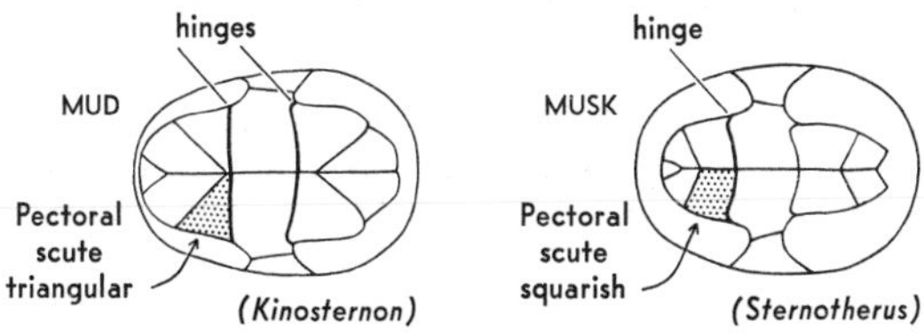

barbels (downward fleshy projections) on the chin and smaller ones on the neck; and (b) the marginal scutes, including the nuchal, are almost always 23 in number (most other turtles have 25). At hatching the young of most species vary from about ¾ to 1 in. (1.9 to 2.5 cm) in carapace length.

These turtles are often mistaken for young snappers, but the Snapping Turtle has a long tail with saw-toothed projections on top. Musk and mud turtles have short tails, but these are useful in distinguishing sexes. Males have longer, stouter tails with a clawlike tip; in females the tails may be little more than nubbins. Males of most species also have 2 rough patches of skin on each hind leg; the patches touch each other when the knee is flexed.

STINKPOT   *Sternotherus odoratus*   **Pls. 4, 5**
Identification: 3¼–4½ in. (8–11.5 cm); record 5⅜ in. (13.7 cm). The only musk turtle occurring north of "Dixie." Two characteristics distinguish it from all other musk turtles: (a) 2 light stripes on head; and (b) barbels on chin *and throat.* Dark pigment may at least partly obscure the head stripes, and in extreme cases the head may be uniformly black. The smooth carapace varies from light olive-brown to almost black and may be irregularly streaked or spotted with dark pigment. Plastron *small* and with *single* hinge. *Male:* Broad areas of soft skin showing between scutes of plastron; tail thick and terminating in a blunt, horny nail. *Female:* Only small areas of skin showing between plastral scutes; tail very small and with or without a sharp, horny nail. *Young:* Carapace dark gray to black, rough in texture, and with a prominent middorsal keel; a smaller keel on each side varying in size from a mere trace to as prominent as in Loggerhead Musk Turtle (Fig. 5, p. 41); keels gradually disappear with age; head stripes prominent; light spot on each marginal (Plate 5).

Extraordinarily abundant in many bodies of water, but not often observed except in shallow, clear-water lakes, ponds, and rivers. In these it may be seen leisurely patrolling the bottom in search of food, its shell looking like a rounded stone, and the illusion being heightened by the green algae that grow on many specimens. Still waters are preferred.

If a turtle ever falls on your head or drops into your canoe, it probably will be this or one of the other musk turtles. Slanting boles of relatively slender trees are occasionally ascended by several species of turtles in wooded swamps, along watercourses, or at edges of marshes, where horizontal basking places are at a premium. Because of small size of plastron and consequent greater mobility of legs, members of the genus *Sternotherus* can most easily negotiate such difficult ascents, and among them the Stinkpot has been recorded as climbing the highest, sometimes 6 or more feet (2 m) above the surface of the water. Sleepy ones may not drop off until your boat passes below them.

Similar species: (1) All other Musk Turtles share the following: (a) heads with *dark* spots, stripes, or streaks on a light ground color; and (b) barbels on chin *only*. (2) Mud Turtles have *large* plastrons with 2 hinges. (3) Snappers have long stout tails.

Range: New England and s. Ontario to s. Florida; west to Wisconsin and Texas; an isolated record from El Sauz, Chihuahua. The Stinkpot occurs in many of the larger, more sluggish streams that penetrate the eastern mts., but is lacking at the higher elevations. Map 7

RAZOR-BACKED MUSK TURTLE Pl. 4; Fig. 7, p. 46
Sternotherus carinatus

Identification: 4–5 in. (10–12.5 cm); record 5⅞ in. (14.9 cm). The upper shell reminds one of the legendary razor-backed hog. A keel is present in *all* turtles of this species, from newest hatchling to oldest adult, and sides of carapace slope down like a tent (Fig. 5, below). Head with dark spots on light ground color. Carapace with dark spots, streaks, or blotches; old adults may lose their patterns and become almost plain horn-colored; scutes slightly overlapping. Plastron *small;* a *single* hinge; *no* gular scute. Barbels on *chin only. Young:* A sharp middorsal keel; shell toothed along each side (Fig. 7, p. 46).

A turtle of the streams and great river swamps of the mid-South. Basks much more frequently than other musk turtles. Margins of carapace are often irregular where bone and overlying tissue have crumbled away. Erosion also occurs in Loggerhead Musk Turtle. In both species it may result from combat between male turtles or from the invasion of damaged tissue by algae or fungi.

Similar species: (1) Stinkpot normally has 2 light lines on head; also has barbels on *throat* as well as chin. (2) Mud Turtles have *large* plastrons with 2 hinges.

Range: Se. Mississippi to e.-cen. Texas; north to cen. Arkansas and se. Oklahoma. Map 9

Fig. 5. TRANSVERSE CROSS SECTIONS OF YOUNG MUSK TURTLES
(Sternotherus)

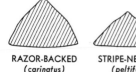

RAZOR-BACKED
(carinatus)
1 keel, sharp slope

STRIPE-NECKED
(peltifer)
1 keel, gentle slope

LOGGERHEAD
(minor)
3 keels

FLATTENED
(depressus)
Blunt keel, low shell

LOGGERHEAD MUSK TURTLE   Pls. 4, 5
Sternotherus minor minor

Identification: 3½–4½ in. (9–11.5 cm); record 5⅚ in. (13.5 cm). This musk turtle has *3 distinct keels* (Fig. 5, p. 41), and distinguishing it would be easy if one could stop right there. But, alas, the keels vanish in old adults, and young Stinkpots sometimes have three well-developed keels. Check the following things first and then allow for sex and age: (a) plastron *small* with *one* hinge and 1 gular scute; (b) barbels on *chin only;* (c) head normally marked with dark spots on a light ground color. *Old male:* Head enormously enlarged. *Female:* Carapace streaked, spotted, or blotched. *Young:* 3 keels that may persist into adulthood; carapace strongly streaked with dark rays; hatchling with *pink* plastron (Plate 5).

A common turtle of the large, clear Florida springs. Like the Stinkpot, it may climb up snags or cypress knees a considerable distance above the water.
Similar species: (1) Stinkpot has barbels on chin *and neck,* and normally 2 light lines on each side of head. (2) Stripe-necked Musk Turtle has only 1 keel. (3) Mud Turtles have *large* plastrons with *2* hinges.
Range: N.-cen. Georgia to se. Alabama and n.-cen. Florida.

Map 8

STRIPE-NECKED MUSK TURTLE   Pl. 4
Sternotherus minor peltifer

Identification: 3–4 in. (7.5–10 cm); record 4½ in. (11.4 cm). Dark stripes on sides of head and neck. A single middorsal keel, prominent in young (Fig. 5, p. 41), but disappearing in older specimens. Carapace gray or brown with dark streaks or spots. Plastron *small,* with *one* hinge; a single gular scute. Barbels on *chin only. Young:* Traces of an additional keel may be evident on each side of carapace.

At home in many streams and rivers of the mid-South. Ascends clear, shallow creeks to elevations of approximately 1000 ft. (300 m) at the edges of the mountains. Feeds chiefly on small snails and insects.
Similar species: (See Fig. 5, p. 41, for shapes of shells.) (1) Sides of head in both Razor-backed and Loggerhead Musk Turtles are marked with dark spots on a light ground color; also, Razor-back has *no* gular scute. (2) Stinkpot has 2 light lines on each side of head and barbels on chin *and* throat. (3) Mud Turtles have *large* plastrons with *2* hinges.
Range: Extr. sw. Virginia and e. Tennessee to the Gulf and the Pearl River, Mississippi.   Map 8

FLATTENED MUSK TURTLE   Pl. 4
Sternotherus depressus

Identification: 3–4 in. (7.5–10 cm); record 4½ in. (11.4 cm). An

extraordinary little turtle that looks almost as though a man
with a heavy foot had trod upon it. In comparison with other
musk turtles the carapace is quite flattened, even in old adults.
In the young there is a blunted dorsal keel and the carapace
flares out at sides (Fig. 5, p. 41); older specimens have flat shells
rounded at edges. Head and neck with network of dark lines
on light ground color. Scutes of carapace slightly overlapping.
Plastron *small*, a gular scute present. Barbels on *chin only*.
Range: Black Warrior River system of nw. Alabama.   Map 9

EASTERN MUD TURTLE   Pls. 4, 5
Kinosternon subrubrum subrubrum

Identification: 3-4 in. (7.5-10 cm); record 4⅞ in. (12.4 cm).
Adults have no distinctive field marks, but throughout most of
its range this is the only mud turtle. Carapace smooth and some
shade of brown, varying from olive horn color to almost black.
The large double-hinged plastron may be plain yellowish brown
or slightly to heavily marked with black or dark brown. A broad
bridge between the shells. Head spotted, mottled, or irregularly
streaked with yellow. *Young* (Plate 5): Carapace rough, black
or very dark brown, and with a middorsal keel; an imperfect
additional keel on each side. Plastron usually black in center
and along the sutures (sometimes virtually solid black); lighter
parts yellow, orange, or reddish; a bright spot on each marginal.

A semiaquatic reptile that wanders away from water much
more often than the Stinkpot. Shallow water preferred —
ditches, wet meadows, small ponds, marshes, etc. This mud
turtle has a strong tolerance for brackish water, and is often
abundant at inner edges of tidal marshes and on many offshore
islands.
Similar species: (1) Striped Mud Turtle has striped head and
carapace. (2) Yellow Mud Turtle has 9th marginal scute much
higher than 8th. (3) Musk Turtles have *small* plastrons with
only a *single* hinge.
Range: Sw. Connecticut and Indiana to Gulf Coast.   Map 13

FLORIDA MUD TURTLE   Fig. 6, p. 44
Kinosternon subrubrum steindachneri

Identification: 3-4 in. (7.5-10 cm); record 4¾ in. (12.1 cm).
Like the Eastern Mud Turtle, but with two main differences:
(a) movable hind lobe of plastron is short, often shorter than
front lobe; and (b) bridge connecting plastron to carapace is
quite narrow (Fig. 6, p. 44). Hence, plastron is proportionately
smaller than in any other mud turtle, and almost as small as
the plastron of a musk turtle. Another point of similarity: many
adult males have greatly enlarged heads, rivaling those of big
male Loggerhead Musk Turtles.

Drainage ditches, marshes, sloughs, ponds, and other small

Fig. 6. PLASTRONS OF MUD TURTLES *(Kinosternon)*

EASTERN
(subrubrum)
Rear lobe large, bridge
broad at abdominal scute

FLORIDA
(steindachneri)
Rear lobe short, bridge
narrow at abdominal scute

YELLOW
(flavescens)
Pectorals pointed,
narrowly in contact

BIG BEND
(murrayi)
Pectorals blunt,
broadly in contact

bodies of water. More aquatic than Eastern Mud Turtle, with which it intergrades in northern Florida.

Similar species: (1) Striped Mud Turtle has light stripes on head and carapace. (2) Musk Turtles have only *one* plastral hinge.

Range: Peninsular Florida; Key Largo and Stock I.   Map 13

MISSISSIPPI MUD TURTLE   Pl. 4
Kinosternon subrubrum hippocrepis

Identification: 3–4¾ in. (7.5–12.1 cm). The distinctive characters of two very different turtles are combined in this mud turtle. It has the large double-hinged plastron of its genus, but also sports 2 light head stripes on each side, like the Stinkpot's. Otherwise, similar to Eastern Mud Turtle, with which it intergrades chiefly east of Mississippi River.

A common turtle of bayous, lagoons, and great swamps of lower Mississippi Valley.

Similar species: In Yellow Mud Turtle the 9th marginal scute is much higher than 8th.

Range: Se. Missouri to e.-cen. Oklahoma and south to the Gulf; extr. w. Florida to cen. Texas.   Map 13

STRIPED MUD TURTLE   *Kinosternon bauri*   Pl. 4
Identification: 3–4 in. (7.5–10 cm); record 4¹³⁄₁₆ in. (12.2 cm). The 3 light stripes on the shell (one down center and another

at each side) may be obscure, particularly in older turtles. If in doubt, also check the head for 2 light stripes on each side. In some specimens scutes of carapace are so nearly transparent that vague outlines of underlying bony structure may be seen through them. *Young:* A narrow middorsal keel; carapace rough; a light spot on each marginal.

Habitats vary from deep drainage canals, sloughs, ponds, and "lettuce" lakes in cypress swamps to wet meadows, ditches, and other small, shallow bodies of water. Often prowls on land, even during the daytime.

Similar species: Musk Turtles have *small* plastrons with only *one* hinge.

Range: S. Georgia to the Florida Keys; an isolated record from S. Carolina.

Subspecies: STRIPED MUD TURTLE, *Kinosternon b. palmarum* (Plate 4). As described above and with lower beak heavily streaked with dark pigment. All of range except Lower Florida Keys. KEY MUD TURTLE, *Kinosternon b. bauri.* Similar but darker; both head and shell stripes may be obscured or almost obliterated by dark pigment; lower jaw not streaked or only slightly so. Lower Florida Keys, from Big Pine Key to Key West.   Map 11

YELLOW MUD TURTLE   Pl. 4; Fig. 7, p. 46
Kinosternon flavescens

Identification: 4–5 in. (10–12.5 cm); record 6⅜ in. (16.2 cm). The *yellowish chin and throat,* that sometimes may be seen from a distance when the turtle is prowling in shallow water or basking at the surface, is a good field character (at least for the wide-ranging western subspecies). But the 9th marginal scute makes identification positive. This scale is distinctly higher than the 8th marginal (10th marginal is also high). Carapace, usually flat or even depressed on top, is olive-brown to olive-green. Pectoral scutes of plastron pointed and only narrowly in contact (Fig. 6, p. 44). Head and neck olive above. *Young:* 9th and 10th marginals as low as 8th (or even lower), except that 9th is always distinctly *peaked* dorsally, with the peak rising above the upper edge of both the 8th and 10th. The 9th and 10th marginals begin to enlarge when shell reaches a length of about 2½ in. (6.4 cm). Small specimens have *bold black dots* at posterior borders of scutes of carapace (Fig. 7, p. 46); 1³⁄₁₆–1³⁄₁₆ in. (2.1–3.0 cm) at hatching.

A common turtle throughout much of its range, occurring in a wide variety of bodies of water, but usually those with muddy bottoms. Toward the west it also utilizes such artificial habitats as cattle tanks, irrigation ditches, cisterns, and sewer drains. May appear on land during rains, while migrating when pools are drying up, or when merely foraging.

Similar species: (1) In all our other Mud Turtles, 9th marginal scute is same height or only slightly higher than 8th. (2) Musk Turtles have *small* plastrons with only *one* hinge. (3) In western Texas also see Big Bend Mud Turtle.

Range: Illinois to n. Mexico.

Subspecies: YELLOW MUD TURTLE, *Kinosternon f. flavescens* (Plate 4). As described above. S. Nebraska to n. Mexico and west to Arizona; isolated colonies in sw. Missouri and adj. Kansas. Mexican subspecies. ILLINOIS MUD TURTLE, *Kinosternon f. spooneri*. Similar but with soft parts black or dark gray, carapace dark brown, and yellow pigment restricted to barbels and front half of lower jaw. Sand prairies of cen. and nw. Illinois; adj. Iowa and Missouri.   Map 10

Fig. 7
CARAPACES OF
BABY MUD AND
MUSK TURTLES

YELLOW MUD
(K. flavescens)
Dark spot on each
large scute; shell
smooth and rounded

RAZOR-BACKED MUSK
(S. carinatus)
A middorsal keel;
shell toothed
along each side

BIG BEND MUD TURTLE   Pl. 4
Kinosternon hirtipes murrayi

Identification: 3¾–6¹¹⁄₁₆ in. (9.5–17.0 cm). Superficially similar to the Eastern Mud Turtle, but larger and more elongated. *Tenth marginal scute distinctly higher than all other marginals.* A faint middorsal keel at all ages. Carapace olive-brown to almost black, each scute narrowly bordered by black. Plastron yellowish; seams bordered by black or dark brown; pectoral scutes broadly in contact (Fig. 6, p. 44). Head brown or olive, profusely marked with small dark spots and streaks.

This Mexican turtle barely enters western Texas, where it has been found in cattle tanks. It probably also occurs in the Rio Grande.

Similar species: Yellow Mud Turtle has a yellow throat, a flattened carapace, the *9th marginal distinctly higher than the 8th,* and the pectoral scutes meeting at a point or only narrowly in contact (Fig. 6, p. 44).

Range: Presidio Co., Texas; the Río Conchos and desert basin drainages of n. Chihuahua south to Zacatecas. Mexican subspecies.   Map 12

Box and Water Turtles:
Family Emydidae

THE largest of all turtle families with representatives in every habitable continent except Australia, and with many kinds in the eastern and central United States and Canada (genera *Clemmys,* this page, to *Emydoidea,* p. 71, inclusive).

Spotted, Bog, and Wood Turtles:
Genus *Clemmys*

THESE are residents chiefly of the Northeast; other members of the genus occur in Europe, Asia, and North Africa, and one lives in our Pacific states.

SPOTTED TURTLE   *Clemmys guttata*   **Pls. 5, 7**
Identification: 3½–4½ in. (9–11.5 cm); record 5 in. (12.7 cm). The "polka-dot turtle." The yellow spots are extremely variable in number. Hatchlings usually have 1 spot on each large scute, but older turtles may be well sprinkled, their spots totaling 100 or more. Conversely, spots on carapace may be few or (rarely) lacking entirely. In such cases, examine head and neck for several yellow or orange spots. *Male:* Horny portion of both jaws almost completely covered with dark pigment. *Female:* Horny portions of both jaws yellowish and virtually unmarked. *Young* (Plate 5): About 1⅛ in. (2.9 cm) at hatching.
     At home in marshy meadows, bogs, swamps, small ponds, ditches, or other shallow bodies of water. Seldom in a hurry. Basking specimens usually enter the water rather leisurely when disturbed, hiding themselves nearby in mud or debris at bottom. *Much* more frequently seen in spring than at other seasons.
Similar species: (1) Bog Turtle has a large orange head patch. (2) Blanding's Turtle has great numbers of yellow spots and a *hinged plastron.*
Range: S. Maine and extr. s. Quebec to extr. e. Illinois; south in the East to n. Florida.   Map 6

BOG TURTLE   *Clemmys muhlenbergi*   **Pl. 7**
Identification: 3–3½ in. (7.6–8.9 cm); record 4½ in. (11.4 cm). Formerly called "Muhlenberg's turtle." The head patch sometimes is yellow or split in 2 parts. Large scutes of carapace may have yellowish or reddish centers. *Young:* About 1 in. (2.5 cm) at hatching.

Although the Bog Turtle still occurs in certain areas, it is rare or completely absent in many regions where it once was fairly abundant. Sphagnum bogs, swamps, and clear, slow-moving meadow streams with muddy bottoms are preferred. Man's propensity for draining and reclaiming such habitats has contributed to its disappearance.

Similar species: Spotted Turtles, a rare few of which completely lack yellow dots on their shells, have many separate yellow or orange spots on their heads and necks.

Range: New York to w. N. Carolina in disjunct colonies; from near sea level in the North to 4000 ft. (1200 m) in the southern mts.   Map 4

WOOD TURTLE   *Clemmys insculpta*   **Pls. 5, 7**
Identification: 5½–7½ in. (14–19 cm); record 9 in. (22.9 cm). The "sculptured turtle." Shell very rough; each large scute in the form of an irregular pyramid rising upward in series of concentric grooves and ridges. Orange on neck and limbs led to vernacular name of "redleg" when this turtle was sold for human food during the early years of the century. *Young* (Plate 5): Shell broad and low, brown or grayish brown; no orange on neck or legs; tail almost as long as carapace; 1 3⁄16–1 5⁄8 in. (3.0–4.1 cm) at hatching.

Next to gopher tortoises and box turtles, this is our most terrestrial turtle. Although quite at home in water and hibernating there, it frequently wanders far afield through woods and meadows, across farmlands, and — often with fatal results — on roads and highways.

Similar species: (1) Both other "land turtles" occurring within the range of Wood Turtle (Blanding's and Eastern Box) have strongly *hinged* plastrons. (2) Adult Diamondbacks are also sculptured, but are restricted to maritime marshes and their environs along the coast; baby Diamondbacks are strongly patterned (Plate 6).

Range: Nova Scotia to e. Minnesota; south in the East to the Virginias.   Map 5

Box Turtles: Genus *Terrapene*

THESE are the "dry-land turtles" that close their shells tightly when danger threatens. Their hallmark is a broad hinge across the plastron, providing movable lobes both fore and aft (Fig. 47, opp. Pl. 7); these fit so neatly against the upper shell that in many individuals not even a knife blade could be inserted between them. With such close-fitting armor, box turtles are well adapted for a terrestrial life, even though they are much more closely related to some of the water turtles than to the gopher tortoises they superficially resemble. The upper jaw ends in a down-turned beak. In hatchlings — average 1⅛ to 1¼ in. (2.9 to 3.2 cm) — the hinge is not functional. The young have a median dorsal ridge, evidences of which may persist in adults. Box turtles, which are strictly North American, range widely over the eastern and central United States and into the Southwest, and they also occur in many parts of Mexico.

As adults, box turtles are kept more frequently as pets than any other turtles. Most adapt themselves readily to captivity, requiring only a backyard or a box of dirt for digging and a shallow pan of water for an occasional soaking. They are omnivorous, and are fond of fruits, berries, and raw hamburger. Canned dog food is a good staple diet. Ages of 30 and 40 years are common, and a very few may reach the century mark.

EASTERN BOX TURTLE   Pls. 5, 7
Terrapene carolina carolina

Identification: 4½–6 in. (11–15 cm); record 7¹³⁄₁₆ in. (19.8 cm). A "land turtle" with a high, domelike shell and an extremely variable coloration and pattern. Both upper and lower shells may be yellow, orange, or olive on black or brown; either dark or light colors may predominate. Four toes on each hind foot. *Male:* Rear lobe of plastron with central concave area; eyes sometimes red. *Female:* Plastron flat or slightly convex; eyes normally brown. *Young* (Plate 5): Shell much flatter; mostly plain grayish brown, but with spot of yellow on each large scute.

Although essentially terrestrial, these turtles sometimes soak themselves by the hour (or day) in mud or water. During hot, dry weather they burrow beneath logs or rotting vegetation, but sharp summer showers usually bring them out of hiding, often in numbers.

Similar species: (1) Top of carapace is flattened in Ornate Box Turtle. (2) Gopher Tortoises have no plastral hinges. (3) Blanding's Turtle has flatter shell, profusion of light dots, and plastral lobes that don't shut tight. Obese Box Turtles also cannot close tight (thus leaving themselves vulnerable to enemies); but, by pushing down one lobe at a time with the fingers, you can check on whether the closure in the turtle's younger and slimmer days would have been complete.

Range: Se. New Hampshire to Georgia, west to Michigan, Illinois, and Tennessee. Within the U.S. this and all other races of *Terrapene carolina* intergrade with one another in most areas where their ranges come in contact; two other races occur in Mexico.

Subspecies: GULF COAST BOX TURTLE, *Terrapene c. major.* Largest of living box turtles — record 8½ in. (21.6 cm). Rear margin of carapace flaring outward and sometimes turning upward to form a gutter instead of extending almost straight downward as in Eastern Box Turtle. Has 4 toes on each hind foot, but no distinctive pattern of its own; some individuals resemble Florida or Three-toed Box Turtles; some adults have white or white-blotched heads. Deep concavity in plastron of males. Occurs in coastal marshes and palmetto-pine forests. Lower Apalachicola region of Florida panhandle. The influence of *major* is evident along a large part of the Gulf Coast where it intergrades with other races from vicinity of Mobile Bay to s. Florida and the lower Keys, and with *triunguis* in s. Louisiana.   Map 28

FLORIDA BOX TURTLE   Pls. 5, 7
Terrapene carolina bauri
Identification: 5–6½ in. (12.5–16.5 cm); record 6⅞ in. (17.5 cm). The light radiating lines may be broken or irregular, at least on some scutes. Also the 2 head lines may be interrupted or incomplete. Usually 3 toes on each hind foot. Deep concavity in plastron of males. *Young:* Yellowish middorsal stripe, involving keel; pattern mottled, yellowish or greenish on dark brown (see Plate 5).
Range: Florida peninsula.   Map 28

THREE-TOED BOX TURTLE   Pl. 7
Terrapene carolina triunguis
Identification: 4½–5 in. (11.5–12.5 cm); record 6½ in. (16.5 cm). Don't depend entirely on the toes—it sometimes has 4! The Florida Box Turtle also usually has only 3 toes on each hind foot, and so do occasional specimens of all other subspecies. Concavity in plastron of males very shallow or absent. A marked tendency for pattern to be replaced (sometimes completely) by plain olive- or horn-colored areas; plastron often plain yellow or horn-colored. Orange or yellow spots usually conspicuous on both head and forelimbs.
Similar species: In Ornate Box Turtle carapace is flattened on top and the pattern of radiating yellow lines is quite constant. Habitat will often separate the two: Ornate most often occurs in open, treeless areas; Three-toed, like its related subspecies, in woodlands, thickets, etc.
Range: Missouri to Texas and sw. Georgia.   Map 28

ORNATE BOX TURTLE *Terrapene ornata ornata* Pl. 7
Identification: 4–5 in. (10–12.5 cm); record 5¾ in. (14.6 cm). Well ornamented above and below and showing far less variation in pattern and coloration than other box turtles. Light lines radiate downward from 3 centers on each side of carapace; 5 to 9 light stripes on 2nd costal scute (Fig. 8, p. 51), but these are sometimes broken into rows of light spots. The strong plastral pattern is characteristic. Other features distinguishing the

Ornate from the *carolina* box turtles are: (a) carapace flat on top, sometimes dished-in, and seldom with any traces of a keel; and (b) plastron large, usually as long as, or longer than, carapace. *Male:* Inner hind toe capable of turning inward at a sharp angle and used in clasping shell of female during mating. Males of *carolina* box turtles lack this feature.

A turtle of the plains and prairies, often found in sandy areas and able to tolerate more arid conditions than its eastern relatives. Burrows to escape heat; rainstorms sometimes result in the sudden appearance of large numbers. Feeds largely on insects, including those found in cattle dung.

Similar species: (1) Three-toed and (2) Eastern Box Turtles, aside from their different patterns, also have high, arched shells and usually retain evidences of a dorsal keel.

Range: Indiana to se. Wyoming, south through Texas and into the coastal prairies of Louisiana; range discontinuous toward northeast.   Map 30

Fig. 8.
RADIATING
LINES IN ORNATE
BOX TURTLES

(2nd costal scute
in each)

ORNATE
(*ornata*)
A few wide lines

DESERT
(*luteola*)
Many narrow lines

DESERT BOX TURTLE   Fig. 8, above
Terrapene ornata luteola

Identification: 4–5 in. (10–12.5 cm); record 5⅞ in. (14.9 cm). Also called "yellow box turtle," a name derived from the tendency for specimens to lose their patterns and to become uniformly yellowish, straw- or horn-colored with age. Younger specimens (and some adults) have an abundance of radiating lines that number 11 to 14 on the 2nd costal scute (Fig. 8, above). In other respects this race resembles Ornate Box Turtle.

A resident of arid grasslands, oak-savannah habitats, and (occasionally) the edges of forests with open herbaceous vegetation.

Range: Northern portions of the Chihuahuan and Sonoran Deserts; intergrades with the Ornate Box Turtle in e.-cen. New Mexico and in a narrow band through the Big Bend region of Texas.   Map 30

Diamondback Terrapins:
Genus *Malaclemys*

MOST celebrated of American turtles. Their succulent flesh, when properly (and laboriously) prepared, rates high on the gourmet's list. During the heyday of the terrapin fad, market hunting seriously reduced them in numbers, but their popularity has waned and they have made a strong comeback in many areas. Terrapins are reptiles of the coastal marshes, rarely straying from salt or brackish water. Their food includes fish, crustaceans, mollusks, and insects. Seven races are recognized, all of a single species, and ranging, collectively, from Massachusetts at least to southern Texas.

Concentric grooves and ridges or concentric dark and light markings on each of the large scutes of the carapace are characteristic. So are the flecked or spotted heads and legs. The carapace has a central keel, low and inconspicuous in the Atlantic Coast races, but prominent and often knobbed in the subspecies along the Gulf of Mexico. Individual variation is great, and some forms are confusingly alike; therefore it is well to lean heavily on geography (the place where the turtle is found) in making identifications.

Females grow considerably larger than males. The sizes given in the text are the standard full lengths of the carapace (see back endpaper). Terrapin marketers used a different system — the length of the *plastron* from its front end to the bottom of the notch at the rear.

NORTHERN DIAMONDBACK TERRAPIN   Pls. 6, 7
Malaclemys terrapin terrapin
  Identification: Adult females 6–9 in. (15–22.9 cm); males 4–5½ in. (10–14.0 cm). The salt-marsh or brackish-water habitat is a good field character. Concentric rings or ridges and spotted head and limbs clinch identification when turtle is at hand. Coloration extremely variable: some specimens have carapace boldly patterned with dark rings on a ground of light gray or light brown, others have shell uniform black or dark brown; plastron orange or yellowish- to greenish-gray, and with or without bold dark markings. In this race the carapace is wedge-shaped when viewed from above, with widest part in rear half; plastron has nearly parallel sides. *Young* (Plate 6): More brightly patterned than most adults; about 1 1⁄16–1¼ in. (2.7–3.2 cm) at hatching.
  Coastal marshes, tidal flats, coves, estuaries, inner edges of barrier beaches — in general, any sheltered and unpolluted body of salt or brackish water.
Similar species: (1) The rough-shelled Wood Turtle has or-

ange on neck and limbs, and it avoids salt water. (2) Snappers and Mud Turtles frequently enter brackish water; Snapper has a long saw-toothed tail, Mud Turtles have hinged plastrons. **Range:** Coastal strip, Cape Cod to Cape Hatteras.

Subspecies: CAROLINA DIAMONDBACK TERRAPIN, *Malaclemys t. centrata.* Very similar, but with sides of carapace more nearly parallel, and sides of plastron tending to curve inward toward rear. Coastal strip, Cape Hatteras to n. Florida. FLORIDA EAST COAST TERRAPIN, *Malaclemys t. tequesta.* Carapace dark or horn-colored and without a pattern of concentric circles; centers of large scutes only a little lighter than areas surrounding them. East coast of Florida. MANGROVE TERRAPIN, *Malaclemys t. rhizophorarum.* Dark spots on neck fused together, producing boldly streaked appearance; bulbous bumps on dorsal keel; has striped "pants." The Florida Keys, chiefly among mangroves.

Map 20

ORNATE DIAMONDBACK TERRAPIN Pl. 7
Malaclemys terrapin macrospilota

Identification: Adult females 6–8 in. (15–20.3 cm); males 4–5½ in. (10–14.0 cm). The orange or yellow centers of the large scutes distinguish this diamondback from all other races. Bulbous bumps or tubercles on middorsal keel are evident in many specimens, juveniles and males especially. *Young:* Entire shell light horn color, except that dorsal scutes are narrowly bordered with black; tubercles also black.

At home in salt or brackish coastal streams and passes, especially those bordered by mangroves. Also may wander offshore or take refuge in the tall stiff grasses that characterize many Gulf beaches.

Range: Florida west coast, Florida Bay to the panhandle.

Subspecies: MISSISSIPPI DIAMONDBACK TERRAPIN, *Malaclemys t. pileata.* A dark turtle; carapace usually uniform black or brown; skin very dark; plastron yellow, often clouded with a dusky shade; a strongly tuberculate central keel; edges of shell orange or yellow and turned upward; most males and some females with a black "mustache" on upper jaw. Averages larger, the record size (an enormous female) 9⅜ in. (23.8 cm). Marshes and estuaries of Gulf Coast from Florida panhandle to w. Louisiana. TEXAS DIAMONDBACK TERRAPIN, *Malaclemys t. littoralis.* Similar to Mississippi Diamondback, but with a deeper shell that has its highest point toward rear of carapace; skin greenish gray, heavily marked with black spots; plastron nearly white; "mustache" usually missing. Coast of Texas and possibly south along the Mexican littoral. Map 20

Map Turtles and Sawbacks:
Genus *Graptemys*

THESE are lake and river turtles. They are shy, quick to plunge from their basking places, and usually difficult to capture. Among them are some of our most beautifully marked and grotesquely adorned turtles. There are ten species, all found in the eastern United States, but several are confined to single river systems emptying into the Gulf of Mexico. All have dorsal keels; in several there are projections upward from the keel (hence the name Sawbacks). Hatching size varies from 1⅛ to 1½ in. (2.9 to 3.8 cm). In the young, the patterns are brightest and the spines best developed; males tend to retain most of the juvenile characteristics; females lose many of them and are often smudged with dark pigment. The heads of adults are quite broad in four species (Map, Mississippi, Alabama, and Barbour's); adult females of the last two have enormously enlarged heads that are efficient machines for crushing the shells of snails and freshwater clams.

The limbs and heads of these turtles are patterned with what may seem at first glance to be a veritable maze of light and dark stripes, whorls, and curlicues. The light head markings, which often take the form of spots or crescents, are useful in making identifications, and so also, in some species, are the light markings on the chins. Although they are subject to considerable individual variation, the chin markings diagrammed on Fig. 9, p. 56 are usually evident. Note that in several of them the characteristic light figures are bordered by *double* dark lines.

The populations of several species of *Graptemys* have been severely decimated by the pollution or channelization (or both) of many southern rivers.

MAP TURTLE *Graptemys geographica*   **Pls. 5, 8**
  Identification: Adult females 7–10¾ in. (18–27.3 cm); males 4–6¼ in. (10–15.9 cm). A young or well-marked specimen carries a map on its back; the light markings resemble an intricate system of canals or waterways laid out on a chart. Shell moderately low; keel may have mere suggestions of knobs on it. A more or less longitudinal yellow spot behind eye, variable in size and shape, but usually largest in specimens from southern part of range. *Female:* Head considerably enlarged; pattern obscure. *Young:* Dorsal keel pronounced; plastral pattern consisting of dark lines bordering seams between the scutes (see Plate 5). Adults have virtually plain plastrons.

The Map Turtle prefers large bodies of water — rivers rather than creeks and lakes rather than ponds. A confirmed but wary basker; slow to retreat into hibernation. In northern lakes it may sometimes be seen walking about in slow motion under ice after early cold snaps. Snails and crayfish are the chief foods. **Similar species:** (1) In False Map Turtle traces of upward projections are usually evident along keel, and head is relatively small. (2) Mississippi Map Turtle has yellow crescent behind eye. (3) Painted Turtles have *unkeeled* shells. (4) In Cooters and Sliders the crushing surface in roof of mouth is ridged (smooth in Map Turtle). Tap turtle gently on snout to make it open mouth. Use a stick, *not* your fingers!

Range: Lakes George and Champlain, westward through St. Lawrence and Great Lakes drainage to Wisconsin; Mississippi drainage from e.-cen. Minnesota south to ne. Louisiana and n. Alabama; Susquehanna drainage, New York to Maryland; introduced in Delaware River.   Map 15

BARBOUR'S MAP TURTLE   Pls. 5, 8
Graptemys barbouri

Identification: Adult females 7–12¾ in. (18–32.4 cm); males 3½–5 in. (9–12.7 cm). The male is a dwarf compared with his mate. Females attain really imposing dimensions, and their heads are enormously enlarged. Adult males retain most markings of young, but big females become smudged and blotched with dark pigment that effectively hides their patterns. *Young:* Strong sawteeth on back; small longitudinal keel on each costal plate; *broad* olive area between and behind eyes. Light markings on marginals, if present, are *narrow;* all the light curved markings on carapace of juvenile illustrated on Plate 5 are reduced or completely absent in many specimens. Light bar *across* or paralleling curve of chin (Fig. 9, p. 56). Half-grown individuals have *deep* plastrons (viewed in profile). Plastral spines present.

Named for Thomas Barbour, herpetologist and long director of Harvard's Museum of Comparative Zoology.

Similar species: (1) Alabama Map Turtle has *longitudinal* light bar running back from point of chin (Fig. 9, p. 56), *broad* light markings on marginals, and no plastral spines. (2) Mississippi Map Turtle has narrow light crescent behind eye.

Range: Apalachicola system (Florida panhandle and adj. Georgia and Alabama).   Map 18

ALABAMA MAP TURTLE   *Graptemys pulchra*   Pl. 8

Identification: Adult females 7–11½ in. (18–29.2 cm); males 3½–5 in. (9–12.7 cm). Big females have grotesquely enlarged heads and strongly resemble females of Barbour's Map Turtle, even to being smudged and blotched with dark pigment. Adult males retain most markings of juveniles. *Young:* A middorsal black line involving the spines; a *broad* olive area between and behind eyes. Light markings on marginals *wide and prominent.*

A *longitudinal* light bar running back from point of chin (Fig. 9, below). Half-grown specimens have *shallow* plastrons (viewed in profile).

This and other map turtles feed to a large extent on snails and other mollusks, the shells of which are crushed by the broad surfaces of the jaws. Aquatic insects also figure largely in the diet, especially of males, which do not have such powerful shell crackers as females.

Similar species: (1) Barbour's Map Turtle has a light bar *across* or following curve of chin (Fig. 9, below), and the light markings on marginals are narrow or obscure. (2) Mississippi Map Turtle has narrow light crescent behind eye.

Range: Streams flowing into Gulf of Mexico — from the Escambia and Alabama River systems to the Pearl River system (extr. w. Florida to extr. e. Louisiana) and well northward into Mississippi and Alabama.   Map 16

MISSISSIPPI MAP TURTLE   Pls. 5, 8
Graptemys kohni

Identification: Adult females 6–10 in. (15–25.4 cm); males 3½–5 in. (9–12.7 cm). The *crescent behind the eye* is the best feature. This sometimes is broken into 2 or 3 parts, but fragmented or whole it cuts off the narrow yellow head stripes from the eye. The eye, on gross inspection, is a wide white ring with black center. *Head large,* especially in females. Toenails on forefeet of large males are elongated. *Young:* These and young of the False Map Turtle, although they have brownish carapaces, have long had the name of "graybacks" in the pet trade. Babies are saw-backed, the rear margin of the carapace is

Fig. 9. CHINS OF MAP TURTLES *(Graptemys)*

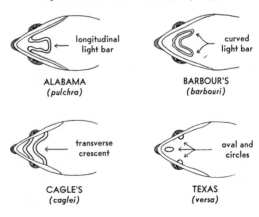

ALABAMA
(pulchra)

longitudinal
light bar

BARBOUR'S
(barbouri)

curved
light bar

CAGLE'S
(caglei)

transverse
crescent

TEXAS
(versa)

oval and
circles

toothed, and there is an intricate design of double dark lines on the plastron (Plate 5).

Similar species: (1) In races of the False Map Turtle one or more light neck stripes reach eye. (2) In Texas Map Turtle the enlarged light postocular stripe extends *backward.*

Presumed distribution: Missouri and portions of adjacent states south to the Gulf, chiefly west of Mississippi River.

Note: The relationships of the turtles of the *Graptemys kohni-pseudogeographica* complex are badly confused. The two species live together and maintain their identities in some areas, notably in Texas and parts of Louisiana, but elsewhere they may hybridize, and every conceivable combination of characters may appear in local populations. Map 19 does not show the range of *kohni;* instead it approximates the general area within which turtles identifiable as *kohni* have been found; hybridization also occurs over a large part of this same area.   Map 19

FALSE MAP TURTLE   Pl. 8
Graptemys pseudogeographica

Identification: Adult females 5–10¾ in. (12.5–27.3 cm); males 3½–5¾ in. (9–14.6 cm). Variable, but usually with this combination of characters: (a) carapace brown; (b) middorsal keel with suggestions of knobs; and (c) light spot or line behind eye. Some of light neck stripes *reach eye.* Head relatively small. *Male:* Greatly elongated toenails on forelegs. *Young:* Saw-backed, spines black; rear of shell toothed; a well-developed plastral pattern. Adults retain indications of the spines, but the teeth of the shell and the plastral pattern become much reduced as turtles grow older.

These reptiles and their close relatives often choose basking spots shunned by other turtles, attempting seemingly impossible climbs up slippery snags that rise at steep angles from the surface of the water.

Similar species: (1) In Mississippi Map Turtle a light crescent prevents neck stripes from reaching the eye. (2) In Map Turtle the keel is lower, and knobs are weak or lacking; head broader and plastral pattern much reduced or absent.

Range: Mississippi drainage from W. Virginia, Ohio, Wisconsin, Minnesota, and s. N. Dakota to Louisiana; Sabine River drainage, Texas and Louisiana. Distribution disjunct toward the northeast.

Subspecies: OUACHITA MAP TURTLE, *Graptemys p. ouachitensis* (Plate 8). A prominent squarish or rectangular light spot behind eye; 1 to 3 light neck lines reach eye; a pair of light spots on jaws, one under the eye and another similar one on chin (Fig. 10, p. 58). Occupies most of the range of the species. SABINE MAP TURTLE, *Graptemys p. sabinensis.* Similar, but with postocular light spot oval or elongate; 5 to 9 light neck stripes reach

OUACHITA
MAP TURTLE
Light spot behind the
eye and 2 below it

Fig. 10

(Graptemys p. ouachitensis)

BIG BEND TURTLE
A large light spot on
side of head, small
one back of eye

(Chrysemys s. gaigeae)

eye; transverse bands under chin; plastron (in juveniles) with
more and finer lines. Sabine River and adjacent drainages.
FALSE MAP TURTLE, *Graptemys p. pseudogeographica.* Yellow
postocular line narrow; no enlarged spots on mandibles; fewer
lines on legs. Attains maximum size of the species; the other
races average considerably smaller. Probably existing as a pure
population only at extreme northern edge of range of species;
intergrades with Ouachita Map Turtle throughout a very large
area.

Note: The subspecies of this turtle are poorly defined, partly
because of individual variation and partly because of hybridization with *Graptemys kohni.* (See *Note* under that species.)

Map 14

TEXAS MAP TURTLE   *Graptemys versa*   **Pl. 8**
   Identification: Adult females 4–5 in. (10–12.7 cm); males
   2¾–3½ in. (7.0–8.9 cm). Smallest of the map turtles. A light
   yellow or orange line (often J-shaped) extending *backward* from
   eye. Chin marked with a light oval near its point and a small,
   light, round spot farther back on each side (Fig. 9, p. 56). The
   more anterior plates of carapace have a quilted effect; they are
   high and rounded at their centers, the sutures forming rather
   deep grooves between them.
   Similar species: Texas Slider has broad light stripes, spots, or
   vertical bars on its head.
   Range: Colorado River system, Texas.   Map 21

CAGLE'S MAP TURTLE   *Graptemys caglei*   **Fig. 9, p. 56**
   Identification: Adult females to 6⅜ in. (16.2 cm); males
   2¾–3⅝ in. (7.0–9.2 cm). Similar in general appearance to Texas
   Map Turtle, but with a dark-edged, cream-colored crescent or
   band across chin (Fig. 9, p. 56). A bold light V-shaped marking
   on top of head, each arm of which often forms a crescent behind
   eye (as in Mississippi Map Turtle). Carapace predominantly
   green (olive in Texas Map Turtle). *Male:* Usually with black
   flecking on light parts of plastron.
      Named for Fred R. Cagle, an authority on turtles and an
   administrator of Tulane University.
   Range: San Antonio–Guadalupe River system of s.-cen. Texas.
                                                          Map 21

RINGED SAWBACK *Graptemys oculifera*   **Pl. 8**
Identification: Adult females 5–8½ in. (12.5–21.6 cm); males 3–4 in. (7.5–10.2 cm). *Broad* light rings on costal plates of carapace. Head has a clownish appearance, as though smeared with grease paint — light mandibles, large postocular yellow spot, and 2 broad light neck stripes entering eye. This and next two species are the spiniest of our turtles. Dorsal spines very conspicuous in the young and adult males, somewhat less so in large females. Also in big females, the light rings may be partially obscured by dark pigment. In juveniles the rear corners of the marginals project outward to give shell a saw-toothed appearance.

The jaws, scissorlike in action, are useful in dismembering insects, which, with mollusks, constitute the principal food of all three sawbacks.
Similar species: The head markings are similar in (1) Black-knobbed and (2) Yellow-blotched Sawbacks, but their names describe those two. In Black-knob, spines are widened and flattened, and rings on carapace are narrow. In Yellow-blotch, light shell markings are of solid colors or are invaded by ground color of shell; they do not form a series of broad, symmetrical rings.
Range: Pearl River system, s. Mississippi and adj. Louisiana.
Map 17

YELLOW-BLOTCHED SAWBACK   **Pl. 8**
Graptemys flavimaculata
Identification: Adult females 4–6⅞ in. (10–17.5 cm); males 3–4 in. (7.5–10.2 cm). *Solid* areas of yellow or orange in each of the large scutes of the carapace. These may be invaded by or surround areas of the dark ground color, but they do not form a series of symmetrical rings. Head markings and gross anatomy are similar to those of Ringed Sawback.
Range: Pascagoula River system, Mississippi.   Map 17

BLACK-KNOBBED SAWBACK   **Pl. 8**
Graptemys nigrinoda
Identification: Adult females 4–7½ in. (10–19.1 cm); males 3–4 in. (7.5–10.2 cm). The spines are broadly knobbed at their tips, like metal spikes struck by a heavy hammer. Light rings on carapace are *narrow*. Specimens from the southwestern part of the range attain the largest sizes and they have a darker and larger plastral pattern than do individuals from farther north and east.

This turtle and the other two sawbacks are most common in streams with moderate current, a bottom of sand or clay, and an abundance of brush, logs, and flood-stranded debris.
Range: Alabama–Tombigbee–Black Warrior River system, Alabama and Mississippi.   Map 17

Cooters, Sliders, and Their Allies:
Genus *Chrysemys*

EXCEPT for the map turtles, many of which are equally addicted to taking the sun, members of this genus are usually the most conspicuous and abundant of all our basking turtles. In spring or autumn, or at any time when the weather is not too hot or too cold, they may rest by the hour on logs, stumps, snags, or rocks. If such "hauling out" places are at a premium, they may stack themselves two and three deep as the late comers climb atop their fellows. A few kinds can be identified through binoculars, especially if their heads are outstretched, but details of carapacial patterns become inconspicuous as their shells dry out in the sun. Check them from a distance or from your car. If you step out the door or approach them on foot the entire assemblage will plunge into the water and out of sight.

The genus *Chrysemys* includes the painted turtles (see pp. 68–69) as well as the big basking turtles, an abundant group in ponds and streams of the Southeast, where people call them cooters,* and the Mississippi Valley, where they are known as sliders. Regardless of which name is applied to any one of the big baskers, they are brown or olive in general appearance with streaks, whorls, or circles of brown or black on a lighter ground color. The carapaces of adults are usually wrinkled with numerous, chiefly longitudinal furrows, and their rear margins are saw-toothed. The head stripes are usually yellowish. Only a few have good field marks. Even in hand they are difficult to identify, particularly since hybridization between species is of frequent occurrence. There are four groups, whose chief characteristics are as follows:

1. **Pond Sliders** (*scripta*). Usually a prominent patch (or patches) of red or yellow on side of head. Lower jaw rounded (flat in all other groups — see Fig. 11, p. 61). Includes Yellow-bellied, Red-eared, Cumberland, and Big Bend Turtles.

2. **River Cooters and Sliders** (*concinna*). A light C-shaped figure on 2nd costal scute (Fig. 12, p. 61). Undersurfaces with numerous dark markings—on plastron, bridge, and marginals. Includes River, Suwannee, and Mobile Cooters and the Slider and Texas Slider.

3. **Coastal Plain Cooters and Sliders** (*floridana*). Light vertical line (or lines) on 2nd costal scute (Fig. 50, opp. Pl. 10). Plastron unmarked or only lightly patterned; dark markings on

---

* Derived from *kuta,* a word for turtle in several African dialects and brought to America during early slave days.

Fig. 11. JAWS OF COOTERS AND SLIDERS *(Chrysemys)*

POND SLIDERS
(scripta)
Rounded lower jaw

**ALL OTHER
GROUPS**
Flattened lower jaw

bridge and marginals fewer and less conspicuous than in the river species. Includes Florida and Peninsula Cooters and Missouri Slider.

4. **Red-bellied Turtles** (*rubriventris* group). Plastron usually red, orange, or coral, at least around edges. Light arrow (Fig. 50, opp. Pl. 10) at front of head (also shared by the pond sliders). Sharp notch at tip of upper jaw bordered on each side by a pronounced cusp (Fig. 50, opp. Pl. 10). Cutting edges of jaws saw-toothed. Includes Red-bellied, Florida Red-bellied, and Alabama Red-bellied Turtles.

Fig. 12

2nd costal scute (arrow).
Turtles of the River Cooter
group have a light "C" on this
scute; those of the Coastal
Plain Cooter group lack it.

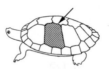

COASTAL PLAIN
(floridana group)

RIVER
(concinna group)

Adult males have greatly elongated nails on their forelimbs (except in Big Bend Turtle — p. 63), and their shells are rather flat compared with the well-arched shells of females. Males, especially of pond sliders and red-bellied turtles, also tend to become dark and to lose their patterns at a smaller size than their mates. Females grow the larger. Hatchlings have a carapace length ranging from about ⅞–1½ in. (2.2–3.8 cm); the babies are strongly and colorfully marked, and have long been popular in the pet trade.

All cooters and sliders are largely vegetarian. Captives should be provided with natural aquatic plants or, in their absence, with lettuce, carrot tops, or other greens. Most of them will also eat raw meat, fish, shellfish, worms, insects, etc.

The genus *Chrysemys* ranges from southern Canada to Argentina. Because so many of its members are similar in appearance, it is advisable to rely heavily on geography, eliminating those species and subspecies not known to occur in your own region (see Maps 22 to 25 and 27 and 29).

YELLOW-BELLIED TURTLE   Pls. 6, 9
Chrysemys scripta scripta
   Identification: 5–8 in. (12.5–20 cm); record 11⅜ in. (28.9 cm).
The yellow blotch behind the eye is the most conspicuous field
mark, but this is strongly evident only in the young and in many
females. Vertical yellow bands on carapace show best when
shell is wet. Yellow underside of both shells marked with round
dusky smudges, one toward rear of each marginal and others
on forward part of plastron. These markings may be reduced
or obscure in older individuals, especially in adult males, which
may completely lose their original patterns, becoming dark and
mottled like old male Red-eared Turtles. Vertical stripes on
"seat of the pants," and *narrow* yellow stripes along front surface of forelegs (Fig. 49, opp. Pl. 9). *Young* (Plate 6): Smudges
or eyelike spots on marginals, bridge, and forepart of plastron.
Such markings may appear all over the plastron, but in that
case the anterior ones are darker and better formed.
   A common turtle of the Southeast. Utilizes a wide variety
of habitats, including rivers, ditches, sloughs, lakes, and ponds.
   Similar species: (1) Chicken Turtle also has striped "pants,"
but yellow stripe on each foreleg is *broad,* and carapace is long
and narrow. (2) See also introductory section on Cooters and
Sliders (pp. 60–61).
   Range: Se. Virginia to n. Florida. Intergrades with Red-eared
Turtle through most of Alabama and parts of adj. states.

Map 25

RED-EARED TURTLE   *Chrysemys scripta elegans*   **Pls. 6, 9**
   Identification: 5–8 in. (12.5–20 cm); record 11 in. (27.9 cm).
The broad *reddish stripe* behind the eye is unique among North
American turtles, but not all Red-ears have it. Rarely, the red
is replaced by yellow. Most trouble will result in trying to
identify adult specimens in which development of dark pigment
(melanism) is advanced. This is a phenomenon in which black
appears on both shells in the form of bars, spots, or blotches.
These spread and run together, obliterating details of original
pattern, and in extreme cases producing a nearly uniform black
or very dark turtle. Even limbs, head, and tail become dark.
Change may start at any age from young adulthood onward,
but males are more susceptible to melanism than females.
Young: Carapace green and with a low keel; plastron profusely
marked with dark eyelike spots (see Plate 6).
   The Red-eared Turtle prefers quiet water with a muddy bottom and a profusion of vegetation. Basks on logs or other
projections above water or in masses of floating plants, but
seldom hauls out on banks.
   Similar species: See introductory section on Cooters and Sliders (pp. 60–61).

Range: Indiana to New Mexico and south to the Gulf and extr. ne. Mexico. Relict colonies in Ohio, W. Virginia, and Kentucky, and introduced and established in many localities through the escape or liberation of captives.

Subspecies: CUMBERLAND TURTLE, *Chrysemys s. troosti.* Similar but with a narrower *yellow* stripe behind eye, fewer and much wider stripes on legs, neck, and head; dark spots under marginals smaller in diameter than light spaces between them. Upper portions of the Cumberland and Tennessee River Valleys from extr. sw. Virginia to extr. ne. Alabama.   Map 25

BIG BEND TURTLE   Fig. 10, p. 58
Chrysemys scripta gaigeae

Identification: 5–8 in. (12.5–20 cm); record 8¾ in. (22.2 cm). A large black-bordered orange spot on the side of the head is a good field character. A second much smaller spot directly behind eye (Fig. 10, p. 58). Carapace pale olive-brown with numerous pale orange curved lines, including one on each marginal. Plastron pale orange and olive with a median series of elongated, concentric dark lines; eyelike spots on underside of marginals. Melanism develops rapidly with age, and large adults, males especially, may have the pattern largely or completely obliterated. The pale head spot may remain in evidence, however. Only race of *C. scripta* north of Mexico in which the nails on the forelimbs of males are not enlarged.

The common pond slider of the Rio Grande and some of its tributaries, occurring in the streams themselves, where there is permanent water; also in nearby ponds, tanks, sloughs, and canals.

Similar species: In Western Painted Turtle there is no large head spot, and plastron is marked with a large dark figure.

Range: Rio Grande in Big Bend region of Texas and Río Conchos system in Chihuahua; Rio Grande valley in s.-cen. New Mexico. Mexican subspecies.   Map 25

RIVER COOTER   *Chrysemys concinna concinna*   Pl. 10

Identification: 9–12 in. (23–30.5 cm); record 12¾ in. (32.4 cm). The *light C on the 2nd costal scute* (Fig. 12, p. 61) rarely can be picked out through binoculars, especially if the turtle has basked long enough for its shell to dry. It must be at hand for accurate checking. Concentric circles are usually well developed in conjunction with the C as well as on the other scutes. The dark plastral pattern tends to follow the seams between the plastral scutes. All (or almost all) marginals have dark spots under them, usually doughnut-shaped, and some may touch the dark markings on the bridge between the shells.

Indigenous to streams of the Piedmont and following such streams to the Atlantic Coast. Hybridization between this species and the Florida Cooter happens so frequently within the Coastal Plain and in other localities that many specimens show some of the characters of both. Because of this and the great difficulty of capturing such wary turtles in the turbid, silt-laden rivers of the region, it is usually practical to list sight records merely as cooters.

Similar species: See Florida Cooter.

Range: S.-cen. and e. Virginia to e. Alabama.   Map 23

SUWANNEE COOTER   Pl. 10
Chrysemys concinna suwanniensis

Identification: 9–13 in. (23–33 cm); record 16⅜ in. (41.6 cm). Darkest and largest of the cooters. Out of water, upper shell may look virtually plain black. Ground color of legs and head also very dark, but head stripes are whitish- to greenish-yellow. Characteristic ventral markings of the river group are strongly evident, with marginal dark spots in contact with dark markings on bridge. Ground color of plastron usually yellow, but brightly tinged with orange in some parts of range. *Young:* Hatchling has dark gray blotches on a pale gray ground, but blotches change within a few days to brownish green separated by a network of yellowish green. Pale C clearly defined. Plastron citron-colored with pattern of grayish brown along seams.

A turtle of the clear spring runs of Florida's upper west coast, and sometimes wandering into the big springs themselves. Also occurs in Gulf of Mexico in the turtle-grass flats off mouths of streams, and occasionally appears far out in the Gulf, its shell encrusted with barnacles.

Similar species: (1) Peninsula Cooter has light "hairpins" on head (Fig. 50, opp. Pl. 10) and *lacks a C;* also, its ventral markings are greatly reduced. (2) Florida Red-bellied Turtle also *lacks a C;* there is an arrow on its head, and the upper jaws have a notch and cusps (Fig. 50, opp. Pl. 10). (3) See also Pond Sliders (p. 60).

Range: W. Florida, Apalachicola River region to vicinity of Tampa Bay.

Subspecies: MOBILE COOTER, *Chrysemys c. mobilensis.* Similar but somewhat smaller and with the ground color of carapace, head, and legs much lighter; head stripes orange-yellow or reddish. Gulf Coast streams, Florida panhandle to extr. se. Texas.
                                                           Map 23

SLIDER   *Chrysemys concinna hieroglyphica*   **Pls. 6, 10**
Identification: 9–13 in. (23–33 cm); record 14¾ in. (37.5 cm). The Mississippi Valley representative of the river group of cooters and sliders. A *light C* (Fig. 12, p. 61) and a strong plastral pattern are in evidence. Many individuals have shell "pinched in" anterior to hind legs.

Like other basking turtles, this one slides into water at the least sign of danger. Hybridization with Missouri Slider occurs frequently; the baby Slider depicted on Plate 6 is somewhat intermediate between the two species.

Similar species: (1) Missouri Sliders *lack the C* and their plastrons are only slightly patterned, if at all. (2) Red-eared Turtles have an oval reddish patch on side of head; old darkened Red-ears may be distinguished by rounded shape of lower jaw (flat in Sliders – see Fig. 11, p. 61). (3) Map Turtles and Saw-backs have strong keels or projections down their backs. (4) In Painted Turtles, rear margin of carapace is smooth (not notched or saw-toothed).

Range: S. Illinois and se. Kansas to cen. Alabama, n. Louisiana, and adj. Texas.   Map 23

TEXAS SLIDER   *Chrysemys concinna texana*   **Pl. 10**
  Identification: 7–10 in. (18–25 cm); record 10¾ in. (27.3 cm). Head markings exceedingly variable, but broad yellowish stripes, spots, or vertical bars are always present, either joined together or separated by dark pigment. The ventral pattern is typical of the river group, but is represented by narrow lines that become dim as the turtle grows and may disappear altogether in old adults. Upper jaw has a notch flanked by a cusp at each side, as in Florida Red-bellied Turtle (Fig. 50, opp. Pl. 10). *Old male:* Shell, head, and limbs rather uniformly mottled, completely obscuring original pattern. (Some females approach this mottled condition.) A pair of swollen ridges extends downward from nostrils and terminates in the cusps.

  Rivers constitute the chief habitat, but this turtle is also found in ditches and cattle tanks.
  Similar species: (1) Red-eared and Big Bend Turtles have rounded lower jaws (flat in Sliders — see Fig. 11, p. 61). (2) Texas Map Turtle has keel down back and carapace has a quilted effect. (3) See also Cagle's Map Turtle.
  Range: Most of cen. Texas and Pecos River into extr. se. New Mexico and south into Coahuila; extr. s. Texas.   Map 23

FLORIDA COOTER   *Chrysemys floridana floridana*   **Pl. 10**
  Identification: 9–13 in. (23–33 cm); record 15⅝ in. (39.7 cm). The unmarked plastron and the dark "doughnuts" or thick, hollow ovals on underside of the marginals are characteristic. Numerous stripes on head, but they normally do not join to form "hairpins" except in regions where intergradation takes place with Peninsula Cooter. One or more vertical light stripes on 2nd costal scute (Fig. 50, opp. Pl. 10).

  A turtle of the Coastal Plain, a resident of permanent bodies of water — ponds, lakes, big swamps or marshes, *and* rivers.

(Except in times of flood, Coastal Plain streams are quiet and sluggish and similar to lakes in many respects.) This turtle will frequently be seen basking, but it is extremely wary and is seldom caught.

Similar species: (1) River Cooter and its subspecies have heavy ventral markings (Plate 10) and a C on the 2nd costal scute (Fig. 12, p. 61). (2) Yellow-bellied Turtle has striped "pants" (Fig. 49, opp. Pl. 9), and there may be a large yellow patch on side of head. (3) Chicken Turtle also has striped "pants" and its carapace is marked with network of light lines. (4) Red-eared Turtle has a reddish oval on each side of head. (5) In Painted Turtles the rear margin of carapace is smooth (not notched or saw-toothed).

Range: Coastal Plain from Virginia to Alabama, but excluding peninsular Florida; established (introduced?) in isolated colonies in N. Carolina and W. Virginia.

Subspecies: MISSOURI SLIDER, *Chrysemys f. hoyi.* Similar but smaller — maximum about 12 in. (30.5 cm); shell relatively short and broad; head stripes numerous and often broken or twisted. S. Illinois, s. Missouri, and se. Kansas to the Gulf.   Map 24

PENINSULA COOTER   Pls. 6, 10
Chrysemys floridana peninsularis

Identification: 9–13 in. (23–33 cm); record 15⅞ in. (40.3 cm). The only cooter with a pair of light "hairpins" atop the head (Fig. 50, opp. Pl. 10). One or both of these may be broken or incomplete. (Submerge turtle in water to make its head come out.) Plastron usually completely unmarked, but marginal spots may be stronger and more numerous than shown on Plate 10. *Young* (Plate 6): Plastron yellow or with slight tinge of orange; never strongly orange or reddish.

A turtle of lakes, sloughs, wet prairies, canals, and Florida's great springs and spring runs; also lives in the Everglades north of Tamiami Trail. Although extremely wary at or above water's surface, it can be closely approached when submerged. Divers equipped with face masks usually find this and other turtles easy to observe under banks of clear streams and springs.

Similar species: (1) Suwannee Cooter has all the characteristics of River Cooters and Sliders — a light C on 2nd costal (Fig. 12, p. 61) and heavy dark ventral markings. (2) Florida Cooter has dark "doughnuts" on the marginals. (3) Plastron of Florida Red-bellied Turtle is reddish, orange, or coral and almost always marked with at least some dark pigment. Peninsula Cooter occasionally hybridizes with both Suwannee Cooter and Florida Redbelly, and it intergrades with Florida Cooter where their respective ranges meet.

Range: Florida peninsula, but excluding southern tip.

Map 24

RED-BELLIED TURTLE *Chrysemys rubriventris* **Pl. 9**
Identification: 10–12½ in. (25–32 cm); record 15¾ in. (40.0 cm). The only *big basking* turtle throughout most of its range. Much larger than painted turtles, with which it often suns on logs or snags. A notch in upper jaw is flanked by a cusp at each side as in Florida Redbelly (Fig. 50, opp. Pl. 10). Adult females with vertical reddish line on each of first 3 costal scutes. Old males mottled with reddish brown. Coloration and pattern highly variable, and melanism is almost universal among large adults in some areas, notably in southern New Jersey. Among the virtually black specimens, the reddish markings usually persist, however, although they may be quite vague. (You may have to wet the shell to see them.) Ground color of plastron yellow, marked with large gray smudges and bordered by a wash of pink or orange-red. Plastrons of old males often mottled with pink and light charcoal-gray. *Young:* Carapace with slight keel and patterned (with yellow or olive on green) in same basic design as in adult female illustrated. Plastron with large dark pattern on coral-red ground color (Fig. 13, below), and often strongly resembling that of Western Painted Turtle (see Plate 6).
    A turtle of ponds, rivers, and, in general, relatively large bodies of fresh water.
Similar species: (1) In both River Cooter and Florida Cooter, upper jaw is rounded and lacks both notch and cusps. (2) In Painted Turtles there are 2 bright yellow spots on each side of head.
Range: S. New Jersey and extr. e. W. Virginia to ne. N. Carolina; Plymouth Co. and Naushon I., Massachusetts.   Map 27

FLORIDA RED-BELLIED TURTLE   **Pl. 10**
Chrysemys nelsoni
    Identification: 8–12 in. (20–30.5 cm); record 13⅜ in. (34.0 cm). Many of these turtles have a distinctly reddish appearance (quite noticeable when submerged in clear water) that contrasts with the darker Peninsula and Suwannee Cooters. Other specimens may be darker and more somber, but plastron is almost always strongly tinted with orange, red, or coral, at least around margins. Light vertical band on the 2nd costal is variable in width from quite wide (Fig. 50, opp. Pl. 10) to relatively narrow.

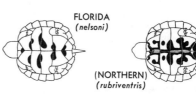

Fig. 13
PLASTRAL PATTERNS OF BABY RED-BELLIED TURTLES

FLORIDA
(nelsoni)

(NORTHERN)
(rubriventris)

The light head stripes are few in number, but they include a *slender arrow* with its shaft between the eyes and its point at the turtle's snout; also the notch in upper jaw is flanked by a strong cusp on each side (Fig. 50, opp. Pl. 10). *Young:* Plastron orange to scarlet-orange (rarely yellow); dark plastral markings tend to be in form of solid semicircles with flat sides along seams between scutes (Fig. 13, p. 67).

A turtle of streams, ponds, lakes, ditches, sloughs, marshes, and mangrove-bordered creeks.

Similar species: (1) Peninsula and (2) Suwannee Cooters *lack:* (a) notch and cusps; and (b) arrow on head.

Range: Florida peninsula and Apalachicola region in the panhandle.

Related species: ALABAMA RED-BELLIED TURTLE, *Chrysemys alabamensis.* Similar, but with numerous head stripes, including the arrow. Mobile Bay and vicinity, Alabama.   Map 29

Painted Turtles:
The Races of *Chrysemys picta*

THESE are readily identified by their *smooth, unkeeled shells* and attractive patterns of *red, yellow,* and *black* (or olive). They live chiefly where the water is shallow, the aquatic vegetation profuse, and the bottom soft and muddy — in ponds, marshes, ditches, edges of lakes, backwaters of streams, and (westward) in prairie sloughs, cattle tanks, and river pools. Their food in nature consists largely of aquatic vegetation, insects, crayfish, and small mollusks.

The shells often become encrusted with a red or brownish deposit (easily scraped away by thumbnail or knife) that may hide the true coloration. Females average larger than their mates. Fully adult males have very long nails on their forefeet. Hatchlings are usually 1 in. (2.5 cm) or less in shell length; *their* carapaces are keeled.

There is only one species, but four distinct subspecies. Where the ranges of these approach one another there are broad areas of overlap in which individual turtles may *combine* the characteristics of different subspecies.

Painted turtles range from coast to coast through the northern states and southern Canada, but they also occur southward virtually (in fresh water) to the Gulf of Mexico from Louisiana to extreme southwestern Alabama. In many northern localities they are the only conspicuous basking turtles.

EASTERN PAINTED TURTLE   Pls. 6, 9
Chrysemys picta picta
Identification: 4½–6 in. (11.5–15 cm); record 7⅛ in. (18.1 cm).

A unique turtle, our only one in which the large scutes of the carapace are in more or less *straight rows across* the back. In other turtles the plates are arranged in alternating fashion across the back. The olive front edges of the large scutes collectively form light bands across carapace — a good field mark easily seen through binoculars when the turtle floats at the surface in clear water. Look also for bright yellow spots on head (2 on each side). For basking specimens, red and black margins of shell are also good checks. Plastron is plain yellow or with a small dark spot or two. (See Plate 6 for young.)

Range: Nova Scotia to Alabama, but intergrading with the Midland Painted Turtle throughout a large area in the Northeast. Map 22

MIDLAND PAINTED TURTLE   Pls. 6, 9
Chrysemys picta marginata

Identification: 4½–5½ in. (11.5–14 cm); record 7⅜ in. (18.7 cm). Very similar to Eastern Painted Turtle, but with large scutes of back alternating instead of running straight across. There is also a dark plastral blotch that is variable in size, shape, and intensity from one turtle to the next. Typically it is oval, involves all, or nearly all, of the scutes, is half or less than width of plastron, and does not normally send out extensions along the seams. (See Plate 6 for young.)

Range: S. Quebec and s. Ontario to Tennessee.   Map 22

SOUTHERN PAINTED TURTLE   Pls. 6, 9
Chrysemys picta dorsalis

Identification: 4–5 in. (10–12.5 cm); record 6⅛ in. (15.6 cm). A *broad* red stripe down the back and normally a plain yellow plastron. Stripe is sometimes yellow; plastron may show 1 or 2 small black spots. (See Plate 6 for young.)

Range: Extr. s. Illinois to the Gulf; w. Alabama to extr. se. Oklahoma. Map 22

WESTERN PAINTED TURTLE   Pls. 6, 9
Chrysemys picta belli

Identification: 5–7 in. (12.5–18 cm); record 9⅞ in. (25.1 cm). Largest of the painted turtles and the one with the most intricate pattern. Not much red on marginals; light, irregular lines appear on carapace, these sometimes so extensive as to form a netlike pattern. Males from North Dakota sometimes have a fine black reticulation superimposed over the normal pattern. Most of plastron occupied by a large dark figure that sends branches out along seams of scutes. (See Plate 6 for young.)

Range: Sw. Ontario and Missouri to the Pacific Northwest; disjunct colonies in the Southwest. Map 22

Chicken and Blanding's Turtles:
Genera *Deirochelys* and *Emydoidea*

DESPITE the marked differences in their patterns, coloration, and plastrons, these two genera are closely related. Their members have the longest necks of any of our turtles except the softshells, and the first vertebral scute is in contact with four marginals and the nuchal. In all other members of the Family Emydidae within our area only two marginals and the nuchal normally are in broad contact with the first vertebral. The Chicken Turtle is southern in distribution and it has a rigid plastron. Blanding's Turtle is northern and its plastron is hinged, an adaptation that has developed in turtles of many genera in many parts of the world.

CHICKEN TURTLE   *Deirochelys reticularia*   **Pls. 6, 9**
Identification: 4–6 in. (10–15 cm); record 10 in. (25.4 cm). The light netlike pattern on the carapace and the extra-long, strongly striped neck are good characters, but they may be invisible if the shell is coated with mud or algae or if the turtle refuses to stick out its neck. In the case of timid specimens, look at the "seat of the pants." The hind legs are *vertically striped* (Fig. 49, opp. Pl. 9). Also look at the forelegs; each one has a *broad* yellow stripe along its front surface. Many specimens have a longitudinal dark bar, spot, or spots on bridge. Carapace is sculptured with small linelike ridges, is much longer than wide, and is widest over the hind legs. *Young* (Plate 6): Carapace with a slight keel; about 1⅛ in. (2.9 cm) at hatching.
   An inhabitant of still water — ponds, marshes, sloughs, and ditches. Frequently walks about on land.
Similar species: Yellow-bellied Turtle also has striped "pants," but yellow lines on forelegs are *narrow* and carapace is much rounder.
Range: Chiefly the Coastal Plain from se. Virginia to e. Texas.
Subspecies: FLORIDA CHICKEN TURTLE, *Deirochelys r. chrysea* (Plate 9). Netlike pattern orange or yellow, bold and broad in younger specimens, but less conspicuous in old ones; rim of carapace boldly edged with orange; plastron orange or bright yellow, unpatterned. Florida peninsula. EASTERN CHICKEN TURTLE, *Deirochelys r. reticularia* (young illustrated on Plate 6). Similar but with the netlike lines greenish or brownish and much narrower; entire turtle less brightly colored. N. Carolina to Mississippi River; well established (introduced?) in Virginia Beach region of se. Virginia. WESTERN CHICKEN TURTLE, *Deirochelys r. miaria*. This race has a rather flat appearance; netlike lines broad, but only a little lighter than the ground color be-

tween them; plastron with dark markings along seams; *under-side* of neck unpatterned in adults. Extr. se. Missouri and se. Oklahoma south to Louisiana and e. Texas.   Map 31

BLANDING'S TURTLE   *Emydoidea blandingi*   **Pls. 5, 7**
   Identification: 5–7½ in. (12.5–19 cm); record 10⁹⁄₁₆ in. (26.8 cm). The "semi-box turtle." Hinge across plastron permits the movable lobes to be pulled well upward toward carapace, but closure is far less complete than in box turtles. The profuse light spots often tend to run together, forming bars or streaks. *Bright yellow on chin and throat* is a good field character that is easily seen through binoculars when turtle basks or floats at water's surface. *Young* (Plate 5): Carapace virtually plain gray or grayish brown; plastron blackish with an edging of yellow; tail much longer proportionately than in adults. About 1⅛–1⅜ in. (2.9–3.5 cm) at hatching.
   Essentially aquatic, but often wanders about on land, although seldom far from marshes, bogs, lakes, or small streams. Usually hisses sharply when picked up in the field. Named for William Blanding, an early Philadelphia naturalist.
   Similar species: (1) Spotted Turtle has fewer and well-separated spots and *no plastral hinge.* (2) Box Turtles can close up tightly, and they have hooklike beaks.
   Range: Nova Scotia to Nebraska; range discontinuous and spotty east of Ohio and Ontario.   Map 26

Gopher Tortoises: Family Testudinidae

THE only tortoises native to the United States. The feet are stumpy, the hind ones elephant-like. The heavily scaled forelimbs, when folded, close the opening of the shell and provide good protection for the head and neck. Carapace high and rounded, each scute with or without a light center. Captives eat grass, lettuce, and a variety of other vegetables and fruit; some show interest in meat. Of the four known species one is confined to the Southeast, two are shared by the United States and Mexico, and one occurs only in arid north central Mexico. The family is represented in all the continents except Australia, and it includes the giant Galápagos and Aldabra tortoises.

GOPHER TORTOISE   *Gopherus polyphemus*   **Pl. 4**
   Identification: 6–9½ in. (15–24 cm); record 14½ in. (36.8 cm). This is the "gopher" of the Deep South. The stumpy feet,

completely without webs, and the rigid, unhinged plastron make
identification easy. Carapace brown or tan; plastron dull yellowish, soft parts grayish brown. Old adults are virtually
smooth, but younger ones have conspicuous growth rings. Compared with the Texas Tortoise, the Gopher Tortoise's carapace
is longer and lower in proportion to its width, its hind feet are
smaller, and the front of its head, when viewed from above, is
rounded (wedge-shaped in Texas Tortoise). *Young:* Considerable orange or yellow on soft parts, plastron, and marginals;
each large carapace scute yellowish but bordered by brown;
about 1¾ in. (4.4 cm) at hatching.

An accomplished burrower. Its tunnels slope downward from
the surface and then usually level off underground. An excavation may be as long as 35 ft. (about 10 m), and wide enough
so the turtle can turn around at any point along its length.
Many other animals seek shelter or live permanently in
"gopher" burrows, these running the gamut from insects to
burrowing owls, raccoons, and opossums. Gopher frogs, indigo
snakes, and diamondback rattlers are frequent guests — a good
point to remember before you start probing into a tunnel.

Tortoises emerge daily in warm weather (usually in the morning before the heat is too great) to forage on grass, leaves, and
such wild fruits or berries as they can find.

Similar Species: Box Turtles have a hinge across plastron.
Range: Sandy regions of Coastal Plain from s. S. Carolina
to extr. e. Louisiana and most of Florida; introduced on Cumberland I., Georgia.   Map 34

TEXAS TORTOISE *Gopherus berlandieri*   **Pl. 4**
Identification: 5½–8 in. (14–20 cm); record 8¾ in. (22.2 cm).
The rounded carapace may be nearly as broad as long, and its
coloration varies from tan to dark brown. Specimens showing
growth rings have a finely sculptured appearance. Feet stumpy;
plastron rigid. Gular scutes of plastron may be greatly elongated, forked, and curved upward, especially in adult males,
which are thus equipped with a weapon useful in overturning
masculine opponents during breeding activities. *Young:* Each
large scute of carapace with a yellow center, and each marginal
edged with same color; about 1½–2 in. (3.8–5.1 cm) at hatching
(both lengthwise and crosswise).

An arid-land counterpart of the Gopher Tortoise that prowls
actively in hot weather, but usually in early morning or late
afternoon. Burrows sometimes are constructed in sandy soil,
but Texas Tortoises normally spend their resting time in shallow
forms or pallets made by scraping away the ground litter and
soil at the base of a bush or clump of grass or cactus. Such
simple shelters may conceal them only partially, but they often
enter mammal burrows. Food consists mainly of grass and the

pads, flowers, and fruits (*tunas*) of the prickly pear, but other vegetation also is eaten.

Similar species: Box Turtles have a hinge across plastron.

Range: S. Texas and ne. Mexico. Map 32

Sea Turtles: Families Cheloniidae and Dermochelyidae

LARGE turtles of tropical seas whose limbs are modified into flippers. They may turn up on beaches, in bays, or at sea, and some kinds nest along the Gulf and Atlantic shores of our southern states. Many travel northward through the warm waters of the Gulf Stream to North Carolina and then continue up the coast to appear during the summer months offshore and in estuaries as far north as New England, Nova Scotia, and Newfoundland. Some apparently follow the Stream to northern Europe. All five kinds have relatives in the Pacific Ocean.

Measurements and weights for larger specimens are often unreliable because of the difficulty of lifting and maneuvering such huge animals, varying techniques of measuring, and estimates which, although sheer guesswork when made, get mellowed by time and repetition and are finally accepted as truth. Adult sea turtles often are battered or encrusted with barnacles, making identification more difficult. If in doubt, be sure to check the scute and headplate diagrams. Be careful in handling or approaching large specimens. They bite and their flippers can deliver punishing blows.

All the sea turtles are in trouble because of overhunting (especially the Green and Hawksbill) and the destruction of enormous numbers of their eggs for human food and for use as an imagined, but worthless, aphrodisiac. A number of turtle nesting beaches, both in the United States and in the tropics, are now given protection during the laying and incubating seasons.

ATLANTIC GREEN TURTLE Pl. 11
Chelonia mydas mydas

Identification: 36–48 in. (91–122 cm); record 55+ in. (140+ cm). Weight 250–450 lbs. (113–204 kg); record 650+ lbs. (295+ kg). General coloration brown. (This turtle's name derives from the greenish fat of the body.) Carapace light or dark brown, sometimes shaded with olive; often with radiating mottled or wavy dark markings or large dark brown blotches. Only 4 costal plates on each side of carapace, the 1st *not* touching the nuchal. *One* pair of prefrontal plates between eyes (Fig. 14, p. 74). Large scutes of carapace do not overlap. *Young:* Dorsum dark brown; venter white except for ends of flippers, which are black but edged with white; a keel down center of back and a pair of keels down plastron; about 2 in. (5.1 cm) at hatching. Hatchlings are black above, but they become much paler by the age of 6 months.

A turtle greatly reduced in numbers because of its succulent flesh and its possession of "calipee" and "calipash." These two ingredients, esteemed for producing a gelatinous consistency in green-turtle soup, are derived from cartilaginous portions of the shell.

Similar species: (1) Hawksbill has *2 pairs* of prefrontals and large scutes on carapace may overlap. (2) In both Loggerhead and Ridley the 1st costal touches the nuchal.

Range: Warmer parts of Atlantic, but straggling north to Massachusetts and south to n. Argentina.

Fig. 14. HEAD PLATES OF SEA TURTLES

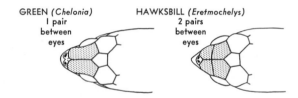

GREEN *(Chelonia)*
1 pair
between
eyes

HAWKSBILL *(Eretmochelys)*
2 pairs
between
eyes

ATLANTIC HAWKSBILL   Pl. 11
Eretmochelys imbricata imbricata

Identification: 30–35 in. (76–89 cm); record 36+ in. (91+ cm). Weight 95–165 lbs. (43–75 kg); record 280 lbs. (127.0 kg). The large scutes of the carapace overlap, except in very old individuals in which they lie side by side as in most other turtles. A keel down center of carapace. General coloration brown. Some specimens, smaller ones especially, show a tortoise-shell pattern. Four costal plates on each side of carapace, the 1st *not* touching the nuchal; *2 pairs* of prefrontals between eyes (Fig. 14, above). *Young:* Black or very dark brown above and below except for raised ridges, edges of shell, and areas on neck and flippers — all of which are light brown; 1 middorsal and 2 plastral keels; about 1½–1¾ in. (3.8–4.4 cm) at hatching.

Source of the tortoise shell of commerce, and still in demand as a luxury item even though plastics have replaced many of its former uses.

Similar species: (1) Green Turtle has only *one pair* of prefrontals between eyes, and scutes do not overlap (except in very young). (2) In Loggerhead and Ridley there are 5 or more costals on each side of carapace, the 1st touching the nuchal.

Range: Warmer parts of Atlantic, but straggling north to s. New England and south to s. Brazil.

ATLANTIC LOGGERHEAD   Pl. 11
Caretta caretta caretta

Identification: 31–45 in. (79–114 cm); record 48+ in. (122+ cm). Weight 170–350 lbs. (77–159 kg); record 500+ lbs. (227+ kg). Reddish-brown coloration offers quickest clue, but also check arrangement of the scutes. Number of costals on each side of carapace is 5 or more, and the 1st one always *touches* the nuchal. There are 3 (usually) or 4 large scutes on bridge between shells (see Fig. 51, opp. Pl. 11), but these are poreless. There is also a middorsal keel, but this becomes low and inconspicuous in large specimens. *Young:* Brown above and whitish, yellowish, or tan beneath; 3 dorsal keels and 2 plastral keels; 1⅝–1⅞ in. (4.1–4.8 cm) at hatching.

Similar species: (1) The Ridley is smaller, has an almost circular olive-green carapace (gray in young specimens), usually has an interanal scute, and almost always has 4 large, pored scutes on bridge. (2) In both Hawksbill and Green Turtles the 1st costal does *not* touch the nuchal.

Range: Warm waters of Atlantic Ocean, but frequently appearing in summer as far north as New England and occasionally even the Canadian Maritime Provinces; also south to Argentina. Nests regularly north to the beaches of the Carolinas and (rarely) to Maryland and New Jersey.

ATLANTIC RIDLEY *Lepidochelys kempi*   Pl. 11

Identification: 23–27½ in. (58–70 cm); record 29½ in. (74.9 cm). Weight 80–100 lbs. (36–45 kg); record 110 lbs. (49.9 kg). Our only sea turtle with an almost circular carapace; olive-green above and yellow below (gray above in smaller specimens). Five costals on each side of carapace, the 1st one *touching* the nuchal. Almost invariably *4* (rarely 5) enlarged scutes on bridge, *each pierced by a pore near the posterior edge;* usually an interanal scute (Fig. 51, opp. Pl. 11) at posterior tip of plastron. *Young:* Almost completely dark gray; a short streak of light gray along rear edge of front flipper; 3 tuberculate dorsal ridges and 4 plastral ones; about 1½–1¾ in. (3.8–4.4 cm) at hatching.

Smallest of the Atlantic sea turtles and widely known as the "bastard turtle" because of the erroneous belief it is a cross between the Loggerhead and Green Turtle.

Similar species: (1) The much larger Loggerhead is reddish brown, it lacks an interanal scute, and the 3 or 4 large scutes on bridge are poreless. (2) In both the Hawksbill and Green Turtle the 1st costal does *not* touch the nuchal.

Range: Chiefly Gulf of Mexico, but often appearing in summer

along the Atlantic Coast to New England and Nova Scotia.
Note: The Indo-Pacific Ridley, *Lepidochelys olivacea,* may eventually appear in Florida waters. Nesting colonies, apparently derived from migrants across the Atlantic Ocean from West Africa, occur along several beaches of the Guianas and Trinidad, and stray specimens are known from Puerto Rico and the northern coast of Cuba. In *olivacea* there are usually 6 or 7 costals (sometimes as many as 9) on each side of the carapace, instead of the usual 5 as in *kempi;* the middle marginals are mostly wider than long in *kempi* (longer than wide in *olivacea*).

ATLANTIC LEATHERBACK   Pl. 11
Dermochelys coriacea coriacea

Identification: 54–70 in. (137–178 cm); record 72+ in. (183+ cm). Weight 650–1200 lbs. (295–544 kg); record 1500± lbs. (680± kg). Largest of all living turtles. *Seven prominent longitudinal ridges on carapace.* Five similar ridges on plastron. Carapace and plastron have no scutes, but are covered instead by a smooth, slaty-black to dark bluish-black skin. Irregular patches of white or pink may appear almost anywhere; white predominates on the plastron. *Young:* Black and white and much more conspicuously marked than adults; covered with great numbers of small, beady scales, which later are shed; tail keeled above; about 2½–3 in. (6.4–7.6 cm) at hatching.

A strong and powerful swimmer that uses its jaws and flippers with telling effect if attacked or restrained. When hurt it emits cries that have been likened to groans, roars, and bellows. Despite its great size the Leatherback feeds chiefly on jellyfish. Long, backward-projecting spines that line both the mouth and esophagus help in swallowing such soft and slimy food. This turtle has the extraordinary ability to maintain its deep body temperature at a considerably higher level than that of the cold water in which it is found along our northern coasts during summer.

Range: Open seas — chiefly warmer parts of Atlantic Ocean, but frequently appearing in New England waters and north to Newfoundland during the summer months. Nests along the east coast of Florida and on several beaches around the Gulf of Mexico.

Softshell Turtles:
Family Trionychidae

THESE animated pancakes belie the traditional slowness of the turtle. They are powerful swimmers, and they can run on land with startling speed and agility. The shell is soft and leathery, bends freely at the sides and rear, and is completely devoid of scales or scutes. Vague outlines of the underlying bony structure often show through the skin of the plastron.

All species are aquatic. They may bask ashore, but only where they can slide or dash into the water in literally a split second. A frequent habit is to lie buried in mud or sand in shallow water with only the eyes and snout exposed and where, when the long neck is extended, the nostrils can reach the surface for a breath of air. The Florida Softshell lives chiefly in lakes; all the others are river turtles to a large degree.

Identification is hampered by changes associated with age and sex. Young softshells are about as well patterned as they will ever be. Males tend to retain the juvenile pattern and coloration, but the females, which grow very large in comparison with their mates, undergo marked changes, the original pattern being replaced and eventually obliterated completely by mottlings and blotches. (An exception to the general rule is the Florida Softshell, in which both sexes become drab and retain only traces of pattern.) Males have much longer and stouter tails than females. The young in all our species average about 1 ¼ to 1 ¾ in. (3.2 to 4.4 cm) at hatching time.

Handle softshells with caution. Their sharp claws and mandibles deserve respect.

The Family Trionychidae occurs in Africa, Asia, and the East Indies, as well as in North America.

SMOOTH SOFTSHELL *Trionyx muticus*   **Pls. 6, 12**
Identification: Adult females 7–14 in. (18–35.6 cm); males 5–7 in. (12.5–17.8 cm). Sometimes called the "spineless softshell," which is not very complimentary to a turtle that can bite and scratch with vigor, but this is a good way to remember an important fact. Our only softshell *without* spines, bumps, or sandpapery projections on carapace. Shell is quite smooth. Also, only softshell *without* ridges in nostrils (see Fig. 52, opp. Pl. 12). To complete the roster of negative characters, the feet are *not* strongly streaked or spotted. *Male and young:* Carapace olive-gray or brown, marked with dots and dashes only a little darker than ground color. *Adult female:* Mottled with various shades of gray, brown, or olive. *Young:* Plastron paler than underside of carapace (see Plate 6).

Essentially a river turtle, an inhabitant of streams ranging in size from creeks to the mighty Mississippi. Occurs in lakes less frequently than the members of the spiny softshell group, and often is missing where they are abundant, and vice versa. **Similar species:** (1) Florida Softshell (p. 81) has a bumpy carapace, and (2) all races of the Spiny Softshell have shells that are either sandpapery or with spines on front edge of carapace, or both. (3) All Softshells except Smooth have a ridge in each nostril.
Range: Cen. U.S.; Ohio, Mississippi, and Missouri Rivers and

their tributaries; streams draining to the Gulf of Mexico.

Subspecies: MIDLAND SMOOTH SOFTSHELL, *Trionyx m. muticus* (Plates 6 and 12). Ill-defined pale stripes usually evident on snout in front of eyes; pale postocular stripes with narrow dark borders; otherwise as described above. W. Pennsylvania to extr. n. Alabama, w. Mississippi, and most of Louisiana; west to Kansas and cen. Texas and ascending rivers to Minnesota, N. Dakota, and New Mexico. GULF COAST SMOOTH SOFTSHELL, *Trionyx m. calvatus.* Carapace of young has large, circular, dusky spots that disappear in adult females but persist at least indistinctly in adult males. No stripes on dorsal surface of snout; pale postocular stripe with thick black borders. Streams draining to the Gulf of Mexico from the Escambia River of extr. w. Florida west to the Pearl River and the Florida Parishes of Louisiana. Map 33

EASTERN SPINY SOFTSHELL
Trionyx spiniferus spiniferus

Pls. 6, 12

Identification: Adult females 7–17 in. (18–43.2 cm); males 5–9¼ in. (12.5–23.5 cm). Check three items: (a) feet strongly streaked and spotted; (b) a ridge in each nostril (Fig. 52, opp. Pl. 12); and (c) look or feel for projections on uppersurface of carapace as described for the two sexes. *Male:* Dark eyelike spots (ocelli) on carapace, especially toward center. These quite variable in size — on same turtle and from one specimen to the next. Ground color olive-gray to yellowish brown. Tiny projections on entire surface of carapace in adult males make shell feel like sandpaper; anterior edge of shell has small spinelike projections. *Female:* The circular markings, characteristic of juveniles, begin to break up as female approaches maturity; they are replaced by blotches of brown or olive-brown of varying sizes that produce a camouflage effect. Surface of carapace smooth, but spines or enlarged tubercles are present on and near forward edge of carapace (Fig. 52, opp. Pl. 12), and raised protuberances may appear on other parts of shell. *Young* (Plate 6): Small dark spots or circular markings on a pale yellowish-brown ground color.

Essentially a river turtle, but also occurring in lakes and other quiet bodies of water where sand and mud bars are available. Sometimes floats at surface, where shape identifies it as a softshell. Over a large part of the range this is the only member of the group, but in areas where Smooth Softshells also occur it is usually necessary to capture specimens to be sure of identification.

Similar species: See Smooth Softshell (p. 77).

Range: W. New York to Wisconsin and south to the Tennessee River; intergrading with other races in the lower Mississippi Valley virtually to the Gulf. A disjunct area in Lake Champlain and lower part of Ottawa River, Canada; an old record from e.-cen. New York, and introduced and well established in Maurice River system of s. New Jersey.   Map 36

WESTERN SPINY SOFTSHELL   Pl. 12
Trionyx spiniferus hartwegi
Identification: Adult females 7–18 in. (18–45.7 cm); males 5–7¼ in. (12.5–18.4 cm). A western subspecies characterized by the smallness of the dark markings on the carapace; these are only slightly enlarged toward the center of shell. In other characteristics like Eastern Spiny Softshell.

In western parts of range, where arid or semiarid conditions prevail, rivers offer the only suitable natural habitats for softshells. Farther east a variety of bodies of water are utilized.
Similar species: See Smooth Softshell (p. 77).
Range: Minnesota to Arkansas and west to se. Wyoming, e. Colorado, and ne. New Mexico; an isolated record in e. Wyoming, and a large disjunct area in Missouri River drainage in Montana. This race intergrades with Eastern Spiny Softshell through a broad area paralleling the Mississippi River.

Map 36

GULF COAST SPINY SOFTSHELL   Pl. 12
Trionyx spiniferus asperus
Identification: Adult females 7–17⅞ in. (18–45.4 cm); males 5–8 in. (12.5–20.3 cm). The southern representative of the spiny softshells. Two items of pattern set this off from other subspecies: (a) 2 or more dark lines (or broken lines) parallel the rear margin of shell — in all other races there is only a single dark line; (b) the 2 light bands on head, one extending backward from eye and other from jaw, usually unite on side of head (Fig. 15, below) — in Eastern Spiny Softshell the light bands normally fail to join. All these markings are best seen in juveniles and male specimens; they are obscure or even lacking in old females. In many of the latter, spines on the forward part of shell are developed to a remarkable degree.

A resident of southern rivers and ponds or oxbows associated with rivers.
Similar species: (1) Florida Softshell has: (a) bumps on carapace in form of flattened hemispheres; (b) general coloration dark in both sexes; and (c) a carapace that, proportionately, is

Fig. 15

EASTERN SPINY SOFTSHELL
(*Trionyx s. spiniferus*)
Head lines separate

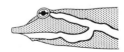

GULF COAST SOFTSHELL
(*Trionyx s. asperus*)
Head lines meet

considerably longer than wide; young Florida Softshell is patterned with large dark spots separated by a network of light areas (Plate 6). (2) See also Smooth Softshell (p. 77).

Range: S.-cen. N. Carolina to the Florida panhandle; west to Mississippi and e. Louisiana. Four races of the species (Eastern, Western, Pallid, and Gulf Coast) come together in the great plexus of rivers and bayous of the lower Mississippi Valley in Arkansas, Louisiana, and Mississippi, and all contribute their characters to a general spiny softshell melting pot. Specimens from those areas should be considered as intergrades. Map 36

GUADALUPE SPINY SOFTSHELL   Pl. 12
Trionyx spiniferus guadalupensis

Identification: Adult females 7–16⅝ in. (18–42.2 cm); males 5–8½ in. (12.5–21.6 cm). Small white spots are present on almost all parts of the carapace, and each spot is often tightly surrounded by a narrow black ring. This is a member of a complex of three subspecies of the spiny softshell group that are characterized by small white spots on the brown or olive carapace. (See **Subspecies** below for ways to distinguish the other two races.) Among all three the spots are usually conspicuous in the young and in many adult males; females, which become mottled like females of our other softshells, usually lack them. Males may be quite sandpapery, but females usually do not have the spines so well developed as in other members of the spiny softshell group.

One might think, from their western distribution, that these turtles are adept at threading their way through arid country by following the streams. That is probably true in some cases, but geological evidence indicates that a large part of the range formerly was much more moist than at present. The turtles have survived only in the more permanent streams and by estivating in mud during periods of drought.

Similar species: See Smooth Softshell (p. 77).

Range: S.-cen. Texas; drainage systems of the Guadalupe–San Antonio and Nueces Rivers; intergrades with the Pallid Spiny Softshell in the Colorado River system.

Subspecies: PALLID SPINY SOFTSHELL, *Trionyx s. pallidus.* White spots more or less confined to posterior half of carapace and not ringed with black. W. Louisiana, s. Oklahoma, and most of n. and e. Texas. TEXAS SPINY SOFTSHELL, *Trionyx s. emoryi.* White spots confined to rear third of carapace; pale rim of carapace conspicuously widened along rear edge, 4 or 5 times wider than pale rim of lateral edges. Rio Grande and Pecos River drainages and south to the Río Purificación, Tamaulipas; also the Gila-Colorado River system (into which it may have been introduced by man) from sw. New Mexico and extr. sw. Utah to the delta at the head of the Gulf of California.

Map 36

FLORIDA SOFTSHELL *Trionyx ferox*   **Pls. 6, 12**
Identification: Adult females 8–19⅝ in. (20–49.8 cm); males
6–11½ in. (15–29.2 cm). Heaviest and bulkiest of North American softshells, but the species with the smallest range. General
appearance is dark brown or dark brownish gray, nearly uniform
in coloration or with vague suggestions of large dark spots.
There are numerous small bumps on the carapace (Fig. 52,
opp. Pl. 12), usually occupying a crescentic area involving
the front of the shell and back along its sides as far as the
forelegs. The bumps are flattened hemispheres — *not* spines or
conical projections. A ridge in each nostril (Fig. 52, opp. Pl. 12)
just as there is in the various members of the spiny softshell
group. *Young:* Carapace with large dark round spots separated
by network of light areas; bright lines and spots on an otherwise
dark head (see Plate 6).
    The lake dweller among the softshells — at home in lakes,
ponds, big springs, canals, and roadside ditches, and occasionally
in quiet portions of rivers. Largely because of the nature of its
habitat, this softshell is the most conspicuous member of the
group, at least when submerged. Often seen moving about in
clear water.
Similar species: Gulf Coast Spiny Softshell has spines or
cone-shaped projections on carapace, and in large individuals
these may be present well back on shell; males and young are
easily identified by yellowish-brown carapace and dark lines or
broken lines paralleling rear margin of shell.
Range: All of Florida except the Keys; s. S. Carolina to Mobile
Bay, Alabama.   Map 35

VII

Lizards

Order Squamata*

Suborder Lacertilia

LIZARDS are abundant in the tropics and many temperate regions, and collectively they range from above the Arctic Circle (in the Old World) to the southern tips of Africa, Australia, and South America. They have also reached many islands — even remote ones — to which they were transported on floating vegetation or inadvertently in the cargoes or personal belongings of mankind. Vertically they occur from sea level to at least 16,000 feet (4900 m) in the tropics. There are in excess of 3000 species, but only two are venomous — the Beaded Lizard, which is confined to Mexico, and the Gila Monster of Mexico and our own Southwest. The latter ranges eastward only to extreme southwestern New Mexico. Despite rumors and reports to the contrary, there is no authentic evidence for the natural occurrence of the Gila Monster in Texas. There are no poisonous lizards in our area.

Many kinds of lizards must be caught for accurate identification, a real challenge in the cases of the more alert, active, and elusive varieties. Nooses, traps, or other devices are often indispensable. Be careful when seizing any lizard to avoid grasping the tail, which, in a great many of our species, may break off at the slightest pinch. The tails, unless they are severed close to the body, soon regenerate, but the new ones are never so long or so perfectly formed as were the originals.

Geckos: Family Gekkonidae

A LARGE family, widespread through the tropics and subtropics of both New and Old Worlds. Geckos are notorious for their ability to establish themselves around buildings and old docks in tropical seaports, and five of the eight species in our area are immigrants that arrived fortuitously, presumably in cargoes of

*The Order Squamata includes the vast majority of all living reptiles. Subdivisions (suborders) are Lacertilia (lizards—this page), Amphisbaenia (amphisbaenians, p. 135), and Serpentes (snakes, p. 136).

fruit, produce, lumber, etc., in Key West, Florida, and other localities in our southern states.

Most of our species have immovable eyelids, and their eyes, like those of snakes, are open all the time. Some kinds are diurnal or crepuscular. Others prowl at night and in these the pupil of the eye, which is a mere vertical slit in bright light, expands widely in the dark. Gecko food includes insects, spiders, and other arthropods.

Many kinds of geckos are as good as flies at walking up and down smooth walls and even across ceilings. This they can do by virtue of their expanded toes, which are covered by brushlike pads or lamellae that bear myriads of tiny bristles or setae. Each bristle (and there may be a million of them in at least one Old World species) ends in as many as 100 to 1000 suction cups so extremely small they are clearly visible only under the scanning electron microscope. No wonder some geckos are marvelous acrobats, with so many "plumber's helpers" to assist them! On rough surfaces, the claws are also useful in climbing.

Geckos as a whole are noted for their vocalizations, and the group derives both its common and scientific names from an oriental species whose cry sounds like *geck'-o.* Coloration may vary considerably in the same individual specimen, at least in some species, in response to such factors as temperature, humidity, amount of light, and degree of activity. The tails of most geckos are *very* easily detached.

Representatives of three subfamilies are found within our area: (1) House Geckos (*Hemidactylus* of the subfamily Gekkoninae); (2) Dwarf and Yellow-headed Geckos (*Sphaerodactylus* and *Gonatodes* of the Sphaerodactylinae); and (3) Banded Geckos (*Coleonyx* of the Eublepharinae). The Banded Geckos have movable eyelids.

MEDITERRANEAN GECKO   Pl. 13
Hemidactylus turcicus turcicus

Identification: 4–5 in. (10–12.7 cm); head–body max. 2⅜ in. (6.0 cm). A pale ghostly lizard with very large eyes, and broad toe pads extending nearly full length of toes (Fig. 53, opp. Pl. 13). Prominent tubercles (wartlike bumps) on head, body, legs, and tail. Both light and dark spots on a pale ground. Dark spots may be brown or gray; pale areas variable from bright pinkish ivory to very pale yellow or whitish.

Almost completely nocturnal. On warm evenings look for it on buildings, window screens, or near lights where insects congregate. It makes itself quite at home around human habitations.

Voice: A faint mouselike squeak repeated at more or less regular intervals.

Range: Established at many localities in the Gulf Coastal states and ne. Mexico, and now known from dozens of places in s. Texas; also introduced into Cuba, Puerto Rico, Panama, and other parts of Mexico. An Old World gecko that ranges from w. India and Somali, chiefly in coastal areas and around both sides of the Mediterranean Basin, to Spain, Morocco, and the Canary Is. The speed with which this gecko has expanded its range in the southern U.S. in recent years is even more remarkable than the spread of the cattle egret. The bird has wings, but the lizard has been distributed, chiefly inadvertently, by mankind.   Map 44

INDO-PACIFIC GECKO *Hemidactylus garnoti*   **Pl. 17**
Identification: 4–5¼ in. (10–13.3 cm); head–body max. 2½ in. (6.4 cm). A brownish-gray gecko with small ovoid dorsal scales and large toe pads (as in the Mediterranean Gecko, Fig. 53, opp. Pl. 13), but *no large tubercles*. Dorsum almost uniformly colored or marbled with darker brown; small whitish dorsal spots that vary in size and shape. *Venter lemon yellow; underside of tail pale red. Young:* About 1⅝–2⅛ in. (4.1–5.4 cm) at hatching.
   Like many of the whiptail lizards this gecko is apparently unisexual. Males are unknown and reproduction is presumably by parthenogenesis (development of an unfertilized egg).
Similar species: Mediterranean Gecko is pinkish or whitish and has conspicuous tubercles on the dorsal surfaces.
Range: Established in the Miami region and on Sanibel I., Florida; native to se. Asia, the East Indies, and many islands of the South Seas; also established in Hawaii.   Map 43

ASHY GECKO *Sphaerodactylus cinereus*   **Pl. 13**
Identification: 2¾–2⅞ in. (7.0–7.3 cm); head–body max. 1⁷⁄₁₆ in. (3.7 cm). A wraith of a lizard that appears on building walls, window screens, or near lights on warm evenings in search of insects attracted by the illumination. Check dorsal pattern. Uppersurfaces with a profusion of tiny white or yellow spots on a darker ground color that varies from reddish brown to pale grayish brown. The spots often tend to run together and form light lines on head. Snout pointed and slightly flattened. Dorsal scales *small and granular.* Small round pad at tip of each toe (Fig. 53, opp. Pl. 13). *Young:* The dark crossbands and reddish tail disappear with age.
   Chiefly crepuscular, but active at night near house and street lights; hides in crevices or under debris or vegetation during daylight hours. Often found in or on walls of cisterns and outhouses.
Similar species: (1) Reef and (2) Ocellated Geckos are brown with *dark* markings, and their dorsal scales are strongly *keeled.* Ocellated Gecko also has light stripes on head and white spots on nape.

Range: Introduced on Key West from where it has spread to other Lower Florida Keys; native to Cuba, Hispaniola, and adj. islands.   Map 39

REEF GECKO *Sphaerodactylus notatus notatus*   **Pl. 13**
Identification: 2–2¼ in. (5.1–5.7 cm); head–body max. 1³⁄₁₆ in. (3.0 cm). A tiny, chubby brown lizard with a pointed, slightly flattened snout. Dorsal scales *strongly keeled,* 41 to 48 around midbody. Small round pad at tip of each toe (Fig. 53, opp. Pl. 13). *Male:* Entire dorsal surface with small dark spots. Old males may be uniformly brown. *Female:* Three broad, dark, light-centered, longitudinal stripes on head. A pair of light spots on the shoulder may or may not be present. *Young:* Like adult female (not strongly crossbanded as in Ashy Gecko).
   The Reef Gecko quickly scurries for the next nearest cover when its shelter (a board, stone, coconut husk, trash, or other debris) is lifted. Chiefly crepuscular. Occurs in pinelands, hammocks, vacant lots, and around buildings.
Similar species: (1) Ashy Gecko has *light* spots on dark ground color and small *granular* dorsal scales. (2) Ocellated Gecko has many *pale* spots on nape and *light lines on head.*
Range: The Dry Tortugas, the Florida Keys, and extr. se. mainland Florida; related races in Cuba, the Bahamas, and on Little Swan I. in western part of Caribbean Sea.   Map 40

OCELLATED GECKO *Sphaerodactylus argus argus*   **Pl. 13**
Identification: 1⅞–2⅜ in. (4.8–6.0 cm); head–body max. 1⁵⁄₁₆ in. (3.3 cm). The tiny white eyelike spots (ocelli) on the nape are far fewer than the hundred eyes of the Argus of mythology, but they give this lizard its scientific name and furnish a quick clue to identification. The ocelli may continue onto the back and some may fuse with one another longitudinally or with the *light lines on the head.* Some specimens are virtually patternless. Dorsal coloration brown to olive-brown, tail brown or reddish. Dorsal scales *keeled,* 57 to 73 around midbody. Small round pad at tip of each toe (as in Reef and Ashy Geckos, Fig. 53, opp. Pl. 13). *Young:* Like adults, but tending to have a more lineate body pattern; about 1¹⁄₁₆ in. (2.7 cm) at hatching.
Similar species: (1) Reef Gecko has only two light spots on nape or none at all, head stripes (if present) are dark, and dorsal scales around midbody are 48 or fewer. (2) Ashy Gecko has granular dorsal scales.
Range: Introduced on Key West, Florida, the Biminis and Nassau in the Bahamas; native to Jamaica, the south coast of Cuba and adjacent offshore islets, and the Corn Is. (Nicaragua). A related subspecies on the Isla de San Andrés in the sw. Caribbean Sea.   Map 41

YELLOW-HEADED GECKO   Pl. 13
Gonatodes albogularis fuscus

Identification: 2½–3½ in. (6.4–8.9 cm); head–body max. 1 9⁄16 in. (4.0 cm). *Adult males:* Head yellow; body, legs, and tail uniformly dark, almost black in sunlight, but bluish (as illustrated) at night or in heavy shade. *Female and young:* Mottled with brown, gray, and yellow; a *narrow light collar* usually present on *one or both sides of neck.* In this species there are no expanded pads on toes (Fig. 53, opp. Pl. 13), and pupils of eyes are round. Tip of tail, unless regenerated, is whitish.

Largely diurnal, in contrast with our other geckos. Occurs in and about abandoned buildings and docks and among debris on vacant land. A favorite habit is to cling upside down beneath a log, board, or other shelter.

Range: Introduced on Key West and in Coconut Grove, Miami, Florida; Cuba (possibly introduced), Grand Cayman I., Cen. America, and Colombia. Related subspecies in s. Mexico, the West Indies, and n. S. America.   Map 42

TEXAS BANDED GECKO *Coleonyx brevis*   Pl. 13
Identification: 4–4⅞ in. (10–12.4 cm); head–body max. 2 5⁄16 in. (5.9 cm). A gecko with *functional eyelids.* No toe pads (Fig. 53, opp. Pl. 13). Scales tiny. A considerable *change in pattern* is associated with age. Juveniles are strongly marked by broad chocolate crossbands that alternate with narrower bands of cream or yellow. But as they grow older dark pigment appears in the light bands and, conversely, light areas develop in the chocolate bands. This produces a mottled effect that increases with age. In many adults the original pattern can be made out only with difficulty. *Young:* See above; about 1¾ in. (4.4 cm) at hatching.

Banded Geckos are terrestrial, climbing but little in comparison with their more acrobatic relatives. They prefer rocky areas, such as canyons, where they can take shelter during daylight hours beneath stones or in crevices. One of the thrills of nighttime driving in Banded Gecko country is to see these pale delicate lizards standing out conspicuously against the dark macadamized paving as they cross the highway during their nocturnal prowlings.

Similar species: See Big Bend Gecko.
Voice: A faint squeak, often heard when a specimen is first picked up or when it is actively moving about in a terrarium.
Range: S. New Mexico to se. Texas and south to Nuevo León and ne. Durango.   Map 37

BIG BEND GECKO *Coleonyx reticulatus*   Fig. 16, p. 87
Identification: 5½–6⅝ in. (14–16.8 cm); head–body max. 3 9⁄16 in. (9.0 cm). Superficially like the Texas Banded Gecko, but differing as follows: (a) enlarged tubercles scattered among the

Fig. 16
DORSAL
SCALATION
IN GECKOS
(*Coleonyx*)

BIG BEND
(*reticulatus*)
Enlarged tubercles

TEXAS BANDED
(*brevis*)
All scales small

tiny scales of the back (Fig. 16, above); (b) dorsum marked with brown spots or streaks on a light brown ground color, and often arranged to suggest a light reticulated (netlike) pattern; (c) attains a much larger size. The *eyelids are functional. Young:* Strongly marked with dark brown crossbands on body and tail.

Nocturnal and secretive. This species was not discovered until 1956 when the first known specimen was caught in a mouse trap. **Voice:** Specimens may squeak when captured.

Range: Brewster and Presidio Cos. in the Big Bend of Texas and probably adj. Mexico.   Map 38

Iguanids: Family Iguanidae

To THIS very large family belong the anoles (*Anolis*), and the following other groups of lizards: collared and leopard (*Crotaphytus*), earless (*Holbrookia*), spiny (*Sceloporus*), tree (*Urosaurus*), side-blotched (*Uta*), curly-tailed (*Leiocephalus*), and horned (*Phrynosoma*). This is chiefly a New World family with many other genera in the tropics, and it ranges from New York and extreme southwestern Canada southward throughout the Americas to Tierra del Fuego. It is also represented in the West Indies, Bermuda (introduced), the Galápagos Islands, Madagascar, and the Fiji and Tonga Islands in Polynesia.

Display patterns, consisting of head-bobbing, nodding, and push-ups and which serve to declare territory, establish sex, aid in species discrimination, or enable a male to challenge another male, are characteristic of most iguanids.

Anoles: Genus *Anolis*

THE anoles, with more than 300 named species and subspecies, constitute the largest genus of reptiles in the Western Hemisphere. They are especially abundant in the tropics, and extend southward to Bolivia and Paraguay. Only one species, the Green Anole, is native to the continental United States; four West Indian species are now well established in Florida.

A striking feature is the throat fan. A flap of skin, attached to the throat and extending onto the chest in some species, is swung forward and downward by a flexible rod of cartilage attached near the middle of the throat. As the fan flares out, the scales become widely separated and a bright color (often red, orange, or yellow) flashes into view. Males have large throat fans; in females they are small or rudimentary. The fan is displayed, often to the accompaniment of push-ups and head-bobbing, during courtship and in defense of territory.

The ability to change color is well developed. The changes are the result of the movement of pigment granules within the cells of the skin and in response to such stimuli as temperature, humidity, emotion, and activity. Our native (and introduced) species, taken collectively, are capable of exhibiting browns, grays, and greens. The measurements that appear in the text immediately following **Identification** are for males; females are smaller.

Anoles have pads on their toes that aid in climbing, but they are less adept at negotiating smooth vertical surfaces than some of the geckos. All our anoles are arboreal, but they also forage on the ground. Their food consists largely of insects and spiders.

GREEN ANOLE *Anolis carolinensis carolinensis*   **Pl. 14**
 Identification: 5–8 in. (13–20.3 cm); head–body max. $2\,^{15}/_{16}$ in. (7.5 cm). The "chameleon." The plain *green* hue and *pink* throat fan (Fig. 17, p. 89), combined with overall small size, distinguish it from all our other lizards. Coloration varies: individuals are green at one time, mottled green and brown at another, and all brown at still another. There may be indications of pattern in the form of dark streaks or spots. Color-changing abilities are poor compared with true chameleons of the Old World. *Young:* About $2\,^{1}/_{16}$–$2\,^{5}/_{8}$ in. (5.2–6.7 cm) at hatching.

An abundant lizard in the South; often seen on fences, around old buildings, on shrubs and vines, or (less often) on ground. Green Anoles climb high into trees, out of which they may tumble — especially when chasing one another — without harmful effects. Easily caught at night when, asleep on leaf or vine, the lizard stands out vividly in the beam of a flashlight.
 Range: N. Carolina to Key West, Florida; west to se. Oklahoma and cen. Texas, and established in lower Rio Grande Valley; also introduced in other localities but may not be established. Subspecies in Cuba and the Bahamas.
 Note: Males from southern Florida are variable. They may be longitudinally streaked with slate gray on the nape and anterior part of the trunk. Throat fans vary from virtually white through pinks and magentas to blues and purples. Whether these anomalies represent variation within the species or whether a sibling complex of two or more species is involved is unknown at this time.   Map 45

BROWN ANOLE *Anolis sagrei*   **Pl. 14**
Identification: 5–8⅜ in. (13–21.3 cm); head–body max. 2½ in.
(6.4 cm). *Male:* A *brown* lizard with a white streak down center
of throat, although it is not always so prominent as in Fig. 17,
below. The streak is the underside of the throat fan, which,
when extended, is brilliant orange-red with a whitish border
sometimes flecked with dark brown. Both throat fan and white
streak are good field marks easily seen through binoculars.
General coloration and pattern variable; same individual may
change from pale to very dark brown. Small yellow spots,
arranged in 6 or more vertical rows, are visible in some specimens. *Female:* Narrow yellowish stripe down center of back,
flanked on each side by a row of dark brown half-circles.

"Ground anoles" would be a good name for these lizards.
They climb, but are far less arboreal than the other anoles in
Florida. When cornered, they make short, erratic hops in their
efforts to escape.
Similar species: (1) Green Anoles turn bright green, whereas
Brown Anoles are always some shade of brown. (2) Bark Anole
is geckolike and has crossbands on tail. (3) See also Large-
headed Anole.
Range: Introduced and established in Florida and in several
coastal localities from s. Mexico to Honduras; Cuba, Jamaica,
and the Bahamas.
Subspecies: CUBAN BROWN ANOLE, *Anolis s. sagrei* (Plate

Fig. 17. HEADS OF ANOLES *(Anolis)*

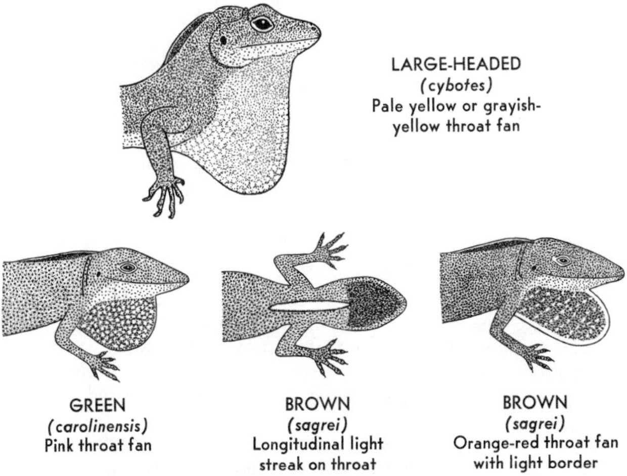

LARGE-HEADED
(cybotes)
Pale yellow or grayish-
yellow throat fan

GREEN
(carolinensis)
Pink throat fan

BROWN
(sagrei)
Longitudinal light
streak on throat

BROWN
(sagrei)
Orange-red throat fan
with light border

14). As described above. Abundant in metropolitan Broward, Dade, and Palm Beach Cos., Florida; also established on many of the Florida Keys and in the Tampa–St. Petersburg region; Cuba, the Isla de Pinos, Jamaica, and Cayman Brac. BAHAMAN BROWN ANOLE, *Anolis s. ordinatus*. Similar, but dorsal coloration from pale brown to pale gray, and throat fan with a mustard-yellow to chocolate ground color. Males of this race usually have a pronounced crest along top of tail. Introduced in the Miami area, at Lake Worth, on Chokoloskee I., and probably in other south Florida localities; the Bahamas. Subspecies on Caribbean Is. (The two Florida east coast localities are indicated on the range map by black dots connected with their proper subspecific symbol, which covers most of the Bahaman archipelago.)   Map 46

LARGE-HEADED ANOLE   **Fig. 17, p. 89**
Anolis cybotes cybotes
  Identification: 7–8 in. (18–20.3 cm); head–body max. 2 $^{15}/_{16}$ in. (7.5 cm). Females considerably smaller than males. A large-headed, stockily-built anole. General coloration brown (never wholly green), but varying through several shades of brown to tan. *Male:* Changeable — often with a pair of greenish longitudinal stripes on each side of body and dark brown crossbands on body, legs, and at least base of tail. An erectile dorsal and nuchal crest, the nuchal one especially prominent. Throat fan pale yellow or grayish yellow, sometimes with a central area of pale orange. *Female:* Nearly plain orange-brown except for a middorsal light stripe that may be smooth-sided or with scalloped or notched edges posteriorly and a pair of small yellowish spots on back and shoulder; head not enlarged.
  Similar species: (1) Brown Anole has keeled ventral scales (smooth in *cybotes*). (2) Bark Anole has a small head and paired rows of snout scales.
  Range: Established in Miami, Florida; Hispaniola and some of its satellite islands. Additional subspecies on Hispaniola.
                                                      Map 49

BARK ANOLE   *Anolis distichus*   **Pl. 14; Fig. 18, p. 91**
  Identification: 3½–5 in. (9–12.7 cm); head–body max. 2 in. (5.1 cm). Resembles a piece of lichen-covered bark that scurries away when approached. Coloration and pattern changeable, but always some shade of gray or brown (never green). When at rest or asleep, lizard may appear putty-colored or almost white; at other times it varies from pale gray to mahogany brown or almost black. A dark line across and between eyes and a crossbanded tail (most pronounced near tip) are almost

always present. A frequently occurring pattern consists of two small, eyelike spots at back of head and four vague chevrons pointing rearward on dorsum (Fig. 18, below). Throat fan yellow, sometimes with an extensive pale orange blush.

This highly arboreal lizard is geckolike in its actions. Once aroused, it can be extremely elusive and difficult to catch.

Range: Miami, Florida, area; Hispaniola and the Bahamas.

Subspecies: FLORIDA BARK ANOLE, *Anolis d. floridanus* (Plate 14 and Fig. 18, below). As described above. Known only from the Miami area. GREEN BARK ANOLE, *Anolis d. dominicensis.* Similar but slightly larger — head-body max. 2¼ in. (5.7 cm) — and dorsal coloration changing from all dark brown to all *green.* Throat fan frequently with a pale orange blush. Introduced at Miami; Hispaniola.   Map 48

Fig. 18
FLORIDA BARK ANOLE
(*Anolis d. floridanus*)
Faint chevronlike
dorsal pattern

KNIGHT ANOLE *Anolis equestris equestris*   **Pl. 14**
Identification: 13–19⅜ in. (33–49.2 cm); head-body max. 7 in. (17.9 cm). This colorful and impressive lizard is one of the giant Cuban anoles, the largest members of the genus. Sheer size, the enormous pink throat fan of the male, and the arboreal habits are sufficient identification, but two white or yellowish longitudinal lines, one on shoulder and the other extending from below eye to ear opening, are also helpful. General coloration bright or apple-green, but sometimes changing to dull grayish brown. Yellow areas may appear and disappear, especially across tail. Small crest on nape is raisable at will.

At home in shade trees in areas where introduced, and called "iguana" by local residents.

Range: Established in the Miami, Florida, area; Habana Province and vicinity in Cuba; related subspecies in other parts of Cuba.   Map 47

Collared and Leopard Lizards:
Genus *Crotaphytus*

DESPITE the marked differences in head shapes — narrow in the leopard lizards and almost grotesquely enlarged in the collared lizards — the members of these two groups are closely related. All are alert, elusive, and pugnacious. The genus as a whole ranges from eastern Missouri to the Pacific States and well south into western Mexico, including virtually all of Baja California and several islands off its coast, both in the Gulf of California and the Pacific Ocean.

COLLARED LIZARD *Crotaphytus collaris*   **Pl. 15**
   Identification: 8–14 in. (20–35.6 cm); head–body max. 4½ in. (11.4 cm). The "mountain boomer," a gangling, big-headed, long-tailed lizard that runs on its hind legs like a miniature dinosaur. The 2 black collar markings (often broken at nape) are constant, but coloration and pattern are variable. Body scales very small. *Male:* General coloration yellowish, greenish, brownish, or bluish; dorsal pattern consisting of a profusion of light spots and (at least in younger specimens) a series of dark crossbands. Very old specimens may lose all their markings except for the black collars and light spots. *Female:* Similar, but less brilliantly colored; in gravid specimens red spots or bars appear on sides of body and similar spots may appear on sides of neck. *Young:* Broad dark crossbands consisting of rows of dark spots alternating with yellowish crossbands (at hatching); later, young of both sexes may develop red bars on body like gravid females; the red is lost when a head–body length of about 3 in. (7.5 cm) is attained. Total length about 3½ in. (8.9 cm) at hatching.
   This reptile has no voice. The name "mountain boomer" may have originated from someone's having seen a Collared Lizard on top of a rock while some other animal, possibly a Barking Frog, called from beneath the same rock. A resident of hilly, rocky, often arid or semiarid regions. Seldom found on the plains, except on rocky hills or in gullies traversing them. Limestone ledges or rock piles, both offering an abundance of hiding places, are favorite habitats. Collared lizards are wary and quick to take cover. When surprised in the open, however, they run first on all fours, not assuming the upright, bipedal type of locomotion until they have attained considerable speed. They are pugnacious, nip hard when caught, and when on the defense hold their mouths open in readiness to bite, exposing the black throat lining to view. Insects of many kinds are eaten; so also are small lizards, including "horned toads." Don't cage collared lizards with other reptiles smaller than themselves. In the field never put two collared lizards in the same collecting bag; in the excitement following capture they may bite each other to death.
   Similar species: Both (1) Blue and (2) Crevice Spiny Lizards have only *one* black band (collar) across the neck, and their dorsal scales are very large and spiny.
   Range: E. and cen. Missouri through cen. Texas to n. San Luis Potosí; west to Utah, Arizona, and Sonora.   Map 51

RETICULATE COLLARED LIZARD   **Pl. 15**
Crotaphytus reticulatus
Identification: 8–16¾ in. (20–42.5 cm); head–body max. 5⅜ in. (13.7 cm). Reticulate means netlike, and the light markings on the dorsum of this large lizard form an open, though often broken, network. This, in conjunction with a series of large black spots across the back, makes identification easy, although the netlike pattern temporarily disappears in specimens chilled by cold weather. *Male:* A bright golden yellow suffusion on chest during breeding season. *Female:* No vertical black bars on neck; during breeding season vertical brick-red bars may appear between lateral rows of black spots and throat may have a pinkish suffusion. *Young:* Hatchlings are light gray marked with 4 to 6 yellow or yellow-orange crossbands interspersed with transverse rows of black spots. About 3½–4 in. (8.9–10.2 cm) at hatching.

An alert, active lizard most often seen sunning atop a rock or found hiding beneath stones or debris or in packrat nests. A resident of thornbrush deserts. Habits similar to those of Collared Lizard.
Range: Rio Grande Valley in s. Texas and adj. Mexico.

Map 52

LEOPARD LIZARD *Crotaphytus wislizeni wislizeni*   **Pl. 15**
Identification: 8½–15⅛ in. (22–38.4 cm); head–body max. 4¹¹⁄₁₆ in. (11.9 cm). Unlike its mammalian namesake this "leopard" can change its spots — or at least their coloration. Spots vary from black through several shades of brown, all in the same lizard, depending on such factors as temperature and activity. Ground color gray or brown, darkest when lizard is cool. In darker phases, narrow whitish lines extend upward on each side of body, from neck to base of tail, usually meeting their partners to form crosslines; they are especially prominent in juveniles. Throat streaked with gray. *Female:* Flanks and underside of tail have salmon-red spots and streaks for a short period before deposition of eggs in spring or summer. *Young:* Spots often reddish. A curved yellow line above each eye, in combination with pale spots on lips, creates illusion lizard is wearing spectacles. About 5 in. (13 cm) at hatching.

A large, speedy resident of arid or semiarid flats where vegetation occurs in clumps with ample running space between them. Almost always found on loose sandy or gravelly soil, and frequently close to a burrow. Characteristically flattens itself after running, and the spotted pattern usually blends so well with the ground that the lizard is difficult to see. Feeds on a large variety of insects and spiders; also eats lizards smaller than itself. Bites hard.
Similar species: Large size and strongly spotted or cross-

banded pattern distinguish this species from all other lizards
within our area. (1) Collared Lizard has 2 black collars and a
much wider head. (2) Most other spotted lizards have spots in
rows, not scattered.

Range: W. Texas, chiefly Trans-Pecos; Idaho and se. Oregon
south to extr. n. Zacatecas, Sonora, and the southern tip of Baja
California; isolated localities in Oregon and on Mexican coastal
islands (not shown on map). Western subspecies.   Map 50

Earless Lizards: Genus *Holbrookia*

THESE lizards have no visible ear openings. There are two folds
across the throat, one strongly indicated, the other weak, irregular,
or both (Fig. 19, below). Several of the species are adapted for
life in regions of dry sandy or loamy soil. Their long legs and
toes are useful for running on the surface, and their heads are
shaped for quick burrowing in sand. They dive in head first and
quickly bury themselves with a shimmying motion. The Texas
and Southwestern Earless Lizards prefer rocky areas. Sexual
dimorphism is pronounced, and males of most species are marked
with a pair of bold black bars on their sides. Such bars are usually
less distinct in adult females or may be lacking entirely. Females
heavy with eggs may bear a bright overwash, often strong, of
orange, reddish orange, pink, or yellow. Food includes insects
and spiders. Members of the genus occur well southward into
Mexico.

The two most wide-ranging species (including their several subspecies) are often called the Greater Earless Lizard (*texana*) and
the Lesser Earless Lizard (*maculata*), respectively.

Fig. 19. THROAT FOLDS OF IGUANID LIZARDS

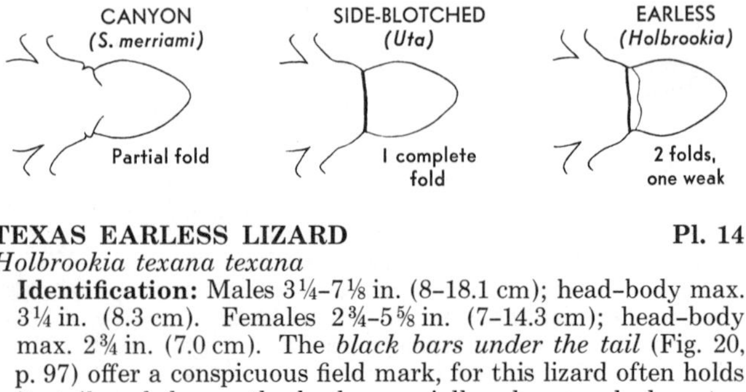

CANYON (S. merriami)	SIDE-BLOTCHED (Uta)	EARLESS (Holbrookia)
Partial fold	1 complete fold	2 folds, one weak

TEXAS EARLESS LIZARD   **Pl. 14**
Holbrookia texana texana
   Identification: Males 3¼–7⅛ in. (8–18.1 cm); head–body max.
3¼ in. (8.3 cm). Females 2¾–5⅝ in. (7–14.3 cm); head–body
max. 2¾ in. (7.0 cm). The *black bars under the tail* (Fig. 20,
p. 97) offer a conspicuous field mark, for this lizard often holds
its tail curled over the back, especially when perched on top

of a boulder. The bars are flashed when running, the tail is curled and waved from side to side as the lizard slows for a halt, or immediately after it stops. (*Caution:* Black bars are lacking under regenerated portions of tails.) Intensity of dark dorsal markings varies in same individual and from one lizard or one geographical locality to the next. Also there is a tendency for the general coloration to resemble that of the habitat: those living in regions of gray soil are often grayish, those living on reddish soil are often reddish, etc. *Male:* The 2 bold, black, crescent-shaped lines near the groin (shared by the Southwestern Earless Lizard) are much longer than in other species of earless lizards. The blue field surrounding them on the belly is usually prominent. *Female:* No black lines or blue field. *Young:* About 2 in. (5.1 cm) at hatching.

Rocky streambeds, sandstone or limestone outcrops, and open, rocky or gravelly areas in general, are typical habitats of this race of the Greater Earless Lizard. Each lizard tends to remain in its own home range, and may dash from one boulder to another and then back again when pursued. The protective coloration of the dorsum is spectacularly evident when one of these lizards runs just a short distance, settles down on a pale-colored rock or sand, and virtually disappears.

Similar species: Spot-tailed Earless Lizard has rounded dark spots under tail instead of crossbars (Fig. 20, p. 97).

Range: N.-cen. Texas and e. New Mexico to ne. Mexico.

Map 59

SOUTHWESTERN EARLESS LIZARD Pl. 14
Holbrookia texana scitula

Identification: Males 3½–7¼ in. (9–18.4 cm); head–body max. 3¼ in. (8.3 cm). Females 2⅝–5⁵⁄₁₆ in. (7–13.5 cm); head–body max. 2½ in. (6.4 cm). Similar to the Texas Earless Lizard, but males much more colorful, and so brilliant during the breeding season that ranchers of the Big Bend region call them "the lizard with the pink shirt and green pants." *Black bars under tail* (Fig. 20, p. 97). A light-bordered *dark stripe on rear of thigh,* often clearly visible when lizard is approached from rear; conspicuous in females and young, but much less so in large males. (This characteristic also shared by Texas Earless Lizard.) *Male:* Two prominent black ventro-lateral crescents bordered by blue or green on belly and by yellowish on flanks. Normal coloration gray with orange markings on forward part of body; hindquarters, legs, and tail green or yellowish. *Female:* Brown to gray, but with a rosy tint along the flanks when heavy with eggs; ventro-lateral crescents faint or absent.

A common and fast-running lizard of rocky desert flats and the vicinity of rocky cliffs and stream beds.

Range: The Big Bend and adj. w. Texas to w.-cen. Arizona;

south to ne. Zacatecas and adj. San Luis Potosí. Mexican subspecies.   Map 59

NORTHERN EARLESS LIZARD   Pl. 14
Holbrookia maculata maculata

Identification: 4–5 in. (10–12.7 cm); head–body max. 2⁷⁄₁₆ in.
(6.2 cm). *Pale longitudinal stripes,* one extending from eye to
base of tail and another faint one from armpit to groin. A single
obscure middorsal stripe. *No black spots under tail. Male:* A
pair of black bars behind armpit, often touched or surrounded
by a small area of blue; dorsal pattern blotched, but not clear-
cut; dorsum usually sprinkled with small white specks. *Female:*
Slightly smaller in size and with lateral black bars much reduced and without blue borders; dorsal spots well defined but
not surrounded by light pigment. Body strongly tinted with
orange or orange red when heavy with eggs, the color brightest
on the two lateral stripes. *Young:* Like female in pattern and
coloration; about 1½ in. (3.8 cm) at hatching.

This race of the Lesser Earless Lizard is a resident of sandy
prairies, either open or with scant vegetational cover. Specific
habitats include sandy grasslands, dry sandbars in streambeds,
and fields under cultivation. These lizards are diurnal and
during the heat of the day keep to shade afforded by bushes
and other plants or take refuge in mammal or other burrows.
Similar species: (1) Texas and Spot-tailed Earless Lizards
have black bars or spots under tail (Fig. 20, p. 97). (2) Desert
Side-blotched Lizard (*Uta*) has ear openings and *only one black
spot* near armpit. (3) See also Keeled Earless Lizard.
Range: S. South Dakota to e.-cen. New Mexico and through
the Texas panhandle.   Map 58

EASTERN EARLESS LIZARD   Pl. 14
Holbrookia maculata perspicua

Identification: 4–5 in. (10–12.7 cm); head–body max. 2¼ in.
(5.7 cm). Similar to Northern Earless Lizard, but males lack
white speckling. In many specimens of both sexes there is a
strong tendency for the dark dorsal blotches to fuse together
so there is only a *single* row of *broad* blotches down each side
of body.

Occurs chiefly in tallgrass or modified tallgrass prairie with
sandy or loamy soils.
Range: Se. Kansas to cen. Texas.   Map 58

SPECKLED EARLESS LIZARD   Pl. 14
Holbrookia maculata approximans

Identification: 4⅛–5⅛ in. (10.5–13.0 cm); head–body max.
2¾ in. (7.0 cm). *Dorsum strongly speckled,* especially in males.
No longitudinal light stripes except on neck. Otherwise similar
to Northern Earless Lizard. *No black spots under tail.*

A western race of the Lesser Earless Lizard that occurs chiefly in desert grasslands and outwash slopes of intermontane basins. **Similar species:** Desert Side-blotched Lizard (*Uta*) has ear openings and *only one black spot* near armpit.
Range: Trans-Pecos Texas, New Mexico, and Arizona south to Jalisco and Guanajuato. Western and Mexican subspecies, including a nearly uniformly white or ash-gray race confined to the White Sands region of New Mexico.   Map 58

SPOT-TAILED EARLESS LIZARD   Pl. 14
Holbrookia lacerata

Identification: 4½–6 in. (11–15.2 cm); head–body max. 2^{13}⁄$_{16}$ in. (7.1 cm). Most conspicuously spotted of all earless lizards. Three separate sets of markings can be checked: (a) dark dorsal spots *surrounded* by light pigment; (b) about 7 rounded dark spots under tail (Fig. 20, below); and (c) dusky to black oval streaks at edge of abdomen (these variable in number — from 4 to only 1, or even absent). Sexes patterned alike. **Young:** Marked like adults; about 1½ in. (3.8 cm) at hatching.

A species of arid, dark-soil flats, mesquite-prickly pear associations, and uplands of Edwards Plateau in central Texas.
Similar species: (1) Texas Earless Lizard has black *bars* extending completely across underside of tail. (2) In female Lesser Earless Lizards (races of *Holbrookia maculata*) the light pigment does *not* surround the dorsal spots and there are *no* dark spots under tail.
Range: Cen. and s. Texas and adj. Mexico.
Subspecies: SOUTHERN SPOT-TAILED EARLESS LIZARD, *Holbrookia l. subcaudalis* (Plate 14). Two distinct rows of dark blotches down each side of back; femoral pores average 16 under each hind leg. S. Texas and adj. Mexico, but not in lower Rio Grande Valley. PLATEAU SPOT-TAILED EARLESS LIZARD, *Holbrookia l. lacerata*. Dark blotches usually fused together in pairs, producing the effect of a single row on each side of back; femoral pores average 13. Edwards Plateau region of cen. Texas.
                    Map 56

Fig. 20. UNDERSURFACES OF TAILS OF EARLESS LIZARDS (*Holbrookia*)

GREATER	SPOT-TAILED	KEELED AND LESSER
(*texana*)	(*lacerata*)	(*propinqua* and *maculata*)
Black crossbars	Dark spots	No markings

KEELED EARLESS LIZARD   Pl. 14
Holbrookia propinqua propinqua

Identification: 4½–5^{9}⁄$_{16}$ in. (11–14.1 cm); head–body max. 2⅜ in. (6.0 cm). This is a *longtailed* earless lizard. The full

original tail is noticeably longer than the head–body length in
males and as long or longer in females. Dorsal scales distinctly
keeled, but so small that a lens is necessary to see them. No
dark spots under tail (Fig. 20, p. 97). *Male:* 2 black lines on
side of body (behind armpit) *not* surrounded by blue; dorsal
pattern variable and not clear-cut — usually a combination of
dark blotches and dark longitudinal stripes covered by many
small light dots. *Female:* Specimens from near the coast lack
any prominent markings, but inland females are darker and
with blotches. *Young:* Well-defined pattern of paired blotches;
about 1½ in. (3.8 cm) long at hatching.

A lizard indigenous to loose, wind-blown sands and dunes and
barrier beach islands of southern Texas and the Mexican coast.
Similar species: Tail in Lesser Earless Lizards (races of *Holbrookia maculata*) is shorter — about as long as head and body
combined, or a little shorter. (*Caution:* Be sure the tail has not
been regenerated. Comparisons must be made upon basis of full
original tail and not on invariably shorter, newly grown replace-
ment.) Lesser Earless males usually have a small patch of blue
touching or surrounding the black bars near the armpit. Some
Lesser Earless Lizards have keeled scales. The two species (*propinqua* and *maculata*) are most easily separated on basis of
range. If in doubt, also check the femoral pores (10 to 21,
average 14 or 15, under each hind leg in Keeled Earless Lizard;
5 to 15, average 11 or 12, in Lesser Earless Lizard).
Range: S. Texas and ne. Mexico. Mexican subspecies.

Map 57

Spiny Lizards: Genus *Sceloporus*

A LARGE and distinctive genus of lizards with *keeled* and pointed
dorsal scales. Some species are so rough they seem almost like
pine cones with legs and tails. Several were formerly called
"swifts." In gross appearance they resemble the tree and side-
blotched lizards (*Urosaurus* and *Uta* — see pp. 108–109), but in
those two genera there is a fold of skin across the throat (Fig.
19, p. 94 and Fig. 54, opp. Pl. 16.)

Most Spiny Lizards within our area are arboreal, at least to
some extent. Rock outcrops or boulders and large rotting stumps
or logs are also favorite habitats. They are best stalked by two
persons working toward them from opposite directions, for they
are adept at keeping a tree trunk or rock between themselves and
a single observer.

These lizards are chiefly insectivorous, but they also eat spiders
and other arthropods, and even smaller lizards, baby mice, etc.
Some kinds reproduce by laying eggs; others bear living young.

Sexual differences are usually well marked. Males of most species have a prominent blue patch at each side of the belly, and

in many there is also some blue on the throat. Under certain conditions, such as during cool weather or before skin shedding, the blue may turn black. Females lack the blue areas or have them only slightly developed. Middorsal dark markings, which are often faint or reduced in size (or both) in males, are normally rather prominent in females.

Counting dorsal scales may be necessary in some cases to distinguish between members of this genus. Counts are stated in the text as the number of scales from "back of head to base of tail." Count in as direct a line as possible down middle of back, starting immediately behind the large head scales and terminating at a point opposite rear margin of thighs. Hold thighs at right angles to lizard's trunk to be sure of correct stopping point. (This is the most practical method. Counting to a point directly above the anal opening, the real base of the tail, is difficult because it is not visible from above and, in turning the specimen back and forth, one can easily lose his place.)

The genus ranges from the Pacific Northwest and extreme southern New York to Panama.

ROSE-BELLIED LIZARD   Pl. 16
Sceloporus variabilis marmoratus

Identification: 3¾–5½ in. (9.5–14.0 cm); head–body max. 2⅛ in. (5.4 cm). Unique in two ways. Our only spiny lizard with: (a) pink belly patches; and (b) a skin pocket behind the thigh (Fig. 21, below). Neither one is a good field mark; the reptile usually must be caught to see them. The *light dorsolateral stripe* and row of brown spots down each side of back are best points to check. General coloration buffy- to olive-brown. *Male:* Large area of pink at each side of belly bordered fore and aft and toward center of belly by dark blue; the dark color extends upward onto sides of body to form a *prominent dark spot in armpit* and another much smaller one in groin. *Young:* About 2 in. (5.1 cm) at birth.

An essentially terrestrial lizard of arid southern Texas. Often seen on fence posts and in clumps of cactus; occasionally on rocks or in mesquite or other scrubby trees.

Similar species: (1) Prairie and Fence Lizards lack skin pocket behind thigh, and color on belly, when present, is blue and not

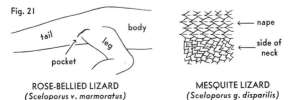

Fig. 21

ROSE-BELLIED LIZARD
(*Sceloporus v. marmoratus*)
Location of skin pocket

MESQUITE LIZARD
(*Sceloporus g. disparilis*)
Scales of neck

pink. (2) Mesquite Lizard lacks dorsolateral light line, and scales on side of neck are abruptly smaller than those on nape (Fig. 21, p. 99). (3) Texas Spiny Lizard grows very large and has only 33 or fewer dorsal scales counted from back of head to base of tail (58 or more in Rose-bellied Lizard). (4) Tree Lizard (*Urosaurus*) has fold of skin across throat (Fig. 54, opp. Pl. 16).

Range: S. Texas and ne. Mexico. Mexican and Cen. American subspecies.   Map 71

MESQUITE LIZARD   Pl. 16
Sceloporus grammicus disparilis

Identification: 4–6⅞ in. (10–17.5 cm); head–body max. 2⅞ in. (7.3 cm). An arboreal and remarkably camouflaged spiny lizard, best identified (at a distance) by habitat and habits. When caught, check on scalation. Only spiny lizard in southern Texas with scales on sides of neck abruptly *much* smaller than those on nape (Fig. 21, p. 99). General coloration gray or olive-gray. *Male:* Dorsum sometimes with a metallic greenish luster; markings obscure; a dark vertical line in front of arm; sides of belly pale blue, the blue bordered by black (toward center of belly); throat mottled with black except the center, which may be flesh color or pale blue. *Female:* 4 or 5 dark wavy lines across back; foreleg distinctly barred. *Young:* About 1⅝–1¹⁵⁄₁₆ in. (4.1–4.9 cm) at birth.

Most quiet and unobtrusive of the spiny lizards. Protective coloration and the habit of dodging to the opposite side of tree limb or bole are so well developed that few people ever see this reptile. Usually retreats to uppermost branches while observer is still far away. Found chiefly in mesquite, but also on other small scrubby trees.

Similar species: (1) Rose-bellied and Southern Prairie Lizards have a light dorsolateral stripe; both also are largely terrestrial. (2) Texas Spiny Lizard grows big and has large dorsal scales, numbering 33 or fewer from back of head to base of tail; dorsal scales are 50 or more in Mesquite Lizard. (3) Tree Lizard (*Urosaurus*) has fold of skin across throat (Fig. 54, opp. Pl. 16).

Range: Extr. s. Texas and n. Mexico. Mexican subspecies.
                                                             Map 70

CREVICE SPINY LIZARD   Pl. 17
Sceloporus poinsetti poinsetti

Identification: 5–11½ in. (13–29.2 cm); head–body max. 4⅝ in. (11.7 cm). The dark band across the neck is an excellent field mark. Tail strongly barred, especially *near tip*. Young, at birth, boldly crossbanded with black from head to tip of tail. Females tend to retain these markings, but in adult males they may virtually disappear, except across neck and on tail. General dorsal coloration gray or greenish gray to orange or reddish. *Male:* Throat bright blue; sides of belly bright blue, the blue bordered on its inner side by a broad black band. *Young:* Sometimes a narrow dark stripe connecting crossbands down center of back; 2½–3 in. (6.4–7.6 cm) at birth.

Boulders and rocky outcrops are favorite habitats, and on these the lizards may stand out conspicuously — at binocular range. Difficult to approach and capture in such places, quickly darting to opposite side or into crevices. Prying them from hiding places unharmed is difficult; the slightest touch makes them wedge themselves even tighter.

Similar species: (1) In Blue Spiny Lizard the tail markings are *not* conspicuous toward tip; light spots are present on nape and back. (2) In Collared Lizard, there are 2 black lines on neck, and scales are very small and smooth.

Range: Edwards Plateau of cen. Texas to sw. New Mexico; south into Chihuahua and to s. Coahuila. Mexican subspecies.
Map 66

BLUE SPINY LIZARD *Sceloporus cyanogenys*   **Pl. 17**
Identification: 5–14¼ in. (13–36.2 cm); head–body max. 5¹³⁄₁₆ in. (14.8 cm). Largest and bluest of the spiny lizards. The dark band across neck, bordered by white and in combination with light spots on nape and back, is a good field mark. Tail markings not conspicuous at tip. *Male:* A brilliant metallic greenish blue over a ground color of brown; upper sides of legs bronzy; entire throat bright blue; a large light blue patch at each side of belly bordered by a black band on inner side. *Female* (and young male): Gray or brown. *Young:* 2½–2¾ in. (6.4–7.0 cm) at birth.

Habitats include boulders, rocky or earthen cliffs, stone bridges, and abandoned houses.

Similar species: (1) In Crevice Spiny Lizard the black bands are conspicuous near *tip* of tail. (2) Collared Lizard has *two* black lines across neck, and scales are smooth and very small.
Range: S. Texas and ne. Mexico.   Map 67

TWIN-SPOTTED SPINY LIZARD   **Pl. 17**
Sceloporus magister bimaculosus
Identification: 7½–13 in. (19–33.0 cm); head–body max. 5½ in. (14.0 cm). A relatively pale, stocky lizard with large pointed scales, a narrow dark line running back from lower corner of eye, and a *black wedge (or blotch) on each side of neck.* Twin spots on back not sharply defined. General coloration pale gray or brown to straw color; some scales on sides may be yellow. Legs finely striped longitudinally with pale and dark gray. *Male:* Groin black; blue-green throat patch; two elongated blue-green belly patches edged with black and often joined

together. Mature males may have a wash of pale blue about 5 scales wide on forepart of back. *Female:* All blue pigment absent or only slightly indicated. *Young:* Markings much more prominent; black wedge bordered by yellow; 4 rows of black spots, a twin row on back and an extra row on each side of body. About 2⅞–3⅜ in. (7.3–8.6 cm) at hatching.

A wary but not especially speedy lizard of arid and semiarid country below 4000 ft. (1200 m) elevation. Seldom found far from dense thickets, rock piles, old buildings, burrows, or other refuges to which it darts when approached. Adults are chiefly terrestrial; young more arboreal. Large ones bite hard and, when held, may move their heads from side to side, forcing the sharp scales against one's fingers.

Similar species: Crevice Spiny Lizards have conspicuously crossbanded tails.

Range: Trans-Pecos Texas; w.-cen. New Mexico and se. Arizona to sw. Coahuila. Western and Mexican subspecies.   Map 65

TEXAS SPINY LIZARD *Sceloporus olivaceus*   **Pl. 17**
Identification: 7½–11 in. (19–27.9 cm); head–body max. 4¾ in. (12.1 cm). The "rusty lizard." Conspicuous field marks are lacking, but this is our only very large, very spiny, tree-inhabiting lizard. A rather vague dorsolateral light stripe (stronger in males) and wavy dark lines across the back (more conspicuous in females). General dorsal coloration gray- to rusty-brown. The very large dorsal scales, counted from back of head to base of tail, are 33 or fewer (average 30). *Male:* Narrow light blue area at each side of belly and *without* a black border. *Young:* 2½–2⅝ in. (6.4–6.7 cm) at hatching.

Usually seen in trees — mesquite, live oak, cottonwood, cedar, etc. They are inconspicuous against the bark and are usually discovered when they move or by the noise they make in climbing. Although essentially arboreal, Texas Spiny Lizards also may be seen on fences, old bridges, abandoned houses, in patches of prickly pear, or in other places that offer shelter in the form of cracks or cavities.

Similar species: Fence Lizard usually has a fairly complete black line running along rear surface of thigh. In Northern Fence and Prairie Lizards the dorsal scales are small; from back of head to base of tail they number 35 or more.

Range: Red River Cos. of n. Texas to ne. Mexico. Records from east of the Trinity River may be based on escaped (liberated?) specimens and not on established populations.   Map 69

FENCE LIZARD *Sceloporus undulatus*   **Pl. 16**
(subspecies *hyacinthinus* and *undulatus*)
Identification: 4–7¼ in. (10–18.4 cm); head–body max. 3¼ in. (8.3 cm). A small gray or brown spiny lizard with strong ar-

boreal tendencies. Females chiefly gray and most conspicuously patterned on top; males usually brown and most heavily marked on bottom. Both sexes have a more or less complete dark line running along rear surface of thigh. *Male:* Sides of belly hyacinth- to greenish-blue, the bright color bordered by black toward center of belly; a broad bluish area at base of throat, the blue surrounded by black and often split in 2 parts; dorsal crosslines indistinct or absent. *Female:* A series of dark wavy (undulating) lines across back; yellow, orange, or reddish at base of tail; belly whitish with scattered black flecks; small amounts of pale blue at sides of belly and throat. *Young:* Patterned like female but darker and duller; averaging 1⅝–2¼ in. (4.1–5.7 cm) at hatching.

Often seen on rail fences or on rotting logs or stumps. The only spiny lizard occurring throughout most of its range. (No other members of genus are found north of Florida or east of Texas.) When surprised on the ground, Fence Lizards usually dash for a nearby tree, climb upward for a short distance, and then remain motionless on the opposite side of the trunk. If approached, they dodge to the opposite side again, but higher up. The performance may be repeated several times, and the lizard soon ascends out of reach. Often called "pine lizard" because of its frequent occurrence in open pine woods.

Similar species (and subspecies): (1) Florida Scrub Lizard has a distinct *dark brown* lateral stripe. (2) Prairie Lizards have light longitudinal stripes, and are largely terrestrial in habits. (3) Texas Spiny Lizard grows much bigger, has very large dorsal scales, and lacks a dark line on rear of thigh.

Range: Se. New York to cen. Florida; west to e. Kansas and cen. Texas.

Subspecies: NORTHERN FENCE LIZARD, *Sceloporus u. hyacinthinus* (Plate 16). As described above. All of general range except the deep Southeast. SOUTHERN FENCE LIZARD, *Sceloporus u. undulatus.* Similar, but averaging slightly larger and with black markings more intense. Undersurfaces of males may be almost entirely black, except for patches of blue. In females the ventral black flecks are more numerous than in the northern race, and some of them may form a broken black line down center of belly. Dorsal scales larger, usually 37 or fewer from back of head to base of tail. In Northern Fence Lizard they are usually 38 or more. S. South Carolina to cen. Florida and e. Louisiana.   Map 72

PRAIRIE LIZARD *Sceloporus undulatus*   **Pl. 16**
(subspecies *garmani* and *consobrinus*)
Identification: 3½–5⅜ in. (9–13.7 cm); head–body max. 2⅛ in. (5.4 cm). The light longitudinal stripes, bold and usually clear-cut, are excellent field marks. (The lower stripe on each side

may be less conspicuous than in the specimens illustrated.)
Dark dorsal markings, so prominent in other subspecies, are
reduced to spots bordering the light dorsolateral stripe. Ground
color light brown to reddish brown; a light brown stripe down
center of back. *Male:* Two long narrow light blue patches, one
at each side of belly, bordered medially with black and well
separated from each other. Throat markings absent or consisting of two small widely separated blue patches. *Female:* Uniform white below, and without the black flecks of the Fence
Lizards. *Young:* About 1¾-2 in. (4.4-5.1 cm) at hatching.

Essentially terrestrial, but occupying a wide variety of habitats — stabilized (non-blowing) sand dunes and other sandy
areas, open prairies (but with weeds, brush, or mammal burrows
for cover), brushy flatlands, etc. Often found under shocks of
wheat. Forages widely for food but scurries to cover when
approached. Northern sandhill-dwelling specimens are awkward at climbing, but southern prairie dwellers commonly ascend into yuccas and other low plants.

Similar species (and subspecies): (1) In Fence Lizard a dorsolateral light stripe is sometimes evident, but it is not well defined
and is crossed by the dark markings of the back. Male Fence
Lizards are conspicuously marked with black on throat and
belly. (2) Texas Spiny Lizard grows much bigger, and its very
large dorsal scales number only 33 or fewer counted from back
of head to base of tail (35 or more in Prairie Lizards). (3) Racerunners, most Whiptail Lizards, and many of the Skinks have
prominent light stripes, but none has large keeled scales.

Range: S. South Dakota to n. Mexico; west through New
Mexico to se. Arizona.

Subspecies: NORTHERN PRAIRIE LIZARD, *Sceloporus u. garmani* (Plate 16). As described above. Gular patches absent or
faint, not black-bordered. S. South Dakota to cen. Oklahoma
and ne. corner of Texas panhandle; isolated populations in extr.
e. New Mexico. SOUTHERN PRAIRIE LIZARD, *Sceloporus u. consobrinus.* Similar but with the light stripes less prominent.
Males have 2 large gular patches, blue and black-bordered, that
often fuse together across throat; females usually have a small
amount of blue on throat. Averages considerably larger than
the northern subspecies, and attains a total length of about 7 in.
(18 cm) and a head–body maximum of 2¾ in. (7.0 cm). A lizard
of the plains and mountains (although it avoids the highest
elevations). Especially common in rocky terrain that furnishes
abundant hiding and basking places. Sw. Oklahoma to extr. se.
Arizona and well south into Mexico. Intergrades with Northern
Fence Lizard over a rather broad area through e.-cen. Texas.
Western subspecies, including a pale gray to almost white, virtually patternless race that is confined to the White Sands region
of New Mexico.   Map 72

RED-CHINNED SCALY LIZARD   Not illus.
Sceloporus undulatus erythrocheilus
Identification: 4–7½ in. (10–19.1 cm); head–body max. 3 in. (7.6 cm). A spiny lizard characterized by the yellow to reddish coloration of the chin anterior to the blue throat patches. The colors are more intense in males than in females and may be bright rusty red during the breeding season.

A rock-face lizard, often found on cliffs, lava flows, gully banks, etc., where cover in the form of vegetation or cracks and fissures is available.

Range: Barely enters our area in extr. w. Oklahoma. Se. Wyoming south through e.-cen. Colorado to ne. New Mexico.

Map 72

FLORIDA SCRUB LIZARD   *Sceloporus woodi*   Pl. 16
Identification: 3¹³⁄₁₆–5¹¹⁄₁₆ in. (10–14.4 cm); head–body max. 2⁵⁄₁₆ in. (5.9 cm). A spiny lizard with a *dark brown* lateral stripe. General coloration brown or gray-brown above, whitish below. *Male:* Middorsal area with few, if any, markings. A long blue patch on each side of belly, bordered by black on inner side; a pair of blue spots at base of throat; rest of throat black except for a median white stripe. *Female:* Seven to 10 dark brown wavy lines across back; rarely, these may be fused or otherwise altered to form dark longitudinal lines. Dark spots often present on chest and undersurface of head; some blue on throat and sides of belly (not bordered by black). *Young:* Similar to female but paler and with the markings darkening with age; about 1¾ in. (4.4 cm) at hatching.

A lizard characteristic of the sand-pine scrub but sometimes found in adjacent beach dune scrub, longleaf pine-turkey oak woodlands, or citrus groves where areas of open sandy ground exist. More terrestrial than the Fence Lizard in foraging and escape behavior, but commonly seen on lower tree trunks.

Similar species: In Southern Fence Lizard the undersurfaces are marked with considerable black pigment, and there may be a *black* lateral stripe, but it is not so clear-cut as the *brown* stripe in the Florida Scrub Lizard. Dorsal scales (counted from back of head to base of tail) in Scrub Lizard average more than 40; in Southern Fence Lizard average is 34.

Range: Apparently restricted to four disjunct areas in cen. and s. Florida.   Map 68

SAGEBRUSH LIZARD   Pl. 16
Sceloporus graciosus graciosus
Identification: 4½–5⅞ in. (11–14.9 cm); head–body max. 2⅝ in. (6.7 cm). A pale brown spiny lizard with 4 longitudinal rows of darker brown spots that may run together to suggest dark longitudinal stripes. Usually 2 pale dorsolateral stripes, one extending backward from each eye and terminating on the tail.

Often an irregular black spot on shoulder. *Small granular scales on rear surface of thigh. Male:* A large elongated blue patch at each side of belly; no blue throat patches, although throat may be mottled with blue. *Young:* About 2½ in. (6.4 cm) at hatching.

Often found in sagebrush, but also occurs on rocks, in open forested areas, or in canyon bottoms. Essentially terrestrial, seldom climbs, and usually remains close to shelter.

Similar species: (1) Other Spiny Lizards have *large keeled scales on rear of thigh.* (2) In Prairie and Red-chinned Scaly Lizards (as among other members of the *S. undulatus* complex) there is a narrow dark line between eyes.

Range: Known in our area only from w. S. Dakota and w. N. Dakota; Montana to nw. New Mexico and west to the Pacific Coast. Western subspecies.   Map 64

SAND DUNE LIZARD   Pl. 16
Sceloporus graciosus arenicolous

Identification: 4½–6 in. (11–15.2 cm); head–body max. 2¾ in. (7.0 cm). A relatively faint grayish-brown stripe, extending from upper edge of ear opening to the tail, is the most conspicuous pattern feature of this very pale lizard. Dorsum light yellowish brown or light golden brown; venter white, cream-colored, or yellowish. *Small granular scales on rear surface of thigh* instead of keeled scales. *Male:* A large, elongated, bright blue patch at each side of belly, bordered midventrally by a band of deeper blue or black. No blue on throat in either sex.

A ghostly streak dashing across the sandhills that usually comes to rest hidden or nearly hidden beneath patches of dwarf shin oak, sand sagebrush, prairie yuccas, or other plants. Most specimens match the sand so closely they virtually disappear when they stop running. If closely pursued, they often hide in leaf litter or burrow in the sand beneath sheltering vegetation.

Similar species: (1) Other Spiny Lizards have large scales on rear surface of thigh. (2) The Side-blotched Lizard has a dark spot posterior to the arm.

Range: Active sand dune areas from Andrews to Crane Cos., Texas, and the Mescalero Sands of se. New Mexico.   Map 64

CANYON LIZARD   *Sceloporus merriami*   Pl. 16
Identification: 4½–6¼ in. (11–15.9 cm); head–body max. 2¼ in. (5.7 cm). A rock-dwelling spiny lizard that usually matches the general coloration of the cliffs and boulders on which it is found (gray, tan, reddish brown, etc.). Four rows of dark spots on back that are most conspicuous in the two westernmost subspecies. A *vertical black bar* on shoulder directly in front of foreleg, but this may be obscured by a fold of skin if the lizard turns its head toward you. *Scales at sides of body tiny* (granular);

dorsal scales, although keeled, are small. Scales on sides of neck abruptly smaller than those on nape, and comparable with change in Mesquite Lizard (Fig. 21, p. 99). A partially developed throat fold (Fig. 19, p. 94). *Male:* Belly with 2 large blue patches that are broadly margined midventrally and posteriorly with black; there may be a white midventral stripe, or the black markings may merge together from the two sides. Blue and black lines on throat. Crosslines may be present under tail. A small but rather conspicuous dewlap. *Female:* Ventral markings much less extensive than those in male; dewlap proportionately smaller. *Young:* About 2 in. (5.1 cm) at hatching.

Boulders, rocky outcrops, and the rocky walls of canyons are the favorite habitats of this small lizard. It is not very wary, and, if frightened, may reappear soon after taking refuge in a crack or crevice.

Similar species: (1) Other Spiny Lizards within range have large keeled scales on sides of body. (2) Tree and Side-blotched Lizards have a fold of skin completely across throat. (3) Whiptail Lizards have tiny dorsal scales and broad rectangular belly plates.

Range: W. Texas from Edwards to Presidio Cos.; s.-cen. Coahuila and canyon of the Río Conchos, Chihuahua.

Subspecies: BIG BEND CANYON LIZARD, *Sceloporus m. annulatus* (Plate 16). Dark dorsal spots well defined; usually 52 or fewer dorsal scales from back of head to base of tail. Ventral markings bold and extensive in males. Higher elevations of Big Bend region of w. Texas. MERRIAM'S CANYON LIZARD, *Sceloporus m. merriami.* A pale, ashen race with dorsal spots faint or absent; usually 58 or more dorsal scales; a narrow white midventral stripe in males; dark ventral markings reduced. Named for C. Hart Merriam, originator and chief of the Bureau of Biological Survey, a forerunner of the U.S. Fish and Wildlife Service. W. Texas from Edwards and Crockett Cos. to s.-cen. Brewster Co. and adj. Mexico. PRESIDIO CANYON LIZARD, *Sceloporus m. longipunctatus.* Dorsal spots comma-shaped, with tails of commas pointing outward; ventral markings paler and less extensive than in subspecies *annulatus.* S. Presidio Co., Texas. Mexican subspecies.   Map 62

Miscellaneous Iguanid Lizards: Genera *Leiocephalus, Urosaurus,* and *Uta*

MEMBERS of these genera bear varying degrees of resemblance to the spiny lizards (*Sceloporus*). The curly-tailed *Leiocephalus,* one species of which has been introduced and is now established in southern Florida, is otherwise confined to the West Indies. Members of the other two genera may be recognized by the fold across their throats and the absence of large, strongly keeled scales over most of their bodies. Both range widely through the southwestern U.S. and into Mexico, the tree lizards (*Urosaurus*) southward to Chiapas and the side-blotched lizards (*Uta*) into the northern Mexican states.

NORTHERN CURLY-TAILED LIZARD   Pl. 17
Leiocephalus carinatus armouri

Identification: 7–10¼ in. (18–26.0 cm); head–body max. 4⅛ in. (10.5 cm). Here is a lizard that signals its identity by holding its tail curled over its back. In other respects it resembles a large, robust spiny lizard.

Curly-tailed lizards of many kinds occur on Cuba, Hispaniola, the Bahamas, and numerous small islands where they occupy a variety of habitats including rocky coasts and beaches and scrub and pine woods. They even invade towns and villages. On islands where English is spoken they are called "lion lizards."

Range: Introduced. Known to occur on Key Biscayne and Virginia Key se. of Miami, on Palm Beach I. and the adjacent mainland, and possibly in other parts of se. Florida. Native to Grand Bahama I., the Abacos, and associated keys of the Little Bahama Bank, Bahama Islands. Numerous Cuban and Bahaman subspecies; other races on the Cayman and Swan Is.

Map 63

TREE LIZARD   *Urosaurus ornatus*   Pl. 16

Identification: 4–5⅝ in. (10–13.7 cm); head–body max. 2 in. (5.1 cm). A small gray or grayish-brown lizard with arboreal tendencies. Back has irregular dark spots or crossbands, some narrowly edged with blue. Check for three things: (a) a fold of skin running across the throat (Fig. 54, opp. Pl. 16); (b) dorsal scales variable in size — some large, some tiny; and (c) 2 long folds of skin on each side of body. The folds give the Tree Lizard a somewhat wrinkled appearance, as though the skin were a little too large for it. Throat yellow or pale orange in adults. *Male:* Three blue patches — one centered under throat and another at each side of belly. *Young:* About 1¼–1¾ in. (3.2–4.4 cm) at hatching.

Almost always seen in trees or on rocks and usually resting in a *vertical* position — "heads up" with tail dangling, or the reverse with head pointing down. Trips to the ground, either to forage or to move from one tree or rock to another, are usually brief. A difficult reptile to observe or catch by hand. When motionless, camouflage is nearly perfect, but the lizard often may reveal itself by indulging in bobbing movements. When pursued, it is adept at dodging, keeping on opposite side of tree trunk or rock and climbing quickly out of reach.

Similar species: Various members of the Spiny Lizard genus (*Sceloporus*), although similar to Tree Lizard in gross appearance, have following distinctive features: (a) *no* fold completely across throat; and (b) dorsal scales all approximately *same size*.

Range: Cen. Texas and Rio Grande Valley; west to se. California and north to Utah and sw. Wyoming; south in w. Mexico to cen. Sinaloa.

Subspecies: EASTERN TREE LIZARD, *Urosaurus o. ornatus* (Plate 16). Enlarged scales of the inner series on each side of dorsum about twice as large as those of outer series. Cen. Texas and Rio Grande Valley. BIG BEND TREE LIZARD, *Urosaurus o. schmidti*. Inner series of enlarged dorsal scales *not* twice as large as outer ones. Usually seen on rocks and boulders and often associated with the Canyon Lizard in desert habitats, but utilizes trees in the mountains. Trans-Pecos Texas and adj. Mexico and New Mexico. Western and Mexican subspecies.   Map 61

DESERT SIDE-BLOTCHED LIZARD   Pl. 15
Uta stansburiana stejnegeri

Identification: 4–5⅜ in. (10–13.7 cm); head–body max. 2⅛ in. (5.4 cm). Our only lizard with a blue-spangled back (chiefly in males) and a *single black spot posterior to the arm pit*. Except in the very young the spot may be readily seen with binoculars, at least at close range. General coloration brown, striped and spotted, or with a profusion of blue flecks on the back and yellow to pale orange-brown spots on the sides. With the lizard at hand check for two things: (a) a single fold of skin across the throat (Fig. 19, p. 94); (b) middorsal scales keeled and larger than the small smooth scales on the sides of the body (use a lens). *Female:* A pale, dark-bordered stripe from eye to base of tail and another stripe or series of pale spots from upper lip to groin. *Adult male:* Pale stripes greatly reduced or absent; throat and lower sides of body washed with pale blue or pale bluish gray. *Young:* About 2⅚₁₆ in. (5.9 cm) at hatching.

An abundant lizard in many areas; often found in sandy regions and on desert flats and foothills. Chiefly terrestrial, but also climbs on rocks or boulders. Less speedy than many other lizards, and seldom wanders far from such shelters as crevices, mammal burrows, or clumps of vegetation.

Similar species: (1) Earless Lizards (*Holbrookia*) may show *2* dark spots behind the foreleg when viewed from the side, but they have *2 folds* of skin under the throat (Fig. 19, p. 94). (2) Spiny Lizards (*Sceloporus*) lack complete throat folds.

Range: Trans-Pecos Texas, the Texas panhandle, and extr. sw. Oklahoma; New Mexico and extr. se. Arizona to w. Coahuila and n. Durango. Western and Mexican subspecies.   Map 60.

Horned Lizards: Genus *Phrynosoma*

THE "horned toads," the majority of them adorned like cactus plants, are the most bizarre of all our lizards. The arrangement of the spines, especially on the head, and the fringe scales at the sides of the abdomen offer the best clues to identification.

Horned lizards are diurnal. They eat spiders, sowbugs, and insects — ants especially — but high temperatures are required to stimulate their appetites. Even when a heat lamp is used, they are difficult to keep in captivity in the North; most of them refuse food during the winter months and die either during cold weather of after their first meal in the spring. Horned lizards are protected by law in many states.

An extraordinary habit is the occasional squirting of blood from the forward corners of the eyes for a distance of several feet. This is associated with an ability to increase blood pressure in the head. Some species lay eggs; others give birth to living young. Despite their spiny garb, horned lizards are eaten by certain birds, such as hawks and roadrunners, and by such reptiles as whipsnakes and collared lizards. The genus ranges from southern Canada to Guatemala and is particularly well represented in the Southwest and in Mexico.

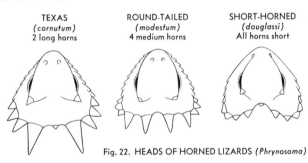

| TEXAS
(*cornutum*)
2 long horns | ROUND-TAILED
(*modestum*)
4 medium horns | SHORT-HORNED
(*douglassi*)
All horns short |

Fig. 22. HEADS OF HORNED LIZARDS (*Phrynosoma*)

TEXAS HORNED LIZARD *Phrynosoma cornutum*   **Pl. 15**
  Identification: 2½-4 in. (6–10 cm); record 7⅛ in. (18.1 cm); head-body max. 5⅛ in. (13.0 cm). This "horned toad" is the species most frequently carried home, often illegally, by tourists or visitors to the Southwest. The 2 central head spines are *much longer* than any of the others (Fig. 22, above). *Two rows* of fringe scales at each side of abdomen. The general coloration is usually some shade of brown — yellowish, reddish, grayish, or tan — but may sometimes be gray. Dark dorsal spots usually conspicuous and with light posterior borders. *Young:* About 1⅛–1¼ in. (2.9–3.2 cm) at hatching.

A lizard typically of flat, open terrain with sparse plant cover; often found in areas of sandy, rocky, or loamy soil. Occurs from sea level to at least 6000 ft. (1800 m). Specimens are usually in evidence only on very warm days. They run surprisingly fast and seek refuge in mammal burrows, rock piles or ledges, or clumps of vegetation.

Similar species: (1) In Round-tailed Horned Lizard: (a) the tail is slender and rounded but broadens abruptly near base; (b) all the longer horns are about equal in length; and (c) there are *no* fringe scales at edge of abdomen. (2) In Short-horned Lizards the horns are greatly reduced in size (Fig. 22, p. 110), and there is *one row* of fringe scales.

Range: Kansas and nw. Louisiana to se. Arizona and n. Mexico; introduced in Florida and other southern states.   Map 55

NORTHERN SHORT-HORNED LIZARD   Pl. 15
Phrynosoma douglassi brevirostre
Identification: 2½–3¾ in. (6–9.5 cm); record 4½ in. (11.4 cm); head–body max. 2½ in. (6.4 cm). Short, stubby horns (Fig. 22, p. 110) and only a *single row* of fringe scales along each side of abdomen. Ground color brown or gray. *Young:* About 1¼ in. (3.2 cm) at birth.

Indigenous to semiarid, shortgrass portions of the northern Great Plains; usually found in rather rough terrain.
Similar species: See Texas Horned Lizard.
Range: Western parts of the Dakotas and Nebraska; Montana and adj. Canada south to e. Colorado and extr. ne. Utah. Formerly believed to range eastward to cen. Kansas, hence old name of "Eastern Short-horned Lizard." Western subspecies. Map 54

MOUNTAIN SHORT-HORNED LIZARD   Pl. 15
Phrynosoma douglassi hernandesi
Identification: 3¾–5 in. (9.5–13 cm); record 5⅞ in. (14.9 cm); head–body max. 4⁵⁄₁₆ in. (10.9 cm). Like the Northern Short-horned Lizard, but larger, and adults usually more colorful, often with much orange or reddish-brown pigment on both dorsum and venter. Short horns and *one row of fringe scales.* *Young:* About 1½ in. (3.8 cm) at birth.

An upland race, found within our area only in or near forested portions of the Guadalupe and Davis Mountains, but it may occur in other forested mountains of western Texas.
Similar species: See Texas Horned Lizard.
Range: W. Texas; Colorado and Utah south to nw. Chihuahua. Mexican subspecies.   Map 54

ROUND-TAILED HORNED LIZARD   Pl. 15
Phrynosoma modestum
Identification: 3–4⅛ in. (8–10.5 cm); head–body max. 2¾ in. (7.0 cm). Three distinct items to check: (a) tail round and slen-

der but broadened abruptly near base; (b) 4 horns at back of head, all about equal in length (Fig. 22, p. 110); and (c) *no* row of fringe scales along side of abdomen. Coloration variable: general tone may be yellowish gray or ash-white or any of several shades of light brown, but adults usually closely match the dominant soil color of the immediate habitat; young and half-grown individuals are less likely to match. The ability to change color is marked, and the intensity of the dark blotches may vary from black to pale hues only a little darker than ground color. *Young:* About 1¼–1½ in. (3.2–3.8 cm) at hatching.

This "horny toad" is so well camouflaged that it can easily be overlooked. Normally it remains motionless when approached and with its body flattened so closely to the ground that it casts almost no shadow — a trait common to all our horned lizards. It may be almost stepped on before it moves. After a short dash, it stops abruptly, virtually vanishing against the background. Habitats include desert flats and washes and arid and semiarid plains with shrubby vegetation.

Similar species: See Texas Horned Lizard.

Range: W.-cen. Texas to se. Arizona and cen. Mexico; isolated records in Oklahoma, s. Texas, and Tamaulipas.   Map 53

Whiptails: Family Teiidae

A LARGE family, confined to the New World and especially abundant and diverse in South America. Only one genus (*Cnemidophorus*) is native to the United States, but there are many species in the West. Nine occur in our area; all are diurnal, and may be recognized as whiptails by their long tails and active, nervous prowling. There are thousands of tiny scales (granules) on their backs and 8 rows of large rectangular scales on their bellies (Fig. 23, below). The tail is rough to the touch.

Distinguishing among the many species is difficult, partly because some look confusingly alike and partly because their patterns change with age and growth. Positive identification often is impossible unless the specimen is in hand, and then the following must be checked: (a) How many light longitudinal stripes are there? (b) Are

Fig. 23. BACK AND BELLY SCALES OF WHIPTAILS AND SKINKS

WHIPTAILS AND RACERUNNERS
(*Cnemidophorus*)
Rows of enlarged scales on belly

SKINKS
(*Eumeces*)
All scales approximately same size

there pale spots in the dark fields between the light stripes? (c) Do the small scales around the inner edge of the supraorbital scales (the supraorbital semicircles) penetrate far forward or do they stop before they reach the frontal plate (Fig. 24, below)? (d) Are the scales directly anterior to the gular fold abruptly enlarged? (e) Is there a patch of enlarged scales on the rear of the forearm (Fig. 25, p. 114)? (f) How many granules are there across the back at midbody? (Use a strong lens or dissecting microscope, and count the granules all the way around the body in as straight a line as possible. Do *not* include the large belly scales.)

Fig. 24. HEAD CHARACTERISTICS OF WHIPTAIL LIZARDS *(Cnemidophorus)*

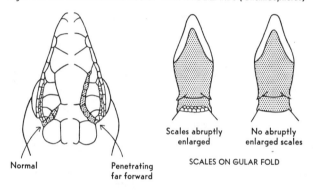

Scales abruptly enlarged

No abruptly enlarged scales

SCALES ON GULAR FOLD

Normal

Penetrating far forward

SUPRAORBITAL SEMICIRCLES

Several kinds of whiptails are unisexual, and reproduction is through parthenogenesis (development of an unfertilized egg). Males are completely unknown in some species; they have been reported in others, but there is some evidence to indicate that such males may be hybrids between the unisexual form and a bisexual species inhabiting the same area. Food consists chiefly of insects, but also includes spiders, scorpions, and other small arthropods. Often these are dug from the ground, suggesting that the sense of smell or hearing may be useful in locating prey. Although whiptails can easily be observed through binoculars and they often approach to within a few feet of a person, they are extremely difficult to catch by hand. Several collectors working together can drive them into a drift fence equipped with a trap; pitfall traps set beneath boards or flat stones may also be successful. Despite their narrow heads they can be noosed if, as soon as they are snared, they are swung continuously until one's free hand can grab them.

Another representative of the Family Teiidae, a member of the genus *Ameiva,* has been introduced and is now established in southern Florida (see p. 120). The species of *Ameiva,* which are es-

Patch of enlarged scales

No enlarged scales

Fig. 25
REAR OF FOREARM
IN WHIPTAIL LIZARDS
(*Cnemidophorus*)

pecially numerous in the West Indies, also range, collectively, from cen. Tamaulipas and Nayarit southward along both coasts of Mexico and through Central and South America to southeastern Brazil.

CHIHUAHUA WHIPTAIL   Pl. 18
Cnemidophorus exsanguis

Identification: 9½–12⅜ in. (24–31.4 cm); head–body max. 3⅞ in. (9.8 cm). A distinctly brownish whiptail with *6 light stripes*. Pale yellowish or whitish spots in the dark fields *and on the stripes*. Dark fields brown or reddish brown; stripes pale brown or gray brown, most conspicuous and often yellowish on sides of body. Tail dark, usually brown, but often with a greenish tinge. Venter whitish or faintly bluish, unmarked. Enlarged scales along anterior edge of gular fold (Fig. 24, p. 113) and on rear of forearm (Fig. 25, above). Supraorbital semicircles normal (Fig. 24, p. 113); 65–79 granules around midbody. Unisexual. *Young:* Stripes yellow or whitish, clean-cut and sharply in contrast with the dark brown or blackish fields; paravertebral stripes wavy. *Pale reddish spots present in hatchlings.* A light middorsal stripe may be present on the nape; this disappears or is only vaguely indicated in adults. Tail blue or greenish. Head–body length about 1⁵⁄₁₆–1⁹⁄₁₆ in. (3.3–4.0 cm) at hatching.

Habitats vary from desert grasslands to forested mountains. This whiptail is usually found in the open, but always near cover — on rocky hillsides, in canyon bottoms or dry washes, and, like the other unisexual whiptails, most often in disturbed areas such as along draws or arroyos where flooding occurs periodically.

Similar species: (1) Spotted Whiptail (*gularis*) is easily confused with Chihuahua Whiptail in Trans-Pecos Texas. Upperside of tail is dark in Chihuahua, but *pink* in Spotted. Also, Spotted Whiptail has pale spots largely confined to the lateral dark fields; spots occur in all dark fields in the Chihuahua. Spotted also has 7 or 8 light stripes, in contrast with 6 in the Chihuahua Whiptail. Males of Spotted have pink on chin and often black on chest. (2) In New Mexico Whiptail (*neomexicanus*) the light stripes are sharply in contrast with the dark fields at all ages, the middorsal light stripe is distinctly wavy, the pale spots in the dark fields are obscure, and the supraorbital semicircles penetrate far forward.

Range: Trans-Pecos Texas to n.-cen. New Mexico and west to se. Arizona; through Chihuahua to ne. Sonora. Map 91

SPOTTED WHIPTAIL   Pl. 18
Cnemidophorus gularis gularis

Identification: 6½–11 in. (16.5–27.9 cm); head–body max. 3½ in. (8.9 cm). A liberally spotted, 7 or 8-striped whiptail. The vertebral (middorsal) stripe is very broad and often splits in two (to give count of 8). Stripes normally whitish or yellowish, but often greenish anteriorly and brownish posteriorly. Pale spots prominent in *lateral* dark fields, but faint or absent in paravertebral dark fields; spots white or pale yellow, changing to brownish toward rear of body. Tail pink, pale orange-brown, or reddish. Enlarged scales along anterior edge of gular fold (Fig. 24, p. 113) and on rear of forearm (Fig. 25, p. 114). Supraorbital semicircles normal (Fig. 24, p. 113); 76–93 granules around midbody. Bisexual. *Male:* Chin pink, red, or orange; chest and belly blue, frequently also with a large black patch. *Female:* Venter unmarked, whitish or cream throughout life. *Young:* Striped, but spotting faint or absent, and confined to lateral dark fields when present; tail pink or reddish; rump reddish. Head–body length about 1⅜ in. (3.5 cm) at hatching.

A lizard of prairie grasslands, river floodplains and washes, grassland reverting to brush, and rocky hillsides. More deliberate in its movements than Prairie Racerunner and generally less wary.

Similar species: (1) Prairie Racerunner (*viridis*) is bright green anteriorly, lacks spots in dark fields, and has a short light stripe extending backward from hind leg. (2) Chihuahua Whiptail (*exsanguis*) has 6 light lines and an unmarked venter at all ages, and pale spots in paravertebral as well as lateral dark fields. Also check number of granules between paravertebral light stripes — 10 to 21 in Spotted Whiptail, 3 to 7 in Chihuahua Whiptail. (3) In Rusty-rumped Whiptail (*scalaris*) dorsal stripes and dark fields both terminate on body.

Range: S. Oklahoma, Texas panhandle, and se. New Mexico to n. Veracruz. Mexican subspecies. Map 86

SEVEN-STRIPED WHIPTAIL   Pl. 18
Cnemidophorus inornatus heptagrammus

Identification: 6½–9⅜ in. (16.5–23.8 cm); head–body max. 2¹³⁄₁₆ in. (7.1 cm). The "blue-tailed whiptail." *Tail bright blue to purplish blue* at all ages. The juvenile pattern of 7 light stripes separated by dark, *unspotted fields* is retained throughout life. Stripes yellow in young, whitish or cream in adults.

Fields black in young, becoming grayish or brownish with age. Scales anterior to gular fold slightly enlarged (Fig. 24, p. 113); approximately two rows of scales on posterior surface of forearm slightly enlarged (Fig. 25, p. 114). Supraorbital semicircles normal (Fig. 24, p. 113); 55–71 granules around midbody. Bisexual. *Male: Venter and sides of head bright blue* (bluish to bluish white in females). *Young:* Less blue below than in adults; head-body length about 1⅛ in. (2.9 cm) at hatching.

Primarily a lizard of the foothills in western Texas, most often found on rocky, grassy slopes and deteriorated grassland or where a rocky knoll pushes upward above flat mesa tops. Sometimes seen on alluvial flats or on sandy-silty soil.

Similar species: (1) Desert-Grassland (*uniparens*) and New Mexico (*neomexicanus*) Whiptails have greenish tails. (2) Spotted Whiptail (*gularis*) has pink tail. (3) New Mexico and Chihuahua (*exsanguis*) Whiptails have pale spots in their dark fields.

Range: Trans-Pecos Texas and adjacent portions of New Mexico, Chihuahua, and Coahuila. Western and Mexican subspecies.   Map 84

NEW MEXICO WHIPTAIL   Pl. 18
Cnemidophorus neomexicanus

Identification: 8–11⅞ in. (20–30.2 cm); head–body max. 3⅜ in. (8.6 cm). A pattern of 7 pale yellow stripes, all equally distinct, but with the *middorsal stripe wavy*. Fields brown to black and obscurely spotted throughout life. Tail *greenish gray*. Venter white to pale blue, unmarked. Usually no abruptly enlarged scales anterior to gular fold (Fig. 24, p. 113) or on posterior surface of forearm (Fig. 25, p. 114). *Supraorbital semicircles penetrating far forward* (Fig. 24, p. 113); 71–85 granules around midbody. Unisexual. *Young:* Strongly striped, yellow on black, and with spots in the dark fields. Tail bright blue in hatchlings. Head–body length about 1⅜–1⅝ in. (3.5–4.1 cm) at hatching.

A lizard of disturbed areas; for example, where periodic flooding at the confluence of arroyos with the Rio Grande provides a perpetually disturbed, sandy habitat. Also occurs around the perimeters of playas, in open sandy places, such as washes and draws, and in terrain altered by human activities.

Similar species: (1) In Desert-Grassland Whiptail (*uniparens*) middorsal light stripe is straight-edged and supraorbital semicircles are normal. (2) See also Chihuahua Whiptail (*exsanguis*), in which the spots are much more numerous and the stripes less well defined. The New Mexico Whiptail (*neomexicanus*) occasionally hybridizes with other kinds, especially the Seven-striped Whiptail (*inornatus*).

Range: Chiefly the Rio Grande Valley from Presidio Co., Texas, to north of Santa Fe, New Mexico.   Map 89

RUSTY-RUMPED WHIPTAIL   Pl. 18
Cnemidophorus scalaris septemvittatus

Identification: 8-12½ in. (20-31.8 cm); head–body max. 4⅛ in. (10.5 cm). Two main pattern characteristics: (a) dorsal stripes terminating toward rear of body; and (b) *rump and base of tail rusty red or orange.* Hind legs may also be rust-colored. The young are patterned with 6 or 7 light stripes; adults retain this basic pattern, but the dark fields become spotted as the lizard grows. Tail brown or gray. Venter white or pale blue; a few black spots on chin and chest in some specimens. Enlarged scales along anterior edge of gular fold (Fig. 24, p. 113) and on rear of forearm (Fig. 25, p. 114). Supraorbital semicircles normal (Fig. 24, p. 113); 77-98 granules around midbody. Bisexual. *Young:* Light stripes inclined to be wavy, with the middorsal one intermittent; fields very dark with pale spots chiefly in lowermost dark field; tail blue or greenish. Head–body length about 1½ in. (3.8 cm) at hatching.

When prowling, this lizard moves slowly and deliberately in comparison with some of the other whiptails. It often roots in ground litter, overturning sticks and stones with its snout. A resident of mountains and desert foothills, of lava flows and canyons. Seldom climbs and is most frequently found in rocky situations with sparse vegetation.

Similar species: (1) The rusty rump distinguishes this species from all our other Whiptails. (2) In the Short-lined Skink the light stripes terminate on the shoulder and the belly scales are approximately same size as dorsal ones (Fig. 23, p. 112).

Range: Big Bend region of Texas; adj. Chihuahua and much of Coahuila. Mexican subspecies.   Map 87

SIX-LINED RACERUNNER   Pl. 18
Cnemidophorus sexlineatus sexlineatus

Identification: 6-9½ in. (15-24.1 cm); head–body max. 3 in. (7.6 cm). The only whiptail in eastern United States. Six light stripes; no spots in dark fields. Stripes yellow, white, pale gray, or pale blue. Dark fields some shade of brown, sometimes almost black. A short light stripe on side of tail, extending backward from hind leg and bordered below by a dark line. Scales anterior to gular fold conspicuously enlarged (Fig. 24, p. 113); scales on rear of forearm only slightly enlarged or not at all (Fig. 25, p. 114). Supraorbital semicircles normal (Fig. 24, p. 113); 89-110 granules around midbody. Bisexual. *Male:* Stripes less intense; belly washed with blue. *Young:* Light blue tail; stripes yellow and sharply in contrast with dark fields; head–body length about 1⅛-1¼ in. (2.9-3.2 cm) at hatching.

An active lizard, conspicuous because of its boldness. Open, well-drained areas are preferred — those covered with sand or loose soil; fields, open woods, thicket margins, rocky outcrops, river floodplains, etc. Racerunners are well named, usually winning the race with the would-be collector. Called "field-streaks" in some parts of range and "sandlappers" in others. When pursued, they take refuge in vegetation, under boards or stones, or in burrows that are sometimes of their own making. **Similar species:** Skinks are shiny, and their ventral scales are like dorsal scales in size and shape.

Range: Maryland to Florida Keys and west to Missouri and e. Texas; north in Illinois River Valley and to dune region of nw. Indiana, and Mississippi River Valley to ne. Minnesota and adj. Wisconsin.   Map 93

PRAIRIE RACERUNNER   Pl. 18
Cnemidophorus sexlineatus viridis

Identification: 6–10½ in. (15–26.7 cm); head–body max. 3⅜ in. (8.6 cm) in some females. Similar to the eastern subspecies (Six-lined Racerunner) except that there are *7 light stripes* and the coloration is *bright green anteriorly.* Scutellation also similar, but dorsal granules are fewer (62–91 around midbody). Bisexual. *Male:* Belly pale blue. *Young:* Head–body length about 1 3/16 in. (3.0 cm) at hatching.

Occupies a variety of habitats — banks and floodplains of rivers, open grasslands with scattered bushes, and the vicinity of rock outcrops; occurs in both lowland and hilly terrain.

Similar species: Other Whiptails within its range have pale spots in the dark fields. (1) Spotted Whiptail (*gularis*) lacks the short light stripe on side of tail, extending backward from hind leg and bordered below by a dark stripe (a characteristic shared by both kinds of Racerunners). (2) In Checkered Whiptail (*tesselatus*) the supraorbital semicircles extend far forward. (3) Seven-striped Whiptail (*inornatus*) has a blue tail and a bluish suffusion over head and sides of body.

Range: S. South Dakota and se. Wyoming south to s. Texas; possibly in adj. Mexico.   Map 93

CHECKERED WHIPTAIL   Pl. 18
Cnemidophorus tesselatus

Identification: 11–15½ in. (28–39.4 cm); head–body max. 4 3/16 in. (10.6 cm). Largest of our whiptails. Many individuals and some entire populations bear checkered patterns, but others have rows of black spots or other modifications. Ground color yellowish to cream. Tail brown to yellow. Venter plain whitish or with some black spots; chin usually unmarked. *Scales anterior to gular fold abruptly enlarged* (Fig. 24, p. 113). No distinctly enlarged scales on rear of forearm (Fig. 25, p. 114). *Supraorbital semicircles extending far forward* (Fig. 24, p. 113) in most Texas specimens; 81–110 granules around midbody. Unisexual. *Young:* Usually with 6 light stripes, but sometimes

7 or 8; small pale spots in dark fields. Middorsal light stripes (if present) often represented by a series of pale dots or dashes that may produce a wavy appearance. As the lizard grows, the light stripes become less conspicuous and may disappear altogether on sides of body, largely because they are invaded by black checks or spots. Head–body length about 1½–1¾ in. (3.8–4.4 cm) at hatching.

A lizard of many habitats — plains, canyons, foothill uplands, and river floodplains (as along the Rio Grande) — but almost always associated in one way or another with rocks. More than any other kind of whiptail this species occurs in isolated local populations or small groups of individuals.

Similar species: (1) In Marbled Whiptail (*tigris*) scales anterior to gular fold are only slightly enlarged, underside of the tail is dark, and, in adults, there are black spots on the peach-colored chin, throat, and chest. (2) In Chihuahua Whiptail (*exsanguis*) the supraorbital semicircles are normal and there is a patch of enlarged scales on the rear of the forearm.

Range: Trans-Pecos Texas and Río Conchos drainage in Chihuahua north to se. Colorado and Texas panhandle. Map 88

MARBLED WHIPTAIL   Pl. 18
Cnemidophorus tigris marmoratus

Identification: 8–12 in. (20–30.5 cm); head–body max. 4 in. (10.2 cm). "Gray whiptail" would be an appropriate name, because the pale markings are gray and seldom in sharp contrast with the darker gray ground color. Pattern extremely variable — marbled, crossbanded, checkerboarded, or with pale spots arranged more or less in longitudinal rows. Some have tiger stripes on the sides of the body; others are virtually uniform gray. (A patternless phase, dorsum uniformly brownish gray and venter white, is known from eastern edge of range in Texas.) Tail gray; dark on its underside. Venter chiefly white or pale yellow, but washed with peach on throat and, in larger individuals, also on chest and sides of abdomen. Chin, throat, and chest with a few black or partly black scales (in adults). Scales anterior to gular fold slightly enlarged (Fig. 24, p. 113), but separated from the fold by a row or more of granules; no enlarged scales on rear of forearm (Fig. 25, p. 114). *Supraorbital semicircles penetrating well forward* (Fig. 24, p. 113), reaching or almost reaching frontal plate; 83–100 granules around midbody. Bisexual. *Young:* Numerous small, pale, often elongated spots arranged in longitudinal rows on a ground color of dark brown to black. Head–body length about 1⅜–1¾ in. (3.5–4.4 cm) at hatching.

At home on desert flats or sandy areas where they prowl incessantly beneath clumps of thorny vegetation in their search for insects. When disturbed they dart into the open and race to another clump of vegetation, looking like a dark streak as they go. If pursued, they flee in similar fashion from clump to clump, but eventually return to a favorite spot where they may disappear down a burrow. One of the few kinds of lizards apt to be encountered at (shade) temperatures of 100°F (38°C) or more.

Similar species: Boldly-marked individuals may be confused with Checkered Whiptails (*tesselatus*) but in the latter the scales anterior to the gular fold are abruptly enlarged, the chin is never peach-colored, and there are rarely any black spots on the chin. Other Whiptails retain at least two pairs of longitudinal light stripes throughout life.

Range: Chiefly the Chihuahuan Desert of w. Texas and adjacent parts of New Mexico, Chihuahua, and Coahuila. Western and Mexican subspecies. Map 85

DESERT-GRASSLAND WHIPTAIL Pl. 18
Cnemidophorus uniparens

Identification: 6½–9⅜ in. (16.5–23.8 cm); head–body max. 2¹⁵⁄₁₆ in. (7.5 cm). A small 6-striped whiptail with *no pale spots in the dark fields*. Usually a suggestion of a seventh (middorsal) light stripe, at least on the neck. Dark fields reddish brown to black. Stripes yellowish; whitish on sides of body. *Tail bluish green or olive-green.* Venter whitish and virtually unmarked; adults often with a bluish wash on chin and sides of neck. Enlarged scales along anterior edge of gular fold (Fig. 24, p. 113) and on rear of forearm (Fig. 25, p. 114). Supraorbital semicircles normal (Fig. 24, p. 113); 59–78 granules around midbody. Unisexual. *Young:* Head–body length about 1⁵⁄₁₆–1⁹⁄₁₆ in. (3.3–4.0 cm) at hatching.

A whiptail of desert and mesquite grassland; chiefly in low desert areas but also ascending river valleys into lower mountainous areas.

Similar species: (1) Seven-striped Whiptail (*inornatus*) has a distinctly *blue tail,* especially on its underside. (2) In New Mexico Whiptail (*neomexicanus*) middorsal stripe is wavy, there are pale spots in the dark fields, and supraorbital semicircles extend far forward.

Range: Vicinity of El Paso, Texas, and north in Rio Grande Valley to cen. New Mexico; n. Chihuahua and ne. Sonora to cen. Arizona. Map 90

GIANT AMEIVA *Ameiva ameiva* Pl. 17
Identification: 15–25 in. (38–63.5 cm); head–body max. 8¼ in. (21.0 cm). A giant relative of the whiptail lizards, but with 10 or 12 rows of large rectangular plates on the belly instead of 8. General coloration dark (often blackish), but with several vertical rows of yellowish circular spots on sides of body, and

bluish spots on the two or three outermost rows of belly plates and anterior surface of hind leg. A brown or yellowish middorsal stripe may be present on posterior two-thirds of body.

An alert, elusive lizard. The Florida population may have been derived from the interbreeding of two tropical American races of this species.

Range: Introduced and established in the Miami, Florida, region; the species as a whole inhabits grasslands, savannahs, and other open areas in Panama and tropical South America, and it also occurs on Trinidad, Tobago, the Isla de Margarita, and the Isla de Providencia, the latter off the coast of Nicaragua.

Map 92

Skinks: Family Scincidae

SMOOTH, shiny, alert, and active lizards that are difficult to catch — and to hold. Yet in most instances they *must* be caught and examined carefully for accurate identification. Watch the tails; they break off *very* easily. The average skink will try to bite, and large ones can pinch painfully hard.

In making identifications be sure to check *all* characters. Many skinks change markedly in coloration and pattern as they grow older (as in the Five-lined species). Others (notably among the Mole Skinks) show a bewildering degree of individual variation. The positions of the longitudinal stripes are important. Count downward from the midline of the back. Thus, *stripe on 3rd row,* for example, indicates that stripes occupy the 3rd row of scales on each side of the midline. Rule out whiptail lizards by checking back and belly scales (Fig. 23, p. 112).

Most skinks are terrestrial, foraging actively by day but taking shelter (at night, in bad weather, or from high temperatures) under stones or in debris, decaying logs, abandoned packrat nests, etc. The Broad-headed Skink and some others are often arboreal. Habitats usually include some evidence of moisture, such as in the form of nearby springs or swamps or underground humid retreats. Insects and other arthropods are the chief food, but large skinks can also manage such sizable prey as baby mice or birds in the nest, or the eggs of such species as sparrows. Captives often do well on a diet of live insects and spiders and will sometimes take bits of meat dipped in raw beaten egg. (Add vitamins and minerals!)

All but two of our skinks belong to the big genus *Eumeces;* the exceptions are the Ground Skink (*Leiolopisma*) and the curious Sand Skink (*Neoseps*). In some of the species of *Eumeces,* tones of red or orange appear on the heads (of males only) during the breeding season; in others the bright colors are retained throughout the year. Females normally guard their eggs during the incubation period.

The family is very large and occurs in all the habitable continents, but the great majority of species are confined to the Eastern Hemisphere.

GROUND SKINK *Leiolopisma laterale*   **Pl. 19**
Identification: 3–5⅛ in. (8–13.0 cm); head–body max. 1¹⁵⁄₁₆ in. (4.9 cm). The "brown-backed skink." A small, smooth, golden-brown to blackish-brown lizard with a *dark* dorsolateral stripe. Shade of brown varies from one locality to another — from reddish or chocolate to light golden brown. In darkest specimens the dark stripe almost blends with ground color. Belly white or yellowish. A "window" in lower eyelid in form of a transparent disc through which lizard may see when eye is closed. *Young:* About 1¾ in. (4.4 cm) at hatching.

An elfin reptile of the woodland floor, quietly but nervously searching for insects among leaves, decaying wood, and detritus, and taking refuge, when approached, beneath the nearest shelter. When running, it makes lateral, snakelike movements. Does not hesitate to enter shallow water to escape. Seldom climbs. Likely to appear almost anywhere in the Deep South, even in towns and gardens.
Similar species: (1) Two-lined Salamanders are similar in coloration and pattern, but they lack claws and scales. (2) Other small brown lizards either have rough scales, indications of *light* stripes, or both.
Range: S. New Jersey to Florida Keys; west to e. Kansas and w.-cen. Texas; an isolated locality in Coahuila.   Map 74

FIVE-LINED SKINK *Eumeces fasciatus*   **Pl. 19**
Identification: 5–8¹⁄₁₆ in. (13–20.5 cm); head–body max. 3⅜ in. (8.6 cm). Highly variable, depending on age and sex. Hatchlings have 5 white or yellowish stripes on a black ground color, and their tails are bright blue. As they grow older and larger, the pattern becomes less conspicuous — the stripes darken and the ground color lightens; the tail turns gray. Females almost always retain some indications of striped pattern, the broad dark band extending backward from eye and along the side of body remaining most prominent. Adult males usually show traces of stripes, but they tend to become nearly uniform brown or olive in coloration; orange-red appears on jaws during spring breeding season. *Young:* See above; about 2–2½ in. (5.1–6.4 cm) at hatching.

Two other species, Broad-headed and Southeastern Five-lined Skinks, are similarly patterned, undergo comparable changes, and have ranges broadly overlapping that of the Five-lined Skink. Therefore it is essential to check scale characters to be sure of identification. Eliminate Southeastern Five-line (*inexpectatus*) by looking under base of tail; all its scales are about same size (middle row enlarged in the other two species — see Fig. 26, below). This species (*fasciatus*) has: (a) 26 to 30 longitudinal rows of scales around center of body; (b) usually 4 labials anterior to the subocular; and (c) 2 enlarged postlabial scales (Fig. 27, below).

Fig. 26. SKINKS *(Eumeces)*: UNDERSURFACES OF TAILS

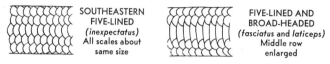

SOUTHEASTERN
FIVE-LINED
(inexpectatus)
All scales about
same size

FIVE-LINED AND
BROAD-HEADED
(fasciatus and *laticeps)*
Middle row
enlarged

Cutover woodlots with many rotting stumps and logs, abandoned board or sawdust piles, rock piles, and decaying debris in or near woods are good places in which to look for these lizards. Habitat is usually damp. Over the greater part of its range, the Five-lined Skink is essentially terrestrial, but it occasionally ascends trees, especially dead and decaying snags where insects are abundant. In Texas, it is distinctly arboreal.

Similar species: (1) Broad-headed Skink usually has: (a) 30 to 32 rows of scales at midbody; (b) 5 labials anterior to the subocular; and (c) no enlarged postlabials (Fig. 27, below). (2) See also Southeastern Five-lined Skink.

Range: New England to n. Florida; west to Wisconsin and eastern parts of Kansas, Oklahoma, and Texas; isolated localities farther west.   Map 75

BROAD-HEADED SKINK *Eumeces laticeps*   **Pl. 19**
Identification: 6½–12¾ in. (16.5–32.4 cm); head–body max. 5⅝ in. (14.3 cm). The red-headed "scorpion" is our second largest skink; only the Great Plains Skink attains a greater length and only a slightly greater bulk. Big, olive-brown males, with their widely swollen jowls and orange-red heads, are impressive reptiles. Pattern and color variations parallel those of Five-lined Skink (*fasciatus*). Broad-headed Skink has: (a) scale rows at midbody usually 30 or 32; (b) usually 5 labials anterior to the

Fig. 27. HEADS OF SKINKS

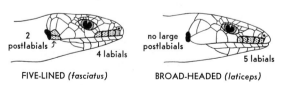

2
postlabials ↑
4 labials

no large
postlabials
5 labials

FIVE-LINED *(fasciatus)*   BROAD-HEADED *(laticeps)*

subocular; and (c) no enlarged postlabials (Fig. 27, p. 123). Middle row of scales under tail wider than others (Fig. 26, p. 123). *Young:* Black with 5 yellow stripes and bright blue tail; in eastern part of range young may show 7 *light stripes;* about 2⅜–3⅜ in. (6.0–8.6 cm) at hatching.

Habitats vary from swamp forests to empty urban lots strewn with debris. This is essentially a woodland species, however, and the most arboreal of our skinks. The lizards make use of hollow trees and tree holes, and sometimes may be seen on rail fences or high among bare branches of dead or decaying trees.

Similar species: (1) Southeastern Five-lined Skink (*inexpectatus*) has the scales under tail all about same size. (2) Five-lined Skink (*fasciatus*) has: (a) scale rows at midbody 26 to 30; (b) usually 4 labials anterior to the subocular; and (c) 2 enlarged postlabials (Fig. 27, p. 123).

Range: Se. Pennsylvania to cen. Florida; west to e. Kansas and e.-cen. Texas. Map 76

SOUTHEASTERN FIVE-LINED SKINK Pl. 19
Eumeces inexpectatus

Identification: 5½–8½ in. (14–21.6 cm); head–body max. 3½ in. (8.9 cm). The only one of the three Five-lined Skinks in which the rows of scales under the tail are all about the same size (Fig. 26, p. 123). (Check only on an original part of tail — not a regenerated portion.) Pattern and coloration run same course of changes as in Five-lined Skink (*fasciatus*). Light stripes, especially middorsal one, tend to be quite narrow. Dorsolateral stripe is on the 5th (or 4th and 5th) row of scales, counting from midline of back. Dark areas between light stripes are black in young, but become brown in older specimens. *Young:* 5 very narrow light stripes that become brighter (often reddish orange) on head; often an additional faint light stripe at each side of belly; tail blue or purple. The juvenile coloration very frequently persists into adulthood, the orange head stripes remaining prominent and, in conjunction with the darker stripes, giving head an overall orange-brown appearance; purplish hues may be seen on tails of even rather large specimens. About 2½ in. (6.4 cm) at hatching.

Found in a great variety of habitats, but able to tolerate drier conditions than the two other 5-striped species. Thrives on many small seashore islands in the Southeast which have no fresh water and little vegetation. Climbs well, but is also quite at home on the ground.

Similar species: In (1) Five-lined Skink (*fasciatus*) and (2) Broad-headed Skink (*laticeps*) middle row of scales under tail is distinctly wider than other rows (Fig. 26, p. 123). Also, the dorsolateral light stripe is on the 3rd and 4th (or 4th only) rows of scales in both of those species.

Range: S. Maryland, Virginia, and Kentucky to the Florida Keys and the Dry Tortugas; west to e. Louisiana.   Map 77

GREAT PLAINS SKINK *Eumeces obsoletus*   Pl. 19
Identification: 6½–13¾ in. (16.5–34.9 cm); head–body max. 5⅝ in. (14.3 cm). Largest of all the skinks occurring within our area, and unique in having scales on sides of body arranged *obliquely* instead of in horizontal rows (Fig. 28, below). The ground color varies from light tan to light gray, and basically each scale is edged with black or dark brown. Distribution of the edging varies so that some specimens have strong indications of longitudinal stripes. Two postmental scales (Fig. 29, p. 127). *Young:* Jet-black; tail blue; white and orange spots on head; about 2½ in. (6.4 cm) at hatching.

Chiefly a grassland species in the Great Plains where it prefers fine-grained soil suitable for burrowing and with sunken rocks for shelter. In the arid Southwest and northern Mexico it occurs along water courses and in other areas where there is permanent or semipermanent moisture. Secretive; seldom seen except when rock slabs or other places of concealment are overturned. Can inflict a painful bite.
Similar species: Young Southern Coal Skinks also may be virtually plain black; their snouts and lips may be reddish, but they lack bold white and orange spots. Check chin — Coal Skinks have only one postmental scale (Fig. 29, p. 127).
Range: S. Nebraska southward and including most of Texas, to n. Nuevo León; west to cen. Arizona; isolated records in Missouri, Chihuahua, and Durango.   Map 79

Fig. 28
SKINKS
(Eumeces):
SIDES OF
BODIES

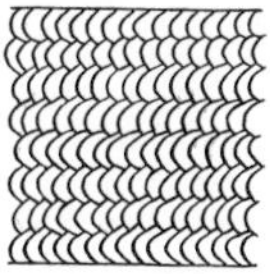

MOST
SPECIES
Scales in
parallel
rows

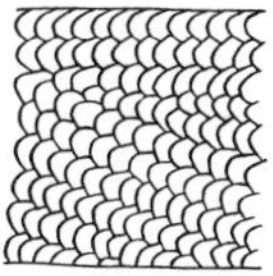

GREAT
PLAINS
(obsoletus)
Scales in
oblique
rows

FOUR-LINED SKINK   Pl. 19
Eumeces tetragrammus tetragrammus
Identification: 5–7⅞ in. (13–20.0 cm); head–body max. 3 in. (7.6 cm). Four light stripes that terminate in the region of the *groin.* A broad black stripe between them on each side of body; dorsal coloration dark gray or gray-brown. In old individuals pattern is less distinct, with dorsum changing to light brown and the black lateral stripe to brown. *Young:* Black with orange head and neck lines and tail bright blue (the adult pattern and coloration are gradually assumed); 1½ in. (3.8 cm) or more at hatching.

At home in the lower Rio Grande Valley, in brush- or grass-lands, and in the gallery forest along the river. Hides under all sorts of debris. Sometimes found by peeling away the dried frond husks at the bases of palm trees.

Similar species and subspecies: (1) In Southern Prairie Skink, light stripes extend onto tail, and the light lateral stripe passes *above* the ear opening onto the head (it crosses the ear opening in both races of *tetragrammus*). (2) In Short-lined Skink, light stripes terminate in *shoulder* region.

Range: S. Texas to n. Veracruz and Querétaro; an isolated colony in Coahuila. Intergrades with the Short-lined Skink in s. Texas.   Map 82

SHORT-LINED SKINK   Pl. 19
Eumeces tetragrammus brevilineatus

Identification: 5–7 in. (13–17.8 cm); head–body max. 2⅝ in. (6.7 cm). The light stripes terminate in the region of the *shoulder.* Dorsal coloration varies from brown or gray to olive- or grayish green. *Male:* Wash of orange at sides of throat. *Young:* Dark band extending backward from eye; tail bright blue; about 2 in. (5.1 cm) at hatching.

A resident of rough, hilly country (as on the Edwards Plateau), in brush- or grasslands with sandy soil, and riparian woodlands (as in the gallery forest of the Nueces River). Elevations range from the Texas lowlands to 7500 ft. (2300 m) in the Chisos Mts. of the Big Bend region. Hides in, and forages near, brush and trash piles, clumps of cactus, or abandoned packrat nests.

Similar species: See Four-lined Skink.

Range: Cen. and sw. Texas south through n. Coahuila and n. Nuevo León; an isolated record from the Sierra del Nido, Chihuahua. Mexican subspecies.   Map 82

COAL SKINK *Eumeces anthracinus*   Pl. 19
Identification: 5–7 in. (13–17.8 cm); head–body max. 2¾ in. (7.0 cm). A 4-lined skink, but with the light stripes extending *onto tail.* Broad dark lateral stripe 2½ to 4 scales wide. *No light lines on top of head.* Dorsolateral light stripe is on the edges of the 3rd and 4th scale rows, counting from midline of back. *One postmental scale* (Fig. 29, p. 127). *Male:* Sides of head reddish during spring breeding season, at least in some parts of range. *Young:* Plain black in one subspecies; patterned like adults in the other; about 1⅞ in. (4.8 cm) at hatching.

The more humid portions of wooded hillsides are favorite habitats; also vicinity of springs and rocky bluffs overlooking creek valleys. When pursued, these lizards (as well as skinks of some other species) do not hesitate to take refuge in shallow water, going to the bottom and hiding under stones or debris.

Fig. 29. CHINS OF SKINKS *(Eumeces)*

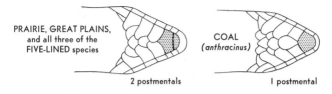

PRAIRIE, GREAT PLAINS, and all three of the FIVE-LINED species

2 postmentals

COAL *(anthracinus)*

I postmental

Similar species: (1) In the two Prairie Skinks the dark lateral stripe is not more than 2 scales wide, and the dorsolateral light stripe is on the 4th (or 4th and 5th) row of scales. (2) In Short-lined and Four-lined Skinks light stripes do not extend onto tail. (3) In juveniles and young adults of the three species of Five-lined Skinks (*fasciatus, inexpectatus,* and *laticeps*) there are 2 light lines on head; in old adults of these, in which the stripes may have faded, check for presence of 2 *postmental scales* (Fig. 29, above). (4) The black young of the Great Plains Skink have bold white and orange spots on their heads; they also have 2 postmental scales (Fig. 29, above).

Range: Discontinuous — see subspecies below.

Subspecies: SOUTHERN COAL SKINK, *Eumeces a. pluvialis* (Plate 19). Posterior supralabials with light centers and dark edges, producing a spotted appearance. Rows of scales around middle of body 26 or more. Young, black and unpatterned, but often with faint suggestions of light stripes or whitish labial spots or both; snout and lips may be reddish; tail blue. Kansas and Missouri to e. Texas and the Florida panhandle, but absent from the Mississippi Alluvial Plain; isolated colonies in Georgia and Alabama; intergrades with Northern Coal Skink in parts of the Southeast. NORTHERN COAL SKINK, *Eumeces a. anthracinus.* A continuous light stripe through posterior supralabials. Rows of scales around midbody usually 25 or fewer. Young with blue tail, but otherwise patterned like adults. Range disjunct from New York to Virginia and Kentucky.   Map 80

NORTHERN PRAIRIE SKINK   Pl. 19
Eumeces septentrionalis septentrionalis
    Identification: 5¼–8⅛ in. (13–20.6 cm); head–body max. 3¼ in. (8.3 cm). A many-striped skink, but with the dorsolateral *light* stripe strongly bordered *both above and below* by dark stripes and extending onto the tail. This light stripe is on the 4th (or 4th and 5th) row of scales, counting from midline of back. A pair of relatively faint dark lines down center of back, or a pale middorsal stripe, or both. Broadest dark stripe not more than *2 scales wide.* Dorsal ground color olive to olive-brown. Two postmental scales (Fig. 29, above). *Male:* Deep reddish orange

on sides of head during breeding season. *Young:* Tail bright blue; about 2 in. (5.1 cm) at hatching.

Seldom seen in the open, but uses shallow burrows and excavations, often of its own making. Usually occurs in areas of soft sands or soils, often in gravelly glacial deposits or their sandy outwashes (in northern localities). Sometimes found in rock or sawdust piles or by overturning objects left undisturbed long enough to be well settled into surface of sod or soil.

Similar species: (1) In Many-lined Skink, the dorsolateral light stripe is *confined* to 3rd row of scales. (2) Coal Skink has: (a) broad dark lateral stripe, *2½ to 4 scales wide;* (b) dorsolateral light stripe on edges of 3rd and 4th scale rows; and (c) a single postmental scale (Fig. 29, p. 127).

Range: Minnesota and w. Wisconsin to Kansas; an isolated area in s. Manitoba.   Map 73

SOUTHERN PRAIRIE SKINK   Pl. 19
Eumeces septentrionalis obtusirostris

Identification: 5–7 in. (13–17.8 cm); head–body max. 2 $^{15}\!/_{16}$ in. (7.5 cm). Similar to the Northern Prairie Skink, but with the middorsal markings greatly reduced or absent. In extreme cases the dark line above the light dorsolateral stripe may even be missing. Occasionally the light stripe along lower sides also is lacking. Dorsolateral light line is on the 4th (or 4th and 5th) row of scales, counting from middorsal line. The broad dark lateral stripe is not more than *2 scales wide.* Two postmental scales (Fig. 29, p. 127).

Often seen foraging near bases of clumps of prickly pear or other vegetation into which it retreats at first sign of danger. **Similar species:** (1) Coal Skink has: (a) the dorsolateral light stripe on edges of the 3rd and 4th scale rows; (b) only one postmental scale; and (c) the broad dark lateral stripe is *2½ to 4 scales wide.* (2) In Short-lined and Four-lined Skinks light lines do not extend onto tail.

Range: S.-cen. Kansas to e.-cen. Texas.   Map 73

MANY-LINED SKINK   Pl. 19
Eumeces multivirgatus multivirgatus

Identification: 5–7⅝ in. (13–19.4 cm); head–body max. 2⅞ in. (7.3 cm). Numerous light and dark stripes, some strong and well defined, others weak and appearing merely as rows of dark dots. This lizard and the southern race (*gaigeae*) are the only skinks of our area with a *prominent light stripe restricted to 3rd row of scales,* counting from midline of back. A well-defined *light* middorsal stripe flanked by *dark* stripes. Tail swollen at base. Stripeless or virtually stripeless individuals occur as rare variants. *Young:* Darker than adults; only the prominent lines present, and these rather dim; the fainter secondary stripes develop later; tail brilliant blue; about 2½ in. (6.4 cm) at hatching.

A lizard of the open plains and sandhills, often occurring in vacant lots and under debris in towns and settlements. Sometimes also found beneath cow chips, where it has taken shelter or is in search of insects.

Similar species: In Northern Prairie Skink, dorsolateral light stripe is on the 4th (or 4th and 5th) row of scales.

Range: Sw. S. Dakota to e.-cen. Colorado.   Map 78

VARIABLE SKINK *Eumeces multivirgatus gaigeae*   **Pl. 19**
Identification: 5-7⅝ in. (13-19.4 cm); head-body max. 2⅞ in. (7.3 cm). A skink with a highly variable pattern; both plain-colored and striped phases occur, and the striped ones change with age. Juveniles of the latter are dark, but they bear a well-defined light middorsal stripe and a vivid dorsolateral stripe on the 3rd row of scales, counting from midline of back. As the lizards grow, the ground color becomes paler, the middorsal stripe disappears, and the dark dorsal stripes are reduced to narrow zigzag lines or they vanish altogether. Meanwhile the broad dark lateral stripe is invaded by the pale ground color and is replaced by 2 or 3 dark lines. Tail may be swollen at base in large adults. *Young:* Tail bright blue; 2-2½ in. (5.1-6.4 cm) at hatching.

Habitats are as variable as the color pattern. They range from high mountains and plateaus, where the striped phase is common, to relatively low creosote bush deserts, where the plain-colored phase is more abundant and blends better with the rocks and soils of the open, arid landscape.

Range: Extr. s. Colorado, se. Utah, and much of Arizona to w. Texas; intergrades with Many-lined Skink in se. Colorado and probably also in w. Texas, although its taxonomic status in the disjunct areas is not clear. *Eumeces multivirgatus* may also occur in sw. Chihuahua.   Map 78

FLORIDA KEYS MOLE SKINK   **Pl. 19**
Eumeces egregius egregius
Identification: 3½-6 in. (9-15.2 cm); head-body max. 2¼ in. (5.7 cm). A combination of red or brownish-red tail plus light stripes that neither widen nor diverge to other scale rows. The lateral stripes usually continue to the groin but the dorsolateral stripes may terminate much farther forward. Ground color varies from gray-brown to dark chocolate-brown. Reddish color of tail *persists throughout life;* it does not fade as does the blue in other species of skinks. Scales around middle of body usually 22 or more. *Male:* With a reddish or orange suffusion that extends onto the venter during the mating season.

Highly secretive; often found in piles of stones or debris. Also in driftwood and tidal wrack along shores of the islands. Mole Skinks in general feed largely on roaches and crickets, but other kinds of insects and spiders are also eaten. Small crustaceans constitute a large part of the diet of some of the insular populations.

Range: Florida Keys and the Dry Tortugas.

Subspecies: NORTHERN MOLE SKINK, *Eumeces e. similis*. Similar but with only 6 upper labials (most frequently 7 in the other races). Scales around middle of body usually 21 or fewer. Tail red, orange, or reddish brown. Length of stripes highly variable. Habitat similar to that of Peninsula Mole Skink, except that dry rocky areas are also utilized. N. Florida and roughly the southern halves of Alabama and Georgia. CEDAR KEY MOLE SKINK, *Eumeces e. insularis*. Slightly larger in size — to 6⅜ in. (16.2 cm); head–body to 2-2½ in. (5.1-6.4 cm). Dorsolateral light stripes inconspicuous; 21 or fewer scale rows around middle of body. Hatchlings almost uniform black in coloration. Cedar and Seahorse Keys, Levy Co., Florida.   Map 81

PENINSULA MOLE SKINK   Pl. 19
Eumeces egregius onocrepis

Identification: 3½-6³⁄₁₆ in. (9-15.7 cm); head–body max. 2⁵⁄₁₆ in. (5.9 cm). A variable race in which the tail may be red, orange, yellow, pinkish, brown, or lavender. Dorsolateral light stripes widen posteriorly or diverge to a different scale row, or both. *Young* (of Mole Skinks in general): 1⅞-2⅜ in. (4.8-6.0 cm) at hatching.

The Mole Skinks are so slender and their legs are so short that they seem almost snakelike in appearance and actions. They are found chiefly in areas of sandy, well-drained soil that support sandhill scrub or dry hammock vegetation. They burrow in loose, dry sand, and frequently "bask" just beneath the surface in mounds pushed up by pocket gophers.

Range: Much of the Florida peninsula.   Map 81

BLUE-TAILED MOLE SKINK   Pl. 19
Eumeces egregius lividus

Identification: 3½-6½ in. (9-16.5 cm); head–body max. 2⁷⁄₁₆ in. (6.2 cm). Distinguished from all other Mole Skinks by the bright blue tail of the young, a coloration that persists in some adults. Tail light blue to salmon in older specimens. Dorsolateral light stripes widen posteriorly or diverge to involve another scale row, or both; invariably 7 upper labials on each side of head.

A sand burrower like the other members of its species. Discovery of this blue-tailed race suggested the advisability of using the more appropriate name of Mole Skinks for the group instead of "Red-tailed Skinks" by which they were previously known.

Range: Essentially confined to the Lake Wales Ridge of Polk and Highlands Cos., Florida.   Map 81

SAND SKINK *Neoseps reynoldsi*   **Pl. 19**
Identification: 4–5⅛ in. (10–13.0 cm); head–body max. 2⁹⁄₁₆ in. (6.5 cm). The legs are greatly reduced in size. Each foreleg fits into a groove on lower side of body; it bears only a single toe and is so tiny as to be easily overlooked. Hind legs are a little larger and each has 2 digits. Other characteristics include a wedge-shaped snout, lower jaw partially countersunk into upper one, a flat or slightly concave belly that meets sides of body at an angle, a tiny eye with built-in "window" in lower lid, and no external ear opening. Coloration varies from dirty white to deep tan. *Young:* About 2⁵⁄₁₆ in. (5.9 cm) at hatching.

An adept burrower that literally "swims" through dry sand. The limbs, of little help underground, are in the evolutionary process of being lost. Food consists mainly of termites and beetle larvae, most of which are caught and eaten while burrowing. Largely restricted to areas of rosemary scrub where moist sand underlies the dry surface sand at a depth of one to a few inches (2.5 cm or more). The Sand Skink may play 'possum when first caught, holding itself rigidly immobile, but it will flop over on its belly if placed upside down on a hard surface.
Range: Apparently confined to two disjunct areas of the Florida peninsula from Marion Co. to Highlands Co.   Map 83

Glass Lizards and Alligator Lizard: Family Anguidae

MEMBERS of this small, but wide-ranging, family have their scales reinforced with bony plates called osteoderms, a characteristic shared by the skinks. Compensation for the resultant stiffening of the body is provided, among the glass lizards and our single form of alligator lizard, by the presence of a deep, flexible groove that runs along each side of the body. The groove is lined with granular scales, and it permits expansion when the body is distended with food or (in females) with eggs.

The legless glass lizards are easily mistaken for snakes. But, *unlike* snakes, they have *movable eyelids* and *external ear openings* (see front endpaper). To the touch they feel stiff, almost brittle, and they lack the suppleness of the serpent. Their tails are very long (up to 2.75 times the head–body length) and are so fragile in both of our wide-ranging species (*ventralis* and *attenuatus*) that full-tailed specimens are not common. The regenerated tip, sharply pointed and of a different color from the remaining part of the original tail, earns them the name of "horn snakes" among country folk. Some people even think such a tip is a stinger. If hit with a flat object, the tail may break in two or more pieces. This is the origin of the "joint snake" legend in which the animal, after fragmentation, is supposed to grow back together again — an obvious impossibility.

Glass lizards are good burrowers, and at least two of the kinds may spend much of their time below ground. Their food includes insects, spiders, snails, birds' eggs, and small snakes and lizards. Captives will usually accept a mixture of chopped raw meat and egg (add vitamins and minerals!). They should have gravel or soil in which to hide, and should not be caged with other reptiles much smaller than themselves. The young average about 6 to 8 inches (15 to 20 cm) at hatching (smaller in *compressus*). Females normally guard their eggs during incubation.

We have three species of glass lizards. Other members of the genus occur in Mexico, Africa, Europe, and Asia.

In contrast with the members of the genus *Ophisaurus,* the alligator lizards, of which there are several genera ranging, collectively, from British Columbia to Panama, have four well-developed legs. The lateral groove is strongly evident in some of them but only weakly in others. North of Mexico they are confined to the West and only one, the Texas Alligator Lizard, occurs in our area.

The family as a whole ranges from extreme southwestern Canada to northern Argentina, and it is also represented in the West Indies and the Old World.

EASTERN GLASS LIZARD *Ophisaurus ventralis*   **Pl. 13**
    Identification: 18–42⅝ in. (46–108.3 cm); head–body max. 12 in. (30.5 cm). *No* dark lengthwise stripes below the lateral groove or under the tail; *no* distinct middorsal dark stripe (Fig. 30, below). White marks on neck, essentially vertical, are highly irregular in shape. White markings on *posterior corners* of

Fig. 30. HEADS OF GLASS LIZARDS *(Ophisaurus)*

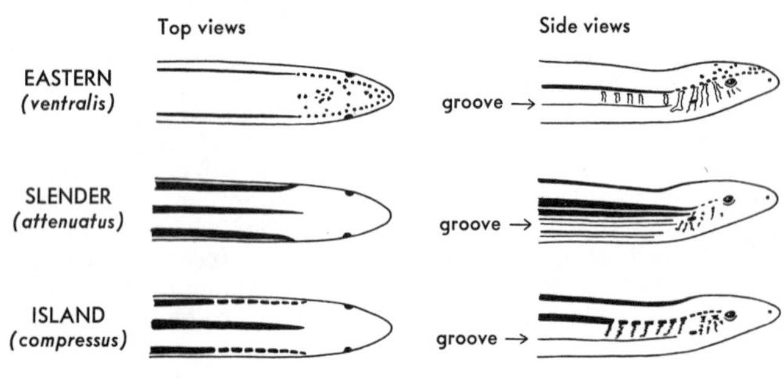

scales. In older specimens there are numerous longitudinal dark lines or dashes on uppersides of body, and sometimes similar parallel lines occupy the entire middorsal area. An old adult (as shown on Plate 13) may be greenish above and yellow below. *Only* glass lizard that may look *green.* Scales along lateral groove number 98 or more. *Young:* Khaki-colored and normally with a broad dark longitudinal stripe on each side of back.

Characteristically an inhabitant of wet meadows and grasslands and pine flatwoods; also occurs in tropical, hardwood hammocks in southern Florida.
Similar species: (1) Slender Glass Lizards always have at least traces of dark stripes below lateral groove. (2) See also Island Glass Lizard.
Range: N. Carolina to s. Florida and west to Louisiana; isolated records in Oklahoma and Missouri.   Map 95

SLENDER GLASS LIZARD *Ophisaurus attenuatus*   **Pl. 13**
  Identification: 22–42 in. (56–106.7 cm); head–body max. 11⅜ in. (28.9 cm). Narrow dark longitudinal stripes *below* the lateral groove and under the tail (Fig. 30, p. 132); these are black in the young, but paler and less prominent (sometimes considerably less) in adults. A dark middorsal stripe or series of dashes in young and medium-sized specimens. Old adults may be brown with irregular light (but dark-bordered) crossbands on the back and tail. White marks on scales occupy *middle* of scales. In some parts of range females are strongly patterned, but males become flecked with whitish when nearing adult size. These markings become more prominent with age, and old males may have a salt-and-pepper appearance. Scales along lateral groove number 98 or more.

Found chiefly in dry grasslands or dry, open woods. Seldom burrows, except for hibernation. Very active when restrained, vigorously trying to escape and sometimes whipping back and forth somewhat as racers and whipsnakes do. Fully capable of snapping off the tail, even if held carefully by the body and when the tail is not touching anything. Glass lizards of the other species are much less energetic in their efforts to escape.
  Similar species: Both (1) Eastern and (2) Island Glass Lizards *lack* dark stripes below lateral groove and under tail.
  Range: Se. Virginia to s. Florida; west to cen. Texas and north in Mississippi Valley to se. Nebraska, s. Wisconsin, and nw. Indiana.
  Subspecies: WESTERN SLENDER GLASS LIZARD, *Ophisaurus a. attenuatus* (Plate 13). Tail (when unregenerated) less than 2.4 times head–body length. Chiefly west of Mississippi River, but crossing into Illinois and adjacent states in the North. EASTERN SLENDER GLASS LIZARD, *Ophisaurus a. longicaudus.* Tail longer (when unregenerated), 2.4 or more times head–body length. Attains a greater length than western subspecies — to 46½ in.

(118.1 cm); head–body max. 12%16 in. (31.9 cm). Se. Virginia to
s. Florida and the Mississippi River.   Map 97

ISLAND GLASS LIZARD   Fig. 30, p. 132
Ophisaurus compressus
Identification: 15–24 in. (38–61.0 cm); head–body max. 6¾ in.
(17.1 cm). The *single* dark solid stripe on each side of the body
is situated on scale rows 3 and 4 above the lateral groove. A
middorsal dark stripe, but this sometimes represented merely
by a series of dark dashes (Fig. 30, p. 132). No dark stripes below
the groove. Undersurfaces pinkish buff or yellowish and unmarked. Numerous more or less vertical light bars on neck,
more numerous and usually more conspicuous than those of
Eastern Glass Lizard. In older specimens the top and sides of
neck are mottled with bronze. Scales along lateral groove number 97 or fewer. Our only glass lizard in which *one or two upper
labials extend upward to the eye;* in the other species the labials
are separated from the eye by a row of scales. Fracture planes
are lacking in the caudal vertebrae, and the tail is not brittle.
Similar species: (1) Slender Glass Lizard has dark stripes
below lateral groove. (2) Both Eastern and Slender Glass Lizards have 98 or more scales along lateral groove.
Range: Coastal areas and offshore islands of S. Carolina,
Georgia, and Florida; scrub pine regions and adjacent flatwoods
of peninsular Florida.   Map 96

TEXAS ALLIGATOR LIZARD   Pl. 13
Gerrhonotus liocephalus infernalis
Identification: 10–16 in. (25–41 cm); record 20 in. (50.8 cm);
head–body max. 8 in. (20.3 cm). Scales large and platelike (suggesting the alligator). Coloration variable, from yellowish- to
reddish-brown. Broken, irregular light lines cross back and tail.
Check for flexible groove that runs along the side from neck
to hind leg. Our only lizard with *both a lateral groove and
legs.* (The alligator lizard illustrated on Plate 13 has puffed
itself up with air — a common reptilian habit — so the groove
is stretched out nearly flat.) *Young:* Much more vividly marked
than adults; ground color dark brown to black and crossed by
narrow whitish crossbands; head tan; about 3½–4 in. (8.9–
10.2 cm) at hatching.
    Essentially terrestrial and usually slow and deliberate in con-
trast with the quick, darting movements of most lizards. Tail
is somewhat prehensile. Food includes insects, spiders, newborn
mice, and small snakes and lizards. Never cage alligator lizards
with smaller reptiles. Large specimens can bite painfully hard.
Range: Edwards Plateau and Big Bend regions of Texas to San
Luis Potosí. Mexican subspecies.   Map 94

Amphisbaenians
Suborder Amphisbaenia
and Family Amphisbaenidae

SNAKELIKE reptiles with rings of scales encircling body and tail. There are no external ear openings, and only a few members of the suborder have visible limbs. Represented in Africa and adjacent parts of Europe and Asia, South America to Mexico, the West Indies, and Florida.

WORM LIZARD *Rhineura floridana*   **Pl. 13**
  Identification: 7–11 in. (18–28 cm); record 16 in. (40.6 cm). Extraordinarily similar to the common earthworm, both in coloration and gross appearance. Body looks segmented, like the worm's, but this reptile has scales and a well-defined, lizard-like head, even though both ends of the animal look superficially alike. Lower jaw countersunk into upper, facilitating burrowing. There are no limbs, no ear openings, and most specimens lack external eyes (internally there are remnants of eyes). Uppersurface of the very short tail is flattened and covered with numerous small bumps (tubercles), forming an effective stopper for tunnels the lizard makes as it burrows through sand or soil. *Young:* About 4 in. (10.2 cm) at hatching.

  Worm Lizards remain underground virtually all their lives, but are sometimes plowed or dug up or may be forced to the surface by heavy rains. Dry, sandy habitats are preferred. Earthworms, spiders, and termites are the principal foods.
  Range: Cen. and n. parts of Florida peninsula.   Map 98

VIII
Snakes
Order Squamata[*]
Suborder Serpentes

SNAKES, of which there are well in excess of 2000 species, are almost as widespread as lizards. They range northward above the Arctic Circle in Scandinavia and to the 60th parallel in North America. Southward they extend through Australia and into Tasmania, to the Cape Region of Africa, and very nearly to the tip of South America. They are absent, however, from many islands where lizards occur, including Ireland, New Zealand, and numerous South Sea archipelagos. Vertically they range from sea level to at least 14,000 feet (4300 m) in Tibet.

Venomous snakes are widespread through the larger land masses and on many islands. No poisonous kinds occur on Madagascar, however, or on any of the West Indian islands except St. Lucia and Martinique. In Australia venomous snakes predominate.

Many snakes are easily recognized by their patterns, behavior, or other characteristics, but a great number of kinds must be caught for close examination. Checking for the presence or absence of certain scales is sometimes necessary, and ventrals or subcaudals (or both occasionally) must be counted for positive identification. Be extremely careful in approaching poisonous snakes. Make no attempt to catch them unless you have had careful coaching on how to do it. Learn to recognize them on sight (study Plates 30, 34, 35, and 36). See Plate 2 and pages 30–33 for instructions on what to do in case of snakebite.

Slender Blind Snakes:
Family Leptotyphlopidae

A LARGE family containing only a single genus (*Leptotyphlops*) of small burrowing, wormlike snakes with vestigial eyes, extremely short tails, and with the dentition reduced to a few teeth in the lower jaw.

[*] The Order Squamata includes the vast majority of all living reptiles. Subdivisions (suborders) are Lacertilia (lizards, p. 82), Amphisbaenia (amphisbaenians, p. 135), and Serpentes (snakes — this page).

Which end is the head in these snakes? The blunt, rounded tail strongly resembles the head, but the latter may be recognized by 2 black dots that show where the eyes are buried beneath translucent scales. Blind snakes are unique among the snakes of our area in having *belly scales the same size as the dorsal scales.* Despite its blunt appearance the tail ends in a tiny spine. Food consists of termites and the larvae and pupae of ants.

The Family Leptotyphlopidae ranges from the south-central United States to Argentina, and also occurs in the West Indies, Africa, and southwestern Asia.

TEXAS BLIND SNAKE *Leptotyphlops dulcis* **Pl. 33**
  Identification: 5–8 in. (13–20 cm); record 10¾ in. (27.3 cm). A wormlike snake, slender as a knitting needle, with no constriction at the neck, *no enlarged ventral scales,* and *3* small scales between the oculars (Fig. 31, p. 138). Coloration pale shiny brown or reddish brown above, and whitish or pinkish below; no markings. May appear silvery after being caught (see below). *Young:* Smallest known specimen 2⁹⁄₁₆ in. (6.5 cm) in total length.

  A largely subterranean resident of the plains and semiarid regions. Occurs on stony hillsides, prairies, and in sandy or rocky deserts, but almost always in areas where some moisture is available. Frequently found beneath stones and small boulders after rains. Most likely to prowl abroad in early evening. When first caught or when attacked by ants these snakes tilt the individual scales, imparting a silvery appearance to their skins. Individuals protect themselves by writhing while they coat their bodies with feces and a clear, viscous liquid discharged from the anus. The coating serves to repel insects and permits the snake to enter columns of ants (and presumably their nests) in its search for food.
  Range: Sw. Kansas to ne. Mexico and west to se. Arizona.
  Similar species: Trans-Pecos Blind Snake has only one scale between the oculars (Fig. 31, p. 138).
  Subspecies: PLAINS BLIND SNAKE, *Leptotyphlops d. dulcis* (Plate 33). A *single* supralabial scale between the enlarged ocular scale (the one containing the eye) and the lower nasal scale (the one containing the nostril) — see Fig. 31, p. 138. S. Oklahoma to ne. Mexico. NEW MEXICO BLIND SNAKE, *Leptotyphlops d. dissectus.* *Two* supralabial scales between ocular and lower nasal scale (Fig. 31, p. 138). Sw. Kansas and cen. Oklahoma to se. Arizona, cen. Chihuahua, and s. Coahuila. Mexican subspecies. Map 122

TRANS-PECOS BLIND SNAKE **Fig. 31, p. 138**
Leptotyphlops humilis segregus
  Identification: 7–10 in. (18–25 cm); record 12⅝ in. (32.1 cm). Similar to our other blind snakes, but with only a *single* scale

on top of the head between the ocular scales (Fig. 31, below). *Belly scales same size as dorsals.* Coloration brown or pale dull purplish above; venter paler, but usually pink or purplish.

A burrower that, like all our blind snakes, has the lower jaw countersunk into the upper one for easy progress through loose soil or sand. A resident of sandy and stony deserts, grassland-desert transition areas, and foothill canyons. By day it is most often found under rocks near streams, springs, or other areas where moisture is present. During warm weather it often prowls in the open at night.

Similar species: In both races of Texas Blind Snake there are *3* scales on top of head between ocular scales (Fig. 31, below).
Range: Kinney Co., Texas, the Big Bend region, and n. Coahuila to se. Arizona. Western and Mexican subspecies.

Map 121

Fig. 31. HEADS OF BLIND SNAKES *(Leptotyphlops)*

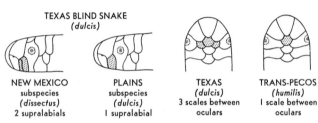

TEXAS BLIND SNAKE
(dulcis)

NEW MEXICO
subspecies
(dissectus)
2 supralabials

PLAINS
subspecies
(dulcis)
1 supralabial

TEXAS
(dulcis)
3 scales between
oculars

TRANS-PECOS
(humilis)
1 scale between
oculars

Colubrids: Family Colubridae

To THIS enormous family belong approximately 75% of all the genera and 78% of the species of snakes of the entire world. Its members predominate on all the continents save Australia, where relatives of the cobras and coral snakes (Family Elapidae) are most numerous. An even greater preponderance is evident in our area, where the colubrids constitute about 87% of the genera and 84% of the species. All the snakes from *Natrix* (below) to *Tantilla* (p. 224), inclusive, belong to the Family Colubridae. They vary in form and size from the stout-bodied hognose snakes to the slender short-tailed and rough green snakes, and from the 7-foot plus (2 m or more) rat, bull, and indigo snakes to the tiny ground and earth snakes.

Most of our colubrids have solid teeth, but some species are equipped with grooved fangs in the rear portions of the upper jaws (see p. 215).

Water Snakes: Genus *Natrix*

HARMLESS, semiaquatic snakes often seen basking on logs, branches, or brush from which they drop or glide into the water at the slightest alarm. They are adept at swimming and diving, and obtain most of their food, including frogs, salamanders, fish, and crayfish, in or near the water. Canned sardines or chopped raw fish (be sure to include the entrails) are readily accepted by captives of many species.

Water snakes have been more maligned than any other non-poisonous serpents, partly because they strike and bite hard when cornered (even a rat would do as much), and partly because biased or uninformed persons resent their predation on fishes. They actually improve good fishing by culling out sick and less vigorous fish and helping to thin out overpopulated lakes and ponds in which the fish otherwise would remain stunted in size.

Most persons confuse the larger, stouter kinds of water snakes with the venomous Cottonmouth, and with good reason. They look much alike, and even the distinctive patterns may be obscured if the snake has been crawling in mud or is soon to shed its skin. Live cottonmouths move more slowly, beating a more dignified retreat; cornered ones hold their mouths open wide in readiness to bite. Dead cottonmouths can be checked for two things: (a) a single row of scales under the tail (double in water snakes); and (b) a deep pit between eye and nostril (absent in all harmless snakes — see Fig. 60, opp. Pl. 34). Be cautious about trying to catch any aquatic serpent within the range of the cottonmouths (Map 173).

Many water snakes flatten their bodies when alarmed. When first seized, they discharge copious quantities of foul-smelling musk from glands at the base of the tail. Females grow larger than males; many that are heavy with young are noticeably distended in girth. Dead or captive water snakes are often most quickly identified by flipping them over and examining their colorful and usually distinctive belly patterns.

Besides occurring in eastern North America and Mexico, the genus *Natrix* is represented in Europe, Africa, Asia, and the Malay Archipelago.

GREEN WATER SNAKE.   Pl. 21
Natrix cyclopion cyclopion
   Identification: 30–45 in. (76–114 cm); record 50 in. (127.0 cm). Although they lack distinctive field marks, the two Green Water Snakes are unique among our *Natrix* in having a row of scales between the eye and lip scales (upper labials) — see Fig. 32, p. 140. This makes identification positive and final, but it means

Fig. 32. HEADS OF WATER SNAKES *(Natrix)*

GREEN AND FLORIDA GREEN
(cyclopion ssp.*)*
Scales between eye and lip plates

BANDED, BROAD-BANDED, AND FLORIDA
(fasciata ssp.*)*
Dark stripe from eye to angle of jaw

having the snake in hand for close-up examination. General dorsal coloration may be greenish or brownish, but usually with at least some faint suggestion of a dark pattern on a lighter ground. Belly marked with *light* spots or half-moons on a ground color of gray or brown. Scales *keeled;* anal *divided. Young:* About 9–10½ in. (23–27 cm) at birth.

A species of quiet waters — edges of lakes and ponds, of swamps, rice fields, or marshes, of bayous and other waterways. Occasionally found in brackish water.

Similar species: (1) Virtually all other large Water Snakes usually have strong indications of pattern — stripes, spots, or blotches — but these may not show well in a basking serpent unless it is wet. (2) Cottonmouth usually moves sluggishly, not dropping or diving into water as fast as Water Snakes.

Range: Mississippi Valley from extr. s. Illinois to the Gulf; extr. sw. Alabama to se. Texas.   Map 105

FLORIDA GREEN WATER SNAKE   Pl. 21
Natrix cyclopion floridana

Identification: 30–55 in. (76–140 cm); record 74 in. (188.0 cm). A large greenish or brownish serpent (sometimes reddish in southern Florida) without any distinctive markings. Belly plain whitish or cream-colored, except near anus and under tail, where it is patterned like the western subspecies, the Green Water Snake. A row of scales between eye and upper lip plates (Fig. 32, above). Scales *keeled;* anal *divided. Young:* Ground color brownish- or greenish-olive with about 50 black or dark brown bars on each side of body and similar but less conspicuous markings on back; belly yellow, but with black markings near and under tail; 8¾–10 in. (22–25 cm) at birth.

Habitats include the Everglades and the Okefenokee region, as well as other swamps, marshes, and quiet bodies of water. Sometimes found in brackish water.

Similar species: (1) Most other Water Snakes have distinctive patterns, either on their backs or bellies or both. (2) Cottonmouth retreats slowly, and often holds mouth open in readiness to bite when closely approached.

Range: S. South Carolina to tip of Florida; west through the Florida panhandle to Mobile Bay, Alabama.   Map 105

BROWN WATER SNAKE *Natrix taxispilota*   **Pl. 21**
Identification: 30–60 in. (76–152 cm); record 69 in. (175.3 cm). Often called the "water-pilot," and one of the easiest of all water snakes to mistake for the venomous Cottonmouth. The pattern consists of a series of large, squarish, dark brown blotches down middle of back and a similar but alternating row on each side (Fig. 33, below). Many specimens are exceptionally dark, being deep chocolate-brown in gross appearance and with blotches only a little darker than ground color. Belly yellow to brown and boldly marked with spots and half-moons of dark brown or black. The head in this species is distinctly wider than the neck, producing a heart-shaped or diamond-headed appearance (viewed from above) that is erroneously alleged to occur only in venomous snakes. Scales *keeled;* anal *divided.* *Young:* 7½–13 in. (19–33 cm) at birth.

Fig. 33. DIAGRAMMATIC DORSAL PATTERNS OF WATER SNAKES
(*Natrix*)

BROWN (*taxispilota*)
Dark squares

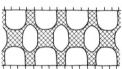

DIAMONDBACK (*rhombifera*)
Dark chainlike pattern

A species chiefly of clear, quiet waters. Largely diurnal and a characteristic resident of the great swamps and rivers of the South. An accomplished swimmer and climber, ascending trees to heights of 20 ft. (6 m) or more. Although they flee from man with alacrity, Brown Water Snakes are spirited fighters when seized or cornered.
Similar species: (1) Cottonmouth is either virtually plain dark brown or marked with broad dark crossbands on a lighter (often greenish or olive) ground color; often holds mouth open in readiness to bite when approached. (2) Green Water Snakes have a row of scales between eye and upper labials (Fig. 32, p. 140). (3) Banded and Florida Water Snakes often have red in their patterns, and usually show a dark stripe from eye to angle of jaw (Fig. 32, p. 140).
Range: Se. Virginia to se. Alabama and south to tip of Florida; chiefly in Coastal Plain, but ascending streams into the Piedmont.   Map 107

DIAMONDBACK WATER SNAKE Pl. 21
Natrix rhombifera rhombifera

Identification: 30–48 in. (76–122 cm); record 63 in. (160.0 cm). The light areas on the back may be vaguely diamond-shaped, but the pattern is best described as consisting of dark brown chainlike markings on a ground color of lighter brown or dirty yellow (Fig. 33, p. 141). Belly yellow, marked with black or dark brown spots or half-moons. *Adult male:* Unique among serpents of our area in having numerous raised protuberances (papillae) under chin (Fig. 34, below). Scales *keeled;* anal *divided. Young:* Strongly patterned, belly often brightly tinged with orange; 9–13⅛ in. (23–33 cm) at birth.

Throughout most of its range this is a ubiquitous serpent, appearing in many types of aquatic habitats from big lakes and rivers to ditches and cattle tanks. Toward the west, it follows rivers far into otherwise arid terrain. During warm weather it becomes strongly nocturnal.

Similar species: Cottonmouth tends to move slowly and often holds mouth open when approached; adult Western Cottonmouths usually are plain black or dark brown, but younger ones are marked with dark crossbands on a lighter ground color.

Range: Mississippi Valley from sw. Indiana and extr. se. Iowa to Kansas and south to the Gulf and ne. Mexico; absent from much of the Interior Highlands region in Missouri and Arkansas. Mexican subspecies. Map 104

RED-BELLIED WATER SNAKE Pl. 20
Natrix erythrogaster erythrogaster

Identification: 30–48 in. (76–122 cm); record 62 in. (157.5 cm). The "copperbelly." Venter plain red or orange-red. Dorsum normally plain brown (pale reddish brown to rich chocolate-brown), but often somewhat grayish or greenish on lower sides of body. Scales *keeled;* anal normally *divided* (single in about 10 percent of the specimens of all subspecies of *Natrix erythrogaster*). *Young:* Boldly patterned, ground color usually pinkish as in young of Blotched Water Snake (top left figure, Plate 20); lateral blotches *alternate* with larger middorsal ones all the way *forward to head* (or nearly so.) Juvenile pattern disappears with

Fig. 34. CHARACTERISTICS OF WATER SNAKES *(Natrix)*

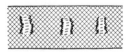

BLOTCHED
(transversa)
Traces of dark-bordered but light
crossbars in middorsal area

DIAMONDBACK
(rhombifera)
Projecting papillae
on chin of male

age, but traces of it often persist well into young adulthood.
About 8½–11½ in. (22–29 cm) at birth.

At home in the great river swamps and numerous other
aquatic habitats of the Southeast. This snake often wanders
well away from water in hot, humid weather, a habit shared
by the several subspecies of *Natrix erythrogaster.*
Similar species: (1) Occasional Water Snakes of other species
may be uniformly brown above, but they normally have
strongly patterned bellies. (2) Certain small serpents, such as
the Red-bellied and Black Swamp Snakes, may have plain dark
dorsal surfaces and crimson venters, but, when fully adult, they
are of a size comparable with the well-patterned young of the
"copperbelly." (3) Kirtland's Water Snake has a row of black
spots down each side of belly.
Range: Extr. s. Delaware to n. Florida and se. Alabama.
Subspecies: NORTHERN COPPERBELLY, *Natrix e. neglecta.*
Similar but darker above (sometimes black); belly often heavily
invaded by dorsal ground color; young with the dorsal spots
often irregular and running together. W. Kentucky and adj.
Tennessee north, chiefly in disjunct colonies in or near swampy
woodlands or river bottoms, to s. Michigan and nw. Ohio.

Map 103

YELLOW-BELLIED WATER SNAKE   Pl. 20
Natrix erythrogaster flavigaster
Identification: 30–48 in. (76–122 cm); record 53⅛ in. (134.9
cm). A "redbelly" without the red — essentially like the Red-
bellied Water Snake except in coloration. Dorsum gray or
greenish gray, usually plain, but sometimes with traces of pattern persisting as light (but dark-bordered) transverse bars
across center of back as in the Blotched Water Snake (Fig. 34,
p. 142). Belly plain yellow, often washed with orange; occasionally with dark pigment on bases or ends of ventral scutes.
Scales *keeled;* anal usually *divided. Young:* Strongly patterned
like young of blotched Water Snake (Plate 20); about 9½–12 in.
(24–30 cm) at birth.

A snake of the wetlands of the lower Mississippi Valley and
adjacent areas. Usually found in or near the larger, more permanent, bodies of water — in river bottoms, swamps, marshes,
edges of ponds and lakes, etc.
Similar species: Adult Water Snakes of other species are
sometimes plain dark above, but their bellies are usually boldly
marked.
Range: N.-cen. Georgia and se. Iowa to e. Texas and the Gulf.

Map 103

BLOTCHED WATER SNAKE   Pl. 20
Natrix erythrogaster transversa
Identification: 30–48 in. (76–122 cm); record 58 in. (147.3 cm).
A race of the "redbelly" in which the blotched pattern of the

young persists into adulthood, or even throughout life. An extremely variable snake; general coloration may be almost any shade of gray or brown, but with markings darker than background. Occasionally the blotched pattern may virtually disappear, but traces of it usually remain in the form of short, light, but dark-bordered, bars across center of back (Fig. 34, p. 142). Belly virtually plain yellow, often with an orange tinge; bases of belly scales may be dark, or the dark coloration of the dorsum may encroach onto edges of the scutes. Underside of tail unpatterned and usually *orange* or *reddish*. Scales *keeled;* anal usually *divided. Young:* Strongly blotched, lateral dark blotches (or spots) alternating with large middorsal blotches all the way forward to the head (or nearly so); 7½–12⅞ in. (19–33 cm) at birth.

Likely to be found wherever permanent or semipermanent water occurs — in ditches, cattle tanks, and along streams. Follows rivers, in western part of its range, into what is otherwise decidedly arid country.
Similar species: (1) In Northern Water Snake the lateral blotches unite with the middorsal ones to form dark crossbands on neck and forepart of body; belly is usually strongly patterned with half-moons or other dark markings, and underside of tail is patterned. (2) In Broad-banded Water Snake dorsal markings are quite large, the venter is boldly patterned, and the head bears a dark stripe from eye to angle of jaw (Fig. 32, p. 140).
Range: W. Missouri and Kansas to ne. Mexico. Intergrades with Yellow-bellied Water Snake over a wide area where their ranges meet, especially in se. Texas and even into extr. sw. Louisiana. Mexican subspecies.   Map 103

NORTHERN WATER SNAKE   Pl. 20
Natrix sipedon sipedon
Identification: 24–42 in. (61–107 cm); record 53 in. (134.6 cm). The only large water snake in most of the northern states, a fortunate thing for northerners, because this reptile exhibits a bewildering array of variations. Farther south, where its range overlaps some of the other species of water snakes, one must check the chief diagnostic characters, which are: (a) dark crossbands on neck and forepart of body, but alternating dorsal and lateral blotches on rest of body; (b) dark markings wider than spaces between them; (c) black or reddish half-moons on belly; and (d) dark pattern continuous to tip of underside of tail. Ground color varies from pale gray to dark brown, markings from bright reddish brown to black. Adults tend to darken so that the pattern becomes obscure; it may disappear altogether, resulting in a plain black or dark brown serpent. (Putting snake in water will often reveal pattern details in what seems like a virtually unicolored specimen.) Half-moons on belly may be

arranged in a regular pattern, scattered at random, represented merely by dusky areas, or be entirely absent. Some specimens have their bellies almost uniformly stippled with gray except for a yellow, orange, or pinkish midventral stripe. Scales *keeled;* anal *divided. Young:* Strongly patterned, black on a ground of pale gray or light brown; about 7½–9 in. (19–23 cm) at birth.

A resident of virtually every swamp, marsh, or bog, of every stream, pond, or lake border within its range. Quiet waters are preferred, but swift-flowing streams and the environs of waterfalls also have their quotas of these water snakes — unless they have been exterminated by man or pollution!

Similar species: (1) Banded Water Snake has crossbands throughout length of body, a dark stripe from eye to corner of mouth (Fig. 32, p. 140), and squarish spots on belly. (2) Northern Copperbelly has bright red belly marked only with black or dark brown, and usually just at edges of ventral scales, but the dark pigment may often heavily invade venter. (3) Blotched Water Snake has virtually plain yellowish belly, and underside of tail is unpatterned and usually orange or reddish.

Range: S. and e. Maine and extr. s. Quebec to N. Carolina and southern uplands; west to Colorado. Intergrades with Midland Water Snake over a broad area where their ranges meet.

Subspecies: LAKE ERIE WATER SNAKE, *Natrix s. insularum.* A pale race in which the pattern is much reduced or completely lacking. General coloration gray (often greenish or brownish); belly white or yellowish and sometimes with a pink or orange tinge down center. Pattern elements, when present, are like those of Northern Water Snake. Islands of Put-in-Bay Archipelago, Lake Erie. CAROLINA SALT MARSH SNAKE, *Natrix s. williamengelsi.* A very dark race; many specimens are almost plain black above. Half-moons on belly solid black except anterior to 50th ventral where some may have brown or reddish centers. A snake adapted to seaside and estuarine conditions that avoids drinking salt water. Outer Banks of e. N. Carolina and mainland shores of Pamlico and Core Sounds.   Map 99

MIDLAND WATER SNAKE   Pl. 20
Natrix sipedon pleuralis

Identification: 22–40 in. (56–102 cm); record 51½ in. (130.8 cm). Patterned basically like the Northern Water Snake — dark crossbands on the neck and alternating blotches farther back. But the dark markings are *smaller* than the spaces between them. Older specimens tend to darken and lose their patterns, but traces, at least of the lateral markings, usually show when snake is submerged in water. Occasionally crossbands continue throughout length of body. General coloration may be brown or gray instead of red, and blotches may even be black. The belly markings tend strongly to be in pairs, and do not so often break up and disappear as they do in Northern Water Snake. Scales *keeled;* anal *divided. Young:* 7½–12 in. (19–30 cm) at birth.

Throughout the bulk of its range this snake utilizes a wide variety of habitats — streams, ponds, swales, marshes, etc. Toward the south, however, it follows river valleys, in some cases all the way to the Gulf Coast.

Similar species: In the Banded Water Snake, crossbands are present throughout length of body, belly markings tend to be squarish and most prominent at sides, and there is a dark stripe from eye to angle of jaw (Fig. 32, p. 140).

Range: Midland America, from Indiana to Oklahoma and the Gulf, and (south of the mountains) to the Carolinas. Map 99

BANDED WATER SNAKE   Pl. 20
Natrix fasciata fasciata
Identification: 24–42 in. (61–107 cm); record 60 in. (152.4 cm). Distinguished by three characteristics: (a) dark crossbands (often black-bordered); (b) squarish spots at sides of belly; and (c) dark stripe from eye to angle of jaw (Fig. 32, p. 140). There is great variation in coloration; crossbands may be red, brown, or black, and ground color gray, tan, yellow, or even reddish. Most specimens darken with age, and black pigment tends to obscure the markings, resulting, in extreme cases, in a virtually all-black snake. Even in one of these, however, patches of red or of other light colors usually appear on lower sides of body. Scales *keeled;* anal *divided. Young:* Crossbands very dark, usually black, and in strong contrast with pale ground color; 7½–9½ in. (19–24 cm) at birth.

Occupies virtually all types of freshwater habitats, including streams, ponds, lakes, and marshes.

Similar species: (1) Northern and Midland Water Snakes normally have dark crossbands only on *forepart* of body; their belly markings include dark or reddish half-moons. (2) See also Cottonmouths (Pl. 34 and Fig. 60).

Range: Coastal Plain, N. Carolina to Mississippi. Hybridizes with the Northern and Midland Water Snakes in a few localities along the Fall Line in Georgia and the Carolinas and with the Carolina Salt Marsh Snake in the Sounds region of e. N. Carolina. Intergrades with Broad-banded Water Snake in se. Louisiana and adj. Mississippi.   Map 100

FLORIDA WATER SNAKE   Pl. 20
Natrix fasciata pictiventris
Identification: 24–42 in. (61–107 cm); record 62½ in. (158.8 cm). The Florida member of the "banded" water snake group. As in the others, there are dark crossbands and a dark stripe from eye to angle of jaw (Fig. 32, p. 140). But it differs in often having secondary dark spots on sides of body (between the

prominent crossbands) and in possessing *wormlike* red or black markings across belly. Coloration and pattern highly variable — black, brown, or reddish markings on a ground color of gray, tan, or reddish. In the redder specimens, black pigment is reduced or even lacking; in darker ones, black obscures the other colors, and virtually plain black specimens are not rare. Scales *keeled;* anal *divided. Young:* Red or black crossbands that are in bold contrast with a light ground color; 7½–10½ in. (19–27 cm) at birth.

A snake chiefly of shallow-water habitats, of Florida's swamps, marshes, flatwoods ponds, cypress bays, borders of lakes and ponds, rivers, and fresh water in general.

Similar species: (1) Florida Green Water Snake has a row of scales between eye and lip plates (Fig. 32, p. 140). (2) See also Florida Cottonmouth (p. 229).

Range: Extr. se. Georgia to southern tip of Florida. Map 100

BROAD-BANDED WATER SNAKE   Pl. 20
Natrix fasciata confluens

Identification: 22–36 in. (56–91 cm); record 45 in. (114.3 cm). None of our other water snakes has such *broad* dark crossbands or so few. They number only 11 to 17 on the body; every other North American *Natrix* has at least 19 and normally many more than that. The dark crossbands are separated by areas of yellow, irregular in shape and arrangement, and they frequently run together; in coloration they vary from black through brown to rich red-brown (or combinations of these). In some parts of range, either the yellow or red may be exceptionally prominent, as is reflected in such colorful local names as "yellow moccasin" and "pink flamingo snake." In lower Mississippi Valley, dark hues predominate, and even the large squarish belly markings are usually black or very dark brown. A dark stripe from eye to angle of mouth (Fig. 32, p. 140). Scales *keeled;* anal *divided. Young:* More brightly patterned; 7–9½ in. (18–24 cm) at birth.

A snake of the great watery wilderness of the Mississippi River delta region and of marshes, swamps, and shallow bodies of water in general throughout its range. Occurs to very edge of salt or brackish water along Gulf Coast.

Similar species: Cottonmouth has broad head and is a stouter, heavier snake with a single row of scales under tail.

Range: Central lowlands from extr. s. Illinois to cen. Texas and Gulf Coast.   Map 100

GULF SALT MARSH SNAKE   Pl. 21
Natrix fasciata clarki

Identification: 15–30 in. (38–76 cm); record 36 in. (91.4 cm). The only *striped* water snake normally occurring in a salt- or brackish-water habitat. There are 2 dark brown stripes and 2 tan or yellowish ones on *each* side of body. The very distinctive belly pattern consists of a central row of large white or yellow spots on a ground color of brown or reddish-brown; in some specimens there is an extra, smaller row of light spots on each side, making 3 rows in all. Dorsal scale rows 21 or 23. Scales *keeled;* anal *divided. Young:* 7¾–9¾ in. (20–25 cm) at birth.

An abundant snake of Gulf coastal salt meadows, swamps, and marshes; only rarely enters freshwater habitats.

Similar species: (1) Other striped Water Snakes (Queen and Graham's) do not have more than 19 scale rows. (2) Garter Snakes have *single* anal plates and only *one* light stripe on each side of body.

Range: Gulf Coast from w.-cen. Florida to s. Texas. Intergrades with Banded and Broad-Banded Water Snakes in many areas where their freshwater habitats blend into brackish ones.

Subspecies: ATLANTIC SALT MARSH SNAKE, *Natrix f. taeniata.* Dorsum striped anteriorly as in Gulf Salt Marsh Snake, but pattern on remainder of body consisting of dark blotches on a light ground color. A row of broad light spots down center of belly. North-central portion of Florida's east coast.

Note: Water snakes from scattered localities in coastal regions may have aberrant patterns that combine the characteristics of two different races. Some, for example, may be partially blotched or spotted (as in the Banded Water Snakes) and partially striped (as in the Gulf Salt Marsh Snake), and the blotch-stripe combinations can occur at random on any part of the body.   Map 101

MANGROVE WATER SNAKE   Pl. 21
Natrix fasciata compressicauda

Identification: 15–30 in. (38–76 cm); record 36¾ in. (93.3 cm). A small water snake of the mangrove swamps of Florida's lower coasts. Pattern and coloration extremely variable. Commonly there are dark spots or crossbands on a greenish ground color. Stripes may appear on the neck. Some specimens are almost plain black, others straw-colored, and one fairly common phase is virtually plain red or orange-red. Scales *keeled;* anal *divided. Young:* 7–9½ in. (18–24 cm) at birth.

Identification is often best accomplished on basis of habitat. Although it occasionally enters fresh water, as in some ponds on the Florida Keys, this is chiefly a serpent of salt and brackish water, an environment not often invaded by other water snakes native to southern Florida.

Similar species: Cottonmouth, which also sometimes occurs in brackish waters, is stout-bodied and has a broad head distinctly wider than neck; often opens mouth in readiness to bite when alarmed.

Range: S. Florida, especially on west coast and the Keys; north coast of Cuba. Intergrades with Gulf Salt Marsh Snake north of Tampa Bay and with Florida Water Snake where salt- and freshwater habitats meet. Map 101

HARTER'S WATER SNAKE *Natrix harteri* **Pl. 21**
Identification: 20–30 in. (51–76 cm); record 35½ in. (90.2 cm). Within its range this is the only water snake with *4 rows of dark spots* on its back (2 rows on each side) and a row of dark dots down each side of a pink or orange belly. (Kirtland's Water Snake, of the north-central region, is similarly patterned.) Dorsal spots brown on a brownish-gray or slightly greenish ground color. Usually 2 rows of small scales between the posterior chin shields. Scales *keeled;* anal *divided. Young:* 8–9 in. (20–23 cm) at birth.
    Locally abundant in fast-flowing, rocky streams or in bushes or grasses along the shores. Its ability to swim in swift water is remarkable. Named for Philip Harter, snake fancier and collector of Palo Pinto Co., Texas, who discovered the species.
Range: Brazos and Concho River systems in cen. Texas.
Subspecies: BRAZOS WATER SNAKE, *Natrix h. harteri* (Plate 21). As described above. Brazos River. CONCHO WATER SNAKE, *Natrix h. paucimaculata.* Similar but more reddish in coloration, the dorsal spots less prominent, and the dark dots on the belly inconspicuous or completely absent. A single row of scales between the posterior chin shields. Known only from the Concho-Colorado River system in cen. Texas. Map 102

QUEEN SNAKE *Natrix septemvittata* **Pl. 21**
Identification: 15–24 in. (38–61 cm); record 36¼ in. (92.1 cm). A slender brown aquatic snake with a yellow stripe along lower side of body (on 2nd scale row and upper half of 1st). Belly yellow but boldly marked with 4 brown stripes: the 2 outer stripes are the larger and are situated on the edges of the belly plates (plus lower half of 1st row of scales). Ventral stripes most prominent toward neck; farther back they tend to run together, especially in adults, and to be obscured by a darkening of the ground color. Three additional very narrow dark stripes run down the back, but are difficult to see except in specimens that have recently shed their skins. Queen Snakes from the South tend to be nearly unicolored, with indications of pattern remaining only in the neck region. Scales *keeled;* anal *divided. Young:* Belly stripes clearly defined, usually all the way to tail; about 7½–9⅛ in. (19–23 cm) at birth.
    The "willow snake" or "leather snake," as it sometimes is called, likes small stony creeks and rivers, especially those abounding in crayfish, but it is by no means confined to such habitats. Queen Snakes are not usually such conspicuous baskers as some of the other (and larger) water snakes, and they are more likely to be seen swimming or discovered beneath rocks or debris at the water's edge. They feed very largely on soft-

shelled crayfish (ones that have just shed), and so are difficult to keep in captivity.

Similar species: (1) Garter Snakes have *single* anal plates, and usually a *middorsal light stripe*. (2) Graham's Water Snake has a broader yellow stripe (on scale rows 1, 2, and 3); its belly is either plain yellow or with a single dark area or row of spots down the center. (3) Glossy Water Snake and Lined Snake each have a *double* row of black belly spots. (4) Gulf Salt Marsh Snakes have brown or black bellies with 1 or 3 rows of yellow spots down center.

Range: S. Great Lakes region and se. Pennsylvania to Gulf Coast; a disjunct area in Arkansas and sw. Missouri.

Map 109

GRAHAM'S WATER SNAKE *Natrix grahami*   **Pl. 21**
Identification: 18–28 in. (46–71 cm); record 47 in. (119.4 cm). Look for two pattern characteristics: (a) broad yellow stripe on scale rows 1, 2, and 3; and (b) narrow black stripe where lower-most row of scales meets belly plates (stripe often zigzag or irregular). Sometimes a dark-bordered, pale stripe down center of back. Belly yellowish, either plain or marked with dark dots or a dull dark area down center. A dark color phase of this snake occurs in Iowa in which entire dorsal surface is brown, and pattern details can be made out only with difficulty; belly is deep olive-buff, chin and throat yellow. Scales *keeled;* anal *divided. Young:* About 8–10 in. (20–25 cm) at birth.

Found at margins of ponds and streams, along sloughs and bayous, and in swamps. Sometimes basks, but is more apt to be found by overturning stones and debris at water's edge. May hide in holes in muddy streambanks or in crayfish chimneys. Food includes crayfish and other crustaceans, plus small amphibians and fish. Named for James Duncan Graham, a professional soldier and engineer, who was in the field with the U.S. and Mexican Boundary Survey in the early 1850's.

Similar species: (1) Queen Snake has 4 brown stripes down belly, and yellow side stripe is on scale rows 1 and 2. (2) Garter Snakes have *single* anal plates and usually a prominent light stripe down center of back.

Range: Iowa and Illinois to Louisiana and Texas; absent from much of the Interior Highlands region in Missouri, Arkansas, and Oklahoma.   Map 110

GLOSSY WATER SNAKE *Natrix rigida*   **Pl. 21**
Identification: 14–24 in. (36–61 cm); record 31⅜ in. (79.7 cm). Shiniest of all the water snakes. A more or less plain brown or olive-brown snake, but dark stripes may be faintly evident on back or (more strongly so) on lower sides of body. The 2 rows of black spots down the belly are bold and distinct even in large specimens, in which the center portion of belly may become clouded with dark pigment. Scales *keeled;* anal *divided.*

A secretive snake of the southern lowlands, rarely seen in the open except at night or after heavy rains. Decidedly aquatic, its habits resembling those of the swamp snakes. Food includes small fish, frogs, salamanders, and crayfish.
Similar species: (1) Garter Snakes, (2) Lined Snakes, (3) Striped Swamp Snake, and (4) striped kinds of Water Snakes have prominent *light* stripes.
Range: Coastal Plain; Virginia to n.-cen. Florida and west to e.-cen. Texas.
Subspecies: EASTERN GLOSSY WATER SNAKE, *Natrix r. rigida* (Plate 21). A pattern of narrow dusky stripes following edges of scales on sides of throat; subcaudals usually 54 or fewer in females; 62 or fewer in males. Atlantic Coastal Plain from Virginia to n.-cen. Florida. GULF GLOSSY WATER SNAKE, *Natrix r. sinicola.* No pattern on sides of throat; subcaudals usually 55 or more in females; 63 or more in males. Gulf Coastal Plain from cen. Georgia to e.-cen. Texas; north into Arkansas and se. Oklahoma. DELTA GLOSSY WATER SNAKE, *Natrix r. deltae.* Only 1 preocular scale on at least one side of head (2 on both sides in other races); number of subcaudals subtracted from number of ventrals usually 81 or more in females; 73 or more in males (fewer in other races). Se. Louisiana and adj. Mississippi.

Map 108

KIRTLAND'S WATER SNAKE *Natrix kirtlandi* **Pl. 22**
Identification: 14–18 in. (36–46 cm); record 24½ in. (62.2 cm). The reddish belly with a prominent row of round black spots down each side is the best check. The 4 rows of dark spots on the back are not always conspicuous. They show best when the skin is stretched, when body, for example, is distended by food or by young (in pregnant females). In a relatively few specimens, the dark spots of the 2 central rows become small and indistinct, especially toward rear of body, and the reddish-brown ground color may appear as a light middorsal stripe. Scales *keeled;* anal *divided. Young:* Dark and virtually unicolored above (unless skin is stretched); belly deep red; about 5–6½ in. (13–17 cm) at birth.

Flattening of the body when alarmed, a trait shared by other water snakes, garter snakes, and their close allies, is developed to a remarkable degree in this species. Some specimens can make themselves almost ribbonlike, and may remain rigidly immobile until touched or otherwise disturbed. Most often found in or near wet meadow and open swamp-forest habitats. Feeds on earthworms and slugs. Named for Jared P. Kirtland, early Ohio physician and naturalist.
Similar species: Red-bellied Snake lacks conspicuous black spots, either above or below.
Range: W. Pennsylvania to ne. Missouri; s. Michigan to n. Kentucky. Map 106

Swamp Snakes:
Genera *Liodytes* and *Seminatrix*

THE swamp snakes probably are now much more abundant than they were before the introduction of the water hyacinth from Venezuela in 1884. The enormous mats formed by these floating plants provide shelter among their roots and leaves for a veritable menagerie of small aquatic and semiaquatic animals, including several kinds of snakes, frogs, and salamanders. The members of these two genera, which are small relatives of the water snakes, occur only in the extreme southeastern United States.

STRIPED SWAMP SNAKE *Liodytes alleni* **Pl. 22**
Identification: 13–20 in. (33–51 cm); record 25¾ in. (65.4 cm). A shiny, brown, chiefly aquatic snake with a broad yellowish stripe along lower side of body. Three relatively inconspicuous dark stripes on back, one middorsal and the others lateral. Belly normally yellowish and virtually unmarked, but it may be orange or orange-brown instead, and the same color may also replace the yellow of the lateral stripe. Dark midventral markings, when present, may vary from a few scattered smudges to a long, well-defined row of spots. Head small in proportion to size of body and with nasal scales arranged in unorthodox fashion; *only one internasal scute* and the two nasal scutes *meet each other* on the middorsal line of the snout. Scales *smooth* except in anal region and on top of tail, where they are keeled. Anal *divided. Young:* Like adults; 6¼–7 in. (16–18 cm) at birth.

At home in dense vegetation in shallow water. Sometimes found by hauling masses of water hyacinths ashore and then sorting through them. Habitats include sloughs and marshes, bayheads and sphagnum bogs. At twilight, especially on rainy or humid evenings, Striped Swamp Snakes sometimes travel overland and may be seen on roads paralleling or traversing wet prairies, marshes, etc. Food consists of crayfish, dwarf sirens, and frogs. The jaws are powerful enough to hold and engulf hard-shelled crayfish. Captives of this species and Black Swamp Snake survive best in aquariums well supplied with aquatic vegetation and several inches of water.
Similar species: (1) Garter and (2) Ribbon Snakes have *keeled* scales and *single* anal plates.
Range: S. Georgia and peninsular Florida. Map 111

BLACK SWAMP SNAKE *Seminatrix pygaea* **Pl. 22**
Identification: 10–15 in. (25–38 cm); record 18½ in. (47.0 cm). A shiny black aquatic snake with a red belly. Scales *smooth,*

but each scale of the 3 to 5 lowermost rows bears a light, longitudinal line that *looks* like a keel. Anal *divided*. *Young:* Like adults; 4¼-5⅜ in. (11-14 cm) at birth.

Often common in areas where water hyacinths abound. Dragging hyacinths ashore is one way to search for them. They often hide under boards and debris at water's edge, and on rainy or dewy nights may wander overland. The environs of cypress ponds are a natural habitat, and probably were one of the most important before the pestiferous hyacinth was introduced. Food includes leeches, small fish, worms, tadpoles, dwarf sirens, and other small salamanders.

Similar species: Red-bellied Snake has *keeled* scales.

Range: Coastal N. Carolina to s. Florida.

Subspecies: NORTH FLORIDA SWAMP SNAKE, *Seminatrix p. pygaea* (Plate 22). Belly plain red or with a pair of black bars on base of each ventral scale; ventrals 118 to 124. N. Florida, extr. se. Alabama, and se. Georgia. SOUTH FLORIDA SWAMP SNAKE, *Seminatrix p. cyclas.* A short triangular black mark at forward edge of each ventral scale; ventrals 117 or fewer. Southern half of Florida peninsula. CAROLINA SWAMP SNAKE, *Seminatrix p. paludis.* A pair of black bars on each ventral scale; ventrals 127 or more. Chiefly the Coastal Plain of S. Carolina to extr. e. N. Carolina.   Map 112

Brown Snakes: Genus *Storeria*

THESE are small secretive snakes, usually brown, but sometimes gray or reddish in dorsal coloration. Scales *keeled,* anal *divided,* and no loreal scale (Fig. 55, opp. Pl. 22). Several other small brown or gray snakes of other genera resemble them, so recourse to checking scale characteristics, especially whether a loreal is present or not, is often necessary.

Brown snakes, like the garter and water snakes to which they are related, may flatten their bodies when alarmed. They also use their anal scent glands when picked up, but the odor is not particularly offensive. Food includes slugs, earthworms, and soft-bodied insects. The genus ranges from Canada to Honduras.

NORTHERN BROWN SNAKE   **Pl. 22**
Storeria dekayi dekayi

Identification: 9-13 in. (23-33 cm); record 19⅜ in. (49.2 cm). Formerly called "DeKay's snake" after James Edward DeKay, an early naturalist of New York. This is the little brown snake with 2 parallel rows of blackish spots down the back. A few of the spots may be linked with their partners across the dorsum by narrow lines of dark pigment. General coloration varies from light yellowish brown or gray to dark brown or deep reddish brown. The middorsal area, for a width of about 4 scales, is almost always lighter in color than sides of body. The small dark lateral spots may be inconspicuous unless skin is stretched. A dark downward streak on side of head (Fig. 35, p. 155). Belly pale yellowish, brownish, or pinkish, unmarked except for 1 or more small black dots at side of each ventral scale. Scales *keeled* and in 17 rows; anal *divided*. *Young:* Conspicuous yellowish collar across neck; general coloration darker than in adults and with spotted pattern scarcely evident; 3⅜–4½ in. (9–11 cm) at birth.

Before the days of bad pollution and the massive use of pesticides this could almost have been called the "city snake" because of the frequency with which it turned up in parks, cemeteries, and beneath trash in empty lots, even in large urban centers. Although still a common snake in some areas, even in close proximity to mankind, it is so adept at hiding that few persons know it, and those who encounter it for the first time may mistake it for a baby garter snake. Habitats (away from cities) include environs of bogs, swamps, freshwater marshes, moist woods, hillsides, etc.

Similar species: (1) Earth Snakes have a long, horizontal loreal scale, whereas Brown Snakes have a vertical preocular scale — see Fig. 55, opp. Pl. 22. (2) Ground Snakes (*Sonora*) and Worm Snakes (*Carphophis*) have *smooth* scales. (3) Red-bellied Snakes have 15 scale rows and (normally) red bellies. (4) Garter Snakes have *single* anal plates and (usually) a light stripe on each side of body. (5) Ringneck Snakes (easily confused with young Brown Snakes) have *smooth* scales.

Range: S. Maine and s. Canada to Virginia. Intergradation among the several races of this species occurs over such enormous areas that accurate delineation of the ranges of subspecies is virtually impossible. (Marsh and Florida Brown Snakes are exceptions.) In some instances it may be practical simply to designate specimens as Brown Snakes without attempting to assign them to subspecies.

Subspecies: MIDLAND BROWN SNAKE, *Storeria d. wrightorum.* Record length 20¾ in. (52.7 cm). Very similar, but with numerous dark crosslines (Fig. 35, p. 155); sum of ventrals and subcaudals 176 or more (175 or fewer in Northern Brown Snake). Wisconsin to the Carolinas and Gulf Coast. TEXAS BROWN SNAKE, *Storeria d. texana.* Similar to the northern subspecies, with 2 rows of dark spots down back; no dark line on temporal scale, but a large dark spot under eye. Also, spot behind head is large and extends downward to belly scales (Fig. 35, p. 155). Minnesota to Texas and ne. Mexico. MARSH BROWN SNAKE, *Storeria d. limnetes.* Record length 16⅛6 in. (40.8 cm). A median dark line through long axis of temporal scale and no dark markings on 6th and 7th upper or lower labials (Fig. 35, p. 155).

Restricted chiefly to the salt marshes of coastal Louisiana and
Texas where it occurs on levees and in muskrat houses; ranges
from Colorado Co., Texas, to (isolated?) colonies near both
Mobile, Alabama, and Pensacola, Florida. These last two localities are shown on the map by black dots connected with their
proper subspecific symbol (in the Gulf of Mexico).   Map 128

Fig. 35. CHARACTERISTICS OF BROWN SNAKES *(Storeria)*

MARSH	TEXAS	NORTHERN
(limnetes)	*(texana)*	*(dekayi)*
Dark line on temporal	Large blotch back of head; spot below eye	Small blotch; dark streak downward on side of head

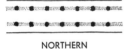

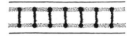

NORTHERN	MIDLAND
(dekayi)	*(wrightorum)*
2 rows of dark spots on dorsum	Dorsum crossed by dark lines

FLORIDA BROWN SNAKE *Storeria dekayi victa*   **Pl. 22**
Identification: 9–13 in. (23–33 cm); record 19 in. (48.3 cm). The
broad light band across the back of the head, heavy dark pigment on the lip scales below the eye, and a double row of small
black spots at each side of the belly are all present in typical
specimens, but this brown snake is subject to many variations.
Some individuals closely resemble Midland Brown Snake in
pattern and coloration, but others have the markings greatly
reduced. *Most constant character* is number of scale rows — 15
as opposed to 17 in all other subspecies of *Storeria dekayi*.
Florida Brown Snake also tends to be more slender than the
others. Scales *keeled;* anal *divided. Young:* Similar to adults,
but much darker; a prominent light band across back of head;
3¾–4¼ in. (10–11 cm) at birth.

A resident of bogs and marshes, of river-bottom swamps, and
environs of ponds and sloughs, but also occurring in upland
hammocks and the pineland-prairie region of southern Florida.
Often hides among water hyacinths. Most likely to be seen
abroad on warm, rainy, or humid nights on roads that traverse
or parallel marshy bodies of water.
Similar species: (1) Pine Woods and Crowned Snakes have
smooth scales. (2) Earth Snakes have a horizontal loreal scale
(Fig. 55, opp. Pl. 22). (3) Florida Red-bellied Snakes (some of

them do not have red bellies!) show a light collar across neck (not back of head) and there is a light spot on the 5th upper lip (labial) scale.

Range: Se. Georgia and peninsular Florida; lower Keys.

Map 128

RED-BELLIED SNAKE *Storeria occipitomaculata*   **Pl. 22**
   Identification: 8–10 in. (20–25 cm); record 16 in. (40.6 cm). The two key characters — a plain red belly and 3 pale-colored nape spots — are usually present, but this small snake is subject to great variation. Dorsum normally plain brown except for indications of 4 narrow dark stripes or a broad, fairly light middorsal stripe, or both. Many specimens are gray; a few are black, and in extreme cases the belly may be blue-black. The belly color, normally bright red, may vary through orange to pale yellow. The 3 light spots may fuse together (especially in the Florida subspecies) to form a light collar across neck. Two preoculars. Scales *keeled* and in 15 rows; anal *divided.* *Young:* Similar but darker than adults; 2¾–4 in. (7–10 cm) at birth.

A secretive snake of spotty distribution, common in some localities but rare or lacking in others that seemingly offer identical habitats. Particularly abundant in many mountainous or upland parts of the Northeast. Often found in or near open woods, but also occurring in or near sphagnum bogs from sea level to high in the mountains.

Similar species: (1) Kirtland's Water Snake has double row of black spots down belly. (2) Black Swamp Snake has *smooth* scales.

Range: Nova Scotia to cen. Florida; west to se. Saskatchewan, the Dakotas, and eastern parts of Kansas, Oklahoma, and Texas; a disjunct area in S. Dakota and Wyoming.

Subspecies: NORTHERN RED-BELLIED SNAKE, *Storeria o. occipitomaculata* (Plate 22). The 3 light nape spots are usually well defined; moderate amount of black pigment on sides and back of head; a light mark on the 5th upper labial, which is *bordered below by black.* All of range except the Black Hills and parts of Florida and Georgia. FLORIDA RED-BELLIED SNAKE, *Storeria o. obscura.* Spots fused to form a light collar across neck; top and sides of head black; a light spot on 5th upper labial extending downward to edge of mouth. N. Florida and s. Georgia. BLACK HILLS RED-BELLIED SNAKE, *Storeria o. pahasapae.* Light nape spots very small or lacking; no light spot on 5th upper labial. Wooded portions of the Black Hills in extr. w. S. Dakota and adj. Wyoming.   Map 127

Garter, Ribbon, and Lined Snakes:
Genera *Thamnophis* and *Tropidoclonion*

LIKE the fancy garters that once were fashionable for supporting a gentleman's socks, most of these snakes are longitudinally striped. The positions of the light lateral stripes (one on each side of the body) and whether they are encroached upon by the dark pattern are useful in telling one species of garter snake from another. To locate the stripe accurately, count upward from the large belly scales (the ventrals). "Stripe on rows 3 and 4," for example, means that the light lateral stripe is on the 3rd and 4th rows of scales above the ventrals. (See Fig. 56, opp. Pl. 24). Count ¼ of the way back on the body. Most garter snakes have 2 very small white or yellow spots on top of their heads.

When alarmed, many specimens flatten their bodies, making the pattern seem particularly vivid. When first captured they discharge musk from glands at the base of the tail which has an unpleasant, sweetish odor. Many are docile, but others may strike and bite vigorously in self-defense.

Natural foods consist chiefly of frogs, toads, salamanders, fish, tadpoles, and earthworms, but other items, including leeches, small mammals, birds, and carrion, are eaten occasionally. Captives usually learn to accept chopped fresh fish. (Be sure to include the entrails.)

Garter and ribbon snakes are closely allied to the water snakes (*Natrix*), but, unlike water snakes, they almost always have *single* anal plates. (See front endpaper.) Members of the group are often found near water, especially in the arid or semiarid West, with the inevitable result of their being called "water snakes" by persons not acquainted with representatives of the genus *Natrix*. In the more humid East, garter (sometimes called "garden") snakes may occur almost anywhere, from sea level to high in the mountains. The genus ranges from coast to coast across both southern Canada and the United States and southward to Costa Rica.

The diminutive Lined Snake, the only member of the genus *Tropidoclonion,* strongly resembles the garter snakes and shares most of their characteristics. It ranges widely across the plains and prairies of the Central United States.

EASTERN GARTER SNAKE   Pl. 23
Thamnophis sirtalis sirtalis

Identification: 18–26 in. (46–66 cm); record 48¾ in. (123.8 cm). The *only* garter snake throughout most of its range with lateral stripes *confined to rows 2 and 3.* Extremely variable in coloration and pattern; either stripes or spots may predominate.

Normally 3 yellowish stripes, but they may be brownish, greenish, or bluish instead. Ground color black, dark brown, green, or olive. Usually a double row of alternating black spots between stripes, the spots sometimes very prominent and invading the stripes; occasional specimens are virtually stripeless. Belly greenish or yellowish, with 2 rows of indistinct black spots partially hidden under overlapping portions of ventrals. Some individuals, especially from western part of range, have red or orange on skin between dorsal scales. Jet-black (melanistic) specimens are found occasionally, especially near shores of Lake Erie. Scales *keeled;* anal *single. Young:* 5–9 in. (13–23 cm) at birth.

A well-known and common snake occupying a wide variety of habitats — meadows, marshes, woodlands, hillsides, along streams and drainage ditches, and sometimes even in city lots, parks, and cemeteries if pollution is not too severe.
Similar species: (1) All other Garter Snakes within the range have lateral stripes involving row 4, at least on neck — except Short-headed Garter Snake which is distinguished by small head and low number (17) of scale rows (19 in Eastern Garter). (2) The striped Water Snakes (Queen, Graham's, and Glossy) and Gulf Salt Marsh Snake all have *divided* anal plates, and most of them have *strongly patterned* bellies. (3) Brown Snakes lack light *lateral* stripes and loreal scale (Fig. 55, opp. Pl. 22).
Range: S. Canada to Gulf of Mexico and west to Minnesota and e. Texas.
Note: Garter snakes from the Canadian Maritime Provinces, Quebec, and adjacent parts of New England, in which spotting is prominent and the light middorsal stripe is lacking or only faintly developed, may eventually be recognized as a separate race, *T. s. pallidula.* The status and range of the complex in that far northeastern area require study.					Map 116

## CHICAGO GARTER SNAKE					Pl. 23
Thamnophis sirtalis semifasciata
Identification: 18–26 in. (46–66 cm); record 35⅝ in. (90.5 cm). The lateral stripes on the forepart of the body are interrupted at regular intervals by vertical black crossbars, which are formed by the fusion of the black spots immediately above and below the light stripe. Also, in many specimens, 1 or more narrow black lines may cross middorsal stripe in neck region. Otherwise similar to eastern Garter Snake.
Range: Ne. Illinois and small adjacent portions of Indiana and Wisconsin.					Map 116

## RED-SIDED GARTER SNAKE					Pl. 24
Thamnophis sirtalis parietalis
Identification: 20–26 in. (51–66 cm); record 48⅞ in. (124.1 cm).

The red or orange bars vary in size and intensity, so some specimens are redder than others. In many, red is largely confined to skin between scales. General ground color olive, brown, or black, the dark pigment sometimes invading much of belly. Lateral stripes on rows 2 and 3; all 3 stripes may be yellow, orange-yellow, bluish, or greenish. Scales *keeled;* anal *single.* *Young:* 7–8 in. (18–20 cm) at birth.

In the eastern part of the range, this snake is widespread and common in such habitats as prairie swales, along ditches paralleling railroads, the environs of ponds, etc. Farther west it may occur wherever water is found, and it follows watercourses, even intermittent ones, far into arid country.
Similar species: (1) All other Garter Snakes within the range of this one lack red bars. (2) Plains Garter and Ribbon Snakes have the light stripes on rows 3 and 4.
Range: Extr. s. Mackenzie and e.-cen. British Columbia to Oklahoma. Western subspecies.   Map 116

NEW MEXICO GARTER SNAKE   Pl. 24
Thamnophis sirtalis dorsalis
Identification: 18–28 in. (46–71 cm); record 51⅝ in. (131.1 cm). Similar to the Red-sided Garter Snake but with the red more subdued and largely confined to the skin between the scales, which may be chiefly black in the middorsal region. In some specimens the red is reduced, the stripes are especially prominent, and the general appearance may be greenish. Lateral stripes on scale rows 2 and 3. Venter bluish or brownish, unmarked or with dark spots on edges. Scales *keeled;* anal *single.* *Young:* Similar but occasionally rusty orange in coloration; about 6–8 in. (15–20 cm) at birth.

Found in marshy swales and depressions and irrigation ditches, less often in running water.
Range: Rio Grande Valley from extr. s. Colorado to vicinity of El Paso, Texas; a disjunct population in the Río Casas Grandes, Chihuahua.   Map 116

TEXAS GARTER SNAKE   Pl. 24
Thamnophis sirtalis annectens
Identification: 18–25 in. (46–64 cm); record 34½ in. (87.6 cm). The unusually broad orange middorsal stripe is characteristic. On forward third of body the lateral stripes involve row 3, *plus* adjacent parts of rows 2 and 4. Scales *keeled;* anal *single.*
Similar species: (1) In Eastern and Red-sided Garter Snakes the lateral stripes do not include row 4. (2) Eastern Black-necked Garter Snake has *single* row of large black spots on each side of neck. (3) Ribbon Snakes are more slender, and lateral stripes do not involve scale row 2. (4) Checkered Garter Snake

has a light curved band behind mouth followed by a broad dark blotch.

Range: E.-cen. Texas; disjunct colonies in sw. Kansas and Texas panhandle.   Map 116

BLUE-STRIPED GARTER SNAKE   Pl. 23
Thamnophis sirtalis similis

Identification: 20–26 in. (51–66 cm); record 39¼ in. (99.7 cm). An extraordinary "mimic" of the Blue-striped Ribbon Snake. Both occur together, and positive identification often requires checking the position of the lateral stripe — on rows 2 and 3 in the garter snake and 3 and 4 in the ribbon snake. Dorsum dark brown or *very* dark brown; middorsal stripe dull tan or yellowish; lateral stripes light blue or bluish white. Scales *keeled;* anal *single. Young:* 7¼–9⅛ in. (18–23 cm) at birth.

Occurs in marshes, pine flatwoods, etc. in the coastal lowlands of northwestern peninsular Florida. Usually far less abundant than the Blue-striped Ribbon Snake.

Range: W. Florida from Wakulla Co. to the Withlacoochee River.   Map 116

PLAINS GARTER SNAKE   *Thamnophis radix*   Pl. 24

Identification: 20–28 in. (51–71 cm); record 40 in. (101.6 cm). This one may be troublesome. First check the stripe — it is on rows 3 and 4. Then look for black markings — black bars on lips, a double alternating row of black spots between stripes, a row of black spots *below* side stripe, and a row of dark, often indefinite, spots down each side of belly. Some specimens are so dark that part of the markings may be obscured. Dorsal stripe may be bright yellow or orange, lateral ones greenish or bluish. Scales *keeled* in a maximum of 21 rows; anal *single. Young:* About 7½ in. (19 cm) at birth.

An abundant snake throughout much of its range, and especially common in river valleys and near prairie ponds and sloughs. Formerly common in open lots and parks in many large cities, but now greatly reduced in numbers in such habitats because of building activities and the widespread use of pesticides by mankind.

Similar species: (1) Lateral stripe involves row 2 and maximum number of scale rows is only 19 in most other Garter Snakes (Eastern, Red-sided, Butler's) occurring within the range of this one. (2) Checkered Garter Snake has a yellow curve or triangle behind mouth followed by a broad dark blotch. (3) Ribbon Snakes, with stripe on rows 3 and 4, are slender and their tails are long — ¼ or more of total length. (4) Wandering Garter Snake has stripe on rows 2 and 3 and 21 rows of scales at midbody.

Range: N.-cen. Ohio; nw. Indiana to Rocky Mts. and from s. Alberta to n. New Mexico.
Subspecies: EASTERN PLAINS GARTER SNAKE, *Thamnophis r. radix* (Plate 24). Ventral scales usually 154 or fewer; scale rows on neck usually 19. Cen. Ohio; nw. Indiana to Iowa and adjacent states. WESTERN PLAINS GARTER SNAKE, *Thamnophis r. haydeni.* Similar, but with black spots between stripes somewhat smaller. Ventral scales usually 155 or more; scale rows on neck usually 21. Minnesota, Iowa, and nw. Missouri to the Rockies; southern plains and prairie parts of Canada to ne. New Mexico and Kansas; nw. Arkansas.   Map 118

BUTLER'S GARTER SNAKE *Thamnophis butleri*   Pl. 23
Identification: 15–20 in. (38–51 cm); record 27¼ in. (69.2 cm). A curious method of crawling when excited — as when trying to escape — is a good field character. The body wriggles vigorously from side to side, but the rather meager forward progress is out of all proportion to the amount of energy expended. Head small; lateral stripe (on neck) on row 3 and adjacent halves of rows 2 and 4. Lateral stripes may be orange. Dorsal ground color variable — olive-brown to black — and it may or may not show a double row of black spots between the stripes. Scales *keeled;* anal *single. Young:* 5–7 in. (13–18 cm) at birth.
  Chiefly a snake of open, prairie-like areas. Common in some localities, but rare or completely lacking over many parts of its range. Named for Amos Butler, early Indiana naturalist.
Similar species: (1) Eastern Garter Snake has stripe on rows 2 and 3. (2) Plains Garter Snake has stripe on rows 3 and 4, and there are usually prominent black spots both above *and below* the lateral stripes. (3) See also Short-headed Garter Snake.
Range: Ohio, extr. s. Ontario, and e. Michigan to cen. Indiana; se. Wisconsin; an unconfirmed record from near western tip of Lake Ontario.   Map 113

SHORT-HEADED GARTER SNAKE   Pl. 23
Thamnophis brachystoma
Identification: 14–18 in. (36–46 cm); record 22 in. (55.9 cm). Smallest of the eastern garter snakes, and the one with the most restricted range. Head short and no wider than neck. A tendency for each lateral stripe to be bordered by a narrow dark line. Lateral stripe (on neck) on rows 2 and 3, but occasionally involving lower part of row 4. Dark spots between stripes, so common in many other kinds of garter snakes, are lacking or only faintly indicated. Scales *keeled;* anal *single. Young:* 5–6 in. (13–15 cm) at birth.
  A snake of the Allegheny High Plateau. Low herbaceous

cover, such as in meadows and old fields, is preferred. Food consists very largely of earthworms.

Similar species: Butler's Garter Snake has the lateral stripe on same scale rows, but head is somewhat larger and a trifle wider than neck; also, dark spots may appear between stripes. If any doubt remains, count dorsal scale rows; maximum number normally is 17 in Short-headed and 19 in both Butler's and Eastern Garter Snakes. The stripe in the latter does *not* involve row 4.

Range: Sw. New York and nw. Pennsylvania; introduced and established at Pittsburgh, and apparently also in Butler and Erie Cos., Pennsylvania.   Map 113

CHECKERED GARTER SNAKE   Pl. 24
Thamnophis marcianus marcianus

Identification: 18–24 in. (46–61 cm); record 42½ in. (108.0 cm). The garter snake with the checkerboard pattern. Black squarish spots often strongly invade the light stripes. On each side of head behind mouth there is a yellowish curve or triangle, followed by a large dark blotch. Lateral stripe on row 3 near head; on rows 2 and 3 farther back. Scales *keeled* in a maximum of 21 rows; anal *single*. *Young:* 8–9¼ in. (20–23.5 cm) at birth.

A snake of the southern plains and the Edwards Plateau; also widely distributed through the arid Southwest where it seldom strays far from streambeds, springs, irrigation ditches, or other places where water may be present — at least beneath the surface.

Similar species: Plains Garter Snake may have suggestion of a yellowish curve behind head, but its lateral stripes involve row 4.

Range: E.-cen. Texas to w.-cen. Kansas and west to extr. se. California; south to n. Zacatecas and extr. n. Veracruz; a disjunct population in the vicinity of Tehuantepec, Oaxaca. Mexican and Cen. American subspecies.   Map 114

WESTERN BLACK-NECKED GARTER SNAKE   Pl. 24
Thamnophis cyrtopsis cyrtopsis

Identification: 16–28 in. (41–71 cm); record 41¾ in. (106.0 cm). *A large black blotch at each side of neck,* usually separated from its partner by the middorsal stripe, which is orange anteriorly but fades to dull yellow posteriorly. Lateral stripes on scale rows 2 and 3; yellowish anteriorly, whitish or pale tan throughout most of length. Head gray (usually bluish gray), its color sharply set off from the black neck blotches. (Specimens from the Big Bend of Texas are chiefly black or very dark brown between the light stripes; large black spots appear when skin is stretched. Those from far western Texas are brown with smudgy black spots.) Venter unmarked, whitish or slightly brownish or greenish. Scales *keeled,* usually in 19 rows at midbody; anal *single*. *Young:* More brightly and contrastingly colored than adults; about 8 in. (20 cm) at birth.

Usually found near water, in permanent or intermittent streams, vicinity of springs, cattle tanks, etc., but often wandering into arid terrain during wet weather. Occurs from low desert flats to forested mountains.

Similar species: (1) Checkered Garter Snake usually has 21 rows of scales at midbody and lateral stripe involves *only scale row 3* near head. (2) New Mexico Garter Snake lacks prominent black blotches at sides of neck, and has red on skin between scales.

Range: Trans-Pecos Texas; se. Utah and s. Colorado south to Sonora, Zacatecas, and San Luis Potosí. Mexican subspecies.

Map 115

EASTERN BLACK-NECKED GARTER SNAKE   Pl. 24
Thamnophis cyrtopsis ocellata

Identification: 16–20 in. (41–51 cm); record 43 in. (109.2 cm). The *single row* of large dark spots on the neck sets this apart from our other garter snakes. The light lateral stripe on rows 2 and 3 is wavy from being partly invaded by the black spots both above and below it. Scales *keeled;* anal *single*.

An inhabitant of rocky hillsides, limestone ledges, and cedar brakes.

Range: Edwards Plateau of s.-cen. Texas west to the Big Bend.

Map 115

WANDERING GARTER SNAKE   Pl. 24
Thamnophis elegans vagrans

Identification: 18–30 in. (46–76 cm); record 35½ in. (90.2 cm). Despite the considerable variation in coloration and pattern, the light middorsal stripe is usually fairly well defined, the dark markings are rounded, and there are usually 8 upper labials and 21 rows of scales at midbody. General coloration brown, brownish green, greenish buff, or gray. Lateral light stripe on scale rows 2 and 3. Scales *keeled;* anal *single*. *Young:* About 7–8 in. (18–20 cm) at birth.

A wide-ranging western garter snake that barely enters our area. Normally found near water, but also wanders well away from it. Food includes lizards, fish, frogs, tadpoles, salamanders, earthworms, slugs, and leeches.

Similar species: (1) Plains Garter Snake has lateral stripe on scale rows 3 and 4. (2) Skin between scales is red in Red-sided Garter Snake. (3) Checkered Garter Snake has lateral stripe confined to scale row 3 near head.

Range: Black Hills of S. Dakota; extr. w. Nebraska and Oklahoma; west to British Columbia, Washington, Oregon, Nevada, and e.-cen. California. Western and Mexican subspecies.

Map 117

EASTERN RIBBON SNAKE   **Pl. 23**
Thamnophis sauritus sauritus
  Identification: 18–26 in. (46–66 cm); record 38 in. (96.5 cm).
  Ribbon snakes are the slimmest, trimmest members of the garter
  snake group. The 3 bright stripes are well set off against the
  dark slender body and tail; stripes normally yellow, but middorsal one sometimes with an orange or greenish tinge. A double
  row of black spots may appear between the stripes when the
  skin is stretched. Lateral stripes on rows 3 and 4. *A dark
  ventrolateral stripe* (usually brown), involving the two lowermost rows of scales and the outer edge of the belly, is characteristic of this and all other races of the Eastern Ribbon Snake
  (*sauritus*). Lips unpatterned; normally 7 upper labials; belly
  plain yellowish or greenish. *Tail exceptionally long,* about ⅓
  total length of snake. Scales *keeled;* anal *single. Young:*
  7¼–9 in. (18–23 cm) at birth.
    This agile, nervous serpent is semiaquatic, seldom wandering
  far from streams, ponds, bogs, or swamps. Swims at surface
  instead of diving as water snakes do. Deep water normally is
  avoided, and fleeing ribbon snakes skirt the shore, threading
  their way through vegetation and getting lost from sight with
  amazing rapidity. Unlike other garter snakes, ribbon snakes
  usually will not eat earthworms but are fond of salamanders,
  frogs, and small fish. Captives remain nervous, and may dart
  out of their cages the instant the lids are opened.
  Similar species: Several other Garter Snakes have stripes that
  also involve row 4, but no other kinds are so thin and have such
  long tails. The tail in other species of *Thamnophis* and in the
  striped Water Snakes is generally less than ¼ total length.
  Range: Southern half of New England to S. Carolina; southwest to extr. se. Illinois, e. Louisiana, and the Florida panhandle.
  Subspecies: NORTHERN RIBBON SNAKE, *Thamnophis s. septentrionalis.* Similar but darker; dorsum velvety black or dark
  brown; yellow middorsal stripe often partly obscured by brown
  pigment; tail usually less than ⅓ total length. Maine to extr.
  ne. Wisconsin, lower peninsula of Michigan, and n. Indiana; a
  disjunct colony in Nova Scotia.   Map 119

PENINSULA RIBBON SNAKE   **Pl. 23**
Thamnophis sauritus sackeni
  Identification: 18–25 in. (46–63.5 cm); record 40 in. (101.6 cm).
  The "southern ribbon snake." A less well patterned counterpart
  of the other ribbon snakes. The general impression is of a tan
  or brown snake with a narrow light stripe on each side involving
  rows 3 and 4. Middorsal stripe less distinct than lateral ones
  and occasionally lacking altogether or represented only by a
  short line on neck. A broad dark ventrolateral stripe; remainder
  of belly plain yellowish white. Upper labials 8. Tail very long.
  Scales *keeled;* anal *single.*

This abundant southern subspecies is semiaquatic and, like other ribbon snakes, often basks on vegetation overhanging water, dropping in at the slightest alarm.
Similar species: Queen, Glossy Water, and Striped Swamp Snakes have *divided* anals and series of dark markings on their bellies.
Range: Extr. s. S. Carolina; south to southern tip of Florida peninsula; the lower Keys (Big Pine and Cudjoe).   Map 119

BLUE-STRIPED RIBBON SNAKE   Pl. 23
Thamnophis sauritus nitae
Identification: 18–25 in. (46–63.5 cm); record 29¾ in. (75.6 cm). Typically a velvety black snake with a narrow sky-blue or bluish-white stripe on each side of body. Dorsum may be black or dark brown; lower sides (scale rows 1 and 2) often somewhat paler; an obscure middorsal stripe sometimes present; lateral stripe involving rows 3 and 4; upper labials 8; tail more than ⅓ total length. Scales *keeled;* anal *single. Young:* About 7–9 in. (18–23 cm) at birth.

Found in and near marshes, pine flatwoods, and hammocks in the Gulf Coastal region of northwestern peninsular Florida.
Similar species: See Blue-striped Garter Snake.
Range: W. Florida from e. Wakulla Co. to the Withlacoochee River.   Map 119

WESTERN RIBBON SNAKE   Pl. 23
Thamnophis proximus proximus
Identification: 20–30 in. (51–76 cm); record 37⅝ in. (95.6 cm). Very similar to the Eastern Ribbon Snake, but with *no ventrolateral dark stripe;* venter unmarked. Lateral light stripe on scale rows 3 and 4. The parietal spots on the head are large, brightly colored, and they touch each other. In the Eastern Ribbon Snake, these spots are faint or lacking and rarely touch. Dorsum black; a narrow orange vertebral stripe. Upper labials usually 8. Tail long, but usually somewhat less than ⅓ total length. Scales *keeled;* anal *single. Young:* About 9–10 in. (23–25 cm) at birth.

Semiaquatic and remaining close to streams and ditches, the edges of lakes and ponds, and other bodies of water.
Similar species: (1) Other Garter Snakes with a stripe on rows 3 and 4 have tails that are generally less than ¼ total length. (2) Glossy Water Snake has a *divided* anal and bold black ventral markings.
Range: Indiana and s. Wisconsin to e. Nebraska and most of Kansas; south to s.-cen. Louisiana and ne. Texas.
Subspecies: GULF COAST RIBBON SNAKE, *Thamnophis p. orarius.* Similar but with an olive-brown dorsum and a broad *gold* vertebral stripe. Gulf Coast, chiefly in the marshes from extr. s. Mississippi to s. Texas. ARID LAND RIBBON SNAKE,

Thamnophis p. diabolicus. Record 48½ in. (123.2 cm). Dorsum olive-gray to olive-brown; vertebral stripe *orange;* a narrow dark ventrolateral stripe. Occurs in streams, cattle tanks, and other bodies of permanent or semipermanent water from extr. se. Colorado southward to ne. Mexico; the Pecos River Valley of New Mexico and Texas. Intergradation between two and even three subspecies is common over a wide area within the range of the *Thamnophis proximus* complex.   Map 120

RED-STRIPED RIBBON SNAKE   Pl. 23
Thamnophis proximus rubrilineatus

Identification: 20–30 in. (51–76 cm); record 48 in. (121.9 cm). The red vertebral stripe may change to orange on the neck in some specimens or, rarely, may be orange throughout its length. Dorsal ground color olive-brown to olive-gray; a narrow dark ventrolateral stripe sometimes present; lateral light stripe on rows 3 and 4. Scales *keeled;* anal *single.*

Confined chiefly to the vicinity of streams, springs, and cattle tanks, but occasionally wanders farther afield during rainy weather.

Range: The Edwards Plateau of cen. Texas and intergrading with the adjacent subspecies over a relatively broad area.

Map 120

LINED SNAKE   *Tropidoclonion lineatum*   Pl. 24

Identification: 8¾–15 in. (22–38 cm); record 21 in. (53.3 cm). It's "bottoms up" for checking this snake. The double row of bold black half-moons down belly plus *single* anal plate should clinch identification.   Middorsal stripe variable in coloration — whitish, yellow, orange, or light gray. Lateral stripe on rows 2 and 3. Scales *keeled. Young:* Averaging 4–4¾ in. (10–12 cm) at birth.

An abundant snake through much of its range, sometimes even appearing in city lots, parks, cemeteries, or abandoned trash dumps that have not been seriously affected by pollution or the use of pesticides. Also occurs on open prairies and in sparsely timbered areas. Usually found by overturning stones, boards, and debris, but it prowls at night or during the breeding season in spring. Earthworms are the favorite food.

Similar species: (1) Some of the Garter Snakes have dark spots on their bellies, but these are not so large, dark, or clearly defined as in the Lined Snake. (2) Glossy Water Snake bears similar belly markings, but its dorsal pattern, if any shows at all, consists of *dark* stripes, and its anal plate is *divided.* (3) Graham's Water Snake also has *divided* anal.

Range: Cen. Illinois to Colorado and New Mexico; se. South Dakota to s.-cen. Texas.

Subspecies: NORTHERN LINED SNAKE, *Tropidoclonion l. line-*

atum. Ventrals 143 or fewer; caudals more than 32 in females and more than 40 in males. CENTRAL LINED SNAKE, *Tropidoclonion l. annectens.* Ventrals more than 143; caudals more than 33 in females and more than 40 in males. TEXAS LINED SNAKE, *Tropidoclonion l. texanum.* Ventrals 143 or fewer; caudals fewer than 34 in females and fewer than 41 in males. See map for individual ranges and areas of intergradation.

Map 123

Earth Snakes: Genus *Virginia*

THESE are small gray, brown, or reddish-brown snakes virtually devoid of any distinctive markings. They must be caught and examined closely to verify identification. Any small nondescript serpent of an earthy color *may* belong to this genus. Earth snakes are highly secretive and, in the North at least, seldom appear above ground except after cool, heavy rains, when they may be found, in addition to other places, hidden beneath stones that have been warmed by the sun. Food includes earthworms and soft-bodied insects and their larvae. The genus occurs only in the eastern United States, and a variety of names have been applied to its members — "ground snakes," "gray snakes," "little brown snakes," etc.

SMOOTH EARTH SNAKE *Virginia valeriae*   **Pl. 22**
  Identification: 7–10 in. (18–25 cm); record 13¼ in. (33.7 cm). Any small gray or reddish-brown snake virtually without markings may be this one (within its geographical range, of course). There may be an indication of a faint light stripe down the back, and many scales may have faint light lines on them that look like keels but aren't. Often a dark shadow from eye to nostril. Belly plain white or yellowish. Upper labials 6; a horizontal loreal scale (Fig. 55, opp. Pl. 22). Scales *smooth or weakly keeled* and in 15 or 17 rows (see subspecies below). Anal *divided.* *Young:* Without markings; 3⅛–4½ in. (8–11 cm) at birth.
  Although considered a rare reptile over much of its range, the Smooth Earth Snake is locally common, and may be much more abundant than it seems. Adept at keeping out of sight. Habitats include abandoned fields, environs of trails and back roads, especially those in or near deciduous forests.
  Similar species: (1) Brown Snakes have *strongly keeled* scales and no loreal (Fig. 55, opp. Pl. 22). (2) Rough Earth Snake has *strong keels* and only 5 upper labials. (3) Worm Snakes have *smooth* scales and a maximum of 13 scale rows. (4) Pine Woods Snake has a dark band running from snout through eye and to angle of jaw, and 7 upper labials.
  Range: New Jersey to n. Florida; west to Iowa, Kansas, and Texas.

Subspecies: EASTERN EARTH SNAKE, *Virginia v. valeriae* (Plate 22). Scale rows 15; scales mostly *smooth,* but faint keels are usually discernible on back near tail. Often there are tiny black spots on dorsum, more or less scattered or arranged in 4 rows. Coloration gray or light brownish gray. New Jersey to n. Florida; west to Ohio, cen. Tennessee, and Alabama. MOUNTAIN EARTH SNAKE, *Virginia v. pulchra.* Scales *weakly keeled,* in 15 rows anteriorly and 17 at midbody and posteriorly. Dorsum reddish brown to dark gray. Unglaciated mountains and high plateaus of w. Pennsylvania and adj. Maryland through W. Virginia to Highland Co., Virginia. WESTERN EARTH SNAKE, *Virginia v. elegans.* Scales *weakly keeled,* in 17 rows. Reddish- to grayish-brown above; venter whitish, with a pale greenish-yellow tint in adults. (Great Plains Ground Snake, range of which overlaps range of Western Earth Snake, has *smooth* scales in 15 rows.) Sw. Indiana and s. Iowa to Mississippi and e.-cen. Texas.   Map 125

ROUGH EARTH SNAKE   *Virginia striatula*   **Pl. 22**
Identification: 7–10 in. (18–25 cm); record 12¾ in. (32.4 cm). A cone-headed snake with a distinctly pointed snout. Plain light gray or brown to reddish brown in coloration. *Upper labials 5;* a horizontal loreal scale (Fig. 55, opp. Pl. 22); *internasals fused together into a single scale.* Scales *keeled;* anal normally *divided,* occasionally single. *Young:* Darker and grayer. The newborn young may have a pale gray to white band across the back of the head, which is lost as maturity is reached. They thus resemble young brown or ringneck snakes both of which, however, have *2 internasals* and *7 or more upper labials.* About 3–4¾ in. (8–12 cm) at birth.
    This small secretive snake is locally common in the South. It feeds chiefly on earthworms.
Similar species: (1) Smooth Earth Snakes have 6 upper labials and *smooth* or *weakly keeled* scales. (2) Brown Snakes have no loreal scale (Fig. 55, opp. Pl. 22). (3) Worm, Ringneck, and Pine Woods Snakes have *smooth* scales.
Range: Virginia to n. Florida; west to se. Kansas, Oklahoma, and Texas.   Map 124

Hognose Snakes: Genus *Heterodon*

SERPENTS of extraordinary behavior. These are the "spreadheads" that flatten their heads and necks, hiss loudly, and inflate their bodies with air, producing a show of hostility that has earned them a bad reputation. If the intruder fails to retreat or prods the snake with a stick, it may soon roll on its back, open its mouth, give a few convulsive movements, and then lie still as though dead.

Turn the snake right side up, and it promptly rolls over again, giving the bluff away.

As a result of their behavior these harmless snakes have earned such dangerous-sounding names as "hissing adder," "blow viper," "spreading adder," "hissing sand snake," and "puff adder."

The upturned snout (in combination with keeled scales) is also a good identification point. The tail is often held in a tight, flat coil. Toads are the principal food. The genus occurs only in North America.

EASTERN HOGNOSE SNAKE   Pl. 25
Heterodon platyrhinos

Identification: 20–33 in. (51–84 cm); record 45½ in. (115.6 cm). The hissing, head- and neck-spreading, and playing 'possum are usually sufficient. Check for the upturned snout, which is keeled above. General coloration quite variable — yellow, brown, gray, olive, orange, or red may predominate. Normally a spotted snake, but jet-black specimens or nearly plain gray ones are common in some areas. Belly mottled, gray or greenish (rarely black) on yellow, light gray, or pinkish. Underside of tail *lighter than belly* — easily checked when the snake is playing 'possum (see Fig. 36, below). Scales *keeled;* anal *divided. Young:* 6¼ to almost 10 in. (16–25 cm) at hatching.

Sandy areas are a favorite habitat. After a short period in captivity, most hognose snakes fail to "perform" any longer. Although toads are the mainstay, frogs also are eaten; young snakes may also eat crickets and other insects.

Similar species: (1) In Southern Hognose, underside of tail is *not* lighter than belly. (2) In all three races of the western species the entire ventral surface is black with white or yellow patches (Fig. 36, below).

Fig. 36. CHARACTERISTICS OF HOGNOSE SNAKES *(Heterodon)*

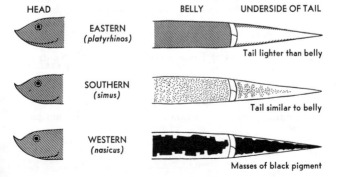

HEAD   BELLY   UNDERSIDE OF TAIL

EASTERN
(platyrhinos)

Tail lighter than belly

SOUTHERN
(simus)

Tail similar to belly

WESTERN
(nasicus)

Masses of black pigment

Range: Extr. s. New Hampshire to s. Florida; west to Minnesota, se. S. Dakota, Kansas, and Texas.   Map 130

SOUTHERN HOGNOSE SNAKE *Heterodon simus*   **Pl. 25**
Identification: 14–20 in. (36–51 cm); record 24 in. (61.0 cm). Smallest of the hognose snakes. Snout sharply upturned (Fig. 36, p. 169) and keeled above. Coloration fairly constant, not highly variable as in Eastern Hognose Snake. Underside of tail *not* conspicuously lighter than belly (Fig. 36, p. 169). Scales *keeled;* anal *divided.*

Habitats include sandy woods, fields, and groves, dry river floodplains, and hardwood hammocks; occasionally plowed out of the ground. Upturned snout is used in burrowing and in digging for spadefoot and other toads.
Similar species: In Eastern Hognose Snake, underside of tail is lighter than belly (Fig. 36, p. 169).
Range: Se. N. Carolina to s.-cen. Florida and s. Mississippi.
          Map 132

WESTERN HOGNOSE SNAKE *Heterodon nasicus*   **Pl. 25**
Identification: 16–25 in. (41–64 cm); record 35¼ in. (89.5 cm). The sharply upturned snout, normally with a keel on top, marks this as a hognose snake, but the belly should be checked for positive species identification (Fig. 36, p. 169). Large jet-black ventral areas, interspersed with white or yellow, are characteristic. Scales *keeled;* anal *divided. Young:* 5½–7¾ in. (14–20 cm) at hatching.

Partial to relatively dry prairie areas, especially sandy ones. The habit of head- and neck-spreading is not so well developed as in the Eastern Hognose Snake, but feigning of death and rolling over occurs almost as frequently. Some Western Hognose Snakes may crawl away without performing or may hide their heads beneath coils of their bodies. Called "prairie rooter" in some parts of range. Amphibians and lizards are the chief foods, but small mammals and ground-nesting birds are also eaten.
Similar species: (1) In Eastern Hognose underside of tail is never black and is usually lighter than belly (Fig. 36, p. 169). (2) The two kinds of Hook-nosed Snakes have smooth scales and there is a depression instead of a raised keel behind the "hook."
Range: Illinois to Alberta; south to se. Arizona and n. Mexico. Isolated, relict populations, indicative of a once much wider distribution, survive in suitable habitats east of main part of range.
Subspecies: DUSTY HOGNOSE SNAKE, *Heterodon n. gloydi* (Plate 25). Dark middorsal blotches, counted from head to a point directly above anus, are fewer than 32 in males; fewer

than 37 in females. Se. Kansas to much of Texas; isolated colonies in se. Missouri and sw. Illinois. PLAINS HOGNOSE SNAKE, *Heterodon n. nasicus.* Similar but with markings darker and in sharper contrast with ground color. Dark body blotches more than 35 in males; more than 40 in females. Minnesota to se. Alberta and south to New Mexico; isolated colonies in Manitoba, Minnesota, and Iowa. Intergrades between *nasicus* and *gloydi* occur in Kansas, Oklahoma, and nw. Missouri, and in isolated colonies in sand prairies of w. Illinois and adj. Iowa. MEXICAN HOGNOSE SNAKE, *Heterodon n. kennerlyi.* Like Dusty Hognose in coloration and pattern but distinguished by scalation. Two to 6 small scales in the group on top of head directly behind rostral plate. The Plains and Dusty subspecies have 9 or more. (These are called azygous scales.) Extr. s. Texas to se. Arizona and n. Mexico.   Map 129

Small Woodland Snakes:
Genera *Diadophis, Carphophis,* and *Rhadinaea*

SECRETIVE snakes that are usually discovered by overturning boards, flat stones, or debris or by tearing apart decaying logs or stumps. Ringneck snakes (*Diadophis*) have yellow bellies that, in many southern and western populations, turn to red under and near the tail. The presence or absence and arrangement of the black spots on the venter are useful in distinguishing among subspecies. Ringnecks are noted for the habit of twisting their tails into tight coils and elevating them to show the bright undersurfaces, thus earning the names of "corkscrew" and "thimble" snakes. Curiously, the display occurs only in populations with red tails — in Regal and Prairie Ringnecks, in Mississippi Ringnecks from extreme southern Mississippi, and Southern Ringnecks from the Florida Peninsula. Exceptions are where the two types of coloration come together and where both red- or yellow-tailed snakes show this behavior. When a ringneck is held, drops of saliva may appear at the corners of its mouth. The musk is pungent, clinging, and unpleasant.

Worm snakes (*Carphophis*) and our single member of the pine woods snake group (*Rhadinaea*) are more plainly and less colorfully marked than the ringnecks, and they neither twist their tails nor exhibit other spectacular behavior.

The range of the genus *Diadophis* extends from coast to coast except for large gaps in the arid West where it is confined to uplands and the vicinity of streams; it also occurs far south into Mexico where future studies will probably show it to be absent from most basin and lowland habitats. *Carphophis* occupies a large part of the eastern and central United States. Our lone representative of *Rhadinaea* is confined to the Southeast, but the genus as a whole, with a large number of species, ranges south through Mexico and the American tropics to Uruguay and northern Argentina.

NORTHERN RINGNECK SNAKE   Pl. 25
Diadophis punctatus edwardsi

   Identification: 10–15 in. (25–38 cm); record 24⅝ in. (62.5 cm). A plain dark slender snake with a golden collar (Fig. 38, p. 174). Dorsal coloration variable — bluish black, bluish gray, slate, or brownish. Belly uniform yellow (Fig. 37, below) or occasionally with a row or partial row of small black dots down center. Scales *smooth;* anal *divided. Young:* Darker than adults; 4–5½ in. (10–14 cm) at hatching.

   A secretive woodland snake, usually most common in cutover areas that include an abundance of hiding places in the form of stones, logs, bark slabs, or other rotting wood. Rocky, wooded hillsides are also favored. Many people believe ringnecks are young racers. Small salamanders are an important food, but earthworms and small snakes, lizards, and frogs also are eaten. **Similar species:** Juvenile Brown Snakes have neck rings, but they also have *keeled* scales. (A lens may be needed to see them.)
   Range: Nova Scotia to Wisconsin; south through uplands to n. Georgia and in Mississippi Valley to Illinois.   Map 133

SOUTHERN RINGNECK SNAKE   Pl. 25
Diadophis punctatus punctatus

   Identification: 10–14 in. (25–36 cm); record 18½ in. (47.0 cm). A ringneck with a spotted belly. The black spots are large, shaped like half-moons, and in a *central row* (Fig. 37, below).

Fig. 37. BELLY PATTERNS OF RINGNECK SNAKES *(Diadophis)*

PRAIRIE
(arnyi)
Spots numerous, irregularly placed

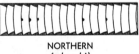

NORTHERN
(edwardsi)
Unmarked or with few black dots

MISSISSIPPI
(stictogenys)
Paired black spots down the center

SOUTHERN
(punctatus)
Row of bold black half-moons

Neck ring normally interrupted by dark pigment (Fig. 38, p. 174). Small black spots on chin and lower lips. Dorsal coloration light brown to nearly black; venter yellow, changing to red posteriorly and under tail in Florida peninsula. Scales *smooth;* anal *divided. Young:* 3½–4 in. (9–10 cm) at hatching.

Although not aquatic, ringnecks are most often found where there are evidences of moisture — near swamps, springs, on damp wooded hillsides, in flat, poorly-drained pine woods, etc. — but almost invariably under shelter. Prowling occurs chiefly at night. Specimens from peninsular Florida twist tails, exposing their red undersurfaces.

Range: S. New Jersey to Upper Florida Keys; west to the Appalachian Mts. in the South, and to cen. Alabama. (The entire population in s. New Jersey and the Delmarva Peninsula is intermediate between the northern and southern races.)

Subspecies: MISSISSIPPI RINGNECK SNAKE, *Diadophis p. stictogenys.* Neck ring narrow, often interrupted; belly spots irregular but usually grouped along midline in attached or separate pairs (Fig. 37, p. 172). Extr. s. Illinois to the Gulf; w. Alabama to e. Texas. KEY RINGNECK SNAKE, *Diadophis p. acricus.* Virtually no neck ring; head pale grayish brown; chin and labials only faintly spotted. Known only from Big Pine Key, but may also occur on some of the other Lower Florida Keys that support pine and scrub vegetation.   Map 133

PRAIRIE RINGNECK SNAKE   Fig. 37, p. 172
Diadophis punctatus arnyi

Identification: 10–14 in. (25–36 cm); record 16½ in. (41.9 cm). Dark head coloration extending around or across angle of jaw and slightly forward on lower jaw; neck ring sometimes interrupted; belly spots numerous and highly irregular (Fig. 37, p. 172); scale rows usually 17 on forward part of body (normally 15 on the four eastern subspecies). Scales *smooth;* anal *divided.*

Rocky hillsides in open woods are a favorite habitat. Like the Eastern and Southern Ringnecks, members of this race may occur in large colonies in some localities, but may be rare or absent in others that seem to offer identical conditions for hiding and finding food. Twists tail, exposing red undersurface. Often feigns death, a behavior shared by the Regal Ringneck.

Range: Extr. se. Minnesota and extr. se. S. Dakota to s.-cen. Texas.   Map 133

REGAL RINGNECK SNAKE   Fig. 38, p. 174
Diadophis punctatus regalis

Identification: 15–18 in. (38–46 cm); record 19¼ in. (48.9 cm); to 30 in. (76 cm) or more west of our area. Neck ring usually absent, but sometimes partially indicated or even complete (in

Fig. 38. TYPICAL NECK PATTERNS IN RINGNECK SNAKES *(Diadophis)*

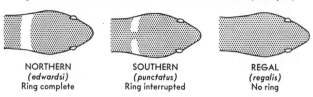

NORTHERN	SOUTHERN	REGAL
(edwardsi)	*(punctatus)*	*(regalis)*
Ring complete	Ring interrupted	No ring

Trans-Pecos Texas populations). Dorsum plain greenish, brownish, or pale slate-gray; pale bluish gray in young. Yellow pigment on 1st scale row or 1st and 2nd rows. Belly yellow, irregularly spotted with black, but turning to bright orange-red near and under tail. Scale rows usually 17 anteriorly and at midbody. (Strictly speaking, the entire Trans-Pecos population is intermediate between the subspecies *arnyi* and *regalis*, but closer to *regalis*.)

Less generally distributed than the eastern races. Partial to moist habitats — forested mountains, vicinity of water courses, etc. Food consists chiefly of lizards, small snakes, and invertebrates. Twists tail into spiral when caught or pinned down, exposing the reddish coloration to view.

Range: W.-cen. New Mexico to w.-cen. Arizona and south to San Luis Potosí; disjunct populations from se. Idaho to se. California. The large Regal Ringneck and smaller Prairie Ringneck intergrade in w. and cen. Texas despite their disparity in size. The two occur together and maintain their identities in the Guadalupe Mts. of the Texas–New Mexico border region. Western and Mexican subspecies.   Map 133

EASTERN WORM SNAKE   Pl. 25
Carphophis amoenus amoenus
Identification: 7½–11 in. (19–28 cm); record 13¼ in. (33.7 cm). A serpentine imitation of the common earthworm. Plain brown above; belly and adjacent 1 or 2 rows of dorsal scales pink. Head pointed. Two prefrontal and 2 internasal scales (Fig. 39, p. 175). Scales *smooth and opalescent;* anal *divided. Young:* Darker than adults; 3½–4 in. (9–10 cm) at hatching.

Almost never seen in the open, but usually discovered under stones or boards, in rotting logs, during digging operations, etc. Partial to moist earth and disappears deep underground in dry weather. When held in the hand, worm snakes attempt to push their way between one's fingers with both the head and spinelike tail tip. Food includes earthworms and soft-bodied insects.

Similar species: Other small brown snakes either have keeled scales or the belly color doesn't extend upward to involve a full row or more of dorsal scales.

Range: S. New England to S. Carolina, cen. Georgia, and cen. Alabama.

Subspecies: MIDWEST WORM SNAKE, *Carphophis a. helenae.* Very similar, but with each prefrontal scale fused with corresponding internasal (Fig. 39, below). S. Ohio to s. Illinois and south to the Gulf. Intergrades with the eastern subspecies (*amoenus*) in several broad areas where their ranges meet.

Map 131

Fig. 39. HEAD SCALES OF WORM SNAKES *(Carphophis)*

EASTERN
(amoenus)
Prefrontals and
internasals
separate

MIDWEST
(helenae)
Each prefrontal
fused with the
corresponding
internasal

WESTERN WORM SNAKE   Pl. 25
Carphophis amoenus vermis

Identification: 7½–11 in. (19–28 cm); record 14¾ in. (37.5 cm). Plain purplish black above; pink of belly extends upward on the sides to the 3rd row of scales. Head pointed. Scales *smooth and opalescent;* anal *divided.*

Essentially a woodland snake that follows stream valleys westward through prairie areas. Secretive and usually found under moist logs, stones, etc.

Range: Extr. s. Iowa and se. Nebraska to nw. Louisiana; w. Illinois near the Mississippi River. Intergrades with the subspecies *helenae* in a disjunct area in ne. Louisiana.   Map 131

PINE WOODS SNAKE   *Rhadinaea flavilata*   Pl. 25

Identification: 10–13 in. (25–33 cm); record 15⅞ in. (40.3 cm). The "Yellow-lipped Snake." Dorsal coloration varying from rich golden brown to light reddish brown, but becoming paler on the lower sides. Head darker. *Dark line through eye.* Often a suggestion of a narrow dark stripe down center of .back and another on each side of body on scale rows 2 and 3 (3rd only toward tail). Belly plain white, pale yellow, or yellow-green. Lip (labial) scales virtually plain white or yellowish in most Florida specimens, but usually speckled with dark pigment in the western and especially the northern part of the range. Usually 7 upper labials. Scales *smooth;* anal *divided. Young:* About 6½ in. (17 cm) at hatching.

A snake of damp woodlands, chiefly pine flatwoods but also occasionally in hardwood hammocks and on coastal islands. Secretive and found under logs, boards, or leaves, in woodpiles or loose soil, but most frequently under bark and in the decaying interiors of pine logs and stumps. Food includes small frogs and lizards; captives also have eaten salamanders and small snakes. **Range:** A narrow coastal strip, N. Carolina to e. Louisiana, and most of Florida.   Map 126

Mud and Rainbow Snakes: Genus *Farancia*

THESE large, smooth-scaled snakes are fully as aquatic as the keel-scaled water snakes (*Natrix*), and they are best kept in aquariums. They are specialized for overpowering and eating slippery aquatic prey, eel-like salamanders and true eels in the cases of the mud and rainbow snakes, respectively. The tongue is noticeably small for such large serpents, and, prior to shedding, the skin in both becomes a translucent blue that obscures the normal color pattern. Both are confined to the southeastern United States where their ranges widely overlap each other.

MUD SNAKE *Farancia abacura*   **Pl. 25**
  Identification: 40–54 in. (102–137 cm); record 81 in. (205.7 cm). A shiny, iridescent black and red (or pink) snake. Scales *smooth,* except in the supra-anal region where they are keeled. Anal normally *divided,* occasionally single. *Young:* Tail tip sharp, in contrast with blunt tip of adult; 6¼–9½ in. (16–24 cm) at hatching.
  A snake of southern swamps and lowlands. A burrower, but also thoroughly at home in water. Feeds chiefly on eel-like salamanders (amphiumas), which are maneuvered into better swallowing positions by being pricked with the snake's stiff but harmless tail tip. (A young mud snake, when bitten by an amphiuma it has seized to eat, may stab the amphibian with its sharp tail tip to make it let go.) When mud snakes are first caught, the tail also may press against the collector's hands. This behavior earns it the names of "horn snake" or "stinging snake," and the habit of lying in a loose horizontal coil associates this species with the fabled "hoop snake." Sirens, other amphibians, and fish also are eaten.
  Range: Southern lowlands (see subspecies below).
  Subspecies: WESTERN MUD SNAKE, *Farancia a. reinwardti* (Plate 25). Belly color extends upward on lower sides to form 52 or fewer red bars with rounded tops. (Count on body only; omit tail.) Alabama to e. Texas and north in Mississippi Valley to s. Illinois. EASTERN MUD SNAKE, *Farancia a. abacura.* Like the western subspecies, but with red bars more numerous (53 or more), extending farther upward, and in the shape of trian-

gles. In some, the young especially, the upward red extensions from the points of the triangles may cross back of neck. Se. Virginia to s. Florida and se. Alabama.   Map 138

RAINBOW SNAKE   *Farancia erytrogramma*   **Pl. 25**
Identification: 36–48 in. (91–122 cm); record 66 in. (167.6 cm). An iridescent, glossy snake with red and black stripes. Often an extra row of small black spots between the 2 main rows on the belly. Scales *smooth,* but some specimens may have supra-anal keels. Anal normally *divided,* but sometimes single, especially in Virginia populations. *Young:* 7¾–8½ in. (20–22 cm) at hatching.

This handsome snake is usually found in or near water; streams passing through cypress swamps are a favorite habitat. It swims well and is so adept at catching eels, its principal food, that many country people in the South call it the "eel moccasin." Young ones also eat small frogs and salamanders, and especially tadpoles. In the northern part of the range it burrows in sandy fields near water and is sometimes turned up by plowing. Specimens are usually inoffensive when handled, but when first caught the hind part of the body may thrash about, and the harmless tail may stab at the collector's hands.
Range: S. Maryland to s.-cen. Florida and e. Louisiana.
Subspecies: RAINBOW SNAKE, *Farancia e. erytrogramma* (Pl. 25). As described above. All of range except for vicinity of Lake Okeechobee, Florida. SOUTH FLORIDA RAINBOW SNAKE, *Farancia e. seminola.* Similar except that black pigment predominates on the venter and extends upward onto lower rows of dorsal scales. S.-cen. Florida.   Map 137

Racers and Whipsnakes:
Genera *Coluber* and *Masticophis*

THESE are slender, fast-moving snakes — often mere streaks in the grass as they dash away. Adults of most kinds are more or less uniformly colored or longitudinally striped. Young racers are blotched or spotted, juvenile coachwhips are crosslined, and baby whipsnakes, in general, resemble their parents. The scales are *smooth;* anal *divided.*

When alarmed or on the defensive, many of these snakes rapidly vibrate the tips of their tails, and, if they are in dry weeds or leaves, they produce a buzzing sound suggestive of a rattlesnake. When held by the neck, with the body dangling, they characteristically lash vigorously back and forth in an effort to shake themselves free. All are diurnal; many are partially arboreal, ascending into shrubs, cactus, or low trees. Rodents, small birds, lizards, snakes, frogs, and insects are included on their menus. Food is not constricted. A loop of the body is thrown over the struggling victim, pressing it down. Eggs of whipsnakes, racers, and indigo snakes are coated with small nodules resembling hard dry grains of salt. Racers range from about 10–13 in. (25–33 cm) at hatching; coachwhips 12–16 in. (30–41 cm); and whipsnakes 10–16 in. (25–41 cm).

These snakes are subject to considerable individual and local variation, especially in regions where two or more subspecies intergrade. Whipsnakes (*Masticophis*) range from the United States to northern South America. Racers (*Coluber*) occur from southern Canada to Guatemala; there are related species in southern Europe, northern Africa, and parts of Asia.

NORTHERN BLACK RACER   Pl. 26
Coluber constrictor constrictor

Identification: 36–60 in. (91–152 cm); record 73 in. (185.4 cm). A slender, satiny snake that is plain black *both* above and below. Usually some white on chin and throat. Iris of eye brown or dark amber. Scales *smooth;* anal *divided. Young:* Strongly patterned with a middorsal row of dark gray, brown, or reddish-brown blotches on a ground color of gray or bluish gray; small dark spots on flanks and venter (Fig. 40, p. 180); tail virtually unpatterned. As snake grows older, pattern becomes less distinct and uppersurface darkens; at length of 30 inches (76 cm) virtually all traces of pattern have usually disappeared.

An alert, active, locally abundant serpent that is quick to flee when approached but fights fiercely when cornered. Often retreats *upward* into bushes or low branches of trees when closely pursued. Normally makes a poor captive, seldom settling down and often falling victim to parasites and infections.

Similar species: (1) Black Rat Snake has *keels* on middorsal scales and is shaped like a loaf of bread in cross section (Fig. 58, opp. Pl. 28). (2) Black phase of Eastern Coachwhip may show slight indications of light pigment toward rear of dorsum, and sides of tail often are reddish; check number of scale rows just anterior to the tail — 13 in Coachwhips, 15 in Racers. (3) Melanistic specimens of Eastern Garter Snake have *keeled* scales and *single* anal plates. (4) Young Rat Snakes have conspicuous dark blotches on tails.

Range: S. Maine to cen. Alabama. (Old "records" for Black Racers in the Canadian Maritime Provinces cannot be substantiated; they may have been based on melanistic or dark-colored snakes of other species.)

Subspecies: SOUTHERN BLACK RACER, *Coluber c. priapus.* Very similar to Northern Black Racer, but with internal anatomical differences. (Enlarged basal hemipenial spine 3 or more times length of its predecessor in same row. Spine is less than 3 times

as long in Northern Black Racer.) Florida specimens usually
have considerable white on chin and throat, and their irises may
be bright red or orange. Young also similar to those of Northern
Black Racer, but juveniles from Florida may have reddish dorsal
blotches and their bellies may be reddish or pinkish toward tail.
Southeastern states and north and west in Mississippi Valley
to s. Indiana and se. Oklahoma; Lower Florida Keys. BROWN-
CHINNED RACER, *Coluber c. helvigularis.* Uniform black above
and below except for chin and lips, which are light tan or brown
or mottled or suffused with those colors. Lower Chipola and
Apalachicola River Valleys in Florida panhandle and adj.
Georgia.   Map 139

BLUE RACER   *Coluber constrictor foxi*   **Pl. 26**
Identification: 36–60 in. (91–152 cm); record 72 in. (182.9 cm).
Plain blue above, the head darker and very often with an even
darker area extending backward from the eye. Shade of blue
varies; it may be greenish, grayish, or much darker than in the
illustration. Chin and throat white, unspotted. Belly bluish,
paler than back. Scales *smooth; * anal *divided. Young:* Similar
to young of Northern Black Racer.
   Prairies, open woodlands, environs of lakes and tamarack-
sphagnum bogs, and more or less open habitats in general.
Range: Extr. s. Ontario and nw. Ohio to e. Iowa and se. Minnesota; an isolated record from Menominee Co., Michigan. Intergrades through a broad area with Eastern Yellow-bellied Racer.
Subspecies: EVERGLADES RACER, *Coluber c. paludicola.* A pale
bluish-, greenish-, or brownish-gray snake. Bluish ones look
very much like Blue Racer of the north-central region, and they
will check out to that subspecies when compared with Plate 26.
Belly whitish and usually with pale cloudy markings of whitish
gray or powder blue. Iris of eye red or (rarely) yellow or reddish
brown. *Young:* Similar to those of Black Racers, but with a
decidedly reddish cast; dorsal spots light chestnut, reddish, or
pinkish; belly spots reddish or orange. The Everglades and the
Miami rim rock of se. Florida; also Cape Canaveral region of
e. Florida.   Map 139

EASTERN YELLOW-BELLIED RACER   **Pl. 26**
Coluber constrictor flaviventris
   Identification: 30–50 in. (76–127 cm); record 70 in. (177.8 cm).
Averages considerably smaller than the Black or the Blue
Racer. Highly variable in coloration. Dorsum plain brown,
gray, olive, or dull to dark blue. Belly plain yellowish, varying
from pale cream in some parts of range to bright lemon-yellow
in others. Scales *smooth; * anal *divided. Young:* Similar to
young of Northern Black Racer.
   At home in fields and grasslands, brushy areas, and open

woods. More likely to forage actively through the day than most other snakes. Like other small animals of plains and prairies, it takes refuge in clumps of vegetation, glides into mammal burrows, or hides in stone or rock piles.

Similar species: Could be mistaken for one of the Green Snakes: (1) Rough Green Snake has *keeled* scales. (2) Smooth Green Snake has a maximum of 15 rows of dorsal scales (17 in the Racers). Most confusion will occur with young. Scales must be checked; combination of *smooth* scales, *divided* anals, and maximum of 17 scale rows will distinguish juveniles from any of the several other spotted snakes occurring within its range.

Range: Montana, w. N. Dakota, and Iowa to Texas and extr. sw. Louisiana.

Subspecies: BLACK-MASKED RACER, *Coluber c. latrunculus.* Dorsum slate-gray, venter grayish blue; *a black postocular stripe.* Bottomland hardwoods and cypress region of se. Louisiana. Western subspecies.   Map 139

MEXICAN RACER   Fig. 40, below
Coluber constrictor oaxaca

Identification: 20–40 in. (51–101.6 cm). The "dwarf" or "Rio Grande" racer. Middorsal area plain green or greenish gray, sides of body much lighter, and belly plain yellow to yellow-green. Upper labials usually 8 (normally 7 in Eastern Yellow-bellied Racer). Scales *smooth;* anal *divided. Young:* Scattered small dark spots on a greenish ground color, the spots joining together to form dark crossbands on neck and forward part of body (Fig. 40, below); body becoming uniform dark olive-green toward tail.

Often arboreal, foraging in shrubs and bushes where it may remain immobile when approached, and where its coloration makes detection difficult.

Range: S. Texas and Coahuila to cen. Veracruz; isolated records

Fig. 40. PATTERNS OF RACERS *(Coluber)* AND WHIPSNAKES *(Masticophis)*
(Each diagram shows a section of skin removed from the animal)

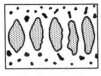  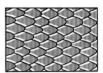

YOUNG RACERS *(C. constrictor)* of most subspecies. Middorsal blotches

YOUNG MEXICAN RACER *(C. c. oaxaca)* Spots and crossbands

SCHOTT'S AND RUTH-VEN'S WHIPSNAKES Scales of middorsal rows with light edges

in Durango, Colima, Oaxaca, Chiapas, and Guatemala. Specimens from w. and s.-cen. Texas and se. New Mexico are intermediate between *oaxaca* and *flaviventris*. Map 139

BUTTERMILK SNAKE Pl. 26
Coluber constrictor anthicus

Identification: 36–60 in. (91–152 cm); record 70 in. (177.8 cm). This racer looks almost as though it had been spattered by a bleaching compound. Numerous scales are the "wrong" color — white, yellow, buff, or pale blue — and scattered about indiscriminately. No two specimens are marked alike; some are only slightly spotted, but others are heavily speckled. Ground color may be black, bluish, or olive. Scales *smooth;* anal *divided.*

Usually found in open areas, such as old fields, but also occurs at forest edges.

Similar species: (1) Speckled Kingsnake is shiny, has a *single* anal plate, and the specks are small (several would fit on one scale). (2) Speckled Racer has several rows of scales *weakly keeled.*

Range: Louisiana and e. Texas.

Subspecies: TAN RACER, *Coluber c. etheridgei.* Similar; the pale spots variable in number but with the dorsal ground color light tan. Longleaf pine flatwoods in extr. w.-cen. Louisiana and adj. Texas. Map 139

EASTERN COACHWHIP Pl. 26
Masticophis flagellum flagellum

Identification: 42–60 in. (107–152 cm); record 102± in. (259± cm). The marked change from black or dark brown "forward" to light brown "aft" is unique among our snakes, but the amount of dark pigment is variable. Some specimens have only their heads and necks dark, others may be half-and-half, and still others may show light pigment only on the tail and rear of body. Coloration of belly corresponds with that of back. Scalation of the long slender tail suggests a braided whip. *Black phase:* In parts of northwestern Arkansas and adjacent Oklahoma and Missouri, coachwhips may be virtually plain black all over, or with tail and rear of body distinctly reddish. Even in the blackest specimens, however, sides of tail are often reddish, and there may be traces of lighter pigment toward rear of dorsum, plus a considerable light area under tail. *Pale phase:* Coachwhips from several parts of southern Georgia and northern and western Florida have the dark pigment reduced to narrow dark brown crossbands on a pale tan ground color. Minimum number of scale rows (just anterior to anus) is 13 (15 in racers). Scales *smooth;* anal *divided. Young:* Similar to young of Western Coachwhip (see Plate 26), but with dark crosslines closer together.

An active, fast-moving serpent that sometimes prowls with head raised well above ground. Normally escapes the would-be collector with a burst of speed, but fights savagely when cornered. Many habitats are utilized, ranging from dry, sandy flatwoods to swamps, creek valleys, and the rugged terrain of western Arkansas. Coachwhips make nervous captives and are prone to strike repeatedly at persons passing their cages. In biting, they embed their teeth and then yank away, producing lacerations instead of puncture wounds.

Range: N. Carolina to s. Florida and west to Texas, Oklahoma, and Kansas; apparently absent from a large portion of the lower Mississippi River Valley.   Map 141

WESTERN COACHWHIP   Pl. 26
Masticophis flagellum testaceus

Identification: 42–60 in. (107–152 cm); record 80 in. (203.2 cm). A highly variable snake, light yellow-brown to dark brown in coloration and with head and neck same color as body and tail. Occurs in three distinct pattern phases: (a) unicolored, with virtually no markings; (b) narrow-banded, with narrow dark crossbands like those seen in the young; and (c) broad-banded, marked with several broad crossbands, 10 to 15 scales wide, that are somewhat darker than and alternate with similar broad bands of the ground color. Among these the narrow-banded phase is the commonest and the broad-banded phase the least abundant. Some of the populations in Trans-Pecos Texas, east-central New Mexico, and southeastern Colorado, include numerous reddish-colored individuals (see Plate 26). Scales *smooth;* anal *divided.* *Young:* Dark crosslines 1 or 2 scales wide and separated from one another by about the width of 3 or more scales. Head often distinctly darker than body.

A snake of grasslands, mesquite savannas, arid brushlands, and numerous other more or less open habitats. Called "prairie runner" in some parts of its range.

Similar species: (1) Racers have 15 dorsal scale rows immediately in front of anus; Coachwhips have 13. (2) Ruthven's Whipsnake has only 15 dorsal rows on forward part of body; Coachwhips have 17.

Range: Sw. Nebraska, e. Colorado, and w. Kansas to ne. Mexico. Western and Mexican subspecies.

Note: Specimens from the vicinity of El Paso, Texas, may show some of the characteristics of the LINED WHIPSNAKE, *Masticophis f. lineatulus,* that occurs in adjacent Chihuahua. In these there may be a central longitudinal dark streak on each anterior dorsal scale, and the underside of the tail and posterior portion of the venter may be salmon-pink.   Map 141

CENTRAL TEXAS WHIPSNAKE   Pl. 26
Masticophis taeniatus ornatus
Identification: 42–60 in. (107–152 cm); record 72 in. (182.9 cm). The only "black snake" with longitudinal white patches on the sides. These are about equally spaced, but are strongest on neck and become gradually less prominent farther back. Effect is similar to that produced by an automobile tire that runs over a freshly painted white line on highway and then prints an ever weakening white spot with each turn of the wheel. In some parts of range white markings may be strongly evident throughout length of body and may produce a crossbanded effect. Large scales atop head usually outlined with light pigment. General dorsal coloration variable from black to reddish brown. Underside of tail bright coral-pink. Scales *smooth;* anal *divided.* *Young:* No white patches, except for narrow light crossband just behind head; longitudinal stripes present on lower sides, the most prominent being a light one on scale rows 3 and 4; usually a reddish overwash.

Also called "cedar racer" and "ornate whipsnake." An alert, fast-moving snake of brakes and valleys of Edwards Plateau and mountains and basins of Trans-Pecos Texas; occurs at least to 5800 ft. (1800 m). Retreats among rocks, thorny vegetation, or other shelter when approached.
Range: Cen. and w. Texas; south on Mexican plateau to Guanajuato.
Subspecies: DESERT STRIPED WHIPSNAKE, *Masticophis t. taeniatus.* Similar but with the white patches absent. Longitudinal white stripes strongly developed, 2 on each side of body, and the upper stripe actually a double one with the two halves separated by a black line that runs along center of 4th scale row. A western race that barely enters our area. Northern part of Trans-Pecos Texas; west and north to California and Washington.   Map 140

SCHOTT'S WHIPSNAKE   Pl. 26
Masticophis taeniatus schotti
Identification: 40–56 in. (102–142 cm); record 66 in. (167.6 cm). The only *strongly* striped whipsnake in southern Texas. The 2 light longitudinal stripes on each side, one at edge of belly scales and the other on scale rows 3 and 4, are the most conspicuous features of the pattern. General coloration varies from bluish- to greenish-gray. Sides of neck reddish orange. Belly whitish anteriorly, stippled with bluish gray farther back; underside of tail pink or salmon. The light anterior edgings of 7 or 8 middorsal rows of scales (Fig. 40, p. 180) are best seen when scales are spread slightly apart (easily checked on living specimens). Scales *smooth;* anal *divided.* *Young:* Like adults but with reddish overwash.

An alert, elusive resident of the arid brush country of southern Texas. Named for Arthur Schott, who collected the type specimen while a member of the U.S. and Mexican Boundary Survey soon after the termination of the Mexican War.

Similar species: (1) Texas Patch-nosed Snake has a light *middorsal* stripe flanked by dark stripes. (2) Ruthven's Whipsnake has only faint indications of light stripes.

Range: Texas, south of San Antonio; west into adj. Mexico.

Map 140

RUTHVEN'S WHIPSNAKE   Pl. 26
Masticophis taeniatus ruthveni

Identification: 40–56 in. (102–142 cm); record 66 ⅛ in. (168.0 cm). Typical specimens show very little pattern, except for traces of narrow light stripes on neck or sides. Throat dotted with dark orange; belly bright yellow anteriorly, light bluish gray or olive at midbody, and pink posteriorly; underside of tail bright red. Light anterior edges on 7 or 8 of the middorsal rows of scales (Fig. 40, p. 180). Scales *smooth;* anal *divided. Young:* Like adult, but with neck stripes better indicated.

An agile serpent of arid brushlands. Named for Alexander Grant Ruthven, herpetologist and long-time president of the University of Michigan.

Similar species: (1) Mexican Racer has maximum of 17 scale rows; Whipsnakes have only 15. (2) Rough Green Snake has *keeled* scales.

Range: Extr. s. Texas and ne. Mexico. Intergrades with Schott's Whipsnake in lower Rio Grande Valley. (Specimen illustrated on Plate 26 is actually an intergrade, and shows more indications of stripes than do typical individuals from Mexico.)

Map 140

Green Snakes: Genus *Opheodrys*

Two green snakes occur within our area, the terrestrial Smooth Green Snake and the more arboreal Rough Green Snake, which gets its name from its keeled scales. The bright green coloration is fleeting after death, a good point to remember if you ever find a dull blue snake that has been run over on the road. Postmortem changes from green to blue occur rather quickly. The genus *Opheodrys* ranges from southern Canada to Florida and northeastern Mexico, and from the Maritime Provinces to the Rocky Mountains. It also occurs in Asia.

ROUGH GREEN SNAKE   *Opheodrys aestivus*   Pl. 25
Identification: 22–32 in. (56–81 cm); record 45 ⅝ in. (115.9 cm). The "vine snake." This dainty, slender serpent is plain light

green above and plain white, yellow, or pale greenish below. Scales *keeled;* anal *divided. Young:* Grayish green; about 7 or 8 in. (18–20 cm) at hatching.

An excellent climber that, when foraging amid vines or shrubs, blends with the background so well it is virtually invisible. At times it is almost semiaquatic, freely entering shallow bodies of water. A frequent habitat is in the dense growth of vegetation overhanging a stream or lake border. Crickets, grasshoppers, larvae of moths and butterflies, and spiders constitute the bulk of the food.

Similar species: (1) The very similar Smooth Green Snakes have *smooth* scales; (2) so also does the greenish Mexican Racer.
Range: S. New Jersey to Florida Keys; west to Kansas and Texas; south in Mexico to Tampico. Several old records allegedly from Trans-Pecos Texas and New Mexico need confirmation.   Map 135

SMOOTH GREEN SNAKE *Opheodrys vernalis*   **Pl. 25**
Identification: 14–20 in. (36–51 cm); record 26 in. (66.0 cm). The "green grass snake." A gentle little reptile that is plain bright green above and plain white or washed with pale yellow below. Scales *smooth;* anal *divided. Young:* Dark olive- or bluish-gray; 4–6½ in. (10–16.5 cm) at hatching.

In eastern and far western parts of its range this is an upland snake, but it occupies the lowlands in the north-central portion of the country and in southeastern Texas. (See comments under subspecies below.) Largely terrestrial, showing little inclination to climb. Spiders and insects are eaten.

Similar species: (1) Rough Green Snake is more slender, grows to a much greater length, and has *keeled* scales; its range is more southern, only partially overlapping that of Smooth Green Snake. (2) Greenish specimens of the Yellow-bellied Racer are usually longer than the largest Smooth Green Snake by the time they become unicolored. If in doubt check the nostril. In Green Snakes (both species) the nostril is centered in a single scale; in Racers it lies between 2 scales.
Range: Maritime Provinces of Canada to se. Saskatchewan and the Rocky Mts.; south to N. Carolina, Texas, and Chihuahua.
Subspecies: EASTERN SMOOTH GREEN SNAKE, *Opheodrys v. vernalis* (Plate 25). Males have 130 or fewer ventrals; females 139 or fewer. A snake chiefly of high altitudes or relatively high latitudes. Often found in mountain glades and in grassy or rocky meadows. Eastern and northern part of range. WESTERN SMOOTH GREEN SNAKE, *Opheodrys v. blanchardi.* Males have 131 or more ventrals; females 140 or more. Occupies a wide variety of habitats, including moist grassy portions of plains and prairies, but now scarce in such areas because of the destruction

of habitats by agriculture and other human activities. Range largely disjunct in the west and confined chiefly to upland areas from the Black Hills of S. Dakota and adj. Wyoming to extr. se. Idaho and south to Chihuahua. Specimens from the Black Hills have the low ventral counts of the Eastern Smooth Green Snake. Members of the disjunct population in the grasslands of se. Texas may be light brown with an olive wash instead of green.   Map 134

Speckled Racer and Indigo Snakes: Genera *Drymobius* and *Drymarchon*

ESSENTIALLY these are tropical snakes. There are several species of *Drymobius* and they, together, range from extreme southern Texas to Peru and Venezuela. The genus *Drymarchon,* which includes the indigo snakes, has only a single species, but its many races extend, collectively, from the southeastern United States to Argentina.   One subspecies (*melanurus*) attains a known length of 116⅛ in. (295.0 cm), the greatest measurement for any member of the Family Colubridae in the New World.

SPECKLED RACER   Pl. 32
Drymobius margaritiferus margaritiferus
   Identification: 30–40 in. (76–102 cm); record 50 in. (127.0 cm). A black stripe behind the eye, and a yellow spot near the center of each dorsal scale. Base of each scale blue and this, in combination with the yellow spots, produces the illusion of a greenish overwash along sides of body. Outer part of each scale black. Belly plain whitish or yellowish. Subcaudal scales black-edged posteriorly; ventrals may be similarly marked. Scales of several middorsal rows *weakly keeled;* outer rows smooth. Anal *divided. Young:* Similar but with colors less vivid.
   A rarity north of the Rio Grande. Often found near water or in thickets of dense natural vegetation. Frogs are relished.
   Range: Low to moderate elevations from extr. s. Texas and Coahuila south along the Caribbean coast to n. S. America. Mexican and Cen. American subspecies.   Map 142

EASTERN INDIGO SNAKE   Pl. 27
Drymarchon corais couperi
   Identification: 60–84 in. (152–213 cm); record 103½ in. (262.9 cm). This large, handsome serpent is entirely shiny bluish black, belly included, except that chin and sides of head may be reddish- or orange-brown. Scales *smooth;* anal *single.* Third from last upper labial wedge-shaped and cut off above by contact between adjacent labials (Fig. 41, p. 187). *Young:* Like

adults, but often with much more reddish on head and forward part of belly; 19–24 in. (48–61 cm) at hatching.

When cornered, the Indigo Snake flattens its neck vertically (not horizontally as in the hognose snakes), hisses, and vibrates its tail, producing a rattling sound. When caught, it seldom attempts to bite. Captives are usually restless and keep on the move when handled. Food includes small mammals, birds, frogs, and snakes — even cottonmouths and rattlers are eaten. Not a constrictor. A snake chiefly of large unsettled areas.

Indigo snakes of several races, including imported tropical ones, were long popular with snake charmers and carnival "pit" shows, in which they were exhibited as "blue bullsnakes" or "blue gophers." These alternate common names are still in use in some areas.

Similar species: All other plain black snakes within its range have *keeled* scales, a *divided* anal plate, or both.

Range: Se. Georgia, peninsular Florida and lower Keys; disjunct colonies in w. Florida and s. Alabama.   Map 144

Fig. 41. HEADS OF INDIGO SNAKES (*Drymarchon*)

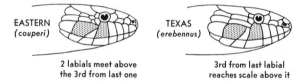

EASTERN (*couperi*) — 2 labials meet above the 3rd from last one

TEXAS (*erebennus*) — 3rd from last labial reaches scale above it

TEXAS INDIGO SNAKE   Pl. 27
Drymarchon corais erebennus

Identification: 60–78 in. (152–198 cm); record 100¼ in. (254.6 cm). Like the Eastern Indigo Snake except for: (a) prominent dark lines downward from eye; (b) tendency for forepart of body to be brownish and with some indications of pattern; (c) 3rd from last upper labial reaching the scale above it (Fig. 41, above); and (d) almost always 14 rows of dorsal scales on hindmost part of body instead of 15 as in eastern race. Scales *smooth;* anal *single.* Hisses and vibrates tail.

Range: Arid s. Texas to Veracruz and Hidalgo.   Map 144

Patch-nosed Snakes: Genus *Salvadora*

THE curious snout, which may facilitate digging in loose sand, is characteristic of these diurnal snakes. The rostral is large, curved upward, and notched below, and has a free, slightly-projecting flap at each side. The pale middorsal stripe, flanked by broad dark stripes will also distinguish the patch-nosed snakes from any other smooth-scaled species within our area. (Keels may appear, however, on a few scales above the anal region in adult males and large females). Some individuals strike repeatedly when first caught, and may vibrate their tails. Food includes lizards and snakes (and their eggs) and small rodents. The young are patterned like the adults, and are about 8¼ to 10 in. (21 to 25 cm) at hatching. Members of the genus occur from Texas to California and southward through Mexico to Chiapas.

MOUNTAIN PATCH-NOSED SNAKE   Pl. 31
Salvadora grahamiae grahamiae
Identification: 22–30 in. (56–76 cm); record 37½ in. (95.3 cm). A pale gray or slightly olive or brownish snake with 2 fairly broad, dark olive-brown, often nearly black, dorsolateral stripes running the length of the body. Pale middorsal stripe matching or only a little brighter than coloration on sides of body. Some specimens have a *faint* narrow dark line on the 3rd row of scales. Posterior chin shields touching each other or separated only by width of 1 scale (Fig. 42, p. 189). Scales *smooth;* anal *divided.*

A snake of isolated mountain areas, foothills, and mesas. Usually occurs at higher elevations than the Big Bend Patch-nosed Snake.
Similar species: (1) Garter and Ribbon Snakes have *keeled* scales and *single* anals. (2) Big Bend Patch-nosed Snake has a dark stripe on *4th* row of scales and 2 or 3 small scales between posterior chin shields (Fig. 42, p. 189).
Range: Trans-Pecos region of Texas to n.-cen. New Mexico and se. Arizona; intergrades with Texas Patch-nosed Snake in cen. Chihuahua and east of the Big Bend in Texas.   Map 146

TEXAS PATCH-NOSED SNAKE   Pl. 31
Salvadora grahamiae lineata
Identification: 26–40 in. (66–102 cm); record 47 in. (119.4 cm). The middorsal stripe varies in coloration from one specimen to another through several tones of yellow or pale orange, and the broad dark stripes that border it are brown to almost black. A narrow, but sharply distinct, dark line on *3rd row of scales* (on 2nd row toward tail). Posterior chin shields touching each other or separated only by width of 1 scale (Fig. 42, p. 189). Scales *smooth;* anal *divided.*

An essentially terrestrial relative of the racers that utilizes a variety of habitats, including prairies, rugged, rocky terrain of the Edwards Plateau in central Texas, arid brushlands farther south, and cultivated country of the lower Rio Grande Valley.
Similar species: Garter and Ribbon Snakes have *keeled* scales and *single* anals.

Range: N.-cen. Texas in the east and s. Chihuahua in the west and southward to Hidalgo. Map 146

BIG BEND PATCH-NOSED SNAKE Pl. 31
Salvadora deserticola

Identification: 24–32 in. (61–81 cm); record 40 in. (101.6 cm). Check for two things: (a) a narrow dark line on the *4th* row of scales (it may encroach on the 3rd anteriorly and shifts entirely to the 3rd near the tail); and (b) 2 or 3 small scales between the posterior chin shields (Fig. 42, below). Middorsal stripe varies from brownish orange in some specimens to tan in others; dark stripes black or dark brown. Lateral ground color pale gray, but with orange-brown encroaching on anterior corner of each scale. Belly peach-colored. Scales *smooth;* anal *divided.*

Fig. 42. CHINS OF PATCH-NOSED SNAKES *(Salvadora)*

BIG BEND
(deserticola)

2 or 3 scales between
posterior chin shields

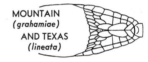

MOUNTAIN
(grahamiae)
AND TEXAS
(lineata)

Posterior chin shields touching
or separated by only 1 scale

At home on desert flats and washes, but also ascending into the foothills and mesas surrounding the higher mountains. The habitats of this species and the Mountain Patch-nosed Snake overlap in some areas, and they occasionally are found together. **Similar species:** (1) Garter and Ribbon Snakes have *keeled* scales and *single* anals. (2) In Mountain Patch-nosed Snake the narrow dark line, if present, is on *3rd* row of scales, and posterior chin shields are separated by width of only 1 scale (Fig. 42, above).

Range: Big Bend region of Texas to se. Arizona; south to s. Sinaloa. Map 143

Rat Snakes: Genus *Elaphe*

THESE large handsome snakes in cross section are shaped like a loaf of bread, the flat belly meeting the sides of the body at an angle (Fig. 58, opp. Pl. 28). Adults have several of the mid-dorsal rows of scales weakly *keeled* and the others smooth; keels are only slightly developed or lacking altogether in the young. The anal plate is *divided.*

Hatchling rat snakes are boldly patterned with dark spots or blotches; some kinds retain these markings throughout life, in others they vanish with age. Some develop 4 dark longitudinal stripes, and similar stripes may appear in individual specimens of kinds that normally are not striped at all.

When cornered in the field, many of these snakes literally stand up and fight, with the fore portion of the body reared upward, the head drawn back in an S-curve, and the mouth held open in readiness to strike. Sometimes they hiss as they lunge forward. All the rat snakes vibrate their tails rapidly when alarmed. All are good climbers, the angles in their belly scales helping to grip irregularities on the boles of trees, faces of cliffs, etc. With proper care most of them thrive in captivity. They constrict mice, young rats, or small birds in their strong coils. Young rat snakes also eat lizards and frogs, treefrogs especially. Young of the fox and corn snake groups vary from about 9 to 14 in. (23 to 36 cm) at hatching; members of the black rat snake (*obsoleta*) group from about 11 to 17 in. (28 to 43 cm).

The genus *Elaphe* ranges southward to Costa Rica and is also represented in Europe, Asia, and the Malay Archipelago.

Fig. 43. UNDERSURFACES OF YOUNG RAT SNAKES *(Elaphe)*

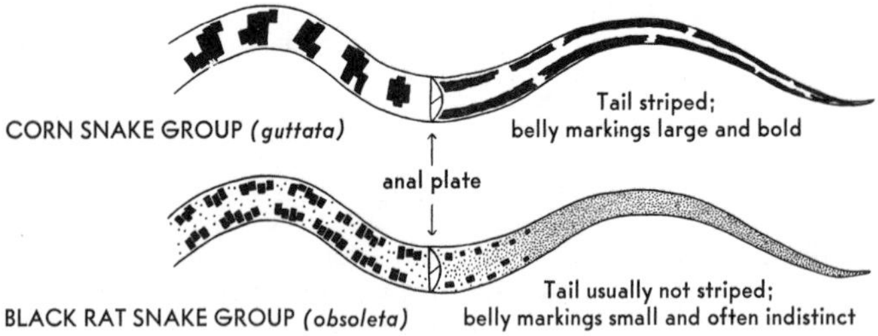

CORN SNAKE GROUP *(guttata)*   Tail striped; belly markings large and bold

anal plate

BLACK RAT SNAKE GROUP *(obsoleta)*   Tail usually not striped; belly markings small and often indistinct

CORN SNAKE *Elaphe guttata guttata*   **Pl. 28**
  Identification: 30–48 in. (76–122 cm); record 72 in. (182.9 cm). The "red rat snake." The belly is boldly checkered with black on whitish, and the underside of the tail is usually striped (Fig. 43, above). A beautiful red or orange snake, but subject to considerable individual variation in color. Some specimens trend strongly to browns, especially those from upland habitats. Ground color variable from orange to gray. Dorsal spots and blotches boldly outlined with black. First blotch on neck divided into 2 branches that extend forward and meet in a spearpoint between eyes (Fig. 44, p. 191). Dorsum occasionally with 4 dusky longitudinal stripes. Scales weakly *keeled;* anal *divided. Young:* Blotches dark, usually rich reddish brown; patches of orange between blotches along middorsal line. The stripe extending

backward from eye has dark borders and usually continues past mouth line and onto neck (Fig. 45, p. 193).

The Corn Snake climbs well, but is most likely to be found in terrestrial habitats — in pine barrens or wood lots, on rocky hillsides, etc. More common in many areas than it appears, spending much time underground, resting in or prowling through rodent burrows or other subterranean passageways.

Similar species: (1) Milk Snakes and Mole Snake have *single* anal plates and *smooth* scales, and *lack* striping under tails. (2) In young Rat Snakes of the races of *Elaphe obsoleta* (Black, Yellow, Gray, etc.) there is no dark spearpoint between the eyes, and the postocular dark stripe stops at the mouth line (Fig. 45, p. 193).

Range: S. New Jersey to s. Florida and s. Louisiana; isolated localities in Kentucky.   Map 150

ROSY RAT SNAKE *Elaphe guttata rosacea*   Pl. 28
Identification: 30–48 in. (76–122 cm); record 66 in. (167.6 cm). A subspecies of the Corn Snake in which the black pigment is greatly reduced, both on the back and belly. Amount of black in pattern varies from specimen to specimen, but is never so intense or extensive as in Corn Snake, nor is belly so heavily checkerboarded. General dorsal coloration usually reddish orange. Scales weakly *keeled;* anal *divided.*

Besides hiding beneath logs and debris, the Rosy Rat Snake both climbs and burrows. Often ascends trees in search of food.
Range: Lower Florida Keys; intergrading with the Corn Snake on the upper Keys.   Map 150

GREAT PLAINS RAT SNAKE   Pl. 28
Elaphe guttata emoryi
Identification: 24–36 in. (61–91 cm); record 60¼ in. (153.0 cm). A western and rather drab subspecies of the Corn Snake, but similar in all essentials of pattern, including a spearpoint between eyes (Fig. 44, below) and striping under tail (Fig. 43, p.

Fig. 44. HEADS OF ADULT RAT SNAKES *(Elaphe)*

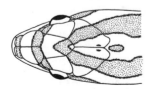

CORN AND GREAT PLAINS RAT SNAKE
(guttata and *emoryi)*
Dark neck lines unite to form
a spearpoint between the eyes

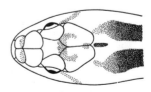

FOX SNAKE
(vulpina)
No spearpoint; head brown
or reddish

190). In very old adults the head markings are usually faint. Four dusky longitudinal stripes may be present. Blotches dark gray, brown, or olive-brown on a ground color of light gray. (In northern part of range blotches are much more numerous and so narrowed that they resemble transverse bands.) Scales weakly *keeled;* anal *divided.*

Secretive and essentially nocturnal during warm weather; hides beneath stones and in rock crevices, caves, etc., by day. More likely to be found in canyons or rocky draws or on hillsides than on open plains or prairies. Often occurs along water courses or near springs in arid country.

Similar species: (1) Bullsnake has *strongly keeled* scales and a *single* anal plate. (2) Prairie Kingsnake and Glossy Snake have *single* anals plus *smooth* scales. (3) Black, Texas, and Baird's Rat Snakes and Fox Snake (Fig. 44, p. 191) all lack a spearpoint between eyes.

Range: Sw. Illinois to se. Colorado and e. New Mexico and south through Texas and n. Mexico to San Luis Potosí and n. Veracruz; a disjunct area in w. Colorado and e. Utah. Intergrades with the Corn Snake through a broad area from s. Arkansas to the Gulf.   Map 150

FOX SNAKE   *Elaphe vulpina*   **Pl. 28**
Identification: 36–54 in. (91–137 cm); record 70½ in. (179.1 cm). A boldly blotched snake of the north-central region. Ground color varies from yellowish to light brown, and the dark spots and blotches from chocolate to black. The head, usually devoid of any really conspicuous markings (Fig. 44, p. 191), varies from brown to distinctly reddish. Belly yellow, strongly checkered with black. Scales weakly *keeled;* anal *divided. Young:* Ground color paler than in adults; blotches rich brown and narrowly edged with black or dark brown; head markings bold, including a dark transverse line anterior to eyes and a dark line from eye to angle of jaw. Dark lines on head fade and become difficult to define as the snake approaches adulthood.

A serpent with many aliases — a "timber snake" in Ohio and parts of Michigan, a "pine snake" in Wisconsin and adjacent states, and a "spotted adder" to many who cannot think of a better name. The reddish head frequently causes it to be killed as a copperhead, and the black and yellowish coloration plus the habit of vibrating the tail cause it to be slain as a rattler. Actually harmless and normally quite inoffensive. Toward the west, it occurs in farmlands, prairies, stream valleys, woods, and dune country, but the eastern subspecies is essentially a resident of the extensive marshes bordering Lakes Erie and Huron and their immediate environs.

Similar species: (1) Corn Snake and Great Plains Rat Snake have a spearpoint atop head (Fig. 44, p. 191). (2) Milk Snakes and Prairie Kingsnake have *smooth* scales and *single* anal plates. (3) Bullsnake, a great hisser, has pointed snout, *strongly keeled* scales, and a *single* anal. (4) Hognose Snakes have up-turned snouts. (5) Juvenile Black Rat Snakes will be trouble-some, for they are as strongly spotted as young Fox Snakes; only safe check is to count ventral scutes — 221 or more in Black Rat Snake and 216 or fewer in Fox Snake.

Range: S. Ontario to Nebraska; upper peninsula of Michigan to cen. Illinois and n. Missouri.

Subspecies: WESTERN FOX SNAKE, *Elaphe v. vulpina* (Plate 28). Large dorsal blotches average 41 in number (counted on body only). Most of range outlined above. EASTERN FOX SNAKE, *Elaphe v. gloydi*. Dorsal blotches larger and fewer, averaging 34. Head very likely to be reddish. S. Ontario, e. Michigan, and n.-cen. Ohio.   Map 148

BLACK RAT SNAKE *Elaphe obsoleta obsoleta*   **Pl. 28**
Identification: 42–72 in. (107–183 cm); record 101 in. (256.5 cm). Typically a plain shiny black snake, but sometimes showing traces of a spotted pattern when the skin is distended (as after a heavy meal) or in portions of the range near where intergradation takes place with related subspecies. Light areas, chiefly confined to *skin between scales,* may be white, yellow, orange, or red. Belly diffused or clouded with gray or brown on white or yellowish, but usually with some indications of checkerboarding, at least toward head. Chin and throat plain white or cream. Scales weakly *keeled;* anal *divided.* *Young:* Strongly patterned dorsally on body *and tail* with gray or brown blotches on a pale gray ground color and looking like the adult Gray Rat Snake illustrated on Plate 28. Darkening occurs rapidly as the animal grows, and a specimen roughly 3 ft. (1 m) long may have only traces of pattern remaining. The dark stripe extending backward from eye normally terminates at mouth line (Fig. 45, below). Some young Black Rat Snakes may have indications of dark stripes beneath the tail, but these

Fig. 45. HEADS OF YOUNG RAT SNAKES *(Elaphe)*

CORN SNAKE GROUP *(guttata)*
Postocular stripe has dark border,
extends onto neck

BLACK RAT SNAKE GROUP *(obsoleta)*
Postocular stripe entirely dark,
stops at mouth line

are usually not so prominent as those in corn snake group (Fig. 43, p. 190), and usually fade out rapidly as snake grows older and larger.

The so-called "pilot" or "mountain black snake." Occurs virtually at sea level and to considerable altitudes in parts of the Appalachian mountain chain. Habitats range from rocky, timbered hillsides to flat farmlands of the Coastal Plain. An excellent climber, sometimes establishing residence in cavities high up in hollow trees.

Similar species: (1) Black Racers and Coachwhips have *smooth* scales and their bodies are round in cross section — not shaped like a loaf of bread (Fig. 58, opp. Pl. 28). Juvenile Racers have no pattern on tail, or only traces of one. (2) Water Snakes have *strongly keeled* scales, and many of them flatten their bodies when alarmed. (3) Fox Snakes have 216 or fewer ventrals (221 or more in Black Rat Snake). (4) Milk Snakes and King-snakes have *smooth* scales and *single* anal plates. (5) See also Hognose Snakes, p. 168. Most confusion will occur in trying to identify young Black Rat Snakes. In young (and adults) of Corn Snake and Great Plains Rat Snake there is a spearpoint on head (Fig. 44, p. 191), and the postocular stripe continues onto neck (Fig. 45, p. 193).

Range: Sw. New England and e. Ontario to Georgia in the East; sw. Wisconsin to Oklahoma and n. Louisiana in the Midwest.
Map 149

YELLOW RAT SNAKE   Pl. 28
Elaphe obsoleta quadrivittata

Identification: 42–72 in. (107–183 cm); record 84 in. (213.4 cm). The 4 dark stripes are always strongly defined, but the ground color is subject to considerable variation. The brightest, most golden-yellow specimens come from peninsular Florida; from farther north they are darker, less brilliant yellow. (The "green-ish rat snake" on Plate 28 is an intergrade between the Black and Yellow Rat Snakes from along the extreme northern portion of latter's range.) *Tongue black.* Scales weakly *keeled;* anal *divided. Young:* Strongly blotched and similar in general appearance to an adult Gray Rat Snake (Plate 28); stripes absent or only slightly indicated. Blotches fade and the dark stripes develop as the young serpent grows.

A common and characteristic snake of the great river swamps of the South, foraging high into cypress and other trees. Also occurs in a wide variety of other habitats, including live-oak hammocks, cutover woods, fallow fields, and around barns and abandoned buildings.

Similar species: For ways of telling the blotched young from other blotched or spotted snakes see Black Rat Snake (p. 193).
Range: S. N. Carolina to s. Florida.   Map 149

EVERGLADES RAT SNAKE   Pl. 28
Elaphe obsoleta rossalleni
   Identification: 48–78 in. (122–198 cm); record 87 in. (221.0 cm).
"Orange rat snake," would be a good alternate name for this
handsome serpent. The ground color, usually bright orange,
may be orange-yellow or orange-brown instead. The grayish
longitudinal stripes are not clear-cut and are often vague or
almost lacking. Belly bright orange or orange-yellow. *Tongue
red.* Scales weakly *keeled;* anal *divided. Young:* Ground color
pinkish buff or pinkish orange; blotches light grayish brown and
not sharply in contrast with ground color.
   A resident of the Kissimmee Prairie and the Everglades where
it is found in the great waving seas of sawgrass, on open prairies
within the 'Glades, in trees or shrubs, and along the waterways,
taking readily to the water and swimming skillfully when
alarmed. Often seen in the Australian pine (*Casuarina*) trees
that have been planted along roads of the region.
   Range: S. Florida, chiefly in the Everglades.
   Subspecies: KEY RAT SNAKE, *Elaphe o. deckerti.* A striped *and*
spotted race, stripes gray-brown to blackish and better defined
than in Everglades Rat Snake; dorsal ground color tan, dull
orange, or some shade of brown; dark dorsal spots, remnants
of juvenile pattern, are usually distinctly evident; belly suffused
with light gray, at least posteriorly. *Tongue black.* Upper Florida Keys from Elliott Key to Grassy Key.   Map 149

GRAY RAT SNAKE *Elaphe obsoleta spiloides*   Pl. 28
   Identification: 42–72 in. (107–183 cm); record 84¼ in. (214.0
cm). Called the "oak snake" in some parts of the South.
This rat snake retains the strongly blotched juvenile pattern
throughout life, but there is much variation in its intensity. The
ground color may be dark or medium gray in some specimens
but pale brown or gray, sometimes almost white, in others.
Blotches may be either brown or gray and varying from pale
to very dark, but always in contrast with the lighter ground
color. Scales weakly *keeled;* anal *divided.*
   Habits of this serpent are similar to those of the Black Rat
Snake, which it replaces in the South. The two intergrade over
a fairly broad zone where their ranges meet except in parts of
the Southeast, where they may occur virtually side by side but
apparently still retain their full identities. Intergrades in some
areas are often chocolate-brown with the blotches not much
darker than ground color.
   Similar species: See (1) Black Rat Snake (p. 193), and (2)
general discussion of Rat Snakes (p. 189).
   Range: Sw. Georgia to Mississippi and north in Mississippi
Valley to extr. s. Illinois; overlaps range of Black Rat Snake
in e. Tennessee and n. Alabama.

Subspecies: GULF HAMMOCK RAT SNAKE, *Elaphe o. williamsi.*
Blotched like Gray Rat Snake, but also with 4 dark longitudinal
stripes; ground color whitish and with dark markings standing
out strongly against it. Northwestern portion of peninsular
Florida.   Map 149

TEXAS RAT SNAKE *Elaphe obsoleta lindheimeri*   **Pl. 28**
   Identification: 42–72 in. (107–183 cm); record 84¾ in. (215.3
   cm). A blotched rat snake but often with less contrast between pattern and ground color than in Gray Rat Snake.
   Blotches usually brownish- or bluish-black; ground color gray
   or yellowish. Head often black. There may be red on the skin
   between scales, and this color often encroaches on edges of the
   scales themselves. This race is subject to considerable individual
   variation in both coloration and pattern. Scales weakly *keeled;*
   anal *divided. Young:* A pattern of bold dark blotches that are
   considerably larger than the spaces between them. Ground color
   gray — much darker than in the young of other races of *Elaphe
   obsoleta.*
      A snake with a variety of habitats, ranging from bayou and
   swampy country of Louisiana and eastern Texas through woods
   and stream valleys to rocky canyons in western part of range.
   Similar species: See (1) Black Rat Snake (p. 193), and (2)
   general section on Rat Snakes (p. 189).
   Range: From the Pearl and Mississippi Rivers west through
   Louisiana to cen. Texas.   Map 149

BAIRD'S RAT SNAKE   *Elaphe obsoleta bairdi*   **Pl. 28**
   Identification: 33–54 in. (84–137 cm); record 62 in. (157.5 cm).
   The 4 longitudinal stripes, all rather vague but with the 2 center
   ones the darkest, are the most conspicuous markings in large
   adults. Traces of dorsal and lateral spots, remnants of the
   juvenile pattern, are often faintly discernible, but very large
   specimens may be patternless. The general dorsal coloration is
   grayish brown, but edges of the scales are yellow or orange-
   yellow on forepart of body and deeper orange toward rear, giving
   snake a rich overwash of bright coloration. Scales weakly
   keeled; anal *divided. Young:* 48 or more brown crossbands on
   back, and additional ones on tail; an alternating row of smaller
   dark spots along each side of body; a dark band across head
   anterior to eyes, and a dark postocular stripe that stops at
   mouth line.
      A resident of rocky, wooded canyons and of forested uplands
   (as in Chisos Mountains of the Big Bend). Named for Spencer
   Fullerton Baird, zoologist and administrator of the Smithsonian
   Institution during the nineteenth century.
   Range: Cen. Texas to the Big Bend and south to Tamaulipas.
                                                             Map 149

TRANS-PECOS RAT SNAKE   *Elaphe subocularis*   **Pl. 32**
Identification: 36–54 in. (91–137 cm); record 66 in. (167.6 cm). This is the "H-snake," a name derived from large, black or dark brown, H-shaped markings on a tan, yellow, or olive-yellow dorsum. The arms of the H's form parts of 2 longitudinal stripes that, anteriorly, are bold and black and terminate on the neck. No pattern of any kind on the olive or tan-colored head. Venter whitish, virtually unmarked except for indications of dusky stripes under tail. *A row of scales between eye and upper labials.* Scales *keeled;* anal *divided. Young:* Dorsal markings similar but paler; ground color yellow with a slightly grayish tinge; about 11 in. (28 cm) at hatching.

The rat snake of the Chihuahuan Desert. This large, slightly popeyed serpent is locally common in areas where it can hide by day in rock piles or mammal burrows. Like other residents of the desert, it prowls at night when the rodents that constitute the bulk of its food are abroad. It also feeds on bats and birds. Lizards are an important item in the diet of the young.
Similar species: Adults of Baird's Rat Snake have 4 rather vague dark stripes and no blotches; the young of that form are marked with rounded or rectangular (not H-shaped) blotches.
Range: S. New Mexico to Durango and Nuevo León.

Map 151

Glossy Snakes: Genus *Arizona*

THE genus *Arizona* includes only a single species, but there are many races, all of which are sometimes called "faded snakes" because of their pale, washed-out appearance. The snakes of this group are related to the bull and gopher snakes, but they differ in being mainly nocturnal or crepuscular and in having smooth scales and only 2 prefrontals. (Some Mexican members of the genus *Pituophis* also have only 2 prefrontals.) The glossy snakes range collectively from Kansas, Oklahoma, and southeastern Texas to California and south to San Luis Potosí, Aguascalientes, Sinaloa, and central Baja California.

TEXAS GLOSSY SNAKE   **Pl. 27**
Arizona elegans arenicola
Identification: 27–36 in. (69–91 cm); record 54⅝ in. (138.7 cm). A shiny, brownish "bullsnake." Blotches brown and dark-edged, usually 50 or fewer on body. Ground color cream or buff. In large adults the sides of the body may become so heavily suffused with brown or gray that the lateral spots are obscured, and the pale ground color may be restricted to small middorsal patches between the large blotches. Belly white or pale buff,

unmarked. Pupil of eye slightly elliptical. Only 2 prefrontals (Fig. 57, opp. Pl. 27). Ventrals usually 212 or more in males and 221 or more in females. Scales *smooth; anal single. Young:* about 11 in. (28 cm) at hatching.

Chiefly nocturnal or crepuscular, but also may be abroad during morning hours. Vibrates tail when alarmed. Partial to sandy areas and adept at burrowing. Food includes small mammals and lizards.

Similar species: (1) Great Plains and Texas Rat Snakes have *keeled* scales and *divided* anals. (2) In Prairie Kingsnake belly is normally marked with squarish blotches of brown on a yellowish ground color, but sometimes it is plain *except* that the lowermost lateral spots encroach on ends of ventrals.

Range: S. Texas.

Subspecies: KANSAS GLOSSY SNAKE, *Arizona e. elegans.* Similar but usually with more than 50 large body blotches; ventrals 211 or fewer in males and 220 or fewer in females. Extr. sw. Nebraska and cen. Kansas through w. Texas and southeast to Tamaulipas. PAINTED DESERT GLOSSY SNAKE, *Arizona e. philipi.* Maximum number of scale rows usually 27 (29 or more in eastern races); body blotches usually 62 or more. El Paso, Texas, region; New Mexico, Arizona, and adj. Mexico. Western and Mexican subspecies.   Map 145

Pine, Bull, and Gopher Snakes: Genus *Pituophis*

LARGE, powerful, constricting snakes that hiss loudly, vibrate their tails rapidly, and are apt to strike vigorously when first encountered. The head appears disproportionately small, especially among the pine snakes. In our species there are 4 prefrontal scales (Fig. 57, opp. Pl. 27) instead of 2 as in most other snakes of the Family Colubridae. The snout is somewhat pointed and the rostral plate extends upward between the internasals. Scales *keeled; anal single.*

Snakes of this group are good burrowers; they are chiefly diurnal except during hot weather, and are useful in controlling rodents. Their food consists largely of small mammals, but they also eat birds and their eggs, and the smaller snakes prey on lizards. Some make good captives, but they tend to be nervous and wriggly when handled. The young vary from 14 to 21½ in. (36 to 55 cm) at hatching. Our single species (*melanoleucus*) occurs in a variety of subspecies ranging collectively from coast to coast; members are called pine snakes in the East, bullsnakes from the plains and prairie states westward, and gopher snakes in the Pacific states. The genus *Pituophis* as a whole ranges from New Jersey,

Wisconsin, Minnesota, and southwestern Canada to Guatemala and the southern tip of Baja California.

NORTHERN PINE SNAKE   Pl. 27
Pituophis melanoleucus melanoleucus

Identification: 48–66 in. (122–168 cm); record 83 in. (210.8 cm). A large black and white snake with a *noisy hiss.* Dark blotches are black toward front of body, but they may be brown near and on tail. Ground color dull white, yellowish, or light gray. Scales *keeled;* anal *single. Young:* Pattern like that of adults, but with ground color paler and with a pink or orange tinge.

A snake of flat, sandy pine barrens, sandhills, and dry mountain ridges, most often in or near pine woods. Climbs occasionally, but is much addicted to burrowing and is so secretive that its presence may be unsuspected even by persons who have lived in the same region with it for years.

Similar species: Gray Rat Snakes and juvenile Black Rat Snakes have *divided* anals and only 2 prefrontals (4 in Pine and Bullsnakes — see Fig. 57, opp. Pl. 27).

Range: S. New Jersey; Coastal Plain and Piedmont in the Carolinas; mountain areas from Virginia to Georgia; west into Kentucky, Tennessee, and n. Alabama. Intergrades with Florida Pine Snake through a broad area in S. Carolina and along the Fall Line in Georgia.   Map 147

FLORIDA PINE SNAKE   Pl. 27
Pituophis melanoleucus mugitus

Identification: 48–66 in. (122–168 cm); record 90 in. (228.6 cm). A tan or rusty-brown snake with an indistinct pattern. Might be likened to a Northern Pine Snake coated with a thin layer of dried mud and through which dark markings are vaguely visible. Amount of pattern quite variable, but the markings are never so clean-cut and sharply defined as in the northern race. The dark blotches are clearly distinct on only the hind part of the body and on the tail. *Hisses loudly.* Scales *keeled;* anal *single. Young:* Patterned much as in the Northern Pine Snake, but with the blotches brown instead of black.

Often found in dry, sandy areas, in stands of oak or pine, abandoned fields, etc. An accomplished burrower, adept at pursuing pocket gophers, a favorite food.

Similar species: (1) Eastern Coachwhip has *smooth* scales and *divided* anal. (2) Rat Snakes have *divided* anals and a few middorsal rows of scales *weakly* keeled.

Range: S. South Carolina to Alabama and s. Florida.
                                              Map 147

BLACK PINE SNAKE   Pl. 27
Pituophis melanoleucus lodingi

Identification: 48–64 in. (122–163 cm); record 74 in. (188.0 cm).

A melanistic pine snake. Plain (or nearly plain) black or dark brown, both above and below. Faint indications of blotches may be evident on or near tail, and a few irregular white spots may be present on throat or belly. Snout and lips often dark russet-brown. *Hisses loudly.* Scales *keeled;* anal *single.*

Similar species: (1) Racers and Whipsnakes have *smooth* scales and *divided* anals. (2) Eastern Indigo Snake has *smooth* scales.

Range: Chiefly in sandy areas of longleaf pine belt from sw. Alabama to extr. e. Louisiana.   Map 147

LOUISIANA PINE SNAKE   Pl. 27
Pituophis melanoleucus ruthveni

Identification: 48–56 in. (122–142 cm); record 70¼ in. (178.4 cm). Markings conspicuously different at opposite ends of body: (a) blotches *near head* dark brown, obscuring ground color and often running together; and (b) blotches *near and on tail,* brown or russet, clear-cut, and well separated. Total number of *body* blotches (in middorsal row) usually 40 or fewer. Ground color buff, changing to yellowish on and near tail. Head buff and profusely spotted or splotched with dark brown. Belly boldly marked with black. *Hisses loudly.* Scales *keeled;* anal *single.*

Range: Chiefly sandy, longleaf pine woods of w.-cen. Louisiana and e. Texas.   Map 147

BULLSNAKE   *Pituophis melanoleucus sayi*   Pl. 27

Identification: 50–72 in. (127–183 cm); record 100 in. (254.0 cm). A large yellowish snake marked with a series of black, brown, or reddish-brown dorsal blotches, which are darkest and in strongest contrast with the ground color at *both* ends of the snake — near the head and near and on the tail. Some specimens, especially those from eastern part of range, have all the blotches dark; in arid regions the general appearance is more pallid. *Body* blotches (in middorsal row) usually 41 or more. Belly yellow with bold black spots, especially toward sides. Usually a *dark band* extending from eye to angle of jaw, and with a parallel yellow band above it. *Hisses loudly.* Scales *keeled;* anal *single.*

At home on plains and prairies; also occurring from sand prairies in Illinois and Indiana southwestward to the desert and semi-arid portions of southern and western Texas and adjacent Mexico. Clumps of vegetation and mammal burrows are favorite lurking places, both for the Bullsnake and its rodent food. Birds and their eggs are also eaten.

Similar species: Texas Rat Snake, Glossy Snake, and Prairie Kingsnake have only 2 prefrontals (4 in the Bullsnakes — see Fig. 57, opp. Pl. 27).

Range: W. Indiana and Wisconsin to s. Alberta, and south to Texas and ne. Mexico. Map 147

SONORA GOPHER SNAKE Not illus.
Pituophis melanoleucus affinis
Identification: 50–72 in. (127–183 cm); record 92 in. (233.7 cm). Similar to the Bullsnake but with the blotches all brown or reddish-brown on the forepart of the body; the blotches are strikingly darker on and near the tail where they may be almost black.

Some specimens are extraordinarily belligerent when first encountered. They raise and draw back their heads, inflate their throats, hiss and strike repeatedly, and glide toward a person, meanwhile beating a lively tattoo with their tails. Similar behavior occurs (rarely) in the Bullsnake.
Range: Extr. w. Texas to se. California and south to Zacatecas and s. Sinaloa. Western and Mexican subspecies. Map 147

Kingsnakes and Milk Snakes: Genus *Lampropeltis*

THESE are shiny snakes with *smooth* scales and *single* anal plates. All are powerful constrictors, and their killing and eating of other serpents, including venomous ones, is well known. They should not be kept with other reptiles smaller than themselves, even of their own species. In fact, they must be fed in separate cages or watched very closely. Otherwise two of them may start to eat at opposite ends of the same food animal and, when their heads meet, one snake will engulf the other! Besides snakes, they also eat lizards, rodents, small birds and their eggs, and turtle eggs.

The kingsnakes are essentially black (or dark brown) with white or yellowish spots on their scales, but the size and arrangement of the spots vary from one subspecies to the next. When first encountered they vibrate their tails rapidly and may hiss and strike but, once caught, the majority become calm almost immediately. Contrary to popular opinion, they do not prowl about looking for rattlers to fight. Any snake is simply a meal, but they apparently are immune to the venoms of our *native* poisonous snakes. Young kingsnakes vary from about 9 to 12 in. (23 to 30 cm) at hatching.

The milk snakes are basically tricolored, with red (or brown), black, and white (or yellow) in the form of transverse rings. In some kinds there are rows of blotches instead of rings, but in all cases the reddish parts of the pattern are surrounded by black. Milk snakes also vibrate their tails and hiss and strike, but many remain belligerent in captivity; some have a habit, when handled, of biting without warning. The name of the group derives from the nonsensical old-wives' tale that snakes milk cows. Milk snakes feed largely on mice and are among our most beneficial serpents; small snakes and lizards also are eaten. Young milk snakes are about 7 to 10 in. (18 to 25 cm) at hatching.

The Prairie Kingsnake and the Mole Snake are marked with brown or reddish-brown blotches outlined with black on a ground color of light brown or tan. The Gray-banded Kingsnake has a gray ground color, black crossbands, and may or may not also have coral-colored markings.

The genus occurs from southeastern Canada and Montana to Ecuador, and so does the milk snake, *Lampropeltis triangulum,* which has one of the largest ranges of any species of snake in the world. It is also one of the most variable, with 23 allopatric races, including 8 within our area and another 15 distributed, collectively, from Mexico to Ecuador.

EASTERN KINGSNAKE   Pl. 29
Lampropeltis getulus getulus

Identification: 36–48 in. (91–122 cm); record 82 in. (208.3 cm). The "chain snake" — a shiny black serpent clad with large, bold links of white or cream. Specimens from southern part of range may be dark brown instead of black. Scales *smooth;* anal *single. Young:* Patterned like adults.

A handsome snake of the eastern seaboard's pine belt, but one that also crosses the Piedmont and even enters mountain valleys. Habitat is chiefly terrestrial, but it shows a distinct liking for streambanks and borders of swamps, possibly because water snakes and turtle eggs, two important foods, may be abundant there. Kingsnakes swim readily. They are often secretive, hiding under boards, logs, or debris; they bask in the open occasionally in spring or autumn, and may prowl by day, especially in early morning or at twilight, but are largely nocturnal in hot weather. Other vernacular names are "thunder snake" and "swamp wamper."

Similar species: (1) Northern Pine Snake has black or dark brown blotches on a *whitish* ground color and *strongly keeled* scales. (2) Young Black Rat Snakes and young Black Racers, which bear a superficial resemblance to young Kingsnakes, have *divided* anals.

Range: S. New Jersey to n. Florida; west to the Appalachians and s. Alabama.

Subspecies: OUTER BANKS KINGSNAKE, *Lampropeltis g. sticticeps.* Similar but usually brown instead of black; white speckles present in dark interspaces between chainlike markings; a robust, tapering head with the rostral exceptionally large (its dorsal length exceeds length of suture between internasal scales). Outer Banks of N. Carolina from Cape Hatteras to Cape Lookout.   Map 156

FLORIDA KINGSNAKE   Pl. 29
Lampropeltis getulus floridana
Identification: 36–48 in. (91–122 cm); record 66 in. (167.6 cm).
Palest of the large kingsnakes. Each individual dorsal scale is
yellowish or cream-colored at base and brown at apex. Indications of light crosslines are usually present, especially in neck
region. Belly is cream to pale yellow with spots of tan or pinkish
brown. Scales *smooth;* anal *single. Young:* A chainlike pattern
similar to that of Eastern Kingsnake. Dorsal crossbands
cream-colored, yellow, or reddish yellow on a ground color of
brown; many scales in the dark dorsal areas have reddish-brown
centers; light areas on sides have bright red centers.
Range: S. Florida from vicinity of Tampa Bay to southern tip
of peninsula; intergrades with the Eastern Kingsnake over much
of Florida, including a large part of the peninsula, and in disjunct areas in the panhandle and along the border with se.
Georgia. Two types of intergradation are illustrated on Pl. 29,
one labelled "peninsula" and the other, from the panhandle
population, labelled "blotched."   Map 156

BLACK KINGSNAKE *Lampropeltis getulus niger*   Pl. 29
Identification: 36–45 in. (91–114 cm); record 58 in. (147.3 cm).
Similar to the Eastern Kingsnake, but with the chainlike pattern greatly reduced and indicated only by small white or yellowish spots. Some specimens are almost plain black; others,
especially those from near the region of intergradation with the
Speckled Kingsnake, may have numerous yellowish spots on
sides of body. Scales *smooth;* anal *single. Young:* Chainlike
pattern clearly distinct.
   Habitats include dry, rocky hills, open woods, dry prairies,
and stream valleys.
Similar species: Black Racers and Black Rat Snakes both
have *divided* anal plates; Rat Snakes also have *keeled* scales.
Range: S. Ohio and adj. W. Virginia to se. Illinois; south to
cen. Alabama.   Map 156

SPECKLED KINGSNAKE   Pl. 29
Lampropeltis getulus holbrooki
Identification: 36–48 in. (91–122 cm); record 72 in. (182.9 cm).
The "salt-and-pepper snake" with a white or yellowish spot
centered in each (or most) of the black or dark brown dorsal
scales. The light spots often form narrow whitish rows across
the back. Scales *smooth;* anal *single. Young:* Distinct light
dorsal crossbands with little or no spotting between them; sides
of body spotted.
   This kingsnake makes use of a greater variety of habitats than
any of the related subspecies. It is at home in the great river
swamps of the lower Mississippi Valley, in coastal marshes, in

upland wooded areas like the Ozarks, and in stream valleys across the open plains and prairies. Shelters, such as logs, rocks, ledges, thick clumps of vegetation, etc., are utilized as hiding places.

Similar species: Buttermilk Snake has light spots that vary both in coloration and size, and its anal plate is *divided*.

Range: S. Iowa south to the Gulf of Mexico; intergrades with the Desert Kingsnake throughout a wide area from Nebraska to Texas.   Map 156

DESERT KINGSNAKE   Pl. 29
Lampropeltis getulus splendida

Identification: 36–45 in. (91–114 cm); record 60 in. (152.4 cm). A profusion of white or yellowish dots on the sides, but with a middorsal series of plain black or dark brown spots. Each such spot is separated from its neighbor by a row of light dots across the back. *Belly chiefly black.* Scales *smooth;* anal *single. Young:* Less dark pigment; middorsal dark spots boldly outlined with yellow; a row of dark spots on each side of body. The speckled flanks and overall dark appearance develop with age.

A kingsnake of the arid Southwest which, in order to avoid high temperatures and desiccation, is largely nocturnal — like other serpents of the region. Often found near streams or irrigation ditches. (Formerly called "Sonora Kingsnake.")

Similar species: Speckled Racer has *divided* anal plate and the middle rows of dorsal scales are *weakly* keeled. Also, Speckled Racer has conspicuously large eyes and a black stripe extending backward from eye.

Range: Cen. Texas to e. Sonora and n.-cen. Mexico. Western and Mexican subspecies.   Map 156

EASTERN MILK SNAKE   Pl. 30
Lampropeltis triangulum triangulum

Identification: 24–36 in. (61–91 cm); record 52 in. (132.1 cm). A rather slender, strongly blotched snake with a Y-shaped or V-shaped light patch on the nape. There are 3 (sometimes 5) rows of brown or reddish-brown, black-bordered blotches down the body, the middorsal ones quite large and alternating in position with the smaller lateral ones. Ground color gray to tan. Belly checkerboarded (often very irregularly) with black on white (Fig. 65, p. 207). Not too much trust should be placed in the Y or V marking, because it is subject to variation; in extreme cases it may even be replaced by a light collar like those found in other races of milk snakes. Scales *smooth;* anal *single. Young:* Blotches bright red and forming basis for the name "red adder."

A frequent victim of the ridiculous belief that it milks cows. Also killed because of its superficial resemblance to the Copper-

Plates

Symbols and Explanation of Scale

♂ means male and ♀ means female

These symbols, universally used in zoology and which appear frequently on the plates and legend pages that follow, are borrowed from astronomy. The ♂ represents the shield and spear of Mars and the ♀ the looking glass of Venus. Both symbols have long been used in referring to the planets bearing those two names.

Ssp. (for subspecies)

This designation signifies that the species (or subspecies) illustrated has one or more additional races that are not shown on the plates, but which are discussed in the text. Only subspecies that occur within the area encompassed by this book (see map on p. xx) are included. Many of the reptiles and amphibians of the eastern and central United States and Canada have extralimital subspecies, the ranges of which are indicated in part on the maps (pp. 363–412) as Western or Mexican subspecies.

Scale

All the animals depicted on any one plate are shown in scale with one another. But a black line across a plate denotes a change in scale, as in the case of the young crocodilians on Plate 3, which are shown proportionately larger than the adults.

Plate 1

HANDLING THE CATCH

CAUTION: Don't attempt to catch or handle venomous snakes unless you have received professional coaching and are prepared to suffer the serious consequences of a snakebite accident.

1. **A Bullfrog,** like other amphibians, is slippery. Encircle its waist with your fingers so it won't kick itself free. Any large or medium-sized frogs may be held in the same way, but small frogs are best grasped by the hind legs.

2. **A Snapper's tail** makes a good handle, but keep the head aimed away from your leg.

3. **Large salamanders** should be held firmly but gently with the entire hand. Let the head protrude. Small salamanders can be caged briefly within your clenched fist.

4. **Lizards** are best immobilized by holding their feet, but the body should also be gripped to prevent sudden lunges. Make it a practice *never* to grab or hold a lizard by the tail, for it may break right off in your hands.

5. **Softshell turtles** are difficult to hold. Pressing against the neck with your fingers will help keep the head from protruding far enough to turn around and bite at you. Also watch out for flailing legs with their sharp claws. *Large* snappers should be carried in this same fashion.

6. **Carrying a snake bag.** With your hand well above the knot and the bag held away from your leg, a venomous snake may be safely transported. In the case of a harmless species, the knot and the empty part of the bag may be thrust upward under your belt, letting the snake dangle there until you return to your car or base. This leaves both hands free.

7. **Glass jars** are safest for transporting small fragile specimens. They retain moisture and may save your catch from injury. More than one collector has sat or stepped on a collecting bag with fatal consequences to the specimens inside.

8. **A stevedore's hook** works well on logs, boards, and smaller rocks, but it requires stooping. An advantage is that it can be thrust under your belt when not in use.

9. **A potato rake** or similar tool is useful for overturning rocks. The long handle lets you stand erect and keeps you well away if by chance you should uncover a poisonous snake.

Additional collecting equipment is described on pp. 17 to 21 and illustrated in Fig. 1, p. 16.

Plate 2

FIRST AID FOR SNAKEBITE

What to do for snakebite should be part of the mental equipment of everyone who spends much time out of doors. If you work, live, or play where venomous snakes are prevalent, buy yourself a snakebite suction kit and keep it handy.

In case of a bite, keep calm. Assure the victim he has an excellent chance of recovery. Make him sit or lie still. Remove rings or bracelets at once if bite is on hand, wrist, or arm. Send someone to summon a doctor or to arrange transportation to a hospital or clinic. If it is obvious that you will be unable to get medical help within 30 minutes, follow the steps shown on the opposite page.

1. **Apply constriction band** a few inches above the bite. It must impede superficial blood and lymph flow, but not deep blood flow.

2. **Test its tightness** by forcing a finger under it. If it is adjusted properly it doesn't need to be loosened periodically.

3. **Sterilize** razor blade or sharp knife, using flame or antiseptic. If neither is available, omit sterilization rather than incision.

4. **Make a cut** not more than ⅛″ deep and ¼″ long (3 and 6 mm) through each fang puncture and parallel to the long axis of the limb.

5. **Apply suction cup** over wound, first squeezing air from bulb. Apply for 3 to 5 minutes, then remove cup, squeeze it out, and apply again. Continue this routine for at least an hour, even while en route to a hospital or doctor's office. If no kit is available, use your mouth for suction provided it is free of cuts, abrasions, lesions, etc., and your gums are healthy.

6. **Move constriction band** upward as swelling advances. When suction is discontinued cover wound with a wet compress.

7. **Rubber bulb kit,** components of which are shown in use in illustrations 1 through 6.

8. **Plastic suction kit.** Snakebite kits of several varieties are available through first-class drug stores.

Use a necktie, belt, etc. if no regular constriction band is at hand. *Avoid use of alcoholic beverages.* Antivenin (snakebite serum) must be administered by a doctor or under his direction.

Be sure that a poisonous snake was involved before starting first aid. For additional and *important* information on the snakebite problem see pages 30 to 33.

1. Apply constriction band

2. Test its tightness

3. Sterilize

4. Make a cut

5. Apply suction cup

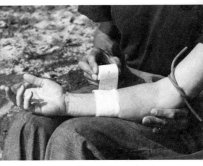

6. Move constriction band

7. Rubber bulb kit

8. Plastic suction kit

Plate 3

CROCODILIANS

Young

AMERICAN ALLIGATOR, *Alligator mississippiensis*   1   35
Black with yellowish lines. Head smooth in front of
eyes (as in photograph of adult Alligator).

SPECTACLED CAIMAN, *Caiman crocodilus*   36
Gray with dark brown crossbands. A curved, bony,
crosswise ridge in front of eyes (Fig. 46).

AMERICAN CROCODILE, *Crocodylus acutus*   1   34
Gray or greenish gray with black crossbands or rows
of spots. Head tapering toward snout (as in photograph of adult Crocodile).

Adults

AMERICAN CROCODILE   1   34
Tapering head; 4th tooth of lower jaw fitting into
a groove in upper jaw and remaining visible when
mouth is closed (Fig. 46).

AMERICAN ALLIGATOR   1   35
Broadly rounded snout.

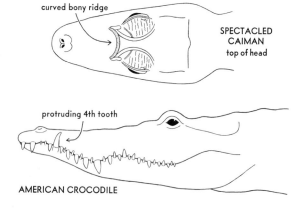

Fig. 46. CHARACTERISTICS OF CROCODILIANS

curved bony ridge

SPECTACLED
CAIMAN
top of head

protruding 4th tooth

AMERICAN CROCODILE

YOUNG

ALLIGATOR

CAIMAN

CROCODILE

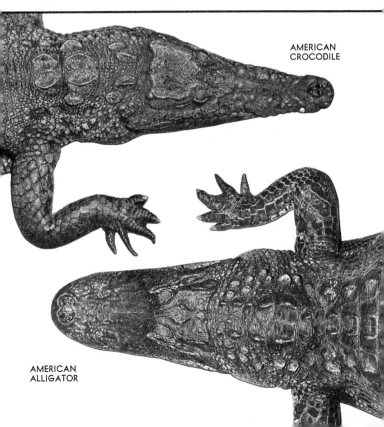

AMERICAN CROCODILE

AMERICAN ALLIGATOR

Plate 4

MUSK TURTLES (*Sternotherus*)

	Map	Text
STINKPOT, *S. odoratus*	7	40

2 light lines on head; plastron small. ♂: Large areas of skin between plastral scutes; large, stout tail. ♀: Plastral scutes close together.

STRIPE-NECKED MUSK TURTLE, *S. minor peltifer*   8   42
Head and neck striped; a dorsal keel (Fig. 5, p. 41).

RAZOR-BACKED MUSK TURTLE, *S. carinatus*   9   41
Head spotted; strong dorsal keel (Fig. 5, p. 41).

FLATTENED MUSK TURTLE, *S. depressus*   9   42
Netlike head pattern; shell flattened (Fig. 5, p. 41).

LOGGERHEAD MUSK TURTLE, *S. minor minor*   8   42
♂: Very large head. ♀: Head moderate; shell streaked, spotted, or blotched. *Young:* Shell streaked; 3 keels (Fig. 5, p. 41).

MUD TURTLES (*Kinosternon*)

STRIPED MUD TURTLE, *K. bauri* (ssp.)   11   44
Shell and head striped.

MISSISSIPPI MUD TURTLE, *K. subrubrum hippocrepis*   13   44
2 light lines on head; plastron large.

EASTERN MUD TURTLE, *K. subrubrum subrubrum*   13   43
Nondescript; rounded shell; plastron large.

YELLOW MUD TURTLE, *K. flavescens* (ssp.)   10   45
Throat plain yellow; 9th marginal higher than 8th; pectoral scutes narrowly in contact (Fig. 6, p. 44).

BIG BEND MUD TURTLE, *K. hirtipes murrayi*   12   46
Head spotted; 10th marginal higher than 9th; pectoral scutes broadly in contact (Fig. 6, p. 44).

GOPHER TORTOISES (*Gopherus*)

GOPHER TORTOISE, *G. polyphemus*   34   71
Foot elephant-like; shell relatively long.

TEXAS TORTOISE, *G. berlandieri*   32   72
Foot elephant-like; shell relatively short.

4

STINKPOT

plastron ♀   plastron ♂

STRIPE-NECKED MUSK

RAZOR-BACKED MUSK

FLATTENED MUSK

young

old ♀

♂

LOGGERHEAD MUSK

STRIPED MUD

MISSISSIPPI MUD

EASTERN MUD

plastron

YELLOW MUD

BIG BEND MUD

GOPHER TORTOISE

TEXAS TORTOISE

Plate 5

YOUNG TURTLES (1)

	Map	Text
STINKPOT, *Sternotherus odoratus*	7	40
Light head lines; edge of shell with light spots.		
LOGGERHEAD MUSK TURTLE,	8	42
Sternotherus minor minor		
3 keels along top of shell. *Plastron:* Pink.		
EASTERN MUD TURTLE,	13	43
Kinosternon subrubrum subrubrum		
No lines on head. *Plastron:* Orange to pale yellow, dark at center.		
MAP TURTLE, *Graptemys geographica*	15	54
Yellow spot behind eye; maplike lines on shell. *Plastron:* Dark lines along seams.		
MISSISSIPPI MAP TURTLE, *Graptemys kohni*	19	56
Yellowish crescent behind eye. *Plastron:* Broad dark markings with open centers.		
BARBOUR'S MAP TURTLE, *Graptemys barbouri*	18	55
Saw-backed; broad light area behind eye and another across chin.		
WOOD TURTLE, *Clemmys insculpta*	5	48
Shell rough; head dark, unmarked; long tail.		
BLANDING'S TURTLE, *Emydoidea blandingi*	26	71
Light marks on head; chin yellow; long tail.		
FLORIDA BOX TURTLE, *Terrapene carolina bauri*	28	50
Yellow middorsal stripe; mottled pattern.		
EASTERN BOX TURTLE, *Terrapene carolina carolina*	28	49
Light spot in each large scute. *Plastron:* Dark pigment concentrated toward center.		
SPOTTED TURTLE, *Clemmys guttata*	6	47
Light spot in each large scute *and spots on head.* *Plastron:* Dark pigment toward center.		
ALLIGATOR SNAPPING TURTLE,	2	38
Macroclemys temmincki		
Shell extremely rough; beak strongly hooked; long tail.		
SNAPPING TURTLE, *Chelydra serpentina*	3	37
Shell rough, edged with light spots; long tail.		

5

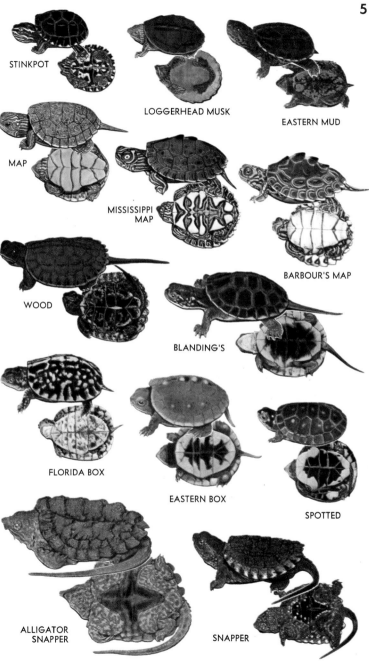

Plate 6
YOUNG TURTLES (2)

	Map	Text

WESTERN PAINTED TURTLE, *Chrysemys picta belli* — Map 22, Text 69
  Pale wormlike markings. *Plastron:* Dark area large and with outward extensions.

MIDLAND PAINTED TURTLE, — Map 22, Text 69
Chrysemys picta marginata
  No bold markings. *Plastron:* Dark central blotch.

SOUTHERN PAINTED TURTLE, — Map 22, Text 69
Chrysemys picta dorsalis
  Broad red, orange, or yellow stripe.

EASTERN PAINTED TURTLE, *Chrysemys picta picta* — Map 22, Text 68
  The large scutes have light borders. *Plastron:* Usually unmarked.

NORTHERN DIAMONDBACK TERRAPIN, — Map 20, Text 52
Malaclemys terrapin terrapin
  Dark lines parallel edges of scutes (both shells).

RED-EARED TURTLE, *Chrysemys scripta elegans* — Map 25, Text 62
  Red patch or stripe behind eye. *Plastron:* Circular markings large and involving all parts of shell.

YELLOW-BELLIED TURTLE, *Chrysemys scripta scripta* — Map 25, Text 62
  Large yellow patch behind eye. *Plastron:* Circular markings on forepart of shell.

PENINSULA COOTER, — Map 24, Text 66
Chrysemys floridana peninsularis
  Curved lines on shell. *Plastron:* Unmarked. Dark spots on anterior marginals.

SLIDER, *Chrysemys concinna hieroglyphica* — Map 23, Text 64
  Markings circular, especially on marginals. *Plastron:* Markings chiefly along seams.

CHICKEN TURTLE, *Deirochelys reticularia* — Map 31, Text 70
  Network of light lines; has striped "pants" (Fig. 49, opp. Pl. 9).

FLORIDA SOFTSHELL, *Trionyx ferox* — Map 35, Text 81
  Head striped; large round spots. *Plastron:* Dark.

EASTERN SPINY SOFTSHELL, — Map 36, Text 78
Trionyx spiniferus spiniferus
  Small circular spots. *Plastron:* Light and nearly matching underside of carapace.

SMOOTH SOFTSHELL, *Trionyx muticus* — Map 33, Text 77
  Indistinct dots and dashes. *Plastron:* Light. (Underside of carapace brown.)

6

WESTERN PAINTED

MIDLAND PAINTED

SOUTHERN PAINTED

EASTERN PAINTED

NORTHERN DIAMONDBACK

RED-EARED

YELLOW-BELLIED

PENINSULA COOTER

SLIDER

CHICKEN

FLORIDA SOFTSHELL

EASTERN SPINY SOFTSHELL

SMOOTH SOFTSHELL

Plate 7

BOX, WOOD, AND SPOTTED TURTLES; DIAMONDBACKS

	Map	Text

ORNATE BOX TURTLE, *Terrapene ornata ornata* — Map 30, Text 50
Carapace: Flattened or depressed on top; radiating light lines. *Plastron:* Transverse hinge; bold light lines.

EASTERN BOX TURTLE, — Map 28, Text 49
Terrapene carolina carolina (ssp.)
Carapace: High, domeline; yellow, orange, or olive markings on dark brown or black. *Plastron:* Transverse hinge; pattern variable.

FLORIDA BOX TURTLE, *Terrapene carolina bauri* — Map 28, Text 50
Shell arched, highest toward rear, and with radiating light lines; 2 yellow stripes on head.

THREE-TOED BOX TURTLE, — Map 28, Text 50
Terrapene carolina triunguis
Orange on head (and often on forelimbs); 3 toes on *hind* foot; shell pattern much reduced or absent.

BOG TURTLE, *Clemmys muhlenbergi* — Map 4, Text 47
Orange head patch; small size.

SPOTTED TURTLE, *Clemmys guttata* — Map 6, Text 47
Scattered yellow spots; orange or yellow spots on head.

BLANDING'S TURTLE, *Emydoidea blandingi* — Map 26, Text 71
Carapace: Profuse light spots. *Plastron:* Transverse hinge. *Bright yellow throat.*

WOOD TURTLE, *Clemmys insculpta* — Map 5, Text 48
Orange on neck and legs; shell rough, sculptured.

ORNATE DIAMONDBACK TERRAPIN, — Map 20, Text 53
Malaclemys terrapin macrospilota (ssp.)
Orange or yellow in center of each large scute. Salt and brackish water only.

NORTHERN DIAMONDBACK TERRAPIN, — Map 20, Text 52
Malaclemys terrapin terrapin (ssp.)
Concentric rings on each large scute. Salt and brackish water only.

hinge

Fig. 47. BLANDING'S and the BOX TURTLES have a hinge across the plastron.

7

ORNATE BOX

plastron

EASTERN BOX

plastron

FLORIDA BOX

THREE-
TOED
BOX

BOG

BLANDING'S

SPOTTED

plastron

WOOD

NORTHERN
DIAMONDBACK

ORNATE DIAMONDBACK

Plate 8

MAP TURTLES AND SAWBACKS
(*Graptemys*)

Females of all species grow larger than males.

	Map	Text
TEXAS MAP TURTLE, *G. versa*	21	58

Horizontal or J-shaped line behind eye; anterior scutes of carapace distinctly convex (examine closely).

BLACK-KNOBBED SAWBACK, *G. nigrinoda* 17 59
Rounded black knobs; narrow light rings.

RINGED SAWBACK, *G. oculifera* 17 59
Broad light rings.

YELLOW-BLOTCHED SAWBACK, *G. flavimaculata* 17 59
Solid orange or yellow spots.

ALABAMA MAP TURTLE, *G. pulchra* 16 55
Broad light bars on marginals; *longitudinal* light bar under chin (Fig. 9, p. 56). ♀: Large and big-headed like Barbour's Map Turtle.

BARBOUR'S MAP TURTLE, *G. barbouri* 18 55
Narrow light markings on marginals; a *curved* or transverse bar under chin (Fig. 9, p. 56). *Mature* ♀: Very large; head enormous; pattern obscure.

MISSISSIPPI MAP TURTLE, *G. kohni* 19 56
Yellow crescent, cutting off neck stripes from eye.

FALSE MAP TURTLE, *G. pseudogeographica* (ssp.) 14 57
Yellow spot behind eye; neck stripes reach eye; middorsal spines conspicuous.

MAP TURTLE, *G. geographica* 15 54
Yellowish spot behind eye; maplike pattern, middorsal spines not prominent.

Fig. 48. Basking FALSE MAP TURTLE

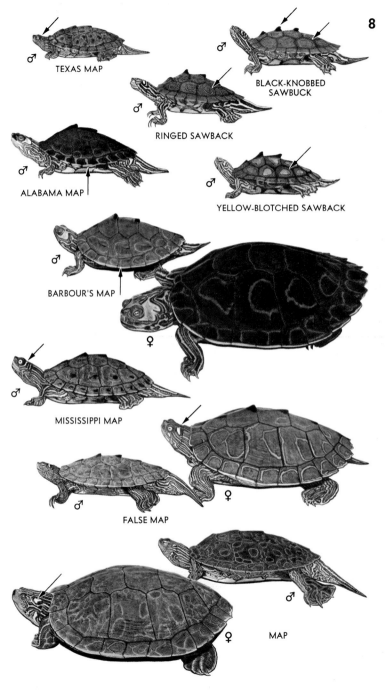

8

TEXAS MAP ♂

BLACK-KNOBBED SAWBUCK ♂

RINGED SAWBACK ♂

ALABAMA MAP ♂

YELLOW-BLOTCHED SAWBACK ♂

BARBOUR'S MAP ♂ ♀

MISSISSIPPI MAP ♂

FALSE MAP ♂ ♀

MAP ♂ ♀

Plate 9

PAINTED AND CHICKEN TURTLES; POND SLIDERS (chiefly *Chrysemys*)

See Plate 6 for the young of many of these turtles.

	Map	*Text*

MIDLAND PAINTED TURTLE, *C. picta marginata* — Map 22, Text 69
Large scutes arranged in alternating fashion.

EASTERN PAINTED TURTLE, *C. picta picta* — Map 22, Text 68
Large scutes with broad olive edges and arranged more or less in straight rows *across* back.

WESTERN PAINTED TURTLE, *C. picta belli* — Map 22, Text 69
Light wormlike or netlike lines on carapace; bars on marginals.

SOUTHERN PAINTED TURTLE, *C. picta dorsalis* — Map 22, Text 69
Broad red stripe (sometimes yellowish).

YELLOW-BELLIED TURTLE, *C. scripta scripta* — Map 25, Text 62
Yellow head blotch; vertical yellowish bars on shell; leg stripes *narrow;* has striped "pants" (Fig. 49).

CHICKEN TURTLE, *Deirochelys reticularia* (ssp.) — Map 31, Text 70
Long striped neck; light network on shell; leg stripe *broad;* has striped "pants" (Fig. 49).

RED-EARED TURTLE, *C. scripta elegans* (ssp.) — Map 25, Text 62
♀ *and young:* Reddish stripe behind eye. ♂: Reddish stripe reduced; completely obscured in old specimens (see text).

RED-BELLIED TURTLE, *C. rubriventris* — Map 27, Text 67
♀: Vertical reddish markings (persisting even in very dark specimens). ♂: Dark; markings irregular (see text).

Fig. 49. YELLOW-BELLIED AND CHICKEN TURTLES

YELLOW-BELLIED
Narrow leg stripes

BOTH
Striped "pants"

CHICKEN
Broad leg stripe

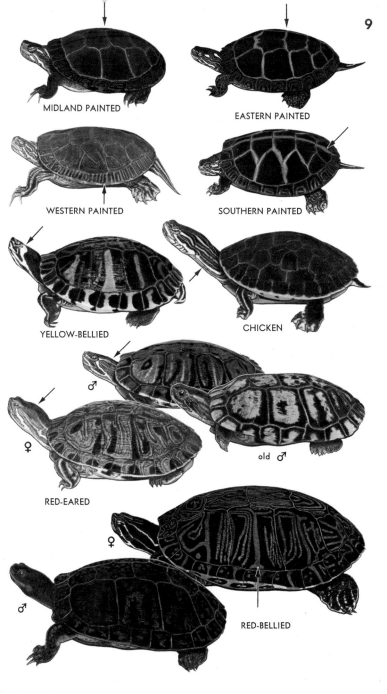

9

MIDLAND PAINTED

EASTERN PAINTED

WESTERN PAINTED

SOUTHERN PAINTED

YELLOW-BELLIED

CHICKEN

♂

♀

RED-EARED

old ♂

♀

♂

RED-BELLIED

Plate 10
COOTERS AND SLIDERS (*Chrysemys*)

	Map	Text
PENINSULA COOTER, *C. floridana peninsularis*	24	66

"Hairpins" on head; dark marginal smudges; plastron unmarked.

| **FLORIDA RED-BELLIED TURTLE,** *C. nelsoni* | 29 | 67 |

Light vertical band; few stripes on head (Fig. 50).

| **RIVER COOTER,** *C. concinna concinna* | 23 | 63 |

A figure C; undersurfaces heavily marked.

| **FLORIDA COOTER,** *C. floridana floridana* (ssp.) | 24 | 65 |

No "hairpins"; hollow circles on marginals; plastron as in Peninsula Cooter.

| **TEXAS SLIDER,** *C. concinna texana* | 23 | 65 |

Broad head markings; undersurfaces basically like River Cooter's but reduced to narrow dark lines.

| **SUWANNEE COOTER,** *C. concinna suwanniensis* (ssp.) | 23 | 64 |

A figure C; carapace dark; venter like River Cooter's.

| **SLIDER,** *C. concinna hieroglyphica* | 23 | 64 |

A figure C; shell pinched inward in front of hind legs; undersurfaces like River Cooter's.

Note: Patterns, often obscure in large specimens, are best seen if the turtle is submerged in water. The illustrations of the River Cooter and Texas Slider are of relatively young individuals, chosen to show the distinctive markings that fade or even disappear in old adults. These two turtles are reproduced at the scale of large adults. Note that their heads are disproportionately large.

Fig. 50. HEAD AND SCUTE PATTERNS

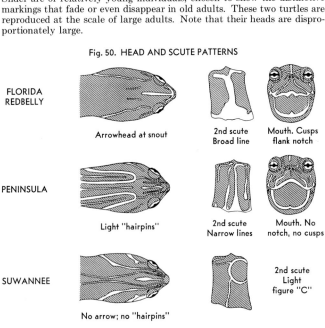

FLORIDA
REDBELLY

Arrowhead at snout

2nd scute
Broad line

Mouth. Cusps
flank notch

PENINSULA

Light "hairpins"

2nd scute
Narrow lines

Mouth. No
notch, no cusps

SUWANNEE

No arrow; no "hairpins"

2nd scute
Light
figure "C"

10

♂

PENINSULA
COOTER

plastron

♀

FLORIDA
RED-BELLIED
TURTLE

RIVER
COOTER

plastron

♀

FLORIDA
COOTER

♂

SUWANNEE COOTER

TEXAS
SLIDER

♂

SLIDER

Plate 11

SNAPPERS

Macroclemys temmincki
    Extra row of scutes at side of carapace; 3 prominent
    ridges along back; head very large, beaks strongly
    hooked.

    Long, saw-toothed tail.

SEA TURTLES

    Reddish brown; 5 (or more) costal plates, 1st touch-
    ing the nuchal; 3 or 4 bridge scutes.

    Gray; 5 costal plates, 1st touching the nuchal; an
    interanal scute; usually 4 bridge scutes (Fig. 51).

    4 costal plates, 1st *not* touching the nuchal; 1 pair
    of plates between eyes (Fig. 14, p. 74).

Dermochelys coriacea coriacea
    Prominent ridges along back; no scutes; smooth skin.

Eretmochelys imbricata imbricata
    Tortoise-shell pattern; scutes overlap (varies — see
    text); 2 pairs of plates between eyes (Fig. 14, p. 74).

Fig. 51. SCUTES OF SEA TURTLES

GREEN TURTLE
Nuchal separated from costal

LOGGERHEAD AND RIDLEY
Nuchal touches 1st costal

RIDLEY

Interanal scute →

Bridge has
4 scutes

LOGGERHEAD

Bridge has
3 scutes

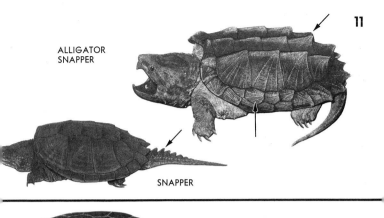

11

ALLIGATOR SNAPPER

SNAPPER

LOGGERHEAD

GREEN

RIDLEY

HAWKSBILL

LEATHERBACK

Plate 12

SOFTSHELL TURTLES (*Trionyx*)

Consult text for descriptions of females not illustrated.

	Map	Text

WESTERN SPINY SOFTSHELL, *T. spiniferus hartwegi* 36 79
  ♂: Shell with dark spots and small eyelike marks; feet
  strongly streaked and spotted. Top of shell rough;
  feels like sandpaper, at least toward rear.

SMOOTH SOFTSHELL, *T. muticus* (ssp.) 33 77
  Feet *not* strongly patterned. Shell smooth; no spines
  or bumps. No ridge in nostril (Fig. 52). ♂: Vague dots
  and dashes. ♀: An indefinite mottled pattern.

EASTERN SPINY SOFTSHELL, *T. spiniferus spiniferus* 36 78
  Feet strongly patterned. ♂: Large eyelike spots; top
  of shell sandpapery. ♀: Pattern vague (see text);
  spines at front of shell.

GULF COAST SPINY SOFTSHELL, *T. spiniferus asperus* 36 79
  ♂: 2 or more rows of curved black lines bordering rear
  edge of shell. Light lines on head usually meet (Fig.
  15, p. 79).

GUADALUPE SPINY SOFTSHELL, 36 80
T. spiniferus guadalupensis (ssp.)
  ♂: Numerous light dots.

FLORIDA SOFTSHELL, *T. ferox* 35 81
  Shell proportionately longer than in other species.
  Anterior surface of shell with numerous small bumps
  in form of flattened hemispheres.

Fig. 52. NOSTRILS AND CARAPACES

TIPS OF SNOUTS

SMOOTH SOFTSHELL   ALL OTHER SOFTSHELLS
Nostrils round   A ridge in each nostril

FRONT EDGES OF CARAPACES

SMOOTH   FLORIDA   SPINY GROUP
No projections   Flattened hemispheres   Spines or cones

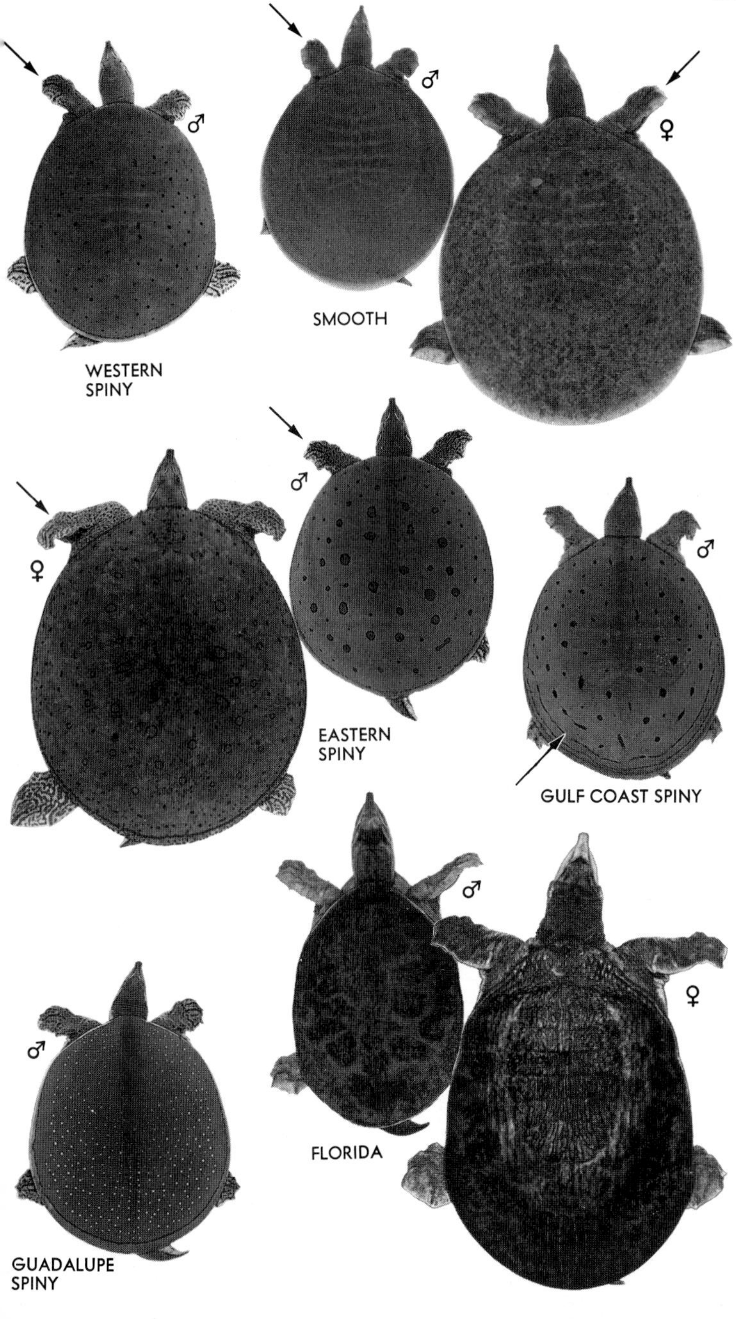

12

WESTERN
SPINY

♂

SMOOTH

♂

♀

♀

EASTERN
SPINY

♂

♂

GULF COAST SPINY

GUADALUPE
SPINY

♂

FLORIDA

♂

♀

Plate 13

GECKOS; GLASS, WORM, AND ALLIGATOR LIZARDS

(See also Plate 17)

	Map	*Text*
ASHY GECKO, *Sphaerodactylus cinereus*	39	84

ASHY GECKO, *Sphaerodactylus cinereus*   39   84
  Adult: Tiny *light* spots on a dark ground color.
  Young: Dark crossbands; reddish tail.

REEF GECKO, *Sphaerodactylus notatus notatus*   40   85
  Dark markings on a lighter ground color. ♂: Numerous small dark spots. ♀: Dark head stripes; often 2 light spots on shoulder.

OCELLATED GECKO, *Sphaerodactylus argus argus*   41   85
  Numerous white spots; tail light brown or reddish.

YELLOW-HEADED GECKO,   42   86
Gonatodes albogularis fuscus
  Adult ♂: Yellowish head; body bluish (or black).
  ♀ *and young:* Light collar; body mottled.

TEXAS BANDED GECKO, *Coleonyx brevis*   37   86
  Light crossbands (or mottlings) on a brown ground color; *movable eyelids.*

MEDITERRANEAN GECKO,   44   83
Hemidactylus turcicus turcicus
  Toe pads *broad* (Fig. 53); dorsum warty.

WORM LIZARD, *Rhineura floridana*   98   135
  Like an earthworm; head scales distinctly evident when examined at close range.

SLENDER GLASS LIZARD,   97   133
Ophisaurus attenuatus (ssp.)*
  No legs; middorsal dark stripe; dark stripes on lower sides.

EASTERN GLASS LIZARD, *Ophisaurus ventralis**   95   132
  No legs; no distinct middorsal dark stripe; greenish coloration. (Tip of tail regenerated.)

TEXAS ALLIGATOR LIZARD,   94   134
Gerrhonotus liocephalus infernalis
  Large scales; irregular light crosslines.

*There are three species of Glass Lizards, all confusingly alike. See text and Fig. 30, p. 132.

Fig. 53. TOES OF GECKOS

Side views   Bottom views

TEXAS BANDED

YELLOW-HEADED

REEF AND ASHY

MEDITERRANEAN

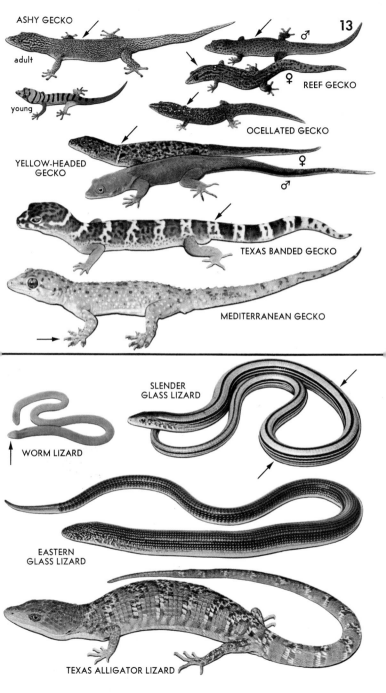

13

ASHY GECKO

adult

young

REEF GECKO ♂ ♀

OCELLATED GECKO

YELLOW-HEADED GECKO ♀ ♂

TEXAS BANDED GECKO

MEDITERRANEAN GECKO

WORM LIZARD

SLENDER GLASS LIZARD

EASTERN GLASS LIZARD

TEXAS ALLIGATOR LIZARD

Plate 14

EARLESS LIZARDS (*Holbrookia*)

TEXAS EARLESS LIZARD, *H. texana texana* — Map 59, Text 94
Black crossbars under tail. ♂: 2 black lines on lower side near groin and invading a blue field on belly.

SOUTHWESTERN EARLESS LIZARD, *H. texana scitula* — Map 59, Text 95
Black ventro-lateral bars broad; body color different from that of hind legs and tail.

SPOT-TAILED EARLESS LIZARD, *H. lacerata* (ssp.) — Map 56, Text 97
Dark dorsal blotches with light borders; dark streaks at edge of abdomen; dark spots under tail (Fig. 20, p. 97).

KEELED EARLESS LIZARD, *H. propinqua propinqua* — Map 57, Text 97
Tail long. ♂: 2 short black lines near armpit. ♀: Markings absent or indistinct; variable (see text).

NORTHERN EARLESS LIZARD, *H. maculata maculata* — Map 58, Text 96
Tail short. ♂: 2 short lines near armpit; faint longitudinal stripes; pale specklings faint and indistinct.

EASTERN EARLESS LIZARD, *H. maculata perspicua* — Map 58, Text 96
♀: Distinct blotches or spots on back; suggestion of black lines near armpit; faint longitudinal stripes.

SPECKLED EARLESS LIZARD, — Map 58, Text 96
H. maculata approximans
Tail short. No stripes on body; dorsum with pale specklings, especially prominent in male.

ANOLES (*Anolis*)

BROWN ANOLE, *A. sagrei* (ssp.) — Map 46, Text 89
Always brown. ♂: Vertical rows of yellowish spots; extends orange-red throat fan (Fig. 17, p. 89). ♀: Light middorsal stripe with scalloped edges.

GREEN ANOLE, *A. carolinensis carolinensis* — Map 45, Text 88
Green or brown or mottled with both. ♂: Extends pink throat fan (Fig. 17, p. 89).

BARK ANOLE, *A. distichus* (ssp.) — Map 48, Text 90
Crossbanded tail and dark line between eyes.

KNIGHT ANOLE, *A. equestris equestris* — Map 47, Text 91
Great size; yellowish lines on shoulder and from beneath eye to ear opening. ♂: Extends very large pink throat fan.

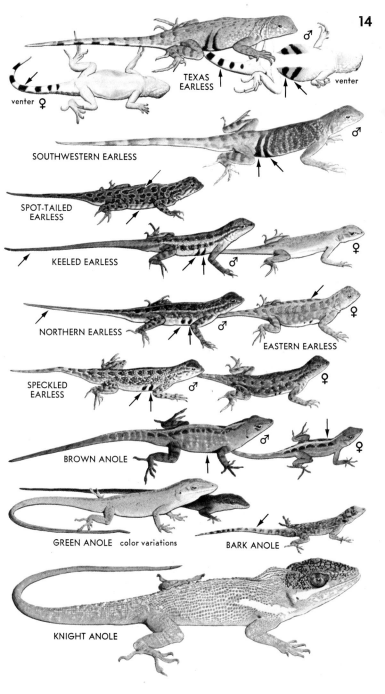

14

TEXAS EARLESS

venter ♀ venter ♂

SOUTHWESTERN EARLESS ♂

SPOT-TAILED EARLESS

KEELED EARLESS ♂ ♀

NORTHERN EARLESS ♂ EASTERN EARLESS ♀

SPECKLED EARLESS ♂ ♀

BROWN ANOLE ♂ ♀

GREEN ANOLE color variations BARK ANOLE

KNIGHT ANOLE

Plate 15

SIDE-BLOTCHED, HORNED, LEOPARD, AND COLLARED LIZARDS

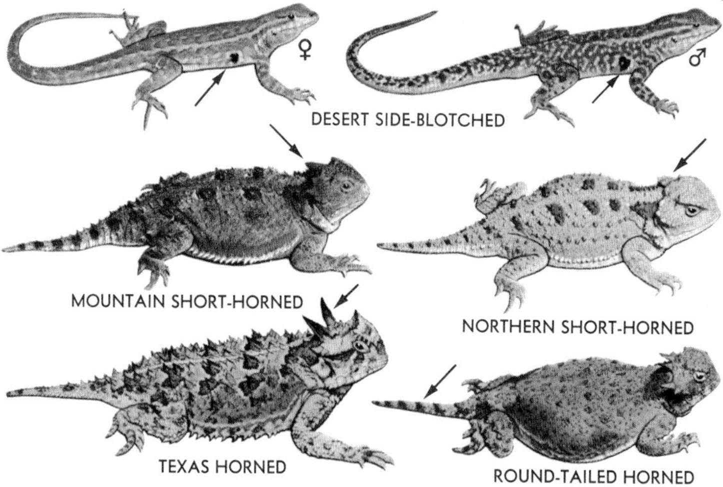

15

DESERT SIDE-BLOTCHED

MOUNTAIN SHORT-HORNED

NORTHERN SHORT-HORNED

TEXAS HORNED

ROUND-TAILED HORNED

LEOPARD
young

RETICULATE
COLLARED

COLLARED

Plate 16

TREE AND SPINY LIZARDS
(*Urosaurus* and *Sceloporus*)
(See also Plate 17)

Males of most species have a blue patch at each side of belly.

	Map	*Text*

TREE LIZARD, *U. ornatus* (ssp.) — Map 61, Text 108
Irregular dark spots; dorsal scales variable — some large, some tiny; a fold across throat (Fig. 54).

ROSE-BELLIED LIZARD, *S. variabilis marmoratus* — Map 71, Text 99
Row of dark spots bordered below by a light stripe; a pocket at rear of thigh (Fig. 21, p. 99). ♂: Dark spot above armpit; large *pink* patch on each side of belly.

MESQUITE LIZARD, *S. grammicus disparilis* — Map 70, Text 100
Wavy dark crosslines (in ♀); scales at sides of neck much smaller than scales on nape (Fig. 21, p. 99).

FENCE LIZARD, *S. undulatus hyacinthinus* (ssp.) — Map 72, Text 102
♀: Wavy dark crosslines. ♂: Nearly unicolored above; blue throat patch surrounded by black.

PRAIRIE LIZARD, *S. undulatus garmani* (ssp.) — Map 72, Text 103
A row of small dark spots bordered below by a *bold* light stripe; secondary light stripe along lower side of body.

CANYON LIZARD, *S. merriami* (ssp.) — Map 62, Text 106
A vertical black bar in front of foreleg; a partially developed throat fold (Fig. 19, p. 94).

SAND DUNE LIZARD, *S. graciosus arenicolous* — Map 64, Text 106
Pale, nearly unicolored; small granular scales on rear surface of thigh.

SAGEBRUSH LIZARD, *S. graciosus graciosus* — Map 64, Text 105
Four rows of dark longitudinal spots that may coalesce to form stripes; small granular scales on rear of thigh.

FLORIDA SCRUB LIZARD, *S. woodi* — Map 68, Text 105
A prominent dark *brown* stripe. ♀: Dark wavy lines across back.

Fig. 54. THROAT FOLD — PRESENT OR ABSENT
(See also Figure 19)

SPINY LIZARD   TREE LIZARD

No fold across throat   Fold across throat

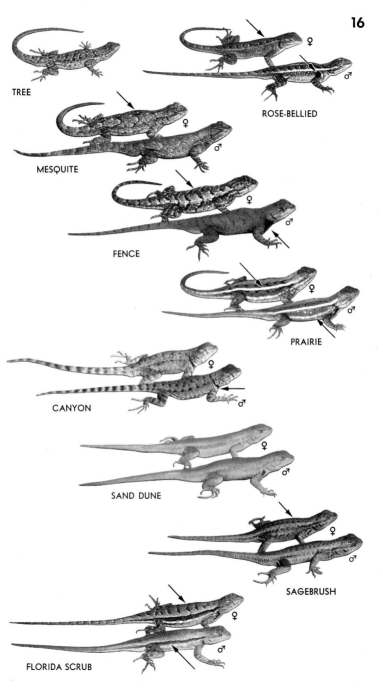

16

TREE

ROSE-BELLIED
♀
♂

MESQUITE
♀
♂

FENCE
♀
♂

PRAIRIE
♀
♂

CANYON
♀
♂

SAND DUNE
♀
♂

SAGEBRUSH
♀
♂

FLORIDA SCRUB
♀
♂

Plate 17
LARGE SPINY LIZARDS (*Sceloporus*)
(See also Plate 16)

Males have a blue or blue-green patch at each side of belly.

	Map	Text

TEXAS SPINY LIZARD, *S. olivaceus*   69   102
    Pale longitudinal stripe not sharply defined.

TWIN-SPOTTED SPINY LIZARD,   65   101
S. magister bimaculosus
    Black wedge or blotch on shoulder; twin spots on
    back not sharply defined.

CREVICE SPINY LIZARD, *S. poinsetti poinsetti*   66   100
    Dark collar; tail strongly patterned near tip. ♀ *and*
    young: Dark bands across back.

BLUE SPINY LIZARD, *S. cyanogenys*
    Dark collar; tail markings not clear-cut.   67   101

SOME FLORIDA INTRODUCTIONS

NORTHERN CURLY-TAILED LIZARD,   63   108
Leiocephalus carinatus armouri
    Habitually carries tail arched above back.

INDO-PACIFIC GECKO, *Hemidactylus garnoti*   43   84
    Toe pads broad like those of Mediterranean Gecko
    (Fig. 53, opp. Pl. 13); dorsum smooth; belly lemon-
    yellow; pale red under tail.

GIANT AMEIVA, *Ameiva ameiva*   92   120
    Like an enormous Whiptail Lizard but with 12 rows
    of large rectangular plates on belly.

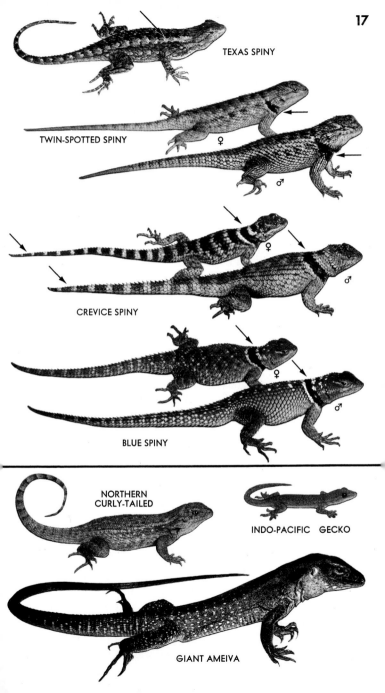

17

TEXAS SPINY

TWIN-SPOTTED SPINY ♀ ♂

CREVICE SPINY ♀ ♂

BLUE SPINY ♀ ♂

NORTHERN CURLY-TAILED

INDO-PACIFIC GECKO

GIANT AMEIVA

Plate 18

WHIPTAILS (*Cnemidophorus*)

	Map	Text
SIX-LINED RACERUNNER,	93	117

C. sexlineatus sexlineatus
   6 light stripes; dark stripes solid. (Only eastern Whiptail.)

PRAIRIE RACERUNNER, *C. sexlineatus viridis*   93   118
   Bright green coloration.

RUSTY-RUMPED WHIPTAIL,   87   117
C. scalaris septemvittatus
   Rump and base of tail rust-colored.

SPOTTED WHIPTAIL, *C. gularis gularis*   86   115
   Prominent light spots in the dark lateral fields. Tail pink, pale orange-brown, or reddish.

DESERT-GRASSLAND WHIPTAIL, *C. uniparens*   90   120
   6 light stripes; no light spots in dark fields.

NEW MEXICO WHIPTAIL, *C. neomexicanus*   89   116
   7 light stripes, the center one *wavy*. Obscure light spots in dark fields.

SEVEN-STRIPED WHIPTAIL,   84   115
C. inornatus heptagrammus
   Blue tail. ♂: Blue on belly and sides of head.

CHIHUAHUA WHIPTAIL, *C. exsanguis*   91   114
   6 light stripes; pale spots on *both* the dark fields *and* light stripes. *Young:* Light stripes in strong contrast with dark fields.

MARBLED WHIPTAIL, *C. tigris marmoratus*   85   119
   A "gray" Whiptail. Highly variable; pattern may be striped, crossbanded, mottled, etc. (see text).

CHECKERED WHIPTAIL, *C. tesselatus*   88   118
   Black spots or squares on a tan or yellowish ground color.

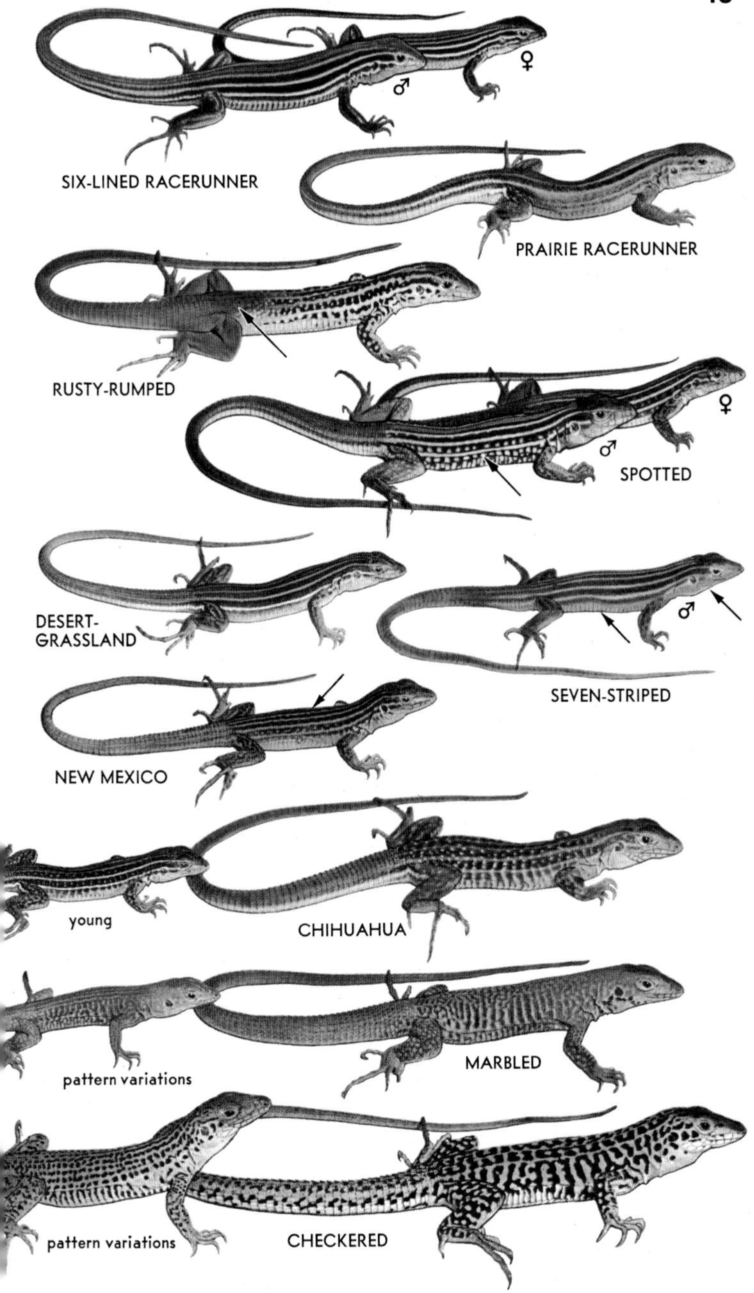

18

SIX-LINED RACERUNNER

♂ ♀

PRAIRIE RACERUNNER

RUSTY-RUMPED

SPOTTED

♀ ♂

DESERT-GRASSLAND

SEVEN-STRIPED

♂

NEW MEXICO

young

CHIHUAHUA

pattern variations

MARBLED

pattern variations

CHECKERED

Plate 19

SKINKS (chiefly *Eumeces*)

	Map	Text
GREAT PLAINS SKINK, *E. obsoletus*	79	125

Dark-edged scales; suggestion of striping.   *Young:* Black; bright head spots; blue tail.

| **SAND SKINK,** *Neoseps reynoldsi* | 83 | 131 |

Tiny legs; only 1 or 2 toes.

| **GROUND SKINK,** *Leiolopisma laterale* | 74 | 122 |

Dark stripe; no light stripes.

| **MOLE SKINKS,** *E. egregius* (ssp.) | 81 | 129 |
| | | 130 |

Slender bodies; short legs. Variable (see text). Representatives of 3 subspecies illustrated: PENINSULA, *onocrepis;* FLORIDA KEYS, *egregius;* BLUE-TAILED, *lividus.*

| **SHORT-LINED SKINK,** *E. tetragrammus brevilineatus* | 82 | 126 |

Light stripes end at shoulder. *Young:* Blue tail.

| **FOUR-LINED SKINK,** *E. tetragrammus tetragrammus* | 82 | 125 |

Light stripes end near hind legs.

| **COAL SKINK,** *E. anthracinus* (ssp.) | 80 | 126 |

Light stripes extend onto tail; broad dark stripe 2½ to 4 scales wide.

| **SOUTHERN PRAIRIE SKINK,** | 73 | 128 |

E. septentrionalis obtusirostris
Middorsal area plain or only weakly patterned; broad dark stripe not more than 2 scales wide.

| **NORTHERN PRAIRIE SKINK,** | 73 | 127 |

E. septentrionalis septentrionalis
Stripes in middorsal area; broad dark stripe not more than 2 scales wide.

| **MANY-LINED SKINK,** | 78 | 128 |

E. multivirgatus multivirgatus
Middorsal light stripe flanked by bold dark stripes; tail swollen at base.

| **VARIABLE SKINK,** *E. multivirgatus gaigeae* | 78 | 129 |

Unicolored or striped. Variable (see text).

| **FIVE-LINED SKINK,** *E. fasciatus* | 75 | 122 |

♀: 5 broad light stripes. ♂: Traces of stripes; reddish on head. *Young:* Blue tail.

| **SOUTHEASTERN FIVE-LINED SKINK,** *E. inexpectatus* | 77 | 124 |

♀: 5 light stripes, middle one narrow; *male and young:* Similar to Five-lined Skink.

| **BROAD-HEADED SKINK,** *E. laticeps* | 76 | 123 |

♂: Body olive-brown; head reddish; grows very large. *Female and young:* Like Five-lined Skink.

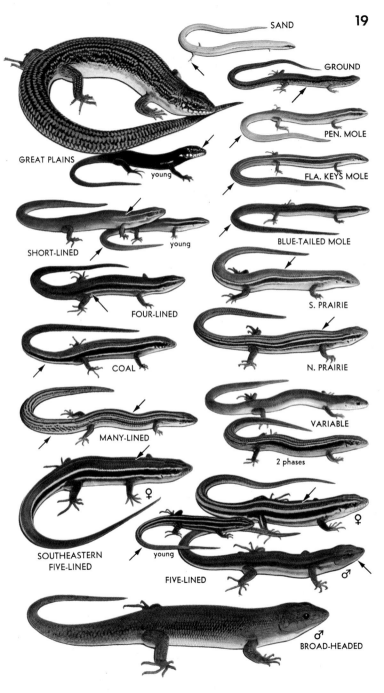

19

GREAT PLAINS

young

SAND

GROUND

PEN. MOLE

FLA. KEYS MOLE

BLUE-TAILED MOLE

SHORT-LINED

young

FOUR-LINED

COAL

S. PRAIRIE

N. PRAIRIE

MANY-LINED

VARIABLE

2 phases

SOUTHEASTERN
FIVE-LINED

♀

FIVE-LINED

young

♀

♂

BROAD-HEADED

♂

Plate 20

WATER SNAKES (*Natrix*) (1)

(See also Plate 21)

Keeled scales and divided anal plates. The rectangles
show belly colors and patterns.

	Map	Text
BLOTCHED WATER SNAKE (young)	103	143

Dark spots on neck alternate with dorsal blotches.

NORTHERN WATER SNAKE (young) — 99 — 144

Dark spots on neck join dorsal blotches to form
crossbands.

MIDLAND WATER SNAKE, *N. sipedon pleuralis* — 99 — 145

Dark markings *smaller* than spaces between them.
Belly: Double row of half-moons or crescents.

NORTHERN WATER SNAKE, *N. sipedon sipedon* (ssp.) — 99 — 144

Dark markings *larger* than spaces between them.
Belly: Highly variable; half-moons paired, scattered,
or virtually absent.

FLORIDA WATER SNAKE, *N. fasciata pictiventris* — 100 — 146

Eye stripe (Fig. 32, p. 140); black, brown, or red
crossbands; often secondary dark spots on sides.
Belly: Wavy, wormlike crosslines.

BANDED WATER SNAKE, *N. fasciata fasciata* — 100 — 146

Eye stripe (Fig. 32, p. 140); black, brown, or red
crossbands throughout length of body. *Belly:* Largest
markings squarish.
Black phase: Usually some red showing on sides.

BROAD-BANDED WATER SNAKE, — 100 — 147

N. fasciata confluens

Eye stripe (Fig. 32, p. 140); dark crossbands *much*
wider than light interspaces. *Belly:* Large squarish
markings, red to black in coloration.

RED-BELLIED WATER SNAKE, — 103 — 142

N. erythrogaster erythrogaster (ssp.)

Plain brown above. *Belly:* Red or orange.

BLOTCHED WATER SNAKE, — 103 — 143

N. erythrogaster transversa

Dark lateral spots alternate with dorsal blotches
throughout length of body. *Belly:* Yellow with faint
suggestions of spots.

YELLOW-BELLIED WATER SNAKE, — 103 — 143

N. erythrogaster flavigaster

Plain gray or greenish above. *Belly:* Yellow.

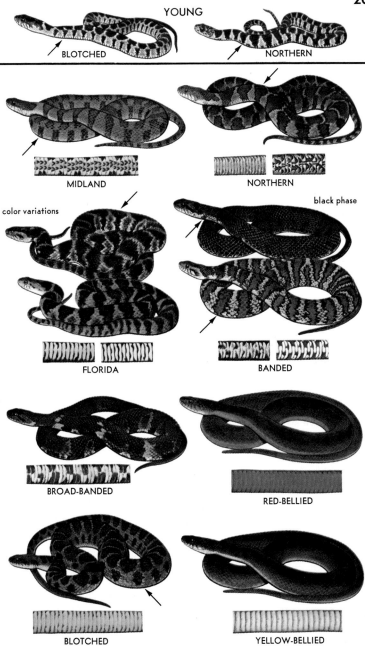

20

YOUNG

BLOTCHED

NORTHERN

MIDLAND

NORTHERN

color variations

FLORIDA

black phase

BANDED

BROAD-BANDED

RED-BELLIED

BLOTCHED

YELLOW-BELLIED

Plate 21
WATER SNAKES (*Natrix*) (2)
(See also Plate 20)

Keeled scales and divided anal plates. The rectangles
show belly colors and patterns.

	Map	Text

GRAHAM'S WATER SNAKE, *N. grahami* — Map 110, Text 150
Broad yellowish stripe. *Belly:* Plain or with a central
row of dark dots.

QUEEN SNAKE, *N. septemvittata* — Map 109, Text 149
Yellowish stripe. *Belly:* 4 brown stripes.

GLOSSY WATER SNAKE, *N. rigida* (ssp.) — Map 108, Text 150
Shiny, often with traces of stripes. *Belly:* Double row
of large black half-moons.

MANGROVE WATER SNAKE, — Map 101, Text 148
N. fasciata compressicauda
Irregular dark markings above and below; highly
variable (see text).
Red phase: Red or orange-red on both back and
belly.

GULF SALT MARSH SNAKE, *N. fasciata clarki* (ssp.) — Map 101, Text 147
2 *dark* stripes on each side of body. *Belly:* A row
of light spots (sometimes 3 rows).

HARTER'S WATER SNAKE, *N. harteri* (ssp.) — Map 102, Text 149
2 rows of spots on each side of body. *Belly:* Pink
center; row of dark dots down each side, but inconspicuous or even absent in one subspecies (see text).

GREEN WATER SNAKE, *N. cyclopion cyclopion* — Map 105, Text 139
No distinctive pattern; a row of scales between lip
plates and eye (Fig. 32, p. 140). *Belly:* Light half-
moons on dark ground.

FLORIDA GREEN WATER SNAKE, — Map 105, Text 140
N. cyclopion floridana
No distinctive pattern; a row of scales between lip
plates and eye (Fig. 32, p. 140). *Belly:* Light, virtually
unicolored.

DIAMONDBACK WATER SNAKE, — Map 104, Text 142
N. rhombifera rhombifera
Dark chainlike pattern (Fig. 33, p. 141). *Belly:*
Yellow, largest dark spots concentrated chiefly at
sides.

BROWN WATER SNAKE, *N. taxispilota* — Map 107, Text 141
Dark middorsal blotches separate from lateral
blotches (Fig. 33, p. 141). *Belly:* Heavy dark markings on yellow ground color.

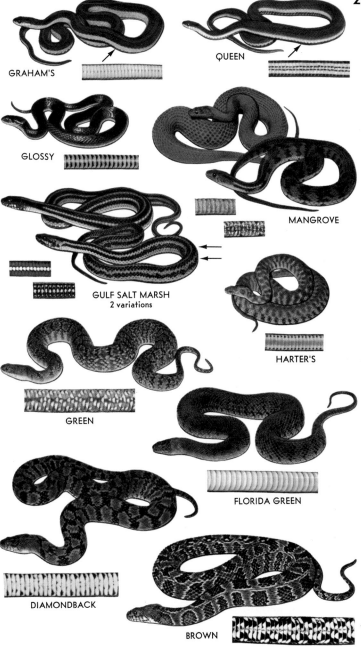

21

GRAHAM'S

QUEEN

GLOSSY

MANGROVE

GULF SALT MARSH
2 variations

HARTER'S

GREEN

FLORIDA GREEN

DIAMONDBACK

BROWN

Plate 22

SWAMP, BROWN, AND EARTH SNAKES

All have divided anal plates.

Map *Text*

KIRTLAND'S WATER SNAKE, *Natrix kirtlandi*   106   151
2 rows of large dark spots on each side of body; scales *keeled. Venter:* Brick-red with flanking rows of black spots.

SMOOTH EARTH SNAKE, *Virginia valeriae* (ssp.)   125   167
Tiny black dots on a plain gray or brown dorsum; loreal scale horizontal and touching eye (Fig. 55); scales *smooth* or *weakly keeled.*

ROUGH EARTH SNAKE, *Virginia striatula*   124   168
Head pointed; loreal scale horizontal and touching eye (Fig. 55); scales *keeled.*

NORTHERN BROWN SNAKE,   128   153
Storeria dekayi dekayi (ssp.)
Dark downward streak on side of head; no loreal (Fig. 55); scales *keeled. Young:* Light band across neck.

FLORIDA BROWN SNAKE, *Storeria dekayi victa*   128   155
Light band across head; no loreal (Fig. 55); scales *keeled.*

RED-BELLIED SNAKE,   127   156
Storeria occipitomaculata (ssp.)
Light spots on nape; coloration highly variable (see text); scales *keeled. Venter:* Bright red or orange-red.

BLACK SWAMP SNAKE, *Seminatrix pygaea* (ssp.)   112   152
Shiny black; scales *smooth* but with pale streaks that *look* like keels. *Venter:* Red; black encroaching on ends of ventral scales.

STRIPED SWAMP SNAKE, *Liodytes alleni*   111   152
A broad yellowish stripe on lower side; a dark stripe down back and another on each side of body; scales *smooth. Venter:* Plain yellow or orange or with a midventral row of dark spots (see text).

Fig. 55. LOREAL SCALES — PRESENT OR ABSENT

EARTH SNAKE
Loreal scale
horizontal and
touching eye

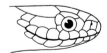

BROWN SNAKE
No loreal;
postnasal scale
touches preocular

GROUND SNAKE
A loreal scale
between postnasal
and preocular

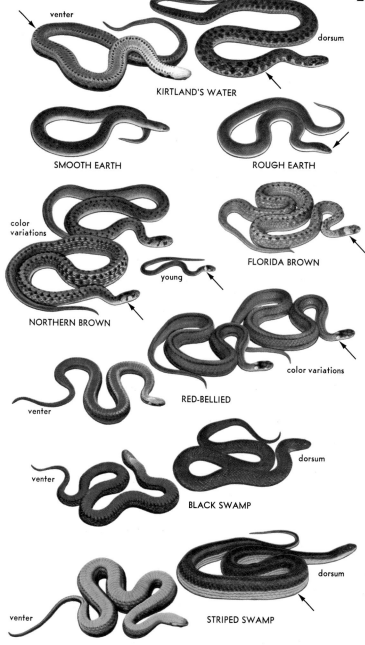

venter

dorsum

KIRTLAND'S WATER

SMOOTH EARTH

ROUGH EARTH

color variations

young

FLORIDA BROWN

NORTHERN BROWN

venter

color variations

RED-BELLIED

venter

dorsum

BLACK SWAMP

venter

dorsum

STRIPED SWAMP

Plate 23

GARTER AND RIBBON SNAKES
(*Thamnophis*)
(See also Plate 24)

Keeled scales and single anal plates. Ribbon Snakes are slender and their lateral stripes are on rows 3 and 4.

	Map	*Text*
EASTERN GARTER SNAKE, *T. sirtalis sirtalis* Stripe on rows 2 and 3; either stripes or spots may predominate. Some specimens are stripeless.	116	157
CHICAGO GARTER SNAKE, *T. sirtalis semifasciata* Black bars cross lateral stripe in neck region.	116	158
BLUE-STRIPED GARTER SNAKE, *T. sirtalis similis* Blue stripe on rows 2 and 3.	116	160
BUTLER'S GARTER SNAKE, *T. butleri* Small head; stripe on rows 2, 3, 4; scale rows 19.	113	161
SHORT-HEADED GARTER SNAKE, *T. brachystoma* Very small head; scale rows 17.	113	161
EASTERN RIBBON SNAKE, *T. sauritus sauritus* (ssp.) Long slender tail; stripe on rows 3 and 4; a dark ventrolateral stripe (see text).	119	164
WESTERN RIBBON SNAKE, *T. proximus proximus* (ssp). Like Eastern Ribbon Snake but without a dark ventrolateral stripe (see text).	120	165
RED-STRIPED RIBBON SNAKE, *T. proximus rubrilineatus* Red middorsal stripe.	120	166
BLUE-STRIPED RIBBON SNAKE, *T. sauritus nitae* Blue stripe on rows 3 and 4; an obscure middorsal stripe sometimes present.	119	165
PENINSULA RIBBON SNAKE, *T. sauritus sackeni* Dorsal stripe fainter than lateral stripes, or even lacking.	119	164

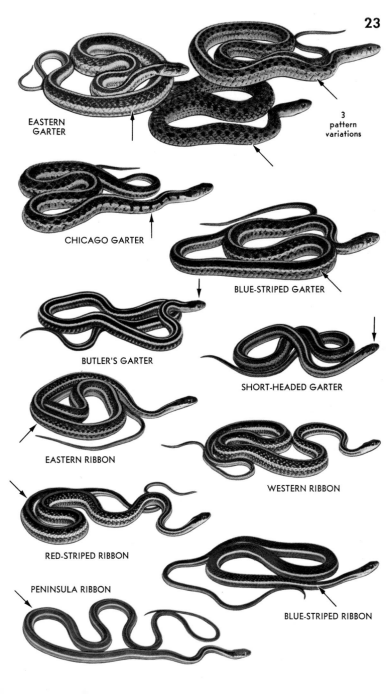

23

EASTERN
GARTER

3
pattern
variations

CHICAGO GARTER

BLUE-STRIPED GARTER

BUTLER'S GARTER

SHORT-HEADED GARTER

EASTERN RIBBON

WESTERN RIBBON

RED-STRIPED RIBBON

PENINSULA RIBBON

BLUE-STRIPED RIBBON

Plate 24
WESTERN GARTER SNAKES (*Thamnophis*)
(See also Plate 23)

Keeled scales and single anal plates.

	Map	Text

RED-SIDED GARTER SNAKE, *T. sirtalis parietalis*   116 158
  Red or orange bars; stripe on rows 2 and 3.

TEXAS GARTER SNAKE, *T. sirtalis annectens*   116 159
  Broad orange dorsal stripe; stripe on rows 2, 3, 4.

NEW MEXICO GARTER SNAKE, *T. sirtalis dorsalis*   116 159
  Red subdued and largely confined to skin between
  scales.

PLAINS GARTER SNAKE, *T. radix* (ssp.)   118 160
  Black bars on lips; stripe on rows 3 and 4.

CHECKERED GARTER SNAKE,   114 162
T. marcianus marcianus
  Checkerboard of black spots; light curved band
  behind mouth followed by broad black blotch.

WESTERN BLACK-NECKED GARTER SNAKE,   115 162
T. cyrtopsis cyrtopsis
  Black blotch at side of neck; lateral stripe on rows
  2 and 3.

EASTERN BLACK-NECKED GARTER SNAKE,   115 163
T. cyrtopsis ocellata
  Large black spots on neck; lateral stripe wavy.

WANDERING GARTER SNAKE, *T. elegans vagrans*   117 163
  8 upper labials and 21 scale rows at midbody. Variable; may be striped or spotted (see text).

LINED SNAKE, *Tropidoclonion lineatum* (ssp.)   123 166
  Double row of black half-moons on belly; small
  head; stripe on rows 2 and 3.

Fig. 56. POSITIONS OF LATERAL STRIPES (Numbers refer to scale rows)

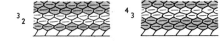 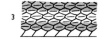

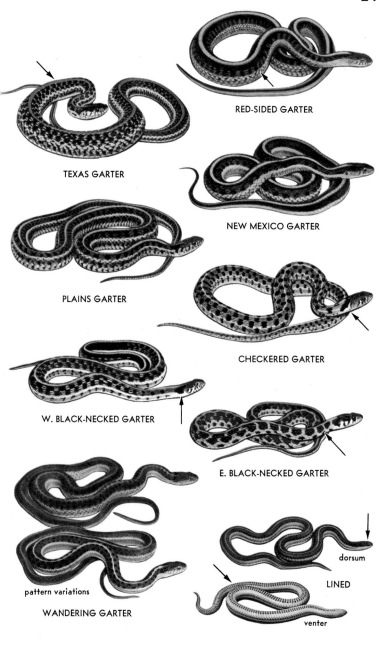

24

TEXAS GARTER

RED-SIDED GARTER

NEW MEXICO GARTER

PLAINS GARTER

CHECKERED GARTER

W. BLACK-NECKED GARTER

E. BLACK-NECKED GARTER

pattern variations

WANDERING GARTER

dorsum

LINED

venter

Plate 25

WOODLAND, HOGNOSE, AND MUD SNAKES

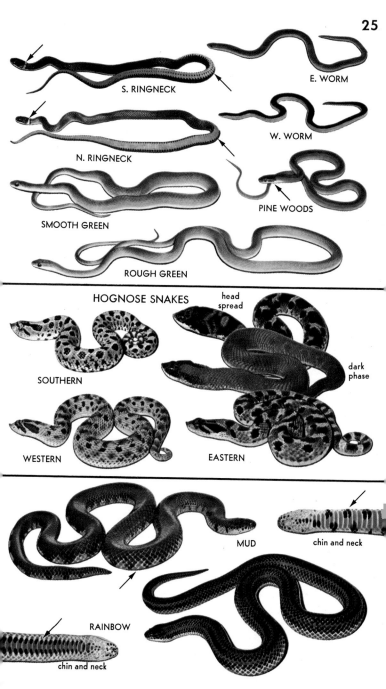

S. RINGNECK

E. WORM

N. RINGNECK

W. WORM

SMOOTH GREEN

PINE WOODS

ROUGH GREEN

HOGNOSE SNAKES

head spread

SOUTHERN

dark phase

WESTERN

EASTERN

MUD

chin and neck

RAINBOW

chin and neck

Plate 26

RACERS AND WHIPSNAKES
(*Coluber* and *Masticophis*)

All have smooth scales and divided anal plates.

	Map	Text

NORTHERN BLACK RACER (young)   139   178
  Dark middorsal blotches.

WESTERN COACHWHIP (young)   141   182
  Dark crosslines.

NORTHERN BLACK RACER,   139   178
C. constrictor constrictor (ssp.)
  Plain black above and below; some white on chin.

BLUE RACER, *C. constrictor foxi* (ssp.)   139   179
  Blue above, belly paler; dark area on side of head.
  (Everglades Racer may be very similar — see p. 179.)

EASTERN YELLOW-BELLIED RACER,   139   179
C. constrictor flaviventris (ssp.)
  Venter yellow; dorsal coloration variable (see text).

BUTTERMILK SNAKE, *C. constrictor anthicus* (ssp.)   139   181
  Irregular white, buff, or blue spots.

WESTERN COACHWHIP, *M. flagellum testaceus*   141   182
  Essentially plain brown above, but varying (see text);
  reddish in some parts of range, as in Texas Big Bend
  region. Tail like a braided whip.

EASTERN COACHWHIP, *M. flagellum flagellum*   141   181
  Head and body black or dark brown, changing to
  light brown posteriorly, but varying (see text).
  Black phase: Traces of light pattern; reddish on tail
  (see text).

CENTRAL TEXAS WHIPSNAKE,   140   183
M. taeniatus ornatus (ssp.)
  Longitudinal white patches on sides.

SCHOTT'S WHIPSNAKE, *M. taeniatus schotti*   140   183
  Striped on sides; reddish on neck; dorsal scales with
  light edges (Fig. 40, p. 180).

RUTHVEN'S WHIPSNAKE, *M. taeniatus ruthveni*   140   184
  Suggestion of stripes on sides; dorsal scales with light
  edges (Fig. 40, p. 180).

26

YOUNG

N. BLACK RACER

W. COACHWHIP

N. BLACK RACER

BLUE RACER

E. YELLOW-BELLIED RACER

BUTTERMILK

red phase

W. COACHWHIP

black phase

E. COACHWHIP

CENTRAL TEXAS WHIPSNAKE

SCHOTT'S WHIPSNAKE

RUTHVEN'S WHIPSNAKE

Plate 27

PINE, BULL, GLOSSY, AND INDIGO SNAKES

All have single anal plates.

| | Map | Text |

TEXAS GLOSSY SNAKE, — 145 197
Arizona elegans arenicola (ssp.)
    Brown blotches on ground of cream or buff; superficially like Bullsnake; scales *smooth*.

NORTHERN PINE SNAKE, — 147 199
Pituophis melanoleucus melanoleucus
    Black spots on white, yellowish, or pale gray; scales *keeled*.

BLACK PINE SNAKE, — 147 199
Pituophis melanoleucus lodingi
    Uniform black or dark brown; scales *keeled*.

FLORIDA PINE SNAKE, — 147 199
Pituophis melanoleucus mugitus
    Rusty-brown or brownish gray; blotches obscure toward front of body; scales *keeled*.

LOUISIANA PINE SNAKE, — 147 200
Pituophis melanoleucus ruthveni
    40 or fewer dark body blotches, these obscure and dark toward front of body, but clear-cut and often reddish on and near tail; no conspicuous head markings; scales *keeled*.

BULLSNAKE, *Pituophis melanoleucus sayi* — 147 200
    Dark line from eye to angle of jaw; 41 or more black or brown body blotches on a ground color of yellow; scales *keeled*.

TEXAS INDIGO SNAKE, — 144 187
Drymarchon corais erebennus
    Black lines on upper lip; traces of pattern on forepart of body; scales *smooth*.

EASTERN INDIGO SNAKE, — 144 186
Drymarchon corais couperi
    Plain shiny bluish black (chin and sides of head may be reddish- or orange-brown); scales *smooth*.

Fig. 57. PREFRONTAL SCALES

GLOSSY SNAKE

BULL AND PINE SNAKES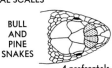

2 prefrontals   4 prefrontals

TEXAS GLOSSY

NORTHERN PINE

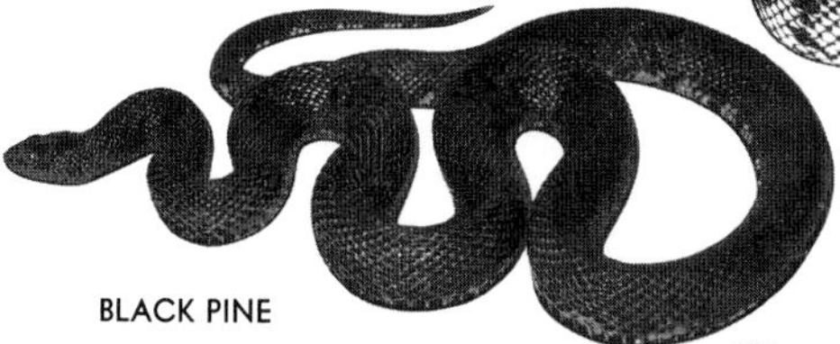

BLACK PINE

FLORIDA PINE

LOUISIANA PINE

BULL

TEXAS INDIGO

EASTERN INDIGO

Plate 28

RAT SNAKES (*Elaphe*)

(See also Plate 32)

All have weakly keeled scales and divided anal plates.

	Map	*Text*

CORN SNAKE, *E. guttata guttata* — Map 150, Text 190
Reddish blotches with black borders on a ground of gray, tan, yellow, or orange.

ROSY RAT SNAKE, *E. guttata rosacea* — Map 150, Text 191
Like Corn Snake but with black greatly reduced or absent.

GREAT PLAINS RAT SNAKE, *E. guttata emoryi* — Map 150, Text 191
Brown blotches on a gray ground; neck lines unite to form a spearpoint on head (Fig. 44, p. 191).

FOX SNAKE, *E. vulpina* (ssp.) — Map 148, Text 192
Dark brown blotches on a yellowish ground; no spearpoint on head (Fig. 44, p. 191).

BLACK RAT SNAKE, *E. obsoleta obsoleta* — Map 149, Text 193
Uniform black or with faint traces of spotted pattern; throat light. *Young:* Patterned like Gray Rat Snake (below).

"GREENISH RAT SNAKE" — Text 194
(Intergrade: *obsoleta* × *quadrivittata*)
4 dark stripes on a ground of dark olive-gray.

YELLOW RAT SNAKE, *E. obsoleta quadrivittata* — Map 149, Text 194
4 dark stripes on a ground of yellow to olive.

EVERGLADES RAT SNAKE, — Map 149, Text 195
E. obsoleta rossalleni (ssp.)
4 dark stripes on a ground of orange.

BAIRD'S RAT SNAKE, *E. obsoleta bairdi* — Map 149, Text 196
4 poorly defined dark stripes on a dark ground.

TEXAS RAT SNAKE, *E. obsoleta lindheimeri* — Map 149, Text 196
Brownish- or bluish-black blotches on a ground color of yellow or gray.

GRAY RAT SNAKE, *E. obsoleta spiloides* (ssp.) — Map 149, Text 195
Grayish in general appearance, but coloration variable (see text).

Fig. 58.
CROSS SECTIONS
OF SNAKES

RAT SNAKES
Like a
loaf of
bread

MOST OTHER
SNAKES
Body more
rounded

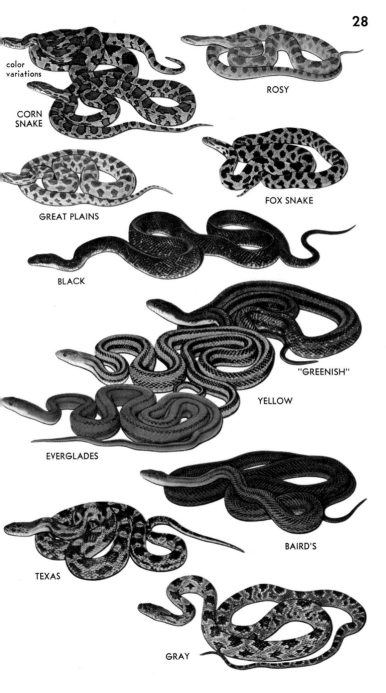

color variations

CORN SNAKE

ROSY

GREAT PLAINS

FOX SNAKE

BLACK

"GREENISH"

YELLOW

EVERGLADES

BAIRD'S

TEXAS

GRAY

Plate 29

KINGSNAKES (*Lampropeltis*)

All have smooth scales and single anal plates.

Spotted phase: Brown or reddish-brown blotches arranged in middorsal and flanking rows.
Dark phase: Pattern similar but obscure; a slight suggestion of dark longitudinal stripes.

Uniform brown or with well-separated dark spots; variable (see text).

Shiny black or dark brown with a bold chainlike pattern.

(Intergrade: *getulus* × *floridana*)
Light bands very wide; dark blotches broad and few in number. (Northern Florida and extreme southern Georgia)

(Intergrade: *getulus* × *floridana*)
Dark blotches small and numerous; highly variable (see text). (Florida peninsula)

Pale coloration; crosslined pattern only faintly indicated.

Salt-and-pepper effect.

Shiny black with a chainlike pattern faintly or incompletely indicated by white or yellow dots.

Black or dark brown dorsal blotches; sides of body speckled.

29

PRAIRIE

dark phase

spotted phase

MOLE SNAKE

EASTERN

"BLOTCHED"

"PENINSULA"

FLORIDA

SPECKLED

BLACK

DESERT

Plate 30

MILK SNAKES (*Lampropeltis*)

All have smooth scales and single anal plates.

	Map	Text

EASTERN MILK SNAKE, *L. triangulum triangulum* 153 205
A light Y or V at back of head; large dorsal blotches alternating with smaller lateral ones. *Young:* Blotches red.

"COASTAL PLAIN MILK SNAKE" 153 206
(Intergrade: *triangulum* × *elapsoides*)
A light collar; dorsal blotches reach belly scales on forepart of body; highly variable. (Mid-Atlantic region)

RED MILK SNAKE, *L. triangulum syspila* 153 206
A light collar; lateral blotches greatly reduced or absent. (Midwest)

LOUISIANA MILK SNAKE, *L. triangulum amaura* 153 208
Red rings broad (13 to 25); head black, snout normally light.

MEXICAN MILK SNAKE, *L. triangulum annulata* 153 208
Red rings broad (14 to 26); snout black; belly chiefly black.

CENTRAL PLAINS MILK SNAKE, 153 206
L. triangulum gentilis (ssp.)
Reddish rings narrow (20 to 39); head black, snout light.

CORAL SNAKE AND "MIMICS"

EASTERN CORAL SNAKE, *Micrurus fulvius fulvius** 175 224
Red and yellow rings touch; snout black.

SCARLET SNAKE, *Cemophora coccinea* (ssp.) 152 211
Red and yellow separated by black; belly whitish, unpatterned; snout red. (See also Plate 31.)

SCARLET KINGSNAKE, 153 209
Lampropeltis triangulum elapsoides
Red and yellow rings separated by black; rings enter upon or cross belly; snout red.

* Venomous.

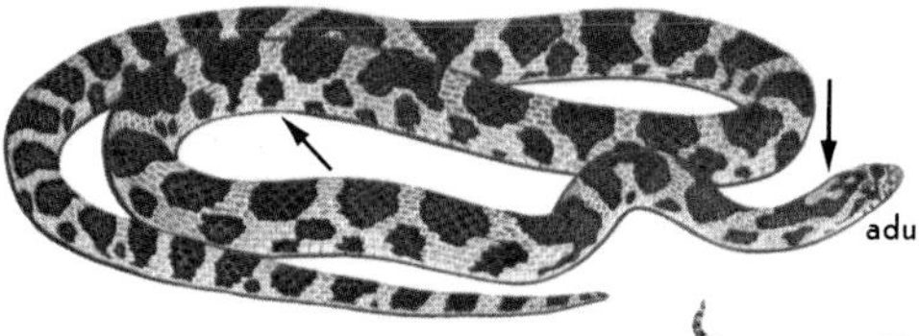

30

30

EASTERN

adult

young

"COASTAL PLAIN"

RED

LOUISIANA

CENTRAL
PLAINS

MEXICAN

EASTERN
CORAL

SCARLET

SCARLET
KING

Plate 31
GROUND, SHORT-TAILED, SCARLET, AND LONG-NOSED SNAKES

PATCH-NOSED SNAKES (*Salvadora*)

All have a slightly projecting flap at each side of rostral.

31

GROUND

3 variations

TRANS-PECOS GROUND

2 variations

MOLE
young

SHORT-TAILED

SCARLET

TEXAS LONG-NOSED

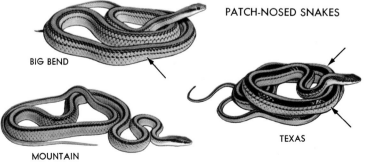

PATCH-NOSED SNAKES

BIG BEND

MOUNTAIN

TEXAS

Plate 32

SOME TEXAS SNAKE SPECIALTIES

    Head unicolored; black stripes on neck; dark
blotches posteriorly. (Western Texas)

Lampropeltis mexicana alterna
    Gray crossbands; varying amounts of red or orange
(these colors sometimes absent). (Western Texas)
Dark phase: Gray crossbands very dark.

Trimorphodon biscutatus vilkinsoni
    Dark brown saddles on a light brown (or gray)
ground color. Pupil elliptical in daylight. (Chihuahuan Desert)

Leptodeira septentrionalis septentrionalis
    Body crossed by bold black (or dark brown) saddles;
ground color often yellow, but variable from cream
to reddish tan. Pupil elliptical in daylight. (Extreme
southern Texas)

Drymobius margaritiferus margaritiferus
    Scales with light centers; dark stripe behind eye; a
few middorsal rows of scales with faint keels. (Extreme southern Texas)

Fig. 59. Several Mexican snakes enter Texas in the Chihuahuan
Desert of the Pecos River and Big Bend regions, and in
The Valley of the Rio Grande in the extreme south.

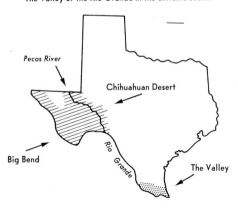

Pecos River

Chihuahuan Desert

Big Bend

Rio Grande

The Valley

32

TRANS-PECOS
RAT SNAKE

3 pattern variations

GRAY-BANDED
KINGSNAKE

TEXAS LYRE SNAKE

NORTHERN
CAT-EYED SNAKE

SPECKLED RACER

Plate 33
BLIND AND REAR-FANGED SNAKES
All have smooth scales.

Map Text

TEXAS BLIND SNAKE, *Leptotyphlops dulcis* (ssp.)   122 137
Wormlike; tail blunt; belly scales same size as those
on dorsum.

WESTERN HOOK-NOSED SNAKE, *Gyalopion canum*   161 217
Snout upturned; head strongly crossbanded.

MEXICAN HOOK-NOSED SNAKE, *Ficimia streckeri*   160 216
Snout upturned; head virtually unpatterned.

FLAT-HEADED SNAKE, *Tantilla gracilis*   169 221
Head nearly same color as body or only slightly
darker; upper labials usually 6.

SOUTHEASTERN CROWNED SNAKE,   163 219
Tantilla coronata
Light band across rear of head.

FLORIDA CROWNED SNAKE, *Tantilla relicta neilli*   164 220
No light band; black cap extends far back of head
scales.

PLAINS BLACK-HEADED SNAKE,   166 222
Tantilla nigriceps (ssp.)
Black pigmentation rounded or pointed on nape and
normally without dark downward extensions; upper
labials usually 7.

BLACK-HOODED SNAKE, *Tantilla rubra cucullata*   167 224
Black hood covers both dorsal and ventral surfaces
of head. Also has an interrupted ring-necked phase
(see text). (Trans-Pecos Texas)

DEVILS RIVER BLACK-HEADED SNAKE,   167 223
Tantilla rubra diabola
Light band across rear of head. (Western Texas)

MEXICAN BLACK-HEADED SNAKE, *Tantilla atriceps*   168 223
Rear of short black cap runs straight across.

SPOTTED NIGHT SNAKE,   170 217
Hypsiglena torquata ochrorhyncha
Dark neck blotch; general coloration pale.

TEXAS NIGHT SNAKE, *Hypsiglena torquata texana*   170 217
Dark neck blotch; profuse dark spots.

BLACK-STRIPED SNAKE,   136 216
Coniophanes imperialis imperialis
3 black (or dark brown) stripes on a ground color
of light brown; belly bright red or orange.

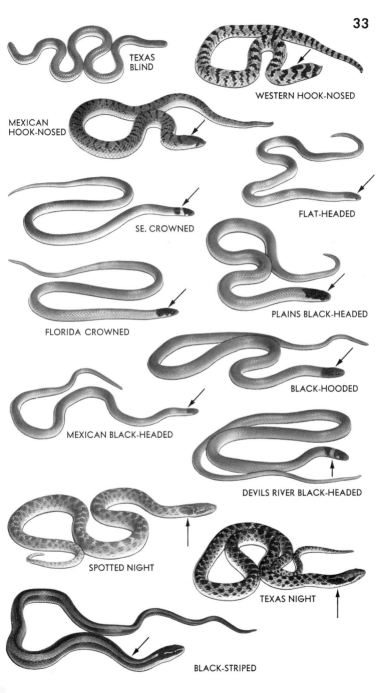

33

TEXAS BLIND

WESTERN HOOK-NOSED

MEXICAN HOOK-NOSED

SE. CROWNED

FLAT-HEADED

FLORIDA CROWNED

PLAINS BLACK-HEADED

BLACK-HOODED

MEXICAN BLACK-HEADED

DEVILS RIVER BLACK-HEADED

SPOTTED NIGHT

TEXAS NIGHT

BLACK-STRIPED

Plate 34

COPPERHEADS AND COTTONMOUTHS
(Agkistrodon)

	Map	Text

SOUTHERN COPPERHEAD, *A. contortrix contortrix* 174 227
Bands narrow along midline of back, often failing to meet; ground color pale.

NORTHERN COPPERHEAD, 174 226
A. contortrix mokasen (ssp.)
Coppery-red head; bands wide at sides of body, narrow across back.

BROAD-BANDED COPPERHEAD, 174 228
A. contortrix laticinctus
Bands broad, nearly as wide across back as on sides.

TRANS-PECOS COPPERHEAD, 174 228
A. contortrix pictigaster
Pale area at base of each broad band; belly strongly patterned.

FLORIDA COTTONMOUTH (young)* 173 229
Yellow tail tip; *broad* dark band through eye.

NORTHERN COPPERHEAD (young) 174 226
Yellow tail tip; *narrow* dark line through eye.

FLORIDA COTTONMOUTH, *A. piscivorus conanti** 173 229
Head markings well defined.

WESTERN COTTONMOUTH, 173 229
*A. piscivorus leucostoma**
Head markings obscure or absent; general coloration usually dark and body pattern indistinct.

EASTERN COTTONMOUTH, 173 228
*A. piscivorus piscivorus**
Head markings obscure; coloration variable — may be brown, black, or olive.

*Cottonmouths resemble many of the Water Snakes. On dead or captive specimens check heads and undersurfaces of tails (Fig. 60).

Fig. 60. COTTONMOUTH AND WATER SNAKES (*Natrix*)

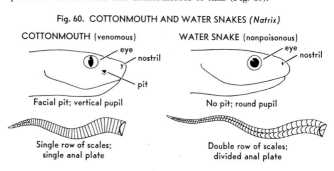

COTTONMOUTH (venomous)
eye
nostril
pit
Facial pit; vertical pupil

WATER SNAKE (nonpoisonous)
eye
nostril
No pit; round pupil

Single row of scales; single anal plate

Double row of scales; divided anal plate

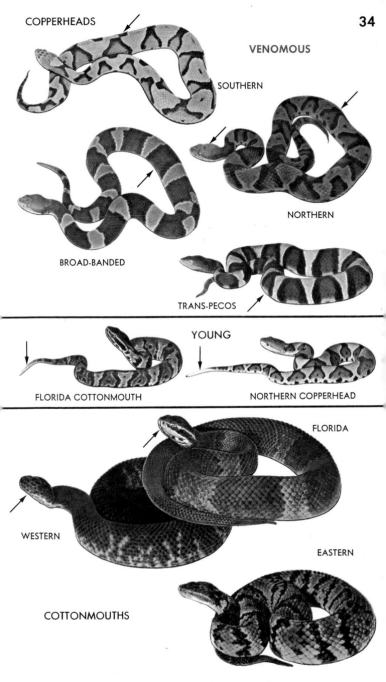

34

COPPERHEADS

VENOMOUS

SOUTHERN

NORTHERN

BROAD-BANDED

TRANS-PECOS

YOUNG

FLORIDA COTTONMOUTH

NORTHERN COPPERHEAD

FLORIDA

WESTERN

EASTERN

COTTONMOUTHS

Plate 35

RATTLESNAKES (*Sistrurus and Crotalus*)

(See also Plate 36)

	Map	Text

WESTERN PYGMY RATTLESNAKE,   177   233
S. miliarius streckeri
  Tiny rattle; slender tail; dark bars.

DUSKY PYGMY RATTLESNAKE, *S. miliarius barbouri*   177   233
  Tiny rattle; slender tail; rounded spots; dusty appearance.

CAROLINA PYGMY RATTLESNAKE,   177   232
S. miliarius miliarius
  Tiny rattle; slender tail; markings clear-cut; gray or reddish (see text).

WESTERN MASSASAUGA,   176   231
S. catenatus tergeminus (ssp.)
  Large rounded spots on a *pale* ground color; belly light (Fig. 71, p. 232).

EASTERN MASSASAUGA, *S. catenatus catenatus*   176   231
  Large rounded spots on a *medium to dark gray* ground color; belly mostly black (Fig. 71, p. 232).

EASTERN DIAMONDBACK RATTLESNAKE,   184   235
C. adamanteus
  Large, clear-cut, strongly outlined diamonds.

CANEBRAKE RATTLESNAKE, *C. horridus atricaudatus*   178   234
  Reddish-brown stripe; dark crossbands; dark postocular line (Fig. 72, p. 235).

TIMBER RATTLESNAKE, *C. horridus horridus*   178   233
  Yellow phase: Dark spots or crossbands; no head markings (Fig. 72, p. 235).
  Black phase: Black predominates (often all black).

Fig. 61. THE RATTLE — HALLMARK OF THE GROUP

| Button | Young rattle, tapering in size, button still retained | Old rattle, terminal joints broken off | Cross section showing interlinking arrangement |

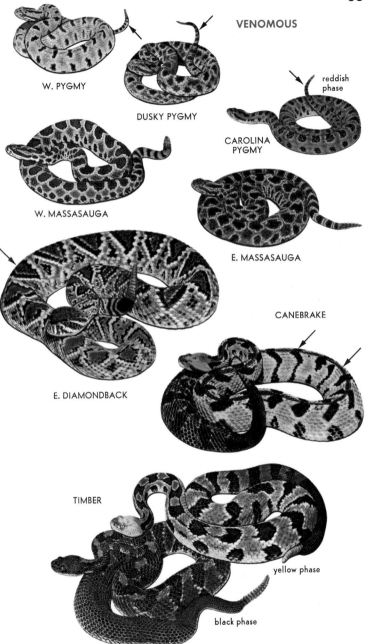

35

VENOMOUS

W. PYGMY

DUSKY PYGMY

CAROLINA PYGMY

reddish phase

W. MASSASAUGA

E. MASSASAUGA

E. DIAMONDBACK

CANEBRAKE

TIMBER

yellow phase

black phase

Plate 36
WESTERN RATTLESNAKES (*Crotalus*)
AND CORAL SNAKE
(See also Plate 35)

	Map	Text

BANDED ROCK RATTLESNAKE, *C. lepidus klauberi* 182 238
Conspicuous dark crossbars throughout length of
body; no dark stripe from eye to angle of mouth.

MOTTLED ROCK RATTLESNAKE, *C. lepidus lepidus* 182 238
Dark crossbars conspicuous only on rear of body;
dark stripe from eye to angle of mouth; coloration
variable (see text).

BLACK-TAILED RATTLESNAKE, *C. molossus molossus* 180 237
Black tail in strong contrast with body coloration.

PRAIRIE RATTLESNAKE, *C. viridis viridis* 179 237
Dark crossbars on rear of body; postocular light line
passes *above* corner of mouth (Fig. 72, p. 235).

MOJAVE RATTLESNAKE, *C. scutulatus scutulatus* 181 236
Black rings on tail much narrower than white rings;
postocular light line passes *above* corner of mouth
(Fig. 72, p. 235).

WESTERN DIAMONDBACK RATTLESNAKE, *C. atrox* 183 236
Black tail rings relatively broad; diamonds not clear-
cut; postocular light line reaches mouth in front of
back corner (Fig. 72, p. 235).

TEXAS CORAL SNAKE, *Micrurus fulvius tenere* 175 225
Red and yellow rings touch; snout black. (See also
Plate 30.)

36

BANDED ROCK

VENOMOUS

MOTTLED ROCK

color variations

BLACK-TAILED

color variations

MOJAVE

PRAIRIE

WESTERN DIAMONDBACK

TEXAS CORAL

Plate 37

GIANT SALAMANDERS

Waterdogs and Mudpuppy (*Necturus*)

All have external gills and 4 well-developed legs.

	Map	Text

GULF COAST WATERDOG, *N. beyeri*   195   244
Dark spots numerous and close together.

DWARF WATERDOG, *N. punctatus*   194   245
Almost uniformly dark above; paler below.

MUDPUPPY, *N. maculosus* (ssp.)   192   241
Dark spots few and well separated.

Sirens and Amphiuma

Eel-like salamanders with 2 or 4 legs.

LESSER SIREN, *Siren intermedia* (ssp.)   186   247
Tiny front legs; external gills; small size (see text).

GREATER SIREN, *Siren lacertina*   185   247
Small front legs; external gills; large size.

AMPHIUMA, *Amphiuma*   189   245
Tiny front *and* hind legs; no external gills. (Three 190   246
species, all virtually identical in gross appear- 191
ance — count number of toes on any one foot — see
text.)

Hellbenders (*Cryptobranchus*)

Broad, flat heads; folds of skin along sides.

HELLBENDER, *C. alleganiensis alleganiensis*   188   240
Dark markings few and small.

OZARK HELLBENDER, *C. alleganiensis bishopi*   188   241
Dark markings large and blotchlike.

Fig. 62. LARVAE OF MUDPUPPIES AND A WATERDOG

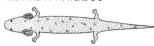

MUDPUPPY GROUP
(*maculosus*)
Striped

GULF COAST WATERDOG
(*beyeri*)
Spotted

37

GULF COAST WATERDOG

DWARF WATERDOG

MUDPUPPY

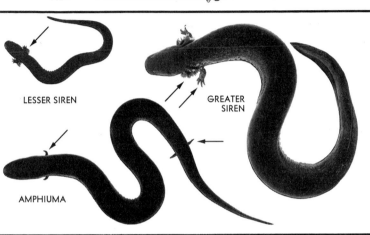

LESSER SIREN

GREATER SIREN

AMPHIUMA

HELLBENDER

OZARK HELLBENDER

Plate 38

MOLE SALAMANDERS (*Ambystoma*)

	Map	Text

FLATWOODS SALAMANDER, *A. cingulatum*   204 252
Variable: (a) irregularly "frosted," (b) narrow light
rings, or (c) tendency to form a netlike pattern.

MOLE SALAMANDER, *A. talpoideum*   200 251
Short, chunky body; large head.

MABEE'S SALAMANDER, *A. mabeei*   203 253
Profuse light speckling on sides; small head.

MARBLED SALAMANDER, *A. opacum*   211 251
White or silvery crossbars; black on lower sides and
belly.

SMALL-MOUTHED SALAMANDER, *A. texanum*   201 253
Very short snout; pattern variable.
Dark phase: Markings indistinct.
Speckled phase: Profuse lichenlike markings.

BLUE-SPOTTED SALAMANDER, *A. laterale*   208 254
Long toes; numerous blue or bluish-white spots and
flecks.

JEFFERSON SALAMANDER, *A. jeffersonianum*   206 254
Long toes; long snout; a few bluish flecks on sides.

RINGED SALAMANDER, *A. annulatum*   202 252
Bold light crossbands; light lateral stripe; head small.

SPOTTED SALAMANDER, *A. maculatum*   210 255
Round light spots in irregular dorsolateral row.

BARRED TIGER SALAMANDER,   205 256
A. tigrinum mavortium (ssp.)
Large light bars or blotches.

EASTERN TIGER SALAMANDER,   205 255
A. tigrinum tigrinum
Light markings small, not forming definite pattern.

Fig. 63. NEOTENIC ("AXOLOTL") FORM OF THE
BARRED TIGER SALAMANDER

38

FLATWOODS pattern variations

MOLE

MABEE'S

MARBLED

SMALL-MOUTHED

speckled phase

dark phase

BLUE-SPOTTED

JEFFERSON

RINGED

SPOTTED

BARRED TIGER

EASTERN TIGER

Plate 39

NEWTS (*Notophthalmus*)

	Map	Text
RED-SPOTTED NEWT, *N. viridescens viridescens*	198	257

RED-SPOTTED NEWT, *N. viridescens viridescens*   198   257
Red spots in all phases. *Red Eft* (land form): Red or orange, transforming to dark olive (or other colors — see text). *Aquatic ♀:* Olive; belly yellow, spotted with black. *Aquatic ♂* (in breeding condition): High tail fin; black horny growths on hind legs and toes.

BLACK-SPOTTED NEWT,   199   259
N. meridionalis meridionalis
Large scattered black spots; irregular yellowish stripes; orange venter.

STRIPED NEWT, *N. perstriatus*   197   259
Red stripe.

BROKEN-STRIPED NEWT, *N. viridescens dorsalis*   198   258
Red stripe broken into dots and dashes.

CENTRAL NEWT, *N. viridescens louisianensis*   198   258
Dorsal and ventral coloration in sharp contrast; normally no red markings.

PENINSULA NEWT, *N. viridescens piaropicola*   198   258
Dorsum very dark; belly peppered with black.

NEOTENIC SALAMANDERS

TEXAS BLIND SALAMANDER, *Typhlomolge rathbuni*   251   295
Toothpick legs; pale coloration; gills evident.

GROTTO SALAMANDER, *Typhlotriton spelaeus*   248   296
Pale coloration; no gills. *Larva:* High tail fin; longitudinal streaks on sides; gills evident.

SAN MARCOS SALAMANDER, *Eurycea nana*   250   293
Brown; a row of small light spots; gills evident.

TEXAS SALAMANDER, *Eurycea neotenes* (ssp.)   247   293
Yellowish; rows of light spots; gills evident.

OKLAHOMA SALAMANDER, *Eurycea tynerensis*   245   292
Gray above, lighter below; gills evident.

SLENDER DWARF SIREN,   187   250
Pseudobranchus striatus spheniscus (ssp.)
Tiny forelimbs; no hind limbs; gills evident; yellowish side stripes; darker stripes above.

NARROW-STRIPED DWARF SIREN,   187   249
Pseudobranchus striatus axanthus
Similar to Slender Dwarf Siren, but general coloration grayish with faint stripes.

TENNESSEE CAVE SALAMANDER,   223   285
Gyrinophilus palleucus (ssp.)
Flesh-colored; gills evident; large tail fin.

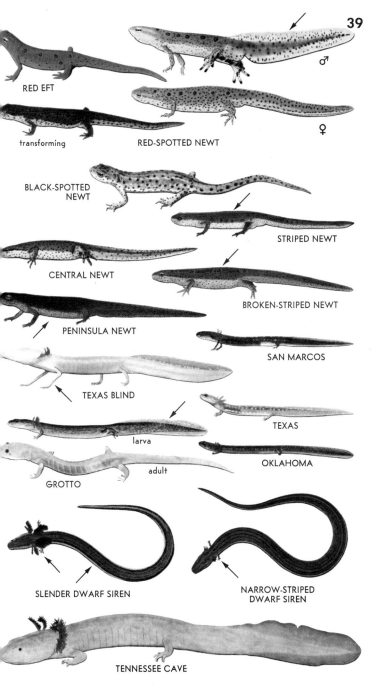

39

RED EFT

♂

♀

transforming

RED-SPOTTED NEWT

BLACK-SPOTTED NEWT

STRIPED NEWT

CENTRAL NEWT

BROKEN-STRIPED NEWT

PENINSULA NEWT

SAN MARCOS

TEXAS BLIND

TEXAS

larva

OKLAHOMA

adult

GROTTO

SLENDER DWARF SIREN

NARROW-STRIPED DWARF SIREN

TENNESSEE CAVE

Plate 40
WOODLAND SALAMANDERS
(chiefly *Plethodon*)

Extremely variable. Includes "Clemson," "Metcalf's," "Red-legged," "Red-cheeked," and other pattern phases that were previously assigned to subspecific status (see text).

(a pattern phase of *Desmognathus ochrophaeus*)
Light cheek patch; suggestion of line from eye to angle of jaw. Seepage areas or wet environment.

4 toes on *hind* foot; constriction at base of tail; belly white with black spots (Fig. 86, p. 274).

Gold or silver blotches.

Numerous small gold flecks; belly *black.*

Salt-and-pepper effect on belly (Fig. 86, p. 274).
Lead-backed: Dorsum nearly plain dark.
Red-backed: Straight-edged middorsal stripe.

Zigzag or irregular middorsal stripe.

Salt-and-pepper effect. Identify by range.

Chestnut with white specks; variable (see text).

Varying amounts of chestnut; light lateral stripe bordered above chiefly by dark pigment.

Red or chestnut dorsum; light lateral stripe.

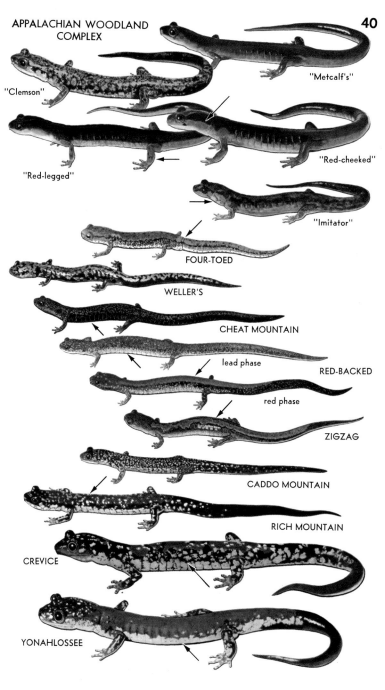

APPALACHIAN WOODLAND COMPLEX

40

"Clemson"

"Metcalf's"

"Red-legged"

"Red-cheeked"

"Imitator"

FOUR-TOED

WELLER'S

CHEAT MOUNTAIN

lead phase

RED-BACKED

red phase

ZIGZAG

CADDO MOUNTAIN

RICH MOUNTAIN

CREVICE

YONAHLOSSEE

Plate 41

WOODLAND AND DUSKY SALAMANDERS

Woodland Species (*Plethodon*)

Most of these are blackish with light markings.

	Map	Text

WEHRLE'S SALAMANDER, *P. wehrlei* — 232 277
White, bluish-white, or yellow spots along sides.
Dixie Caverns phase: Small white flecks and bronzy mottling on purplish-brown background.

RAVINE SALAMANDER, *P. richmondi* — 231 274
Long, slender body; no conspicuous markings; belly dark (Fig. 86, p. 274).

WHITE-THROATED SLIMY SALAMANDER, — 230 277
P. glutinosus albagula
Bulk of white spots along sides; throat light.

SLIMY SALAMANDER, *P. glutinosus glutinosus* — 230 276
Numerous white spots or brassy flecks or both; throat dark.

Dusky (*Desmognathus*) and Allied Species

Usually a diagonal light line behind eye in most species.

SEAL SALAMANDER, *D. monticola* (ssp.) — 216 265
Heavy dark markings on dorsum; venter pale.

NORTHERN DUSKY SALAMANDER, *D. fuscus fuscus* — 213 261
Markings extremely variable (see text); venter lightly pigmented.

BLACK-BELLIED SALAMANDER, *D. quadramaculatus* — 214 266
2 rows of light dots on sides; venter black.

SHOVEL-NOSED SALAMANDER, — 226 270
Leurognathus marmoratus
Spotted or blotched, but markings extremely variable (see text). Check internal openings of nostrils if in doubt (Fig. 84, p. 270).

RED HILLS SALAMANDER, *Phaeognathus hubrichti* — 227 271
Very long body; small legs; uniformly very dark brown with no markings of any kind.

Fig. 64. BASIC DIFFERENCES BETWEEN THE TWO GENERA

WOODLAND SALAMANDER
Legs approximately
same size

DUSKY SALAMANDER
Hind legs larger than forelegs;
light line from eye to angle of jaw

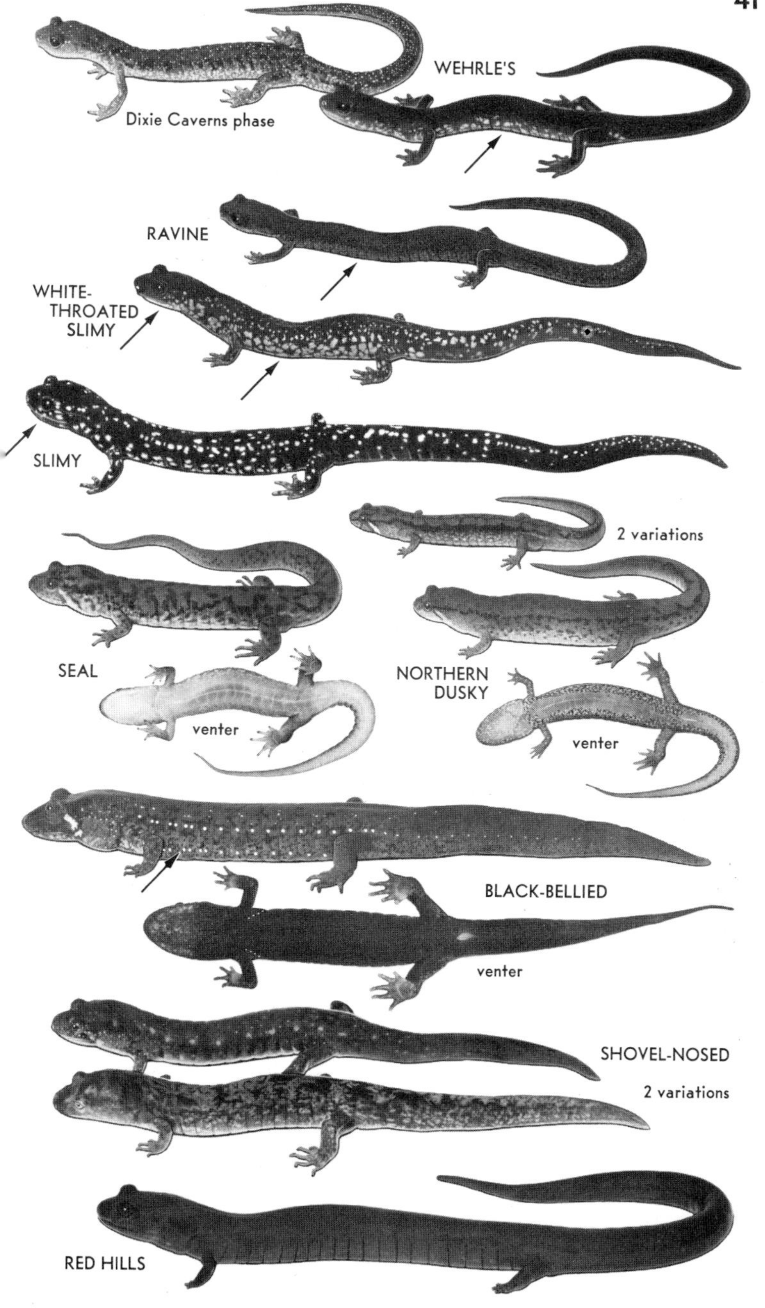

WEHRLE'S

Dixie Caverns phase

RAVINE

WHITE-
THROATED
SLIMY

SLIMY

SEAL

NORTHERN
DUSKY

2 variations

venter

venter

BLACK-BELLIED

venter

SHOVEL-NOSED

2 variations

RED HILLS

Plate 42

DUSKY SALAMANDERS (*Desmognathus*)

RED AND MUD SALAMANDERS (*Pseudotriton*)

SPRING SALAMANDERS (*Gyrinophilus*)

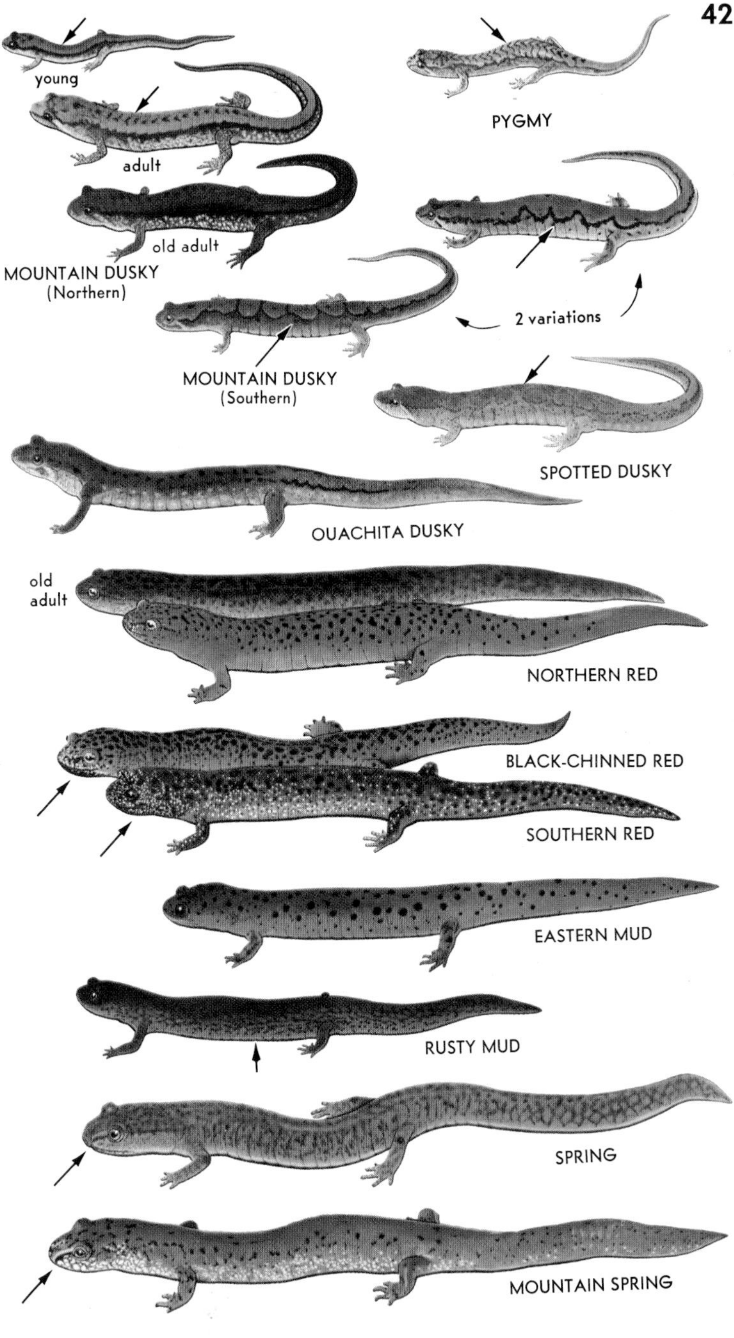

42

young

adult

old adult

MOUNTAIN DUSKY
(Northern)

MOUNTAIN DUSKY
(Southern)

PYGMY

2 variations

SPOTTED DUSKY

OUACHITA DUSKY

old adult

NORTHERN RED

BLACK-CHINNED RED

SOUTHERN RED

EASTERN MUD

RUSTY MUD

SPRING

MOUNTAIN SPRING

Plate 43

BROOK SALAMANDERS (*Eurycea*)

	Map	Text

BLUE RIDGE TWO-LINED SALAMANDER,   240   289
E. bislineata wilderae
    Bright coloration; dark lines clear-cut. ♂: Conspicuous downward projection from nostril.

NORTHERN TWO-LINED SALAMANDER,   240   288
E. bislineata bislineata (ssp.)
    Dark line from eye to tail; belly yellow.

BROWN-BACKED SALAMANDER, *E. aquatica*   241   290
    Brown back; dusky-black sides; relatively short tail.

MANY-RIBBED SALAMANDER,   242   290
E. multiplicata multiplicata
    Light spots in dark lateral stripe (see text).

GRAY-BELLIED SALAMANDER,   242   290
E. multiplicata griseogaster
    Dark venter; trace of tan on dorsum (see text).

DWARF SALAMANDER, *E. quadridigitata*   246   292
    4 toes on *hind* foot; dark dorsolateral stripe.

CAVE SALAMANDER, *E. lucifuga*   243   292
    Tail long; black spots on orange or reddish ground color.

LONG-TAILED SALAMANDER,   244   291
E. longicauda longicauda
    Tail long, with "dumbbells" or herringbone pattern.

DARK-SIDED SALAMANDER,   244   291
E. longicauda melanopleura
    Tail long; sides marked with gray and yellow.

THREE-LINED SALAMANDER,   244   291
E. longicauda guttolineata
    Tail long; a middorsal dark stripe.

GREEN AND MANY-LINED SALAMANDERS

GREEN SALAMANDER, *Aneides aeneus*   221   283
    Green, lichenlike markings.

MANY-LINED SALAMANDER,   228   282
Stereochilus marginatus
    Light and dark streaks on lower sides; small head; short tail.

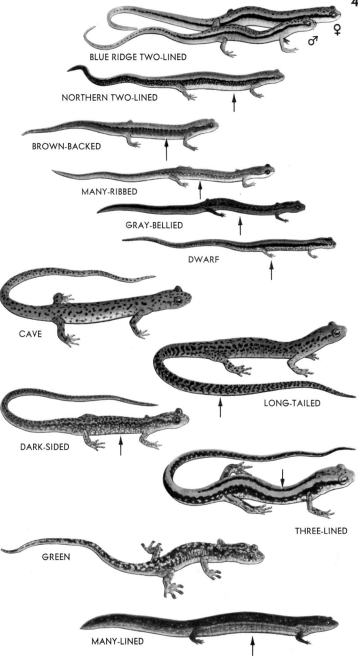

43

BLUE RIDGE TWO-LINED

♀
♂

NORTHERN TWO-LINED

BROWN-BACKED

MANY-RIBBED

GRAY-BELLIED

DWARF

CAVE

LONG-TAILED

DARK-SIDED

THREE-LINED

GREEN

MANY-LINED

Plate 44

SPADEFOOT TOADS (*Scaphiopus*)

A single sharp-edged spade under each hind foot.

	Map	Text
COUCH'S SPADEFOOT, *S. couchi*	256	300
Dark irregular pattern on yellowish or greenish ground color; variable (see text).		
HURTER'S SPADEFOOT, *S. holbrooki hurteri*	253	299
Light dorsal lines; boss between eyes (Fig. 92, p. 301).		
EASTERN SPADEFOOT, *S. holbrooki holbrooki*	253	299
Light lines in form of lyre.		
PLAINS SPADEFOOT, *S. bombifrons*	252	301
Faint longitudinal light stripes; boss between eyes (Fig. 92, p. 301).		
WESTERN SPADEFOOT, *S. hammondi*	254	301
Gray or brown with small dark markings.		

TRUE TOADS (*Bufo*)

(See also Plate 46)

Two tubercles under hind foot — spadelike in some species.

SOUTHERN TOAD, *B. terrestris*	263	307
Prominent cranial knobs (Fig. 95, p. 308).		
AMERICAN TOAD, *B. americanus* (ssp.)	261	306
1 or 2 large warts in each dark spot.		
CANADIAN TOAD, *B. hemiophrys hemiophrys*	260	309
Boss between eyes (Fig. 92, p. 301).		
GULF COAST TOAD, *B. valliceps*	270	311
Broad dark lateral stripe bordered above by light stripe.		
FOWLER'S TOAD, *B. woodhousei fowleri*	265	310
3 or more warts in each dark spot.		
WOODHOUSE'S TOAD,	265	309
B. woodhousei woodhousei (ssp.)		
Warts in dark spots variable in number (see text).		
RED-SPOTTED TOAD, *B. punctatus*	269	314
Parotoid rounded; no middorsal light stripe.		
TEXAS TOAD, *B. speciosus*	268	313
Parotoid oval; no middorsal light stripe.		
GREAT PLAINS TOAD, *B. cognatus*	266	312
Large dark blotches with light borders.		
GIANT TOAD, *B. marinus*	264	315
Parotoid enormously enlarged.		

SPADEFOOT TOADS

44

COUCH'S

HURTER'S

EASTERN

PLAINS

WESTERN

SOUTHERN

AMERICAN

CANADIAN

GULF COAST

FOWLER'S

WOODHOUSE'S

RED-SPOTTED

TEXAS

GREAT PLAINS

GIANT

Plate 45

NARROW-MOUTHED TOADS AND TROPICAL FROGS

	Map	Text

GREAT PLAINS NARROW-MOUTHED TOAD, — 258 335
Gastrophryne olivacea
  Plain gray, tan, or greenish and with or without small black spots.

EASTERN NARROW-MOUTHED TOAD, — 255 334
Gastrophryne carolinensis
  Broad light dorsolateral stripe; center of back dark. *Key West phases:* Dorsolateral stripe reddish; dorsum brown or tan.

SHEEP FROG, *Hypopachus variolosus* — 259 336
  Yellow streak down back.

MEXICAN BURROWING TOAD, — 257 297
Rhinophrynus dorsalis
  Rotund body; orange middorsal stripe (buff in young).

MEXICAN CLIFF FROG, *Syrrhophus guttilatus* — 296 304
  Dark bar between eyes; wormlike dark pattern. (Big Bend of Texas)

CLIFF FROG, *Syrrhophus marnocki* — 295 304
  Pale greenish; numerous dark markings but no definite pattern; skin smooth.

RIO GRANDE FROG, — 297 304
Syrrhophus cystignathoides campi
  Usually grayish brown or grayish olive; dark shadow from eye to nostril; legs crossbarred.

GREENHOUSE FROG, — 294 303
Eleutherodactylus planirostris planirostris
  Reddish; pattern striped or spotted.

BARKING FROG, *Hylactophryne augusti latrans* — 293 303
  Toadlike but no warts; very large forearm; a lateral fold.

WHITE-LIPPED FROG, *Leptodactylus labialis* — 298 302
  Light line on lip; a ventral disc (Fig. 93, p. 302).

NARROW-MOUTHED TOADS

45

GREAT PLAINS

EASTERN   EASTERN – Key West phases

SHEEP FROG

MEXICAN BURROWING TOAD

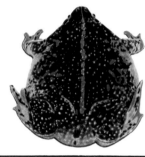

pattern phases

MEXICAN CLIFF   CLIFF   RIO GRANDE   GREENHOUSE

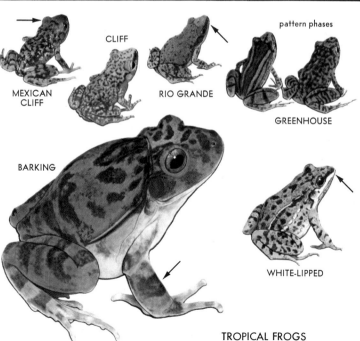

BARKING

WHITE-LIPPED

TROPICAL FROGS

Plate 46

CHORUS FROGS (*Pseudacris*)

	Map	Text
BOREAL CHORUS FROG, *P. triseriata maculata*	289	329

BOREAL CHORUS FROG, *P. triseriata maculata*   289   329
Pattern striped; leg short.

WESTERN CHORUS FROG,   289   327
P. triseriata triseriata (ssp.)
Pattern striped (Fig. 98, p. 328); leg long.

BRIMLEY'S CHORUS FROG, *P. brimleyi*   290   331
Side stripe black; dorsal stripes brown or gray; dark spots on chest.

UPLAND CHORUS FROG, *P. triseriata feriarum*   289   329
Pattern spotted or weakly striped (Fig. 98, p. 328).

SOUTHERN CHORUS FROG, *P. nigrita nigrita*   288   330
White line on lip; dorsal stripes broad but broken.

FLORIDA CHORUS FROG, *P. nigrita verrucosa*   288   330
3 rows of black spots; lip spotted black and white.

MOUNTAIN CHORUS FROG, *P. brachyphona*   285   332
Dorsal stripes curved and bending toward center (Fig. 98, p. 328); triangle between eyes.

ORNATE CHORUS FROG, *P. ornata*   287   332
Bold black spots on side and near groin.

SPOTTED CHORUS FROG, *P. clarki*   286   331
Markings green; triangle between eyes; pattern usually spotted, rarely striped.

STRECKER'S CHORUS FROG, *P. streckeri* (ssp.)   284   333
Dark spot below eye; foreleg very stout.

CRICKET FROGS (*Acris*)

NORTHERN CRICKET FROG, *A. crepitans crepitans*   291   317
Short leg; dark triangle between eyes.

SOUTHERN CRICKET FROG, *A. gryllus gryllus*   292   317
Long leg; dark triangle between eyes.

BLANCHARD'S CRICKET FROG,   291   318
A. crepitans blanchardi
Plump, stocky body; dark triangle between eyes.

TOADS (*Bufo*)
(See also Plate 44)

WESTERN GREEN TOAD, *B. debilis insidior*   267   314
Green; a black netlike pattern on at least part of body; skin warty.

EASTERN GREEN TOAD, *B. debilis debilis*   267   314
Green, spotted with black and yellow; skin warty.

OAK TOAD, *B. quercicus*   271   312
Paired black spots, light middorsal stripe.

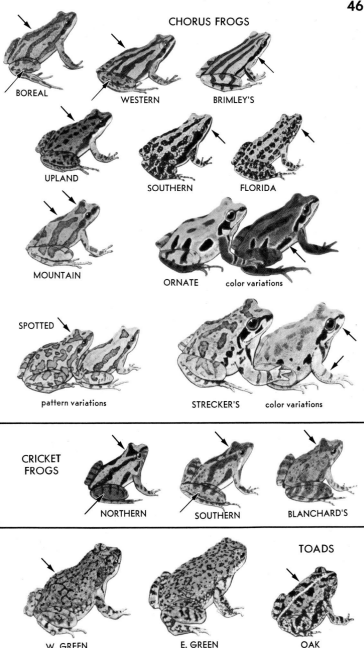

46

CHORUS FROGS

BOREAL

WESTERN

BRIMLEY'S

UPLAND

SOUTHERN

FLORIDA

MOUNTAIN

ORNATE   color variations

SPOTTED

pattern variations

STRECKER'S   color variations

CRICKET FROGS

NORTHERN

SOUTHERN

BLANCHARD'S

TOADS

W. GREEN

E. GREEN

OAK

Plate 47

TREEFROGS (chiefly *Hyla*)

	Map	Text
PINE WOODS TREEFROG, *H. femoralis*	277	322

Dark dorsal blotches; light spots on concealed surface of thigh (Fig. 96, p. 316).

	Map	Text
SQUIRREL TREEFROG, *H. squirella*	276	322

Green or brown or combinations of both; highly variable (see text).

	Map	Text
SPRING PEEPER, *H. crucifer* (ssp.)	273	319

Dark X-shaped mark on back.

	Map	Text
PINE BARRENS TREEFROG, *H. andersoni*	279	320

Whitish (or yellowish) and purplish stripes.

	Map	Text
GREEN TREEFROG, *H. cinerea*	274	320

Light stripe on body highly variable in length; completely absent in some individuals.

	Map	Text
GRAY TREEFROG,	278	323

H. versicolor and *H. chrysoscelis*
Light spot below eye; concealed surfaces of hind legs washed with orange.

	Map	Text
BIRD-VOICED TREEFROG, *H. avivoca* (ssp.)	275	324

Light spot below eye; concealed surfaces of hind legs washed with green or yellowish white.

	Map	Text
CANYON TREEFROG, *H. arenicolor*	280	325

Dark bar below eye. (Trans-Pecos Texas)

	Map	Text
BARKING TREEFROG, *H. gratiosa*	272	321

Profusion of dark rounded spots.

	Map	Text
CUBAN TREEFROG, *H. septentrionalis*	282	325

Large toe discs; warty skin.

	Map	Text
MEXICAN TREEFROG, *Smilisca baudini*	281	326

Light spot below eye; black patch on shoulder behind eardrum.

	Map	Text
LITTLE GRASS FROG, *Limnaoedus ocularis*	283	326

Tiny size; dark line through eye; pattern and coloration variable (see text).

47

PINE WOODS SQUIRREL color variations SPRING PEEPER

PINE BARRENS

GREEN

pattern variations

GRAY

BIRD-VOICED

CANYON

pattern variations

BARKING

color variations

CUBAN

MEXICAN

LITTLE GRASS FROG

Plate 48

TRUE FROGS (Rana)

Most of these have dorsolateral ridges — see back endpaper.

	Map	Text
CARPENTER FROG, *R. virgatipes** 2 golden-brown lateral stripes.	311	340
MINK FROG, *R. septentrionalis** Mottled or spotted pattern (Fig. 103, p. 342); often no ridges; musky odor. (Far northern range)	308	342
WOOD FROG, *R. sylvatica* Dark mask through eye.	309	343
PICKEREL FROG, *R. palustris* Squarish dark spots; bright yellow or orange on concealed surfaces of hind legs.	307	347
NORTHERN LEOPARD FROG, *R. pipiens* Rounded dark spots; variable (see text).	303	344
SOUTHERN LEOPARD FROG, *R. utricularia* Often a light spot on eardrum; pointed snout.	305	345
RIO GRANDE LEOPARD FROG, *R. berlandieri* Pallid coloration; dorsolateral ridges offset (Fig. 104, p. 346).	306	346
FLORIDA GOPHER FROG, *R. areolata aesopus* Stubby; irregular markings on light ground.	310	349
DUSKY GOPHER FROG, *R. areolata sevosa* (ssp.) Stubby, dark; venter spotted (Fig. 105, p. 348).	310	349
CRAWFISH FROG, *R. areolata* (ssp.) Stubby; dark spots rounded and with light borders; venter mostly without markings (Fig. 105, p. 348).	310	348
BRONZE FROG, *R. clamitans clamitans** General bronzy coloration.	299	340
GREEN FROG, *R. clamitans melanota** Bright green and brown; highly variable (see text).	299	341
RIVER FROG, *R. heckscheri** Dark appearance; white spots on lips; no ridges; river-swamp habitat. (See also Fig. 102, p. 339.)	300	339
PIG FROG, *R. grylio** Pointed snout; 4th toe extends only slightly beyond webbing (Fig. 101, p. 338); no ridges.	301	339
BULLFROG, *R. catesbeiana** 4th toe extends well beyond webbing (Fig. 101, p. 338); no ridges; pattern variable (see text).	302	338

* The tympanum (eardrum) is larger than the eye in males, and only the size of the eye or smaller in females.

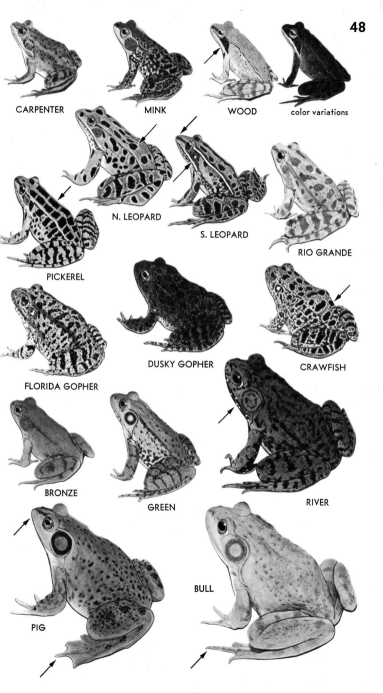

48

CARPENTER

MINK

WOOD

color variations

N. LEOPARD

S. LEOPARD

RIO GRANDE

PICKEREL

DUSKY GOPHER

CRAWFISH

FLORIDA GOPHER

BRONZE

GREEN

RIVER

PIG

BULL

head — and the vernacular name "adder" doesn't help, either. Sometimes called "house snake," but "barn snake" would be more descriptive, because it would reflect the frequency with which farm buildings are entered in search of rodents. Many habitats are utilized — fields, woodlands, rocky hillsides, river bottoms, etc., from virtually sea level to high up in mountains. Usually secretive and found hiding under logs, boards, stones, etc.

Similar species: (1) Copperhead has coppery, virtually unmarked head, single row of dorsal crossbands, and a belly that is *not* checkerboarded. (2) Water Snakes have *keeled* scales and *divided* anals. (3) Racers and Rat Snakes, the young of which are spotted, have *divided* anals. (4) Scarlet Snake has plain (unpatterned) belly. (5) Dark markings of Mole Snake are well separated from one another (Plates 29 and 31).

Range: Maine to Minnesota; south in uplands to n. Alabama. Intergrades with Scarlet Kingsnake from s. New Jersey to ne. N. Carolina (see p. 209); specimens from that area exhibit a wide variety of patterns and various shades of reds and browns; one is illustrated on Plate 30 as the "coastal plain milk snake."

Map 153

RED MILK SNAKE   Pl. 30
Lampropeltis triangulum syspila
Identification: 21–28 in. (53–71 cm); record 42 in. (106.7 cm). Also called "red snake" and "candy-cane snake." A reddish serpent with larger and fewer markings than Eastern Milk Snake. The middorsal blotches extend well down onto sides of body and the lateral blotches are small or virtually absent, at least in the neck region. Whitish or yellowish collar usually conspicuous. Belly boldly checked with black on white. Scales *smooth;* anal *single.*

Habitats vary from woodlands and rocky hillsides to open farming country.

Similar species: (1) In Corn Snake and Great Plains Rat Snake there is a spearpoint between the eyes (Fig. 44, p. 191), and underside of tail is striped (Fig. 43, p. 190). (2) In Prairie Kingsnake, blotches are brown, and belly markings are brown or yellowish brown. (3) See also **Similar species** under Eastern Milk Snake (above).

Range: Midland America from s. Indiana to nw. Mississippi and west to a line extending from extr. se. S. Dakota to e. Oklahoma.

Map 153

CENTRAL PLAINS MILK SNAKE   Pl. 30
Lampropeltis triangulum gentilis
Identification: 16–24 in. (41–61 cm); record 36 in. (91.4 cm). This "Western Milk Snake" has a higher average number of red or orange rings (20 to 39) on the body than either the Louisiana

Milk Snake or Mexican Milk Snake. The light rings vary from pale gray to yellow or greenish yellow, or are sometimes nearly white. The black pigment crosses the red rings on the belly (Fig. 65, below), and in some specimens it also cuts (sometimes completely) across the red rings middorsally, especially on posterior part of body. Head black; snout light. Scales *smooth,* in 21 or more rows at midbody; anal *single.*

Occupies a wide range of habitats — open prairies, wooded stream valleys, rocky canyons, mountain slopes, etc.

Similar species: (1) The 2 warning colors — red and yellow — touch in Coral Snake. (2) Scarlet Snake has plain whitish belly. (3) Long-nosed Snake has broad black markings sprinkled with yellow spots, and its subcaudals are mostly in a single row (in two rows in Milk Snakes and most other snakes). (4) Ground Snake has 15 rows of scales at midbody.

Range: Most of Kansas and Oklahoma to cen. Colorado.

Subspecies: PALE MILK SNAKE, *Lampropeltis t. multistrata.* Similar but paler, the black areas reduced in size and the red replaced by orange (rings 22 to 38); snout orange, with scattered black flecks; midventral area immaculate white or whitish with

Fig. 65. DIAGRAMMATIC VENTRAL PATTERNS OF SNAKES
BOLDLY RINGED OR BLOTCHED
WITH RED, YELLOW, AND BLACK

Red
(or orange)

Yellow
(or white)

Black

CORAL
(Micrurus fulvius)
Danger! Red and yellow touch

EASTERN MILK
(Lampropeltis t. triangulum)
Checkerboard effect

SCARLET KING
(L. t. elapsoides)
Red and yellow separated by black

CENTRAL PLAINS MILK
(L. t. gentilis)
H-shaped effect

LOUISIANA MILK
(L. t. amaura)
Pattern may not cross belly

MEXICAN MILK
(L. t. annulata)
Black predominates

SCARLET
(Cemophora coccinea)
Belly plain whitish

only a few scattered black markings. An inhabitant of sand dunes, open prairies, and high plains. Most of Nebraska to cen. Montana. BIG BEND MILK SNAKE, *Lampropeltis t. celaenops.* Black rings widen in middorsal area, but normally do not cross venter; red rings 17 to 30; snout mottled with black and white. Occurs chiefly in wooded mountains, from shin oak associations to 7000 ft. (2100 m) in juniper-pinyon pine forests. Big Bend Region; w. Texas and e. and n. New Mexico. Western and Mexican subspecies.   Map 153

MEXICAN MILK SNAKE   Pl. 30
Lampropeltis triangulum annulata

Identification: 24–30 in. (61–76 cm); record 39 in. (99.1 cm). A ringed milk snake with an abundance of black pigment. Black rings rather wide and not narrowing on the 1st row of scales. Red rings broad (14 to 26 in number). Belly mostly black (Fig. 65, p. 207). Snout black (or virtually so). Scales *smooth;* anal *single.*

Found in a variety of habitats ranging from sand dunes to cultivated fields.

Similar species: (1) Coral Snake has 2 warning colors — red and yellow — touching each other. Black separates the other colors in Mexican Milk Snake. (2) Scarlet Snake and Ground Snakes have plain light bellies. (3) Long-nosed Snake has the black areas sprinkled with yellow spots.

Range: Cen. Texas through ne. Mexico. Mexican and Cen. and S. American subspecies.   Map 153

LOUISIANA MILK SNAKE   Pl. 30
Lampropeltis triangulum amaura

Identification: 16–22 in. (41–56 cm); record 31 in. (78.7 cm). A brilliantly marked "mimic" of the venomous Coral Snake with 13 to 25 broad red crossbands on body. The red areas may cross the belly or may be encircled by black (Fig. 65, p. 207); in the latter case they are best described as black-bordered red saddles extending well downward onto edges of belly plates. Snout mottled or speckled with black and white; rarely it may be as black as a Coral Snake's snout. Scales *smooth* and in 21 rows at midbody; anal *single.*

Usually found abroad only at night. Hides in such places as beneath stones or under the bark of rotting logs or stumps.

Similar species: (1) The warning colors — red and yellow — touch in Coral Snake; in Louisiana Milk Snake the black separates the other colors. (2) Scarlet and Ground Snakes have plain whitish bellies. (3) Scarlet Kingsnake has plain red snout and only 19 rows of scales at midbody.

Range: Sw. Arkansas and se. Oklahoma to Gulf Coast.
                                                    Map 153

SCARLET KINGSNAKE   **Pl. 30**
Lampropeltis triangulum elapsoides
   Identification: 14–20 in. (36–51 cm); record 27 in. (68.6 cm). An
   extraordinary "mimic" of the venomous Coral Snake. But the
   snout is *red,* and the yellow rings are separated from the red
   by black. In southern Florida the black rings may be enlarged
   middorsally and cross the red rings. Rings normally continue
   across belly (Fig. 65, p. 207). Scales *smooth,* in 19 rows at
   midbody; anal *single. Young:* 5–8 in. (13–20 cm) at hatching.
      Secretive and adept at working its way beneath bark, logs,
   or other hiding places; seldom seen in the open except at night
   or after heavy rains. Commonly found in or near woodland
   habitats, pine especially. Often winters in pine stumps in the
   South. Food includes small snakes and lizards, baby mice, small
   fish, insects, and earthworms.
   Similar species: (1) In Coral Snake (see Plate 30) the 2 warning colors — red and yellow — touch each other; also the *snout
   is black.* (2) In Scarlet Snake the belly is plain white.
   (3) Ringed varieties of Milk Snakes have 21 or more scale rows
   at midbody.
   Range: N. Carolina to the tip of Florida (also Key West) and
   west to Mississippi River, thus chiefly in Coastal Plain but also
   occurring in more inland localities and to elevations of at least
   2000 ft. (600 m) around edges of Appalachians; penetrates north
   into Tennessee and Kentucky.
   Note: The relationship of the Scarlet Kingsnake to the Eastern
   Milk Snake is highly unusual. In the Cumberland and Interior
   Low Plateaus of Tennessee and Kentucky, and around the edges
   of the southern Appalachians, the Scarlet Kingsnake and the
   Eastern Milk Snake occur together and maintain their identities. Conversely, they intergrade to produce a wide variety of
   color and pattern combinations in the lowlands and Piedmont
   from southern New Jersey to northeastern North Carolina. The
   most frequently occurring variation was formerly recognized as
   the "coastal plain milk snake" (Plate 30).   Map 153

PRAIRIE KINGSNAKE   **Pl. 29**
Lampropeltis calligaster calligaster
   Identification: 30–42 in. (76–107 cm); record 52⅛ in. (132.4
   cm). A blotched snake and one that may be troublesome
   to identify. Typically, back and tail are patterned with about
   60 brown, reddish, or greenish, black-edged markings. Occasionally these are split in two down the back. There are 2
   alternating rows of smaller dark markings on each side, but pairs
   of these may fuse together. The ground color is brownish gray
   to tan. In many older specimens the ground color darkens and
   the pattern becomes quite obscure, producing the *dark phase*
   that often is further characterized by the development of 4

longitudinal dusky stripes. Belly yellowish with squarish brown blotches. Scales *smooth;* anal *single. Young:* Strongly spotted; about 9–11 in. (23–28 cm) at hatching.

A resident of grassland prairies, open woodlands, and (farther east) patches of prairie and savanna in the midst of essentially forested country.

Similar species: (1) Great Plains Rat Snake bears a strong superficial resemblance to Prairie Kingsnake, but Rat Snakes have *keeled* scales and *divided* anals. (2) Glossy Snakes have plain white bellies. (3) In Milk Snakes the reddish blotches or rings are boldly surrounded by black, and there are *black* markings on belly.

Range: W. Indiana, cen. Kentucky, nw. Mississippi, and Louisiana west through most of Kansas, Oklahoma, and e. Texas.

Map 155

MOLE SNAKE   **Pls. 29, 31**
Lampropeltis calligaster rhombomaculata

   Identification: 30–40 in. (76–102 cm); record 47 in. (119.4 cm). A shiny, *smooth*-scaled serpent that may be patterned or not! Typical specimens have about 55 rather small, *well-separated,* reddish-brown, dark-edged spots down back and tail, and smaller and fainter spots on sides of body. The ground color is light to dark brown, sometimes with a greenish tinge, but changing to a more yellowish hue on sides of body. Older specimens may lose virtually all their markings, resulting in a plain "brown kingsnake." Dusky lengthwise stripes may also develop, as in Prairie Kingsnake. Belly white or yellowish and checked, spotted, or clouded with brown. Scales *smooth;* anal *single. Young:* Boldly marked with well-separated brown or red spots (see Plate 31); 2 lengthwise dark streaks on neck; about 8 or 9 in. (20–23 cm) at hatching.

   An accomplished burrower often turned up by the plow or during excavations. Occasionally appears on the surface, especially after heavy spring or summer rains. Ranges from Coastal Plain to at least the lower parts of Appalachians. Habitats include thickets, woodlots, cultivated fields, and even back yards in some suburban areas.

Similar species: (1) Corn Snake has *divided* anal, *keeled* scales, and underside of tail is usually striped (Fig. 43, p. 190). (2) In Milk Snakes the dorsal blotches are large and close together, and belly is boldly marked with black.

Range: Vicinity of Baltimore, Maryland, to the Florida panhandle; west to cen. Tennessee and s. Mississippi.   Map 155

GRAY-BANDED KINGSNAKE   **Pl. 32**
Lampropeltis mexicana alterna

   Identification: 20–36 in. (51–91 cm); record 47½ in. (120.7 cm). The gray crossbands on the body are the most constant feature of this highly variable snake. Other markings may consist solely of narrow black crossbands, or the black may be expanded, sometimes greatly, and it may include varying amounts of red or orange pigment. The narrow white lines bordering the black areas may be strikingly evident. Some specimens tend toward melanism like the darkest of the three varieties shown on Plate 32. Belly with black blotches that may fuse together. Eyes slightly protuberant; head noticeably wider than neck. Scales *smooth;* anal *single. Young:* Similar to adults, about 10 in. (25 cm) at hatching.

This resident of the Chihuahuan Desert region lives in arid to semihumid habitats ranging from desert flats and canyons into mountains. Once considered rare, it is now known to be abundant, but is seldom seen because of its secretive and nocturnal habits. Food includes lizards, snakes, frogs, and small rodents. This handsome serpent has a foul-smelling musk and a tendency to jerk spasmodically when handled.

Similar species: (1) In Texas Lyre Snake pupil of eye is vertically elliptical in daylight, and anal plate is *divided.* (2) Milk Snakes have black-bordered red rings separated by areas of white or yellow (not gray).

Range: Trans-Pecos region east to Edwards Co., Texas; south to Durango and extr. n. Zacatecas. Mexican subspecies.

Map 154

Scarlet, Long-nosed, and Short-tailed Snakes: Genera *Cemophora, Rhinocheilus,* and *Stilosoma*

THESE serpents are allied to the members of the genus *Lampropeltis,* and the resemblance of the scarlet snakes in coloration and pattern to the ringed milk snakes is strikingly evident. Even the long-nosed snakes are similar, despite their speckled markings. The ranges of two of the genera are mutually exclusive (except in southern Texas), with *Cemophora* in the Southeast and *Rhinocheilus* in the West. The races of the latter extend, collectively, to California and Baja California and south to San Luis Potosí and Nayarit. The curiously attenuated *Stilosoma* is endemic to Florida.

SCARLET SNAKE   *Cemophora coccinea*   **Pls. 30, 31**
   Identification: 14–20 in. (36–51 cm); record 32¼ in. (81.9 cm). The Coral Snake "mimic" with the plain whitish (or yellowish) belly. Snout *red* and pointed. The pattern is clean-cut in younger specimens; in adults, dark pigment may appear as small

spots in the red and especially the whitish areas. Scales *smooth;* anal *single. Young:* About 5½ in. (14 cm) at hatching.

Usually found in or near soils suitable for burrowing (sandy, loamy, etc.), in logs, beneath bark, etc.; seldom seen above ground except at night or after heavy rains. Occasionally unearthed during plowing or excavation work. Young mice and small snakes and lizards are killed by constriction. Snake eggs also are eaten. Small ones are swallowed whole, but larger eggs are seized at one end by the snake's jaws, which advance until the enlarged posterior maxillary teeth pierce the shell. A combination of vigorous chewing and pressure on the egg from a fold of the snake's body placed above it expels the egg's contents.

Similar species: (1) In venomous Coral Snakes red and yellow rings touch and snout is *black* (Plates 30 and 36). (2) In Scarlet Kingsnake and all Milk Snakes within its range, belly is heavily invaded by black pigment (Fig. 65, p. 207).

Range: S. New Jersey to tip of Florida; west to Louisiana, e. Oklahoma, and extr. e. Texas; disjunct colonies in s. Texas and in several areas north of main body of range.

Subspecies: NORTHERN SCARLET SNAKE, *Cemophora c. copei* (Plates 30 and 31). Upper labials normally 6; first black body blotch usually touching parietal scutes (at least in Atlantic coastal states). All of range except peninsular Florida and s. Texas. FLORIDA SCARLET SNAKE, *Cemophora c. coccinea.* Similar but usually with 7 upper labials; first black body blotch separated from parietals by 1 to 4 scales. Peninsular Florida. SOUTH TEXAS SCARLET SNAKE, *Cemophora c. lineri.* Ventrals 184 or more (usually fewer in the other races); red blotches less brilliant than in eastern subspecies and with no black along their lower edges. Extr. s. Texas.   Map 152

TEXAS LONG-NOSED SNAKE   Pl. 31
Rhinocheilus lecontei tessellatus

Identification: 22–32 in. (56–81 cm); record 41 in. (104.1 cm). A red, black, and yellow snake with a strongly speckled appearance. Head mostly black; snout red or pink and pointed, protruding, or even upturned; belly yellow or whitish with a few dark spots. *Scales under tail essentially in a single row,* but some are divided. Scales *smooth;* anal *single.* Vibrates tail when alarmed. *Young:* Speckling on sides of body may be only partially developed or virtually absent. Coloration paler in general than in adults — pink instead of red and whitish instead of yellow. About 6½–8½ in. (17–22 cm) at hatching.

A resident chiefly of deserts and dry prairies. Nocturnal to a large extent, spending daylight hours secreted among rocks or debris or in mammal burrows or other underground retreats. Captives should be given shelters beneath which to hide, or sand in which to burrow. Lizards are the chief food, but small rodents, lizard eggs, and insects are also eaten.

Occasional specimens perform a presumed defense display that may include a shifting of coils, twisting of body, and a smearing of blood, feces, and musk gland secretions over the snake and the captor's hands. Another behavioral display includes hiding the head beneath a body coil and waving the partially raised tail, which may concurrently smear a bloody fluid from the cloacal region onto the snake's body.

Similar species: (1) Scarlet Snake pattern consists of red saddles with black borders. (2) In the ringed Milk Snakes within its range, black pigment strongly invades the belly and there is no speckling on sides of body. Also, in *all* these snakes there is a *double row of scales under tail.*

Range: Sw. Kansas to San Luis Potosí and west through New Mexico and ne. Chihuahua. Western and Mexican subspecies.

Map 159

SHORT-TAILED SNAKE *Stilosoma extenuatum*   Pl. 31
  Identification: 14–20 in. (36–51 cm); record 25¾ in. (65.4 cm). An exceptionally slender spotted snake with a tail only 7 to 10 percent of total length. The small dark blotches, black or brown in coloration, are separated along midline of back by areas of yellow, orange, or red. Belly strongly blotched with brown or black. Scales *smooth;* anal *single.*

  A secretive burrower occurring chiefly in the dry "high" pine woods of central Florida. Similar in habits to the Milk Snakes — vibrates tail when alarmed, strikes with a sneezelike hiss, is a constrictor, and eats small snakes and lizards.

Range: Florida from Suwannee Co. south to Polk Co.

Map 162

Ground Snakes: Genus *Sonora*

DIFFICULT little snakes is a good way to describe this group. Its members show great individual variation in pattern and are easily confused with small snakes of other genera. Scales must be checked in many cases to be sure of identification. The genus *Sonora* ranges from southwestern Missouri and Kansas to northeastern Mexico, and in the West from Idaho and Oregon to Baja California (probably to its southern tip), Guerrero, and the Distrito Federal.

GROUND SNAKE *Sonora episcopa*   Pl. 31
  Identification: 9–12 in. (23–30 cm); record 15⅛ in. (38.4 cm). One of the most strikingly variable snakes within our area. Plain, crossbanded, black-collared, or longitudinally streaked specimens sometimes are found under the same rock, and all

of this one species. Three common variations are shown on Plate 31. Crossbands usually black or orange; ground color gray or brown, often with a strong red or orange tinge. Belly plain white or yellowish; underside of tail plain or with suggestions of crossbands. Collared and crossbanded individuals are easily identified, but plain ones will be troublesome. The head is slightly wider than the neck, and this will help in distinguishing the Ground Snake from some of the other small brown or gray snakes. If a series of specimens is available (including well-patterned ones), use them to compare head and body shapes, belly color, etc. Scales usually must be checked, however. The loreal scale (see Fig. 66, p. 215), is present 90 percent of the time, but it may be fused with one of the adjacent scales. Scales *smooth,* usually in 15 rows throughout length of body; anal *divided. Young:* 3⅛–4⅜ in. (8–11 cm) at hatching.

Found chiefly in the great open spaces — in terms of general environment; actually a secretive snake most often discovered by overturning stones on rocky hillsides or boards or trash in suburban areas. Feeds on small scorpions, centipedes, spiders, and insects.

Similar species: (1) Flat-headed Snake has: (a) bright pink venter; (b) distinctly small head no wider than neck; and (c) no loreal scale. (2) Western Earth Snake, Rough Earth Snake, and Brown Snakes have keeled scales. (3) In Texas Blind Snake, ventral scales are same size as dorsal scales. (4) See also Trans-Pecos Ground Snake.

Range: Kansas and sw. Missouri to ne. Mexico and the Big Bend of Texas.

Subspecies: GREAT PLAINS GROUND SNAKE, *Sonora e. episcopa* (described above and illustrated on Plate 31). All of range except extr. se. part. SOUTH TEXAS GROUND SNAKE, *Sonora e. taylori.* Like the nearly plain brown form of the Great Plains Ground Snake, but sometimes with a darkening across back of head; scales in 13 rows, occasionally 14 at midbody. S. Texas and extr. ne. Mexico.   Map 158

TRANS-PECOS GROUND SNAKE   Pl. 31
Sonora semiannulata blanchardi

Identification: 9–12 in. (23–30 cm); record 16⅜ in. (41.6 cm). Another snake with extraordinarily variable patterns. Many individuals are plain brown or gray with or without a darkened head; others are crossbanded with black or dark brown or are marked with a broad reddish middorsal stripe or both. There is a tendency for each dorsal scale to be slightly darker (longitudinally) along its center. Belly plain whitish or yellowish; underside of tail often more colorful and sometimes crossbanded. Loreal scale usually present (see Fig. 66, p. 215). Caudals usually 51 or more in males and 45 or more in females. Scales *smooth,* in 15 rows anteriorly but usually only 14 rows posteriorly; anal *divided.*

This secretive snake of arid western Texas is seldom seen except when it prowls at night or if it is uncovered by overturning rocks or other shelters.

Similar species: (1) Within its range apt to be confused only with the more eastwardly ranging Ground Snake (*episcopa*). Ground Snake has: (a) 15 rows of scales throughout length of body in most specimens; and (b) fewer caudals — usually 50 or fewer in males and 44 or fewer in females. (2) Among the several kinds of Black-headed Snakes (*Tantilla*) of the Trans-Pecos region, the heads are black, the loreal scale is lacking (Fig. 66, below), and there are never any dark crossbands on body.

Range: S.-cen. New Mexico to s. Coahuila and adj. Nuevo León. Western subspecies.   Map 157

Fig. 66. HEADS OF GROUND AND BLACK-HEADED SNAKES

GROUND SNAKE
(Sonora)
A loreal scale
separates 2nd labial
from prefrontal scale

BLACK-HEADED SNAKE
(Tantilla)
No loreal; 2nd labial
contacts, or almost contacts,
prefrontal scale (see text)

Rear-fanged Snakes:
Genera *Coniophanes, Ficimia, Gyalopion, Hypsiglena, Leptodeira, Tantilla,* and *Trimorphodon*

FANGS have evolved in the rear of the upper jaw, apparently independently, in a number of unrelated genera of the Family Colubridae in many parts of the world. Fortunately for us, none of ours is so dangerous as the back-fanged Boomslang and Twig Snake of Africa, bites from both of which have caused deaths in human beings. Some of ours, like the black-striped, lyre, and cat-eyed snakes, are venomous but scarcely dangerous to man; others, like the hook-nosed and black-headed snakes, have grooved teeth but no well-developed venom system; still others, like the night snakes, have venom but no grooves, or only slight indications of them. These represent various stages in the evolutionary development of the venom apparatus which, even in the dangerously poisonous serpents, functions chiefly in the procurement of food.

The ranges of all these genera extend south into Mexico, and most of them go much farther — *Coniophanes* to Peru, *Ficimia* to Honduras, *Hypsiglena* to Costa Rica, *Leptodeira* to northern Argentina and Paraguay, *Tantilla* to northern Argentina, and *Trimorphodon* to Costa Rica.

BLACK-STRIPED SNAKE   Pl. 33
Coniophanes imperialis imperialis

Identification: 12–18 in. (30–46 cm); record 20 in. (50.8 cm). The broad black or dark brown stripes alternate with stripes of tan or brown that brighten abruptly at their anterior ends. A thin, whitish or yellowish line, extending from snout through top of eye, terminates near rear of head. These markings, plus a bright red or orange venter, assure identification. Scales *smooth;* anal *divided.*

A secretive, rear-fanged snake best sought by overturning piles of debris, heaps of rotting cactus, palm fronds, etc. It also takes refuge in deep cracks that form when soil dries out quickly under the torrid sun. Food includes small frogs, toads, lizards, and baby mice.

Range: Extr. s. Texas to n. Veracruz. Mexican and Cen. American subspecies.   Map 136

MEXICAN HOOK-NOSED SNAKE   Pl. 33
Ficimia streckeri

Identification: 7–11 in. (18–28 cm); record 19 in. (48.3 cm). A combination of upturned snout, *smooth* scales, and relatively little head pattern identifies this species. Ground color pale to medium brown or gray. A dorsal pattern of narrow brown or olive crossbands numbering 37 to 45 on body; crossbands in many specimens reduced to transverse rows of small dark spots. In both hook-nosed snakes the snout, posterior to the "hook," is flattened or somewhat concave instead of bearing a dorsal keel as it does among the hognose snakes. Rostral in broad contact with frontal. Anal *divided.*

This nocturnal, burrowing serpent occasionally is seen above ground after rains, on freshly sprinkled lawns, along irrigation ditches, or in other places where water is present. Hook-nosed snakes (of both species) make rather unsatisfactory captives. They should be provided with an inch or more of dry sand, into which they will promptly burrow out of sight. Food consists largely of spiders, but centipedes are also eaten.

Similar species: (1) Hognose Snakes have *keeled* scales. (2) In Western Hook-nosed Snake dorsal markings are fewer in number but more prominent, the head is conspicuously patterned,

and the rostral penetrates posteriorly to the *pre*frontals only.
Range: S. Texas to Hidalgo and n. Veracruz.   Map 160

WESTERN HOOK-NOSED SNAKE   Pl. 33
Gyalopion canum

Identification: 7–11 in. (18–28 cm); record 14 in. (35.6 cm).
Check for three things: (a) upturned snout; (b) *smooth* scales;
and (c) a strongly marked pattern with the crossbands on head
particularly prominent. There are 30 or more brown, dark-edged
crossbars on body and 8 to 12 on tail. Ground color pale brown.
Rostral in contact with *pre*frontals. Anal *divided.*

Largely a desert species, often found in areas where mesquite,
creosote bush, and agave are dominant plants, but also ascending into mountains at least to the pinyon-juniper zone. Food
consists chiefly of spiders, but scorpions and centipedes also are
eaten. Nocturnal and crepuscular.

A burrowing snake with the extraordinary habit of anal "popping." When touched in the field, it may undergo a series of
gyrations as though writhing in agony, meanwhile extruding
and retracting the lining of the cloaca through the vent to the
accompaniment of a bubbling or popping sound.

Similar species: (1) Hognose Snakes have *keeled* scales. (2)
Mexican Hook-nosed Snake has narrower, but more numerous, crossbands, its head markings are meager or virtually absent, and the rostral extends all the way to the frontal.

Range: W. Texas and n.-cen. New Mexico to se. Arizona and
south to Nayarit and San Luis Potosí.   Map 161

TEXAS NIGHT SNAKE   Pl. 33
Hypsiglena torquata texana

Identification: 14–16 in. (36–41 cm); record 20 in. (50.8 cm). A
spotted snake with a bold elongated blotch on each side of the
neck and another on the nape. A dark band backward and
downward from eye. Pupil *vertically elliptical.* Body spots
brown or dark gray; ground color light brown or grayish. Belly
immaculate white or yellowish. Scales *smooth;* anal *divided.*
Young: About 6–7 in. (15–18 cm) at hatching.

A resident of arid or semiarid country, prowling chiefly at
night and often frequenting rocky regions. Small lizards are the
principal food. Captives should be given sand or fairly dry soil
in which to burrow, or stones or bark under which to hide.

Range: Sw. Kansas and se. Colorado through New Mexico and
Texas to ne. Mexico.   Map 170

SPOTTED NIGHT SNAKE   Pl. 33
Hypsiglena torquata ochrorhyncha

Identification: 14–16 in. (36–41 cm); record 19⅝ in. (49.8 cm).
Similar to the Texas Night Snake but with the ground color

distinctly paler. Dark middorsal spots surrounded by pale pigmentation and each spot involving fewer than 20 scales (22 or more scales in Texas Night Snake). Pupil *vertically elliptical.* Scales *smooth;* anal *divided. Young:* About 6¼–7½ in. (16–19 cm) at hatching.

Habitats vary from low creosote bush deserts to moist, grass-sedge mountain meadows. Has been taken as high as 8750 ft. (2700 m) in the Graham Mountains of Arizona.

Range: Southern and western portions of Big Bend of Texas; Arizona and w. New Mexico to Jalisco. Western and Mexican subspecies.   .   Map 170

NORTHERN CAT-EYED SNAKE   Pl. 32
Leptodeira septentrionalis septentrionalis
Identification: 18–24 in. (46–61 cm); record 38¾ in. (98.4 cm). The broad crossbands (saddles) of dark brown or black extend almost completely across the back, and are usually in strong contrast with the light ground color, which varies from cream through yellow to reddish tan. Head broad, much wider than neck. Eye with a *vertically elliptical* pupil (cat-eyed). Scales *smooth;* anal *divided. Young:* More boldly patterned than adults; ground color orange-tan; about 8½–9½ in. (22–24 cm) at hatching.

This snake, the northernmost representative of the genus *Leptodeira,* is equipped with grooved fangs toward the rear of the upper jaw for introducing venom into prey after it has been seized. The venom tends to benumb and immobilize the prey. The Cat-eyed Snake is big enough so that theoretically it might cause trouble if it swallowed a person's finger far enough to bring the fangs into play — a quite unlikely occurrence. It is best to handle it with care, however. When the head is held in the usual manner (p. 17), the fangs are dangerously close to one's thumb and middle finger! Nocturnal, and likely to be found prowling in search of frogs near streams or other bodies of water. Sometimes climbs into bushes.

Range: Extr. s. Texas to Veracruz and Hidalgo; an isolated record in Coahuila. Related subspecies range southward through Mexico, Cen. America, and nw. S. America to Peru.
                    Map 172

TEXAS LYRE SNAKE   Pl. 32
Trimorphodon biscutatus vilkinsoni
Identification: 18–30 in. (46–76 cm); record 41 in. (104.1 cm). The dark brown body saddles, 17 to 24 in number, are widest over the back, but they narrow to the width of only a scale or two on the lower sides. Similar but narrower markings on tail. Dorsal ground color light brown or gray. A few dark smudges on head represent remnants of the lyre-shaped pattern that is well developed in some of the related subspecies. Belly

white or gray to yellowish brown, and with a row of dark blotches down each side. *Pupil of eye vertically elliptical* and contracting to a tiny black slit in bright light. Only snake in our area with an extra scale (the lorilabial) between the loreal and upper labials. Scales *smooth;* anal *divided. Young:* Similar to adults but more boldly patterned; smallest known juveniles about 11½ in. (29 cm) long.

Another rear-fanged species that also should be handled with caution. A resident of rock piles and slides, rocky slopes and canyons, hiding in crevices by day and prowling by night. Lizards are the chief food, but small mammals and birds are also eaten. Vibrates tail when first caught.

Similar species: In Gray-banded Kingsnake pupil is circular and *anal is single.*

Range: Big Bend region of Texas to s. New Mexico and ne. Chihuahua. Western and Mexican subspecies.   Map 171

Crowned and Black-headed Snakes: Genus *Tantilla*

THESE small, secretive snakes have 15 rows of *smooth* scales throughout the length of the body, a *divided* anal, and most of them have black caps on their heads. There is no loreal, and the prefrontal scale may extend downward to meet the 2nd labial (Fig. 66, p. 215). In other cases the tip of the postnasal may extend backward to meet the preocular, thus narrowly separating the 2nd labial from the prefrontal. The two conditions may occur in the same snake, one on each side of the head. Food includes centipedes and the larvae of insects that live underground. The genus ranges from the southern United States to northern Argentina.

SOUTHEASTERN CROWNED SNAKE   Pl. 33
Tantilla coronata

Identification: 8–10 in. (20–25 cm); record 13 in. (33.0 cm). This black-headed snake not only has a black head cap but also a light band across rear of head, followed by a black collar 3 to 5 scales wide (Fig. 67, p. 222). Remainder of dorsum is plain light brown or reddish brown; belly white or with a pinkish or yellowish tinge. Dark pigment usually extends downward from the head cap to or almost to the mouth, both under the eye and near back of head. Scales *smooth;* anal *divided.*

Habitats vary from the environs of swamps to dry wooded hillsides, and from wilderness areas to back yards. This snake is where you find it, and then almost always in hiding — under stones, in rotting logs, etc. Occurs at elevations from virtually sea level to 2000 ft. (600 m) or more in the southern Appalachians.

Similar species: (1) Most apt to be confused with Florida Brown Snake and *young* of other Brown Snakes, all of which also have dark heads followed by a light crossband, *but they have keeled scales* (a lens may be needed to see the keels in very small specimens). (2) Ringneck Snakes have brightly colored venters — yellow, orange, or red — boldly marked with black spots (at least in southern races).

Range: S.-cen. Virginia and s. Indiana to the Florida panhandle and the Florida parishes of Louisiana.   Map 163

PENINSULA CROWNED SNAKE   Fig. 67, p. 222
Tantilla relicta relicta

Identification: 7–9 in. (18–22.9 cm). Usually with a light crossband separating black head cap from black collar on neck (as in the Southeastern Crowned Snake — see Fig. 67, p. 222), but crossband often interrupted by black at midline. Most of head black, including labials. Head pointed and lower jaw partly countersunk into upper jaw. Scales *smooth;* anal *divided.*

Similar species: See **Similar species** under Southeastern Crowned Snake.

Range: Peninsular Florida in scrub areas from Lake George, Marion Co., south along central ridge and sandhills to Highlands Co.; isolated colonies in coastal scrub areas of Charlotte and Sarasota Cos. and on Seahorse Key, Levy Co.   Map 164

FLORIDA CROWNED SNAKE   Pl. 33
Tantilla relicta neilli

Identification: 7–9 in. (18–23 cm); record 9½ in. (24.1 cm). Black of head and neck continuous; black extends 3 to 8 scales behind parietal scutes (Fig. 67, p. 222). Labials may be all black or with a whitish area posterior to eye. Head narrowly rounded (not pointed). Lower jaw not noticeably countersunk into upper jaw. Only one basal hook on each hemipenis (in males), a characteristic shared by all races of *relicta.* Scales *smooth;* anal *divided.*

A secretive snake of the sandhills and moist hammocks of north-central Florida.

Range: Peninsular Florida, Suwannee River south to n. Polk Co. and the Hillsborough River; east at least to the St. Johns River.   Map 164

COASTAL DUNES CROWNED SNAKE   Fig. 67, p. 222
Tantilla relicta pamlica

Identification: 7–8½ in. (18–21.6 cm). The crowned snake with the most white on its head. In addition to the light crossband there are usually light areas on the snout, the temporal and parietal scutes, and the posterior labials. Black collar on neck about 3 scales wide. Dorsum reddish brown. Head pointed; lower jaw countersunk into upper. Scales *smooth;* anal *divided.*

A resident of relatively isolated coastal dunes and scrub areas of southeastern Florida.
Range: Vicinity of Cape Canaveral south to s. Palm Beach Co., Florida.   Map 164

RIM ROCK CROWNED SNAKE   Not illus.
Tantilla oolitica
Identification: 7–9 in. (18–23 cm); record 11½ in. (29.2 cm). Best identified by range; the only member of the black-headed snake group (*Tantilla*) in extreme southern Florida. Head pattern similar to that of Florida Crowned Snake (Fig. 67, p. 222). Black of head continuous from snout to neck, except that specimens from Key Largo may have a broken light crossband separating a black head cap from a black collar. Each hemipenis (in males) with two basal hooks instead of one as in all other kinds of *Tantilla* from the Florida Peninsula. Scales *smooth;* anal *divided.*

A secretive snake more or less confined to the rim rock (oölitic limestone) area paralleling the coast of extreme southeastern Florida.
Range: Dade Co. and Key Largo, Florida.   Map 165

FLAT-HEADED SNAKE *Tantilla gracilis*   Pl. 33
Identification: 7–8 in. (18–20 cm); record 9⅝ in. (24.4 cm). A black-headed snake that usually doesn't have a black head! Head normally slightly darker than body, but occasional specimens do have quite dark heads; cap is *concave* at its posterior end (Fig. 67, p. 222). A slender, shiny snake with a plain (unpatterned) dorsum of some shade of brown — golden- or gray-brown to reddish brown. *Belly salmon pink.* Upper labial scales 6. Scales *smooth;* anal *divided. Young:* Gray or brownish gray; about 3–3½ in. (7.6–8.9 cm) at hatching.

A small, secretive, almost wormlike snake, completely inoffensive but adept at forcing its way through the fingers when held in the hand. Normally found under rocks below which there is at least some moisture.
Similar species: Lack of dorsal pattern makes this snake easy to confuse with several other plain brown species. (1) Brown Snakes and the Rough Earth Snake have *keeled* scales. (2) Western Earth Snake has weak *keels* on at least some middorsal scales. (3) Ground Snake has cream or whitish belly and also usually has a loreal scale (Fig. 66, p. 215). (4) Blind Snakes have belly scales same size as dorsal scales. (5) Plains Black-headed Snake has 7 upper labials and the black cap, almost invariably prominent, usually extends farther posteriorly and is *convex* or pointed at rear (Fig. 68, p. 223).
Range: Extr. sw. Illinois, Missouri, and e. Kansas to s. Texas and Coahuila.   Map 169

Fig. 67. HEADS OF CROWNED AND FLAT-HEADED SNAKES *(Tantilla)*

SOUTHEAST *(coronata)*	DUNES *(pamlica)*	PENINSULA *(relicta)*	FLORIDA *(neilli)*	FLATHEAD *(gracilis)*
Light collar, with or without black to mouth line	Much white on head and labials	Most of head and labials black	Cap extends far beyond head scales	Cap pale; concave at rear

PLAINS BLACK-HEADED SNAKE   Pl. 33
Tantilla nigriceps

Identification: 7–10 in. (18–25 cm); record 14¾ in. (37.5 cm). The black cap is convex or even pointed at the rear, and it extends backward 2 to 5 scale lengths from the parietals (Fig. 68, p. 223). Dorsum plain yellowish brown to brownish gray; belly whitish with a broad midventral pink area. Upper labial scales 7. First lower labials usually meet beneath chin (Fig. 69, p. 223). Scales *smooth;* anal *divided.*

A black-headed snake of the southern Great Plains and arid lands to the south and west. Found under rocks, debris, etc., and only rarely in the open.

Similar species: (1) In Flat-headed Snake upper labials are 6, and in the few Flatheads with black caps the rear of the dark area is *concave.* (2) In Mexican Black-headed Snake the first lower labials usually fail to meet beneath chin (Fig. 69, p. 223), and posterior border of black cap usually runs straighter across. (3) Devils River Black-headed Snake has a white collar followed by a broad black band. (4) In Black-hooded Snake the white collar is strongly interrupted by black or the entire head is black (Fig. 68, p. 223).

Range: Nebraska to Arizona and n. Mexico.

Subspecies: TEXAS BLACK-HEADED SNAKE, *Tantilla n. fumiceps* (Plate 33). Ventrals usually 145 or fewer. Sw. Oklahoma to extr. s. Texas and extr. n. Tamaulipas. PLAINS BLACK-HEADED SNAKE, *Tantilla n. nigriceps.* Ventrals 146 or more. Sw. Nebraska and Kansas to se. Arizona and n. Durango.   Map 166

MEXICAN BLACK-HEADED SNAKE   Pl. 33
Tantilla atriceps

Identification: 5–8 in. (13–20 cm); record 9⅝ in. (24.4 cm). The black or dark brown head cap usually extends only the width of 1 or 2 scales behind the parietals and its posterior border usually runs straight across or is somewhat convex (Fig. 68, p. 223). Often a faint light line across neck immediately posterior to dark cap. Dorsum brown or grayish brown; a bright orange-red area extending most of length of belly and under

Fig. 68. HEADS OF BLACK-HEADED SNAKES *(Tantilla)*

| MEXICAN
(atriceps) | PLAINS
(nigriceps) | DEVILS RIVER
(diabola) | BLACK-HOODED
(cucullata) | |

Rear of cap straight; close to head scales | Rear of cap convex or pointed | Light collar continuous across head | Light collar interrupted at midline | Head all black, above and below

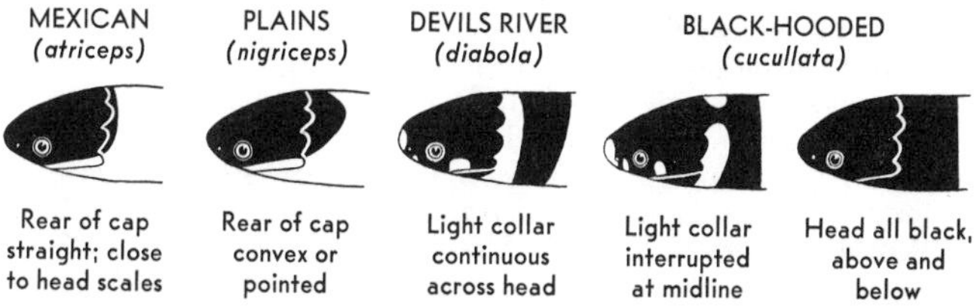

tail. First lower labials usually fail to meet beneath chin (Fig. 69, below). Scales *smooth;* anal *divided.*

This small, secretive snake occurs in a variety of habitats, ranging from wooded mountain canyons to desert flats. Moisture and shelter are necessities. After summer rains look for it beneath flat rocks, logs, or decaying vegetation.

Similar species: (1) In Plains Black-headed Snake the first lower labials usually meet beneath the chin (Fig. 69, below), and the rear of the black cap, which extends farther posteriorly, is convex or pointed (Fig. 68, above). (2) See also Black-hooded Snake and Devils River Black-headed Snake.

Range: Sutton Co., Texas, the Trans-Pecos region, and south to San Luis Potosí; west to Arizona and Sonora; an isolated record in Kleberg Co., Texas.   Map 168

DEVILS RIVER BLACK-HEADED SNAKE   Pl. 33
Tantilla rubra diabola

Identification: 8½–15 in. (22–38 cm); record 21¾ in. (55.2 cm). This black-headed snake not only has a black head cap but also a light band or collar across rear of head, followed by a black band 3½ to 4½ scales wide. A whitish spot on upper labials posterior to eye (Fig. 68, above). Rest of dorsum plain light brown or grayish brown. Scales *smooth;* anal *divided.*

Range: Known only from arid environs of the Devils and Pecos Rivers, sw. Texas, but almost surely also occurring in adjacent parts of Texas and Coahuila. Mexican subspecies. Map 167

Fig. 69. CHINS OF BLACK-HEADED SNAKES *(Tantilla)*

MEXICAN
(atriceps)

1st lower labials fail to meet

PLAINS
(nigriceps)

1st lower labials make contact at midline

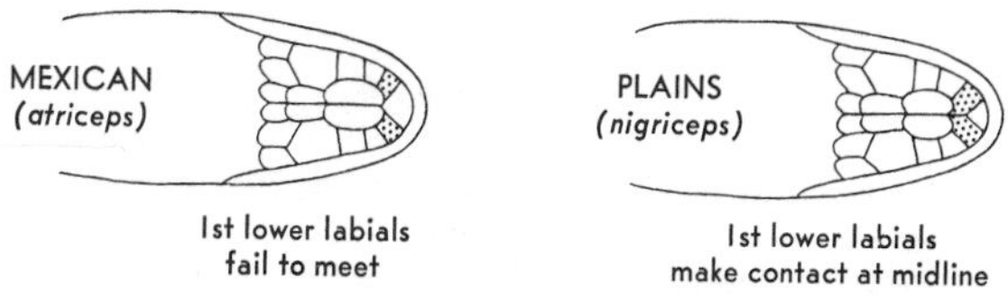

BLACK-HOODED SNAKE *Tantilla rubra cucullata*   **Pl. 33**
   Identification: 8½–15 in. (22–38 cm); record 17¼ in. (43.8 cm).
A black-headed snake with at least two sharply different head
patterns: (a) a black hood that covers both the dorsal and
ventral surfaces of the head; and (b) a ring-necked phase that
resembles the Devils River Black-headed Snake except that the
light neck ring is interrupted by black at its midpoint (Fig. 68,
p. 223). Remainder of dorsum plain light brown or grayish
brown. Scales *smooth;* anal *divided.*
   Range: Chisos and Davis Mountains regions in Trans-Pecos
Texas.   Map 167

Coral Snakes: Family Elapidae

THESE snakes are dangerously poisonous. Although their small
mouths and relatively short fangs make it difficult for them to
bite most parts of the human anatomy (fingers or toes are vulnerable), their venoms are potent. They are strongly ringed with red,
yellow, and black, or in the tropics with black and red or black
and yellow. Coral snakes range from the southern United States
to northern Argentina. The family is also widespread in the Old
World, where it includes such notorious members as cobras, mam-
bas, kraits, and tiger snakes.

EASTERN CORAL SNAKE   **Pl. 30**
Micrurus fulvius fulvius
   Identification: 20–30 in. (51–76 cm); record 47½ in. (120.7 cm).
A shiny, "candystick" snake whose colored rings completely
encircle the body. *Red and yellow rings touch.* End of snout
black, followed by a yellow band across head. Black ring on
neck not touching the parietal scutes. Red rings dotted or
spotted with black, the dark markings often concentrated into
a pair of fairly large black spots in each red ring. Some specimens from southern Florida may lack dark spots in the red rings
entirely. *Young:* Similarly patterned and colored; 7–9 in.
(18–23 cm) at hatching.
   Coral snakes are usually secretive, but when they prowl it
is normally by day, especially in early morning. Sometimes they
may be discovered hiding under leaves or debris, in logs, palmetto stumps, etc. Habitats vary from well-drained pine woods
and open, dry, or sandy areas to such moister environments as
pond and lake borders and in the (often) dense and jungly
growths of hardwoods known in the South (Florida especially)
as hammocks. Coral snakes eat snakes, lizards, and frogs. When
suddenly restrained, a coral snake may thrust its tail upward
with the tip curled into a ball that may momentarily be mistaken for the head.

Similar species: The venomous Coral Snakes are well imitated serpents. Several of our harmless snakes also sport rings (or near-rings) of red, black, and yellow (or white). In all of them, however, black separates red from yellow. Think of a traffic light; red means *stop,* yellow means *caution.* If these two warning colors touch on the snake's body, it is poisonous. "Mimics" include the Scarlet Snake, Scarlet Kingsnake, and several of the Milk Snakes (Plate 30).
Range: Se. N. Carolina south, chiefly in lowlands, to extr. s. Florida and Key Largo; west through Gulf States to w.-cen. Mississippi and extr. e. Louisiana. Coral snakes apparently are absent from much of the delta region of the lower Mississippi Valley.   Map 175

TEXAS CORAL SNAKE *Micrurus fulvius tenere*   **Pl. 36**
  Identification: 20–30 in. (51–76 cm); record 44¼ in. (112.4 cm). Similar to the Eastern Coral Snake except that in the Texas subspecies the black pigment in the red rings is more widely scattered, and the black neck band extends far enough forward to involve the posterior tips of the parietal scutes.
    In addition to inhabiting lowland areas, this race ascends onto the Edwards Plateau of central Texas, where it may be found in cedar brakes or rocky canyons, or on rocky hillsides.
  Similar species: (1) See the "mimics" and the Louisiana and Mexican Milk Snakes on Plate 30. (2) The crossbanded phases of the two Ground Snakes (Plate 31) bear a remote resemblance to a Coral Snake, but they lack the black snout and the broad black rings of the venomous species, and their bellies are unmarked. (3) Long-nosed Snake has a *red* snout and only a *single row of scales under tail.*
  Range: S. Arkansas and Louisiana to w.-cen. Texas; south into Mexico. Mexican subspecies.   Map 175

Family Viperidae
Pit Vipers: Subfamily Crotalinae

ALL our dangerously poisonous serpents except the coral snakes belong to this group. Copperheads, cottonmouths, and rattlesnakes are members.
  The subfamily name is derived from the deep facial pit on each side of the head situated a little below midway between eye and nostril (Fig. 60, opp. Pl. 34). It is a sensory organ that helps the snake to aim in striking at warm-blooded prey. *Any serpent with such a pit is poisonous,* but this can be checked only on dead or caged specimens. Don't approach live ones in the field close

enough to see the pit. Also beware of handling freshly killed snakes. Reflex action is marked; even decapitated heads have been known to bite!

The scales under the tail are in only 1 row, at least anteriorly; the heads are distinctly wider than the necks; and the pupils of the eyes are vertically elliptical. A few nonpoisonous and rear-fanged snakes also have one or more of these characteristics.

Pit vipers range from southern Canada to northern Argentina and Uruguay and from extreme southeastern Europe through southern and central Asia and Malaysia. They and the true vipers of the Old World constitute the Family Viperidae.

Copperheads and Cottonmouths: Genus *Agkistrodon*

THESE are the venomous "moccasins" — copperheads being the so-called "highland moccasins" and cottonmouths the "water moccasins." In referring to these snakes, however, the name "moccasin" should be studiously avoided, for it is misleading. Ignorant or uninformed persons apply the same term to the nonpoisonous water snakes. Members of the genus *Agkistrodon* have facial pits and all the other characteristics of the pit vipers. Scales are *weakly keeled;* anal *single.* When alarmed they rapidly vibrate their tails, producing a lively tattoo against a leaf, vegetation, or even the ground — whatever the tail may touch. The young at birth have bright yellow tail tips. The genus is represented in North and Central America, Asia, Malaysia, and extreme southeastern Europe.

NORTHERN COPPERHEAD   Pl. 34
Agkistrodon contortrix mokasen

Identification: 24–36 in. (61–91 cm); record 53 in. (134.6 cm). A coppery-red head and an hourglass pattern. Viewed from above, the dark chestnut crossbands are wide on the sides and narrow at the center of the back. Small dark spots are frequently present between crossbands. Dark rounded spots at sides of belly. Scales *weakly keeled;* anal *single;* a single row of scales under tail, at least anteriorly. *Young:* Paler; tail tip yellow; a *narrow* dark line through eye that divides the dark head from the pale lips; 8–9¾ in. (20–25 cm) at birth.

The Copperhead has many aliases — "chunkhead," "highland moccasin," "pilot," "adder," etc. Natural camouflage renders it inconspicuous. Normally a quiet, almost lethargic snake, content to lie motionless or beat a dignified retreat. Once aroused, it strikes vigorously and may rapidly vibrate the tail. Rocky, wooded hillsides and mountainous areas are favorite habitats. Abandoned and rotting slab or sawdust piles, left in the wake of the itinerant, portable sawmill, are another; in these, copperheads as well as other reptiles find shelter, food, and moisture. Copperheads are gregarious, especially in autumn, when they assemble at hibernating dens or denning areas, often in company with other species of snakes. Mice are the principal food, but small birds, frogs, and insects also are eaten.

Similar species: (1) In Milk Snakes the large dorsal markings are *wide* at center of back; belly markings black and squarish. Eastern Milk Snake usually has *checkerboard* belly. (2) Hognose Snakes, besides having turned-up snouts, hiss and flatten their heads and necks. (3) Water Snakes seldom wander far from water and retreat into it when alarmed; their scales are *strongly* keeled. (4) In Fox Snakes the markings consist of a series of large dark blotches flanked by a series of smaller blotches on each side. Great numbers of harmless snakes are killed in the mistaken belief they are Copperheads. If snake is dead, check for the facial pits. (See also Plate 34 and *Young* under Eastern Cottonmouth, p. 228.)

Range: Massachusetts to Illinois and w. Tennessee; south in uplands to Georgia and Alabama.

Subspecies: OSAGE COPPERHEAD, *Agkistrodon c. phaeogaster.* Similar, but with the dark crossbands in sharper contrast with the ground color, and without small dark spots between them. Tip of tail yellowish green (yellow in young). The gray to black belly markings blend together to produce a dusky, marbled, or clouded venter. N. and cen. Missouri, e. Kansas, and corners of adjacent states.   Map 174

SOUTHERN COPPERHEAD   Pl. 34
Agkistrodon contortrix contortrix

Identification: 24–36 in. (61–91 cm); record 52 in. (132.1 cm). A paler, pinker counterpart of the Northern Copperhead. The dark markings are quite narrow across the back, giving the hourglasses a more wasp-waist appearance than in the northern race. Very often they are broken at middorsum, the two halves failing to meet. Scales *weakly keeled;* anal *single. Young:* Similar to young of Northern Copperhead, but with pinched, often-broken markings.

This is mainly a snake of the lowlands, of low ground near swamps and cypress-bordered streams, but it also ascends into hilly regions.

Similar species: Baby Cottonmouths have a *broad* dark band through eye, and their body hues consist largely of dark browns.

Range: E. N. Carolina to the Florida panhandle and west to e. Texas and e. Oklahoma; north in Mississippi Valley to s. Illinois and s. Missouri. Areas of intergradation (not shown on map) with adjacent subspecies are relatively wide in some parts of range.   Map 174

BROAD-BANDED COPPERHEAD   Pl. 34
Agkistrodon contortrix laticinctus

Identification: 22–30 in. (56–76 cm); record 36¼ in. (92.1 cm). The rich reddish-brown or chestnut-brown crossbands are almost as broad on the back as on the sides of the body. Tip of tail greenish gray. Scales *weakly keeled;* anal *single. Young:* Pattern contrasty, but of grays rather than rich browns; tip of tail yellow or greenish yellow; 8⅛–10 in. (21–25 cm) at birth. **Range:** Extr. s. Kansas south through Oklahoma to s.-cen. Texas.   Map 174

TRANS-PECOS COPPERHEAD   Pl. 34
Agkistrodon contortrix pictigaster

Identification: 20–30 in. (51–76 cm); record 32⅞ in. (83.5 cm). Superficially this race resembles the Broad-banded Copperhead, but it differs chiefly in having a dark and strikingly patterned belly. Undersurface rich chestnut to almost black, but in sharp contrast with pale areas that: (a) extend downward from the dorsal ground color; and (b) appear in the form of inverted U's beneath each dark dorsal crossband.

This westernmost subspecies of the Copperhead lives in oases in the Chihuahuan Desert, in isolated populations that are relicts of a former, much wider, distribution. It normally occurs near permanent springs, in well-watered canyons, and in river-cane jungles bordering the Rio Grande, but it occasionally wanders into the adjacent desert during the rainy season. **Range:** W. Texas from Crockett and Val Verde Cos. through the Big Bend region and the Davis Mts.   Map 174

EASTERN COTTONMOUTH   Pl. 34
Agkistrodon piscivorus piscivorus

Identification: 30–48 in. (76–122 cm); record 74 in. (188.0 cm). A large semiaquatic snake. Olive, brown, or black above; belly lighter. Crossbands with dark, more or less distinct borders; centers of crossbands often invaded by the lighter ground color. Details of pattern most evident in young and subadults; old adults may be completely dark and unpatterned. A dead specimen is easily distinguished from a water snake by its facial pits, *single* anal plate, and *single* row of scales under tail (Fig. 60, opp. Pl. 34). *Don't ever handle a live one!* Dorsal scales *weakly keeled. Young:* Strongly patterned with light-centered dark brown to brilliant reddish-brown crossbands; a *broad dark band* through eye; tip of tail yellow; 10–13 in. (25–33 cm) at birth.

Beware of any semiaquatic serpent within the range of the cottonmouths. These very dangerous snakes closely resemble several of the nonpoisonous water snakes (*Natrix*) and are difficult to tell from them in the field. Behavior offers some of the best clues. Cottonmouths often stand their ground or crawl slowly away. Water snakes usually flee quickly or drop with a splash into the water. Cottonmouths vibrate tails when excited; water snakes do not. A thoroughly aroused cottonmouth throws its head upward and backward and holds its mouth wide open, revealing a white interior — origin of the name cottonmouth.

This is a snake of southern lowlands, a denizen of swamps, lakes, and rivers, of rice fields and ditches. Suns itself on branches, logs, or stones at water's edge and sometimes wanders away from its normal habitat in pursuit of food. Fish, frogs, salamanders, snakes, lizards, small turtles, baby alligators, birds, and small mammals are included on the menu.

Similar species: (1) The nonpoisonous water snakes (*Natrix*) have *divided* anal plates, a *double* row of scales under tail, and *no* facial pits (Fig. 60, opp. Pl. 34). (2) Young Copperheads are more reddish than baby Cottonmouths, and they have a *narrow* dark line through eye.

Range: Se. Virginia to e.-cen. Alabama.   Map 173

FLORIDA COTTONMOUTH   Pl. 34
Agkistrodon piscivorus conanti

Identification: 30–48 in. (76–122 cm); record 74½ in. (189.2 cm). Similar to the Eastern Cottonmouth, but with conspicuous head markings — even in most large, dark individuals. A dark brown cheek stripe bordered above and below by a narrow light line. Also a pair of dark stripes at front of lower jaw, and a pair of dark vertical lines at tip of snout. Behavior and habitat similar to that of Eastern Cottonmouth.

Similar species: See Fig. 60, opp. Pl. 34.

Range: S. Georgia, se. Alabama, and all of Florida including virtually all adjacent islands; apparently missing from the lower Keys despite an old record from Key West.   Map 173

WESTERN COTTONMOUTH   Pl. 34
Agkistrodon piscivorus leucostoma

Identification: 30–42 in. (76–107 cm); record 55½ in. (141.0 cm). A smaller, darker, less well patterned subspecies of the Cottonmouth. Belly dark brown or black, the dark dorsal crossbands (when evident) uniform or with dusky centers, and snout without clear-cut markings. Many specimens are plain black or dark brown with little or no trace of a pattern. *Young:* Strongly and brightly marked, but all pattern elements, including the dark cheek stripe, rapidly become far less conspicuous as the snake grows. A rare few retain markings into adulthood; most specimens become almost uniformly dark at an early age. From 6–11 in. (15–28 cm) at birth; tip of tail yellow.

Behavior the same as in Eastern Cottonmouth. The habit

of holding the mouth open has earned it the names of "gapper" and "trapjaw," the latter in reference to speed with which mouth snaps shut if anything touches it. These names are prevalent in the Ozarks and adjacent regions. An extremely abundant snake in the swamps and bayous of Louisiana and other southern states. Also invades certain more upland areas of the Central Highlands and may be found in company of or hibernating with rattlesnakes and copperheads.

Similar species: See Fig. 60, opp. Pl. 34.

Range: Extr. s. Illinois and w.-cen. Kentucky to Alabama; west to s.-cen. Oklahoma and cen. Texas. An isolated colony in n.-cen. Missouri.   Map 173

Rattlesnakes: Genera *Sistrurus* and *Crotalus*

THE rattle is the hallmark of these snakes. In adults it is an organ of loosely attached horny segments that strike against one another to produce a buzzing sound when the tail is vibrated rapidly. In the very young the rattle is represented by a button. Later a new segment is added at each shedding time, the segments becoming progressively larger until the snake reaches adult size. Two to 4 new segments are normally added each year. The button remains at the end of the string unless it is lost through wear or breaking of the rather fragile rattle (see Fig. 61, opp. Pl. 35).

Because of the great disparity in size, the sounds made by the different species vary greatly. In general, the largest rattlesnakes produce the loudest, most sonorous tones. Buzzing is the best way to describe them, but the sounds have also been likened to those of escaping steam and the noise produced by cicadas ("locusts"). Rarely, a rattlesnake may have no rattle — if the end of the tail has been chopped off by a man wielding a hoe or severed by some other enemy. Many other serpents, including cottonmouths, copperheads, and numerous nonpoisonous kinds vibrate their tails rapidly when brought to bay. If their tails brush against dry leaves or other vegetation, the resultant sound is suggestive of a rattlesnake.

The pygmy rattlers and massasaugas (*Sistrurus*) have a set of 9 plates on the crowns of their heads, as do most nonpoisonous snakes. All our other rattlers (*Crotalus*) have their heads largely covered with small scales (see Fig. 70, p. 231). The dorsal scales are *keeled* and the anal plate is *single*.

Rodents and birds are the chief foods, but frogs, lizards, etc., are also eaten, especially by the smaller kinds. Rattlesnakes occur only in the New World. There are 31 species distributed from southern Canada to northern Argentina and Uruguay. They are found in all 48 of the contiguous states except Maine and Delaware, but are most numerous, in variety of species and subspecies, in Mexico and the southwestern United States.

In measuring rattlesnakes the length of the rattle is *not* included.

EASTERN MASSASAUGA   Pl. 35
Sistrurus catenatus catenatus

Identification: 20–30 in. (51–76 cm); record 39½ in. (100.3 cm).
The "swamp rattler" or "black snapper." A spotted rattler with
a row of large black or dark brown blotches down the back and
3 rows of smaller dark spots on each side of body. Ground color
gray or brownish gray. Belly black, irregularly marked with
white or yellowish (Fig. 71, p. 232). Some adults are jet-black,
both above and below, with no trace of pattern save for a few
light marks on chin and throat. Nine *plates* on crown of head
(Fig. 70, below). *Young:* Well patterned but paler than adults;
7½–9½ in. (19–24 cm) at birth.

Fig. 70. TOPS OF HEADS OF RATTLESNAKES *(Sistrurus and Crotalus)*

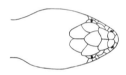

PYGMIES AND MASSASAUGAS   RATTLESNAKES
(Sistrurus)   *(Crotalus)*
A group of 9 large scales   Crown of head with a mixture
(plates) on crown of head   of large and small scales

Wet prairies are the preferred habitat toward the western part
of the range and bogs and swamps toward the east, but these
snakes also occur in dry woodlands. Many individuals are
mild-mannered, seldom rattling until thoroughly aroused. They
may hide in crayfish holes or other underground cavities. At
harvest times massasaugas often turn up, sometimes in numbers, under shocks of grain where mice have congregated. Other
food includes small birds, frogs, and snakes.
Similar species: Timber Rattlesnake has small scales on crown
of head (Fig. 70, above).
Range: Cen. New York and s. Ontario to Iowa and Missouri.
Map 176

WESTERN MASSASAUGA   Pl. 35
Sistrurus catenatus tergeminus

Identification: 18–26 in. (46–66 cm); record 34¾ in. (88.3 cm).
Similar to Eastern Massasauga, but paler in coloration, and with
the dark brown blotches in strong contrast with the light gray

or tan-gray ground color. Belly light with a few dark markings (Fig. 71, below). *Young:* Similar but often pinkish on venter and toward tip of tail; 7–9½ in. (18–24 cm) at birth.

A snake of the plains and prairies, taking advantage of boggy areas and rocky outcrops where they exist. Lizards, small snakes, frogs, mice, and shrews have been recorded as food.

Similar species: (1) Western Pygmy Rattlesnake has a tiny rattle, slender tail, and usually a reddish stripe down center of back. (2) From all other Rattlers within its range, the Western Massasauga may be distinguished by the group of *9 plates* on the crown of its head (Fig. 70, p. 231).

Range: Sw. Iowa and adj. Missouri southwestward and through cen. Texas to the Gulf; intergrades with Desert Massasauga in se. Colorado and adj. areas.

Subspecies: DESERT MASSASAUGA, *Sistrurus c. edwardsi.* Smaller and more slender; max. about 21 in. (53 cm). Similarly patterned but paler, and with ventral surface nearly white and virtually (or completely) unmarked. Scale rows at midbody 23 (25 in Western Massasauga). Chiefly desert grasslands from w. Texas to se. Arizona; also extr. s. Texas and adj. Tamaulipas, and an aberrant, isolated population in Coahuila.   Map 176

CAROLINA PYGMY RATTLESNAKE   Pl. 35
Sistrurus miliarius miliarius

Identification: 15–21 in. (38–53 cm); record 25 in. (63.5 cm). The tiny rattle, sounding like the buzz of an insect, is scarcely audible more than a few feet away. It and the slender tail identify the pygmy or "ground rattlers." In this race the markings are clear-cut, there are 1 or 2 rows of dark lateral spots, and the venter is cream-colored, moderately flecked with brown or gray. Dorsal coloration brown or light gray; a middorsal russet stripe in many specimens. *Reddish phase:* In eastern North Carolina, chiefly between Pamlico and Albemarle Sounds, the majority of specimens are reddish, ranging from orange or pinkish to brick red. Nine *plates* on crown of head (Fig. 70, p. 231). *Young:* Tip of tail sulfur-yellow; 5⅞–7½ in. (15–19 cm) at birth.

Behavior varies, depending on such factors as temperature

Fig. 71. BELLIES OF MASSASAUGAS *(Sistrurus catenatus)*

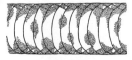

WESTERN
(tergeminus)
Light in coloration

EASTERN
(catenatus)
Chiefly black

and temperament. Some strike furiously; others are lethargic
and do not even sound the rattle. Occurs in longleaf pine-scrub
oak and longleaf-loblolly pine flatwood areas on the Atlantic
Coastal Plain and in pine-oak woods farther west. Food (of all
pygmy rattlers) includes mice, lizards, snakes, and frogs.
Range: E. N. Carolina to cen. Alabama.   Map 177

DUSKY PYGMY RATTLESNAKE   Pl. 35
Sistrurus miliarius barbouri
Identification: 15–22 in. (38–56 cm); record 31 in. (78.7 cm).
This subspecies of the Pygmy Rattler has a dusted appearance
caused by dark stippling that may largely obscure the markings,
especially those on the head. A reddish-brown middorsal stripe,
prominent in many specimens, is subdued or only evident in
the neck region in others. Usually 3 rows of dark lateral spots.
Venter whitish, heavily blotched or flecked with black or dark
brown; sometimes uniform brownish black, at least posteriorly.
Nine *plates* on crown of head (Fig. 70, p. 231). *Young:* Tail tip
yellow; about 6¼–7 in. (16–18 cm) at birth.
    At home in flatwoods and in virtually all types of terrain
where lakes and marshes abound. Especially abundant in the
prairie portions of the Everglades.
Range: Extr. s. S. Carolina to se. Mississippi and south to tip
of Florida.   Map 177

WESTERN PYGMY RATTLESNAKE   Pl. 35
Sistrurus miliarius streckeri
Identification: 15–20 in. (38–51 cm); record 25⅛ in. (63.8 cm).
Tiny rattle and skinny tail. Ground color light, usually pale
grayish brown. The middorsal dark spots may be highly irregular in shape, but they often tend to form short transverse bars.
One or 2 conspicuous rows of dark spots on each side of body.
Reddish dorsal stripe sometimes absent. Nine *plates* on crown
of head (Fig. 70, p. 231). *Young:* About 5⅛–7 in. (13–18 cm) at
birth.
    Habitats are usually in areas where water is nearby — in river
floodplains, swamps, marshes, and wet prairies.
Similar species: (1) Western Massasauga has much larger
rattle and a tail of moderate size. (2) All other Rattlesnakes
occurring within Western Pygmy's range have small scales on
crown of head (Fig. 70, p. 231).
Range: S. Missouri and e. Oklahoma to the Gulf; an eastward
extension into w. Tennessee and sw. Kentucky.   Map 177

TIMBER RATTLESNAKE   Pl. 35
Crotalus horridus horridus
Identification: 36–54 in. (91–137 cm); record 74 in. (188.0 cm).
Sometimes called the "banded" or "velvet-tail rattler." Two
major color patterns: (a) *yellow phase* — black or dark brown

crossbands on a ground color of yellow, brown, or gray; the crossbands, which may be V-shaped, break up anteriorly to form a row of dark spots down the back plus a row along each side of body; (b) *black phase* — a heavy stippling of black or very dark brown that hides much of lighter pigment; completely black specimens are not unusual in uplands of the Northeast. *Young:* Always crossbanded as in yellow phase, but with colors more somber; 11 or 12 in. (28–30 cm) at birth.

The only rattlesnake in most of the populous Northeast. Still common in some mountainous regions but completely extirpated in many areas where it once was numerous. During winter, timber rattlers may congregate in dens to hibernate, together with copperheads and other snakes. Such dens, which may include a hundred or more rattlers, usually are in or near wooded rocky ledges with southern exposures, where they can sun themselves in spring and autumn. During summer they scatter over the surrounding countryside but return to den in the fall. This is a snake of timbered terrain, usually most common in second-growth where rodents abound. Toward the west it follows wooded stream valleys that extend out into the prairies.

Similar species: Eastern Massasauga, which also is sometimes completely black, has *9 plates* on crown of head instead of numerous small scales (Fig. 70, p. 231).

Range: S. New Hampshire and the Lake Champlain region to n. Georgia and west, north of the Mississippi embayment, to Illinois; sw. Wisconsin to nw. Arkansas and ne. Texas. (Map 178 indicates the general distribution of the Timber Rattlesnake, and does not take into account areas in which it has been exterminated by the activities of mankind.)   Map 178

CANEBRAKE RATTLESNAKE   Pl. 35
Crotalus horridus atricaudatus

Identification: 42–60 in. (107–152 cm); record 74½ in. (189.2 cm). The broad dark stripe, running backward from the eye, is one of the most reliable characters (Fig. 72, p. 235). The reddish middorsal stripe splits the black crossbands in half on forward part of body. Ground color ranges from pale grayish brown to pinkish buff. *Young:* Strongly patterned but paler; 11–16 in. (28–41 cm) at birth.

A lowland counterpart of the Timber Rattler that is at home in cane thickets and swamplands of the South.

Similar species: (1) Timber Rattler normally lacks dark stripe behind eye; eastern Timbers usually lack reddish-brown middorsal stripe, but specimens in western part of range may have it. (2) The two Diamondback Rattlers have diamond markings instead of dark crossbands. (3) Pygmies and Massasaugas have *9 plates* on crowns of heads instead of small scales (Fig. 70, p. 231).

Range: Lowlands of se. Virginia to n. Florida and west to cen. Texas; north in Mississippi Valley to s. Illinois.   Map 178

Fig. 72. SIDES OF HEADS OF RATTLESNAKES *(Crotalus)*

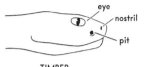

TIMBER
(horridus)
Head markings are
normally lacking

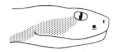

CANEBRAKE
(atricaudatus)
Dark stripe from eye to
angle of jaw and beyond

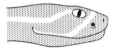

PRAIRIE *(viridis)* AND
MOJAVE *(scutulatus)*
Rear light stripe passes
above mouth line

WESTERN DIAMONDBACK
(atrox)
Rear light stripe meets mouth
line in front of angle of jaw

EASTERN DIAMONDBACK RATTLESNAKE   Pl. 35
Crotalus adamanteus

Identification: 33–72 in. (84–183 cm); record 96 in. (243.8 cm). An ominously impressive snake to meet in the field; suddenly finding yourself in close proximity to the compact coils, broad head, and loud buzzing rattle is almost certain to raise the hair on the nape of your neck. The diamonds, dark brown or black in color, are strongly outlined by a row of cream-colored or yellowish scales. Ground color olive, brown, or almost black. Pattern and colors vivid in freshly shed specimens; dull and quite dark in those preparing to shed. Only rattler within its range with 2 prominent light lines on face and vertical light lines on snout. *Young:* 12–14 in. (30–36 cm) at birth.

At home in the palmetto flatwoods and dry pinelands of the South. Occasionally ventures into salt water, swimming to outlying Keys off the Florida coast. Individual dispositions vary. Some snakes will permit close approach without making a sound, whereas others, completely concealed in palmettos or other vegetation, will rattle when dogs or persons are 20 or 30 feet (6–9 m) away. Many stand their ground, but when hard pressed they back away, rattling vigorously but still facing the intruder. Frequently they take refuge in burrows of gopher tortoises, in holes beneath stumps, etc. Rabbits, rodents, and birds are eaten.

Range: Coastal lowlands from se. N. Carolina to extr. e. Louisiana; all of Florida, including the Keys.   Map 184

WESTERN DIAMONDBACK RATTLESNAKE   Pl. 36
Crotalus atrox

Identification: 30–72 in. (76–183 cm); record 83⅞ in. (213.0 cm). Great size, a tendency to stand its ground, and the loud, buzzing rattle usually are sufficient identification. When fully aroused, it may raise the head and a loop of the neck high above the coils, gaining elevation for aiming and striking. The diamonds are not clear-cut, and the entire head and body may have a dusty appearance. General coloration brown or gray, but sometimes with strong reddish or yellowish tones. Light stripe behind eye meets mouth line in front of angle of jaw (Fig. 72, p. 235). *Tail strongly ringed* with black and white or light gray ("coontail rattler"). *Young:* Diamonds more sharply defined; 10–14 in. (25–36 cm) at birth.

A snake of the arid Southwest, occurring chiefly in the lowlands, but also ascending into mountains to altitudes of 5000 ft. (1500 m) or more. At home on desert flats as well as in rocky cliffs and canyons. Food includes rabbits and such rodents as rats, mice, gophers, and ground squirrels. The Western Diamondback is responsible for more serious snakebites and fatalities than any other North American serpent. From the standpoint of sheer size, it and the Eastern Diamondback rank among the world's largest and most dangerous snakes.

Similar species: (1) In extreme western Texas (and westward) the Western Diamondback may be confused with the very similar Mojave Rattlesnake, which see for characteristics distinguishing the two species. (2) Prairie Rattler has light line behind eye passing *above* corner of mouth (Fig. 72, p. 235).

Range: Cen. Arkansas and Texas to se. California; south into n. Mexico; isolated populations in s. Mexico.   Map 183

MOJAVE RATTLESNAKE   Pl. 36
Crotalus scutulatus scutulatus

Identification: 24–36 in. (61–91 cm); record 51 in. (129.5 cm). Likely to be confused only with the Western Diamondback Rattler, but the Mojave normally has: (a) *black tail rings much narrower than white rings;* (b) light line behind eye passing above and beyond corner of mouth (Fig. 72, p. 235); (c) whitish scales surrounding dark diamonds largely unicolored; (d) lower half of proximal (basal) segment of rattle paler than upper half; and (e) enlarged scales on snout and between supraoculars. Coloration variable; general appearance may be gray, greenish, or brownish, some specimens pale and others relatively dark. *Young:* About 10½ in. (27 cm) at birth.

A snake of the desert; often found on open, brush- or grass-covered flats and on mountain slopes. Despite its similarity to the Western Diamondback, its venom is much more virulent, a fact that makes the Mojave Rattler one of the most dangerous poisonous snakes in the United States. (See p. 30.)

Similar species: (1) Western Diamondback Rattlesnake has: (a) wider black tail rings; (b) light line from eye meeting mouth line (Fig. 72, p. 235); (c) a diamond pattern that is often not clear-cut; (d) proximal segment of rattle same color throughout; and (e) small scales on snout and between supraoculars. Mojave Rattlesnakes in western Texas are often aberrant and one or more identification characters may approximate those of Western Diamondback. (2) Prairie Rattlesnake lacks "coontail" appearance of tail.

Range: Extr. w. Texas including Big Bend region; s. Nevada and adj. California to Querétaro. Mexican subspecies.

Map 181

PRAIRIE RATTLESNAKE *Crotalus viridis viridis* Pl. 36

Identification: 35–45 in. (89–114 cm); record 57 in. (144.8 cm). A blotched rattlesnake with the blotches broad anteriorly, but narrow and joining with the lateral markings to form crossbands near the tail. Ground color usually greenish gray, olive-green, or greenish brown, but sometimes light brown or yellowish. The dark brown blotches are narrowly bordered with white. Two oblique light lines on head, the one behind eye passing *above* corner of mouth (Fig. 72, p. 235). *Young:* About 8½–11 in. (22–28 cm) at birth.

A very abundant rattler (in some areas) that lives in the grasslands of the Great Plains, but retreats in winter to dens in rocky outcrops and ledges. Also ascends into mountains, but only rarely above 8000 ft. (2400 m). This is the snake supposed to live in harmony with prairie dogs and burrowing owls, but, alas for the writers of fanciful fiction, young prairie dogs and owls make excellent meals for prairie rattlers.

Similar species: (1) Tails of Mojave and Western Diamondback Rattlesnakes are strongly ringed with black and white. (2) In Western Diamondback light line behind eye meets mouth line in front of angle of jaw (Fig. 72, p. 235). (3) Western Massasauga has *9 plates* on crown of head instead of small scales (Fig. 70, p. 231). (4) Rock Rattlesnakes have the dark crossbands far apart.

Range: Extr. w. Iowa to the Rockies and beyond; s. Canada to n. Mexico. Western subspecies. Map 179

BLACK-TAILED RATTLESNAKE Pl. 36
Crotalus molossus molossus

Identification: 30–42 in. (76–107 cm); record 49½ in. (125.7 cm). The "green rattler" of the central Texas uplands and westward. Characterized by three unique features: (a) black of the tail ends abruptly at body; (b) patches of light scales in dark crossbands; and (c) each scale unicolored. In most other rattlers the pattern cuts across the scales, so that many individual scales may be half dark and half light, etc. Populations from upland areas, such as the Davis and Chisos Mountains of western Texas, tend to be dark in coloration. Specimens from farther west are often greenish yellow. *Young:* Similar, but with dark crossbands visible on tail; about 9–11¾ in. (23–30 cm) at birth.

An inhabitant of rock piles and slides, wooded canyons, and the vicinity of cliffs.

Range: The Edwards Plateau of cen. Texas west to Arizona and n. Mexico. Mexican subspecies.   Map 180

MOTTLED ROCK RATTLESNAKE   Pl. 36
Crotalus lepidus lepidus
   Identification: 18–24 in. (46–61 cm); record 30¼ in. (76.8 cm). A dusty-looking snake, the mottled effect being produced by a profuse stippling of dark pigment that may be so intense as to form pseudo-crossbands between the dark crossbars. General coloration may be gray, bluish gray, greenish gray, tan, brown, or pinkish. The dark crosslines, inconspicuous on forepart of body but progressively more prominent toward tail, may be brown or black but they vary in intensity from one specimen to the next. *A dark stripe from eye to angle of mouth. Young:* About 6¾–8 in. (17–20 cm) at birth.

A montane, rock-inhabiting rattler. Its menu is extremely varied; small rodents, lizards, small snakes, frogs, salamanders, and insects are included.

Range: S.-cen. Texas west through Trans-Pecos region and south to San Luis Potosí; se. New Mexico. Mexican subspecies.
                    Map 182

BANDED ROCK RATTLESNAKE   Pl. 36
Crotalus lepidus klauberi
   Identification: 15–24 in. (38–61 cm); record 32⅝ in. (82.9 cm). *A pattern of widely-spaced black or brown crossbars* throughout length of body and in strong contrast with the greenish, bluish-green, or bluish-gray ground color. Relatively little dark spotting between crossbars (in comparison with the eastern subspecies, the Mottled Rock Rattlesnake). *No dark stripe from eye to angle of mouth. Young:* About 7¾ in. (20 cm) at birth; tail bright yellow at tip.

An inhabitant of rock slides and rocky hillsides, gorges, or stream beds in arid or semiarid terrain, chiefly in mountains.

Range: Extr. w. Texas to w.-cen. New Mexico and from se. Arizona to Jalisco. Mexican subspecies.   Map 182

IX

Salamanders
Order Caudata

THE Americas have far more kinds of salamanders than all the rest of the world put together. Those in our area range in size from dwarf species scarcely 2 inches long (5 cm), to giants like the amphiumas that attain lengths of nearly 4 feet (1.2 m). The enormous family of lungless salamanders (Plethodontidae), almost exclusively confined to the New World, accounts for more than 180 of the 300-odd species of salamanders known to science.

Moisture is an absolute necessity. Some kinds, including all the larger ones, are aquatic, but even the terrestrial species can survive only in damp environments. They hide by day and prowl by night. Observing salamanders consists largely of examining small streams and wet woodlands at night with flashlight or headlamp or, during daylight hours, overturning stones, logs, or other objects beneath which they may hide.

Lizards are easily confused with salamanders, but lizards have scales on their bodies and claws on their toes. Salamanders have smooth or warty skins, and are clawless. Because the tail is frequently damaged by accident or encounters with predators, herpetologists, in accumulating data for comparative studies, measure the *standard length,* the distance from tip of snout to posterior angle of vent (same as head–body length — see rear endpaper). Salamanders, which are widely used for fish bait, are frequently liberated by anglers or bait dealers, and that often accounts for finding a species outside its normal range.

Counting costal grooves (see rear endpaper) may be necessary for identifying some kinds of salamanders. Adpressing the toes (Fig. 73, below) is helpful in distinguishing between kinds that look alike but which have long legs and toes or both in one species and short ones in the other.

Fig. 73. ADPRESSED TOES IN SALAMANDERS

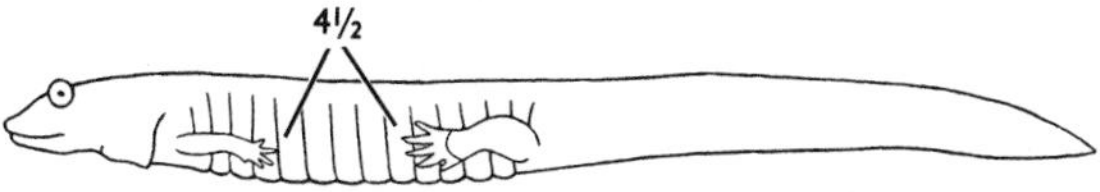

To count intercostal spaces, press limbs firmly against body.

The best way of identifying many kinds of salamander larvae is to raise them until they transform into adults. They do well in aquariums (a minimum of one gallon of water for each specimen) if they are fed frequently with small, live, aquatic invertebrates, supplemented by crumbs of ground beef or canned dog food rich in meat. Large larvae are cannibalistic.

Giant Salamanders: Families Cryptobranchidae, Necturidae, Amphiumidae, and Sirenidae

NORTH America boasts an assortment of big, bizarre salamanders that look more like bad dreams than live animals. Some are long, dark, and slender and resemble eels. Some permanently retain the larval form, bearing external gills throughout their lives. Others are flattened and are suggestive of weird creatures crawling forth from the antediluvian slime. Since all are aquatic and nocturnal, few persons other than fishermen ever meet them in person. Periodically one or the other is reported in the press as an animal "new to science." The erroneous belief that they are poisonous is widespread.

Many of these salamanders thrive in aquariums, but they should be provided with shelter in the form of flat rocks under which to crawl, or aquatic vegetation in which to hide. As in the care of aquarium fishes, the water must be kept from fouling and free from chlorine. A screened lid, tied or weighted down, should be provided; many specimens are persistent in their efforts to escape, at least during the first day or two. Many soon learn to eat small pieces of meat or liver or canned dog food.

Three of the families (Amphiumidae, Necturidae, and Sirenidae) are confined to North America. The Cryptobranchidae (hellbenders) has representatives in the Far East, including the enormous Japanese Salamander that grows to a length of 5 feet (1.5 m). Not all members of these families are large: the dwarf sirens (*Pseudobranchus*) are tiny (up to about 10 inches (25 cm) long) compared with their close relative, the Greater Siren, that attains a length in excess of 3 feet (.9 m).

The classification of the genus *Necturus,* several members of which are confusingly alike, needs study.

HELLBENDER   **Pl. 37**
Cryptobranchus alleganiensis alleganiensis
   Identification: 11½–20 in. (29–51 cm). Records: Males 27 in. (68.6 cm); females 29⅛ in. (74.0 cm). A huge, grotesque, thor-

oughly aquatic salamander. Head flattened and each side of body with a wrinkled, fleshy fold of skin. Ground color usually gray, but varying from yellowish brown to almost black. Vague, scattered, and irregular dark or light spots may often be seen. No external gills in adult. *Young:* Numerous irregular dark spots that are conspicuous against light ground color; usually between 4 and 5 in. (10–13 cm) when they lose their external gills.

Almost always found in rivers and larger streams where water is running and ample shelter is available in the form of large rocks, snags, or debris. Hellbenders sometimes may be caught by *slowly* overturning or moving large rocks in clear, relatively shallow streams, and taking them by dip net or by hand. Since they are exceedingly slimy, the fingers must encircle the neck *and* immobilize both front legs on the first grab. Quite harmless, but many fishermen, believing them to be poisonous, will cut their lines and sacrifice their gear rather than unhook them. Captives will eat crayfish, earthworms, aquatic insects, and sometimes even pieces of meat.

Similar species: Adult Mudpuppies and Waterdogs have external gills, and so do larval specimens of other species.

Range: Susquehanna River drainage from se. New York to head of Chesapeake Bay and southwestward to s. Illinois, extr. ne. Mississippi, and northern parts of Alabama and Georgia; cen. and sw. Missouri and possibly adj. Kansas.   Map 188

OZARK HELLBENDER   Pl. 37
Cryptobranchus alleganiensis bishopi

Identification: 11–22⅜ in. (28–56.8 cm). Much like the wide-ranging Hellbender but with the dark markings on the back much more conspicuous and in the form of blotches rather than spots. Lower lips heavily spotted with black (only lightly spotted or not at all in Hellbender). There are also minor anatomical differences. This form is best identified on basis of geography.

Range: Sections of Black River system and North Fork of White River in se. Missouri and adj. Arkansas.   Map 188

MUDPUPPY *Necturus maculosus*   Pl. 37

Identification: 8–13 in. (20–33 cm); record 17 in. (43.2 cm). The gills, at maximum development, are like miniature ostrich plumes, dyed maroon and waving gracefully in the current. This, like all other members of its genus, is a permanent larva, retaining gills throughout life. *Four* toes on each of the 4 feet. Dark stripe through eye. General coloration gray to rust-brown, dorsum normally marked with rather indistinct, scattered, rounded, blue-black spots. Sometimes the spots are few in number, or, rarely, absent altogether; occasionally they fuse to form dorsolateral stripes. Belly grayish, with dark spots (Fig. 74, p. 243) or sometimes plain gray. Tail fins often tinged with orange or reddish. *Larvae and young:* Normally striped; a broad middorsal dark stripe flanked on each side by a yellowish stripe (Fig. 62, opp. Pl. 37); a conspicuous dark stripe on side of body from gills to tip of tail. Occasionally the young are uniformly gray, without markings.

This salamander is a mudpuppy in the North, but southerners, not to be outdone in coining colorful names, refer to it and all its relatives as waterdogs. Throughout much of Dixieland, mudpuppy is also used by country folk, but they reserve the name for adults of any of the mole salamanders (*Ambystoma*). Both names owe their origin, at least in part, to the erroneous belief that these animals bark.

Habitats include lakes, ponds, rivers, streams, and other permanent bodies of water. Essentially nocturnal, but may also be active by day in muddy or weed-choked waters. Almost any small aquatic animal may be taken as food — fish, fish eggs, crayfish, aquatic insects, mollusks, etc. Size and condition of gills, although subject to individual variation, usually reflect environment. They are most likely to be large, bushy, and kept in motion if the water is foul or warm; usually they are small and contracted if the water is cool and contains considerable oxygen in solution.

Similar species: (1) Hellbenders have flat heads, folds of skin along sides, and adults lack external gills. (2) Gulf Coast Waterdog has very numerous dorsal spots, and dark stripe through eye may be absent or poorly developed. (3) Larvae of some Mole Salamanders (*Ambystoma*) grow large enough to be mistaken for Mudpuppies or Waterdogs (*Necturus*), but Mole Salamanders have 5 toes on each *hind* foot.

Range: S. Quebec, Lake Champlain drainage, and e. New York to se. Manitoba and south to e. Kansas, s. Missouri, and Tennessee River system; introduced in several places in New England.

Subspecies: MUDPUPPY, *Necturus m. maculosus* (Plate 37). As described and with range indicated above. LAKE WINNEBAGO MUDPUPPY, *Necturus m. stictus.* A very dark race, dark gray to almost black, with dorsum, head especially, marked with scattered black or dark brown dots; tiny flecks of tan may partially obscure ground color; occasionally there may be a few large dark blotches on back and sides; record length 19⅛ in. (48.6 cm). Ne. Wisconsin and adj. Michigan; taken at a record depth of 90 ft. (27.4 m) in Green Bay. LOUISIANA WATERDOG, *Necturus m. louisianensis.* Ground color light yellowish brown or tan and with a broad, fairly distinct light stripe on each side of a darker middorsal area. These markings are remnants of the juvenile pattern, which is striped like that of a young Mudpuppy. Dark spots begin to develop at an early age. Dorsum becomes gray in largest specimens, but dark spots remain clearly evident. Dark stripe through eye, extending from nostril to base of gills; center of venter grayish white, unmarked but tinged with pink (Fig. 74, below). Averages smaller than Mudpuppy; maximum length about 11 in. (28 cm). Arkansas River and associated and adjacent drainage systems from s. Missouri to n.-cen. Louisiana.   Map 192

Fig. 74. VENTRAL PATTERNS OF SEVERAL WATERDOGS
AND THE MUDPUPPY (Necturus)

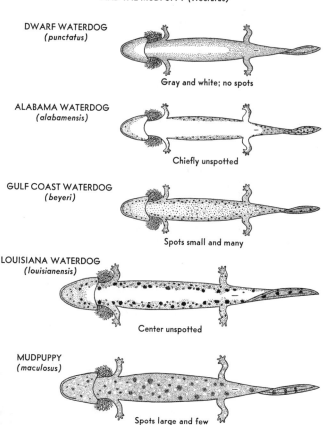

DWARF WATERDOG
(punctatus)

Gray and white; no spots

ALABAMA WATERDOG
(alabamensis)

Chiefly unspotted

GULF COAST WATERDOG
(beyeri)

Spots small and many

LOUISIANA WATERDOG
(louisianensis)

Center unspotted

MUDPUPPY
(maculosus)

Spots large and few

NEUSE RIVER WATERDOG
Necturus lewisi

Fig. 75, below

Identification: 6–9 in. (15–23 cm); record 10⅞ in. (27.6 cm). This waterdog is strongly spotted both above *and below,* but markings tend to be fewer and smaller on the undersurfaces (Fig. 75, below). Spots dark brown or bluish black. Dorsal ground color rusty brown; ventral ground color dull brown or slate-colored. Dark line through eye. *Four* toes on all 4 feet. *Young:* Spotted, never plain or striped.

Similar species: (1) Dwarf Waterdog is almost uniformly dark above and plain bluish white down center of belly (Fig. 74, p. 243). (2) Larvae of Mole Salamanders have 5 toes on each *hind* foot.

Range: Neuse and Tar River systems, N. Carolina.   Map 193

Fig. 75. NEUSE RIVER WATERDOG *(Necturus lewisi)*

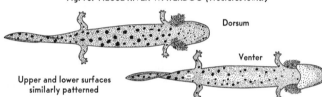

Dorsum

Venter

Upper and lower surfaces
similarly patterned

GULF COAST WATERDOG *Necturus beyeri*

Pl. 37

Identification: 6¼–8¾ in. (16–22.2 cm). A profusely spotted waterdog. Ground color dark brown, but appearing much lighter because of a multiplicity of tan spots that join to form an overlying, fine-meshed, netlike pattern. The round or oval spots, dark brown to almost black in color, are arranged in irregular rows or scattered at random. Belly invaded by spots and by dorsal ground color (Fig. 74, p. 243). Dark stripe through eye in some specimens, absent in others. *Four* toes on all 4 feet. *Larvae and young:* Spotted, never striped (Fig. 62, opp. Pl. 37); dull yellow spots on head and body and in rows on edges of tail fin; dark spots develop as animal grows.

Chiefly in sandy, spring-fed streams.

Similar species: (1) Alabama and Louisiana Waterdogs both have at least the center of the venter unspotted. (2) Larvae of Mole Salamanders have 5 toes on each *hind* foot.

Range: E. Texas to cen. Louisiana; also through the Florida Parishes of Louisiana northward to cen. Mississippi. Map 195

ALABAMA WATERDOG
Necturus alabamensis

Fig. 74, p. 243

Identification: 6–8½ in. (15–21.6 cm). A highly variable salamander in coloration and degree of spotting, depending both on age and geographic locality. Dorsum often reddish brown, but some individuals are russet, others are dark brown, and some may even be slaty black. Patternwise they may be nearly uniformly dark or have a spotted or mottled appearance. Dark spots fairly conspicuous in younger specimens (or in adults that have been poorly or long preserved), but they tend to coalesce and blend with the general dorsal ground color in older individuals. Small scattered light spots often present. Coloration paler on sides of body. *Center of belly unmarked* (Fig. 74, p. 243) white to bluish white. Tips of digits whitish. Tail relatively short; dorsal fin low.

Found chiefly in medium- to large-sized streams that have an abundance of hiding places — stones, bottom debris, and sunken snags and logs.

Similar species: (1) Gulf Coast Waterdog has the *entire venter spotted.* (2) Dwarf Waterdog lacks conspicuous markings of any kind. (3) Larvae of Mole Salamanders have 5 toes on each *hind* foot.

Range: W.-cen. Georgia and the Florida panhandle to e. and sw. Mississippi.   Map 196

DWARF WATERDOG *Necturus punctatus*   **Pl. 37**
Identification: 4½–6¼ in. (11–16 cm); record 7 ⁷⁄₁₆ in. (18.9 cm). A southeastern waterdog with no conspicuous markings of any kind. Dorsum slate-gray to dark brown or black (sometimes purplish black) with a few small pale spots. Throat whitish. Central portion of belly bluish white, plain or partly invaded by the dorsal color (Fig. 74, p. 243). *Four* toes on all 4 feet. *Young:* Always brownish, even if adults from the same populations are gray.

Found in sluggish streams; prefers areas where the bottom is composed of masses of leaf litter and similar debris.
Similar species: (1) Neuse River Waterdog is conspicuously spotted. (2) Larvae of Mole Salamanders have 5 toes on each *hind* foot.
Range: Coastal Plain from se. Virginia to s.-cen. Georgia.
                                                             Map 194

TWO-TOED AMPHIUMA *Amphiuma means*   **Pl. 37**
Identification: 18–30 in. (46–76 cm); record 45¾ in. (116.2 cm). An "eel" with 2 pairs of tiny, useless-looking legs. *Two toes* on each limb. Dorsum dark brown or black; venter dark gray. No sharp change of color between back and belly. This is the "congo (conger) eel," "lamper eel," or "ditch eel" of fishermen and country folk. (The same names are often applied to the other species of *Amphiuma* and to both species of *Siren.*)

Almost completely aquatic, but occasionally moves overland through swamps on rainy nights. Habitats include ditches, sloughs, pools, ponds, rice fields, swamps, streams, etc. Many specimens utilize lairs in mud or jumbles of bottom debris, protruding their heads a short distance upward or outward from their hiding places while waiting for crayfish or other food to come along. Best sought at night in shallow water. A dip net with a deep bag, although rather awkward to use on such slippery, elongated animals, is the safest tool with which to catch them unharmed. They can bite savagely. Another technique is to cover your hand with burlap sacking or wear a stout glove, grab the amphiuma at midbody, and sling it out on land where you can work it into a bag. Food includes worms, insects, mollusks, crustaceans, small fish, snakes, frogs, and smaller amphiumas.

Similar species: (1) See the other two kinds of Amphiumas — count toes. (2) Sirens have external gills and *no hind legs.* (3) True eels (fishes) have a fin at each side of head and no legs.
Range: Coastal Plain from se. Virginia to the southern tip of Florida and west to se. Mississippi and extr. e. Louisiana.

Map 191

THREE-TOED AMPHIUMA   Pl. 37
Amphiuma tridactylum

Identification: 18–30 in. (46–76 cm); record 41¾ in. (106.0 cm). The Mississippi Valley representative of the amphiuma group of species. *Three toes* on each limb. Dorsum dark brown and sharply set off from the much paler (light gray) venter. A dark throat patch.

An abundant salamander of bayous and ditches of the Mississippi delta region, of ox-bows, lakes, and ponds, and in fact of almost any unpolluted muddy or mucky habitat throughout its range.
Similar species: See **Similar species** under Two-toed Amphiuma.
Range: Se. Missouri, adj. Kentucky, and extr. se. Oklahoma to Gulf of Mexico.   Map 190

ONE-TOED AMPHIUMA   *Amphiuma pholeter*   Pl. 37
Identification: 8½–12½ in. (22–32 cm); record 13 in. (33.0 cm). A dwarf amphiuma with only one toe on each foot. Limbs and head proportionately shorter and eye proportionately smaller than in the other amphiumas. Venter dusky and virtually same color as dorsum.

A secretive salamander of muck-bottomed stream floodplains and other mucky habitats.
Similar species: In both the Two-toed and Three-toed Amphiumas the dorsum is distinctly darker than the venter. Occasional specimens of the two larger species may have only a single toe on one or more feet as a result of injury or fighting, but in such cases the maimed or regenerated condition of the limb is usually recognizable.

Range: The Gulf Hammock region of the Florida Peninsula, the adjacent panhandle, and sw. Georgia.   Map 189

GREATER SIREN *Siren lacertina*   **Pl. 37**
Identification: 20–30 in. (51–76 cm); record 38½ in. (97.8 cm). An "eel" with forelegs and external gills; these appendages are crowded together instead of being spread out along the slender body. The legs, so small that they are easily hidden by the gills, have *four* toes each. General coloration olive to light gray, the back darker than sides, and the latter with rather faint greenish or yellowish dots and dashes. In some specimens circular, well-defined black spots may be seen on top of head, back, and sides. Belly with numerous small greenish or yellowish flecks. *Young:* A prominent light stripe on side of body plus a light dorsal fin make juveniles look superficially like dwarf sirens. Light markings disappear and young become almost uniformly dark as they approach maturity.

Lives in a large variety of essentially shallow water habitats — ditches, weed-choked or muddy ponds, rice fields, streams with clear to turbid water, lakes, etc. Often these salamanders may be observed at night with the aid of a flashlight as they forage. Young ones sometimes abound amid roots of water hyacinths. Sirens may yelp when caught, making a sound similar to that of a Green Treefrog heard calling in the distance. Crayfish, worms, mollusks, etc., are eaten, but sirens also engulf quantities of aquatic vegetation in the course of swallowing animal food.

Similar species: (1) True eels (which are fishes) have a fin at each side of neck and no legs or external gills. (2) Amphiumas also lack external gills, but they have *four* small legs, a pair aft as well as forward. (3) Dwarf Sirens have only *three* toes on each leg. (4) Difficulty will inevitably arise in trying to distinguish small Greater Sirens from adults of Eastern Lesser Siren — even experts have trouble. Eastern Lesser Siren lacks any pronounced light markings; counting costal grooves will help, these being 36 to 39 in Greater Siren (from armpit to anus), and from 31 to 34 in Eastern Lesser Siren. Checking on costal grooves is always difficult on a live salamander. Let your Siren settle down in a flat-sided aquarium and don't touch it when you count.

Range: Vicinity of Washington, D.C., to extr. s. Florida and s. Alabama.   Map 185

LESSER SIREN *Siren intermedia*   **Pl. 37**
Identification: 7–27 in. (18–68.6 cm). Size varies — see subspecies. Similar to the Greater Siren in general appearance and in having external gills and 2 tiny front legs, each with *4* toes. General dorsal coloration dark brown to bluish black, sometimes olive-green. Darker specimens are virtually without markings,

but in the lighter ones irregularly scattered black dots are discernible. *Young:* A red band across snout and along side of head. These markings disappear with age; older juveniles may be olive-green with tiny brown spots.

This eel-like salamander spends the daylight hours burrowed in debris that accumulates at bottoms of ditches, ponds, and other bodies of shallow water. When and if the water dries up it descends into the mud, and when that, in turn, dries over, the siren becomes entombed and must wait, sometimes for months, until the coming of rains. In preparation for estivation, skin glands secrete a substance that forms a dry, inelastic, parchmentlike cocoon covering the entire body (except the mouth) and which protects the animal from desiccation.

Sirens were named for a temptress of mythology, and not for the warning device used by emergency vehicles. They do make sounds, however, consisting of series of faint clicks that are emitted when other sirens approach or when a specimen partially leaves a burrow in shallow water to gulp air at the surface. They also may utter shrill cries of distress, as when seized by a water snake. Food similar to that of Greater Siren.

Similar species: See Greater Siren.

Range: N. Carolina to s.-cen. Florida; west to e. and s. Texas and north in Mississippi Valley to Indiana and Illinois; sw. Michigan (introduced?).

Subspecies: EASTERN LESSER SIREN, *Siren i. intermedia* (Plate 37). Plain black or brown above or with minute black dots sprinkled over dorsal surface and tail; venter uniformly dark but paler than dorsum; costal grooves 31 to 34; averages small, with a maximum length of 15 in. (38.1 cm). S. Atlantic and Gulf Coastal Plains to se. Mississippi. WESTERN LESSER SIREN, *Siren i. nettingi*. Olive or gray above with scattered, minute black spots; venter dark with numerous *light spots;* costal grooves 34 to 36; averages larger — record 19¾ in. (50.2 cm). Mississippi Valley; east to s.-cen. Alabama and west to e. Texas. RIO GRANDE SIREN, *Siren i. texana*. Gray or brownish gray above and marked with tiny black flecks; venter light gray but paler under gills and limbs, and behind the angles of jaws; costal grooves 36 to 38; size large — record 27 in. (68.6 cm). Lower Rio Grande Valley and n. Tamaulipas; intergrading with *nettingi* along and near Texas coast.   Map 186

Dwarf Sirens: Genus *Pseudobranchus*

THESE are small, aquatic, eel-like salamanders with external gills and tiny forelegs. Each foot bears *three* toes. All are patterned with longitudinal stripes. Just as is true among the waterdogs, the size of the gills depends on temperature and other conditions. Males are seldom found.

This is one of the groups of animals that has prospered by the introduction of the water hyacinth. Dwarf sirens find food and shelter among the roots of these floating pests. A good collecting technique is to roll up masses of hyacinths or slide a large boxlike sieve of fine-mesh wire under a patch of them and carry them ashore. Careful sorting through the lot often may reveal dwarf sirens. (There is a good chance of finding small aquatic snakes at the same time.) When picked up or pinched dwarf sirens may yelp faintly. Food includes aquatic insects and other invertebrates. The genus *Pseudobranchus* occurs only in the extreme southeastern United States. There is a single species, but there are several races.

NARROW-STRIPED DWARF SIREN   Pl. 39
Pseudobranchus striatus axanthus

Identification: 4¾–7½ in. (12–19 cm); record 9⅞ in. (25.1 cm). The only dwarf siren in which there are no sharply defined light stripes (Fig. 76, below). Entire animal looks muddy and pattern details are obscure. Head terminates in a bluntly rounded snout. *Three* toes on each foot.

Similar species: Both Greater and Lesser Sirens have *4* toes on each foot.

Range: Ne. and cen. Florida and the Okefenokee region, Georgia. This subspecies intergrades with all four other races.

Map 187

Fig. 76. PATTERNS OF DWARF SIRENS *(Pseudobranchus)*

(Each diagram shows a section of skin removed from the animal and flattened out — dorsum in center, venter at the sides)

BROAD-STRIPED
(striatus)
Dark middorsal stripe flanked by broad yellow one

SLENDER
(spheniscus)
2 tan or yellow stripes on each side

EVERGLADES
(belli)
Lateral stripe buff; belly gray

GULF HAMMOCK
(lustricolus)
3 narrow yellow stripes in dark middorsal region; belly blackish

NARROW-STRIPED
(axanthus)
Dark stripes narrow, subdued

SLENDER DWARF SIREN   **Pl. 39**
Pseudobranchus striatus spheniscus
>   **Identification:** 4–6 in. (10–15.2 cm). A tiny, slender "eel" with
>   a narrow, wedge-shaped snout, and 2 bright tan or yellow stripes
>   on sides of body.
>   Dwarf sirens of all kinds occur in a variety of shallow, fresh-
>   water habitats, including swamps, marshes, lime-sink ponds, and
>   ditches, particularly those choked with vegetation. Best found
>   by seining up and examining detritus from pond bottoms or by
>   sifting through hyacinths.
>   **Similar species:** Greater and Lesser Sirens have *4* toes on each
>   foot. Dwarf Sirens have only *3*.
>   **Range:** Sw. Georgia and eastern half of Florida panhandle.
>   **Subspecies:** All of these are strongly striped (Fig. 76, p. 249).
>   The stripes are most easily seen when the salamanders are
>   submerged in water. Put them in a flat-sided aquarium when
>   trying to identify the various subspecies. BROAD-STRIPED
>   DWARF SIREN, *Pseudobranchus s. striatus.* Most strikingly pat-
>   terned of all the races; a broad dark brown middorsal stripe
>   with a vague light line down its center and flanked on each side
>   by a broad yellow stripe; belly dark but heavily mottled with
>   yellow. Body short and stocky. Total length up to 6 in.
>   (15.2 cm). S. South Carolina and se. Georgia. GULF HAMMOCK
>   DWARF SIREN, *Pseudobranchus s. lustricolus.* A broad dark
>   middorsal stripe containing *within itself* 3 narrow light stripes,
>   the central one down ridge of back; 2 broad, sharply defined light
>   stripes on each side of body, upper one orange-brown in colora-
>   tion and lower one silvery white; belly black with light mottling;
>   body relatively stout, snout blunt; length up to 8½ in.
>   (21.6 cm). Gulf Hammock region on northwestern side of Florida
>   peninsula. EVERGLADES DWARF SIREN, *Pseudobranchus s. belli.*
>   Similar in stripe pattern to Gulf Hammock race, but with the
>   broad light stripes buff in color and belly gray; a small, slender
>   subspecies with length up to 6 in. (15.2 cm). Southern third of
>   Florida peninsula.   Map 187

Mole Salamanders:
Family Ambystomatidae

LIKE moles, these amphibians stay underground most of their
lives. But they congregate in numbers in temporary pools and
ponds after early spring rains for courtship and deposition of eggs,
activities that may be completed in one or just a few nights. The
eggs may be laid in large clusters or in small groups, floating at
the surface of the water or submerged and attached to sticks or

debris. The method depends on the species. Some kinds breed in autumn; in the South, most egg-laying takes place in winter.

Finding specimens before or after the breeding season is largely a matter of chance. They may wander on rainy nights, but they take shelter before morning beneath boards, logs, stones, etc., unless they accidentally tumble into cellar window wells or ditches.

The larvae of some kinds grow to large size, retain their gills, remain permanently aquatic, and breed without developing all the adult characteristics. Such specimens technically are said to be neotenic; the Mexican Indians have given us the name "axolotl" for them (Fig. 63, opp. Pl. 38). Newly transformed salamanders of this genus are often difficult to identify.

Some of the mole salamanders bear a resemblance to certain of the lungless salamanders (Plethodontidae), but members of the latter family have a groove running from the nostril down to the lip — see back endpaper. (A lens may be necessary to check this characteristic.) Mole salamanders have 5 toes on each hind foot and 4 on each front foot.

The Family Ambystomatidae occurs throughout most of the United States and ranges from extreme southeastern Alaska, James Bay, and southern Labrador to the southern edge of the Mexican Plateau. Its members are widely studied as laboratory animals. In captivity adults are easily maintained in terrariums equipped with a few inches of damp earth. They will eat live earthworms and other invertebrates, and some can be trained to accept small pieces of meat. Larvae are easily raised in aquariums.

MOLE SALAMANDER *Ambystoma talpoideum* **Pl. 38**
Identification: 3-4 in. (8-10 cm); record 4 $1\frac{3}{16}$ in. (12.2 cm). Looks like a case of arrested growth, with head and feet too large for the rest of the animal. Ground color black, brown, or gray; pale flecks bluish white.

A confirmed burrower, but occasionally found under logs or other objects in damp places. Chiefly confined to lowlands and valleys. Occasionally neotenic.
Range: S. Carolina to n. Florida and west to e. Texas; north in Mississippi Valley to s. Illinois; disjunct populations from w. N. Carolina to se. Oklahoma. Map 200

MARBLED SALAMANDER *Ambystoma opacum* **Pl. 38**
Identification: 3½-4¼ in. (9-11 cm); record 5 in. (12.7 cm). "Banded salamander" would be a good alternate name. The light markings, basically crossbands, are variable, being sometimes incomplete, running together, or enclosing dark spots. On rare occasions there may be a light stripe along or parallel to the middorsal line. Markings gray in females, white in males; in both sexes they contrast strongly with the black components

of the pattern and the plain black belly. *Newly transformed juveniles:* Scattered light flecks on a dorsal ground color of dull brown to black.

This rather chunky salamander occurs in a variety of habitats, ranging from moist sandy areas to dry hillsides. Breeds in *autumn,* the female depositing her eggs in a low depression, which will be filled by the next good rain. Eggs, laid in a group but unattached to one another, do not hatch until covered with water. Until then they are guarded by female.

Similar species: Ringed and Flatwoods Salamanders are more slender, and their light rings or crossbands are narrow.

Range: S. New England to n. Florida and west to s. Illinois, e. Oklahoma, and e. Texas; disjunct colonies near southern perimeter of Lake Michigan.   Map 211

RINGED SALAMANDER *Ambystoma annulatum*   **Pl. 38**
  Identification: 5½–7 in. (14–18 cm); record 9¼ in. (23.5 cm). Any of the rings may be incomplete, interrupted across the back, or represented solely by vertical light bars or elongated spots. Coloration variable from medium dark brown to almost black; rings may be buff, yellow, or whitish, sometimes not all same color on same animal. A light gray, rather irregular stripe along lower side of body. Belly slate-colored, with small whitish spots. Head small.

  Seldom encountered except during or following medium to heavy autumn rains. These stimulate the salamanders into forming breeding congresses of scores or even hundreds in pools or shallow ponds.

  Similar species: (1) Marbled Salamander is a shorter, stouter amphibian with a plain black belly, and its crossbands are broader and usually have a silvery appearance. (2) In Barred Tiger Salamander (and Marbled) black pigment extends uninterruptedly from back to belly.

  Range: Cen. Missouri, w. Arkansas, and e. Oklahoma.

                                                      Map 202

FLATWOODS SALAMANDER   **Pl. 38**
Ambystoma cingulatum
  Identification: 3½–5¹⁄₁₆ in. (9–12.9 cm). The dorsal markings are highly variable, ranging from a "frosted" or lichenlike appearance to a netlike (reticulated) pattern or a tendency to form series of narrow light rings. Ground color black to chocolate-black; markings gray or brownish gray. Belly black with scattered pearl-gray spots or with great numbers of tiny gray flecks that produce a salt-and-pepper appearance.

  An inhabitant of slashpine-wiregrass flatwoods. Often found under objects near the small shallow cypress ponds characteristic of such areas.

Similar species: (1) Mabee's Salamander is often brownish and with the light flecks most conspicuous along the sides; not patterned all over as in the Flatwoods. If in doubt check jaw teeth; they are in a single row in Mabee's, in multiple rows in the Flatwoods Salamander. (2) Slimy Salamander has a groove from nostril to lip and its skin-gland secretions stick like glue to one's fingers.
Range: S. South Carolina to n. Florida and e. Mississippi.
Map 204

MABEE'S SALAMANDER *Ambystoma mabeei*   **Pl. 38**
Identification: 3–4 in. (8–10.2 cm). The light specks are palest and most conspicuous along the sides. Dorsal ground color chiefly deep brown to black; belly dark brown or gray. Note long toes and small head. Jaw teeth are in a single row.
Named for W. B. Mabee, who collected the first specimen made known to science.
Similar species: (1) Mole Salamander has a conspicuously large head. (2) Slimy Salamander has groove from nostril to lip. (3) Flatwoods Salamander is "frosted" or patterned all over, not just conspicuously along sides; if in doubt, check jaw teeth, which in the Flatwoods are in multiple rows.
Range: Coastal Plain of the Carolinas.   Map 203

SMALL-MOUTHED SALAMANDER   **Pl. 38**
Ambystoma texanum
Identification: 4½–5½ in. (11–14 cm); record 7 in. (17.8 cm). Well named; both mouth and head are small. Ground color black or very dark brown. Usually a pattern of grayish lichen-like markings, but these are extremely variable in intensity. Many specimens have the markings concentrated on the back and upper sides. Some, especially toward northeastern part of range, are almost plain black. Texas specimens are very heavily speckled, with the light markings especially large and prominent on the lower sides.
A spring breeder and frequently found at that season under logs, boards, or other debris near ponds or swamps, in river bottoms, or other situations where moisture is abundant.
Similar species: (1) Jefferson and Blue-spotted Salamanders have *much* longer toes and a longer snout and head. (2) Mole Salamander has a conspicuously large head. (3) Rule out any Lungless Salamander that may be similarly marked or colored by checking for groove from nostril to lip.
Range: Extr. se. Michigan and Pelee Island, Ontario (in Lake Erie), west to s. Iowa and south to the Gulf. Absent from much of the Central Highlands area in Missouri and Arkansas.
Map 201

JEFFERSON SALAMANDER   Pl. 38
Ambystoma jeffersonianum

Identification: 4¼–7 in. (11–18 cm); record 8¼ in. (21.0 cm). The long toes and relatively slender build are the best things to look for in distinguishing this otherwise nondescript salamander from other members of the genus *Ambystoma*. Dorsal ground color dark brown or gray, the belly paler. Small bluish flecks, chiefly on limbs and lower sides of body, are usually present. Bluish markings conspicuous on small adults; they may be virtually absent on large adults. *Area around vent usually gray.*

An early spring breeder. Named for Jefferson College, Canonsburg, Pennsylvania, hence indirectly for the excellent naturalist who attained the Presidency — Thomas Jefferson.

Similar species: See Blue-spotted Salamander.

Range: W. New England to w. New York; southwestward to w.-cen. Virginia, cen. Kentucky, and s. Indiana.

Note: Two kinds of salamanders, one resembling the Jefferson and the other the Blue-spotted Salamander range, collectively, over a wide area from the Maritime Provinces and New England to Wisconsin and south to the Ohio River (see Maps 207 and 209). These, to which the names Silvery Salamander, *Ambystoma platineum* (similar to *jeffersonianum*), and Tremblay's Salamander, *A. tremblayi* (similar to *laterale*), have been given, are triploids of hybrid origin; they consist almost exclusively of females. They are identified by their chromosome numbers and the size of their red blood cells, which can be determined only from living specimens and in the laboratory. For detailed information on this species complex see a paper by Thomas M. Uzzell, Jr., in the journal *Copeia* (1964, pp. 257–300).

Map 206

BLUE-SPOTTED SALAMANDER   Pl. 38
Ambystoma laterale

Identification: 4–5⅛ in. (10–13.0 cm). Many specimens would match the enamelware pots and dishpans of yesteryear, with their flecks and spots of white and blue on bluish black. The relatively long toes, relatively long snout, blue to bluish-white flecks on back, and bluish-white spots on sides of trunk and tail, will usually distinguish this species from all others except the Jefferson Salamander (see below). Dorsal ground color black or grayish black; venter paler. *Area around vent is black.*

Breeds in spring in small ponds, ditches, etc., and occurs farther north than any other mole salamander in eastern North America.

Similar species: (1) Small-mouthed Salamander has short snout and short toes. (2) Slimy Salamander has groove from nostril to lip. (3) Jefferson Salamander has proportionately

longer toes and grows much larger — to 8¼ in. (21.0 cm). The Blue-spot normally is profusely marked with *spots,* whereas light markings in the virtually unicolored Jefferson are confined to bluish *flecks* on the limbs and along the sides. The Blue-spot is a dark animal (ground color black or nearly so); the Jefferson may be dark brown, but it tends to be paler — brownish gray or lead-colored. Examine the vent, which is surrounded by *black in the Blue-spot — usually by gray in the Jefferson.*
Range: Northern shore of Gulf of St. Lawrence across s. Canada to Lake Winnipeg and south to New England, New York, and the northernmost parts of Ohio, Indiana, and Illinois; disjunct (relict?) colonies in Labrador, Long Island, n. New Jersey, and Iowa.   Map 208

SPOTTED SALAMANDER *Ambystoma maculatum*   **Pl. 38**
   Identification: 6–7¾ in. (15–20 cm); record 9¾ in. (24.8 cm). The round light spots, yellow or orange in coloration, are arranged in an irregular *row* along each side of the back, from eye to tail tip. Dorsal ground color black, slate, or bluish black; *belly slate-gray.* Unspotted individuals are rare but probably occur throughout the range of the species.
   An early spring breeder which, under stimulus of warm rains, sometimes makes mass migrations to woodland ponds. Occasionally found (from spring to autumn) beneath stones or boards in moist environments or during wet weather.
   Similar species: Light spots on Eastern Tiger Salamander are irregular, often elongated, and extend far down on sides. The Tiger also has an *olive-yellow belly.*
   Range: Nova Scotia and the Gaspé Peninsula to s.-cen. Ontario; south to Georgia and e. Texas. Absent from the Prairie Peninsula in Illinois and from most of s. New Jersey and the Delmarva Peninsula.   Map 210

EASTERN TIGER SALAMANDER   **Pl. 38**
Ambystoma tigrinum tigrinum
   Identification: 7–8¼ in. (18–21 cm); record 13 in. (33.0 cm). The light spots, olive- or yellowish-brown, are highly irregular in shape and distribution, and extend well downward on the sides. Dorsal ground color dull black to deep brown; *belly olive-yellow,* marbled with darker pigment.
   A very early spring breeder, usually congregating in deeper water than does the Spotted Salamander. Larvae are often common in farm ponds — until such ponds are stocked with fish!
   Similar species: In the Spotted Salamander the light spots form an irregular *row* and belly is gray.
   Range: Long Island to n. Florida; Ohio to Minnesota and south to the Gulf; absent from most of Appalachian uplands and

much of lower Mississippi delta region; records sparse and widely scattered in many parts of range.   Map 205

BARRED TIGER SALAMANDER   Pl. 38
Ambystoma tigrinum mavortium

Identification: 6–8½ in. (15–22 cm); record 12¼ in. (31.1 cm). Typically with light vertical bars running upward from belly to midline of back. Highly variable, however, the light markings taking many shapes and forms, but in general being larger in size and fewer in number than the light markings on the Eastern Tiger. Ground color black or dark brown; markings yellowish, bright on sides but diffused with darker pigment on back. Belly black and yellow.

Occasionally neotenic, especially toward the west, where the immediate environs of a pond may become completely dry and inhospitable for a salamander.

Similar species: (1) Some specimens resemble Ringed Salamanders. In the Barred Tiger the head is larger and the dark pigment extends all the way from back to belly; in the Ringed, the black is interrupted by a light grayish stripe along lower side of body. (2) Marbled Salamander has a solid black belly; Barred Tiger has a black and yellow belly.

Range: Cen. Nebraska to s. Texas and probably ne. Mexico.

Subspecies: BLOTCHED TIGER SALAMANDER, *Ambystoma t. melanostictum.* A race in which the dark ground color (brown to black) is reduced to a network; light areas dull yellow and with indefinite borders. Slightly smaller on the average than the Barred Tiger. Frequently neotenic. Nebraska to Washington and s.-cen. Alberta. GRAY TIGER SALAMANDER, *Ambystoma t. diaboli.* Ground color light olive to dark brown; scattered small dark brown to black spots on back and sides. Frequently neotenic. Sw. Minnesota to s. Manitoba and s. Saskatchewan. Western subspecies.

Note: Tiger Salamanders, which have been widely transported as fish bait, are now established in so many localities that it is difficult to define natural ranges, particularly of the western races.   Map 205

Newts: Family Salamandridae

NEWTS are not so slippery as most salamanders. Their skins are rougher and not slimy, and they do not slide easily through your fingers when you try to handle them. The costal grooves, which are prominent in most other salamanders, are indistinct.

Most newts are essentially aquatic, but there is also a land stage, like the Red Eft form of the Red-spotted Newt. The larvae transform into efts, which remain ashore for one to three years; they then return to the water and change into the aquatic adults. Sometimes the land stage is omitted, and the larvae transform directly into adults, in which case remnants of the external gills may be retained. The tails of efts are almost round in cross section, and their skins are quite rough; the tails of adults are vertically compressed and their skins are much smoother.

Natural food includes insects, leeches, worms, tiny mollusks and crustaceans, young amphibians, and frogs' eggs. Captive aquatic adults will eat small pieces of meat, but crumbs of canned dog food make a better balanced diet. Efts respond most readily to live insects. Few predators will eat newts, for their skin-gland secretions are toxic or at least irritating to mucous membranes.

There are three species in eastern North America. Other members of this large family occur in British Columbia and the Pacific states (southeastern Alaska to southern California), in Europe, North Africa, and Asia.

RED-SPOTTED NEWT   Pl. 39
Notophthalmus viridescens viridescens

Identification: 2⅞–4 in. (7–10 cm); record 5½ in. (14.0 cm). The red spots are variable in number and position, but are present at all stages of the complex life history. The aquatic adults, although normally olive-green, may vary from yellowish brown to dark greenish brown. Their venters are yellow with small black spots. *Male:* Both the high tail fin and black excrescences on the hind legs disappear after the spring breeding season, but they may develop again as early as the following autumn. *Red Eft:* 1⅜–3⅜ in. (3.5–8.6 cm). Bright orange-red to dull red or orange, the most brilliantly colored ones usually occurring in moist forested mountains or other upland habitats. Individuals recently transformed from the larval to eft stage may be yellowish brown or dull reddish brown. Specimens transforming to adult form (or aquatic adults that have had to live out of water, as when ponds dry up) may be very dark, even almost black. Neoteny is rare.

Ponds, small lakes, marshes, ditches, quiet portions of streams, or other shallow permanent or semipermanent bodies of unpolluted water are the most frequent habitats during aquatic stages. Adults may be seen resting motionless or swimming about slowly in open water or crawling on the bottom or through vegetation. Often they remain active all winter and may be observed through the ice. The terrestrial efts, although avoiding direct sunlight, are extraordinarily bold, often walking about in the open on the forest floor in broad daylight. After summer showers in mountainous regions they sometimes may be seen by scores or even hundreds. In many areas, notably on the Coastal Plain, the land stage may be omitted.

Similar species: Most other small salamanders have slimy skins and conspicuous costal grooves.
Range: Maritime Provinces to Great Lakes and south to cen. Georgia and Alabama.   Map 198

CENTRAL NEWT   Pl. 39
Notophthalmus viridescens louisianensis
Identification: 2½–4 in. (6–10.2 cm). A small, more slender race of the Red-spotted Newt, but normally *without red spots.* If such spots are present they are small or only partly outlined by black. The dorsal ground color varies from olive-green to yellowish- or olive-brown, and is sharply cut off from the yellow venter.

A newt of swales and swamplands, of woodland ponds and ditches, and of river bottoms in the South. The eft or land stage is uncommon in many areas in comparison with its abundance in the Red-spotted Newt. Neoteny is frequent on the southeastern Coastal Plain.
Similar species: See Red-spotted Newt.
Range: Lake Superior region to e. Texas and east to s. S. Carolina. This race intergrades with the Red-spotted subspecies over a broad area from Michigan to and through the Deep South.   Map 198

PENINSULA NEWT   Pl. 39
Notophthalmus viridescens piaropicola
Identification: 3–4⅛ in. (8–10.5 cm). This is a dusky newt from Florida with a dark olive, dark brown, or almost black dorsum, and a venter finely peppered with black specks on a ground color of yellow or orange-yellow.

An inhabitant of ponds, ditches, swamps, and virtually any other standing body of water. Often abundant in canals or sloughs choked with hyacinths, or in submerged aquatic vegetation of cypress-bordered ponds. Terrestrial individuals, which are rare, may be found ashore under logs or debris. Neoteny is common.
Range: Peninsular Florida.   Map 198

BROKEN-STRIPED NEWT   Pl. 39
Notophthalmus viridescens dorsalis
Identification: 2½–3¾ in. (6.4–9.5 cm). The black-bordered red dorsolateral stripe is broken in at least 1 or 2 places on head and trunk; it rarely extends onto tail. There may also be a row of small red spots on lower sides of body and a light line down center of back. *Eft:* Reddish brown; red stripes not so strongly bordered by black as in the adults.

Found in pools, ponds, ditches, quiet portions of streams, etc.;

the efts under logs, boards, or other shelters in damp places.
Range: Coastal Plain in the Carolinas.   Map 198

STRIPED NEWT *Notophthalmus perstriatus*   **Pl. 39**
Identification: 2-4⅛ in. (5-10.5 cm). The red dorsolateral
stripe is continuous on the trunk, but it may break into frag-
ments on the head and tail. It varies in coloration from bright
to dull red, but the red may be partly obscured by dusky pigment. The stripe is dark-bordered, but not so boldly and evenly
as in Broken-striped Newt. There may be a row of red spots
along the side of body and a faint light stripe down center of
back. Dorsal ground color olive-green to dark brown. Venter
yellow, usually sparsely marked with black specks. *Eft:*
Orange-red but also with red stripes like those of the adults.
    Generally to be found in almost any body of shallow, standing
water; the efts remain ashore but usually near such habitats.
Neoteny occurs frequently.
Range: S. Georgia and n. Florida.   Map 197

BLACK-SPOTTED NEWT   **Pl. 39**
Notophthalmus meridionalis meridionalis
Identification: 3-4⁵⁄₁₆ in. (8-11.0 cm). The large black spots —
on both dorsum and venter — give this salamander its name.
The yellowish stripes are wavy or uneven, and often there is
a suggestion of a brown or russet stripe down the center of
the back. No red spots. Venter bright orange to yellow-orange.
    A resident of ponds, lagoons, and swampy areas — habitats
that are not abundant in its rather arid homeland.
Similar species: Central Newt has much smaller dark spots
and *no stripes*.
Range: S. Texas and adj. Mexico. Mexican subspecies.
                                                      Map 199

Lungless Salamanders:
Family Plethodontidae

LUNGS are absent and respiration is accomplished through the skin
and the lining of the mouth. There is a groove extending downward from the nostril to the edge of the mouth (the naso-labial
groove — see back endpaper), but this is so small that a lens may
be needed to reveal it. In some forms there are cirri, downward
projections from the nostrils beyond the mouth line, and the
groove follows these.
    To this family belong such abundant groups as the dusky,
brook, and woodland salamanders and their allies (genera *Des-*

mognathus, below, through *Haideotriton,* p. 296, inclusive). The family ranges from southern Canada to Bolivia, and is also represented in Europe.

There are two subfamilies. One, the Desmognathinae, includes the Dusky (*Desmognathus*), Shovel-nosed (*Leurognathus*), and Red Hills (*Phaeognathus*) Salamanders. In all of these the lower jaw is relatively immovable, thus stiffening the forward portion of the body so the animal can more readily force its way under things. The salamander opens its mouth in large part by lifting the upper jaw and head. All other members of the group are classified in the Subfamily Plethodontinae.

Dusky Salamanders: Genus *Desmognathus*

IDENTIFYING these salamanders is like working with fall warblers — only worse! Added to changes in coloration and pattern, associated with age and size, are bewildering individual variations plus differences between one local population and the next. Short cuts toward identification can be taken by ignoring color patterns at first and concentrating on three other things: (a) the shape of the tail; (b) sizes (of transformed animals); and (c) geography. Pay strict attention to ranges to eliminate species not found in your vicinity. *Then,* check patterns and do what professional herpetologists do — collect a small series to learn how much the population varies in the immediate area. Among them may be a specimen or two that will match the illustrations closely enough to furnish a clue.

There is usually *a pale diagonal line from eye to angle of jaw* (Fig. 64, opp. Pl. 41). This may be absent, however, in old, dark adults or in those specimens where it is obscured by dark *or* light pigment. The hind legs are larger and stouter than the forelegs; the body is relatively short and stout. Dusky salamanders are accomplished jumpers, often leaping several times their own length in their efforts to escape.

Members of this genus are found most commonly in or near brooks, rills, mountain cascades, springs, or seeps, but are usually absent from larger streams where predatory fish occur. Collectively, they reach their greatest abundance in the Appalachian region. The Mountain Dusky Salamander frequently wanders far out into humid forest areas, especially during wet weather. The Pygmy Salamander is terrestrial.

Similar species: (1) In the Woodland Salamanders (*Plethodon*) the body is long and slender, there is no light line from eye to angle of jaw, and the hind legs are about the same size as the forelegs (Fig. 64, opp. Pl. 41). (2) The Shovel-nosed Salamander (*Leurognathus*) has smaller eyes and a more wedge-shaped head. (3) The Red Hills Salamander (*Phaeognathus*) has no light line from eye to angle of jaw, and it has 20 to 22 costal grooves (only 13 to 15 in Dusky and Shovel-nosed Salamanders). (4) The Mole Salamanders (*Ambystoma*) lack the naso-labial groove common to *Desmognathus* and all other Lungless Salamanders (Family Plethodontidae) — see illustrations on back endpaper.

NORTHERN DUSKY SALAMANDER
Pl. 41;
Desmognathus fuscus fuscus
Fig. 78, p. 262

Identification: 2½–4½ in. (6–11 cm); record 5⁹⁄₁₆ in. (14.1 cm). A medium-sized *Desmognathus* with a *keeled tail;* tail a little less than ½ total length, compressed and knife-edged above, and higher than wide at posterior edge of vent. Mouth line of adult males only slightly sinuous (Fig. 77, below). General coloration gray or brown, markings often not much darker than ground color. Pattern changes with age. The very young have 5 to 8 pairs of round yellowish dorsal spots bordered by a dark *wavy* band (Fig. 78, p. 262); similar markings continue onto tail. The pattern breaks up as the animal ages, the darker remnants of it appearing as spots or streaks. Base of tail usually lighter (olive, yellowish, or bright chestnut) than rest of dorsum and bordered by dark scallops. Venter variable, but usually lightly mottled with gray or brown, sometimes heavily; dark pigment of sides of body may encroach on edges of belly.

Abundant in many localities, occurring in brooks, near springs, and in seepage areas. Perhaps most common along edges of small woodland streams where stones, chunks of wood, and miscellaneous debris provide ample shelter both for the salamanders and their food. Seldom wanders far from running or trickling water.

Similar species: See main heading for Dusky Salamanders (p. 260) for ways of distinguishing *Desmognathus* from species of other genera. Other members of Dusky group may be confusingly similar: (1) In the Mountain Dusky Salamander the *tail is round* (not knife-edged on top) and more tapering, and the mouth line in adult males is more sinuous (Fig. 77, below). (2) Seal Salamanders are larger as adults, and they usually have heavy black or dark brown dorsal spots and pale venters. (3) Black-bellied Salamander grows larger, and has an ebony venter and 2 rows of conspicuous light dots on each side of body.

Fig. 77. MOUTH LINES OF ADULT MALE DUSKY SALAMANDERS
(Desmognathus)

MOUNTAIN
(ochrophaeus)

NORTHERN
AND SPOTTED
(fuscus)

Strongly sinuous   Less sinuous

(4) Shovel-nosed Salamander is strictly aquatic. Check ranges; Northern Dusky is the only member of its genus occurring in many parts of the North.

Range: S. New Brunswick and s. Quebec to se. Indiana and the Carolinas; distribution sporadic in the southern Appalachians. Altitudinally, from virtually sea level to high in the mountains. Map 213

Fig. 78. DORSAL PATTERNS OF YOUNG DUSKY SALAMANDERS
(Desmognathus)

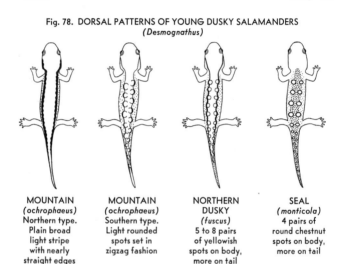

| MOUNTAIN *(ochrophaeus)* Northern type. Plain broad light stripe with nearly straight edges | MOUNTAIN *(ochrophaeus)* Southern type. Light rounded spots set in zigzag fashion | NORTHERN DUSKY *(fuscus)* 5 to 8 pairs of yellowish spots on body, more on tail | SEAL *(monticola)* 4 pairs of round chestnut spots on body, more on tail |

SPOTTED DUSKY SALAMANDER Pl. 42
Desmognathus fuscus conanti

Identification: 2½–5 in. (6–12.7 cm). Anatomically similar to the Northern Dusky Salamander — size medium and with the tail moderately keeled above. More colorful and usually much more strongly patterned than northern race, and with remnants of the spotted juvenile pattern often evident in the adults. Frequently 6 to 8 pairs of golden or reddish-golden dorsal spots that are normally separate from one another, but which may fuse to form a light dorsal band with saw-toothed, wavy, or even straight dark margins. Coloration variable; specimens from some localities are much darker and with the dark markings much more prominent than in the one illustrated on Plate 42. Line from eye to angle of jaw yellow or orange. Venter light but mottled with black and white (or gold) flecks.

Similar species: In specimens from southern localities check the gap between the adpressed toes (Fig. 73, p. 239). In any

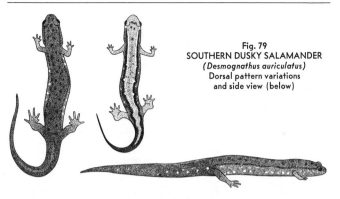

Fig. 79
SOUTHERN DUSKY SALAMANDER
(Desmognathus auriculatus)
Dorsal pattern variations
and side view (below)

Southern Dusky Salamander (*auriculatus*) with a head–body length of 2 in. (5 cm) or more there are 4½ to 5½ costal folds between the adpressed toes; in the Spotted Dusky (*conanti*) there are 2 to 4.

Range: Extr. s. Illinois, w. Kentucky, and w. Tennessee to the Gulf of Mexico and east to the Florida panhandle and to the Fall Line in Georgia; also on Crowley's Ridge in ne. Arkansas and in the Ouachita–Red River rolling lands of Louisiana and extr. s. Arkansas.   Map 213

SOUTHERN DUSKY SALAMANDER   Fig. 79, above
Desmognathus auriculatus

Identification: 3–5 in. (8–13 cm); record 6⅜ in. (16.3 cm). Tail stout at base; compressed posteriorly and knife-edged above. Best characterized as a dark salamander with a row of "portholes" between front and hind leg and along each side of tail. These consist of whitish or reddish spots, but they may be irregular in placement, arranged in a double row, or even obscure in the darkest specimens. General dorsal coloration dark brown or black; belly black or very dark brown, but sprinkled with distinct white dots. There is much local variation in this salamander, and in some populations, notably among those living in ravine or spring habitats in peninsular Florida, certain individuals bear a reddish dorsal wash, producing the effect of a light middorsal stripe (a variation formerly called the "Peninsula Dusky Salamander"). In many areas in the South this species occurs sympatrically with the Dusky Salamander (*fuscus*); elsewhere they occupy different habitats; in a number of areas, especially on the Outer Coastal Plain, the two species may hybridize.

Usually found near cypress ponds or in stagnant or nearly stagnant pools in river flood plains and coastal swamps; the environment is usually mucky and acidic from decomposition of organic material.

Range: Chiefly on the Outer Coastal Plain; se. Virginia to cen. Florida and west to e. Texas.

Note: The relationship between *auriculatus* and the two races of *fuscus* is not clear. The two species occur together and maintain their identities in Mississippi, for example, but they apparently hybridize (intergrade?) in numerous localities through a wide area in the Southeast. A dashed line is used on maps 213 and 215, which, in part, approximates the Fall Line, to indicate that the limits of their ranges in the region cannot be plotted with accuracy. Map 215

Fig. 80
OUACHITA
DUSKY SALAMANDER
(*Desmognathus
brimleyorum*)

OUACHITA DUSKY SALAMANDER

Desmognathus brimleyorum Pl. 42; Fig. 80, above

Identification: 3⅛–5½ in. (8–14 cm); record 7 in. (17.8 cm). A large, robust *Desmognathus* with the tail distinctly keeled and compressed near the tip. Young specimens look superficially like the Northern Dusky Salamander. Usually a row of faint pale spots along each side of body (Fig. 80, above) and another parallel row extending from foreleg to hind leg. General dorsal coloration brown or gray; belly pale and virtually unmarked, varying from pinkish white to yellowish, but faintly stippled with very pale brownish pigment. *Large adult male:* Dorsum uniform dark brown.

Juveniles and larvae hide under stones or in wet gravel at or below water level at streamside, and also in piles of small rocks. Adults are most often found in water beneath large boulders, in large rock piles, or along wet, rocky banks. This salamander is much more aquatic than terrestrial. Many specimens are infested with mites of the family Trombiculidae, which may cause loss or fusing of toes or both.

Range: Ouachita Mountains of Arkansas and Oklahoma.

Map 217

BLACK MOUNTAIN DUSKY SALAMANDER Not illus.

Desmognathus welteri

Identification: 3–5 in. (8–13 cm); record 6¹¹⁄₁₆ in. (17.0 cm). A rather chubby salamander. Tail less than ½ total length, stout at base, but compressed and knife-edged above on posterior half. Resembles Seal Salamander, but belly is usually finely to heavily stippled with gray or brownish pigment on a whitish ground color. Dorsum pale to medium brown and patterned with small dark brown spots or streaks that, in some specimens, tend to surround paler areas. *No sharp lateral separation* of dorsal and ventral ground colors; the dark dorsal pigmentation fading gradually into the paler venter. A line of faint pale dots between legs on each side of body. *Tips of toes usually dark,* except in very young specimens.

An aquatic salamander of mountain brooks, spring runs, and roadside puddles in wooded mountainous terrain.

Similar species: Seal Salamander usually has: (a) a distinct lateral separation between the dorsal and ventral coloration; and (b) venter lightly pigmented.

Range: Big Black Mountain, Harlan Co., Kentucky, and adjacent parts of Kentucky and Virginia; also Warren Co. in w.-cen. Kentucky.   Map 218

SEAL SALAMANDER
Desmognathus monticola

Pl. 41;
Fig. 78, p. 262

Identification: 3¼–5 in. (8–13 cm); record 5⅞ in. (14.9 cm). A stout-bodied salamander. Tail compressed and knife-edged above near tip; approximately ½ total length. Most specimens are boldly patterned above, but plain and quite pale below; usually a distinct lateral separation between dorsal and ventral pigmentation. Dorsum with strong black or dark brown markings on a ground of buff, gray, or light brown, the markings extremely variable — wormlike, netlike, or surrounding roughly circular areas of ground color. Some specimens patterned simply with scattered dark or light spots or streaks. Markings usually more strongly evident toward western part of range, and least so toward south where adults may lose virtually all traces of pattern. Venter white in juveniles, but becoming lightly and usually *uniformly* pigmented with gray or brown in old adults. Sometimes a *single* row of light dots on sides between legs. Old adults may be purplish brown, with dark markings few and obscure. *Young:* About 4 pairs of rounded chestnut or orange-brown spots down back (Fig. 78, p. 262).

Boggy spots in cool, well-shaded ravines and banks of mountain brooks are among the varied habitats utilized by this large, active species. Hides by day and may be found by overturning stones, bark, etc. At night, poised at the entrance to a burrow or perched atop a wet rock and illuminated by the observer's flashlight, its appearance suggests a miniature seal. Sometimes appears in the open in shady spots during daylight. The name Seal is a translation of the Latin specific name *phoca* that was incorrectly applied to this species for many years.

Similar species: (1) Northern Dusky Salamander has a light but mottled undersurface; also it is less pop-eyed than Seal

Salamander. (2) Black-bellied Salamander has a black venter and 2 rows of small white dots along each side of body. (3) See also Black Mountain Dusky Salamander.

Range: Mountainous and hilly regions from sw. Pennsylvania to Georgia and Alabama; southwestward into the hill country of sw. Alabama and to extreme western tip of Florida panhandle.

Subspecies: APPALACHIAN SEAL SALAMANDER, *Desmognathus m. monticola* (Plate 41). As described above and occurring throughout most of range. VIRGINIA SEAL SALAMANDER, *Desmognathus m. jeffersoni.* Similar but with dark markings much reduced, these being round, scattered, and about size of salamander's eye. Some adults virtually patternless. Blue Ridge Mountains of Virginia.   Map 216

BLACK-BELLIED SALAMANDER   Pl. 41
Desmognathus quadramaculatus

Identification: 4–6⅞ in. (10–17 cm); record 8¼ in. (21.0 cm). A large robust salamander of cascading southern mountain streams. Tail very stout at base, less than ½ total length, and knife-edged above. *Belly black* in adults; dark, but flecked with yellow in young. (Put your specimen in a bottle to see its underside.) Usually a conspicuous *double row of light dots* along each side of body. *Young:* Snout and feet often light in color, especially in southern part of range.

This salamander, the heaviest and bulkiest of the lungless group within our territory, is daring enough to pause in the open occasionally on a wet rock, even in sunshine! Abundant in boulder-strewn brooks; also found near waterfalls or other places where cold water drips or flows. Usually seeks shelter under rocks during daylight, but when these are lifted it dashes off instantly to plunge beneath the next nearest stone or to swim vigorously away with *or against* the current. Trying to catch these agile amphibians is like going fishing with your bare hands.

Similar species: (1) Old adults of other members of Dusky Salamander group may be almost uniformly dark (bellies included), but they do not attain so large a size and their tails are proportionately longer. (2) Shovel-nosed Salamander has long-sloping snout and small eyes.

Range: S.-cen. W. Virginia through mountains to n. Georgia; isolated colonies south to cen. Georgia that may have originated from the release of specimens distributed commercially as fish bait.   Map 214

MOUNTAIN DUSKY SALAMANDER   Pl. 42;
Desmognathus ochrophaeus   **Figs. 78, p. 262; 81, p. 267**

Identification: 2¾–4 in. (7–10 cm); record 4⅜ in. (11.1 cm). A medium-sized *Desmognathus* with *a round tail;* tail about ½ total length and as wide as or even wider than its height at posterior edge of vent. Mouth line of adult males very sinuous

(Fig. 77 p. 261). Extraordinarily variable in coloration and pattern (several phases are shown on Plate 42 and in Fig. 81, below). *A light line from eye to angle of jaw.*

In northern part of range specimens, including juveniles (Fig. 78, p. 262), typically have a *straight-edged* light stripe down back and tail. The stripe may be yellow, orange, olive, gray, tan, brown, or reddish; it is flanked by very dark, sometimes black, pigment that usually fades into the mottled lower sides. A row of dark, often *chevronlike,* spots down center of back. Old individuals may be nearly plain dark brown and virtually without pattern. (Formerly called "Allegheny Mountain Salamander.")

In southern part of range *ochrophaeus* is highly variable. Some individuals resemble northern specimens, but the great majority have a *wavy* or *irregular* dorsal stripe and they may be marked with large light areas that are remnants of the light spots set in paired or zigzag fashion down the backs of southern juveniles (Fig. 78, p. 262). Coloration as diverse as in northern populations. (Includes the former "Blue Ridge Mountain," "Cliffside," and "Ocoee Salamanders.")

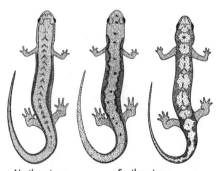

Fig. 81
MOUNTAIN DUSKY
SALAMANDER
(ochrophaeus)
Variations in
dorsal patterns

Northern type   Southern types

An amazing variation of this amphibian, that may have cheek patches of yellow, orange, or reddish, is illustrated on Plate 40 as the "Imitator Salamander." It thus resembles the "red-cheeked" phase of the Appalachian Woodland Salamander (*Plethodon jordani*). Another variation resembles the "red-legged" phase of the same species, and some specimens have both red cheeks and red legs. These "imitators" occur in scattered localities in the southern Appalachians and often with the woodland salamanders they resemble.

More terrestrial than most other dusky salamanders, sometimes wandering far out into the woods during wet weather. Normally found under stones, logs, leaves, etc., near springs, seepage areas, or streams, not actually in the water but where the ground is saturated. Often congregates in winter in large numbers in shaly seepage areas or near springs. Frequently found abroad at night, when it may climb trees and shrubs while foraging.

Similar species: (1) Two-lined Salamanders have bright yellow bellies and laterally compressed tails. (2) Woodland Salamanders (including *jordani*) have smaller hind legs and lack light line from eye to angle of jaw (Fig. 64, opp. Pl. 41). (3) Dusky (*fuscus*) and Seal (*monticola*) Salamanders have tails that are knife-edged above (no dorsal keel in *ochrophaeus*); mouth line of adult male Duskies is only slightly sinuous (Fig. 77, p. 261).

Range: Chiefly upland areas from Adirondack Mountains, New York, to n. Georgia and ne. Alabama. Occurs from a few hundred feet above sea level to the coniferous forests of the highest peaks of the southern Appalachians.   Map 212

PYGMY SALAMANDER   Pl. 42; Fig. 82, below
Desmognathus wrighti

Identification: 1½–2 in. (3.8–5.1 cm). A tiny, bronzy mite of a salamander; one of our smallest species and a strictly terrestrial one. Tail rounded; less than ½ total length. A broad light middorsal stripe, varying from reddish brown to tan in coloration; usually with a dark *herringbone* pattern down its center (Fig. 82, below). Silvery pigment along sides of body. Venter flesh-colored and unmarked except for gold pigment under the heart. *Top of head rugose,* snout especially. *Male:* Mental gland U-shaped (Fig. 83, p. 269).

A resident chiefly of high spruce-fir forests of the Southern Appalachians. Best sought by day under moss and bark on rotting logs or beneath rotting wood or litter on the forest floor near seepage areas. At night, especially in foggy or rainy weather, it may become "arboreal," ascending trunks of trees as much as 6 or 7 ft. (2 ± m) above ground. There is no aquatic larval stage; transformation of larva takes place within the egg.

Fig. 82
DORSAL PATTERNS
IN SEEPAGE AND
PYGMY SALAMANDERS
(*Desmognathus*)

SEEPAGE (*aeneus*)   PYGMY
2 variations   (*wrighti*)

Similar species: In Seepage Salamanders *top of head is smooth* and mental gland (males only) is kidney-shaped (Fig. 83, below).

Range: Elevations of 2750 to over 6500 ft. (800 to 2000+ m) from sw. Virginia to near the Georgia line in sw. N. Carolina; known from Mt. Rogers, Whitetop, Grandfather, and Roan Mts., the Black Mts., Great Smoky, Plott Balsam, and Great Balsam Mts., Wayah Bald, and Standing Indian Mt., all of which are within area shown on map. Map 220

Fig. 83. CHINS OF MALE PYGMY AND SEEPAGE SALAMANDERS
(Desmognathus)

PYGMY
(wrighti)
Mental gland
large, U-shaped

SEEPAGE
(aeneus)
Mental gland small,
kidney-shaped

SEEPAGE SALAMANDER Fig. 82, p. 268
Desmognathus aeneus

Identification: 1¾–2¼ in. (4.4–5.7 cm). Another tiny salamander, and an especially slender one. Tail rounded; about ½ total length. A wide, wavy to almost straight-sided pale dorsal stripe varying in coloration from yellow or tan to reddish brown. Stripe may be flecked or smudged with darker pigment that may suggest a herringbone pattern; sometimes a dark middorsal line that is continuous with a Y-shaped mark on head (Fig. 82, p. 268). Sides dark where they meet the dorsal stripe, paler toward belly. Undersurfaces plain to mottled with brown and white. *Top of head smooth. Male:* Mental gland kidney-shaped (Fig. 83, above).

Most often encountered beneath damp leaf mold on the forest floor, near seepages, springs, or small streams. There is no aquatic larval stage; terrestrial larvae transform in only a few days. (Includes the former "Cherokee" and "Alabama Salamanders.")

Similar species: See Pygmy Salamander.

Range: Elevations of 700 to 4500 ft. (210 to 1400 m) from extr. sw. N. Carolina to e.-cen. Alabama; as low as 100 ft. (30 m) in w.-cen. Alabama. Map 219

Shovel-nosed and Red Hills Salamanders: Genera *Leurognathus* and *Phaeognathus*

SALAMANDERS of these two genera, together with the many kinds of dusky salamanders (*Desmognathus*), constitute the Subfamily Desmognathinae (see p. 260). The genus *Leurognathus* was de-

scribed in 1899, but the first specimen of *Phaeognathus* was not
discovered until 1960 despite the fact that it attains the greatest
length of any lungless salamander of our area. Both genera are
confined to the southeastern United States.

SHOVEL-NOSED SALAMANDER   Pl. 41
Leurognathus marmoratus

Identification: 3½–5 in. (9–13 cm); record 5¾ in. (14.6 cm).
Pattern and coloration dull and variable, but blending beautifully with pebbles, leaves, and debris on bottoms of rocky
streams. Dorsum black, brown, or gray and usually with two
rows of irregular, often weakly indicated, pale-colored spots or
blotches that vary in size, intensity, and coloration (gray, olive,
yellowish, or whitish) from one local population to another. A
pale, often poorly defined, line from eye to angle of jaws. Tail
less than ½ total length, compressed, and knife-edged above.
Head flattened and wedge-shaped, the slope starting downward
from a point *well behind* the rather small eyes.

An aquatic amphibian of mountain brooks that vary in size
and amount of flow from trout streams to rills, but all of which
offer an abundance of stones beneath which to hide. Small
brooks with sandy or gravelly bottoms are a favorite habitat.
In clear, quiet waters, if care is taken not to disturb it unduly
(by lifting rocks slowly, for example), the Shovelnose tends to
remain still or walk slowly and deliberately to another shelter.
The Black-bellied Salamander, often present in same streams,
normally *dashes* away. Food consists principally of the larval
or nymphal stages of aquatic insects.

Similar species: Black-bellied Salamander and other members
of the Dusky group tend to be more pop-eyed, and usually have
a more conspicuous light line from eye to jaw. Check roof of
mouth if in doubt. Internal openings of nostrils are rounded
and clearly evident in Dusky Salamanders (*Desmognathus*);
they are slitlike and scarcely noticeable in Shovel-nosed Salamanders (Fig. 84, below). If you have to open a mouth, lift or
prod the upper jaw *gently;* you are liable to damage the lower
jaw or its musculature if you try to force it downward (see p. 260).

Range: Elevations from 1000 to 5500 ft. (300 to 1700 m) from
Whitetop Mountain in sw. Virginia through w. N. Carolina to
extr. ne. Georgia and adj. S. Carolina; also Floyd Co., Virginia.
Map 226

Fig 84. ROOFS OF MOUTHS OF LUNGLESS SALAMANDERS

DUSKY
(*Desmognathus*)
Internal openings
of nostrils
clearly visible

SHOVEL-NOSED
(*Leurognathus*)
Narrow slitlike
openings
(often not visible)

RED HILLS SALAMANDER   Pl. 41
Phaeognathus hubrichti

Identification: 4–8 in. (10–20 cm); record 10¹⁄₁₆ in. (25.6 cm). This amphibian, the longest member of the Subfamily Desmognathinae, totally lacks distinctive markings. It is deep dark brown all over except that the snout, jaws, and soles of the limbs are slightly paler. Body elongate, legs short; 20 to 22 costal grooves, and about 14 costal folds between the toes of the adpressed limbs; no light line from eye to angle of jaw.

A fossorial salamander that apparently is confined to cool, moist, forested ravines. It is rarely seen except at night at the mouths of its burrows, which are excavated chiefly in sandy loam over and around claystone rock.

Similar species: (1) Shovel-nosed and Dusky Salamanders are marked with a pale line from eye to angle of jaw and they have only 13 to 15 costal grooves. (2) Slimy Salamanders are usually well sprinkled with light spots and they normally have only 16 costal grooves.

Range: The Red Hills formations of Alabama between the Alabama and Conecuh Rivers.   Map 227

Woodland Salamanders: Genus *Plethodon*

THIS group is widespread and abundant through the forested portions of eastern North America. In high, humid mountains in the South, specimens may be encountered at almost all seasons (except midwinter), but elsewhere they are easiest to find after spring or autumn rains. During hot, dry weather they either estivate or seek optimum conditions of moisture in rock crevices or below the surface of the ground. When it is damp or rainy, woodland salamanders prowl at night, and they often can be observed with the aid of a flashlight or headlamp. By day they hide in burrows, under stones or damp boards, or beneath a variety of other shelters where there is little danger of desiccation.

The woodland salamanders feed on a large variety of invertebrates, including earthworms and many kinds of insects, among them beetles with hard shells, ants with sharp stings, and bugs with bad smells. Most captives readily accept tubifex worms, which are procurable at almost any tropical-fish supply store.

Eggs are laid in small clusters in damp logs, moss, etc., and complete development takes place within the egg; there is no aquatic larval stage as is the case among most other salamanders. Adult males of some species have a prominent large circular gland (the mental gland) under their chins.

The genus is strictly North American, with a large number of forms in our area and others in forested portions of far-western states from northwestern California to British Columbia; also in mountains of northern Idaho and adjacent Montana and in north central New Mexico.

Similar species: (1) Mole Salamanders (*Ambystoma*) all *lack* the groove from nostril to lip (use a lens). (2) Dusky Salamanders (*Desmognathus*), especially the kinds that wander far out into the forest, are often confused with Woodland Salamanders. Dusky Salamanders usually have a light line from eye to angle of jaw, and their hind legs are larger and stouter than their forelegs. Woodland Salamanders lack the light line, and *all 4* limbs are about the same size (Fig. 64, opp. Pl. 41).

RED-BACKED SALAMANDER   Pl. 40; Fig. 85, below
Plethodon cinereus cinereus

Identification: 2¼–3⅝ in. (5.7–9.2 cm); record 5 in. (12.7 cm). *Two distinct colorations:* (a) *red-backed* — a straight-edged reddish stripe down back from base of head to tail, and bordered by dark pigment that extends downward onto sides of body; (b) *lead-backed* — uniformly dark gray to almost black. (Some individuals are intermediate between the two types.) In red-backed phase, the stripe may be orange, yellow, or even light gray instead of red. Usually the stripe *narrows* slightly on base of tail. In some areas, red-backed and lead-backed specimens are equally abundant; in others, one or the other may predominate; leadbacks may be rare or absent at high elevations. Both phases have one outstanding character in common — bellies mottled with approximately equal parts of black and white (or yellow), producing a *salt-and-pepper* effect (Fig. 86, p. 274). An all-red phase is found occasionally. Costal grooves 19 over most of range, but 20 in some populations from Long Island to North

Fig. 85. DORSAL PATTERNS OF RED-BACKED AND ALLIED SALAMANDERS
(Plethodon)

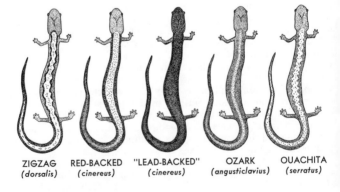

ZIGZAG   RED-BACKED   "LEAD-BACKED"   OZARK   OUACHITA
(dorsalis)   *(cinereus)*   *(cinereus)*   *(angusticlavius)*   *(serratus)*

Carolina and 18 in Missouri and on the Appalachian Plateau from southwestern New York to central West Virginia.

A terrestrial salamander, confined more or less to wooded or forested areas. Hides beneath all manner of objects, including chunks of tar paper or other trash, as well as logs, bark, stones, etc. The most ubiquitous salamander throughout the greater part of its range.

Similar species: (1) Ravine and Valley and Ridge Salamanders (colored as a leadback) are more slender and their bellies look almost *uniformly dark* (Fig. 86, p. 274). (2) See also Zigzag Salamander.

Range: S. Quebec and the Maritime Provinces to Minnesota; south to N. Carolina and se. Missouri.

Subspecies: GEORGIA RED-BACKED SALAMANDER, *Plethodon c. polycentratus.* Virtually identical in appearance with Red-backed Salamander, and occurring in both red-backed and lead-backed phases; differs in having tiny specks of red on sides of body in lead-backed phase, and in having more costal grooves (20 to 22) than in most populations of other subspecies. Identify by range — Piedmont of w. Georgia and adj. Alabama.

Map 233

OUACHITA RED-BACKED SALAMANDER
Plethodon cinereus serratus   **Fig. 85, p. 272**
Identification: 2¾-4 in. (7-10.2 cm). A light middorsal stripe with saw-toothed edges; "teeth" correspond with costal grooves (stripe widest above each groove and narrowest between them). Stripe may be orange or reddish, rest of body dark gray to almost black — coloration, in general, like Red-backed Salamander's; occasional individuals may be dark and unpatterned (lead-backed). Red pigment is mixed with dark pigment on sides but not on venter. Costal grooves usually 18 or 19.
Similar species: Ozark Salamander has red pigment as well as black and white on venter.
Range: Forested mts. of w.-cen. Arkansas and adj. Oklahoma; also w.-cen. Louisiana.   Map 233

ZIGZAG SALAMANDER   **Pl. 40; Fig. 85, p. 272**
Plethodon dorsalis dorsalis
Identification: 2½-3½ in. (6.4-8.9 cm); record 4⅜ in. (11.1 cm). "Zigzag" well describes the light dorsal stripe in many specimens; in others the angles are not so sharp, and lobed or wavy would be more accurate. The stripe varies from red to yellowish in coloration, and may be straight for at least part of its length; it is *broadly* continued on tail. *Venter includes a mottling of orange or reddish pigment.* This salamander also occurs in a dark phase. Costal grooves usually 18.

Sometimes a woodland species, but more likely to be found

in rock slides or in or near mouths of caves. Ascends to elevations of 2500 ft. (760 m) in western approaches to Blue Ridge Mountains.

Similar species: Red-backed Salamander has a straight dorsal stripe that *narrows* slightly on base of tail. Dark phases of Zigzag and Redback will offer difficulties. Unpatterned Zigzags have the dark pigment diffused, as though the dark borders of the light stripe had broken down and spread about. The dorsal coloration may be uniformly dark brown, reddish brown, or gray; dark Redbacks (leadbacks) are much darker, usually dark gray to black, and they have *salt-and-pepper* bellies without a mottling of red or orange pigment.

Range: Cen. Indiana to cen. Alabama; also several isolated localities.   Map 235

OZARK SALAMANDER   Fig. 85, p. 272
Plethodon dorsalis angusticlavius
Identification: 2⅜–3⅞ in. (6.0–9.8 cm). General coloration similar to that of the Zigzag Salamander. The slender orange or reddish middorsal stripe has indistinct edges, and it varies in width from one specimen to the next. Some individuals are uniformly dark.

Usually in or near caves of the Central Highlands.
Similar species: See Ouachita Red-backed Salamander.
Range: Sw. Missouri, n. Arkansas, and ne. Oklahoma.
                                                          Map 235

RAVINE SALAMANDER   *Plethodon richmondi*   Pl. 41
Identification: 3–4½ in. (8–11 cm); record 5⅝ in. (14.3 cm). Like a lead-colored Red-backed Salamander, but with a virtually plain dark venter (Fig. 86, below). A longer, more slender, shorter-legged species — almost a worm with legs. Dorsal color-

Fig. 86. VENTRAL PATTERNS OF SMALL LUNGLESS SALAMANDERS

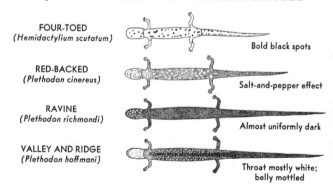

FOUR-TOED
(*Hemidactylium scutatum*)
Bold black spots

RED-BACKED
(*Plethodon cinereus*)
Salt-and-pepper effect

RAVINE
(*Plethodon richmondi*)
Almost uniformly dark

VALLEY AND RIDGE
(*Plethodon hoffmani*)
Throat mostly white; belly mottled

ation seal-brown to nearly black, but sprinkled with minute silvery-white and bronzy or brassy specks; very small, irregular white blotches on lower sides. Costal grooves 19 to 22.

Wooded *slopes* of valleys and ravines are preferred. Frequently found at high elevations in southern part of range.
Similar species: (1) Red-backed Salamander has a *salt-and-pepper* venter (Fig. 86, p. 274). (2) Zigzag Salamander, even in its dark phase, usually has some reddish or orange pigment showing on the undersurfaces. (3) Wehrle's Salamander and members of the Appalachian Woodland Salamander complex are much stouter-bodied and have proportionately larger legs.
Range: W. Pennsylvania to se. Indiana; south to extr. nw. N. Carolina and adj. Tennessee.   Map 231

VALLEY AND RIDGE SALAMANDER   Fig. 86, p. 274
Plethodon hoffmani
Identification: 3-4½ in. (8-11 cm); record 5⅜ in. (13.7 cm). Similar to the Ravine Salamander, but with throat mostly white; belly dark, but with a moderate amount of white mottling. Costal grooves usually 21.
Range: Chiefly the Valley and Ridge physiographic province from the Susquehanna River Valley in Pennsylvania to the New River in Virginia.   Map 231

CHEAT MOUNTAIN SALAMANDER   Pl. 40
Plethodon nettingi nettingi
Identification: 3-4 in. (8-10 cm); record 4⅜ in. (11.1 cm). Dorsal surface strongly sprinkled with *small brassy flecks* that extend to the tail but are most numerous on or near the head. Dorsal ground color black; belly plain dark slaty gray to black; throat paler. Brassy flecks disappear in preserved specimens. Costal grooves 18.

Found in cool, shady ravines and spruce forests at elevations of 3550 ft. (1100 m) or more in the Cheat Mountains of West Virginia.
Similar species: (1) Ravine Salamander has fewer and smaller brassy flecks, and is a longer, more slender animal, with 19 to 22 costal grooves. (2) Red-backed Salamanders collected high in the Cheat Mountains have all been red-backed (not lead-backed), so reddish stripe will distinguish these.
Range: E.-cen. W. Virginia.
Subspecies: PEAKS OF OTTER SALAMANDER, *Plethodon n. hubrichti*. More elongated and larger — to 4¹³⁄₁₆ in. (12.2 cm). Dorsal metallic pigment more abundant and in form of spots, blotches, or a roughly continuous stripe (instead of flecking or lacy mottling). Newly-hatched young with a reddish dorsal stripe. Costal grooves usually 19. Cool, moist forests of Peaks of Otter region ne. of Roanoke, Virginia; type locality 3160 ft.

(960 m). SHENANDOAH SALAMANDER, *Plethodon n. shenandoah.*
Occurs in two pattern phases: (a) a narrow red middorsal
stripe; and (b) a uniformly dark dorsum except for a small
amount of brassy flecking, and usually with tiny red spots in
middorsal region. *Belly black.* Costal grooves usually 18.
(Redbacks, *cinereus,* from same area, have paler bellies, usually
19 costal grooves, a wide red stripe in striped phase, and brassy
flecking may be heavy in lead-backed phase.) Talus slopes
of highest peaks in Shenandoah National Park, nw. Virginia.
Map 229

WELLER'S SALAMANDER   *Plethodon welleri*   **Pl. 40**
Identification: 2½–3⅛ in. (6.4–7.9 cm). Like a small "leadback" (Red-backed Salamander) in size and shape. Upper surfaces with a profusion of dull golden or silvery blotches on a
ground color of black. Venter plain black or spotted with white.
Costal grooves usually 16.
    Named for Worth Hamilton Weller, a promising young Cin-
cinnati naturalist who lost his life while collecting salamanders
on Grandfather Mountain in 1931.
Range: Tri-state area — extreme ne. Tennessee, Whitetop and
Mt. Rogers, Virginia, and nw. N. Carolina. From 2500 ft. (760 m)
upward, but chiefly in spruce forests above 5000 ft. (1500 m).
Subspecies: SPOT-BELLIED SALAMANDER, *Plethodon w. ventro-
maculatum* (Plate 40). Venter and lower flanks of body spotted
with white. All of range except Grandfather Mt. WELLER'S
SALAMANDER, *Plethodon w. welleri.* Venter virtually uniform
black. Grandfather Mt., N. Carolina.   Map 234

SLIMY SALAMANDER   **Pl. 41**
Plethodon glutinosus glutinosus
    Identification: 4¾–6¾ in. (12–17 cm); record 8⅛ in. (20.6 cm).
A large black salamander generally well sprinkled with silvery
white spots or brassy flecks or both. Extent of sprinkling extremely variable; there are innumerable modifications, some
confined to individual specimens and others evident throughout
local populations. Spotting or speckling may be restricted to
certain portions of dorsum, concentrated along sides of body,
greatly reduced, or even absent. Undersurfaces normally plain
slate color; chin and throat definitely dark, although usually
paler than remainder of venter. Costal grooves usually 16.
    This is the "sticky salamander" whose skin-gland secretions
cling to your hands like glue and almost have to wear off. (Some
of the other large woodland salamanders are almost as bad.)
Moist wooded ravines or hillsides are favorite habitats. Apparently the Slimy needs more moisture than its smaller com-
patriot, the Redback.
Similar species: Combination of dark throat and widely scat-

tered light spots will usually distinguish this species from other dark salamanders that resemble it. Like all its relatives, it has a groove running downward from nostril to lip; the Jefferson and the other Mole Salamanders (*Ambystoma*) lack this.

Range: Extr. s. New Hampshire, extr. w. Connecticut, and cen. New York to cen. Florida and west to Missouri, Oklahoma, and Texas. Hybridizes with the Appalachian Woodland Salamander (*P. jordani*) in southwestern part of latter's range, especially in the Nantahala River Valley of sw. N. Carolina.   Map 230

WHITE-THROATED SLIMY SALAMANDER   Pl. 41
Plethodon glutinosus albagula
Identification: 5¼–6 in. (13–15.2 cm). The throat is light and the bulk of the light spotting is along the sides of the body in this otherwise black salamander. Depend largely on geography in making identification; similar lateral concentrations of light pigment appear in some populations of the wide-ranging eastern subspecies, the Slimy Salamander.

Found in wooded ravines and caves in the eastern part of the Edwards Plateau.

Range: S.-cen. Texas.   Map 230

WEHRLE'S SALAMANDER   *Plethodon wehrlei*   Pl. 41
Identification: 4–5¼ in. (10–13 cm); record 6⁹⁄₁₆ in. (16.0 cm). Dark gray or dark brown with a row of irregular white, bluish-white, or yellowish spots and dashes along each side of body. Brassy flecking and a few very small white dots usually present. The middorsal area may lack conspicuous markings or it may be patterned with small *red* or *orange-red* spots, these often arranged in pairs. Specimens from the northern and western parts of the range usually are plain-backed, but those from farther south, the young especially, tend to be red-spotted. *Throat white or blotched with white;* white spots frequently extending backward onto breast. Belly and underside of tail uniform gray. Webbing on hind foot often extending almost to tips of first two toes. *Dixie Caverns phase:* Ground color purplish brown and entire dorsum profusely frosted with small light flecks and bronzy mottling. Known only from Dixie Caverns and Blankenship Cave near Roanoke, Virginia.

At home in upland forests; found under stones, in rotting logs, in deep rock crevices, or the twilight zones of caves. Named for R. W. Wehrle, of Indiana, Pennsylvania, who collected many of the specimens from which the species was first described.

Similar species: (1) Easily confused with Slimy Salamander, which (at least within range of Wehrle's Salamander) normally has larger white spots scattered all over dorsum — not just along sides; also, Slimy's dark throat may be gray, but *not white*.

(2) **Appalachian Woodland Salamander** (*jordani*) has less extensive webbing on hind foot. (3) **Jefferson** and other Mole Salamanders (*Ambystoma*) lack the groove from nostril to lip that is common to all Woodland Salamanders.

Range: Extr. sw. New York to sw. Virginia and adj. N. Carolina.
                                                                    Map 232

COW KNOB SALAMANDER   Fig. 87, below
Plethodon punctatus

Identification: 4–5 in. (10–13 cm); record 6³⁄₁₆ in. (15.7 cm). A close relative of Wehrle's Salamander, but lacking the brassy flecking and red spots of that species. Numerous white or yellowish-white dorsal spots. Throat light, pinkish in life. Costal grooves 17 or 18 (usually 17 in Wehrle's and 16 in Slimy Salamanders, respectively).

Similar species: Slimy Salamander has a darker throat (much darker in some populations). Double-check by counting costal grooves (see above).

Range: North and Shenandoah Mts. on the Virginia–W. Virginia line.   Map 232

Fig. 87. DORSAL PATTERNS OF WOODLAND SALAMANDERS
(*Plethodon*) WITH RESTRICTED RANGES

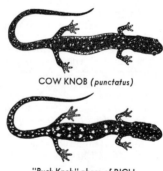

COW KNOB (*punctatus*)

"Buck Knob" phase of RICH
MOUNTAIN SALAMANDER (*ouachitae*)

YONAHLOSSEE SALAMANDER   Pl. 40
Plethodon yonahlossee

Identification: 4½–6½ in. (11–17 cm); record 7½ in. (19.0 cm). An extremely handsome salamander in life, but usually fading rapidly to almost uniform dull gray in preservatives. A broad *red or chestnut stripe* down back, extending from neck well onto base of tail. (Black sometimes invades the red stripe to an appreciable extent.) A stripe of light gray or whitish pigment *directly below* red stripe. Head plain black or marked with light specks. Tail black. Underparts dark gray, belly often mottled with light spots. *Young:* 4 to 6 pairs of red dorsal spots on a dark ground color; belly light.

One of our most agile salamanders, darting away into the forest litter, under any nearby shelter, or down the long burrows it utilizes to move about beneath the surface. Named for the old Yonahlossee Road on Grandfather Mountain, North Carolina.

Similar species: (1) Other red- or chestnut-backed salamanders (Red-backed and some individuals of Mountain Dusky Salamander) occurring within the range of the Yonahlossee Salamander have the red flanked on each side by *dark* instead of light pigment. (2) See also Crevice Salamander.

Range: Southern Blue Ridge Mountains, east and north of French Broad River in sw. Virginia, w. N. Carolina, and extr. e. Tennessee; elevations from 2500 to 5700 ft. (760 to 1700 m).
Map 236

CREVICE SALAMANDER *Plethodon longicrus*   **Pl. 40**

Identification: 5–7 in. (13–18 cm); record 8$\frac{11}{16}$ in. (22.1 cm). The amount of chestnut on the dorsum in this large, handsome salamander is variable, and it may be confined to scattered flecks or blotches or both (often far less extensive than shown on Plate 40). The pale spotting, which may appear anywhere on the head, body, limbs, and base of tail, is most strongly concentrated on the sides in large individuals. Venter dark gray with scattered pale spotting; soles of feet pink. A downward projection from naso-labial groove, especially in males. *Young:* 3 to 7 small chestnut spots on dorsum; venter, including soles, gray.

The vertical surfaces of rock outcrops and their associated fissures and crevices are favored. Little light filters through the dense forest canopy, and the microhabitat is both cool and moist.

Similar species: In Yonahlossee Salamander the chestnut (or red) is more extensive, usually forms a broad dorsal stripe, and is in contact with a gray stripe along lower side of body.

Range: Known from several localities in Rutherford Co., N. Carolina; elevations 1400 to 2600 ft. (430 to 790 m).   Map 236

RICH MOUNTAIN SALAMANDER   Pl. 40; Fig. 87, p. 278
Plethodon ouachitae

Identification: 4–5 in. (10–13 cm); record 6$\frac{1}{4}$ in. (15.9 cm). Extremely variable in coloration. The typical adult from Rich Mountain has varying amounts of chestnut pigment overlying the black of the dorsal ground color, numerous small white specks, and metallic-looking (brassy) flecks. Any one of these pattern elements may be missing, however, and the chestnut is totally lacking in populations from some of the adjacent mountains and in all juveniles. Throat whitish; *chest dark.* One of the several other pattern variations is illustrated in Fig. 87, p. 278 as the "Buck Knob" phase.

Similar species: (1) Slimy Salamander has a *dark throat.* (2) Caddo Mountain Salamander has a *light chest.*

Range: Rich Mt. and adjacent ridges of the Ouachita Range in w. Arkansas and e. Oklahoma from Buck Knob to Buffalo Mt. Hybridizes with the Slimy Salamander on Kiamichi Mt. south of Big Cedar, Oklahoma.   Map 238

CADDO MOUNTAIN SALAMANDER   Pl. 40
Plethodon caddoensis

Identification: 3½–4 in. (9–10 cm); record 4⅜ in. (11.1 cm). A slender, black-and-white salamander somewhat similar to the Rich Mountain species, but lacking the chestnut pigment of the latter. The black back and sides of the body are profusely marked with whitish spots that stand out less sharply than the Slimy Salamander's spotting and Rich Mountain Salamander's speckling. Brassy flecks scattered over back. *Throat light; chest light* (speckled black and white).

Similar species: (1) Slimy Salamander has a *dark throat.* (2) Rich Mountain Salamander has a *dark chest,* and is a larger, stouter animal.

Range: Caddo Mts. of w. Arkansas.   Map 238

APPALACHIAN WOODLAND SALAMANDER   Pl. 40
Plethodon jordani

Members of this species complex exhibit a bewildering array of color and pattern variations and combinations. Many local populations were originally described as distinct species. Later, as more material became available and intermediates were discovered, they were grouped as subspecies of one relatively wide-ranging species. Recent collecting has demonstrated, however, that the presumed subspecies blend together in so many different ways that trying to sort them out taxonomically is virtually impossible. For example, a red-legged race formerly seemed to be quite distinct from a red-cheeked one; other so-called races appeared to be characterized by white spots, black bellies, or brassy flecking on the dorsum. Now that collectors have penetrated to many of the more remote parts of the southern Appalachians, red legs, red cheeks, white spots, etc. are known to occur in widely scattered localities. The various "races" may have been isolated at one time, but they now freely intermingle and presumably are interbreeding. Samples of some of the more outstanding variations are illustrated on Plate 40. It is best to identify all of these and the various combinations among them simply as members of the *Plethodon jordani* complex.

Identification: 3½–5 in. (9–13 cm); record 7¼ in. (18.4 cm). (Northern individuals tend to be smaller than southern ones.) Specimens that match the "Red-cheeked," "Red-legged," "Metcalf's," and "Clemson" Salamanders illustrated on Plate 40 are easily identified as members of this complex, but others may be confused with the Slimy Salamander (see **Similar species,** below). Many are black, either unmarked or with small white spots on cheeks and sides of body; others, essentially black above, bear tiny white spots on dorsum and minute red spots on legs. General trends are as follows: red cheeks and red legs in the Great Smoky and Nantahala Mountains, respectively; lateral white spots in extreme southwestern part of range; bellies dark in roughly southeastern half of range (bellies paler toward north and west); indications of brassy flecks strongest in northwestern South Carolina.

The humid, forested southern Appalachians are the home of this extraordinarily variable salamander. Habitats, which include forest litter, rotting logs, and mossy stone piles, range from near the summits of the highest mountains to as low as 700 ft. (210 m) in extreme northwestern South Carolina. Northern populations are generally restricted to high altitudes.

Similar species: (1) Slimy Salamander usually is abundantly sprinkled with white spots all over sides and dorsum; it has a dark venter, including chin and throat, and grows to larger size — 8⅛ in. (20.6 cm). Slimy Salamander is also known to hybridize with members of Appalachian Woodland Salamander complex in some parts of southwestern North Carolina. (2) Some Mountain Dusky Salamanders (*Desmognathus ochrophaeus*) also have red, orange, or yellow cheek patches (illustrated as "Imitator Salamander" on Plate 40). These were once considered a distinct subspecies to which the name *imitator* was applied. Other specimens of *ochrophaeus* may have reddish legs. The "mimics" generally have indications of a dorsal pattern, a light line from eye to angle of jaws, and their hind legs are larger than their forelegs (Fig. 64, opp. Pl. 41). Habitat may also help. The red-cheeked and red-legged phases of the *jordani* group are terrestrial and normally shun water; the Mountain Dusky (including the "Imitator") also occurs in woods, but is usually found near springs, edges of streams, in seepage areas, etc.

Range: Highlands of sw. Virginia to extr. ne. Georgia and extr. nw. S. Carolina.   Map 237

Four-toed, Many-lined, and Green Salamanders: Genera *Hemidactylium, Stereochilus,* and *Aneides*

SALAMANDERS of these three genera are not closely related, and they are grouped here only for convenience. The first two are monotypic, with *Hemidactylium* widely distributed in the East and *Stereochilus* restricted to a portion of the southeastern Coastal Plain. The genus *Aneides* is represented in our area only by the Green Salamander, but there are several species in the West that range, collectively, from Vancouver Island, British Columbia, to northern Baja California; another occurs only in mountains of southern New Mexico. The generic common name for *Aneides* is climbing salamanders, in reference to the arboreal and rock-climbing tendencies of several of the species.

FOUR-TOED SALAMANDER   Pl. 40
Hemidactylium scutatum
   Identification: 2–3½ in. (5.1–8.9 cm); record 4 in. (10.2 cm). Look for three things: (a) enamel-white belly boldly marked with *black spots* (unique among our salamanders — see Fig. 86, p. 274); (b) 4 toes on *hind foot* as well as forefoot (most salamanders have 5 on each *hind* foot); (c) *marked constriction* at base of tail (if an enemy seized the tail, this is where it would break away from body).
   Usually associated with sphagnum. Sphagnaceous areas adjacent to woods are common habitats, and so are boggy woodland ponds. The Fourtoe is terrestrial when adult (like woodland salamanders); but its larvae are aquatic (like those of dusky salamanders).
   Similar species: Dwarf Salamander also has 4 toes on all feet, but it lacks characteristics (a) and (c) above.
   Range: Nova Scotia to Wisconsin and Alabama. Distribution spotty; disjunct populations in many states.   Map 239

MANY-LINED SALAMANDER   Pl. 43
Stereochilus marginatus
   Identification: 2½–3¾ in. (6.4–9.5 cm); record 4½ in. (11.4 cm). Nondescript except for a series of narrow, indistinct, dark longitudinal lines on sides of body, and even these may be reduced to a few dark spots. In some specimens there are indistinct dark (or light) markings on the back. Most Many-lined Salamanders tend to be brown in general coloration, others may be dull yellow. Belly yellow with scattered dark specks. The small head and short tail are characteristic.

A denizen of pools and sluggish streams in swampy woodlands, best found by raking out dead leaves and other bottom debris. Essentially aquatic, but sometimes uncovered by overturning logs where the ground is damp.

Range: Coastal Plain from se. Virginia to Georgia.   Map 228

GREEN SALAMANDER *Aneides aeneus*   **Pl. 43**
Identification: 3¼–5 in. (8–13 cm); record 5½ in. (14.0 cm). Our *only really green salamander*. Green lichenlike markings on a dark ground color. Note square-tipped toes.

A cliff dweller. Narrow crevices on rock faces are a favorite habitat, provided rocks are damp but not wet, situated where the atmosphere is humid, and well protected from sun and direct rain. The flattened head and body are admirably adapted for getting about in tight places. Also sometimes found under stones, logs, or loose bark. Occasionally arboreal.

Range: Appalachian region; sw. Pennsylvania, extr. w. Maryland, and s. Ohio to w.-cen. Alabama and extr. ne. Mississippi; a disjunct area in sw. N. Carolina and adjacent states. Map 221

Spring, Red, and Mud Salamanders: Genera *Gyrinophilus* and *Pseudotriton*

THESE are chiefly red or salmon-colored salamanders, most of them patterned with black spots. All are at home in the water, as well as in damp or soggy terrain. The spring salamanders (*Gyrinophilus*) like clear, cool water, and their habitats vary from forested seepage areas to rushing mountain brooks. Formerly they were called "purple salamanders," a name more appropriate for a badly preserved specimen than one of the orange- or salmon-colored living animals. Both the red and mud salamanders (*Pseudotriton*) are red or reddish, and details must be checked carefully to tell them apart. Age also is important; young adults are brilliantly colored, whereas older specimens darken and their patterns become obscure. The reds prefer clear water, but the muds usually are found in muddy places. Both genera occur only in eastern North America.

SPRING SALAMANDER   **Pl. 42**
Gyrinophilus porphyriticus
(subspecies *porphyriticus* and *duryi*)
Identification: 4¾–7½ in. (12–19 cm); record 8⅝ in. (21.9 cm). The light line from eye to nostril is bordered below by gray pigment, but these markings usually are not overly conspicuous. The general dorsal coloration varies from salmon or light brownish pink to reddish. The ground color has a cloudy appearance, and the darker markings are vague — not clear-cut.

These are agile denizens of cool springs and mountain streams, but are also likely to be found in any wet depression beneath logs, stones, or leaves in the surrounding forests.

Similar species (and subspecies): (1) In Mountain Spring Salamander (subspecies *danielsi* and *dunni*) there is a conspicuous light *and dark* line from eye to nostril. (2) In Red and Mud Salamanders such markings are completely absent, and the heads are rounded, thus lacking the distinct angle (canthus rostralis) along which the lines run from eye to nostril in Spring Salamanders.

Range: Sw. Maine and s. Quebec to n. Alabama.

Subspecies: NORTHERN SPRING SALAMANDER, *Gyrinophilus p. porphyriticus* (Plate 42). Salmon or light yellowish brown with reddish tinges, and with a mottled or clouded appearance; sides tend to be darker and to form a netlike pattern enclosing light spots; venter flesh-colored; small, scattered dark spots on belly and throat and especially on margin of lower jaw in old specimens. Recently transformed young are salmon-red and with the darker mottlings not well developed. Specimens from southern localities may show evidences of intergradation with the other races. Most of range of species. KENTUCKY SPRING SALAMANDER, *Gyrinophilus p. duryi.* Smaller; max. length about 6½ in. (16.5 cm). Dorsal coloration salmon-pink to light brownish pink; small black spots usually arranged in a row along each side of body, but sometimes scattered along sides or (in some individuals) over all the dorsal surfaces. (Even when the black spots are widely distributed, they are most strongly concentrated along the sides.) Venter flesh-colored and unmarked except on lower lip and occasionally chin and throat. S. Ohio to extr. sw. Virginia.   Map 222

MOUNTAIN SPRING SALAMANDER   Pl. 42
Gyrinophilus porphyriticus
(subspecies *danielsi* and *dunni*)

Identification: 5–7½ in. (13–19 cm); record 8⅟₁₆ in. (20.5 cm). The white line from eye to nostril, *bordered below* by a conspicuous black or dark brown line, is the distinctive mark of these races. There also may be a dark line above the white line, and in many specimens this, too, is conspicuous. Dorsal coloration clear reddish, salmon, or orange-yellow marked with black or brown spots or flecks.

Turning over a stone at a mountain spring and revealing one of these brightly colored amphibians is an exciting experience. Also found in seepage and wet forest areas, especially near edges of mountain brooks.

Similar species (and subspecies): In the subspecies *porphyriticus* and *duryi* (see Spring Salamander), lines from eyes to nostril are much less prominent; a *light* line is present, but the dark line below it may be obscure or virtually lacking. Such markings are completely absent among Red and Mud Salamanders.

Range: Southern Appalachians and adj. Piedmont from N. Carolina to Alabama.

Subspecies: MOUNTAIN SPRING SALAMANDER, *Gyrinophilus p. danielsi* (Plate 42). Reddish or rich salmon-colored with scattered black spots on the back; specimens from high elevations have heavy dark speckling on chin. The Blue Ridge Province of w. N. Carolina and adj. Tennessee. DUNN'S SPRING SALAMANDER, *Gyrinophilus p. dunni*. Orange-yellow to light reddish, profusely flecked with dark pigment; venter salmon-pink, usually immaculate except for margins of jaws, which are mottled with black and white. Named for Emmett Reid Dunn, a pioneer student of North American salamanders and author of the classic work on *The Salamanders of the Family Plethodontidae*. Southern portion of Blue Ridge Province and the Piedmont from sw. N. Carolina to ne. Alabama.   Map 222

TENNESSEE CAVE SALAMANDER   Pl. 39
Gyrinophilus palleucus

Identification: 3–7¼ in. (8–18.4 cm). A neotenic, cave-dwelling member of the spring salamander genus. External gills always present; eye small; its diameter ¼ or less than distance from anterior corner of eye to tip of snout. (In larvae of spring salamanders diameter of eye is ⅓ or more of distance from eye to snout.) Eyelids lacking as in larval salamanders.

Range: Caves of cen. and se. Tennessee, n. Alabama, and nw. Georgia.

Subspecies: SINKING COVE CAVE SALAMANDER, *Gyrinophilus p. palleucus* (Plate 39). Coloration normally pale flesh-pink, except for the bright red external gills. Body pigmentation lacks dark spots. Caves along southeastern edge of Cumberland Plateau, Tennessee. BIG MOUTH CAVE SALAMANDER, *Gyrinophilus p. necturoides*. Dark and heavily spotted dorsally; ground color russet-brown to deep brownish purple; spots roughly circular and blackish, extending from level of jaw to basal third of tail; venter pearl-gray. Big Mouth Cave, Grundy Co., Tennessee. BERRY CAVE SALAMANDER, *Gyrinophilus p. gulolineatus*. Grows larger, to 8¹⁵⁄₁₆ in. (22.7 cm). Similar but with a wider head, more spatulate snout, and a dark stripe or blotch on forward half of throat. Roane and McMinn Cos., Tennessee. The ranges of the subspecies (not shown on map) have not been worked out in detail.   Map 223

EASTERN MUD SALAMANDER   Pl. 42
Pseudotriton montanus montanus

Identification: 3½–6 in. (9–15 cm); record 8⅛ in. (20.7 cm). A red-colored salamander with a *brown* eye. Black spots round and well separated. Dorsum with a definite ground color that doesn't blend directly into the reddish of the lower sides and belly. Young specimens brightly colored, with sharply distinct spots and virtually unmarked venters. Older ones vary from light reddish brown to chocolate; their dorsal spots are larger and more numerous but tend to be inconspicuous against the darker backgrounds; undersurfaces often spotted or flecked with brown or black.

Occurs in the muddy environs of springs, muddy seeps along small streams, etc. It burrows into the muck in its efforts to escape, and may take refuge in crayfish or other holes.

Similar species: (1) Mud and Red Salamanders are easily confused — even experienced herpetologists have trouble with them. Check color of iris; it normally is yellowish instead of brown in the Reds. Look at shape of head: in the Muds, snout is blunter and shorter in front of eyes. Habitat will help: Mud Salamanders usually live up to their names. (2) Spring Salamanders have a light and dark line from eye to nostril.

Range: S. New Jersey to the Carolinas and ne. Georgia.

Subspecies: MIDLAND MUD SALAMANDER, *Pseudotriton m. diastictus.* The ground color, coral-pink or red to brown, is clearer and brighter than in Eastern Mud Salamander; black spots fewer in number; undersurfaces unmarked except occasionally for a dark line on rim of lower jaw. S. Ohio and W. Virginia to n. Alabama. GULF COAST MUD SALAMANDER, *Pseudotriton m. flavissimus.* Averages smaller and more slender; max. length about 4⅛ in. (10.5 cm). A large number of small, well-separated round spots on a ground of clear, light brownish salmon; underside of head and trunk clear salmon-pink. Extr. s. S. Carolina to extr. e. Louisiana.   Map 225

RUSTY MUD SALAMANDER   Pl. 42
Pseudotriton montanus floridanus

Identification: 2⅞–4¼ in. (7–11 cm); record 4⅝ in. (11.7 cm). The rustiest and one of the smallest of the mud salamanders. The virtually plain dorsum may be slightly mottled with indistinct darker areas and a few small, irregular, light pinkish spots. *No dark dots on back,* but there may be a few scattered ones atop tail. Streaking on sides highly irregular — a mixture of pinkish buff and rust color and sometimes with streaks or specks of black. Undersurfaces buffy and sparsely marked with small, irregular blackish spots.

Habitats include mucky seepage areas and small, shallow streams flowing through hardwood hammocks or mixed forests.

Range: N. Florida and s. Georgia.   Map 225

NORTHERN RED SALAMANDER   Pl. 42
Pseudotriton ruber ruber

Identification: 4¼–6 in. (11–15 cm); record 7⅛ in. (18.1 cm). A red or reddish-orange salamander with the uppersurfaces profusely dotted with irregular, rounded black spots. Iris of eye normally *yellow*. Margin of chin often flecked with black. *Old adults:* Dull purplish brown, the ground color darker and the spots larger and running together; black or brown spots on undersurfaces.

Look for the Red Salamander under moss, stones, or other objects in or near springs or rills, even mere trickles, provided water is clear, cool, and not stagnant. Occurs in streams that flow through open fields and meadows as well as those through woods; streams with bottoms of sand, gravel, or rock usually are preferred.

Similar species: (1) Mud Salamanders have: (a) noticeably fewer and well-separated *circular* (or nearly circular) black spots; (b) their dorsal ground color is more sharply set off from the ventral coloration; and (c) their irises are *brown*. (2) Spring Salamanders have a light and dark line from eye to nostril.

Range: S. New York and Ohio to n. Alabama (except in s. Blue Ridge, where related subspecies occur).

Subspecies: BLUE RIDGE RED SALAMANDER, *Pseudotriton r. nitidus*. Small; max. length about 4⅝ in. (12 cm). Coloration and pattern similar to Northern Red Salamander's, but without black pigment on tip half of tail and little or none on chin; old adults retain their bright appearance. Elevations to more than 5000 ft. (1500 m), north and east of French Broad River, in s. Blue Ridge Mts.; Floyd Co., Virginia.   Map 224

BLACK-CHINNED RED SALAMANDER   Pl. 42
Pseudotriton ruber schencki

Identification: 2¾–4¾ in. (7–12 cm); record 5¾ in. (14.6 cm). A red salamander with a strong concentration of black pigment under the chin. (Black area much heavier and broader than narrow black flecking seen in some individuals of its related subspecies.) Tail spotted almost to tip.

Under logs, stones, moss, etc., in habitats ranging from open pastures to forests.

Range: Elevations to more than 5000 ft. (1500 m), west and south of French Broad River, s. Blue Ridge Mts.   Map 224

SOUTHERN RED SALAMANDER   Pl. 42
Pseudotriton ruber vioscai

Identification: 3⅞–5¾ in. (10–15 cm); record 6⅜ in. (16.2 cm). A purplish, reddish, or salmon-colored salamander with a profusion of white flecks, these largely concentrated on snout and sides of head. The purplish effect is produced by numerous, fairly large blue-black blotches. Undersurfaces light but with a profusion of small dark spots.

In and near springs, small streams, and in rotting, well-saturated logs.

Range: E. Georgia to se. Louisiana and w. Tennessee.

Map 224

Brook Salamanders: Genus *Eurycea*

THESE are salamanders of small brooks, rills, springs, seepage areas, river-bottom swamps, and other small bodies of water where fish are absent or at a minimum. An alternate name might be "yellow salamanders," for yellowish pigment is found in most of them, at least on their undersurfaces. In many there are well-pronounced, downward projections (cirri) from the nostrils, at least in males. All species have aquatic larvae.

The brook salamanders may be readily separated into three groups:

1. Typical "brook" salamanders, such as the Two-lined and Many-ribbed. These frequently wander well out into moist woodlands during wet weather and on humid nights.

2. The "long-tailed salamanders," which in the adult stage have tails considerably more than ½ their total lengths (juveniles have much shorter tails). These salamanders are essentially terrestrial but they swim readily; they include the Three-lined, Long-tailed, Dark-sided, and Cave Salamanders, the last three of which frequently are found in caves.

3. The "neotenic euryceas," which retain the larval form (with external gills) throughout life. These are completely aquatic, and are difficult to distinguish from the larvae of salamanders that normally transform into a gill-less adult form. Several occur in localities along or near the Balcones Escarpment in central Texas, where, fortunately, there are no other larval aquatic salamanders that could be confused with them.

The genus *Eurycea* occurs only in eastern and south central North America.

NORTHERN TWO-LINED SALAMANDER   Pl. 43
Eurycea bislineata bislineata

Identification: 2½–3¾ in. (6.4–9.5 cm); record 4¾ in. (12.1 cm). The common yellow salamander of the Northeast. The 2 dark lines border a broad light middorsal stripe, but often tend to break up into dots or dashes on tail. The dorsal coloration, always essentially yellow, may be brownish, greenish, bronzy, or bordering on orange. The broad light stripe down back is usually peppered with small black spots that may join to form a narrow median dark line. Mottling on side of body varies in intensity from one specimen to the next; it may be so dark that it blends with dorsolateral line or it may be much reduced or virtually absent. Costal grooves 14 to 16.

Essentially a brookside salamander, hiding under all manner of objects at water's edge and running or swimming away vigorously when alarmed. Saturated areas near springs or seeps are also favorite habitats. In warm wet weather, it may wander far out into nearby woodlands.

Similar species: (1) Dusky Salamanders, some populations of which include yellowish specimens, have enlarged hind legs and a light stripe from eye to angle of jaw (Fig. 64, opp. Pl. 41). (2) Adult Long-tailed Salamanders (all races) and Cave Salamanders have tails much more than ½ their total lengths. (3) Brown-backed Salamander has a short tail and 13 costal grooves. (4) Ground Skink (a lizard) has scales on its body and claws on its toes.

Range: Quebec to Virginia and e. Illinois; south to the Tennessee River Valley.

Subspecies: SOUTHERN TWO-LINED SALAMANDER, *Eurycea b. cirrigera.* Smaller; max. length about 4 in. (10 cm), but similar to Northern Twoline. The narrow black lines usually continue without interruption to tip of tail, and most specimens have a row of small circular light spots in the dark and light mottled area along the sides; dorsal coloration yellow to russet; adult males with well-developed projections (cirri) downward from nostrils, as in Blue Ridge Twoline. Chiefly a Coastal Plain and Piedmont race, secretive and hiding beneath all types of sheltering objects, including masses of wet leaves in creek or river swamps. S. Virginia to n. Florida and west to Mississippi River.
Map 240

BLUE RIDGE TWO-LINED SALAMANDER   Pl. 43
Eurycea bislineata wilderae

Identification: 2¾–4¼ in. (7–11 cm); record 4¾ in. (12.1 cm). A montane salamander with the colors and pattern more vivid than in the Northern Two-lined Salamander. Lines *broad* and black and normally breaking up into dots at about middle of tail. Most adult males have conspicuous projections (cirri) downward from nostrils.

Found in and near springs and rills, but wandering far out into the humid forests, at least at higher elevations. Most abundant above 2000 ft. (600 m) and to tops of tallest mountains.

Similar species: (1) Yellowish examples of Mountain Dusky Salamander usually have a light line from eye to angle of jaw (Fig. 64, opp. Pl. 41). (2) Cave and Long-tailed Salamanders are *spotted,* and tails of adults are considerably more than ½ their total lengths. (3) Three-lined Salamander also has long tail.

Range: Southern Blue Ridge Mt. region from sw. Virginia to n. Georgia.
Map 240

BROWN-BACKED SALAMANDER   Pl. 43
Eurycea aquatica

Identification: 2½–3⅝ in. (6.4–9.2 cm). Despite its resemblance to the Two-lined Salamanders, this species may be recognized by its short, stout body, short tail, brownish dorsum, and dusky-black sides. The pale dorsal stripe with its bordering black edges extends to the tip of the tail. Dorsum varies from medium to relatively dark brown; on base of tail it may be greenish yellow. Belly yellow, virtually unmarked; 13 costal grooves.

Range: Springs and small streams of cen. Alabama; may also occur in Georgia, Tennessee, or Mississippi.

Note: Some authorities contend this salamander should not be classified as a distinct species, and that it actually represents aberrant individuals or populations of *Eurycea bislineata*.

Map 241

MANY-RIBBED SALAMANDER   Pl. 43
Eurycea multiplicata multiplicata

Identification: 2½–3¼ in. (6.4–8.3 cm); record 3⁹⁄₁₆ in. (9.0 cm). A yellowish salamander without strong longitudinal dark stripes. Sides of body somewhat darker than middorsal area and often with a row of faint light spots. Undersurfaces plain bright yellow. Costal grooves 19 or 20.

Essentially an aquatic amphibian, hiding beneath stones, logs, and various other objects, both in and out of caves. Wanders short distances afield in wet weather.

Similar species: (1) Dwarf Salamander has only *four* toes on each *hind* foot. (2) Two-lined Salamanders are superficially similar, but their ranges do not overlap range of Many-ribbed. They and Dwarf Salamander have 16 or fewer costal grooves.

Range: N.-cen. Arkansas to se. Oklahoma.   Map 242

GRAY-BELLIED SALAMANDER   Pl. 43
Eurycea multiplicata griseogaster

Identification: 1⅞–3¼ in. (4.8–8.3 cm); record 3¹³⁄₁₆ in. (9.7 cm). A dark subspecies of the Many-ribbed Salamander, with a *gray* instead of yellow belly. Amount of tan on back variable, and middorsal area may consist of a longitudinal stripe paler than the adjacent sides. Costal grooves 19 or 20. Occasionally neotenic.

Similar species: (1) Ouachita Dusky Salamander has light line from eye to angle of jaw. (2) Darker specimens of Dwarf Salamander resemble Graybelly but they have only *four* toes on hind feet.

Range: Sw. Missouri and adj. Arkansas and Oklahoma; extr. se. Kansas.   Map 242

LONG-TAILED SALAMANDER Pl. 43
Eurycea longicauda longicauda

Identification: 4–6¼ in. (10–16 cm); record 7¾ in. (19.7 cm). The only yellowish salamander with vertical black markings on the tail. These, although frequently varying from the herring-bone or "dumbbell" theme, are usually conspicuous. The ground color also varies — from yellow to orange-red or even red. Some individuals, from scattered portions of the range, have the black markings larger and more conspicuous. *Young:* Yellow; tail relatively short.

Found in or under rotting logs, under stones, in shale banks near seepages, under rocks at streamside, and frequently in caves. Also occurs in ponds in the limestone belt of northern New Jersey.

Range: S. New York to n. Alabama and s. Illinois. Map 244

THREE-LINED SALAMANDER Pl. 43
Eurycea longicauda guttolineata

Identification: 4–6¼ in. (10–16 cm); record 7⅞ in. (20.0 cm). This is the southern member of the Long-tailed Salamander group and the only one with three dark stripes. Middorsal stripe may be broken into a series of elongated dark spots. Ground color varies from yellow to tan. Belly mottled with greenish gray on a ground color of dull yellow.

In river-bottom swamps, wet ditches, seepage areas at springs and streamside; sometimes at considerable distances from water, but always in a damp environment.

Range: Virginia to Florida panhandle and Mississippi River.
Map 244

DARK-SIDED SALAMANDER Pl. 43
Eurycea longicauda melanopleura

Identification: 3⅝–5⅞ in. (9–15 cm); record 6⅝ in. (16.8 cm). The dark stripes, one along each side of the body, are in strong contrast with a broad middorsal stripe that is essentially light in color but well marked with dark spots. Coloration varies. Dark pigment on sides is grayish in juveniles but changes to deep reddish brown in old adults. The light flecks and spots in the dark bands vary from light gray to yellow. The middorsal stripe ranges from bright yellow in juveniles through greenish yellow to dull brownish yellow in the largest individuals.

This is a cave salamander, occurring in the twilight zone of caverns and grottoes, but also venturing far afield into the outer world.

Range: Central Highlands and adjacent areas; intergrading with the Long-tailed Salamander in Illinois and se. Missouri.
Map 244

CAVE SALAMANDER   *Eurycea lucifuga*   **Pl. 43**
  Identification: 4–6 in. (10–15 cm); record 7⅛ in. (18.1 cm). A reddish salamander with a *long* tail. Ground color variable, however, and ranging from dull yellow through orange to bright orange-red. (Young tend to be yellow, the adults reddish.) The black spots are usually irregularly scattered, but sometimes they may form 2 or 3 longitudinal rows. Occasional specimens have the black markings especially large and conspicuous. Yellowish undersurfaces normally unspotted. *Young:* Tail relatively short.
  A favorite habitat is in the twilight zone of caves — near entrances, where the light is weak. There these salamanders — excellent climbers — move about on the formations and ledges, sometimes clinging solely by their prehensile tails. They also occur outside caves and may be discovered beneath logs, stones, or debris in wooded or fairly open places.
  Similar species: (1) Three-lined and Dark-sided Salamanders have dark longitudinal markings. (2) Long-tailed Salamander usually has dark "dumbbells" or a herringbone pattern on sides of tail; also, its head is not so broad and flat as Cave Salamander's.
  Range: Limestone areas, Virginia to Oklahoma.   Map 243

DWARF SALAMANDER   *Eurycea quadridigitata*   **Pl. 43**
  Identification: 2⅛–3 in. (5.4–7.6 cm); record 3⁹⁄₁₆ in. (9.0 cm). *Four toes on hind feet* as well as forefeet. (Most other salamanders have *five* on each *hind* foot.) The dark dorsolateral stripe ranges from black through various shades of dark brown, and the amount of dark pigmentation on sides of body is quite variable. Many specimens have a middorsal row of small dark spots; in others the row is short, broken, or absent. *Male:* Often with downward projections (cirri) from nostrils.
  A resident of low swampy areas, where it hides under all types of shelter.
  Similar species: Two-lined and Many-ribbed Salamanders are superficially similar, but both have *five* toes on their *hind* feet.
  Range: Chiefly in Coastal Plain from N. Carolina to Florida and west to e. Texas; disjunct colonies in South Carolina, Missouri, and Arkansas.   Map 246

OKLAHOMA SALAMANDER   *Eurycea tynerensis*   **Pl. 39**
  Identification: 1¾–3⅛ in. (4.4–7.9 cm). The grayish appearance is caused by a heavy stippling and streaking of black over a cream-colored ground. Amount of dark pigment variable; may be densest on sides, leaving a broad light stripe down back, or it may be heavy over all dorsal surfaces. Usually at least 1 row of small light spots appears along each side of body (as many as 3 rows in small specimens). Belly pale, except where viscera or eggs show through body wall. *External gills present.* Tail fin low.

This neotenic salamander lives in small gravelly creeks and springs, and may be found among stones or in vegetation growing in water.

Similar species: Larvae of Grotto Salamander have high tail fin and longitudinal streaks on sides of body.

Range: Ne. Oklahoma and adjacent corners of Arkansas and Missouri. Map 245

SAN MARCOS SALAMANDER *Eurycea nana* Pl. 39

Identification: 1½–2 in. (3.8–5.1 cm). Almost plain brown above, but with a row of yellowish flecks or spots down each side of back. Venter whitish or yellowish except where viscera and eggs (of females in season) show through translucent skin. *External gills present.*

A tiny neotenic species known only from the mats of algae carpeting the big spring pool that is the source of the San Marcos River, at San Marcos, Texas.

Similar species: (1) Texas Salamander is chiefly yellowish rather than brown. (2) Other neotenic salamanders of the general region are virtually white.

Range: San Marcos, Texas. Map 250

TEXAS SALAMANDER Pl. 39; Fig. 88, p. 294
Eurycea neotenes

Identification: 2–4⅛ in. (5–10.5 cm). Light brownish yellow in coloration, but mottled or flecked with darker pigment; a double row of light flecks on each side of body, at least in smaller specimens (lower row fades out in older ones). Belly and lower sides almost always white or cream, except where viscera or eggs may be seen through skin. Local populations vary in coloration, size, robustness, and head shape. Costal grooves 14 to 16. *External gills present.*

This neotenic salamander is a resident of springs, seeps, and small cavern streams along the Balcones Escarpment and on adjacent portions of the Edwards Plateau of south central Texas.

Similar species: (1) Several of the neotenic cave salamanders (*Typhlomolge, Eurycea tridentifera,* and *E. latitans*) are virtually plain white and they have flattened snouts. (2) See also San Marcos and Valdina Farms Salamanders.

Range: Edwards Plateau area from vicinity of Austin to Val Verde Co., Texas.

Subspecies: FERN BANK SALAMANDER, *Eurycea n. pterophila* (Plate 39). Known only from a small spring near Wimberley, Hays Co., Texas. EDWARDS PLATEAU SALAMANDER, *Eurycea n. neotenes.* Numerous localities from vicinities of Austin and San Antonio to Edwards and Val Verde Cos., Texas.

Note: Most of the small neotenic salamanders of the Edwards Plateau and Balcones Escarpment have restricted ranges. Many differ only in minutiae or internal anatomy. Identify them by the general localities in which they are collected. It is virtually certain that other species will eventually be described from the same general region.   Map 247

CASCADE CAVERN SALAMANDER   Fig. 88, below
Eurycea latitans

Identification: 2½–3¼ in. (6.4–8.3 cm); record 4³⁄₁₆ in. (10.6 cm). A whitish salamander with a relatively stout body and legs, a flat snout followed by an abrupt elevation at eye level, and a faint network of dark pigment. Eye moderate in size. Costal grooves 14 or 15. *External gills present.*
Similar species: In Texas Blind, Honey Creek Cave Blind, and Valdina Farms Salamanders the eyes are very small (see Fig. 88, below).
Range: Subterranean water systems near Boerne, Kendall Co., Texas.   Map 250

VALDINA FARMS SALAMANDER   Fig. 88, below
Eurycea troglodytes

Identification: 2–3¹⁄₁₆ in. (5.1–7.8 cm). About midway in general appearance between the Texas Blind Salamander and Texas Salamander. This cave dweller looks white in the beam of a flashlight, but it is better described as grayish. Eyes small and partly or completely covered with skin, legs long and slender, a somewhat flattened forehead, and 13 or 14 costal grooves (14 or 15 grooves in Cascade Cavern Salamander, 14 to 16 in Texas

Fig. 88. NEOTENIC SALAMANDERS FROM TEXAS (*Typhlomolge* and *Eurycea*)

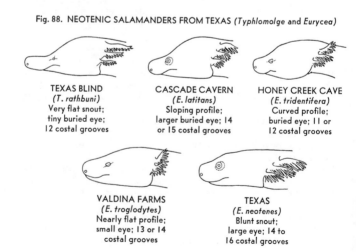

TEXAS BLIND
(*T. rathbuni*)
Very flat snout;
tiny buried eye;
12 costal grooves

CASCADE CAVERN
(*E. latitans*)
Sloping profile;
larger buried eye; 14
or 15 costal grooves

HONEY CREEK CAVE
(*E. tridentifera*)
Curved profile;
buried eye; 11 or
12 costal grooves

VALDINA FARMS
(*E. troglodytes*)
Nearly flat profile;
small eye; 13 or 14
costal grooves

TEXAS
(*E. neotenes*)
Blunt snout;
large eye; 14 to
16 costal grooves

Salamander, and 11 or 12 in Honey Creek Cave Blind Salamander). *External gills present.*
Range: Known only from the Valdina Farms Sinkhole, a cave
in northwestern Medina Co., Texas.   Map 250

HONEY CREEK CAVE BLIND SALAMANDER
Eurycea tridentifera   **Fig. 88, p. 294**
   Identification: 1½–2⅞ in. (3.8–7.3 cm). A white or slightly
yellowish neotenic salamander with pink or red external gills
and a large head that occupies about ⅓ of the entire head–body
length. Snout depressed abruptly at about level of eyes. Traces
of gray pigment in skin. Legs relatively long. Costal grooves
11 or 12. *External gills present.*
   Similar species: (1) In Texas Blind Salamander head is considerably more flattened (Fig. 88, p. 294), snout is much more
truncate (square-cut) when viewed from above, and legs are
longer. (2) Valdina Farms Salamander is grayish and has a
rounded snout and proportionately smaller head.
   Range: Known only from Honey Creek Cave, Comal Co.,
Texas.   Map 250

Blind Salamanders:
Genera *Typhlotriton, Typhlomolge,* and *Haideotriton*

THESE are residents of caves or underground streams that live in
perpetual darkness and have no need for functional eyes. They
are white or pinkish with an iridescent overwash, and their skins
are so translucent that outlines of the darker internal organs are
readily apparent through at least the lower sides and belly. Occasionally they are pumped to the surface or appear in the outflow
from deep wells or springs, but otherwise one must seek them by
becoming a spelunker (cave explorer). Blind salamanders of this
family (Plethodontidae) have been found only in limestone regions
of the southern United States. A similar-looking blind species of
a different family (Proteidae) occurs in Europe.

TEXAS BLIND SALAMANDER   **Pl. 39; Fig. 88, p. 294**
Typhlomolge rathbuni
   Identification: 3¼–4¼ in. (8–11 cm); record 5⅜ in. (13.7 cm).
A ghostly salamander with toothpick legs and a strongly flat-
tened snout (Fig. 88, p. 294). Remnants of·eyes appear as tiny
dark dots buried under the skin. Costal grooves 12. *External
gills present.*
   This weird-looking amphibian occurs in cave waters at San
Marcos, Texas, where a reserve has been set aside for its protec-
tion.

Similar species: (1) Most other neotenic salamanders of same general region bear at least some dark pigment, and their snouts are not so grotesquely flattened. (2) See Cascade Cavern Salamander and Honey Creek Cave Blind Salamander.

Range: Vicinity of San Marcos, Texas.   Map 251

GROTTO SALAMANDER *Typhlotriton spelaeus*   Pl. 39
Identification: 3–4¾ in. (8–12 cm); record 5⁵⁄₁₆ in. (13.5 cm). The "ghost lizard" of Ozark caves and grottoes. The whitish or pinkish adults sometimes have faint traces of orange on tail, feet, and lower sides of body. Eyes show as dark spots beneath fused or partly fused lids. *No* external gills. *Young:* The larvae have functional eyes and external gills; they are rather strongly pigmented, being brownish- or purplish-gray with yellowish longitudinal flecks or dark streaks on the sides; *tail fin high.*

This is an extraordinary salamander that literally has two lives. First, as a larva it resides in mountain brooks and springs, and its activities are not unlike those of larvae of other species. Later it moves into a cave, loses fins and pigment, its eyes cease to function, the eyelids grow shut or nearly so, and it remains a blind troglodyte for the rest of its days.

Similar species: Larvae of several forms of Brook Salamanders (*Eurycea*) live in the same region but all have low tail fins, and their patterns tend to be in the form of stippling, networks, or lichenlike patches.

Range: Central uplands; sw. Missouri and adjacent areas.
                                                        Map 248

GEORGIA BLIND SALAMANDER   Fig. 89, below
Haideotriton wallacei
Identification: 2–3 in. (5.1–7.6 cm). A pinkish-white and slightly opalescent salamander. External gills long, slender, and red. Head broad and long but not greatly flattened. In the young, eyes are represented by tiny dark spots; in adults (Fig. 89, below) they may be invisible or virtually so.

Range: Known from a deep well and several caves in sw. Georgia and adj. Florida.   Map 249

Fig. 89. GEORGIA BLIND SALAMANDER
(Haideotriton wallacei)

Snout rounded; large gills; no eye spots

X

Toads and Frogs
Order Anura

TOADS and frogs, which range, collectively, from above the Arctic Circle to virtually the southern tips of Africa, Australia, and South America and into many islands, including New Zealand, are the most widely distributed of all the amphibians. Nearly 2700 species are known.

The typical toad (*Bufo*) has a warty skin and short legs for hopping, and the typical frog (*Rana*) has a relatively smooth skin and long legs for leaping, but there are numerous variations among the other genera. Common names for members of this group have been acquired through usage. There are no hard and fast rules for distinguishing a "toad" from a "frog."

Our species advertise their presence by their calls, and some kinds are rarely seen except at breeding time. Eggs of most are laid in water. Each species has its own distinctive mating call. These are best learned by listening to the records listed on page 360. (The Folkways Record also includes other sounds made by frogs such as screams that are uttered when they are seized by enemies, territorial and rain calls, and various warning chirps or croaks. The latter are the release calls of males that reveal their sex when, during the excitement of mating time, one male may inadvertently grasp another.)

Most toads and frogs are best observed at night with the aid of a flashlight. Because the color or pattern of the concealed surfaces of the limbs are often of diagnostic value, some kinds must be in hand for identification. In arid regions these amphibians may estivate for months at a time.

MEXICAN BURROWING TOAD   Pl. 45
Rhinophrynus dorsalis
   Identification: 2-2¾ in. (5.1–7.0 cm); record 3½ in. (8.9 cm). The rotund body and the *broad* reddish or orange middorsal stripe (buff in young specimens) are sufficient for identifying this toad, which barely enters the United States. Although it looks somewhat like a narrow-mouthed toad of giant size, it is the only living representative of its family, the Rhinophrynidae.

   When this amphibian is calling or alarmed, the body is so inflated with air that it resembles a miniature, somewhat flattened balloon with a small triangular snout protruding from one

side. Specimens are virtually never seen until heavy rains stimulate them to leave their burrows to form breeding choruses.
Similar species: Sheep Frog has a yellow *threadlike* middorsal line and a similar line on its venter.
Voice: A loud, low-pitched *wh-o-o-o-a,* much like a farmer commanding his mule to stop.
Range: In the lowlands from extr. s. Texas (Starr Co.) to Yucatán and Honduras; west coast from the Río Balsas, Mexico, to Costa Rica.   Map 257

Spadefoot Toads:
Family Pelobatidae

A SINGLE, sharp-edged, black spade on each hind foot enables a spadefoot toad to burrow vertically downward into sandy or other loose soil. This is the hallmark of the genus, but other characteristics include a rather smooth skin, parotoid glands absent or indistinct, and a pupil that is vertically elliptical when exposed to even a moderately bright light (Fig. 90, below).

In contrast, the true toads (*Bufo*) have *two* tubercles on the underside of each hind foot, one of which may be quite spadelike. They also have well-developed warts, ridges, and parotoid glands, and their pupils are horizontally oval (Fig. 90, below).

For distinguishing among the several spadefoot toads, two things should always be checked: (a) is the spade elongated and sickle-shaped or short and wedge-shaped (Fig. 91, p. 300); and (b) is there a raised area (boss) between the eyes? (See Fig. 92, p. 301.)

Spadefoot toads are explosive breeders, appearing suddenly, sometimes in great numbers, after heavy rains and at almost any time during the warm months of the year. In general, they are

Fig. 90. CHARACTERISTICS OF TOADS AND SPADEFOOT TOADS

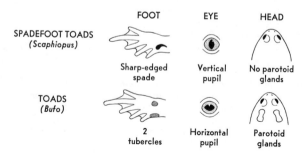

	FOOT	EYE	HEAD
SPADEFOOT TOADS (*Scaphiopus*)	Sharp-edged spade	Vertical pupil	No parotoid glands
TOADS (*Bufo*)	2 tubercles	Horizontal pupil	Parotoid glands

adapted for life in arid regions and can remain underground for weeks or even months at a time, but they often venture forth on damp or rainy nights. Breeding males have black pads or excrescences on their thumbs and first 2 fingers.

Many persons experience strong allergic reactions from handling spadefoot toads. These may take the form of violent sneezing, copious discharge of mucus from the nose, and watering of the eyes. As a precaution, wash your hands with soap or detergent to remove any skin-gland secretions they may have gotten on them from these amphibians, and keep your hands away from your face until you do.

The genus *Scaphiopus,* occurring throughout a large part of the United States and from southwestern Canada to southern Mexico, is the only group of the family in the New World. Other genera are found in Europe, extreme northwestern Africa, Asia, and the East Indies.

EASTERN SPADEFOOT   Pl. 44
Scaphiopus holbrooki holbrooki
Identification: 1¾–2¼ in. (4.4–5.7 cm); record 2⅞ in. (7.3 cm). The only spadefoot toad occurring east of the Mississippi River. Spade elongate and sickle-shaped. No boss between eyes. Two yellowish lines, one originating at each eye and running down back, are usually well in evidence. The 2 lines together may form a lyre-shaped pattern or resemble the outline of a somewhat misshapen hourglass. Normally there is an additional light line on each side of body. Ground color some shade of brown (grayish- or blackish-brown or sepia). Some specimens may be almost uniformly dark gray to almost black.

Although this is a species of the forested East and Southeast, it is usually found in areas characterized by sandy or other loose soils — habitats that in some respects resemble those of the spadefoot toads of more arid regions to the west.
Voice: An explosive grunt, rather low-pitched, short in duration, but repeated at brief intervals. Some persons liken sound to call of a young crow.
Range: S. New England to s. Florida and some of the Keys; west to se. Missouri, ne. Arkansas, and e. Louisiana; absent from most upland areas in the South.   Map 253

HURTER'S SPADEFOOT   Pl. 44
Scaphiopus holbrooki hurteri
Identification: 1¾–2¼ in. (4.4–5.7 cm); record 3¼ in. (8.3 cm). The only spadefoot with a boss between the eyes (Fig. 92, p. 301) *and* an *elongate,* sickle-shaped spade. (The boss is actually a little farther back than the eyes.) General coloration often matches the garrison green uniforms of the U.S. Marine Corps, but it may vary from grayish green to a chocolate- or greenish-brown, or to almost black. The 2 curved light stripes on the

back are often as conspicuous as those of the Eastern Spadefoot.

An inhabitant of wooded and savanna areas, but also occurring in arid terrain in southern Texas. Named for Julius Hurter, Missouri herpetologist.

Similar species: (1) In Couch's and Eastern Spadefoot Toads there is no boss between eyes. (2) In Plains and Western Spadefoot Toads the spade is *short,* rounded, and often wedge-shaped (Fig. 91, below).

Voice: A bleating note, slightly explosive, and short in duration, each bleat lasting less than ½ second.

Range: W. Arkansas and cen. Louisiana to cen. Oklahoma and s. Texas.   Map 253

COUCH'S SPADEFOOT *Scaphiopus couchi*   **Pl. 44**
Identification: 2¼–2⅞ in. (5.7–7.3 cm); record 3½ in. (8.9 cm). A southwestern spadefoot with considerable yellowish pigmentation in the skin. Dorsal ground color varying from bright greenish yellow to dull brownish yellow; marked with a mottling or marbling of black, green, or dark brown. (Dark pattern may fade out during breeding season.) Spade *elongate* and often sickle-shaped. No boss between eyes. Diameter of eyelid about equal to distance between eyes (Fig. 91, below).

A species of shortgrass plains and also of mesquite savannas and other arid or semiarid regions. Named for Darius Nash Couch, a professional soldier who collected many natural-history specimens in northeastern Mexico while on leave of absence from the Army during 1853.

Similar species: (1) Plains and Western Spadefoot Toads have *short* wedge-shaped spades and eyelids noticeably wider than distance between them (Fig. 91, below). (2) Hurter's Spadefoot has boss between eyes (Fig. 92, p. 301).

Voice: A groaning bleat, suggestive of a goat or sheep unhappy at being tied. Each bleat relatively long, lasting ½ to 1 second.

Range: Cen. Texas and adj. Oklahoma to extr. se. California;

Fig. 91. CHARACTERISTICS OF SPADEFOOT TOADS *(Scaphiopus)*

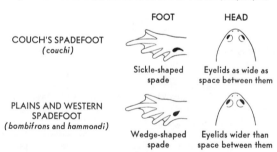

	FOOT	HEAD
COUCH'S SPADEFOOT *(couchi)*	Sickle-shaped spade	Eyelids as wide as space between them
PLAINS AND WESTERN SPADEFOOT *(bombifrons* and *hammondi)*	Wedge-shaped spade	Eyelids wider than space between them

south to tip of Baja California and to Nayarit, Zacatecas, and Querétaro; absent from highlands of w. Mexico.   Map 256

PLAINS SPADEFOOT *Scaphiopus bombifrons*   **Pl. 44**
Identification: 1½–2 in. (3.8–5.1 cm); record 2¼ in. (5.7 cm). Our only spadefoot with a pronounced boss between the eyes *plus* a *short,* rounded, often wedge-shaped spade. General coloration grayish or brownish, often with a greenish tinge; dark markings brown or gray. Small tubercles on the dorsum may be noticeably yellowish or reddish. Four rather vague longitudinal light lines often present on back. Eyelids wider than distance between them (Fig. 91, p. 300).
At home on the Great Plains and in regions of low rainfall; a species of the open grasslands, usually avoiding river bottoms and wooded areas.

Fig. 92. TOPS OF HEADS OF TOADS *(Bufo)* AND
SPADEFOOT TOADS *(Scaphiopus)*

     A raised boss
between the eyes

     No raised boss

CANADIAN TOAD *(hemiophrys)*
PLAINS SPADEFOOT *(bombifrons)*
HURTER'S SPADEFOOT *(hurteri)*

Most other species
of TOADS and
SPADEFOOT TOADS

Similar species: (1) Both Couch's and Western Spadefoot Toads lack a boss between eyes (Fig. 92, above). Also in Couch's Spadefoot the spade is *elongate* and space between eyes is about equal to width of an eyelid (Fig. 91, p. 300). (2) See also Canadian Toad.
Voice: A short rasping bleat repeated at intervals of ½ to a full second, or a rasping snore, rather low-pitched and each trill lasting ½ to ¾ second.
Range: Sw. Manitoba to s. Alberta and south to Chihuahua; follows Missouri River Valley eastward across most of Missouri; a disjunct area in extr. s. Texas and ne. Mexico.   Map 252

WESTERN SPADEFOOT *Scaphiopus hammondi*   **Pl. 44**
Identification: 1½–2 in. (3.8–5.1 cm); record 2½ in. (6.4 cm). The spade is *short* and wedge-shaped, and there is *no* boss between the eyes. General coloration dusky — gray, brown, dusky green, or sometimes almost black — with scattered spots and blotches of a darker color. The small tubercles on the dorsum may be reddish. Occasional specimens may have vague suggestions of longitudinal, light-colored lines. Eyelids wider than distance between them (Fig. 91, p. 300). Skin produces an odor like unroasted peanuts.

At home in shortgrass plains and in playas and alkali flats of arid and semiarid regions; absent from extreme deserts.

Similar species: (1) Plains Spadefoot has boss between eyes (Fig. 92, p. 301). (2) In Couch's Spadefoot the spade is *elongate,* and space between eyes is about equal to width of eyelid (Fig. 91, p. 300).

Voice: A vibrant metallic trill like running a fingernail along the stiff teeth of a large comb. Each trill lasts about ¾ to 1½ seconds.

Range: W. Oklahoma and cen. Texas to Arizona and far south into Mexico; a large disjunct area in the Californias.

Map 254

Tropical Frogs:
Family Leptodactylidae

A VERY large family of the American tropics, but with a few species ranging northward into Texas and the southwestern United States and another introduced into Florida. Although some members of the family deposit their eggs in water, all but one of our species lay their eggs on land and their tadpoles undergo complete metamorphosis in the egg. The exception is the White-lipped Frog that builds a foam nest and has aquatic tadpoles (see p. 303). Three groups occur within our area: Nest-building Frogs (*Leptodactylus*), Robber Frogs (*Eleutherodactylus* and *Hylactophryne*), and Chirping Frogs (*Syrrhophus*). The family also occurs in Mexico, throughout Central and most of South America, and is abundantly represented in the West Indies, Australia, and New Guinea.

WHITE-LIPPED FROG *Leptodactylus labialis*   **Pl. 45**
  Identification: 1⅜–2 in. (3.5–5.1 cm). A white or cream-colored line on the upper lip and a distinct ventral disc (Fig. 93, below). Dorsolateral folds present. Ground color varies from gray to chocolate-brown. Number and size of dark dorsal spots also variable.

  One of the several Mexican amphibians and reptiles that

Fig. 93. VENTRAL DISC IN TROPICAL FROGS

Disc is present in the BARKING FROG *(Hylactophryne a. latrans)* and the WHITE-LIPPED FROG *(Leptodactylus labialis)*

barely enter the United States in extreme southern Texas. Found in a wide variety of habitats, including roadside ditches, irrigated fields, moist meadows, drains, etc.

Similar species: Spotted Chorus Frog has no dorsolateral folds and also lacks a ventral disc.

Voice: *Throw-up, throw-up* repeated continually and with a rising inflection at end of each call. Males call from cavities beneath hummocks of grass or clods of dirt or in small pits as much as 3 in. (8 cm) deep. Breeding begins with onset of rainy season. Eggs are laid in a foam nest constructed of glandular secretions from the frogs, which are whipped into a froth that looks like beaten egg white. The larvae live in the liquefied center of the nest until rains enable them to swim into nearby pools.

Range: Lower Rio Grande Valley, Texas, to n. Venezuela.
Map 298

BARKING FROG *Hylactophryne augusti latrans* **Pl. 45**
   Identification: 2½–3 in. (6.4–7.6 cm); record 3¾ in. (9.5 cm). A frog that looks like a toad, but has a smooth, dry skin (no warts). There is a dorsolateral fold and a ventral disc similar to that of White-lipped Frog (Fig. 93, p. 302). The general coloration may vary from tan to greenish and may include tones of pink or reddish brown. *Young:* Often greenish and with a fawn-colored band across middle of back.

   A resident of limestone caves and ledges that rarely ventures out into the open, even during rains. When captured, as by snake or human being, it puffs itself up prodigiously. Sometimes called the "robber frog."

   Voice: An explosive call, like the bark of a dog when heard at a distance, but more of a guttural *whurr* at close range. The single note may be repeated at regular intervals of 2 to 3 seconds. When females are grasped in the hand they may make a blaring screech. Breeds during rainy periods from late winter to May.

   Range: Cen. Texas to se. New Mexico and n. Coahuila. Mexican subspecies.   Map 293

GREENHOUSE FROG   **Pl. 45**
Eleutherodactylus planirostris planirostris
   Identification: ⅝–1¼ in. (1.6–3.2 cm). A tiny immigrant, probably from Cuba. Two pattern phases: (a) *striped,* with longitudinal light stripes; and (b) *mottled,* with irregular dark and light markings. The general coloration is brown, but usually with distinct reddish tones. *Young:* With a tiny tail at hatching.

   These minute frogs are terrestrial, seeking shelter by day or in dry weather beneath boards, leaves, trash, or other debris where there is some moisture. They normally move about only at night or in rainy weather. Often found in gardens, green-houses, dumps, hardwood hammocks, gopher tortoise burrows, and small stream valleys.

Voice: Short melodious birdlike chirps, usually 4 to 6 in a series. Breeds during summer rainy season (May to September in northern Florida). Only frog east of Texas that lays its eggs on land. They are deposited under damp vegetation or debris. Development takes place entirely in the egg; no free tadpole stage.

Range: Introduced and now widespread in Florida. Native to Cuba; introduced in Jamaica, the Cayman Islands, some of the Bahamas, and the vicinity of Veracruz, Mexico. Subspecies in Cuba and the Bahamas.   Map 294

CLIFF FROG *Syrrhophus marnocki*   **Pl. 45**
Identification: ¾–1½ in. (1.9–3.8 cm). A chirping frog, greenish in coloration, but mottled with brown and clad in a smooth skin. Head proportionately quite large.

The flattened head and body facilitate rapid retreats into cracks and crevices of cliffs that mark the eastern and southern faces and occur in numerous other parts of the Edwards Plateau of central Texas. This small amphibian normally is active only at night. It leaps and hops as do other frogs, but it may also run when seeking shelter.

Similar species: Green Toad has a warty skin.

Voice: A cricketlike chirp or trill that may be heard throughout the year. The mating call, given only when a female is present, is similar but clearer and sharper. Peak of breeding season is in April or May, but egg deposition may occur at any time from late February to early December.

Range: S.-cen. Texas.   Map 295

MEXICAN CLIFF FROG *Syrrhophus guttilatus*   **Pl. 45**
Identification: ¾–1¼ in. (1.9–3.2 cm). Similar to the Cliff Frog, but with a vermiculate (wormlike) dark pattern, a dark bar between the eyes, and a yellowish to brownish ground color.

Occurs in springs, canyons, and caves in the Chisos Mountains, and in other areas where moisture is present in Brewster and Presidio Cos., Texas. Often runs when disturbed, instead of leaping or hopping.

Voice: A sharp, relatively short whistle.

Range: Big Bend region of Texas; also from se. Coahuila to Guanajuato.   Map 296

RIO GRANDE FROG   **Pl. 45**
Syrrhophus cystignathoides campi
Identification: ⅝–1 in. (1.6–2.5 cm). One of the chirping frogs. A nondescript species, brown to grayish- or yellowish-olive and

with no distinctive field marks. But since it barely enters the
United States from Mexico, it will cause little confusion except
in extreme southern Texas. Dark line from nostril through eye
usually not very prominent. Behavior will help. This little frog
not only leaps and hops but also runs, and is very quick and
adept at darting under cover.

An abundant species in the lower Rio Grande Valley that
seems to thrive in the midst of civilization. At night it may
appear on lawns or in flower beds or gutters, especially if some
sprinkling has been going on. By day it hides under boards,
debris, flower boxes, or other objects that offer both moisture
and shelter. More natural habitats include environs of palm
groves, thickets, ditches, and resacas.

Voice: A cricketlike chirp, usually given erratically, not at
regular intervals. Breeds in spring, but may be heard during
any of the warm months when irrigation is in progress.

Range: Extr. s. Texas and ne. Mexico.   Map 297

Toads: Family Bufonidae

THE homely "hoptoad" is readily recognized as such, but telling
the different kinds apart is quite another matter. Recourse must
be made to checking the shapes and sizes of the shoulder (parotoid) glands and cranial ridges, the relative number and promi-
nence of the warts, and differences in coloration and pattern. To
complicate matters, certain species are known to hybridize with
others. This unfortunate state of affairs undoubtedly has been
aggravated by mankind's propensity for altering habitats and thus
bringing animals together that had remained isolated for one
reason or another during prehistoric times.

Toads in general have dry, warty skins and they hop. Frogs
of the genus *Rana,* as well as many other kinds, have moist,
relatively smooth skins and they leap. Only spadefoot toads
(*Scaphiopus*) are likely to be confused with true toads (*Bufo*).
For ways of telling the two genera apart see Fig. 90, p. 298.

One does not get warts from touching toads, but their skin-gland
secretions are irritating to mucous membranes. Wash your hands
after handling them, and keep your fingers away from your mouth
and eyes until you do.

In the North, toads breed in the spring and, depending on
weather conditions, at more or less the same time each year. In
the South, they may mate more than once and, collectively, during
almost any month. In the arid Southwest, where they occur in
greatest variety, deposition of eggs usually depends on the advent
of rain. Breeding males have dark nuptial pads on their thumbs
and inner fingers. Throats of males are usually dark, ranging from

black to dusky. The vocal sac in most species is round when inflated; in others it is sausage-shaped (Fig. 94, below). In most species the females grow larger than their mates. Individual toads may vary considerably in coloration, being dark at one time and light at another, depending on conditions of temperature, animation, etc. Small toads, especially those which have recently transformed, are often virtually impossible to identify.

The natural distribution of the family is nearly worldwide, except for Madagascar, Polynesia, and the Australian and polar regions. Toads of some species, however, notably *Bufo marinus*, have been introduced into various tropical regions by mankind in an effort to control insect pests.

Fig. 94. MALE TOADS *(Bufo)* WITH VOCAL SACS INFLATED
(DIAGRAMMATIC)

Rounded in most
of the species
within our area

Sausage-shaped in the GREAT
PLAINS *(cognatus)*, TEXAS
(speciosus), and OAK
(quercicus) TOADS

AMERICAN TOAD   *Bufo americanus*   Pl. 44

Identification: 2–3½ in. (5.1–8.9 cm); record 4⅜ in. (11.1 cm). The widespread and abundant "hoptoad" of the Northeast. Throughout the great bulk of its range, only Fowler's Toad is likely to be confused with it, but, unfortunately, the two sometimes hybridize. Despite considerable individual and local variation, the following points normally hold for the American Toad: (a) only *one or 2 large warts* in each of largest dark spots; (b) chest and forward part of abdomen *usually spotted* with dark pigment; (c) enlarged warts on tibia; and (d) parotoid gland either separated from the ridge behind the eye, or connected with it by a short spur (Fig. 95, p. 308). A light middorsal stripe may or may not be present. Many American Toads are almost plain brown, but others, females especially, are gaily patterned. The general ground color varies through numerous shades of brown to gray or olive or brick-red, but may be ornamented by patches of yellow or buff or other light colors. Dark spots are brown or black, and warts vary from yellow, orange, or red to dark brown.

Habitats are legion, ranging from suburban back yards to mountain wildernesses. Requisites seem to be shallow bodies of water in which to breed (temporary pools or ditches or shallow portions of streams, for example), hiding places where there is some moisture, and an abundant supply of insects and other invertebrates for food. Toads of this and several other species do well in captivity if they have loose soil in which to burrow, water to soak in occasionally, plenty of live insects, and a minimum of handling.

Similar species: (1) See Fowler's Toad and Southern Toad. (2) Woodhouse's Toad has a plain belly and its warts are more numerous and nearly all same size.

Voice: A rather long musical trill, one of the most pleasant sounds of early spring. Individual calls may last from 6 to 30 seconds; trill rate about 30 to 40 per second. Breeds from March to July (the later dates at high altitudes or latitudes).

Range: Maritime Provinces to se. Manitoba; south to Mississippi and ne. Kansas.

Subspecies: AMERICAN TOAD, *Bufo a. americanus* (Plate 44). As described and with range indicated above. HUDSON BAY TOAD, *Bufo a. copei.* A far-northern race noted for vividness of colors and sharply defined markings, especially on the heavily spotted venter. Coast of Labrador to west of James Bay. Intergrades with *americanus* throughout a wide area from s. Quebec across much of cen. Ontario. DWARF AMERICAN TOAD, *Bufo a. charlesmithi.* Size much smaller; seldom exceeds 2½ in. (6.4 cm). Very often reddish in coloration; dorsal spots, when present, small and including only a single wart; venter only faintly spotted, or not at all. Call pitched about midway between calls of American and Southern Toads. Sw. Indiana and s. Illinois to e. Oklahoma and extr. ne. Louisiana.   Map 261

SOUTHERN TOAD *Bufo terrestris*   Pl. 44

Identification: 1⅝–3 in. (4.1–7.6 cm); record 4⁷⁄₁₆ in. (11.3 cm). Pronounced knobs and high cranial crests give the head a strongly sculptured appearance. Viewed in direct profile, large adults look almost horned. The 2 crests that run forward from the knobs tend to approach each other toward the snout (Fig. 95, p. 308). General coloration usually some shade of brown, but variable from red to black; with or without dark spots that contain 1 or 2 warts, or often more. There may be a light middorsal stripe, but this is often obscure, especially toward rear of back. *Young:* Knobs not well developed, but their future locations indicated by backward extensions from cranial crests.

The common toad of the South, and particularly abundant in sandy areas. Like other toads, it becomes active at twilight, foraging well into the night. Daylight hours are spent chiefly in hiding, often in burrows of the toad's own making.

Similar species: None of our other toads has such pronounced cranial knobs. Most trouble will come in trying to identify young specimens. (1) Fowler's Toad has smaller, less elevated warts, and there are usually 3 or more in each large dark spot. (2) In Oak Toad, cranial crests are inconspicuous, and the light middorsal stripe is prominent. (3) In American Toad, even in young, there are no marked extensions backward from the interorbital crests (Fig. 95, below).

Voice: A shrill musical trill almost an octave higher than that of American Toad. Duration of call varies from about 2 to 8 seconds. Trill rate rapid, about 75 per second. These toads breed in shallow water, and may be heard from March to October, depending on locality and weather conditions.

Range: Coastal Plain from extr. se. Virginia to Mississippi River; south throughout Florida and on some of the lower Keys.

Map 263

HOUSTON TOAD *Bufo houstonensis*   **Fig. 95, below**
Identification: 2–2⅝ in. (5.1–6.7 cm); record 3⅛ in. (7.9 cm). An isolated relative of the American and Southern Toads that resembles them in most details of structure and voice. Cranial ridges quite thickened, especially those running across behind eyes. The dorsum bears a dark mottled pattern that may be arranged in a vague herringbone fashion. The mottling is brown

Fig. 95. CRANIAL CRESTS AND PAROTOID GLANDS OF VARIOUS TOADS (*Bufo*)

FOWLER'S
(*fowleri*)
Parotoid touches
postorbital ridge

AMERICAN
(*americanus*)
Parotoid separate
or connected to
ridge by a spur

SOUTHERN
(*terrestris*)
Pronounced knobs
at rear of inter-
orbital crests

HOUSTON
(*houstonensis*)
Postorbital ridges
thickened

CANADIAN
(*hemiophrys*)
A boss
between eyes

GREAT PLAINS
(*cognatus*)
Interorbital ridges
converge to meet a
boss on the snout

RED-SPOTTED
(*punctatus*)
Parotoid round

GULF COAST
(*valliceps*)
Deep "valley" on
center of head;
parotoid triangular

to black on a ground color of cream to purplish gray and with or without patches of dark green. Usually a middorsal light stripe present. Venter with numerous small dark spots.
Similar species: (1) In Woodhouse's Toad group (including Fowler's Toad) the parotoid gland touches cranial ridge behind eye (Fig. 95, p. 308). (2) Gulf Coast Toad has a pronounced dark stripe along side of body and a deep valley between eyes. (3) In Texas Toad both tubercles beneath hind foot have sharp cutting edges.
Voice: A piercing but rather musical trill, higher pitched than in American Toad, but with about same trill rate (32 per second) and of 4 to 11 seconds' duration.
Range: Se. Texas.   Map 262

CANADIAN TOAD *Bufo hemiophrys hemiophrys*   **Pl. 44**
Identification: 2-3 in. (5.1-7.6 cm); record 3¼ in. (8.3 cm). The "Dakota Toad." A far-northern species with a pronounced boss between eyes (similar to boss of Plains and Hurter's Spadefoot Toads — see Fig. 92, p. 301). The boss, which may be grooved on top, extends from snout as far backward as level of rear margin of eyelids. Borders of parotoid glands indistinct and blending with skin. Ground color brownish or greenish, sometimes reddish. Warts brown or reddish. A light middorsal stripe. *Young:* Cranial crests absent; these develop later, eventually uniting to form the boss.
Considerably more aquatic than most toads. Frequently found along the shores of small lakes in which it may take refuge by swimming well out into the water.
Similar species: (1) Woodhouse's Toad has pronounced cranial crests, but normally lacks boss between eyes (at least in the eastern part of its range). (2) Dark spots of Great Plains Toad are large, contain many warts, and are distinctly light-bordered. (3) In American Toad the cranial crests are strongly evident. (The boss obscures them in Canadian Toad.) (4) In Plains Spadefoot parotoid glands are lacking and pupil of eye is vertical (horizontal in true toads).
Voice: A rather soft, low-pitched trill lasting 2 to 5 seconds and repeated 2 or 3 times a minute. Trill rate very rapid, about 90 per second.
Range: Nw. Minnesota and ne. S. Dakota northwestward to the eastern half of Alberta and into extr. s. District of Mackenzie. Western subspecies.   Map 260

WOODHOUSE'S TOAD   **Pl. 44**
Bufo woodhousei woodhousei
Identification: 2½-4 in. (6-10 cm); record 5 in. (12.7 cm). Because it lacks any really distinctive markings, this large toad is best identified by a process of boiling down — by eliminating

everything it couldn't be (see **Similar species,** below). There is a *light middorsal stripe, cranial crests* are *prominent,* and *parotoid glands* are *elongate.* The dark dorsal spots contain from 1 to several warts, and the spots themselves are irregular and not so prominent as in some other species. Belly whitish or yellowish, usually completely unmarked, but sometimes with a dark breast spot and dark flecks between forelegs. General coloration yellowish brown or gray, sometimes with an olive or greenish cast.

This amphibian, abundant in many localities, ranges from the grasslands of the Great Plains into the arid Southwest. Habitats include marshes and swales, river bottoms, mountain canyons, desert streams, and irrigated areas, plus urban and suburban back yards. It usually appears at night and often near lights, where insects abound and may be had for the gulping. Named for Samuel Washington Woodhouse, surgeon and naturalist of exploration expeditions to the Southwest in the mid-nineteenth century. Formerly called "Rocky Mountain Toad."

Similar species: (1) Texas Toad has *no light middorsal stripe* and no (or virtually no) cranial crests. (2) Red-spotted Toad has *round* parotoids. (3) Canadian Toad has raised *boss* between eyes. (Woodhouse's Toads within our area normally lack such a boss.) (4) In the American Toad there are numerous *dark markings on chest.* (5) Fowler's Toad, related subspecifically to Woodhouse's Toad, has large, dark, well-defined dorsal spots, often 6 in number, and each containing 3 or more warts.
Voice: A nasal *w-a-a-a-h,* lasting 1 to 2½ seconds, and rather like a sheep bleating in the distance. Call very similar to that of Fowler's Toad, but somewhat lower in pitch. Breeds March to July, usually after rains, and wherever there is shallow, standing or slightly moving water.
Range: The Dakotas and Montana to cen. Texas; west of the Rocky Mountains proper from s. Idaho to cen. Arizona; disjunct colonies in several states.
Subspecies: SOUTHWESTERN WOODHOUSE'S TOAD, *Bufo w. australis.* A race with dark markings on the chest and in which the light middorsal stripe normally does not involve the snout. Extr. w. Texas, chiefly in Rio Grande Valley; sw. New Mexico and se. Arizona south into Mexico; a disjunct record from Durango; intergrades with *woodhousei* through a large part of New Mexico and into adjacent states.   Map 265

FOWLER'S TOAD   *Bufo woodhousei fowleri*   **Pl. 44**
Identification: 2–3 in. (5.1–7.6 cm); record 3¾ in. (9.5 cm). A typical Fowler's Toad has: (a) *3 or more warts* in each of the largest dark spots; (b) a virtually *unspotted* chest and belly; (c) no greatly enlarged warts on tibia; and (d) a parotoid gland that touches cranial ridge behind eye (Fig. 95, p. 308). There

is some variation, but usually at least 3 of these characteristics are present. Many specimens have a single dark breast spot on an otherwise immaculate venter. The general dorsal coloration is brown or gray or, more rarely, greenish or brick-red. A light middorsal stripe.

An extremely abundant toad of the Atlantic Coastal Plain from Long Island to North Carolina. Farther inland its distribution is spotty, and it occurs chiefly in sandy areas, around shores of lakes, or in river valleys. In regions where their presence is not even suspected, these toads may appear suddenly in large numbers when warm heavy rains follow a long period of drought. Named for S. P. Fowler, an early Massachusetts naturalist.

Similar species: (1) American Toad has: (a) only *one or 2* large warts in each dark spot; (b) chest *spotted* with dark pigment; (c) enlarged warts on tibia; and (d) parotoid gland either separated from ridge behind eye or connected with it by a short spur. (2) Southern Toad has pronounced knobs at rear of cranial crests (see Fig. 95, p. 308). (3) Gulf Coast Toad has broad dark stripe along the side.

Voice: A short unmusical bleat — a nasal *w-a-a-a-a-h* — lasting 1 to 4 seconds. Breeds from spring to mid-August, and usually later than the American Toad in any given locality. Calls from ditches, temporary pools, or shallow margins of permanent bodies of water.

Range: Cen. New England to Gulf Coast and west to Michigan, ne. Oklahoma, and e. Louisiana; absent from southern part of Atlantic Coastal Plain and most of Florida.

Note: Fowler's Toad is known to hybridize with other species of toads. The offspring may show characteristics of both parents, and the calls of male hybrids may be intermediate, and difficult or impossible to identify. A large and variable toad population, widely distributed through Louisiana, Arkansas, Texas, and southeastern Oklahoma, was formerly recognized, in part, as *Bufo woodhousei velatus,* the "East Texas Toad." Recent studies indicate that the *"velatus"* population is probably of hybrid origin with contributions to its gene pool from toads of both the *americanus* and *woodhousei* groups. This is essentially a dark-breasted toad with a narrow light middorsal stripe, occasionally with vague, lateral stripes, and a dorsum that is more or less uniformly dark, but there are many local variations. The calls also vary. In some populations they consist of repeated trills of 5 to 10 seconds' duration. In others they begin with a whirr and are then prolonged as a single droning note of medium to low pitch.   Map 265

GULF COAST TOAD *Bufo valliceps*   **Pl. 44**
  Identification: 2–4 in. (5–10 cm); record 5⅛ in. (13.0 cm).

The broad dark lateral stripe is usually so prominent that it alone may assure identification. It is bordered above by a light stripe, and there is also a light middorsal stripe. General dorsal coloration variable from almost black, with touches of rich orange, to yellow-brown with whitish spots. Cranial crests strongly developed and bordering a broad, rather deep "valley" down center of head; parotoid glands often triangular (Fig. 95, p. 308). A rather flat toad; the normal resting posture tends to be more squat than in other species. *Male:* Throat clear yellowish green.

Roadside, railroad, or irrigation ditches are frequently utilized, but Gulf Coast Toads also occur in a wide variety of other habitats, including coastal prairies, on barrier beaches bordering the Gulf of Mexico, and in all manner of places in towns and on the outskirts of cities — even in dumps and storm sewers. **Voice:** A short trill, lasting 2 to 6 seconds and repeated several times at intervals of about 1 to 4 seconds. Call similar to that of American and Houston Toads, but less musical. Might be likened to sound of a wooden rattle. Vocal sac a large globular pouch reaching from chin to abdomen when inflated. Breeds March to September.
Range: Extr. s. Arkansas, Louisiana, e.-cen. and s. Texas south to Costa Rica.   Map 270

OAK TOAD *Bufo quercicus*   Pl. 46
Identification: ¾–1 5/16 in. (1.9–3.3 cm). An elfin toad clad in a tapestry of many colors. A conspicuous light middorsal stripe that may be white, cream, yellow, or orange; the 4 or 5 pairs of spots on the back are black or brown. Some warts are red, orange, or reddish brown. The ground color varies from pearl-gray to almost black, so that at times the Oak Toad is almost entirely black with very little pattern in evidence (except for light stripe).

An abundant amphibian of southern pine woods. Hides under all manner of objects, but is much more active by day than other toads.
Voice: Like *peeping* of newly hatched chicks, high-pitched and earsplitting in large choruses. Breeding occurs in shallow pools, ditches, cypress and flatwoods ponds, etc., from April to October, depending on arrival of warm, heavy rains. *Vocal sac sausage-shaped* (Fig. 94, p. 306).
Range: Coastal Plain from se. Virginia to e. Louisiana; south throughout Florida and on some of the lower Keys. Map 271

GREAT PLAINS TOAD *Bufo cognatus*   Pl. 44
Identification: 1⅞–3½ in. (4.8–8.9 cm); record 4½ in. (11.4 cm). Our only toad with *large* dark blotches, each blotch

boldly bordered by light pigment and containing many warts. Ground color gray, brown, greenish, or yellowish. Blotches green, olive, or dark gray and bordered by light pigment. Some specimens have a narrow light middorsal stripe. Cranial crests well apart toward the rear, but extending diagonally forward to meet a boss on the snout (Fig. 95, p. 308). *Young:* Crest between eyes in form of a V; dorsum may be dotted with small red tubercles.

This is a common toad of the "great open spaces," of broad grasslands, and the arid Southwest. It is an accomplished burrower and normally moves about only at night. Often found along irrigation ditches or in river bottoms or flood plains.

Voice: A shrill, piercing, metallic trill, suggestive of a riveting machine, sustained and often lasting 20 seconds or more. (Single calls of more than 50 seconds' duration are on record.) Trill rate 13 to 20 per second. The din of a large chorus is nerve-shattering. *Vocal sac sausage-shaped,* bulking ⅓ size of toad when fully inflated (Fig. 94, p. 306). Breeds April to September, usually May to July in northern part of range.

Range: Great Plains from N. Dakota to se. Alberta and south to n. and w. Texas; e.-cen. Utah to extr. se. California and far south into Mexico; disjunct colonies in Missouri, Colorado, and Arizona.   Map 266

TEXAS TOAD *Bufo speciosus*   **Pl. 44**
Identification: 2–3¼ in. (5.1–8.3 cm); record 3⅝ in. (9.2 cm). A chubby toad without distinctive features except on the underside of the foot, where the 2 tubercles are sharp-edged, often black, and the inner one is *sickle-shaped.* No light middorsal stripe. Cranial crests indistinct or absent. Parotoid gland oval. General coloration gray, but marked with yellowish-green or brown spots and pink, orange, or greenish warts.

Habitats include grasslands, cultivated areas, and mesquite-savanna associations. Sandy soils are preferred. All the obvious breeding sites are utilized — rain pools, cattle tanks, irrigation ditches, etc.

Similar species: (1) Red-spotted Toad has small *round* parotoid glands, and its warts are buff or reddish. (2) In Giant Toad, parotoid gland is *very* large and extends far down on side of body. (3) In Woodhouse's Toad, cranial crests are prominent.
Voice: A continuous series of loud, explosive trills, each ½ second or more in length. Like a high-pitched riveting machine. Trill rate 39 to 57 per second, hence much more rapid than in Great Plains Toad. *Vocal sac sausage-shaped* and ⅓ the bulk of the toad when fully inflated (Fig. 94, p. 306). Breeds April to September (with rains).
Range: Extr. sw. Kansas to Chihuahua, Coahuila, and cen. Tamaulipas.   Map 268

RED-SPOTTED TOAD *Bufo punctatus*   **Pl. 44**
Identification: 1½–2½ in. (3.8–6.4 cm); record 3 in. (7.6 cm).
Our only toad with *round* parotoid glands (Fig. 95, p. 308). Each
gland is small, no larger than the eye. Cranial crests absent or
only slightly developed. General coloration gray, light to medium brown, or pale olive; warts buff or reddish and sometimes
set in small dark blotches. No light stripe down back. Specimens from the limestones of the Edwards Plateau in central
Texas are pale gray and virtually unmarked. A flattish toad,
not so rotund as in most other species.
    In rough, rocky regions and open grasslands. Also a resident
of the desert, but most typically found near springs, seepages,
persistent pools along streams, cattle tanks, etc., throughout the
arid Southwest.
Similar species: Other toads have elongated parotoid glands,
well-defined cranial crests, or both.
Voice: A clear, musical trill, high and essentially on one pitch.
Duration about 4 to 10 seconds; interval variable, sometimes
longer or sometimes shorter than call itself. Breeds April to
September, coincidentally with rains. Usually calls out of water,
frequently on rocks at the water's edge.
Range: Sw. Kansas and cen. Texas to se. California; far south
into mainland Mexico and to the southern tip of Baja California.   Map 269

EASTERN GREEN TOAD *Bufo debilis debilis*   **Pl. 46**
Identification: 1¼–2 in. (3.2–5.1 cm). The bright green coloration, in combination with the flattened head and body, makes
the Green Toads easy to identify. Warts, including black ones,
are numerous on the dorsal surfaces, although less conspicuous
than in many other kinds of toads. Throat black or dusky in
males, yellow or white in females.
    A resident of relatively arid habitats; seldom seen abroad
except during and after periods of heavy rain. Sometimes found
under rocks.
Similar species: (1) Cliff Frog has smooth skin (no warts).
(2) Skins of Strecker's and Spotted Chorus Frogs also lack
prominent warts.
Voice: A shrill trill, almost with the insistence of an irate
policeman's whistle, but not nearly so loud; of 5 to 6 seconds'
duration at intervals of nearly same length. Louder and shriller
than call of Narrow-mouthed Toad. Breeds from March to
September — if rains occur during that period. Often calls at
the bases of clumps of grass.
Range: S. Kansas to ne. Mexico.   Map 267

WESTERN GREEN TOAD *Bufo debilis insidior*   **Pl. 46**
Identification: 1¼–2⅛ in. (3.2–5.4 cm). Similar to the Eastern

Green Toad, but green coloration is often paler. In western race:
(a) black lines connect many of the round black dots on dorsum;
and (b) warts on parotoid glands and upper eyelids have black
points (warts broad and flattened in eastern race).

Occurs in higher — usually above 2500 ft. (760 m) — and drier
areas than its eastern counterpart. A resident largely of subhumid valleys, short grass prairies, and desert flats where it is
seldom seen except after heavy rains.

Similar species: See Eastern Green Toad.

Voice: A cricketlike trill held at one pitch and lasting about
3 to 7 seconds. Some persons liken the sound to that of an
electric buzzer.

Range: Chihuahuan Desert and adjacent regions from sw.
Kansas and se. Arizona to Zacatecas and San Luis Potosí.

Map 267

GIANT TOAD *Bufo marinus*   **Pl. 44**

Identification: 4–6 in. (10–15 cm); record 9⅜ in. (23.8 cm) in S.
America; probably not over 7 in. (17.8 cm) in U.S. A huge brown
toad that barely enters the United States. It is characterized
by immense, deeply pitted parotoid glands extending far down
sides of body.

Pools and arroyos in Rio Grande Valley, but occupying a wide
variety of habitats in the tropics. The skin-gland secretions are
highly toxic to dogs and other animals that may be foolish
enough to bite one of these toads.

Voice: A slow, low-pitched trill, suggestive of the exhaust noise
of a distant tractor. Breeding depends on advent of rains and
may occur from early spring to autumn.

Range: Extr. s. Texas and s. Sonora and south to and through
the Amazon Basin in S. America; introduced into many tropical
parts of the world and also at Miami, Florida, and vicinity,
where it is now abundant in suburban areas and along canals
of the region. Also established on Stock I., near Key West.

Map 264

Treefrogs and Their Allies: Family Hylidae

A LARGE family (450± species) with representatives in all the
habitable continents, including Australia. Within our area there
are five genera: treefrogs (*Hyla, Smilisca,* and *Limnaoedus*),
cricket frogs (*Acris*), and chorus frogs (*Pseudacris*). They are
slim-waisted, usually long-limbed frogs, mostly of small size. Females grow much larger than males.

Cricket Frogs: Genus *Acris*

THESE are small, warty, nonclimbing members of the treefrog family. They are subject to extreme variation in coloration and details of pattern, and may exhibit a myriad of combinations of black, yellow, orange, or red on a base of brown or green. Fortunately there are two pattern details that remain virtually constant: (a) a dark triangle or V-shaped spot between the eyes; and (b) a longitudinal dark stripe (or stripes) on the rear surface of the thigh (Fig. 96, below). Some of the chorus frogs (genus *Pseudacris*) may also show dark triangles between the eyes, but their skins are less warty and their toes are only slightly webbed (Fig. 97, p. 318). The most positive check is the thigh stripe, which requires catching the frog and straightening out the leg to see it. Males have a single vocal pouch under the chin.

Behavior and habitat will help. These small, often very abundant, frogs elude their enemies by a quick succession of erratic hops, usually coming to rest just tantalizingly out of reach. They are at home in or near permanent bodies of shallow water that provide cover in the form of vegetation, either emergent or along the shore, and which are exposed to the sun during the greater part of the day. They also are found on the sandy, gravelly, or muddy bars and banks of small sluggish or intermittent streams.

The genus ranges from southeastern New York, the southern

Fig. 96. THIGH PATTERNS OF CRICKET FROGS *(Acris)*
AND A TREEFROG *(Hyla)*

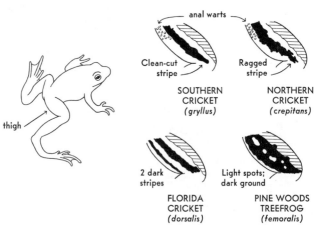

peninsula of Michigan, and Nebraska south to the tip of Florida and northeastern Mexico.

SOUTHERN CRICKET FROG *Acris gryllus gryllus*   Pl. 46

Identification: ⅝–1¼ in. (1.6–3.2 cm). A southern and lowland frog. Dark stripe on thigh usually clean-cut and between 2 well-defined light stripes; anal warts present (Fig. 96, p. 316). Head pointed and legs proportionately longer than in the Northern Cricket Frog. Amount of webbing on toes less than in the northern species; the 1st toe is partly free of webbing and the 4th (longest) toe has the last 3 joints (phalanges) free (Fig. 97, p. 318).

Chiefly a frog of the lowlands, of Coastal Plain bogs and ponds and river-bottom swamps. It follows river valleys northward into more upland regions, however.

Voice: Like a rattle or metal clicker — *gick, gick, gick, gick,* etc., in rapid succession. Breeds February to October, the actual time depending largely on rains.

Range: Se. Virginia to Gulf Coast and Mississippi River.

Map 292

FLORIDA CRICKET FROG   Fig. 96, p. 316

Acris gryllus dorsalis

Identification: ⅝–1 in. (1.6–2.5 cm). Similar to the Southern Cricket Frog except that there are 2 dark lines on rear of thigh and *no* anal warts.

A diminutive frog that makes its presence known by its clicking call. Breeding may occur during any month of the year.

Range: Se. and extr. sw. Georgia to southern tip of Florida.

Map 292

NORTHERN CRICKET FROG   Pl. 46

Acris crepitans crepitans

Identification: ⅝–1⅜ in. (1.6–3.5 cm). A northern and upland frog. Dark stripe on thigh often not clean-cut and it may have ragged edges (Fig. 96, p. 316). Head blunt. Leg short; when it is extended forward along side of body the heel usually fails to reach snout. In the Southern Cricket Frog, heel usually extends beyond snout, but this is an average character and should not be relied upon in itself for separating these two species. Consider geographic origin of the specimen and check amount of webbing on hind foot. In the northern species the 1st toe is completely webbed and only 1½ to 2 joints (phalanges) of the 4th (longest) toe are free (Fig. 97, p. 318).

Voice: *Gick, gick, gick, gick,* etc. Like two pebbles being clicked together, slowly at first but picking up speed and continuing for 20 or 30 or more beats. Breeds April to July; in northern

Fig. 97. WEBBING AND TOE DISCS OF VARIOUS HYLID FROGS
Cricket (*Acris*), Chorus (*Pseudacris*), and Tree (*Hyla*)

| NORTHERN CRICKET (*crepitans*) Webbing extensive | SOUTHERN CRICKET (*gryllus*) Webbing scant | CHORUS FROG (*Pseudacris*) Small discs; small webs | TREEFROG (*Hyla*) Large discs; large webs |

part of range this is one of the last frogs to get into full chorus.
Range: Long Island to the Florida panhandle and e. Texas.
                                                Map 291

BLANCHARD'S CRICKET FROG   Pl. 46
Acris crepitans blanchardi
Identification: ⅝–1½ in. (1.6–3.8 cm). The western member of
the group. Wartier, heavier, and bulkier than other cricket
frogs. Dark stripe on thigh ragged (not clean-cut) and blending
with the dark pigment above it and in the anal region. General
coloration usually some shade of light brown or gray, with a
tendency toward uniformity instead of the wide variety of
strongly contrasting color patterns that are so prevalent in the
other forms. Named for Frank Nelson Blanchard, a herpetologist of the University of Michigan.
Voice: Like the clicking of pebbles in rapid succession. Breeds
from February in southern part of range to late July farther
north.
Range: Michigan and Ohio to Nebraska, extr. e. Colorado, and
most of Texas; the Pecos River Valley in New Mexico and the
Río Sabinas Valley in Coahuila.   Map 291

Treefrogs: Genus *Hyla*

As their name implies, treefrogs (or tree "toads") are well adapted
for an arboreal existence. Their toes end in adhesive discs, and
their long limbs and digits help them cling to twigs and bark.
But only a few of them ascend high into trees. More common
habitats include brushy thickets, swampland vegetation, moist
woodlands, or even on the ground or burrowed in it.

Color changes are pronounced in some species, and the same frog may be gray at one time and green or brown at another, either patterned or plain-colored, depending on conditions of light, moisture, temperature, stress, or general activity. The young of several of the species may exhibit a plain bright green livery for long periods of time, rendering it difficult to tell them apart. It is sometimes helpful to leave a treefrog undisturbed in a collecting bottle or, preferably, a terrarium for a few days; it eventually may change its pattern and coloration to match one of the illustrations on Plate 47. Some species of treefrogs have distinctive markings or coloration on the concealed surfaces of their hind legs, thus making capture imperative for close examination.

Chorus frogs are often mistaken for treefrogs, but their toe discs are smaller and the webbing between the toes is less well developed (Fig. 97, p. 318).

Male treefrogs have a vocal sac that looks like a round balloon under the throat when inflated. The only exceptions among the species in our area are the Mexican and Cuban Treefrogs, in which the single sac inflates more to each side than in the middle, thus producing a suggestion of a double sac.

Many captive treefrogs will survive in terrariums for long periods of time if they are given a variety of live insects and other invertebrates to eat. Members of the genus *Hyla* occur virtually throughout the range of the entire family Hylidae, except in Australia and New Guinea.

SPRING PEEPER *Hyla crucifer*   Pl. 47

Identification: ¾-1¼ in. (1.9-3.2 cm); record 1⅜ in. (3.5 cm). The dark cross on the back is usually in the form of an X, but more often than not an imperfect one. This, the only small treefrog in the North, varies through shades of brown, gray, or olive, but does not exhibit profound changes in pattern and coloration as do some of its relatives.

A frog of the woodlands that is especially abundant in areas of brushy second growth or cutover woodlots, if these are near small, temporary or semipermanent ponds or swamps. In early spring many such habitats — provided they are not polluted — have their quota of peepers. In general these small singers tend to form their choral groups where trees or shrubs are standing in the water, or at least nearby. In contrast, the other small vernal choristers that sing with them throughout a large part of their range — the chorus frogs — usually choose open places for calling stations. There is actually much overlap, however, and the two types of frogs often call from virtually identical situations. Peepers are seldom seen except in the breeding season, but they do occasionally wander through the woods by day in damp or rainy weather.

Similar species: (1) Gray and Bird-voiced Treefrogs have a light spot beneath the eye. (2) Pine Woods Treefrog has rounded light spots on rear of thigh (Fig. 96, p. 316). (3) Most of the Chorus Frogs have a light line along upper lip; Mountain Chorus Frog also usually has a dark triangle between eyes.

Voice: A high, piping whistle, a single clear note repeated at intervals of about a second. There is a terminal upward slur, unlike the piping note of the Ornate Chorus Frog, which ends sharply. A large chorus of peepers heard from a distance sounds like sleigh bells. Some specimens utter a trilling peep that may be heard in the background of small choruses. A winter frog in the South, breeding from late November to March; a spring chorister in the North, beginning with first warm rains and sometimes continuing to call well into June.

Range: Maritime Provinces to n. Florida; west to se. Manitoba and e. Texas; introduced in Cuba.

Subspecies: NORTHERN SPRING PEEPER, *Hyla c. crucifer* (Plate 47). This race, occurring throughout almost all of range of species, is characterized by a plain or virtually plain venter. SOUTHERN SPRING PEEPER, *Hyla c. bartramiana.* Similar, but with venter strongly marked with dark spots. S. Georgia and n. Florida.   Map 273

PINE BARRENS TREEFROG *Hyla andersoni*   **Pl. 47**
Identification: 1⅛–1¾ in. (2.9–4.4 cm); record 2 in. (5.1 cm). The lavender stripes, bordered by white, and set against green make this beautiful little frog easy to identify. Considerable orange on concealed surfaces of legs.

   A resident of the swamps, bogs, and brown, acid waters of the New Jersey pine barrens and the pocosins (shrub bogs) of North Carolina. Rarely seen, however, unless one follows the call of a singing male to its source.

Voice: A nasal *quonk-quonk-quonk* repeated at a rate of about 25 times in 20 seconds (on warm nights; more slowly on cooler ones). Call similar to that of Green Treefrog but lower in pitch and not audible for so great a distance. Breeds in late spring in New Jersey and from April to late August in North Carolina.

Range: S. New Jersey; se. N. Carolina and adj. S. Carolina; isolated colonies in Georgia and the Florida panhandle.

Map 279

GREEN TREEFROG *Hyla cinerea*   **Pl. 47**
Identification: 1¼–2¼ in. (3.2–5.7 cm); record 2½ in. (6.4 cm). Usually bright green, but the coloration is variable; it may be nearly yellow, as it often is when the frog is calling, or a dull greenish- or slate-gray, as when it is hidden and inactive during periods of cool weather. Length of white or yellowish stripe along the side also variable; commonly it extends nearly to groin, but may terminate farther forward or be longer on one

side of body than on other. In some populations the lateral stripe may be very short or lacking entirely. The two Green Treefrogs illustrated on Plate 47 represent the extremes of pattern. Many individuals have tiny golden spots on their backs.

This is a "rain frog," a vernacular name shared by other members of the group, especially the Squirrel Treefrog. Some country people believe these amphibians are weather prophets, but, although they tend to sing mostly during damp weather, they may call as lustily before fair weather as before foul. Habitats include swamps, borders of lakes and streams, floating vegetation, or in fact almost any place well supplied with water or dampness. Occasionally enters brackish water. Green Treefrogs are frequent visitors to windows at night, where they seek insects attracted by lights.

Similar species: (1) Pine Barrens Treefrog is ornamented with lavender stripes and much orange on concealed surfaces of legs. (2) Squirrel Treefrog occasionally has a light lateral stripe, but the stripe's lower border is indistinct and not sharply defined as in Green Treefrog; also Squirrel Treefrog is usually *brown* and will eventually return to that color from its temporary green livery. (3) Treefrogs of many species, especially young ones, may turn bright green, but most of them lack light stripes.

Voice: Bell-like, and the origin of the local names of "bell frog" and "cowbell frog." Call has a ringing quality, but is best expressed as *queenk-queenk-queenk* with a nasal inflection; may be repeated as many as 75 times a minute. Breeding calls may be heard from March to October in the Far South (in spring farther north); the congresses are sometimes enormous, with hundreds or even thousands of males participating.

Range: Delmarva Peninsula to southern tip of Florida and on some of Keys; west through Gulf Coastal Plain to e. and s. Texas; north to extr. s. Illinois and with isolated colonies in Kentucky and Tennessee. Introduced in northwestern corner of Puerto Rico.

Note: The Green and Barking Treefrogs hybridize in some areas; the offspring are stout-bodied, as in the Barking Frog, but they resemble the Green Treefrog in pattern.   Map 274

BARKING TREEFROG *Hyla gratiosa*   Pl. 47

Identification: 2-2⅝ in. (5.1-6.7 cm); record 2¾ in. (7.0 cm). One of the larger, stouter treefrogs — and the spottiest. The profuse round dark markings usually persist, at least in part, through the various color changes, but they may disappear when the frog turns dark brown or bright green or fades to tones of pale gray or yellow. At least some green pigment usually in evidence.

Both a high climber and a burrower, but also uses other habitats between these two extremes. In hot, dry weather often

takes shelter in sand or soil beneath roots or clumps of grass
or other vegetation.

Similar species: Some Southern Leopard Frogs are profusely
spotted, but they lack adhesive discs on toes.

Voice: This frog gets its name from its voice. A barking call
of nine or ten raucous syllables is uttered from high in the
treetops. The breeding call, given in or close to the water, is
a single explosive *doonk* or *toonk* often repeated at intervals
of one or two seconds. Breeds March to August.

Range: Se. Virginia to s. Florida and e. Louisiana, chiefly in
the Coastal Plain but also in many upland areas; isolated
records northward to Kentucky; introduced in s. New Jersey.
                                                    Map 273

PINE WOODS TREEFROG *Hyla femoralis*   Pl. 47

Identification: 1–1½ in. (2.5–3.8 cm); record 1¾ in. (4.4 cm).
Here's a frog that simply must be caught to assure identification. There is a row of small orange, yellow, or whitish spots
on the rear of the thigh (Fig. 96, p. 316), but these are concealed
when the animal is at rest, and when it leaps you cannot see
them either. The deep reddish-brown coloration is perhaps most
common, but this frog may also be gray or greenish gray at
times.

An arboreal acrobat that climbs high in the trees, but also
frequents lower levels, even the ground. Commonly found in
pine flatwoods and in or near cypress swamps.

Similar species: (1) Several other Treefrogs strongly resemble
this one, but they all lack light spots on concealed portion of
thigh. (2) Gray Treefrog and Bird-voiced Treefrog both have
a light spot below eye.

Voice: The dot-and-dash frog. Morse code done with a
snore — no messages, but with the abandon of an amateur playing with a telegraph key. Call much lower pitched than the
dots and dashes we used to hear on our radio or TV sets with
some of the news broadcasts. A large chorus sounds like a series
of riveting machines all operating at once. Breeding calls may
be heard from April to early September (March to October in
Florida).

Range: Coastal Plain, se. Virginia to s. Florida and e. Louisiana.
                                                    Map 277

SQUIRREL TREEFROG *Hyla squirella*   Pl. 47

Identification: ⅞–1⅝ in. (2.2–4.1 cm). Like a "chameleon" in
its myriad variations of coloration and pattern. The same frog
may be brown at one time and green at another, plain or
spotted. Often, but not always, there is a spot or dark bar
between the eyes. Also, there may be a light stripe along side of
body. Identify by a process of elimination, ruling out any species it couldn't be. You had better catch it first!

Called a "rain frog" in many parts of the South. A ubiquitous animal that may appear suddenly in and around houses, even literally "dropping from the sky" as it falls from a tree during acrobatics while in pursuit of insects. Found in gardens, weed or brush tangles, woods, trees, vines — in fact, almost anywhere close to moisture, food, and a hiding place.

Similar species: (1) Pine Woods Treefrog has light round spots on rear of thigh and Cricket Frogs have hidden stripes on theirs (Fig. 96, p. 316). (2) Gray and Bird-voiced Treefrogs have a light spot beneath each eye. (3) Spring Peeper has an X on its back. (4) Cuban Treefrog, in addition to its large size, is warty and has very large toe discs. (5) Ornate Chorus Frog sports a black spot on its flanks, and additional ones rise from groin. (6) Chorus Frogs, in general, have smaller toe discs and less webbing than Treefrogs (Fig. 97, p. 318). (7) See also Green Treefrog.

Voice: Ducklike, but slightly more nasal. A harsh trill or rasp repeated at a rate of 15 to 20 times in 10 seconds (during height of breeding season). The so-called rain call, usually voiced away from water, is a scolding rasp, quite squirrel-like. Breeds from March to October in Florida, April to August farther north.

Range: Se. Virginia to Florida Keys; west to Louisiana and along Texas coast to Corpus Christi Bay; isolated colonies in Alabama, Mississippi, and Oklahoma; introduced and established on Grand Bahama in the Bahama Is.   Map 276

GRAY TREEFROG   Pl. 47
Hyla versicolor and *Hyla chrysoscelis*

Identification: 1¼–2 in. (3.2–5.1 cm); record 2⅜ in. (6.0 cm). These two look-alike species of treefrogs have long masqueraded as one. Only by their voices can you tell them apart in the field. For practical purposes it is sufficient to identify either species as a Gray Treefrog. The following characteristics are shared by both:

Size moderately large in comparison with most other members of the treefrog family within our area. Coloration normally gray (or green), but subject to many variations. An individual frog may be gray, brown, green, pearl-gray, or even almost white, depending, at least in part, on changes in its activities or environment. Light spot beneath eye usually discernible. Concealed surfaces of hind legs *bright orange* (or golden yellow) mottled with black. Skin of back quite warty for a treefrog, the warts very numerous but not so prominent or protuberant as in the average toad (*Bufo*).

Not often seen on ground or at water's edge, except in breeding season. Many forage aloft, chiefly in relatively small trees or shrubs that are near or actually standing in shallow bodies of water. Extremely well camouflaged when clinging to bark of a rough tree trunk, and often their presence is known only when they call.

Similar species: (1) Bird-voiced Treefrog closely resembles members of Gray Treefrog complex, but concealed surfaces of hind legs are washed with green or yellowish white instead of orange. Also, Bird-voiced has a rapid ringing call instead of a trill. (2) The Squirrel Treefrog also resembles Gray Treefrog when both are in green livery; if in doubt allow frogs to rest quietly until colors change or details of pattern appear. (3) See Canyon Treefrog, which occurs west of range of Gray Treefrog.

Voice: The call of the Gray Treefrog (without discriminating between the two species) has been variously likened to a musical trill, a resonant flutelike trill, or a sound similar to the call of the red-bellied woodpecker. The calls of the two species are best described as a slow trill (*versicolor*) and a fast, higher-pitched trill (*chrysoscelis*). When the two are heard together, it is possible to distinguish between the males, but positive identification of the calls at other times depends on making tape recordings and analyzing them in the laboratory in conjunction with temperature data obtained in the field. The speed of the trills in both species is slowed when the weather is cool.

Range: New Brunswick to n. Florida and west to s. Manitoba and cen. Texas. The general limits of the complex as a whole are probably shown fairly accurately on Map 278, but detailed delineation of the distributional patterns of these two sympatric, sibling species must await (a) the accumulation and analysis of calls recorded in the field in a large number of localities and (b) the use of laboratory techniques to determine the chromosome numbers of individual frogs (including females); *versicolor* (tetraploid) has twice as many chromosomes as *chrysoscelis* (diploid).   Map 278

BIRD-VOICED TREEFROG *Hyla avivoca*   **Pl. 47**
Identification: 1⅛–1¾ in. (2.9–4.4 cm); record 2 1/16 in. (5.2 cm). A junior edition of the Gray Treefrog. Both species have a light spot under the eye, but in the Bird-voiced Treefrog the *concealed* portions of the hind legs are washed with pale *yellowish green to greenish- or yellowish-white* instead of orange. General dorsal coloration gray, brown, or green.

A resident of permanent wooded swamps — of tupelo, cypress, birch, buttonbush, and vine tangles — along many of the creeks and larger waterways of the South.
Similar species: See Gray Treefrog.
Voice: A ringing, birdlike whistle, *wit-wit-wit-wit* rapidly repeated 20 or more times. A single frog calling reminds one of whistling for a dog. Breeds from spring to late summer.
Range: Extr. s. Illinois to Louisiana and the Florida panhandle;

e.-cen. Georgia and adj. S. Carolina; an isolated record in extr. se. Oklahoma.

Subspecies: WESTERN BIRD-VOICED TREEFROG, *Hyla a. avivoca* (Plate 47). Concealed surfaces of hind limbs washed with bright green or yellowish green. Swamps along streams of Gulf drainage. EASTERN BIRD-VOICED TREEFROG, *Hyla a. ogechiensis.* Concealed surfaces pale greenish white or yellowish white. Along streams of Atlantic drainage.   Map 275

CANYON TREEFROG *Hyla arenicolor*   Pl. 47
Identification: 1¼–2 in. (3.2–5.1 cm); record 2¼ in. (5.7 cm). A treefrog of boulder-strewn canyon creeks of the arid Southwest and Mexico. General coloration brownish gray, often tinted with pink. Dorsal markings varying from dark or medium brown to greenish. Concealed surfaces of hind limbs orange-yellow. A dark bar below eye. Skin moderately rough. *Male:* Throat gray, brown, or black.

This well-camouflaged frog is sometimes seen at night perched on or between boulders along small, intermittent streams that retain at least some water throughout the year. Essentially an upland species in our area, but it follows streams, such as Limpia Creek in the Davis Mountains of western Texas, into lower and more arid terrain.

Voice: A series of short nasal notes — *ah-ah-ah-ah* — that sound much as a Gray Treefrog would if it called from inside a tin can. Breeds March to July or during autumn rains in drier parts of range.

Range: Chisos and Davis Mountains and canyons of Trans-Pecos Texas; s. Utah and s. Colorado to n. Veracruz and w. Oaxaca.   Map 280

CUBAN TREEFROG *Hyla septentrionalis*   Pl. 47
Identification: Males 1½–3½ in. (3.8–8.9 cm); females 2–5 in. (5–13 cm); record 5½ in. (14.0 cm). An immigrant from the West Indies and the largest of our treefrogs. The extra large toe discs and warty skin suffice for distinguishing adults from other frogs, but smaller specimens may offer trouble. This species has no line or stripe, light or dark, running through or under eye. General coloration variable, mostly through greens and bronzes.

Largely nocturnal, sometimes appearing near lights in search of insects. By day this large amphibian hides where there is moisture — in cisterns, drains, cellars, the axils of palms or banana trees, even on porches of houses in jardinieres or other containers holding potted plants that are watered daily. Don't put a Cuban Treefrog in a cage or terrarium with smaller frogs or toads. It may eat them.

Voice: Very suggestive of the snoring rasp of the Southern Leopard Frog, but less vigorous and usually higher pitched. The

call has been described as a rasping snarl the individual notes of which may vary at least through an octave. Vocal sac of male inflates toward each side to suggest a double pouch.
Range: S. Florida and the Keys; Cuba and the Isla de Pinos, the Bahamas and Cayman Islands; introduced on Puerto Rico.
Map 282

MEXICAN TREEFROG *Smilisca baudini* **Pl. 47**
Identification: 2–2¾ in. (5.1–7.0 cm); record 3⁹⁄₁₆ in. (9.0 cm). The most constant markings are the light spot beneath the eye, a light spot at the base of the arm, and a dark patch running backward from the eardrum onto the shoulder. The dark patch usually persists during the most extreme color changes, changes that may produce a brown, very dark gray, or gray-green frog or, conversely, a pale yellow or pale gray one.
Occurs chiefly in subhumid regions. During dry season takes refuge under ground, in damp tree holes, under tree bark or the outer sheaths of banana trees, etc.
Voice: Like the starting mechanism of an old car; a series of blurred notes — *heck* or *keck* — sometimes interspersed with chuckles. Also described as a series of short, explosive notes — *wonk-wonk-wonk*. Inflated vocal sac of male consists of a pair of bulges protruding downward and sideward from under throat. Breeds with advent of rain.
Range: Atlantic and Pacific lowlands and adjacent areas from extr. s. Texas and s. Sonora to Costa Rica. Map 281

LITTLE GRASS FROG *Limnaoedus ocularis* **Pl. 47**
Identification: ⁷⁄₁₆–⅝ in. (1.1–1.6 cm); record 1¹⁄₁₆ in. (1.7 cm). Tiniest North American frog. The dark line passing through the eye and onto side of body is constant, and although this may be variable in length, it is the most reliable characteristic. Usually a narrow dark middorsal stripe starting as a triangle between eyes and extending to anal region. Another dark narrow stripe separates the middorsal color from the lighter ground color of the sides. General coloration extremely variable — tan, brown, greenish, pink, or reddish. Chest whitish or yellowish. Toes slightly webbed.
An elfin treefrog whose climbing is restricted to low vegetation. Moist, grassy environs of ponds and cypress bays are favorite habitats.
Similar species: Most persons upon seeing or capturing this minute amphibian for the first time mistake it for the young of some other species. (1) A dark lateral stripe passing through the eye is also the most conspicuous pattern element in the larger Brimley's Chorus Frog, but that species usually has a *spotted chest*. (2) Cricket Frogs have stripes on the rear of their thighs (Fig. 96, p. 316).

Voice: A tinkling, insectlike call — *set-see, set-see* — so high and shrill that some people have difficulty hearing it. May breed any month of year in Florida; from January to September farther north.
Range: Se. Virginia to southern tip of Florida; inland to edge of the Piedmont and to extr. se. Alabama.   Map 283

Chorus Frogs: Genus *Pseudacris*

MANY persons hear chorus frogs, but few ever see them. In the North these are vernal choristers that respond to the first warm rains as spring moves northward. In the South they are "winter frogs," their breeding season beginning at any time from November to late winter, but usually in correlation with *cool* rains. They sing day and night in or near shallow, often temporary, bodies of water, sometimes in the open, but more often concealed in a clump of grass or other vegetation where they are extremely difficult to find even when they advertise their presence by calling loudly. They are seldom encountered after the breeding season.

These are the "swamp treefrogs" or "swamp cricket frogs," small members of the treefrog family that climb little and then only into weeds or low shrubs in pursuit of insects. Their toe discs are small, and the toes themselves are only slightly webbed (Fig. 97, p. 318). A light line along the upper lip is common to most of them. Males have a single round vocal pouch that, when collapsed, is gray or brown over a cream or yellowish ground color.

The genus is strictly North American, ranging from the Gulf to New York and southern Ontario in the East and from Arizona almost to the Arctic Circle in the West.

WESTERN CHORUS FROG   Pl. 46; Fig. 98, p. 328
Pseudacris triseriata triseriata
Identification: ¾–1½ in. (1.9–3.8 cm). Normally with 3 dark stripes down the back (Fig. 98, p. 328). These typically are as broad and strong as the dark lateral stripe that runs from snout to groin and passes through the eye, but they are subject to variation. They may be broken or reduced to rows of dark spots or be lacking altogether. Middle stripe often forks into 2 parts posteriorly. A dark triangle or other dark figure *may* be present between eyes. Always a *light line along upper lip*. Dorsal ground color varies from pale gray to dark brown but may also be dull green or olive. Markings are darker gray or brown. Undersurfaces whitish, either plain or with a few dark spots on throat and chest.

Shallow bodies of water are required during the breeding season and for the development of tadpoles, but otherwise this frog survives in a wide variety of habitats, some of them sur-

Fig. 98. DORSAL PATTERNS OF VARIOUS CHORUS FROGS
(Pseudacris)

MOUNTAIN	WESTERN	UPLAND	SOUTHERN	FLORIDA
(brachyphona)	(triseriata)	(feriarum)	(nigrita)	(verrucosa)
Reverse	3 broad	Stripes thin,	Stripes broad,	Rows of
parentheses	stripes	often broken	usually broken	spots

prisingly dry and greatly altered by the activities of man. Originally this was chiefly a frog of the prairies, but it has expanded its range to include agricultural lands, and may even be heard in the environs of large cities and suburban areas, provided pollution is not too severe.

Similar species: (1) Spring Peeper *lacks* light line on lip and usually has a dark X on back. (2) Mountain Chorus Frog has only 2 dark dorsal stripes (Fig. 98, above), and they curve inward and may unite to form a crude X. (3) Spotted Chorus Frog has bright green spots or stripes. (4) Upland Chorus Frog, with which the Western Chorus Frog intergrades along a broad line through Mississippi Valley, will offer trouble. Both are variable, but the Western *usually* is strongly striped, whereas the Upland *usually* is spotted or weakly striped (Fig. 98, above). Striped specimens of Upland Chorus Frog have stripes rather thin and frequently broken, but the lateral stripe (one passing through eye) is broad and strong and usually points up the weakness of the dorsal pattern. In the Western, length of tibia is considerably less than ½ length from snout to vent; in the Upland it is approximately half. Geography (point of origin of specimen) may offer best clue to identification (Map 289).

Voice: A vibrant, regularly repeated *crreek* or *prreep* (roll the *r*'s), speeding up and rising in pitch toward the end. The sound may be roughly imitated by running a finger over approximately the last 20 of the *small* teeth of a good-quality pocket comb, rubbing the shortest teeth last. Breeds from February to June, the latest dates occurring in northernmost parts of range.

Range: Extr. s. Quebec and adj. New York to Kansas and Oklahoma; a disjunct area in New Mexico and Arizona.

Subspecies: NEW JERSEY CHORUS FROG, *Pseudacris t. kalmi.* Very similar, but averaging more robust and usually with broad, well-defined dorsal stripes. Coastal Plain from Staten Island, New York, to southern tip of Delmarva Peninsula, and intergrading with Upland Chorus Frog in n. New Jersey and e. Pennsylvania.   Map 289

UPLAND CHORUS FROG   Pl. 46; Fig. 98, p. 328
Pseudacris triseriata feriarum

Identification: ¾–1 ⅜ in. (1.9–3.5 cm). A frog with an extremely variable pattern. The following are constant: (a) light line along the upper lip; (b) dark stripe from snout to groin and passing through eye. On the other hand, the middorsal pattern may be striped, partly striped, spotted — or even lacking. Basically there are 3 longitudinal dark stripes, but they are usually narrow and often broken up into streaks or rows of small spots (Fig. 98, p. 328). Sometimes there are small scattered spots or virtually no dark markings at all. A dark triangle between eyes (or a suggestion of one) is usually present. General coloration brown or gray. Undersurfaces cream-colored but often with dark stipplings on breast. Length of tibia about ½ length from snout to vent.

Grassy swales, moist woodlands, river-bottom swamps, and environs of ponds, bogs, and marshes are included among the habitats. This is an upland frog in the North, but it deeply invades the lowlands in the South.

Similar species: (1) In Brimley's Chorus Frog the lateral stripe (one passing through eye) is *black* and chest is boldly spotted. (2) In Southern Chorus Frog there are *black* stripes or rows of spots down back. (3) Ornate Chorus Frog has a black stripe from *snout to shoulder* followed by black spots along the side of body. (4) See also **Similar species** under Western Chorus Frog (page 328).

Voice: A regularly repeated *crreek* or *prreep* similar to that of Western Chorus Frog. Usually calls from fairly open situations, as is also the case among all the other races of *triseriata*. Breeds from February to May in the North; during winter or early spring in the South.

Range: N. New Jersey to Florida panhandle; west to e. Texas and se. Oklahoma; an isolated area in S. Carolina.   Map 289

BOREAL CHORUS FROG   Pl. 46
Pseudacris triseriata maculata

Identification: ¾–1 ⁷⁄₁₆ in. (1.9–3.7 cm). Northernmost of all the chorus frogs and the one with the shortest legs. Length of tibia is noticeably shorter than tibia of Western Chorus Frog, which in pattern and gross appearance is very similar. General coloration brown or greenish. The stripes, especially the middorsal one, may break up into rows of spots.

Short legs in frogs seem to be adaptations for life in cold climates. Typical specimens have such abbreviated legs that they hop instead of making long leaps like their more southern relatives. This is a frog of marshy environs of far-northern ponds, lakes, and meadows and of similar habitats in mountainous areas.

Voice: A regularly repeated *prreep, prreep* (roll the *r*'s), much like call of Western Chorus Frog.

Range: N. Ontario to vicinity of Great Bear Lake in nw. Canada; south to Utah and n. New Mexico and intergrading with Western Chorus Frog from n. Wisconsin to Nebraska.   Map 289

SOUTHERN CHORUS FROG   Pl. 46; Fig. 98, p. 328
Pseudacris nigrita nigrita

Identification: ¾–1¼ in. (1.9–3.2 cm). Darkest of all the chorus frogs — the markings are usually black. The black stripe from snout to groin (and passing through eye) is prominent and continuous, but the 3 dorsal stripes have a strong tendency to break up into rows of large spots, especially the middle one, which usually forks into 2 rows posteriorly (Fig. 98, p. 328). Ground color light gray, tan, or silvery and often so pale as to appear almost white in contrast with black markings. *Prominent white line along lip.* The snout in this frog and Florida Chorus Frog tends to be more pointed than snouts of other chorus frogs.

Habitats include pine flatwoods, wet meadows, roadside ditches, moist woodlands, etc.

Similar species: Cricket Frogs have prominent stripes on rear of thigh (Fig. 96, p. 316).

Voice: A trill resembling sound of a rachet but with a musical quality. About 8 or 10 beats to each trill; trills are repeated at regular intervals. Breeds November to April.

Range: E. N. Carolina to n. Florida and s. Mississippi.

Map 288

FLORIDA CHORUS FROG   Pl. 46; Fig. 98, p. 328
Pseudacris nigrita verrucosa

Identification: ¾–1¼ in. (1.9–3.2 cm). The only chorus frog with the upper lip chiefly black instead of white. Normally there is a series of black spots on the lip, but these may join together so that the light pigment is much reduced. The dark dorsal spots, normally arranged in three rows, seldom run together (Fig. 98, p. 328).

A resident of varied habitats — ditches, swales, flatwoods ponds, the prairie lands of south-central Florida, and pine forests and sinkholes on the eastern edge of the Everglades.

Similar species: (1) Florida Cricket Frog has conspicuous stripes on rear of thigh (Fig. 96, p. 316). (2) Young River Frogs have strongly webbed toes.

Voice: A regularly repeated rasping trill. Breeding is usually associated with fairly heavy rains and may occur during any month of year.

Range: Florida Peninsula.   Map 288

SPOTTED CHORUS FROG *Pseudacris clarki*   **Pl. 46**
Identification: ¾-1¼ in. (1.9-3.2 cm). The only chorus frog
garbed with patches of bright green that are rimmed with black.
Two extremes of pattern are illustrated. Spotted specimens are
by far the more common, and the spots are normally scattered,
sometimes very numerous, and not arranged in rows. When
stripes are present, they tend to be longitudinal. Almost always
a green triangle between eyes. Dorsal ground color pale gray
to grayish olive. Belly plain white.
    An amphibian of the grassland prairies. Inactive during dry
weather, but even when conditions of moisture are optimum it
normally ventures abroad only at night or in the early evening.
Similar species: (1) Western Chorus Frog is normally brown
or gray — but sometimes dull green or olive — and is patterned
with stripes or with dark spots arranged in 3 longitudinal rows.
(2) Strecker's Chorus Frog is larger, toadlike, and with a *black*
stripe from snout to shoulder; it also usually has a dark spot
below eye. (3) In the very much larger Crawfish Frog the spots
are dark with *light* borders.
Voice: A rasping trill, *wrrank-wrrank-wrrank,* etc., rapidly
repeated 20 to 30 or more times. Interval between notes is about
equal to duration of notes themselves. Two males singing together, but with their calls alternating, sound like rapid sawing.
Peak of season in April and May, but breeding may follow rains
in virtually any month in southern part of range.
Range: Cen. Kansas to s. Texas and extr. ne. Tamaulipas; an
isolated (introduced?) colony in Chouteau Co., Montana.
                                                    Map 286

BRIMLEY'S CHORUS FROG *Pseudacris brimleyi*   **Pl. 46**
Identification: 1-1¼ in. (2.5-3.2 cm). A very changeable little
frog that may fade to virtually plain brownish yellow except
for the bold black stripe down each side of the body. This stripe,
extending without interruption from snout to groin and passing
through eye, is always strongly evident. Middorsal stripes
brown or gray and frequently much less evident than in frog
shown on Plate 46. Undersurfaces yellow and normally there are
dark spots on chest. Markings on legs tend strongly to be
longitudinal instead of forming crossbands. No dark triangle
between eyes.
    An early singer in the marshes, swamps, ditches, and wet open
woods of the Coastal Plain. Named for Clement S. Brimley,
North Carolina naturalist.
Similar species: (1) In Ornate Chorus Frog, there are bold
black spots on sides and rising from groin. (2) In both Southern
and Upland Chorus Frogs, middorsal stripes or spots are usually
same color as lateral stripes. (3) See also Little Grass Frog.
Voice: A short rasping trill, lasting less than a second and

repeated a dozen times or more. Similar to call of Squirrel Treefrog, but the individual notes are shorter and more strongly accented at end. Breeds from February to April.
Range: Se. Virginia to e. Georgia.   Map 290

MOUNTAIN CHORUS FROG   Pl. 46; Fig. 98, p. 328
Pseudacris brachyphona

Identification: 1–1¼ in. (2.5–3.2 cm); record 1½ in. (3.8 cm). The frog with the reversed parentheses (Fig. 98, p. 328). In some specimens the 2 curved stripes bend inward so far that they touch at center of back, producing a crude dark X. Occasionally, the stripes may be broken into spots. The dark triangle between the eyes is almost invariably present, and there is a white line on upper lip, as in most chorus frogs. Many specimens are "dirty" olive, and thus greener than the one illustrated on Plate 46. Yellow pigment on concealed and lower surfaces of legs.

Like a miniature Wood Frog in habits, leaping power, and gross appearance. A woodland species ranging upward to elevations of at least 3500 ft. (1100 m), occurring chiefly on forested slopes and hilltops, and often at long distances from water. Breeds in small shallow bodies of water in woods or at its edge — in ditches, pools along streams or those that form below hillside springs.

Similar species: (1) Spring Peeper, which normally has a fairly clear-cut dark X on back, lacks white line on lip. (2) In both the Upland and Western Chorus Frogs the dorsal pattern consists basically of *three* longitudinal stripes; if stripes are broken into spots, as is often the case, then the spots are usually arranged in *three* rows. (3) Wood Frog has dorsolateral ridges.
Voice: A rasp like that of Western Chorus Frog, but given more rapidly, higher in pitch, and more nasal in quality. Sounds like a wagon wheel turning without benefit of lubrication. Breeds February to April, depending upon latitude and altitude.
Range: Sw. Pennsylvania and se. Ohio to cen. Alabama; disjunct colonies in extr. e. W. Virginia and extr. ne. Mississippi.
                                                        Map 285

ORNATE CHORUS FROG *Pseudacris ornata*   Pl. 46
Identification: 1–1¼ in. (2.5–3.2 cm); record 1⁷⁄₁₆ in. (3.7 cm). More like the creation of an imaginative artist than a real live frog. A black masklike stripe running through the eye. *Dark spots on sides and near groin.* Yellow in groin and numerous small yellow spots on concealed portions of legs. Coloration highly variable — the individual frog may change from almost plain black to silvery white or to the brilliant colors shown on Plate 46. The reddish-brown coloration is the most common. *Young:* Pattern details not well developed.

Habitats include cypress ponds, pine barren ponds, flooded meadows, and flatwoods ditches — plus their environs.

Similar species: (1) Strecker's Chorus Frog is larger and stouter, more toadlike, with a particularly stout foreleg and a dark spot below eye. (2) Among all other Chorus Frogs whose ranges overlap this species (Brimley's, Upland, Southern, and Florida), the pattern consists of longitudinal dark stripes or rows of spots and there are no conspicuous, light-bordered black spots along sides.

Voice: A series of shrill, birdlike peeps, or like the ring of a steel chisel struck by a hammer, 65 to 80 times a minute. Similar to Spring Peeper's call but quicker and lacking Peeper's terminal slur. Calls during late fall, winter, and early spring.

Range: Coastal Plain from N. Carolina to e. Louisiana; south through much of Florida.   Map 287

STRECKER'S CHORUS FROG   Pl. 46
Pseudacris streckeri

Identification: 1-1⅝ in. (2.5-4.1 cm); record 1⅞ in. (4.8 cm). Largest and chubbiest of the chorus frogs. The stout hand and forearm are quite toadlike. A dark, often black, masklike stripe, from snout to shoulder that may continue as a series of dark spots along the side. General coloration highly variable — gray, hazel, brown, olive, or green, the dorsal markings sometimes even dark brown or black. The dark spot below the eye, present in most specimens, is variable in size; in some it may be little more than an upward bulge from the narrow dark line bordering the upper lip.

This frog utilizes a wide variety of habitats, including moist, shady woods, rocky ravines, environs of streams, lagoons, and cypress swamps, sand prairies, and even cultivated fields. Named for John K. Strecker, a naturalist long associated with Baylor University.

Similar species: In all other Chorus Frogs occurring within the range of this species there is a *continuous* light line along the upper lip.

Voice: Very similar to that of Ornate Chorus Frog. Clear and bell-like, a single and quickly repeated note. In strong chorus the effect is of a rapidly turning pulley wheel badly in need of greasing. Calls during and after rains from November to May, with peak of season in January and February in southern part of range.

Range: N. Oklahoma south through Texas to the Gulf; Arkansas, Missouri, and Illinois.

Subspecies: STRECKER'S CHORUS FROG, *Pseudacris s. streckeri* (Plate 46). Dark stripe through eye and dark spots along side of body in strong contrast with ground color; considerable yellow or orange-yellow pigment in groin. Most of range stated above. ILLINOIS CHORUS FROG, *Pseudacris s. illinoensis.* Dark lateral stripe is usually poorly developed in this pale-colored race; *no* yellow pigment in groin and dorsum never green. The stout forelimbs are well adapted for burrowing in sand, and, unlike toads (*Bufo*) and spadefoot toads (*Scaphiopus*) that dig with their hind limbs and literally drop or back into a hole, the Illinois Chorus Frog uses its hands and goes in head first. Chiefly in sand prairies and cultivated fields of se. Missouri and adj. Arkansas; also in w.-cen. and extr. sw. Illinois.   Map 284

Narrow-mouthed Toads: Family Microhylidae

TWO closely related genera, found only in North and Central America represent this family in our area. These are *Gastrophryne* (narrow-mouthed toads) and *Hypopachus* (sheep frogs). They are small, plump amphibians with short limbs, pointed heads, and a *fold of skin across the back of the head.* Males almost always have dark throats, females light ones. They are very secretive, hiding by day but venturing forth at night when the weather is warm and damp. In trying to escape they usually resort to running instead of leaping, but intersperse their gait with short hops of an inch or two or more. Once fully aroused they are difficult to catch, darting into the nearest crack or crevice and disappearing. Food consists very largely of insects, such as small beetles, termites, and especially ants. They are occasionally found at night feeding at the openings of ant hills. The fold of skin across the head is capable of moving forward to wipe away any insects that may attack the eyes. Other members of the family occur in Mexico, Central and South America, Africa, Asia, the Indo-Australian archipelago, and northeastern Australia.

EASTERN NARROW-MOUTHED TOAD   Pl. 45
Gastrophryne carolinensis
   Identification: ⅞–1¼ in. (2.2–3.2 cm); record 1½ in. (3.8 cm). Shape and general appearance alone are usually enough to identify this small frog. (Confusion could only occur in the broad band where the range overlaps that of the Great Plains Narrow-mouthed Toad.) The general coloration varies through shades of gray, brown, or reddish, and the same frog may change from one color to another, depending on its environment and activities. The pattern illustrated on Plate 45 — a broad dark middorsal area flanked by broad light stripes — is very frequently obscured (often completely) by patches, spots, and mottlings of dark or light pigment. *Venter strongly mottled* (Fig. 99, p. 335). *Key West phases:* Middorsal area only a little darker

Fig. 99. NARROW-MOUTHED TOADS (VENTERS)
(*Hypopachus* and *Gastrophryne*)

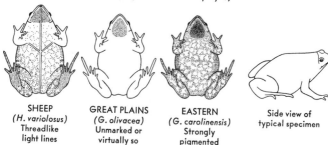

SHEEP	GREAT PLAINS	EASTERN	Side view of
(*H. variolosus*)	(*G. olivacea*)	(*G. carolinensis*)	typical specimen
Threadlike	Unmarked or	Strongly	
light lines	virtually so	pigmented	

than the light dorsolateral stripes, and separated from them by
an irregular dark line. About half the narrow-mouthed toads
on Key West and adjacent Keys are marked in this fashion,
about one-fourth are tan with virtually no pattern (like
olivacea), and the rest are similar to mainland specimens, but
usually much more reddish.

A wide variety of habitats are utilized, but all have two things
in common — shelter and moisture. Margins of bodies of water
are good places in which to look for them. Actually, these toads
are where you find them, and usually as a result of overturning
boards, logs, or other shelters, or raking through vegetable debris, abandoned sawdust piles, etc.

Similar species: (1) Great Plains Narrow-mouthed Toad has
only a few dark spots on its back or no pattern at all; its venter
is unspotted. (2) See also Sheep Frog.

Voice: Like the bleat of a lamb and occasionally with a very
short preliminary *peep*. The call has a vibrant quality, something like an electric buzzer, and lasts for about ½ to 4 seconds.
Breeding sites are chiefly in shallow water, but deep-water situations also are used if covered by a dense floating mat of vegetation. The males usually call from within clumps of plants with
their bodies floating free but with their forelimbs resting on a
stem. Rains initiate breeding, which may occur any time between early April and October in the South, but is limited to
midsummer in northern part of range.

Range: S. Maryland to Florida Keys; west to Missouri and e.
Texas; several disjunct localities along northern and western
borders of range, including one in Iowa and another in extr. s.
Texas.

Map 255

GREAT PLAINS NARROW-MOUTHED TOAD   Pl. 45
Gastrophryne olivacea

Identification: ⅞–1½ in. (2.2–3.8 cm); record 1⅝ in. (4.1 cm).

The oddly shaped body and the absence, or near absence, of pattern make this an easy frog to identify. Adults vary from tan to gray or olive-green, depending on their activities, environment, etc. Dorsum sometimes has scattered small black spots. Venter light and unmarked or virtually so (Fig. 99, p. 335). *Young:* Dark brown with a conspicuous dark leaflike pattern that may occupy half the width of the back. The dark pattern disappears and the general coloration becomes paler as frog grows in size.

A resident of grasslands, marshy sloughs, and rocky, open-wooded slopes. Toward the west it ranges widely through the Chihuahuan and Sonoran Deserts. Hides beneath rocks, boards, debris, etc., in damp places or after rains, but also takes shelter in rodent and reptile burrows and in cracks of drying mud. These Narrow-mouthed Toads sometimes are found in burrows of tarantulas, where they are apparently unmolested and presumably derive protection from the presence of the big spiders. Their skin-gland secretions may be distasteful to potential enemies. Keep your fingers out of your mouth and away from your eyes after handling any narrow-mouthed toad, or you may experience a sharp burning sensation that may last an hour or more. Sometimes called the "ant-eating toad" in reference to its favorite food.

Similar species: (1) Eastern Narrow-mouthed Toad has strongly patterned dorsum, and its venter is mottled with dark pigment. (2) Sheep Frog and Mexican Burrowing Toad have light lines down centers of their backs.

Voice: A distinct but very short *peep* followed by a buzz like that of an angry bee. To some ears the buzz may sound like the bleat of a sheep but higher in pitch and with much less volume. Duration of call about 1 to 4 seconds. Breeding begins upon arrival of heavy rains and may take place at any time from March to September.

Range: Se. Nebraska and Missouri to San Luis Potosí; west through most of Texas and n. Mexico to s. Arizona and south to Durango and Nayarit.   Map 258

SHEEP FROG *Hypopachus variolosus*   Pl. 45

Identification: 1–1½ in. (2.5–3.8 cm); record 1¾ in. (4.4 cm). The narrow-mouthed toad with the yellow streak down its back. There is a similar light threadlike line down the dark mottled belly with extensions outward across the chest toward the arms (Fig. 99, p. 335). *Two prominent metatarsal tubercles* (spades on the heel).

Remains secreted most of the year beneath partly buried objects (such as fallen palm trees), in burrows, or in the trash of packrat nests.

Voice: A sheeplike bleat lasting about 2 seconds and seldom repeated at less than 15-second intervals. Males call while floating in the water, sometimes with their forelimbs resting on a stem. Breeding is initiated by rains or flooding of the frogs' habitat by irrigation.

Similar species: Both Narrow-mouthed Toads have only a *single metatarsal tubercle.*

Range: S. Texas and near Alamos, Sonora; continuous range from cen. Tamaulipas and cen. Sinaloa to Costa Rica. (Some of the Mexican populations lack the yellow stripe.)   Map 259

True Frogs: Family Ranidae

THESE are the typical frogs. In general they are long-legged, narrow-waisted, and rather smooth-skinned, with fingers free and toes joined by webs. Check for the presence or absence of dorsolateral ridges (see back endpaper), which are raised longitudinal folds of glandular tissue. Males of some species have paired vocal pouches, situated at the sides of the throat; others have a pouch or pouches positioned under the throat (Fig. 100, below). Voice is not entirely restricted to males; females of several species scream loudly when captured, and other vocal sounds have been reported. Breeding males have the bases of their thumbs enlarged, and their forearms are swollen. Sex among adults of the bull and green frog groups is easily determined by looking at the tympanum (see footnote opposite Plate 48).

The family occurs in all continents except Antarctica. The big genus *Rana,* with about 250 species and most of them in the Old World, is the only North American representative. From this genus come the frogs' legs of commerce. The leopard and pickerel frogs and the gopher and crawfish frogs are discussed under separate headings.

Fig. 100. TWO TYPES OF VOCAL SACS IN TRUE FROGS *(Rana)*

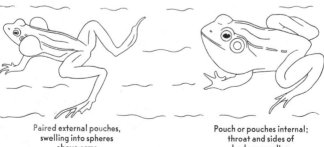

Paired external pouches,
swelling into spheres
above arms

Pouch or pouches internal;
throat and sides of
body expanding

BULLFROG *Rana catesbeiana*   **Pl. 48**
  Identification: 3½–6 in. (9–15 cm); record 8 in. (20.3 cm). Our
  largest frog. Plain or nearly plain green above, or with a netlike
  pattern of gray or brown on a green background. Venter whitish, often mottled with gray, and with a yellowish wash, especially on throats of adult males. *No dorsolateral ridges on
  trunk;* ridges end near eardrum. In the southeastern part of
  its range the Bullfrog may be heavily patterned with dark gray
  or brown; some individuals, especially from Florida, are almost
  black above and heavily mottled below.
    Aquatic and preferring larger bodies of water than most other
  frogs. A resident of lakes, ponds, bogs, sluggish portions of
  streams, cattle tanks, etc.; usually seen at water's edge or amidst
  vegetation or snags among which it can hide. Small streams
  are also utilized where better habitats are lacking.
  Similar species: (1) Green Frog and Bronze Frog have *dorsolateral ridges.* (2) In Pig Frog the hind feet are webbed virtually to tips of toes (Fig. 101, below); the Bullfrog has them less
  fully webbed and the 4th toe extends well beyond the web.
  (3) River Frog has light spots on lips.

Fig. 101. WEBBING IN PIG AND OTHER TRUE FROGS *(Rana)*

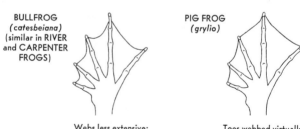

BULLFROG
(catesbeiana)
(similar in RIVER
and CARPENTER
FROGS)

PIG FROG
(grylio)

Webs less extensive;
tip of 4th toe
extending well
beyond web

Toes webbed virtually
to tips; web nearly
straight between
3rd and 4th toes

  Voice: A vibrant, sonorous series of bass notes best stated as
  jug-o'-rum. A single internal vocal sac, forming a flattened
  pouch under the chin when inflated. Breeds May to July; February to October in the South.
  Range: Nova Scotia to cen. Florida; west to Wisconsin and
  across the Great Plains to the Rockies. The natural western
  limits are now hopelessly confused because of the introduction
  of Bullfrogs into a vast number of localities as far west as British
  Columbia and California; also introduced in Mexico, Cuba, etc.
                                                    Map 302

RIVER FROG *Rana heckscheri*   **Pl. 48**
Identification: 3¼-4⅝ in. (8–12 cm); record 5⁵⁄₁₆ in. (13.5 cm).
A large greenish-black frog with *conspicuous light spots on lips,*
these usually largest on lower jaw and often producing a scalloped effect along edge of upper lip. Skin often rugose. Venter
medium to dark gray (sometimes almost black), marked with
light spots or short wavy lines. Usually a pale girdle outlining
groin (Fig. 102, below). *No dorsolateral ridges. Young:* With
reddish eyes.
   A frog of river swamps and swampy shores of ponds and
bayous. Adults are not particularly wary, and are easily observed at night.
Similar species: (1) Pig Frog and Bullfrog lack light lip spots,
and their venters are pale with dark markings; Pig Frog also
has light line or row of light spots along rear of thigh.
(2) Bronze Frog and Green Frog, which often show pale spots
on lips, especially in young adults, have *conspicuous dorsolateral ridges.*
Voice: A deep, sonorous rolling snore; also a snarling, explosive
grunt. Breeds April to August. A single internal vocal pouch.
Range: Se. N. Carolina to n.-cen. Florida and s. Mississippi.
                                        Map 300

Fig. 102. VENTERS OF RIVER AND BULLFROGS *(Rana)*

RIVER
(heckscheri)
Dark with light
markings; pale girdle
in groin

BULL
(catesbeiana)
Light with dark
markings; amount of
pigmentation variable

PIG FROG *Rana grylio*   **Pl. 48**
Identification: 3¼-5½ in. (8–14 cm); record 6⅜ in. (16.2 cm).
A "bullfrog" with a rather narrow and pointed head, and with
the hind feet fully webbed. The *4th toe webbed virtually to its
tip* (Fig. 101, p. 338). Pattern and coloration variable; olive to
blackish brown and with prominent, scattered dark spots.
Venter white or pale yellow with a netlike pattern of brown,
dark gray, or black on thighs; a similar dark pattern extending

well forward on underside of body in some specimens. A light
line or row of light spots across rear of thighs. (Carpenter Frog
has similar markings on rear of thighs.) *No dorsolateral ridges.*
Young: Superficially like adult Carpenter Frogs.

Strongly aquatic; at the edges of lakes, marshes, and cypress
bays, in water-lily prairies, or amid other emergent or floating
vegetation. Shy and difficult to approach except at night with
the aid of a light.

Similar species: (1) In Bullfrog and River and Carpenter
Frogs the webs are less extensive and the *4th toe extends well*
beyond the web (Fig. 101, p. 338). (2) Bronze, Leopard, Pickerel,
and the Gopher Frogs have *dorsolateral ridges.*

Voice: Like the guttural grunt of a pig. Choruses sound like
a herd of swine; very large groups produce a continuous roar.
Males float high in the water when calling. There is only a single
internal vocal pouch, but an extension at each side gives it a
3-sectional effect (with throat and sides expanded somewhat like
right-hand frog in Fig. 100, p. 337).

Range: S. South Carolina to extr. s. Florida and extr. se. Texas.
Map 301

CARPENTER FROG   *Rana virgatipes*   **Pl. 48**
Identification: 1⅝–2⅝ in. (4.1–6.7 cm). The light stripes, 4 in
all, the lack of dorsolateral ridges, and the Coastal Plain distribution are usually sufficient, except within range of Pig Frog
(see **Similar species,** below).

Sometimes called the "sphagnum frog," because of a close
association with sphagnum bogs. It may also be found in stands
of emergent, grasslike vegetation. In such habitats it is difficult
to stalk, especially since its color blends so well with the acid
brown-stained waters of the bogs. In more open habitats it may
be seen at the water's surface with only the head exposed. When
approached, the head vanishes downward but may reappear
seconds later a few feet away.

Similar species: Young Pig Frogs may have suggestions of pale
longitudinal dorsal stripes, but their 4th toes are webbed virtually to their tips; the 4th toe extends well beyond web in Carpenter Frog (Fig. 101, p. 338).

Voice: *Pu-tunk', pu-tunk', pu-tunk.'* Like two carpenters hit-
ting nails a fraction of a second apart. Several variations on
this theme. Large choruses resemble a corps of workmen ham-
mering away. Breeds April to August. Vocal pouches paired,
spherical when inflated (Fig. 100, p. 337).

Range: Coastal Plain, s. New Jersey to Okefenokee Swamp
region of Georgia and adj. Florida; a disjunct colony in Virginia.
Map 311

BRONZE FROG   *Rana clamitans clamitans*   **Pl. 48**
Identification: 2⅛–3 in. (5.4–7.6 cm); record 3⅜ in. (8.6 cm). A
southern frog with a plain brown or bronzy back. The green

of the upper lips is often lacking. Venter white, but with dark wormlike markings. In some males the throat is washed with light yellow. Dorsolateral ridges *ending on body,* not reaching groin. *Young:* Numerous dark dorsal spots; venter with heavy brown or black wormlike markings.

A secretive frog, taking shelter in logs and stumps, in crevices in limestone sinks, etc.; habitats include swamps, bayheads, wet hammocks, and environs of streams.

Similar species: (1) The northern subspecies, the Green Frog, has markings in strong contrast with ground color. (2) Bullfrog, Pig, River, and Carpenter Frogs lack dorsolateral ridges. (3) In Pickerel and Southern Leopard Frogs there is a light line on upper jaw, and dorsolateral ridges extend to groin.

Voice: A twanging, explosive baritone note; usually a single *clung* or *c'tung,* but sometimes repeated rapidly 3 or 4 times. Two (internal) vocal pouches; the throat and sides expand when the frog is calling (Fig. 100, p. 337). Breeds April to August.

Range: Coastal Plain from s. N. Carolina to n.-cen. Florida and west to e. Texas; north in Mississippi Valley to about mouth of Ohio River.   Map 299

GREEN FROG *Rana clamitans melanota*   **Pl. 48**
Identification: 2¼–3½ in. (5.7–8.9 cm); record 4 in. (10.2 cm). Highly variable — may be more brown than green. Green to greenish brown above, dark brown or grayish dorsal spots or blotches usually present and often numerous. Venter white, but usually some dark spots or mottling under legs and head. Throat of adult male bright yellow. Dorsolateral ridges *ending on body,* not reaching groin. *Young:* Numerous small dark dorsal spots; venter mottled.

An abundant frog that throughout a large part of its range may be found wherever there is shallow fresh water — in springs, rills, creeks, and ditches, and along edges of lakes and ponds. In many regions, however, it is characteristically a frog of brooks and small streams.

Similar species: (1) The Bullfrog has no dorsolateral ridges. (2) Leopard and Pickerel Frogs have a light line on upper jaw, and their dorsolateral ridges extend to groin. (3) Check Mink Frog (p. 342). Green Frogs from Canada and northernmost parts of United States are likely to be very dark, with a profusion of black or dark brown markings. Such frogs *strongly resemble* Mink Frog.

Voice: Like a loose banjo string and rather explosive, either a single note or repeated 3 or 4 times, the notes progressively less loud. A pair of vocal pouches, but not evident externally. When the frog is croaking, the throat and sides of body expand considerably (Fig. 100, p. 337). Breeds April to August.

Range: Maritime Provinces to N. Carolina; west to Minnesota and e. Oklahoma, but absent from a large part of Illinois; introduced in Newfoundland, British Columbia, Washington, and Utah.

Note: Green Frogs sometimes are blue. The normal yellow pigment component of the skin may be sparse or lacking, resulting in a partially or almost completely blue dorsum. Blue Leopard Frogs and Bullfrogs have also been reported.

Map 299

MINK FROG   *Rana septentrionalis*   **Pl. 48; Fig. 103, below**
Identification: 1⅞–2¾ in. (4.8–7.0 cm); record 3 in. (7.6 cm). The skin produces an odor like the scent of a mink (or rotten onions) when the frog is rubbed or handled roughly. Webbing on toes of hind feet *extends to last joint of 4th toe and to tip of 5th toe.* The dorsolateral ridges may be absent, partially developed, or even prominent. The dorsal pattern may be mottled or spotted (Fig. 103, below). Dark spots often round and variable in size; in some frogs they dominate the pattern, in others the ground color is most conspicuous. Dark markings on dorsal surfaces of *hind legs* in form of irregular blotches, each with its long axis *more or less paralleling long axis of leg.*

A frog of the North, found along watercourses, but especially partial to borders of ponds and lakes or the cold waters near the mouths of streams that empty into them. Look for it where water lilies are plentiful and where it can venture well out from shore by hopping from pad to pad.

Similar species: Likely to be confused only with Green Frog which often occurs abundantly with and strongly resembles Mink Frog. In Green Frog *hind legs are crossbanded.* That species also lacks minklike odor, always has dorsolateral ridges, and webbing fails to reach tip of 5th toe and barely passes beyond second joint of the 4th.

Voice: A burred and rather deep *cut-cut-cut-cut-cut,* more rapid than but suggestive of the Carpenter Frog's "hammer blows." Breeds June to August. Vocal pouches paired.

Range: Labrador and Maritime Provinces to Minnesota and se. Manitoba; south to n. New York.   Map 308

Fig. 103. DORSAL VARIATION IN MINK FROGS
(Rana septentrionalis)

Spotted and mottled types of pattern
(diagrammatic)

WOOD FROG *Rana sylvatica*   **Pl. 48**
Identification: 1⅜–2¾ in. (3.5–7.0 cm); record 3¼ in. (8.3 cm). The frog with the robber's mask. A dark patch extending backward from the eye is always discernible despite pronounced variations in color. The two illustrations (Plate 48) show dark and light extremes of the same specimen; the gamut runs from pink through various shades of brown to almost black. Specimens from far northern localities (Quebec to British Columbia and Alaska) may have a prominent light middorsal stripe.

Usually encountered in or near moist wooded areas in United States and southern Canada; often wanders considerable distances from water. In the Far North it may occur wherever there is shallow water for breeding, even in tundra ponds.
Voice: A hoarse clacking sound that suggests the quack of a duck. Has little carrying power. Shorter, less loud and less deep, but otherwise resembling voice of Northern Leopard Frog. Appears very early, often heard calling before ice is completely off the ponds. An explosive breeder, the eggs being laid all in the course of a very few days and the adults then disappearing from the ponds instead of lingering, sometimes for weeks, as do many other kinds of frogs. Paired lateral vocal sacs.
Range: Labrador to Alaska; south in the east to the southern Appalachians. Isolated colonies in the Central Highlands, ne. Missouri, and Idaho. Ranges farther north than any other North American amphibian or reptile.
Subspecies: Toward the northern portions of the range, the hind legs of the Wood Frog become proportionately shorter, and specimens resemble toads in appearance and hopping abilities. The change is gradual (clinal), but at least two northern subspecies (*cantabrigensis* and *latiremis*) have been described. Since authorities do not agree on where the range of one presumed race stops and the next begins, no subspecies are here recognized. The virtually identical *Rana maslini* occurs in relict populations in Colorado and Wyoming.   Map 309

Leopard and Pickerel Frogs:
Rana pipiens and Its Relatives;
Rana palustris

FIVE species of frogs belonging to this group, all medium in size and strongly spotted, occur within our area. They maintain their identities in virtually all localities, even where they occur together, but hybridization between some pairs of species has been reported in a few places. The Pickerel Frog, with its squarish spots and bright orange or yellow on the concealed surfaces of the hind legs, can usually be identified with ease. The four leopard frogs are another matter, but fortunately their ranges are almost mutually exclusive, and geography — knowing the place where the specimen was collected — is very helpful. Check the ranges (Maps 303 to 306), and go on from there.

The dorsolateral folds are continuous to the groin in two of the Leopard Frogs; they are interrupted just anterior to the groin and are offset inward in the other two (Fig. 104, p. 346). Further separation of members of the group depends on examination of males or listening to their mating calls. When the vocal sacs are at rest, as they are most of the time, they are invisible in the Northern Leopard Frog, but in the other three species the area surrounding the sac is differentiated by the presence of dark pigment or a roughening of the skin, or the collapsed sac may be clearly visible. (When inflated the vocal sacs form paired pouches in all the leopard frogs — Fig. 100, p. 337.) Mating calls, with approximate pulse rates at 60°F (15.5°C) are given for each of the four leopard frogs. (The rates are more rapid at higher temperatures and less so at lower ones.) Most males in two of the species have vestigial oviducts, whereas males of the other two species lack them. Dissection is required, of course, to check this additional means of identification.

The classification of the leopard frogs has long been in dispute, and more field and laboratory work will be needed before stability is achieved. Studies are also needed on their distribution and ecology. Where two species occur in the same general geographic area do they normally occupy distinctive habitats? Have they been brought together in some places, where they may hybridize, as a result of the disturbance of habitats by mankind? Why are members of the *pipiens* group apparently absent from many sizable areas where *Rana palustris* is widespread, whereas they occur abundantly with the Pickerel Frog in a very large number of localities? Leopard frogs from the southwestern United States and Mexico are also in need of study.

NORTHERN LEOPARD FROG *Rana pipiens*   Pl. 48

Identification: 2–3½ in. (5.1–8.9 cm); record 4⅜ in. (11.1 cm). A brown or green frog with 2 or 3 rows of irregularly placed dark spots between conspicuous dorsolateral ridges. Spots *rounded and with light borders;* adjacent spots may run together. Numerous additional rounded dark spots on sides. A light line on upper jaw. *No* distinct light spot on center of tympanum. *Male:* Vocal sacs visible only when calling; vestigial oviducts usually present.

(In parts of Minnesota and adjacent states, a small percentage of the leopard frog population consists of two aberrant types of patterns: (a) black spots greatly reduced in number or even completely absent, except for a spot behind each elbow; or (b) ground color between spots strongly invaded by dark pigment. These were once thought to be subspecies (*burnsi* and *kandiyohi*), but they are merely mutations of the Northern

Leopard Frog. The spotted one looks superficially like the Northern Crawfish Frog.)

This is the "meadow frog," at least in summertime, a name earned by its wanderings well away from water. Leopard frogs are widely used as laboratory animals.

Similar species: (1) Pickerel Frog has squarish dark spots, and concealed surfaces of its hind legs are bright yellow or orange. (2) Crawfish Frog is squat and stubby in appearance. (3) In other species of Leopard Frogs vocal sacs, when at rest, are visible in males.

Voice: Mating call a long, deep rattling snore interspersed with clucking grunts that may be single or of 2 or more syllables; call duration more than a second (usually 3); pulse rate about 20 a second. Breeds March to May in the more humid parts of its range.

Range: S. Labrador to extr. s. District of Mackenzie; south to Pennsylvania and Kentucky in the East (isolated colonies in Maryland and Illinois); west to Pacific states, and south, in the West, to Nevada, Arizona, and New Mexico (isolated colonies in Oklahoma and New Mexico).   Map 303

SOUTHERN LEOPARD FROG *Rana utricularia*   **Pl. 48**
Identification: 2–3½ in. (5.1–8.9 cm); record 5 in. (12.7 cm). Similar to the Northern Leopard Frog, but differing from the latter as follows: (a) often a light spot in center of tympanum; (b) longer, pointed head; and (c) only a few dark spots on sides of body. A light line along upper jaw. General coloration green or brown or a combination of both. Number of dark dorsal spots highly variable (occasionally completely absent); spots often longitudinally elongated. *Male:* Vocal sacs lie loose at angle of jaw when at rest, but are distinctly spherical when inflated (Fig. 100, p. 337); vestigial oviducts absent, except in males from the Florida peninsula. Also, in Florida males the vocal sacs may fold inward out of sight when not inflated.

In all types of shallow, freshwater habitats, and even entering slightly brackish marshes along coasts. Ventures well away from water in summer, when weeds and other vegetation provide shelter and shade.

Similar species: (1) Pickerel Frog has squarish dark spots, and concealed surfaces of hind legs are bright yellow or orange. (2) Gopher and Crawfish Frogs have fat, chunky bodies and rounded, non-pointed snouts. (3) If specimen is from an area of overlap with one of the other Leopard Frogs, check characteristics of the other species.

Voice: Mating call a short chuckle-like, guttural trill; pulse rate usually fewer than 13 a second. Breeds in early spring toward the north; in any month in the South.

Range: Long Island and extr. s. New York to s. Florida (and some of the *lower* Keys); west to e.-cen. Texas and north in

Mississippi Valley to se. Kansas, Missouri, cen. Illinois, Indiana, and extr. s. Ohio.   Map 305

PLAINS LEOPARD FROG   *Rana blairi*   **Fig. 104, below**
Identification: 2–3¾ in. (5.1–9.5 cm); record 4⅜ in. (11.1 cm). Similar to the Northern Leopard Frog, but averaging stockier and with a relatively shorter head and a *distinct* light line along upper jaw. Nearly always a light spot on tympanum; usually a dark snout spot. Considerable yellow in groin and to some extent on ventral surface of thigh. *Dorsolateral ridges interrupted just anterior to groin and inset medially* (Fig. 104, below). *Male:* Vocal sac area small (when deflated), but longitudinally roughened below light labial stripe; no vestigial oviducts.

The leopard frog of the plains and prairies. Widespread in many parts of its range, but restricted to remnants of the Prairie Peninsula toward the east. Breeds with the onset of warm rains, at least in the less humid parts of the range.
Similar species: See Northern Leopard Frog.
Voice: Mating call usually 2 or 3 distinctly spaced abrupt guttural notes best described as *chuck-chuck* or *chuck-chuck-chuck,* and delivered at a pulse rate of about 3 a second.
Range: W. Indiana to e. Colorado; south in the west to cen. Texas.   Map 304

Fig. 104. DORSOLATERAL RIDGES IN LEOPARD FROGS
(*Rana pipiens* complex)

Interrupted and inset medially
(*blairi* and *berlandieri*)

Not interrupted near groin
(*pipiens* and *utricularia*)

RIO GRANDE LEOPARD FROG   *Rana berlandieri*   **Pl. 48**
Identification: 2¼–4 in. (6–10 cm); record 4½ in. (11.4 cm). Similar to our other leopard frogs, but more pallid. Light line along upper jaw less prominent than in the other species and usually incomplete anterior to eye. *Dorsolateral ridges interrupted just anterior to groin and inset medially* (Fig. 104, above). *Males:* Vocal sacs, when not inflated, collapse inward into a pouch, the external opening of which appears as a dark slit. Vestigial oviducts present, except in specimens from Trans-Pecos Texas.

This frog is well adapted to arid conditions. It is an explosive breeder, ready to take advantage of the rains when they come, hence it may spawn during almost any month of the year. Watercourses, even intermittent ones, and cattle tanks are frequented, but it may appear suddenly, at the onset of rain, in regions where its presence is not even suspected.

Similar species: See Southern and Plains Leopard Frogs.

Voice: Mating call a short, guttural trill, more rapid than that of Southern Leopard Frog and with shorter pulses (13 or more a second).

Range: Cen. and w. Texas and extr. s. New Mexico southward into Mexico. Mexican subspecies (or species?).   Map 306

PICKEREL FROG   *Rana palustris*   **Pl. 48**
Identification: 1¾–3 in. (4.4–7.6 cm); record 3⁷⁄₁₆ in. (8.7 cm). A frog with square spots arranged in 2 parallel rows down the back. These dark markings and similar ones on the sides have the unevenness of squares drawn freehand; the edges are irregular and often curved, but the spots definitely are not circular. Adjacent squares may join to form rectangles or long, longitudinal bars. *Bright yellow or orange on concealed surfaces of hind legs.* A light line along upper jaw. Prominent dorsolateral ridges extending to groin. Venter plain whitish in northern populations, but usually mottled or marbled with dark pigment in Coastal Plain specimens. *Young:* With a metallic luster, but without bright colors under the legs; lower lip clouded with dark pigment.

Typically a species of cool, clear water in the North—in sphagnum bogs, rocky ravines, and meadow streams, but also occupying a wide variety of other habitats. In the South it occurs in the relatively warm, turbid, and often tea-colored waters of Coastal Plain and floodplain swamps. Wanders well out into grassy fields or weed-covered areas in summer. Often found in the twilight zones of caves. Few snakes will eat Pickerel Frogs, probably because the skin-gland secretions make them distasteful.

Similar species: In the Leopard Frogs the dark dorsal spots are circular or oval, and there is no bright yellow or orange on the concealed surfaces of the legs (except in Plains Leopard Frog — see p. 346).

Voice: A steady low-pitched snore of 1 or 2 seconds' duration but with little carrying power. Males very often call while completely submerged in water. Two vocal pouches. Breeds March to May.

Range: Maritime Provinces to the Carolinas; west to Wisconsin and e. Texas; large gaps in the range, especially toward the south and in prairie portions of Ohio, Indiana, and Illinois.

Map 307

Gopher and Crawfish Frogs:
The Races of *Rana areolata*

FROGS of stubby appearance — short, plump bodies, large heads, and relatively short legs. Nocturnal, normally spending the daylight hours underground in burrows or tunnels, in holes beneath stumps, etc. Both the Florida and Dusky Gopher Frogs utilize the burrows of the Gopher Tortoise; the Crawfish Frogs often use the abandoned burrows of the lobsterlike crawfish. The breeding seasons occur in the spring, the dates often being correlated with the occurrence of heavy rains. Males have lateral vocal pouches which are enormous when inflated, each approaching the size of the frog's head.

CRAWFISH FROG   *Rana areolata*   **Pl. 48**
Identification: 2¼–3 in. (5.7–7.6 cm); record 3⅝ in. (9.2 cm). A stubby appearance plus rounded dark dorsal *spots encircled by light borders.* Coloration highly variable, depending on conditions of temperature, activity, etc. Chin and throat unspotted except at sides; belly immaculate whitish (Fig. 105, below). Dorsum often smooth or nearly so. Males may have yellow or greenish yellow on their dorsolateral ridges and on the concealed surfaces of the limbs.
   Not restricted to crawfish holes, but often found in those which have lost their chimneys and contain water. Other habitats include mammal burrows, holes in roadside banks, and in storm or drainage sewers.
Similar species: (1) Leopard Frogs have longer bodies, proportionately longer legs, and lack the stubby, squat appearance of the Crawfish Frogs. (2) Pickerel Frog has squarish spots. (3) The subspecifically related Dusky and Carolina Gopher Frogs have heavily pigmented venters (Fig. 105, below), and lack light-bordered dorsal spots.
Voice: A loud (often chuckling) deep trill with considerable

Fig. 105. VENTERS OF GOPHER FROGS *(Rana areolata)*

CRAWFISH
(areolata and *circulosa)*
Largely unmarked

DUSKY *(sevosa)*
AND CAROLINA *(capito)*
Heavily pigmented

carrying power. Large choruses sound like a sty full of hogs at feeding time. Breeds February to June.

Range: Se. Oklahoma and sw. Arkansas south to the Gulf of Mexico.

Subspecies: SOUTHERN CRAWFISH FROG, *Rana a. areolata* (Plate 48). As described and with range indicated above. NORTHERN CRAWFISH FROG, *Rana a. circulosa.* Somewhat larger; length to 4½ in. (11.4 cm). Head shorter and broader, dorsolateral ridges more prominent, and dorsum rougher. Sw. Indiana to ne. Oklahoma and s.-cen. Mississippi.   Map 310

DUSKY GOPHER FROG *Rana areolata sevosa*   Pl. 48

Identification: 2½–3½ in. (6.4–8.9 cm); record 3⅞ in. (9.8 cm). Warts always prominent, but variable in shape — circular, elongate-oval, or in long ridges. Dorsal coloration also variable, but always dark and ranging from virtually uniform black to a pattern of reddish brown or dark brown spots on a ground of gray or brown. Venter spotted, at least from chin to midbody (Fig. 105, p. 348).

Similar species: (1) River Frog has white spots on lips. (2) In the two Crawfish Frogs the dark dorsal spots are rounded and encircled by *light borders.*

Voice: A deep snore or like the distant roar of an outboard motor; more continuous and hoarser than the guttural notes of the Southern Leopard Frog.

Range: Gulf Coast, w. Florida and adj. Alabama to extr. e. Louisiana.

Subspecies: CAROLINA GOPHER FROG, *Rana a. capito.* Warts smaller, closer together, and almost pavementlike in arrangement (like Belgian blocks on an old-fashioned street, but very much in miniature). Dorsal spots inconspicuous. Venter heavily marked with dark flecks that produce a clouded or marbled pattern. Young with less ventral spotting, especially on abdomen, where it may be lacking entirely. Coastal Plain of the Carolinas and e.-cen. Georgia.   Map 310

FLORIDA GOPHER FROG *Rana areolata aesopus* Pl. 48

Identification: 2¾–3¾ in. (7.0–9.5 cm); record 4¼ in. (10.8 cm). The light ground color has earned this species the name of "white frog." The coloration varies from creamy white to brown through various shades of yellow or purplish. The black or dark brown markings are irregular in shape and not encircled by light borders. Dorsum may be smooth or slightly warty. Chin and throat spotted; belly usually unmarked posteriorly. Males may have yellow on the dorsolateral ridges, on the warts, along upper jaw, and in armpits and groins. Specimens from the Lake Wales Ridge in Polk and Highland Cos., Florida, are dwarfed in size — average length 2½ in. (6.4 cm).

This short, plump frog sometimes may be seen several feet
(1 ± m) back from the entrance of Gopher Tortoise burrows
during daylight hours, but is best sought at night, when it ventures forth to feed.

Voice: A deep roaring snore. Large choruses produce an effect
like that of pounding surf. Breeds in spring toward northern
part of its range, but from February until autumn farther south.

Range: Coastal Plain, s. Georgia to s. Florida.   Map 310

Glossary

For names of scales and other anatomical nomenclature see the endpapers.

Allopatric. A term applied to two or more populations that occupy mutually exclusive, but usually adjacent, geographical areas.

Ambient temperature. The temperature of the environment surrounding the animal in question.

Attenuated. Thin or slender.

Azygous. Odd, not paired.

Barbels. Small, fleshy downward projections from the chins and throats of turtles.

Boss. A raised rounded area; in toads, a rounded eminence on the midline of the head between the eyes or on or near the end of the snout.

Canthus rostralis. The ridge from the eye to the tip of the snout that separates the top of the muzzle from the side.

Cirri. Downward projections from the nostrils in males of certain lungless salamanders. The naso-labial groove extends downward to near the tip of each cirrus.

Cline. A gradual change in a variable characteristic (see p. 9).

Cloaca. The common chamber into which the urinary, digestive, and reproductive canals discharge their contents, and which opens to the exterior through the anus.

Costal grooves. Vertical grooves on the flanks of salamanders. The spaces between grooves are called costal folds.

Cranial crests. The raised ridges on the heads of toads—interorbital (between the eyes) or postorbital (behind the eyes).

Crepuscular. Active at twilight and/or dawn.

Cusp. A toothlike projection on the jaw of a turtle.

Dimorphism. Difference in form, color, or structure between members of the same species. The sexes may be different or there may be two color phases of the same sex (dichromatism).

Dorsal. Of or pertaining to the uppersurface.

Dorsolateral. Neither directly down the center of the back nor at the side of the body, but more or less intermediate between the two.

Dorsum. The entire uppersurface of an animal.

Endemic. Confined to, or indigenous in, a certain area or region.
Estivation. A state of inactivity during prolonged periods of drought or high temperatures, usually while the animal is in seclusion.

Femoral pores. Small openings, containing a waxlike material, on the underside of the thighs in some lizards.
Form. A species or a subspecies; a distinct, identifiable population.
Fossorial. Adapted for digging.

Granules. Very small flat scales.
Gravid. Bearing eggs or young, ordinarily in the oviducts.
Growth rings. Concentric subcircular areas on the scutes of some turtles. Each ring represents a season's growth. Rings, if present, are most evident in young turtles; they are usually not countable in adults.
Gular. On or pertaining to the throat. Also the most anterior scutes (or scute) on a turtle's plastron.

Hemipenis. The copulatory organs of males. There are two such organs in snakes and lizards, but only a single penis in turtles and crocodilians.

Introgression. Incorporation of genes from one species into the gene pool of another.
Introgressive hybridization. Crossbreeding of individuals from two different species that results in introgression.

Keel. A ridge down the back (or along the plastron) of a turtle. Also, a longitudinal ridge on a dorsal scale in certain snakes.

Labial. Of or pertaining to the lip.
Lateral. Of or pertaining to the side.
Littoral. A coastal region.

Melanism. Abundance of black pigment, sometimes resulting in an all-black or nearly all-black animal; opposite of albinism.
Middorsal. Of or pertaining to the center of the back.
Midventral. Of or pertaining to the center of the abdomen.
Monotypic. The only representative of its group, such as a genus with only one species.

Naso-labial groove. A groove extending downward from the nostril and across the lip in the lungless salamanders.
Neotenic. Mature and capable of reproduction but retaining the larval form, appearance, and habits.

Ocelli. Round, eyelike spots.

Papillae. Small nipple-like protuberances.
Paravertebral stripe. A stripe lying to one side but paralleling the midline of the back.

Parotoid. One of a pair of external wartlike glands on the shoulder, neck, or back of the eye in toads; enlarged and prominent in many species.

Parthenogenesis. Reproduction without fertilization by a male element.

Phalanges. The bones of the toes. (Phalanx in the singular.)

Preocular. Anterior to the eye.

Postocular. Behind the eye.

Race. Subspecies.

Rugose. Wrinkled or warty.

Scale pits. Tiny depressions on the posterior portions of the dorsal scales in some kinds of snakes.

Scute. Any enlarged scale on a reptile; sometimes called "shield" or "plate."

Siblings. Offspring of same parents, but not necessarily at same birth.

Sibling species. Two or more species presumably derived from a common parental stock. They often resemble one another closely and may occur together or replace each other geographically.

Spatulate. Flat and rounded at tip; shaped like the blade of a kitchen spatula.

Subcaudals. The scales beneath the tail; in a double row in most snakes, but in a single row in others. Sometimes shortened to "caudals."

Subocular. Beneath the eye.

Supraocular. Above the eye.

Supraorbital semicircle. A row of small scales separating the supra-oculars from the median head scutes in certain lizards.

Suture. A seam; the boundary between scales or scutes.

Sympatric. A term applied to two or more populations that occupy identical or broadly overlapping geographical areas.

Taxonomy. The science of the classification of animals or plants.

Tibia. The leg (of toads and frogs) from heel to knee.

Troglodyte. A cave dweller.

Tubercles. Small knoblike projections.

Tuberculate. With raised projections.

Tympanum. The eardrum.

Venter. The entire undersurface of an animal.

Ventral. Of or pertaining to the lower surface.

Vocal sac. An inflatable pouch on the throat or at the sides of the neck in male toads and frogs; single in most species, but paired in others.

Note: For the definition of other words and terms used in herpetology see: Peters, James A. *Dictionary of Herpetology.* New York: Hafner Publishing Co., 1964.

References

THIS *Field Guide* is designed to present general information about the reptiles and amphibians of our area, but limitations of space prohibit the inclusion of many details that would be of interest to persons wishing to know more about the herpetofauna of their home region or the places they visit on vacation. Many state, regional, and general books and booklets have been published, some of which are readily obtainable through any good bookstore. Others, especially those that are now out of print, must be sought by visiting your local library or the nearest zoo or natural history museum. The list below is a generally comprehensive review of the pertinent literature. It also includes a number of works that are in preparation as this book goes to press.

GENERAL

Bellairs, Angus. The Life of Reptiles. London: Weidenfeld and Nicolson, 1969. 2 vols.

Bishop, Sherman C. Handbook of Salamanders. Ithaca, N.Y.: Comstock, 1947.

Blair, Albert P., and Fred R. Cagle. Vertebrates of the United States, 2nd ed. New York: McGraw-Hill, 1968. (Sections on amphibians and reptiles.)

Carr, Archie. Handbook of Turtles. Ithaca, N.Y.: Cornell Univ. Press, 1952.

———. The Reptiles. New York: Time Inc., 1963.

Cochran, Doris M. Living Amphibians of the World. Garden City, N.Y.: Doubleday, 1961.

———, and Coleman J. Goin. The New Field Book of Reptiles and Amphibians. New York: Putnam, 1970.

Conant, Roger. Reptile Study (merit badge pamphlet). North Brunswick, N.J.: Boy Scouts of America, 1972.

Ernst, Carl H., and Roger W. Barbour. Turtles of the United States. Lexington: Univ. Press of Kentucky, 1973.

Goin, Coleman J., and Olive B. Goin. Introduction to Herpetology, 2nd ed. San Francisco: Freeman, 1971.

Harrison, Hal H. The World of the Snake. Philadelphia and New York: Lippincott, 1971.

Kauffeld, Carl. Snakes: The Keeper and the Kept. New York: Doubleday, 1969.

———. Snakes and Snake Hunting. Garden City, N.Y.: Hanover House, 1957.

Klauber, Laurence M. Rattlesnakes: Their Habits, Life Histories, and
    Influence on Mankind, 2nd ed. Berkeley and Los Angeles: U. of
    California Press, 1972. 2 vols.
Leviton, Alan E. Reptiles and Amphibians of North America. New
    York: Doubleday, 1972.
Minton, Sherman A., Jr., and Madge Rutherford Minton. Giant
    Reptiles. New York: Scribner's, 1973.
———. Venomous Reptiles. New York: Scribner's, 1969.
Oliver, James A. The Natural History of North American Amphibians
    and Reptiles. Princeton: Van Nostrand, 1955.
Pope, Clifford H. The Reptile World, New York: Knopf, 1955.
———. Snakes Alive and How They Live. New York: Viking, 1937.
———. Turtles of the United States & Canada. New York: Knopf,
    1939.
Porter, Kenneth R. Herpetology. Philadelphia: Saunders, 1972.
Pritchard, Peter C. H. Living Turtles of the World. New York:
    T. F. H. Publications, 1967.
Schmidt, Karl P. A Check List of North American Amphibians and
    Reptiles, 6th ed. Chicago: Amer. Soc. of Ichthyologists and Herpe-
    tologists, 1953.
———, and D. Dwight Davis. Field Book of Snakes of the United
    States and Canada. New York: Putnam, 1941.
———, and Robert F. Inger. Living Reptiles of the World. Garden
    City, N.Y.: Hanover House, 1957.
Smith, Hobart M. Handbook of Lizards. Ithaca, N.Y.: Comstock,
    1946.
Wright, Albert Hazen, and Anna Allen Wright. Handbook of Frogs
    and Toads of the United States and Canada, 3rd ed. Ithaca, N.Y.:
    Comstock, 1949.
———. Handbook of Snakes of the United States and Canada.
    Ithaca, N.Y.: Cornell Univ. Press, 1957. 3 vols. (including bibli-
    ography).
Zim, Herbert S., and Hobart M. Smith. Reptiles and Amphibians:
    A Guide to Familiar American Species. New York: Simon &
    Schuster, 1953.

REGIONAL

New England

Babcock, Harold L. Field Guide to New England Turtles. Boston:
    Natural History Guides, No. 2, New England Mus. of Nat. Hist.,
    1938.
———. The Snakes of New England. Boston: Natural History
    Guides, No. 1, Boston Soc. of Nat. Hist., 1929.
———. The Turtles of New England, Memoirs Boston Soc. of Nat.
    Hist., 8 (1919): 323–431.

Northeast

Conant, Roger. Reptiles and Amphibians of the Northeastern States,
    3rd ed. Philadelphia: Zool. Soc. of Philadelphia, 1957.
Pope, Clifford H. Snakes of the Northeastern United States. New
    York: New York Zool. Soc., 1946.

West

Shaw, Charles E., and Sheldon Campbell. Snakes of the American West. New York: Knopf, 1974.

Stebbins, Robert C. Amphibians and Reptiles of Western North America. New York: McGraw-Hill, 1954.

——. Amphibians of Western North America. Berkeley and Los Angeles: U. of California Press, 1951.

——. A Field Guide to Western Reptiles and Amphibians. Boston: Houghton Mifflin, 1966.

Canada

Bleakney, Sherman. The Amphibians and Reptiles of Nova Scotia. Canadian Field-Naturalist, 66 (1952): 125–29. Ottawa.

——. A Zoogeographical Study of the Amphibians and Reptiles of Eastern Canada. Ottawa: Natl. Mus. of Canada, Bull. No. 155, Biol. Ser. 54 (1958).

Cook, Francis R. An Analysis of the Herpetofauna of Prince Edward Island. Ottawa: Natl. Mus. of Canada, Bull. No. 212, Biol. Ser. 75 (1967).

Logier, E. B. S. The Frogs, Toads, and Salamanders of Eastern Canada. Toronto: Clarke, Irwin, 1952.

——. The Snakes of Ontario. Toronto: U. of Toronto Press, 1958.

——, and G. C. Toner. Check List of the Amphibians and Reptiles of Canada and Alaska. Toronto: Contrib. of the Royal Ontario Mus. of Zool. and Palaeon., No. 53 (1961).

Mexico

Smith, Hobart M., and Edward H. Taylor. Herpetology of Mexico: Annotated Checklists and Keys to the Amphibians and Reptiles. Ashton, Md.: Eric Lundberg (1966). (A reprint of Bulletins 187, 194, and 199 of the U.S. National Museum of Natural History with a list of subsequent taxonomic innovations.)

West Indies

Schwartz, Albert, and Richard Thomas. Checklist of West Indian Amphibians and Reptiles. Pittsburgh: Carnegie Museum. (In preparation.)

BY STATES

Alabama

Chermock, Ralph L. A Key to the Amphibians and Reptiles of Alabama. University, Ala.: Geol. Survey of Alabama, Museum Paper No. 33 (1952).

Mount, Robert H. Reptiles and Amphibians of Alabama. (In preparation.)

Arkansas

Dowling, Herndon G. A Review of the Amphibians and Reptiles of Arkansas. Fayetteville: U. of Arkansas Mus. Occasional Papers, No. 3 (1957).

Connecticut

Babbitt, Lewis Hall. The Amphibia of Connecticut. Hartford: State Geol. and Nat. Hist. Survey, Bull. No. 57 (1937).

Lamson, George Herbert. The Reptiles of Connecticut. Hartford: State Geol. and Nat. Hist. Survey, Bull. No. 54 (1935).

Petersen, Richard C. Connecticut's Venomous Snakes. Hartford: State Geol. and Nat. Hist. Survey, Bull. No. 103 (1970).

Delaware

Conant, Roger. Amphibians and Reptiles of New Jersey and the Delmarva Peninsula. (In preparation.)

———. An Annotated Check List of the Amphibians and Reptiles of the Del-Mar-Va Peninsula. Wilmington: Soc. of Nat. Hist. of Delaware, 1945.

Florida

Carr, Archie. A Contribution to the Herpetology of Florida. Gainesville: Univ. of Florida Pub., Vol. 3, No. 1 (1940).

———, and Coleman J. Goin. Guide to the Reptiles, Amphibians, and Fresh-water Fishes of Florida. Gainesville: U. of Florida Press, 1955.

Duellman, William E., and Albert Schwartz. Amphibians and Reptiles of Southern Florida, Bull. of the Florida State Mus., 3 (1958): 181–324. Gainesville.

Georgia

Martof, Bernard S. Amphibians and Reptiles of Georgia, A Guide. Athens: U. of Georgia Press, 1956.

Illinois

Cahn, Alvin R. The Turtles of Illinois. Urbana: U. of Illinois Bull., Vol. 35, No. 1 (1937).

Pope, Clifford H. Amphibians and Reptiles of the Chicago Area. Chicago: Chicago Nat. Hist. Mus., 1944.

Smith, Philip W. The Amphibians and Reptiles of Illinois. Urbana: Illinois Nat. Hist. Survey, Vol. 28, Art. 1, (1961).

Indiana

Minton, Sherman A., Jr., Amphibians and Reptiles of Indiana. Indianapolis: Indiana Academy of Sci., Monog. No. 3 (1972).

Iowa

Guthrie, J. E. The Snakes of Iowa. Ames: Iowa State College of Agric. and Mech. Arts, Agric. Experiment Station, Bull. No. 239 (1926).

Kansas

Collins, Joseph T. Amphibians and Reptiles in Kansas. Lawrence: U. of Kansas Mus. of Nat. Hist., 1974.

Smith, Hobart M. Handbook of Amphibians and Reptiles of Kansas, 2nd ed. Lawrence: U. of Kansas Mus. of Nat. Hist., Misc. Pub. No. 9 (1956).

Kentucky

Barbour, Roger W. Amphibians and Reptiles of Kentucky. Lexington: Univ. Press of Kentucky, 1971.

Louisiana

Dundee, Harold A. and Douglas A. Rossman. Amphibians and Reptiles of Louisiana. (In preparation.)

Keiser, Edmund D., Jr., and Larry David Wilson. Checklist and Key to the Herpetofauna of Louisiana. Lafayette: Lafayette Nat. Hist. Mus., Tech. Bull. No. 1 (1969).

Maryland

Harris, Herbert S., Jr. Distributional Survey: Maryland and the District of Columbia, Bull. of the Maryland Herpetological Soc., 5 (1969): 97–161. Baltimore.

Mansueti, Romeo. A Descriptive Catalogue of the Amphibians and Reptiles Found in and around Baltimore City, Maryland. Baltimore: Nat. Hist. Soc. of Maryland, Proc., No. 7 (1941).

McCauley, Robert H., Jr. The Reptiles of Maryland and the District of Columbia. Hagerstown, Md.: Published by the Author, 1945.

Michigan

Ruthven, Alexander G., Crystal Thompson, and Helen T. Gaige. The Herpetology of Michigan. Ann Arbor: University Museums, U. of Michigan, Handbook Ser., No. 3 (1928).

Minnesota

Breckenridge, W. J. Reptiles and Amphibians of Minnesota. Minneapolis: U. of Minnesota Press, 1970. 3rd printing.

Mississippi

Cook, Fannye A. Snakes of Mississippi (1954); Alligator and Lizards of Mississippi (1957); and Salamanders of Mississippi (1957). Jackson: Mississippi Game and Fish Commission.

Missouri

Anderson, Paul. The Reptiles of Missouri. Columbia: U. of Missouri Press, 1965.

Hurter, Julius, Sr. Herpetology of Missouri, Transactions of the Academy of Sci. of St. Louis, 20 (1911): 59–274.

Nebraska

Hudson, George E. The Amphibians and Reptiles of Nebraska. Lincoln: U. of Nebraska, Nebraska Conservation Bull. No. 24 (1942).

New Hampshire

Oliver, James A., and Joseph R. Bailey. Amphibians and Reptiles of New Hampshire, Biological Survey of the Connecticut Watershed, pp. 195–217 (1939). Concord.

New Jersey

Conant, Roger. Amphibians and Reptiles of New Jersey and the Delmarva Peninsula. (In preparation.)

Trapido, Harold. The Snakes of New Jersey: A Guide. Newark; Newark Mus., 1937.

New York

Bishop, Sherman C. The Salamanders of New York. Albany: U. of the State of New York, New York State Mus. Bull. No. 324 (1941).

North Carolina

Brimley, C. S. The Amphibians and Reptiles of North Carolina. Raleigh: Carolina Tips (printed by author in 32 installments, 1939 to 1943, inclusive).

Huheey, James E., and Arthur Stupka. Amphibians and Reptiles of Great Smoky Mountains National Park. Knoxville: U. of Tennessee Press, 1967.

Palmer, William M. Poisonous Snakes of North Carolina. Raleigh: State Mus. of Nat. Hist. (1974).

——— et al. Amphibians and Reptiles of North Carolina. (In preparation.)

North Dakota

Wheeler, George C., and Jeanette Wheeler. The Amphibians and Reptiles of North Dakota. Grand Forks: U. of North Dakota Press, 1966.

Ohio

Conant, Roger. The Reptiles of Ohio, 2nd ed. Notre Dame, Ind.: The American Midland Naturalist, 1951.

Walker, Charles F. The Amphibians of Ohio: Part I, The Frogs and Toads. Columbus: Ohio State Mus. Sci. Bull. Vol. 1, No. 3 (1946).

Oklahoma

Webb, Robert G. Reptiles of Oklahoma. Norman: U. of Oklahoma Press, 1970.

Pennsylvania

Harrison, Hal. H. Pennsylvania Reptiles & Amphibians. Harrisburg: Reprinted from the Pennsylvania Angler, Pennsylvania Fish Commission, 1949–50.

South Dakota

Fishbeck, Dale W., and James C. Underhill. A Check List of the Amphibians and Reptiles of South Dakota, Proceedings of the South Dakota Academy of Sci., 38 (1959): 107–113. Vermillion.

Over, William H. Amphibians and Reptiles of South Dakota. Vermillion: South Dakota Geol. and Nat. Hist. Survey, Bull. No. 12 (1923).

Tennessee

Gentry, Glenn. An Annotated Check List of the Amphibians and Reptiles of Tennessee, Journal of the Tennessee Academy of Sci., 30 (1955): 168–76 and 31 (1956): 242–51. Knoxville.

Huheey, James E., and Arthur Stupka. Amphibians and Reptiles of

Great Smoky Mountains National Park. Knoxville: U. of Tennessee Press, 1967.

Sinclair, Ralph, Will Hon, and Robert B. Ferguson. Amphibians and Reptiles of Tennessee. Nashville: Tennessee Game and Fish Commission, 1965.

Texas

Brown, Bryce C. An Annotated Check List of the Reptiles and Amphibians of Texas. Waco: Baylor Univ. Press, 1950.

Easterla, David A. The Amphibians and Reptiles of Big Bend National Park, Texas. Big Bend Natural History Association, 1975.

Raun, Gerald G. A Guide to Texas Snakes. Austin: Texas Memorial Mus. Museum Notes No. 9 (1965).

————, and Frederick R. Gehlbach. Amphibians and Reptiles in Texas. Dallas: Dallas Mus. of Nat. Hist. Bull. No. 2 (1972).

Virginia

Mitchell, Joseph C. The Snakes of Virginia. Richmond: Reprinted from Virginia Wildlife, Commission of Game and Inland Fisheries, February and April, 1974.

West Virginia

Green, N. Bayard. The Amphibians and Reptiles of West Virginia, Their Identification, Habits and Distribution. Huntington: Marshall College, 1954.

Wisconsin

Dickinson, W. E. Amphibians and Turtles of Wisconsin. Milwaukee Public Mus., Popular Science Handbook Series, No. 10 (1965).

————. Field Guide to the Lizards and Snakes of Wisconsin. Milwaukee: Milwaukee Public Mus., Popular Science Handbook Ser. No. 2 (1949).

Pope, T. E. B., and W. E. Dickinson. The Amphibians and Reptiles of Wisconsin. Milwaukee: Bull. of the Public Mus. of the City of Milwaukee, Vol. 8, No. 1 (1928).

IDENTIFICATION OF TADPOLES

Altig, Ronald. A Key to the Tadpoles of the Continental United States and Canada, Herpetologica, 26 (1970): 180–207. Lawrence, Kansas.

Orton, Grace L. Key to the Genera of Tadpoles in the United States and Canada, American Midland Naturalist, 47 (1952): 382–395. Notre Dame, Ind.

Stebbins, Robert L. A Field Guide to Western Reptiles and Amphibians. Boston: Houghton Mifflin, 1966. (A number of toads and frogs of our area have ranges extending into the western states; their tadpoles are illustrated in the western *Field Guide*.)

SOUND RECORDINGS OF FROG AND TOAD CALLS

Bogert, Charles M. Sounds of North American Frogs: the Biological

Significance of Voice in Frogs. New York: Folkways Records, 12"
LP record; 92 calls of 50 species of frogs and toads; accompanied
by a profusely illustrated essay on the subject.)

Kellogg, Peter Paul, and Arthur A. Allen. Voices of the Night. Boston: Houghton Mifflin for Cornell Laboratory of Ornithology in the
Sounds of Nature series. (12" LP record; calls of 34 kinds of toads
and frogs of eastern North America.)

Maps

Key to Symbols

✗ or ○		Isolated records.
?		Record questionable or data inadequate.
◀———		Indicates split range or localities apt to be overlooked.
— — — —		Boundary of range uncertain.
		Range boundaries of adjacent western or Mexican subspecies.

To delineate ranges of reptiles and amphibians that occur in the West Indies as well as in Florida, loops are drawn around the Bahamas and along the coasts of Cuba in several cases. These indicate that the species or subspecies in question also occurs on islets of the surrounding banks, which are too tiny to show on the maps.

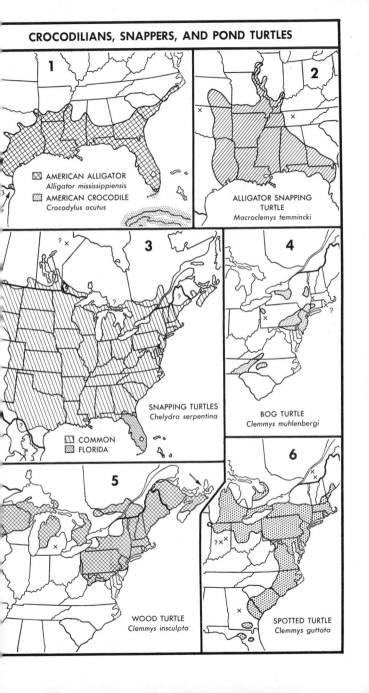

CROCODILIANS, SNAPPERS, AND POND TURTLES

1

☒ AMERICAN ALLIGATOR
Alligator mississippiensis
▦ AMERICAN CROCODILE
Crocodylus acutus

2

ALLIGATOR SNAPPING
TURTLE
Macroclemys temmincki

3

SNAPPING TURTLES
Chelydra serpentina

▨ COMMON
▦ FLORIDA

4

BOG TURTLE
Clemmys muhlenbergi

5

WOOD TURTLE
Clemmys insculpta

6

SPOTTED TURTLE
Clemmys guttata

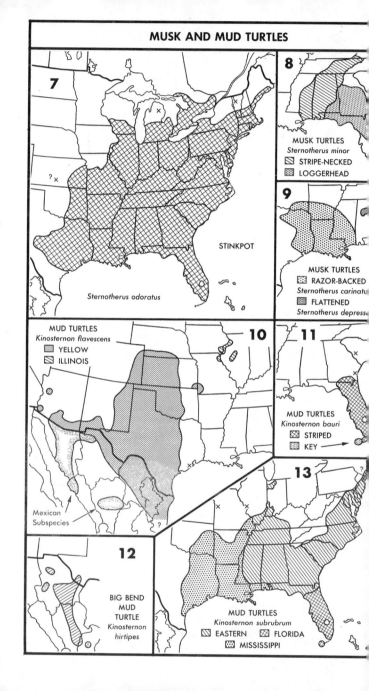

MUSK AND MUD TURTLES

7

STINKPOT

Sternotherus odoratus

8

MUSK TURTLES
Sternotherus minor
⊠ STRIPE-NECKED
▦ LOGGERHEAD

9

MUSK TURTLES
▦ RAZOR-BACKED
Sternotherus carinatus
⊠ FLATTENED
Sternotherus depressus

10

MUD TURTLES
Kinosternon flavescens
▦ YELLOW
⊠ ILLINOIS

Mexican
Subspecies

11

MUD TURTLES
Kinosternon bauri
▦ STRIPED
▦ KEY →

12

BIG BEND
MUD
TURTLE
*Kinosternon
hirtipes*

13

MUD TURTLES
Kinosternon subrubrum
⊠ EASTERN   ▦ FLORIDA
▦ MISSISSIPPI

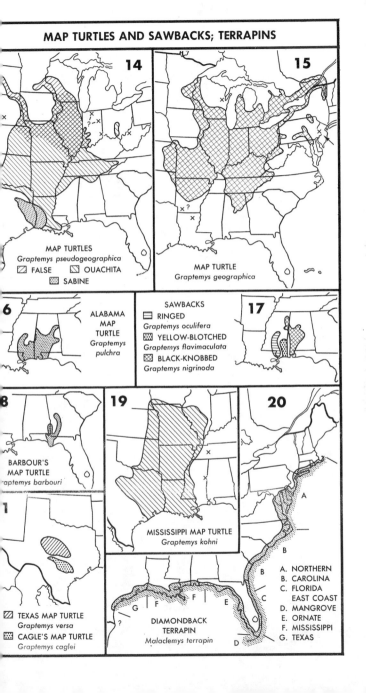

MAP TURTLES AND SAWBACKS; TERRAPINS

14

MAP TURTLES
Graptemys pseudogeographica
☐ FALSE ☐ OUACHITA
☐ SABINE

15

MAP TURTLE
Graptemys geographica

16

ALABAMA
MAP
TURTLE
Graptemys pulchra

17

SAWBACKS
☐ RINGED
Graptemys oculifera
☐ YELLOW-BLOTCHED
Graptemys flavimaculata
☐ BLACK-KNOBBED
Graptemys nigrinoda

18

BARBOUR'S
MAP TURTLE
Graptemys barbouri

21

☐ TEXAS MAP TURTLE
Graptemys versa
☐ CAGLE'S MAP TURTLE
Graptemys caglei

19

MISSISSIPPI MAP TURTLE
Graptemys kohni

20

A. NORTHERN
B. CAROLINA
C. FLORIDA
   EAST COAST
D. MANGROVE
E. ORNATE
F. MISSISSIPPI
G. TEXAS

DIAMONDBACK
TERRAPIN
Malaclemys terrapin

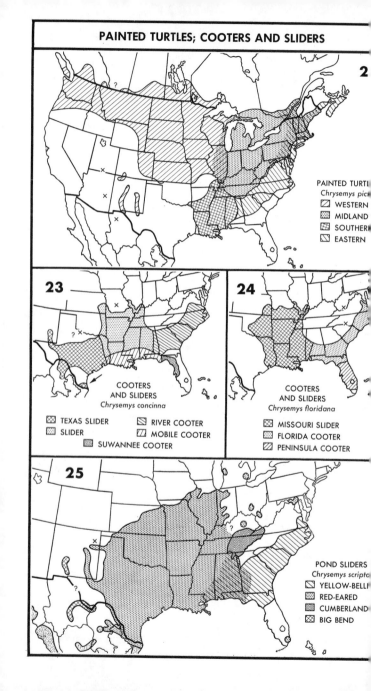

PAINTED TURTLES; COOTERS AND SLIDERS

2

PAINTED TURTLES
Chrysemys picta
- WESTERN
- MIDLAND
- SOUTHERN
- EASTERN

23

COOTERS
AND SLIDERS
Chrysemys concinna

- TEXAS SLIDER
- SLIDER
- SUWANNEE COOTER
- RIVER COOTER
- MOBILE COOTER

24

COOTERS
AND SLIDERS
Chrysemys floridana

- MISSOURI SLIDER
- FLORIDA COOTER
- PENINSULA COOTER

25

POND SLIDERS
Chrysemys scripta
- YELLOW-BELLIED
- RED-EARED
- CUMBERLAND
- BIG BEND

BOX, BLANDING'S, AND RED-BELLIED TURTLES

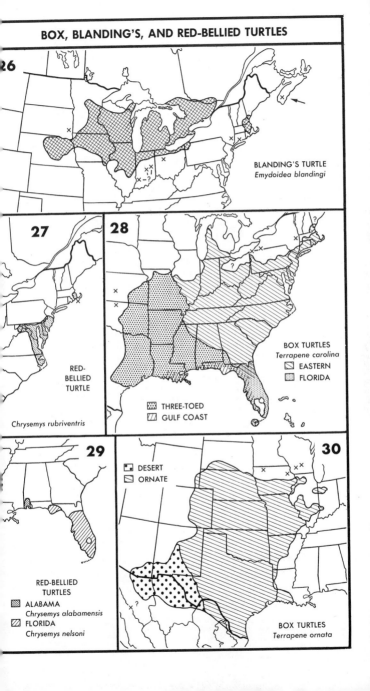

26
BLANDING'S TURTLE
Emydoidea blandingi

27
RED-BELLIED TURTLE
Chrysemys rubriventris

28
BOX TURTLES
Terrapene carolina
◨ EASTERN
▨ FLORIDA
▦ THREE-TOED
▧ GULF COAST

29
RED-BELLIED TURTLES
▨ ALABAMA
Chrysemys alabamensis
▨ FLORIDA
Chrysemys nelsoni

30
▪ DESERT
◨ ORNATE
BOX TURTLES
Terrapene ornata

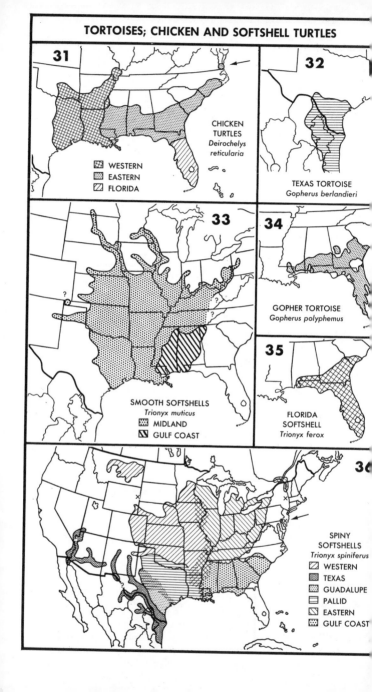

TORTOISES; CHICKEN AND SOFTSHELL TURTLES

31

CHICKEN
TURTLES
*Deirochelys
reticularia*

- ▨ WESTERN
- ▨ EASTERN
- ▨ FLORIDA

32

TEXAS TORTOISE
Gopherus berlandieri

33

SMOOTH SOFTSHELLS
Trionyx muticus
- ▨ MIDLAND
- ▨ GULF COAST

34

GOPHER TORTOISE
Gopherus polyphemus

35

FLORIDA
SOFTSHELL
Trionyx ferox

36

SPINY
SOFTSHELLS
Trionyx spiniferus
- ▨ WESTERN
- ▨ TEXAS
- ▨ GUADALUPE
- ▨ PALLID
- ▨ EASTERN
- ▨ GULF COAST

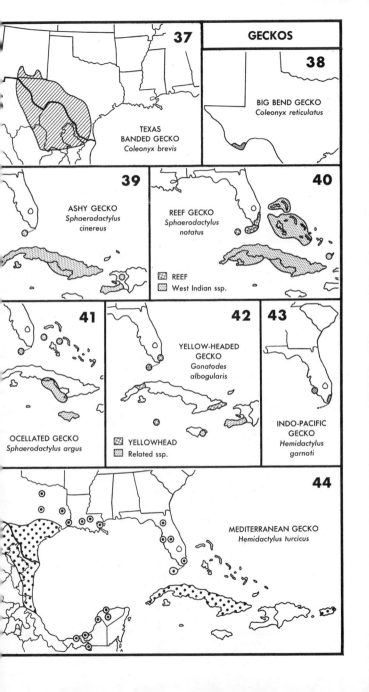

GECKOS

37

38
BIG BEND GECKO
Coleonyx reticulatus

TEXAS
BANDED GECKO
Coleonyx brevis

39
ASHY GECKO
Sphaerodactylus cinereus

40
REEF GECKO
Sphaerodactylus notatus

▨ REEF
▧ West Indian ssp.

41
OCELLATED GECKO
Sphaerodactylus argus

42
YELLOW-HEADED GECKO
Gonatodes albogularis

▨ YELLOWHEAD
▧ Related ssp.

43
INDO-PACIFIC GECKO
Hemidactylus garnoti

44
MEDITERRANEAN GECKO
Hemidactylus turcicus

ANOLES; COLLARED LIZARDS

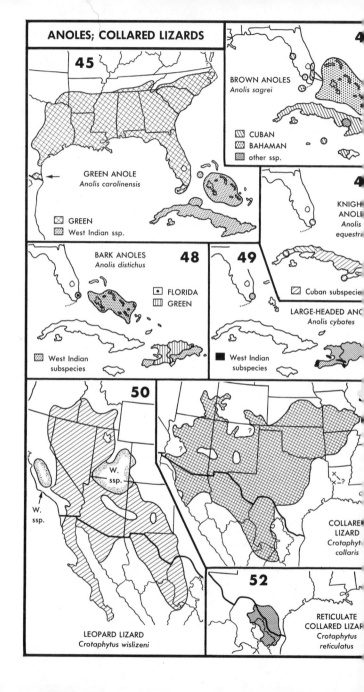

45

GREEN ANOLE
Anolis carolinensis

- ⊠ GREEN
- ▧ West Indian ssp.

4

BROWN ANOLES
Anolis sagrei

- ▨ CUBAN
- ▩ BAHAMAN
- ▧ other ssp.

4

KNIGH
ANOLE
*Anolis
equestr*

48

BARK ANOLES
Anolis distichus

- ⊡ FLORIDA
- ▦ GREEN

- ▨ West Indian subspecies

49

- ▨ Cuban subspecie

LARGE-HEADED ANC
Anolis cybotes

- ■ West Indian subspecies

50

W. ssp.

W. ssp.

LEOPARD LIZARD
Crotaphytus wislizeni

COLLARE
LIZARD
*Crotaphyt
collaris*

52

RETICULATE
COLLARED LIZAR
*Crotaphytus
reticulatus*

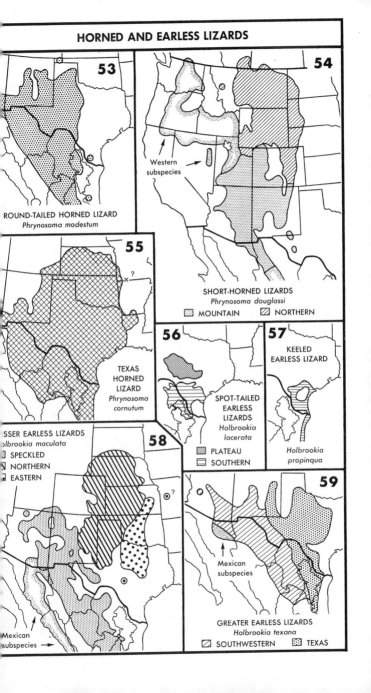

HORNED AND EARLESS LIZARDS

53

ROUND-TAILED HORNED LIZARD
Phrynosoma modestum

54

Western subspecies

SHORT-HORNED LIZARDS
Phrynosoma douglassi

▨ MOUNTAIN   ▨ NORTHERN

55

TEXAS
HORNED
LIZARD
*Phrynosoma
cornutum*

56

57

KEELED
EARLESS LIZARD

SPOT-TAILED
EARLESS
LIZARDS
*Holbrookia
lacerata*

▨ PLATEAU
☰ SOUTHERN

*Holbrookia
propinqua*

SSER EARLESS LIZARDS
olbrookia maculata

▨ SPECKLED
▨ NORTHERN
▨ EASTERN

58

⊙?

Mexican
subspecies →

59

Mexican
subspecies

GREATER EARLESS LIZARDS
Holbrookia texana

▨ SOUTHWESTERN   ▨ TEXAS

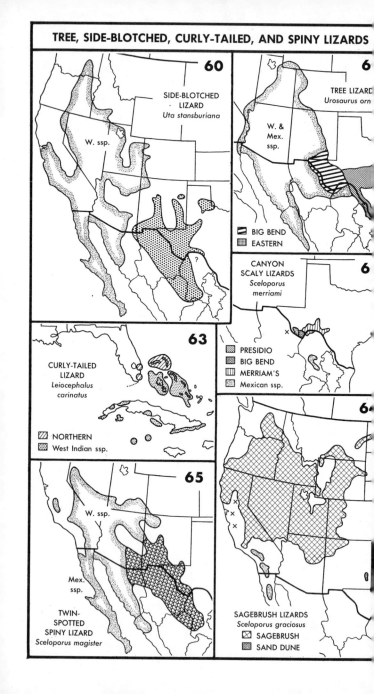

TREE, SIDE-BLOTCHED, CURLY-TAILED, AND SPINY LIZARDS

60

SIDE-BLOTCHED
LIZARD
Uta stansburiana

W. ssp.

?

6

TREE LIZARD
Urosaurus orn

W. &
Mex.
ssp.

▨ BIG BEND
▦ EASTERN

CANYON
SCALY LIZARDS
*Sceloporus
merriami*

6

▨ PRESIDIO
▨ BIG BEND
▥ MERRIAM'S
▨ Mexican ssp.

63

CURLY-TAILED
LIZARD
*Leiocephalus
carinatus*

▨ NORTHERN
▨ West Indian ssp.

65

W. ssp.

Mex.
ssp.

TWIN-
SPOTTED
SPINY LIZARD
Sceloporus magister

6

SAGEBRUSH LIZARDS
Sceloporus graciosus
⊠ SAGEBRUSH
▨ SAND DUNE

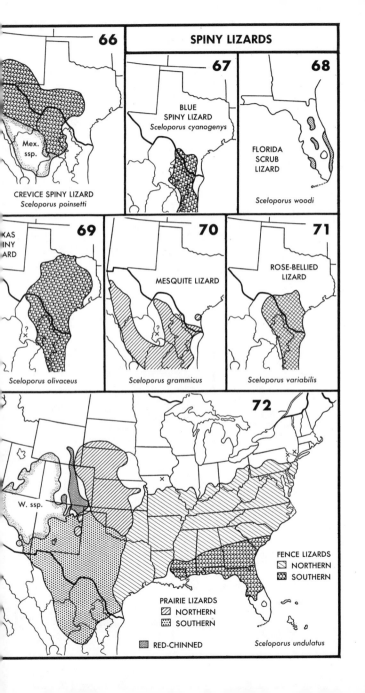

SPINY LIZARDS

66 CREVICE SPINY LIZARD
Sceloporus poinsetti
Mex. ssp.

67 BLUE SPINY LIZARD
Sceloporus cyanogenys

68 FLORIDA SCRUB LIZARD
Sceloporus woodi

69 XAS ︱INY ︱ARD
Sceloporus olivaceus

70 MESQUITE LIZARD
Sceloporus grammicus

71 ROSE-BELLIED LIZARD
Sceloporus variabilis

72
W. ssp.

FENCE LIZARDS
▧ NORTHERN
▨ SOUTHERN

PRAIRIE LIZARDS
▨ NORTHERN
▨ SOUTHERN

▨ RED-CHINNED

Sceloporus undulatus

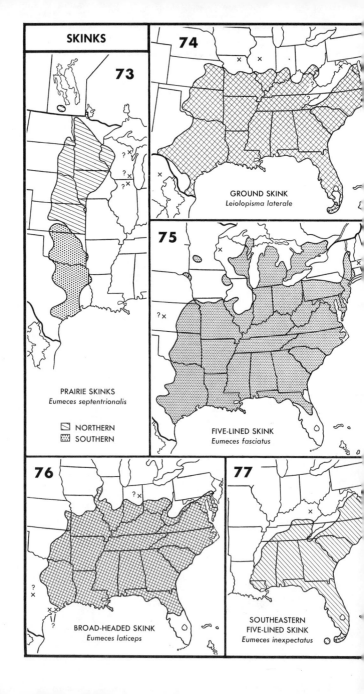

SKINKS

73

PRAIRIE SKINKS
Eumeces septentrionalis

◨ NORTHERN
▨ SOUTHERN

74

GROUND SKINK
Leiolopisma laterale

75

FIVE-LINED SKINK
Eumeces fasciatus

76

BROAD-HEADED SKINK
Eumeces laticeps

77

**SOUTHEASTERN
FIVE-LINED SKINK**
Eumeces inexpectatus

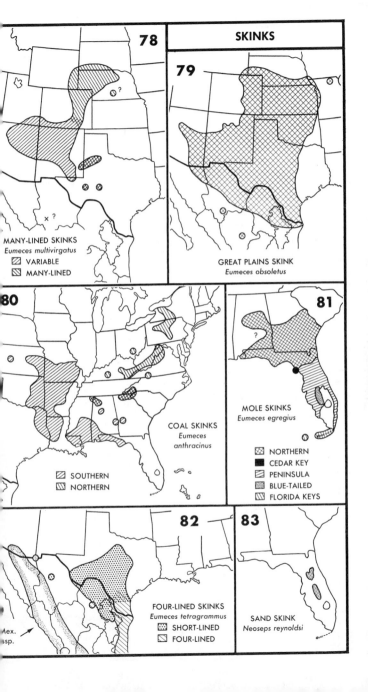

78

MANY-LINED SKINKS
Eumeces multivirgatus
▨ VARIABLE
▨ MANY-LINED

SKINKS

79

GREAT PLAINS SKINK
Eumeces obsoletus

80

COAL SKINK
Eumeces anthracinus
▨ SOUTHERN
▨ NORTHERN

81

MOLE SKINKS
Eumeces egregius
▨ NORTHERN
■ CEDAR KEY
▨ PENINSULA
▨ BLUE-TAILED
▨ FLORIDA KEYS

82

FOUR-LINED SKINKS
Eumeces tetragrammus
▨ SHORT-LINED
▨ FOUR-LINED

Mex.
ssp.

83

SAND SKINK
Neoseps reynoldsi

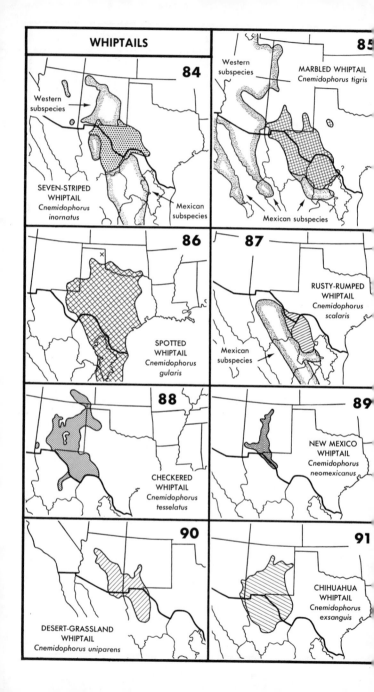

WHIPTAILS

84 Western subspecies

SEVEN-STRIPED WHIPTAIL
Cnemidophorus inornatus

Mexican subspecies

85 Western subspecies

MARBLED WHIPTAIL
Cnemidophorus tigris

Mexican subspecies

86 ×

SPOTTED WHIPTAIL
Cnemidophorus gularis

87

RUSTY-RUMPED WHIPTAIL
Cnemidophorus scalaris

Mexican subspecies

88

CHECKERED WHIPTAIL
Cnemidophorus tesselatus

89

NEW MEXICO WHIPTAIL
Cnemidophorus neomexicanus

90

DESERT-GRASSLAND WHIPTAIL
Cnemidophorus uniparens

91

CHIHUAHUA WHIPTAIL
Cnemidophorus exsanguis

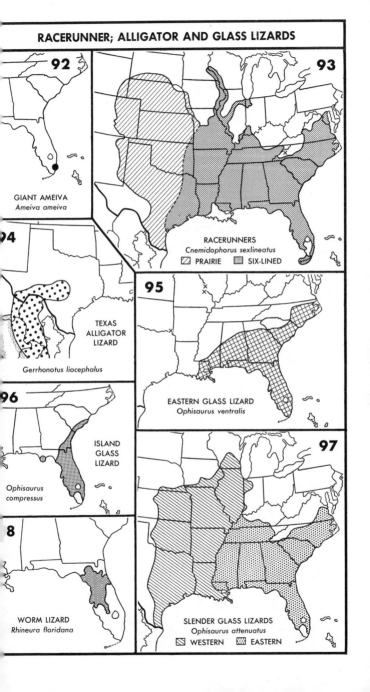

RACERUNNER; ALLIGATOR AND GLASS LIZARDS

92

GIANT AMEIVA
Ameiva ameiva

93

RACERUNNERS
Cnemidophorus sexlineatus
▨ PRAIRIE ▦ SIX-LINED

94

TEXAS ALLIGATOR LIZARD

Gerrhonotus liocephalus

95

EASTERN GLASS LIZARD
Ophisaurus ventralis

96

ISLAND GLASS LIZARD

Ophisaurus compressus

8

WORM LIZARD
Rhineura floridana

97

SLENDER GLASS LIZARDS
Ophisaurus attenuatus
◨ WESTERN ▨ EASTERN

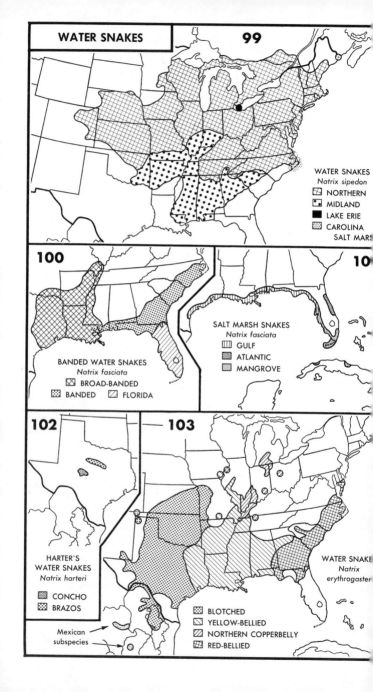

WATER SNAKES 99

WATER SNAKES
Natrix sipedon
▨ NORTHERN
⊡ MIDLAND
■ LAKE ERIE
▦ CAROLINA
SALT MARS

100

BANDED WATER SNAKES
Natrix fasciata
⊠ BROAD-BANDED
▩ BANDED ⧄ FLORIDA

10

SALT MARSH SNAKES
Natrix fasciata
⫴ GULF
▩ ATLANTIC
▦ MANGROVE

102

HARTER'S
WATER SNAKES
Natrix harteri
▨ CONCHO
⊠ BRAZOS

Mexican
subspecies

103

WATER SNAKE
*Natrix
erythrogaster*

▩ BLOTCHED
⧄ YELLOW-BELLIED
▨ NORTHERN COPPERBELLY
⧉ RED-BELLIED

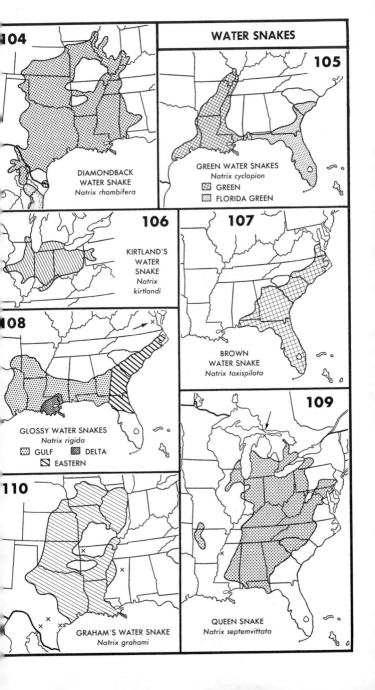

104

DIAMONDBACK
WATER SNAKE
Natrix rhombifera

WATER SNAKES

105

GREEN WATER SNAKES
Natrix cyclopion

▨ GREEN
▦ FLORIDA GREEN

106

KIRTLAND'S
WATER
SNAKE
*Natrix
kirtlandi*

107

BROWN
WATER SNAKE
Natrix taxispilota

108

GLOSSY WATER SNAKES
Natrix rigida

▦ GULF   ▨ DELTA
◩ EASTERN

109

QUEEN SNAKE
Natrix septemvittata

110

GRAHAM'S WATER SNAKE
Natrix grahami

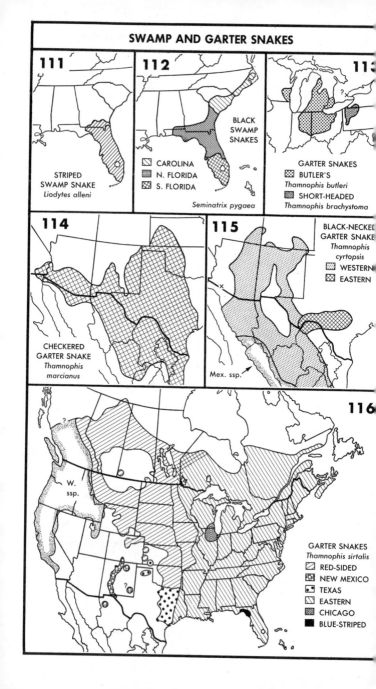

SWAMP AND GARTER SNAKES

111 STRIPED SWAMP SNAKE *Liodytes alleni*

112 BLACK SWAMP SNAKES
◪ CAROLINA
▦ N. FLORIDA
◩ S. FLORIDA
Seminatrix pygaea

113 GARTER SNAKES
▨ BUTLER'S *Thamnophis butleri*
▨ SHORT-HEADED *Thamnophis brachystoma*

114 CHECKERED GARTER SNAKE *Thamnophis marcianus*

115 BLACK-NECKED GARTER SNAKE *Thamnophis cyrtopsis*
▨ WESTERN
▨ EASTERN
Mex. ssp.

116 GARTER SNAKES *Thamnophis sirtalis*
◨ RED-SIDED
▥ NEW MEXICO
▦ TEXAS
◫ EASTERN
▨ CHICAGO
◼ BLUE-STRIPED
W. ssp.

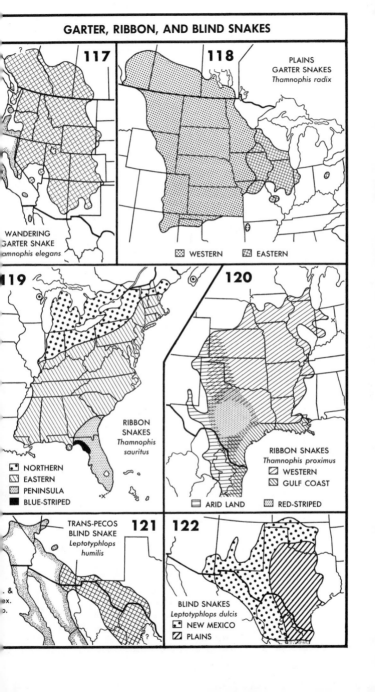

GARTER, RIBBON, AND BLIND SNAKES

117

WANDERING
GARTER SNAKE
Thamnophis elegans

118

PLAINS
GARTER SNAKES
Thamnophis radix

⊠ WESTERN   ⊠ EASTERN

119

RIBBON
SNAKES
*Thamnophis
sauritus*

⊡ NORTHERN
⊠ EASTERN
⊠ PENINSULA
■ BLUE-STRIPED

120

RIBBON SNAKES
Thamnophis proximus
⊘ WESTERN
⊠ GULF COAST

⊟ ARID LAND   ⊞ RED-STRIPED

121

TRANS-PECOS
BLIND SNAKE
*Leptotyphlops
humilis*

122

BLIND SNAKES
Leptotyphlops dulcis
⊡ NEW MEXICO
⊘ PLAINS

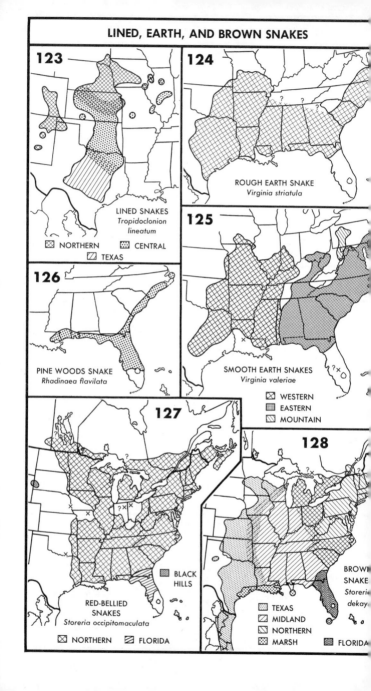

LINED, EARTH, AND BROWN SNAKES

123

LINED SNAKES
Tropidoclonion lineatum

⊠ NORTHERN   ⊞ CENTRAL
▨ TEXAS

124

ROUGH EARTH SNAKE
Virginia striatula

125

SMOOTH EARTH SNAKES
Virginia valeriae

⊠ WESTERN
▦ EASTERN
▧ MOUNTAIN

126

PINE WOODS SNAKE
Rhadinaea flavilata

127

RED-BELLIED
SNAKES
Storeria occipitomaculata

⊠ NORTHERN   ▨ FLORIDA

▤ BLACK
HILLS

128

BROWN
SNAKE
*Storeria
dekayi*

▤ TEXAS
▨ MIDLAND
▧ NORTHERN
⊠ MARSH

▨ FLORIDA

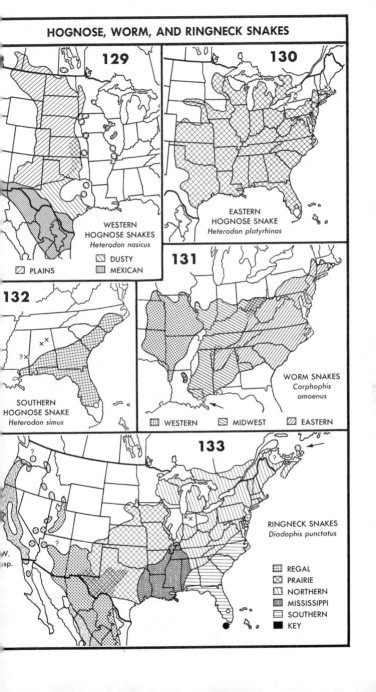

HOGNOSE, WORM, AND RINGNECK SNAKES

129

WESTERN
HOGNOSE SNAKES
Heterodon nasicus

PLAINS   DUSTY
MEXICAN

130

EASTERN
HOGNOSE SNAKE
Heterodon platyrhinos

131

WORM SNAKES
Carphophis amoenus

WESTERN   MIDWEST   EASTERN

132

SOUTHERN
HOGNOSE SNAKE
Heterodon simus

133

RINGNECK SNAKES
Diadophis punctatus

REGAL
PRAIRIE
NORTHERN
MISSISSIPPI
SOUTHERN
KEY

W.
sp.

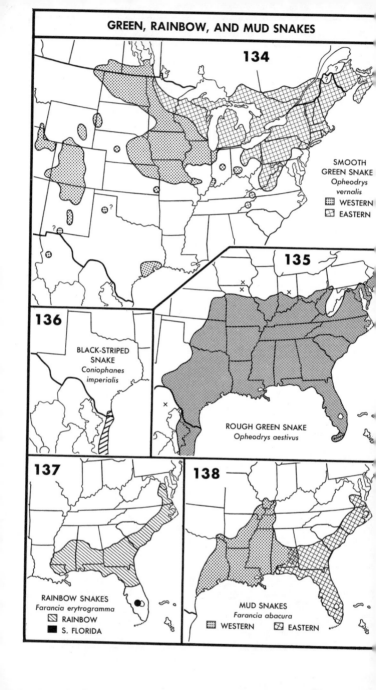

GREEN, RAINBOW, AND MUD SNAKES

134

SMOOTH
GREEN SNAKE
*Opheodrys
vernalis*
⊞ WESTERN
▨ EASTERN

135

ROUGH GREEN SNAKE
Opheodrys aestivus

136

BLACK-STRIPED
SNAKE
*Coniophanes
imperialis*

137

RAINBOW SNAKES
Farancia erytrogramma
▨ RAINBOW
■ S. FLORIDA

138

MUD SNAKES
Farancia abacura
⊞ WESTERN
▨ EASTERN

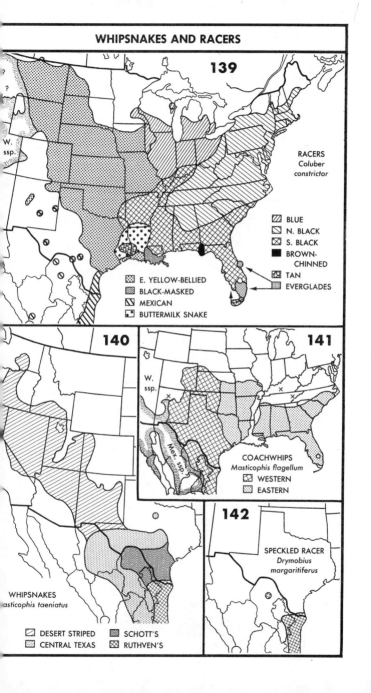

WHIPSNAKES AND RACERS

139

RACERS
*Coluber
constrictor*

W.
ssp.

	BLUE
	N. BLACK
	S. BLACK
	BROWN-CHINNED
	TAN
	EVERGLADES

	E. YELLOW-BELLIED
	BLACK-MASKED
	MEXICAN
	BUTTERMILK SNAKE

140

141

W.
ssp.

Mex. ssp.

COACHWHIPS
Masticophis flagellum
	WESTERN
	EASTERN

142

SPECKLED RACER
*Drymobius
margaritiferus*

WHIPSNAKES
Masticophis taeniatus

	DESERT STRIPED		SCHOTT'S
	CENTRAL TEXAS		RUTHVEN'S

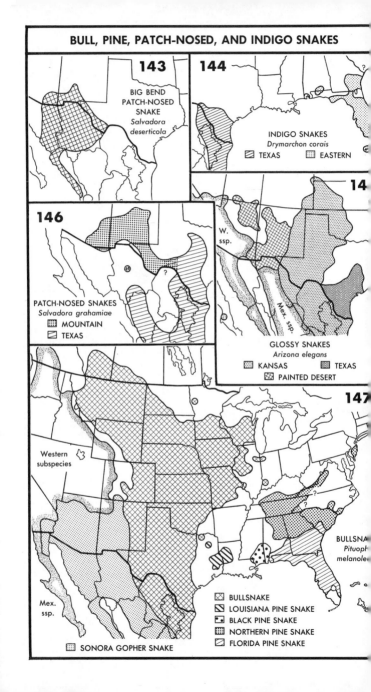

BULL, PINE, PATCH-NOSED, AND INDIGO SNAKES

143
BIG BEND
PATCH-NOSED
SNAKE
*Salvadora
deserticola*

144
INDIGO SNAKES
Drymarchon corais
⊟ TEXAS   ⊞ EASTERN

14
W.
ssp.

Mex. ssp.

GLOSSY SNAKES
Arizona elegans
⊞ KANSAS   ⊟ TEXAS
⊠ PAINTED DESERT

146
PATCH-NOSED SNAKES
Salvadora grahamiae
⊞ MOUNTAIN
⊟ TEXAS
?

147
Western
subspecies

Mex.
ssp.

BULLSNA
*Pituoph
melanole*

⊠ BULLSNAKE
◣ LOUISIANA PINE SNAKE
⬛ BLACK PINE SNAKE
⊞ NORTHERN PINE SNAKE
⊟ FLORIDA PINE SNAKE

⊞ SONORA GOPHER SNAKE

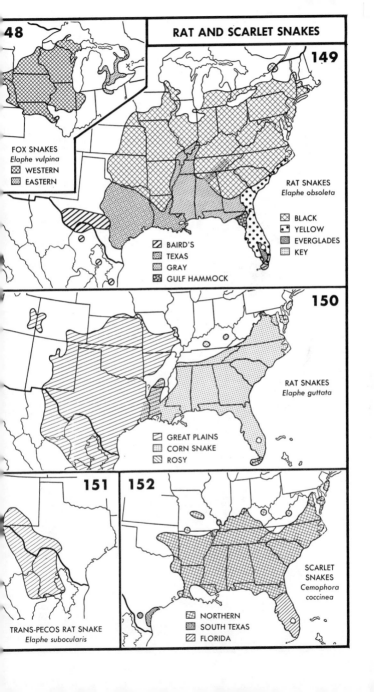

48

RAT AND SCARLET SNAKES

149

FOX SNAKES
Elaphe vulpina
⊠ WESTERN
▨ EASTERN

RAT SNAKES
Elaphe obsoleta

⊠ BLACK
⦂ YELLOW
▨ EVERGLADES
▦ KEY

⧄ BAIRD'S
▨ TEXAS
▨ GRAY
⊠ GULF HAMMOCK

150

RAT SNAKES
Elaphe guttata

⧄ GREAT PLAINS
▨ CORN SNAKE
⧅ ROSY

151

TRANS-PECOS RAT SNAKE
Elaphe subocularis

152

SCARLET
SNAKES
*Cemophora
coccinea*

▨ NORTHERN
▨ SOUTH TEXAS
⧄ FLORIDA

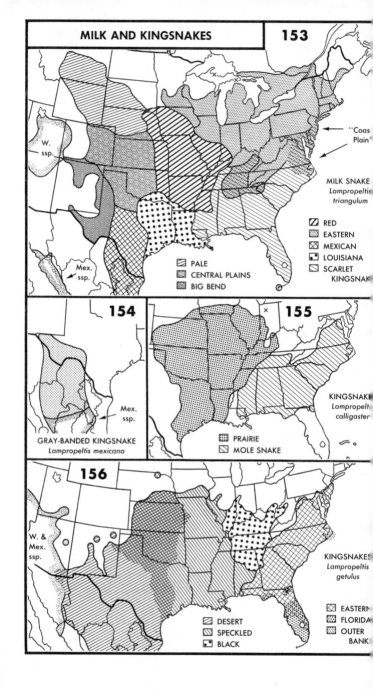

MILK AND KINGSNAKES   **153**

W. ssp.

→ "Coas Plain"

Mex. ssp.

MILK SNAKE
Lampropeltis triangulum

▨ RED
▩ EASTERN
⊠ MEXICAN
⊡ LOUISIANA
◩ SCARLET KINGSNAK

▨ PALE
▩ CENTRAL PLAINS
▧ BIG BEND

154

Mex. ssp. →

GRAY-BANDED KINGSNAKE
Lampropeltis mexicana

× **155**

KINGSNAK
Lampropelt calligaster

⊞ PRAIRIE
◪ MOLE SNAKE

156

W. & Mex. ssp.

KINGSNAKES
Lampropeltis getulus

▨ DESERT
◪ SPECKLED
⊡ BLACK

⊠ EASTERN
▦ FLORIDA
▦ OUTER BANK

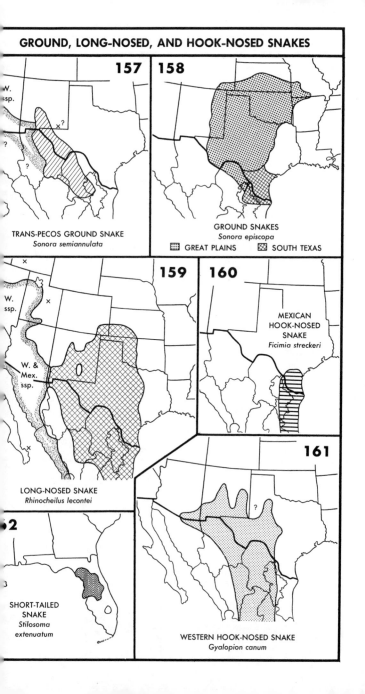

GROUND, LONG-NOSED, AND HOOK-NOSED SNAKES

157

W.
ssp.

x?

?

?

TRANS-PECOS GROUND SNAKE
Sonora semiannulata

158

GROUND SNAKES
Sonora episcopa
▦ GREAT PLAINS   ▨ SOUTH TEXAS

159

×

×

W.
ssp.

W. &
Mex.
ssp.

×

LONG-NOSED SNAKE
Rhinocheilus lecontei

160

MEXICAN
HOOK-NOSED
SNAKE
Ficimia streckeri

161

?

WESTERN HOOK-NOSED SNAKE
Gyalopion canum

2

SHORT-TAILED
SNAKE
*Stilosoma
extenuatum*

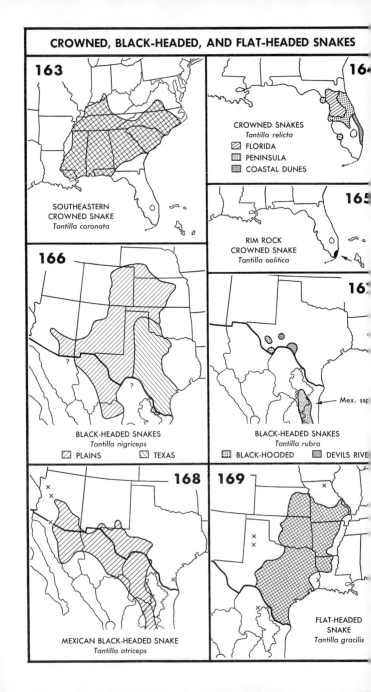

CROWNED, BLACK-HEADED, AND FLAT-HEADED SNAKES

163

SOUTHEASTERN
CROWNED SNAKE
Tantilla coronata

164

CROWNED SNAKES
Tantilla relicta
▨ FLORIDA
▦ PENINSULA
▨ COASTAL DUNES

165

RIM ROCK
CROWNED SNAKE
Tantilla oolitica

166

BLACK-HEADED SNAKES
Tantilla nigriceps
▨ PLAINS   ▨ TEXAS

167

BLACK-HEADED SNAKES
Tantilla rubra
▦ BLACK-HOODED   ▨ DEVILS RIVE

← Mex. ssp

168

MEXICAN BLACK-HEADED SNAKE
Tantilla atriceps

169

FLAT-HEADED
SNAKE
Tantilla gracilis

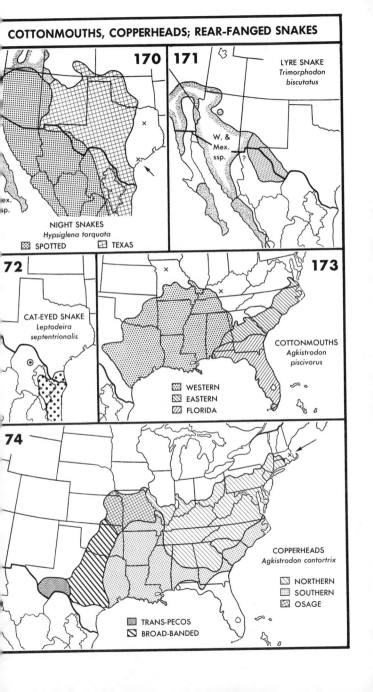

COTTONMOUTHS, COPPERHEADS; REAR-FANGED SNAKES

170

171

LYRE SNAKE
*Trimorphodon
biscutatus*

W. &
Mex.
ssp.
?

NIGHT SNAKES
Hypsiglena torquata

⬚ SPOTTED ⬚ TEXAS

72

CAT-EYED SNAKE
*Leptodeira
septentrionalis*

173

COTTONMOUTHS
*Agkistrodon
piscivorus*

⬚ WESTERN
⬚ EASTERN
⬚ FLORIDA

74

COPPERHEADS
Agkistrodon contortrix

⬚ NORTHERN
⬚ SOUTHERN
⬚ OSAGE

⬚ TRANS-PECOS
⬚ BROAD-BANDED

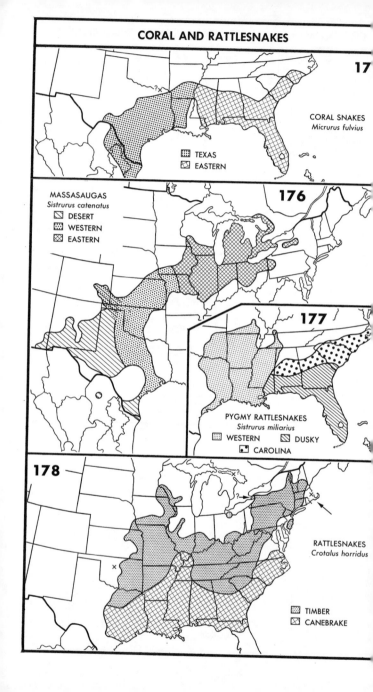

CORAL AND RATTLESNAKES

17

CORAL SNAKES
Micrurus fulvius

▦ TEXAS
▧ EASTERN

176

MASSASAUGAS
Sistrurus catenatus
▨ DESERT
▦ WESTERN
▨ EASTERN

177

PYGMY RATTLESNAKES
Sistrurus miliarius
▦ WESTERN   ▧ DUSKY
▪ CAROLINA

178

RATTLESNAKES
Crotalus horridus

▦ TIMBER
▧ CANEBRAKE

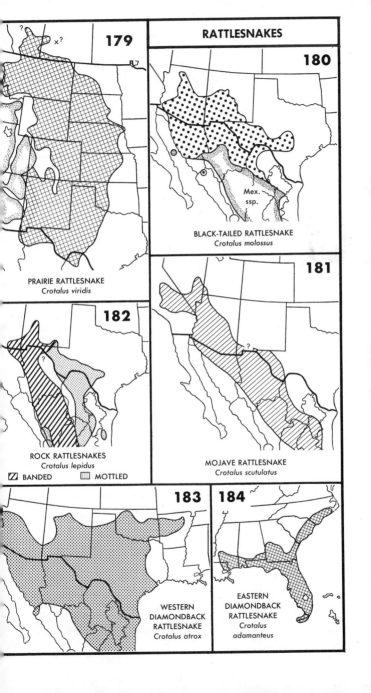

RATTLESNAKES

179

180

PRAIRIE RATTLESNAKE
Crotalus viridis

BLACK-TAILED RATTLESNAKE
Crotalus molossus

Mex.
ssp.

182

181

ROCK RATTLESNAKES
Crotalus lepidus
🔲 BANDED   ▦ MOTTLED

MOJAVE RATTLESNAKE
Crotalus scutulatus

183   **184**

WESTERN
DIAMONDBACK
RATTLESNAKE
Crotalus atrox

EASTERN
DIAMONDBACK
RATTLESNAKE
*Crotalus
adamanteus*

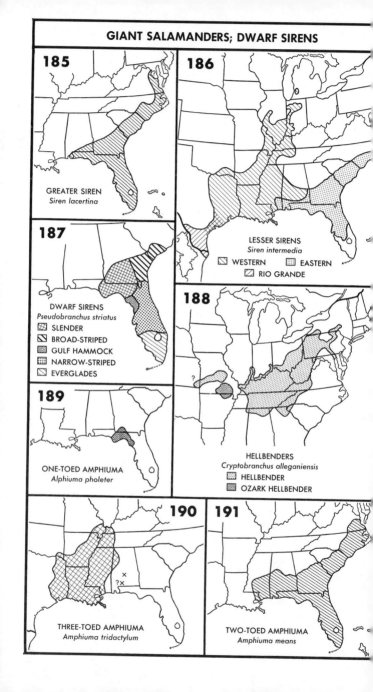

GIANT SALAMANDERS; DWARF SIRENS

185
GREATER SIREN
Siren lacertina

186
LESSER SIRENS
Siren intermedia
◨ WESTERN   ▦ EASTERN
◪ RIO GRANDE

187
DWARF SIRENS
Pseudobranchus striatus
▦ SLENDER
◩ BROAD-STRIPED
◪ GULF HAMMOCK
▦ NARROW-STRIPED
◩ EVERGLADES

188
HELLBENDERS
Cryptobranchus alleganiensis
▦ HELLBENDER
◩ OZARK HELLBENDER

189
ONE-TOED AMPHIUMA
Alphiuma pholeter

190
THREE-TOED AMPHIUMA
Amphiuma tridactylum

191
TWO-TOED AMPHIUMA
Amphiuma means

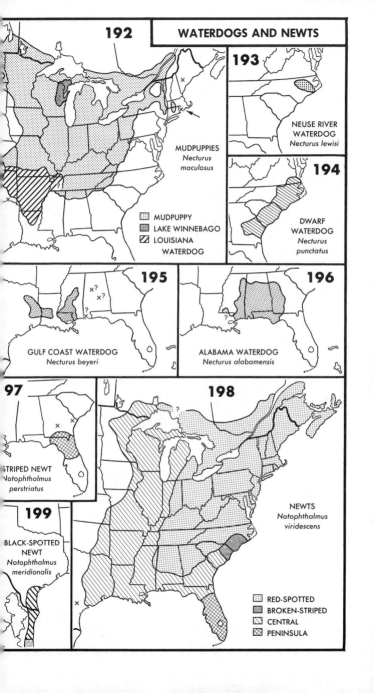

192 | **WATERDOGS AND NEWTS**

MUDPUPPIES
Necturus maculosus

▢ MUDPUPPY
▨ LAKE WINNEBAGO
⧄ LOUISIANA WATERDOG

193
NEUSE RIVER WATERDOG
Necturus lewisi

194
DWARF WATERDOG
Necturus punctatus

195
GULF COAST WATERDOG
Necturus beyeri

196
ALABAMA WATERDOG
Necturus alabamensis

197
STRIPED NEWT
Notophthalmus perstriatus

199
BLACK-SPOTTED NEWT
Notophthalmus meridionalis

198
NEWTS
Notophthalmus viridescens

▢ RED-SPOTTED
▨ BROKEN-STRIPED
⧄ CENTRAL
▧ PENINSULA

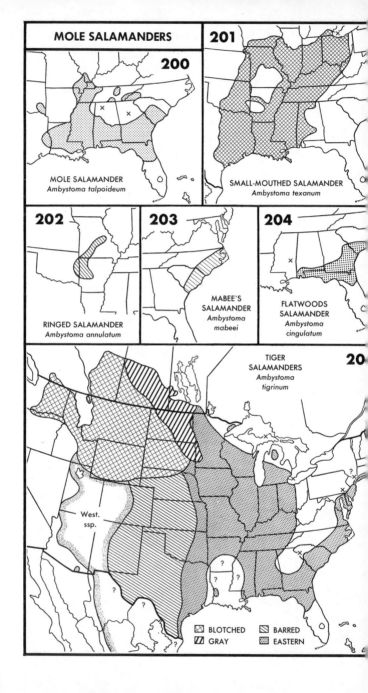

MOLE SALAMANDERS

200

MOLE SALAMANDER
Ambystoma talpoideum

201

SMALL-MOUTHED SALAMANDER
Ambystoma texanum

202

RINGED SALAMANDER
Ambystoma annulatum

203

MABEE'S
SALAMANDER
*Ambystoma
mabeei*

204

FLATWOODS
SALAMANDER
*Ambystoma
cingulatum*

TIGER
SALAMANDERS
*Ambystoma
tigrinum*

20

West.
ssp.

▨ BLOTCHED   ◪ BARRED
▨ GRAY   ▧ EASTERN

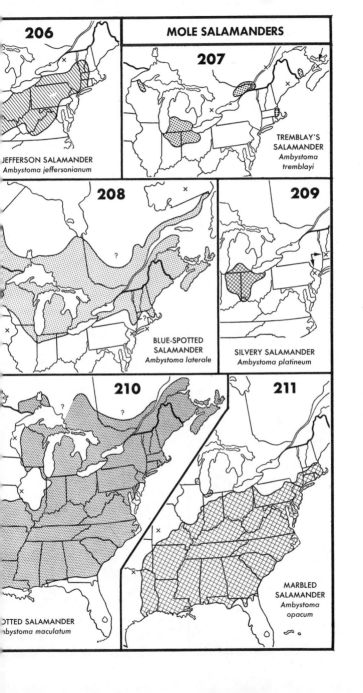

206

JEFFERSON SALAMANDER
Ambystoma jeffersonianum

MOLE SALAMANDERS

207

TREMBLAY'S
SALAMANDER
*Ambystoma
tremblayi*

208

BLUE-SPOTTED
SALAMANDER
Ambystoma laterale

209

SILVERY SALAMANDER
Ambystoma platineum

210

SPOTTED SALAMANDER
Ambystoma maculatum

211

MARBLED
SALAMANDER
*Ambystoma
opacum*

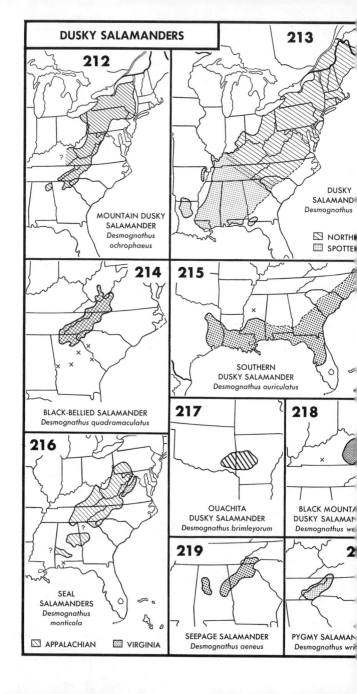

DUSKY SALAMANDERS

212
MOUNTAIN DUSKY SALAMANDER
Desmognathus ochrophaeus

213
DUSKY SALAMAND...
Desmognathus

◩ NORTH...
▦ SPOTTE...

214
BLACK-BELLIED SALAMANDER
Desmognathus quadramaculatus

215
SOUTHERN DUSKY SALAMANDER
Desmognathus auriculatus

216
SEAL SALAMANDERS
Desmognathus monticola

◩ APPALACHIAN ▦ VIRGINIA

217
OUACHITA DUSKY SALAMANDER
Desmognathus brimleyorum

218
BLACK MOUNTA...
DUSKY SALAMAN...
Desmognathus we...

219
SEEPAGE SALAMANDER
Desmognathus aeneus

2...
PYGMY SALAMAN...
Desmognathus wri...

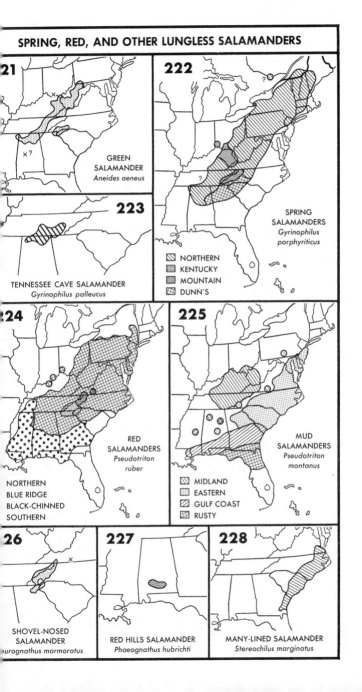

SPRING, RED, AND OTHER LUNGLESS SALAMANDERS

221

222

223

GREEN
SALAMANDER
Aneides aeneus

TENNESSEE CAVE SALAMANDER
Gyrinophilus palleucus

SPRING
SALAMANDERS
*Gyrinophilus
porphyriticus*

- NORTHERN
- KENTUCKY
- MOUNTAIN
- DUNN'S

224

225

RED
SALAMANDERS
*Pseudotriton
ruber*

NORTHERN
BLUE RIDGE
BLACK-CHINNED
SOUTHERN

MUD
SALAMANDERS
*Pseudotriton
montanus*

- MIDLAND
- EASTERN
- GULF COAST
- RUSTY

226

227

228

SHOVEL-NOSED
SALAMANDER
Leurognathus marmoratus

RED HILLS SALAMANDER
Phaeognathus hubrichti

MANY-LINED SALAMANDER
Stereochilus marginatus

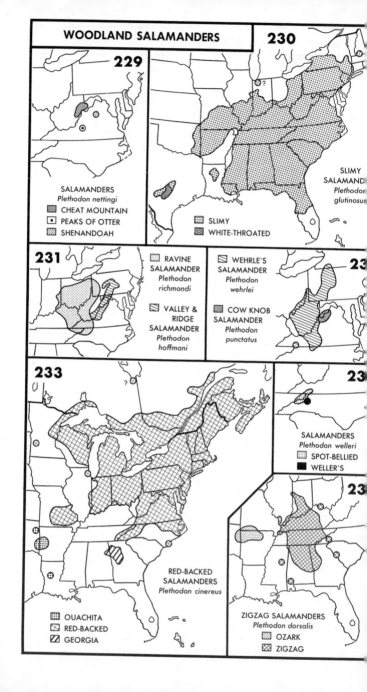

WOODLAND SALAMANDERS

230

229

SALAMANDERS
Plethodon nettingi
⬚ CHEAT MOUNTAIN
⊡ PEAKS OF OTTER
▨ SHENANDOAH

⊞ SLIMY
▧ WHITE-THROATED

SLIMY
SALAMAND
*Plethodon
glutinosus*

231

⊞ RAVINE
SALAMANDER
*Plethodon
richmondi*

◺ VALLEY &
RIDGE
SALAMANDER
*Plethodon
hoffmani*

◺ WEHRLE'S
SALAMANDER
*Plethodon
wehrlei*

▨ COW KNOB
SALAMANDER
*Plethodon
punctatus*

23

233

SALAMANDERS
Plethodon welleri
⊞ SPOT-BELLIED
■ WELLER'S

23

RED-BACKED
SALAMANDERS
Plethodon cinereus

⊞ OUACHITA
◺ RED-BACKED
◿ GEORGIA

23

ZIGZAG SALAMANDERS
Plethodon dorsalis
⊞ OZARK
⊠ ZIGZAG

WOODLAND, FOUR-TOED, AND BROOK SALAMANDERS

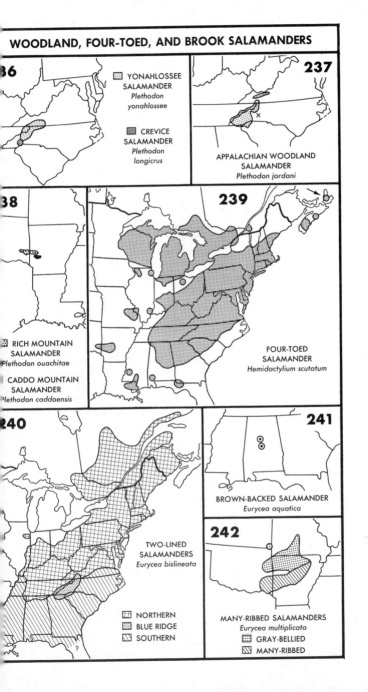

236

YONAHLOSSEE SALAMANDER
Plethodon yonahlossee

CREVICE SALAMANDER
Plethodon longicrus

237

APPALACHIAN WOODLAND SALAMANDER
Plethodon jordani

238

RICH MOUNTAIN SALAMANDER
Plethodon ouachitae

CADDO MOUNTAIN SALAMANDER
Plethodon caddoensis

239

FOUR-TOED SALAMANDER
Hemidactylium scutatum

240

TWO-LINED SALAMANDERS
Eurycea bislineata

NORTHERN
BLUE RIDGE
SOUTHERN

241

BROWN-BACKED SALAMANDER
Eurycea aquatica

242

MANY-RIBBED SALAMANDERS
Eurycea multiplicata

GRAY-BELLIED
MANY-RIBBED

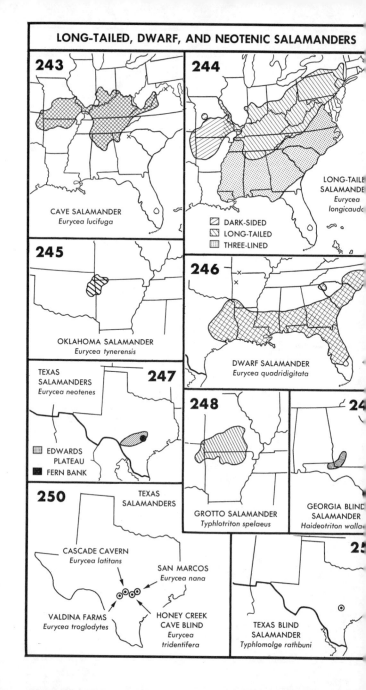

LONG-TAILED, DWARF, AND NEOTENIC SALAMANDERS

243 CAVE SALAMANDER
Eurycea lucifuga

244 LONG-TAILED SALAMANDER
Eurycea longicauda

◪ DARK-SIDED
◪ LONG-TAILED
▦ THREE-LINED

245 OKLAHOMA SALAMANDER
Eurycea tynerensis

246 DWARF SALAMANDER
Eurycea quadridigitata

247 TEXAS SALAMANDERS
Eurycea neotenes

▦ EDWARDS PLATEAU
■ FERN BANK

248 GROTTO SALAMANDER
Typhlotriton spelaeus

24 GEORGIA BLIND SALAMANDER
Haideotriton wallac

250 TEXAS SALAMANDERS

CASCADE CAVERN
Eurycea latitans

SAN MARCOS
Eurycea nana

VALDINA FARMS
Eurycea troglodytes

HONEY CREEK CAVE BLIND
Eurycea tridentifera

25 TEXAS BLIND SALAMANDER
Typhlomolge rathbuni

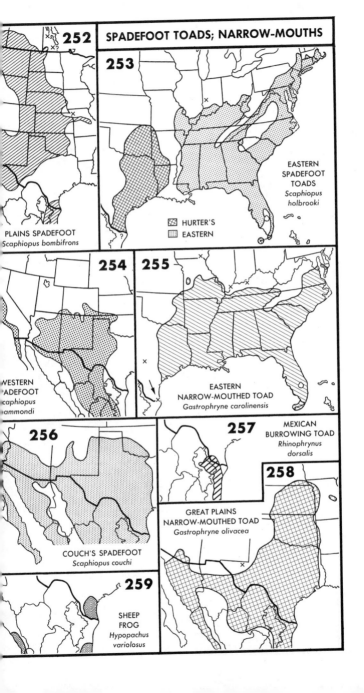

252

253 SPADEFOOT TOADS; NARROW-MOUTHS

EASTERN
SPADEFOOT
TOADS
*Scaphiopus
holbrooki*

⊠ HURTER'S
▦ EASTERN

PLAINS SPADEFOOT
Scaphiopus bombifrons

254

WESTERN
SPADEFOOT
*Scaphiopus
hammondi*

255

EASTERN
NARROW-MOUTHED TOAD
Gastrophryne carolinensis

256

COUCH'S SPADEFOOT
Scaphiopus couchi

257 MEXICAN
BURROWING TOAD
*Rhinophrynus
dorsalis*

258

GREAT PLAINS
NARROW-MOUTHED TOAD
Gastrophryne olivacea

259

SHEEP
FROG
*Hypopachus
variolosus*

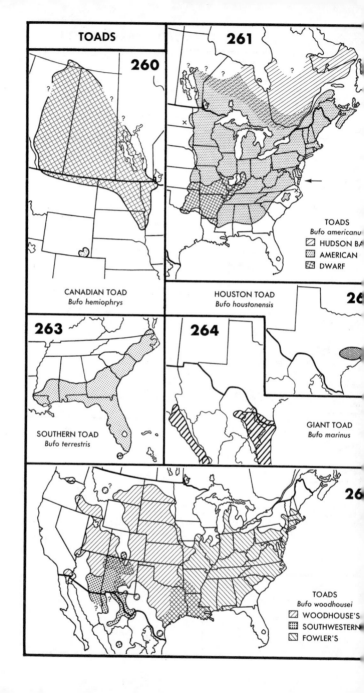

TOADS

260

CANADIAN TOAD
Bufo hemiophrys

261

TOADS
Bufo americanu
- HUDSON BA
- AMERICAN
- DWARF

HOUSTON TOAD
Bufo houstonensis

26

263

SOUTHERN TOAD
Bufo terrestris

264

GIANT TOAD
Bufo marinus

26

TOADS
Bufo woodhousei
- WOODHOUSE'S
- SOUTHWESTERN
- FOWLER'S

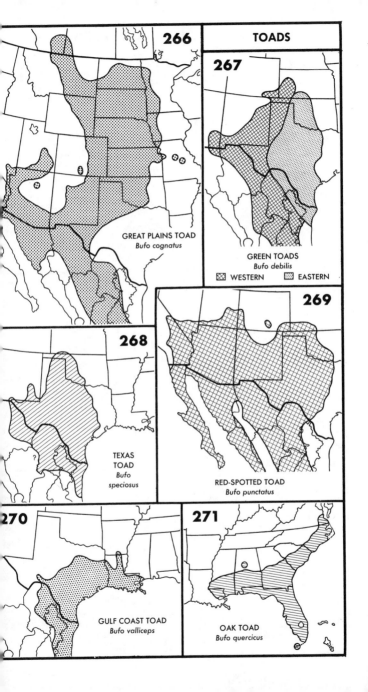

266

GREAT PLAINS TOAD
Bufo cognatus

TOADS

267

GREEN TOADS
Bufo debilis
⊠ WESTERN ⊞ EASTERN

268

TEXAS
TOAD
*Bufo
speciosus*

269

RED-SPOTTED TOAD
Bufo punctatus

270

GULF COAST TOAD
Bufo valliceps

271

OAK TOAD
Bufo quercicus

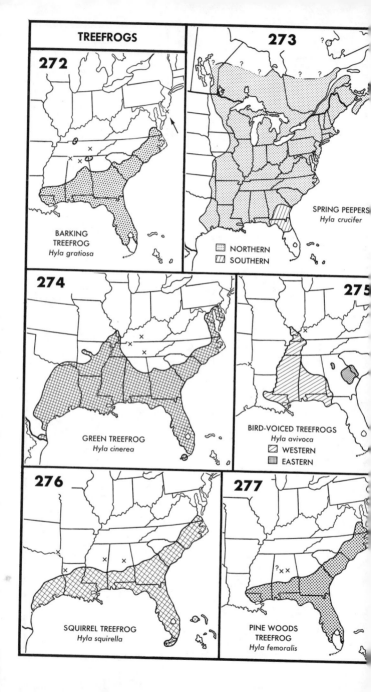

TREEFROGS

272 BARKING TREEFROG
Hyla gratiosa

273 SPRING PEEPERS
Hyla crucifer
▓ NORTHERN
▨ SOUTHERN

274 GREEN TREEFROG
Hyla cinerea

275 BIRD-VOICED TREEFROGS
Hyla avivoca
▨ WESTERN
▦ EASTERN

276 SQUIRREL TREEFROG
Hyla squirella

277 PINE WOODS TREEFROG
Hyla femoralis

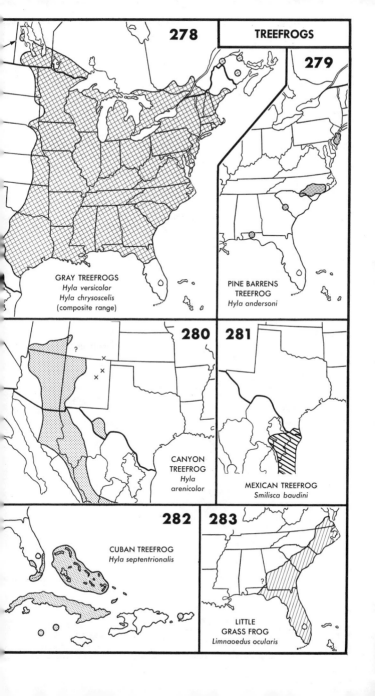

278

TREEFROGS **279**

GRAY TREEFROGS
Hyla versicolor
Hyla chrysoscelis
(composite range)

PINE BARRENS
TREEFROG
Hyla andersoni

280 **281**

CANYON
TREEFROG
Hyla arenicolor

MEXICAN TREEFROG
Smilisca baudini

282 **283**

CUBAN TREEFROG
Hyla septentrionalis

LITTLE
GRASS FROG
Limnaoedus ocularis

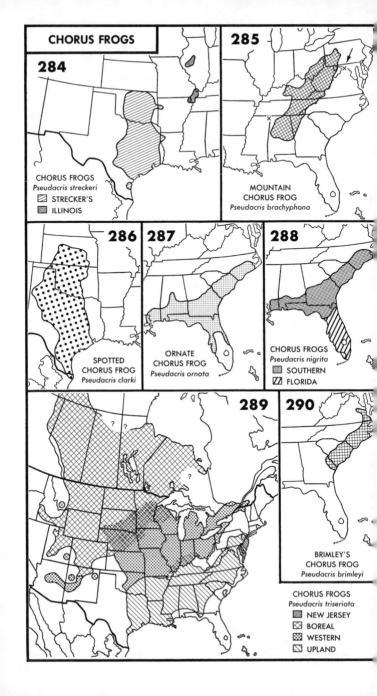

CHORUS FROGS

284

CHORUS FROGS
Pseudacris streckeri
▨ STRECKER'S
▨ ILLINOIS

285

MOUNTAIN
CHORUS FROG
Pseudacris brachyphona

286

SPOTTED
CHORUS FROG
Pseudacris clarki

287

ORNATE
CHORUS FROG
Pseudacris ornata

288

CHORUS FROGS
Pseudacris nigrita
▨ SOUTHERN
▨ FLORIDA

289

290

BRIMLEY'S
CHORUS FROG
Pseudacris brimleyi

CHORUS FROGS
Pseudacris triseriata
▨ NEW JERSEY
▨ BOREAL
▨ WESTERN
▨ UPLAND

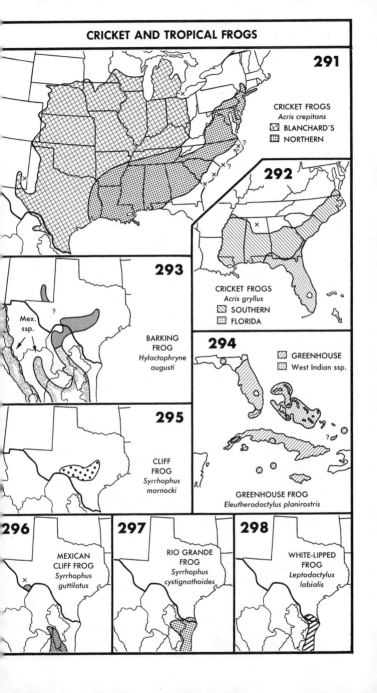

CRICKET AND TROPICAL FROGS

291

CRICKET FROGS
Acris crepitans
⊠ BLANCHARD'S
⊞ NORTHERN

292

CRICKET FROGS
Acris gryllus
⊠ SOUTHERN
⊞ FLORIDA

293

Mex. ssp.

BARKING
FROG
*Hylactophryne
augusti*

294

⊘ GREENHOUSE
⊞ West Indian ssp.

GREENHOUSE FROG
Eleutherodactylus planirostris

295

CLIFF
FROG
*Syrrhophus
marnocki*

296

MEXICAN
CLIFF FROG
*Syrrhophus
guttilatus*

297

RIO GRANDE
FROG
*Syrrhophus
cystignathoides*

298

WHITE-LIPPED
FROG
*Leptodactylus
labialis*

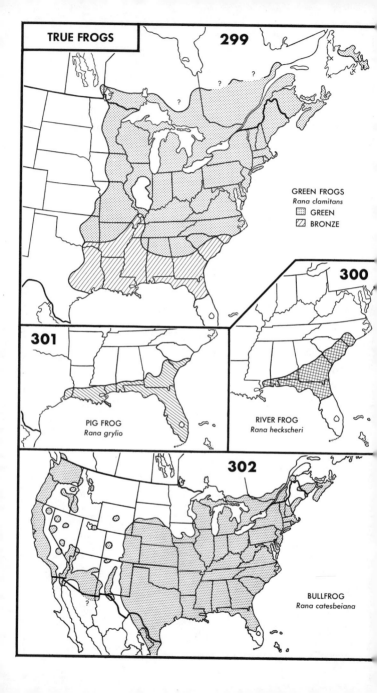

TRUE FROGS

299

GREEN FROGS
Rana clamitans
▦ GREEN
▨ BRONZE

300

301

PIG FROG
Rana grylio

RIVER FROG
Rana heckscheri

302

BULLFROG
Rana catesbeiana

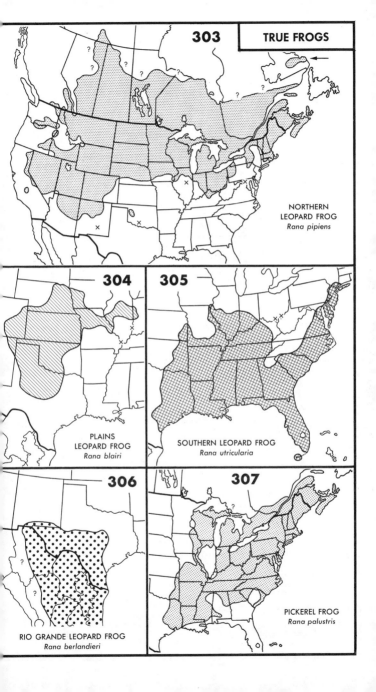

303 | **TRUE FROGS**

NORTHERN
LEOPARD FROG
Rana pipiens

304

PLAINS
LEOPARD FROG
Rana blairi

305

SOUTHERN LEOPARD FROG
Rana utricularia

306

RIO GRANDE LEOPARD FROG
Rana berlandieri

307

PICKEREL FROG
Rana palustris

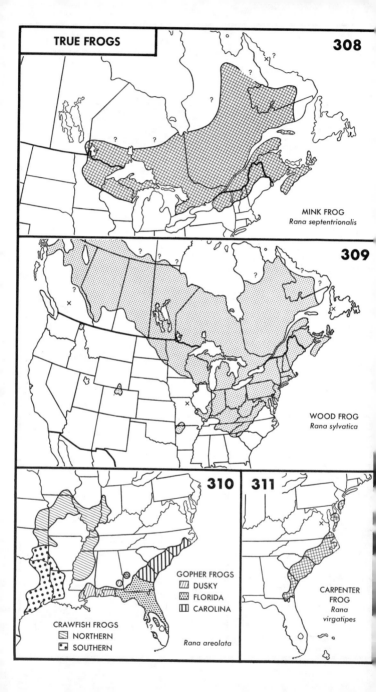

TRUE FROGS | **308**

MINK FROG
Rana septentrionalis

309

WOOD FROG
Rana sylvatica

310 | **311**

GOPHER FROGS
/// DUSKY
⌧ FLORIDA
||| CAROLINA

CRAWFISH FROGS
⌧ NORTHERN
•. SOUTHERN

Rana areolata

CARPENTER
FROG
*Rana
virgatipes*

Index

THIS index has been organized to avoid repetition of such words as "salamander," "turtle," and "lizard" scores of times. In looking for common names, work backward. If you wish to find the entry for "Mountain Dusky Salamander," for example, look under "Salamander" first, then for the subdivision headed "Dusky," and finally for the word "Mountain." In the case of scientific names look for the genus first and then the species or subspecies.

This is primarily a species index, but there are also headings for each order, suborder, family, subfamily, and genus.

References to the text are in lightface type. Plate numbers are in **boldface** and map numbers appear only after the common names of the animals. Colloquial names are not capitalized in the index; official common names follow in parentheses.

SALAMANDERS

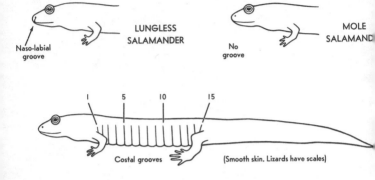

LUNGLESS SALAMANDER

Naso-labial groove

MOLE SALAMAND

No groove

| 1 | 5 | 10 | 15 |

Costal grooves

(Smooth skin. Lizards have scales)

FROGS AND TOADS

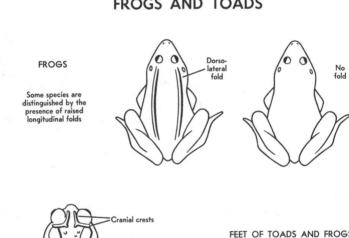

FROGS

Some species are distinguished by the presence of raised longitudinal folds

Dorso-lateral fold

No fold

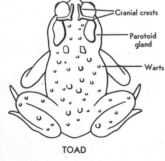

Cranial crests

Parotoid gland

Warts

TOAD

FEET OF TOADS AND FROGS

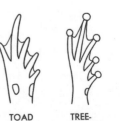

TOAD

TREE-FROG

TRUE FROG

TAKING MEASUREMENTS

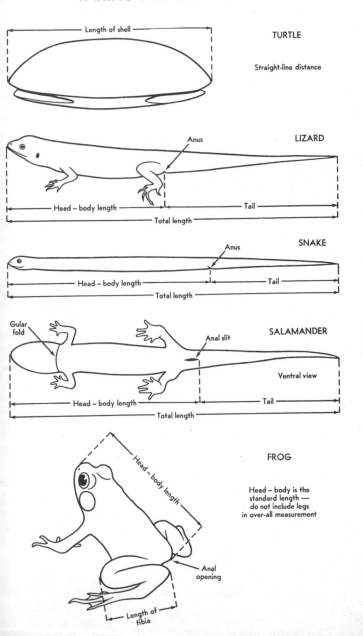

TURTLE

Straight-line distance

LIZARD

SNAKE

SALAMANDER

Ventral view

FROG

Head – body is the
standard length —
do not include legs
in over-all measurement